NOTE

In May 1974 the Twenty-seventh World Health Assembly, after reviewing the Fifth Report on the World Health Situation,[1] requested the Executive Board to consider the question of rationalizing the collection and summarizing of information on the health situation in the various countries, including the intervals at which the information should be published. It also requested the Director-General to continue, pending the Board's recommendations, his preliminary work on preparation of a sixth report on the world health situation, and to present a progress report to a subsequent World Health Assembly.[2]

At its fifty-fifth session, in January 1975, the Executive Board requested the Director-General to study ways of applying, in the preparation of the sixth report on the world health situation, the suggestions he had made in a report to that session, taking into account its discussions on the subject, and to present his proposals to the Board's fifty-seventh session.[3]

After reviewing those proposals, in January 1976, the Executive Board recommended that the future reports on the world health situation should continue to comprise a global analysis and country reviews published by WHO headquarters; should be published every six years, in accordance with the major programme cycle of the Organization (the general programmes of work), with the exception of the sixth report, which should cover the five years 1973–1977, corresponding to the Fifth General Programme of Work; and should be published without prior review by the World Health Assembly.[4]

The Twenty-ninth World Health Assembly, held in May 1976, concurred in those recommendations, and recommended further that the future reports on the world health situation should, at a subsequent Health Assembly, be the subject of discussion bearing particularly on their methodology and content.[5]

The present report is in two volumes. Part I contains the global analysis, with an introduction and chapters on background, health status differentials, health action, research, and the outlook for the future; and Part II the review by country and area, with the additions and amendments submitted by the governments, and an addendum for later submissions.

---

[1] WHO Official Records, No. 225, 1975.
[2] Resolution WHA27.60.
[3] Resolution EB55.R18.
[4] Resolution EB57.R46.
[5] Resolution WHA29.22.

CONTENTS

African Region

Region of the Americas

South-East Asia Region

European Region

CONTENTS

AFRICAN REGION

BOTSWANA

Main health problems

The main problems, as stated in the Fourth National Development Plan (1976–1981), were tuberculosis and respiratory diseases including pneumonia and acute bronchitis, cardiovascular diseases, enteritis, malignant diseases, accidents and injuries, measles and malaria. These accounted for 63.7% of all hospital deaths in 1976.

Tuberculosis continues to be a major problem in five of the health regions. There was, however, a fall in the total number of new cases of tuberculosis admitted. Sexually transmitted diseases have shown an upward trend, from 37 954 cases in 1973 to 63 166 cases in 1976 (however, as a percentage of the total number of outpatients seen, there was a decrease from 11% in 1973 to 8.2% in 1976). Infections of the skin have shown a marked upward trend, from 24 009 cases in 1973 to 75 479 in 1975. This may be accounted for by improved notification from an increased number of health facilities. Accidents have continued to take a steady toll of the population, running at an average of 6% of the total number of hospital inpatients, for the past few years.

It is interesting to note the sex patterns of some conditions. Males predominated in the incidence of cases of gonorrhoea, except in 1975 when there were more cases in females. There was a preponderance of female cases of syphilis in the years 1973 to 1975; however, this finding could be due to the fact that women undergo more examinations and tests than males; for example, tests at antenatal clinics. As a result of their occupations men are more prone to accidents than women. Below 14 years males are more affected by enteritis. More males die during the neonatal period than females.

It is proposed to improve this situation by the development of health education about infectious diseases and the action necessary to combat them, by environmental sanitation to reduce gastroenteritis and other infections, and a communicable diseases programme with an immunization campaign to lower the incidence of infectious diseases such as pertussis, measles and diphtheria. The last case of smallpox was detected in October 1973.

Health policy

The Government is in the process of producing the Fifth National Development Plan, extended to cover a six-year period (1979–1985). In the Fourth (1976–1981) it was stated that the Ministry of Health views an improved health status as a national goal and an important element in an improved quality of life. The long term objective is therefore to provide a comprehensive—personal, family and community—health service integrating curative, preventive and promotive aspects by strengthening basic health services, especially for rural and peri-urban populations, in order to provide personal family care, nutrition and health education, maternal and child care, and family planning.

Health legislation

Since the passing of the 1971 Public Health Act, draft public health regulations have been circulated to other ministries as a preliminary to their presentation to the Cabinet and the National Assembly.

Health planning and programming

There are two planning officers in the Ministry of Health, while the Medical Statistics Unit comprises one statistical officer and 11 assistants. No comprehensive health programming exercise (as defined by WHO) has yet been carried out, but planning work includes appraisals of 10 district plans in preparation for the National Development Plan.

Organization of health services

The provision of health services is a cooperative effort of central Government, local authorities, medical missions, mining companies, private practitioners, and voluntary organizations such as the Red Cross. At the basic health care level, health posts and clinics are run by the local authorities. The Ministry of Health is responsible for the overall planning and supervision of the country's hospitals and health centres.

The missions run their hospitals and health centres in conformity with government policy; they receive a substantial grant from Government to enable them to do this and provide comprehensive services. Thus, for example, at any health post or clinic, curative, preventive and promotive activities are carried out. The specialist units for health education, nutrition, maternal and child health and other special services support the basic health facilities, or train their staff in the necessary skills.

Biomedical and health services research

There is very little research of this nature underway, except for the work of the planning and statistics units.

Education and training of health manpower

A shortage of skilled manpower is one of the most serious constraints facing the development of the country's health sector, and it is the policy of the Government to have as much training as possible done within Botswana. At present the National Health Institute in Gaborone trains registered nurse/midwives, health assistants, pharmacy technicians, and other senior staff; while four other nurse training schools train enrolled nurses. The Institute and schools are in the process of expansion. At the same time the Ministry's Planning Unit is initiating a plan for the health sector in order to assess health manpower needs over the next plan period.

Health establishments

Health posts are the bases for family welfare educators, and it is estimated that there are now about 180. It is planned to build about 100 more by 1985. Clinics (some with maternity wards) provide the next level of health care, and have up to six beds each for curative and maternity care. There are now about 80 clinics in operation, and by 1985 there will be at least 20 more. Next there are seven health centres designed to duplicate on a small scale most of the basic curative functions which are usually provided at hospitals (as well as providing maternity and preventive health care). The highest levels

of health care are provided at the district and referral hospitals, of which there are now 14 (eight general, three mission, two industrial and one psychiatric). By 1985 it is hoped to have a new general hospital in Francistown, when the present general hospital will be converted as a second psychiatric hospital.

Health manpower

Estimates of the main categories of health workers in the various sectors of the health care system are as follows:

	Central Government	Local government	Mission	Private	Total
Doctors	53	—	9	10	72
Enrolled nurses	225	67	52	20	364
General nurses .	190	67	45	45	347
Health assistants . .	65	8	—	—	73
Pharmacists . .	4	—	—	6	10
Health inspectors . .	9	5	—	1	15
Dentists	2	—	2	1	5
Family welfare educators . .	—	280	20	—	300

Production and sale of pharmaceuticals

No pharmaceuticals are manufactured or produced in Botswana, and this position is unlikely to change in the near future. Pharmaceuticals are distributed to the public through three sources: pharmacies under the direct control of the five registered pharmacies in the main towns—two in Gaborone, one in Lobatse, one in Selibe/Pikwe, and one in Francistown; about 100 licensed sellers of non-poisonous medicaments who are not pharmacists, in villages and towns; 22 official Ministry of Agriculture selling points, restricted to the sale of pharmaceuticals for the treatment of domestic animals; and central medical supplies to hospitals and clinics.

Health expenditure

In August 1977 a comprehensive analysis was made of health expenditure. This showed that the total spent (both recurrent and development expenditure) by individuals, organizations and Government on health activities amounted to

15.8 million pula. The breakdown by sources of finance is as follows:

	Total (pula)	
Government (central and local) .	7 212 000	(45.6%)
Employers	607 000	(3.8%)
Charitable organizations	208 000	(1.3%)
Technical cooperation	5 259 000	(33.2%)
Direct payments by recipients .	2 536 000	(16.0%)
	15 822 000	(99.9%)

If, however, the breakdown is made according to services provided, the figures are as follows:

	Development expenditure	Recurrent expenditure	Total (pula)	
Government (central and local)	2 882 000	9 600 000	12 482 000	(78.8%)
Employers	86 000	541 000	627 000	(4.0%)
Charitable organizations . .	50 000	25 000	75 000	(0.5%)
Direct payments by recipients . .		2 059 000	2 059 000	(13.0%)
Missions	78 000	501 000	579 000	(3.7%)

The differences can be ascribed to the following factors: Government provided more services than it paid for from its own funds because of foreign aid and fees charged to patients; employers were also partially reimbursed by employees as patients; charitable organizations' expenditure on health services does not take account of their donations to Government and the missions; recipients paid for drugs, medicines and fees to private doctors, traditional healers, and government health services (all of these are included in the source of finance table, but the latter—payments to Government, missions, and employers—are excluded from the second table); the missions were financed by foreign aid, charitable organizations and government subsidies.

Appraisal of progress made between 1973 and 1977

Under an agreement made with the Norwegian Agency for International Development in 1972, it was planned to construct 161 health posts, 51 clinics, 25 maternity wards, and 60 nurses' houses. At the end of the financial year 1977/78, the following had actually been built under this project: 159 health posts, 45 clinics, 28 maternity wards, and 62 nurses' houses. Thus there has been a very significant increase in the coverage of the health services in rural areas.

Another indicator of the progress made is the reported number of immunizations. In 1973 the estimated numbers of BCG, poliomyelitis, diphtheria, pertussis, tetanus and measles immunizations respectively were 16 000, 13 000, 27 000, and 4000. By 1975 these figures had risen to 120 000, 88 000, 86 000, and 25 000.

Outlook

The Ministry of Health has just produced a paper introducing preparations for the next National Development Plan. This states that the top priority will be given to advancing primary health care, followed by the training of health personnel, the work of various units—such as those for nutrition and health education—and programmes of the Ministry, the improvement of the collection of data and statistics, planning activities, and infrastructure and building.

CENTRAL AFRICAN REPUBLIC

Demographic and health data

At the most recent census, taken in December 1975, the population numbered 3 055 557. The infant mortality rate was between 190 and 290 per 1000, and the population growth rate was 2.7.

Major public health problems

Health coverage, particularly in the rural regions is still incomplete; together with a lack of financial and material resources, it constitutes one of the most important public health problems. The health problems may be grouped into three categories: administrative, resource and medical. The first two problem categories stem from insufficient manpower and logistic support, as well as from the need for better management. The medical infrastructure is adequate, but there is a need for development in primary health care, as well as increased participation by the population.

The National Health Services Development Service is dealing with these problems within the context of the 1976–1980 Plan, confining its activities largely to the health *préfectures.*

The country's major problem in the third category remains the prevalence of infectious diseases which result from unhygienic conditions. Malaria is still the most widespread disease, with more than 134 000 cases reported in 1976. Chemoprophylaxis is the only countermeasure that has been undertaken on an organized basis amongst the most vulnerable groups—women and children. This has been done through the maternal and child health centres in Bangui and in the provinces. The incidence of other parasitic diseases remains high and must be combated by health education and improved sanitary conditions. Respiratory diseases, with 196 000 cases reported, also constitute a serious public health problem.

Action taken

Health policy

The Constitution provides that it shall be the joint task of the State and of public bodies to watch over public health and to promote it within the social context.

Health legislation

This has not yet been developed on a national scale, and the existing texts deal with day-to-day practical questions. A public health code is in the process of being drafted.

Health planning and programming

The Third Socioeconomic Development Plan, 1976–1980, adopted in August 1976, has the following objectives: to provide health coverage for the population through development of the health services; to train personnel at all levels; and to improve working conditions in the health units. These priorities are covered more fully in the 1977 Operational Programme. The first concerns services for family health, environmental sanitation, nutrition, communicable diseases control, and school health. Integrated training was to be provided for doctors, senior health technicians, and paramedical personnel through the Faculty of Health Sciences and internship courses. Working conditions were to be improved by modernization of the operating block, the obstetrics and gynaecology unit and the paediatric unit at the National University Hospital Centre in Bangui, construction of maternity units and improved distribution of medicine and materials. A programming exercise is planned for 1978 in collaboration with WHO.

Organization of public health services

Responsibility for the totality of health services rests with the Ministry of Public Health. At the head is the Minister's cabinet, which is assisted by a technical committee, a technical adviser and the Directorate General. Among the services which report to the Director-General are the Research and Planning Bureau, the Administrative and Financial Affairs Service and the Pharmaceutical Service. The Directorate General covers the Directorate of Urban Health and Hospitals, the Directorate of Training and the Directorate of Rural Health and Major Endemic Diseases. The country has been divided into five sectors for dealing with the major endemic diseases—Bangui, Berberati, Bossangoa, Bambari and Bangassou, each with mobile units for endemic disease control, case-finding and vaccination.

Preventive, curative and health education measures for disease control are also carried out.

Biomedical and health services research

There is still no research centre at the national level. Construction was to begin on the national public health laboratory by the end of 1978. Within the framework of bilateral cooperation, there are the activities with ORSTOM (the French office for scientific and technical research overseas) on the epidemiology of yellow fever and arbovirus, the study of virus vectors and reservoirs, and virological surveillance; and with the Pasteur Institute on enteroviruses, influenza, rabies, vaccinations under tropical conditions, analysis of water, and international vaccination studies.

As regards health services research, continuation of the activities in the Bimbo zone and opening of the Ouham zone with the aid of USAID will allow the elaboration and reinforcement of health strategies and operational methods.

Health manpower development

Training is provided at the Faculty of Health Sciences and at the four annexes in Bimbo, Damara, Bambari and Bouar, for the following categories of health personnel:

Category	Entrance requirements	Length of studies (years)	Number of students as at 31 December 1977
Senior health technicians	Competitive examinations at Baccalaureat level	4	(First graduation in June 1979)
Midwives	BEPC*	3	79
Doctors		6	
State-qualified nurses	BEPC*	3	175
Nursing assistants .		1	275
Registered nurses .	CEP†	2	306
Health aides	Competitive examination	1	73
Midwifery aides . .	Competitive examination	1	84
Sanitary workers . .	Competitive examination	1	66
Community development agents . . .	Competitive examination	2	50

* Brevet d'études secondaires du premier cycle (secondary education, first phase).
† Certificat d'études primaires (Primary school certificate).

In the academic year 1977/78, there was an overall total of 561 students for all these categories.

Health resources

Hospital services

In 1977, in addition to Bangui National University Hospital Centre, which had 700 beds, there were five general hospitals with 650 beds, and 10 *préfecture* hospitals with 610 beds, 40 health centres with 980 beds, 67 health subcentres, 140 health stations, and a number of leper colonies (135 beds). There were also 450 beds in various private units, bringing the total hospital capacity to 3525 beds.

Health manpower resources

In 1977 there were 105 doctors, of whom 32 were local and 73 foreign, 16 pharmacists,

seven local and nine foreign, and three dentists, one local and two foreign. Other health personnel included:

Senior health technicians	30
Supervisors and instructors	11
State-qualified nurses	160
Senior midwives	13
Paramedical specialists	25
State-qualified assistant sanitarians . . .	41
Senior technical agents	17
Technical agents	53
Registered nurses	131
Nurses	330
Assistant nurses	247
Midwifery aides	48
Health aides	37
Medical secretaries	3
Sanitary workers	50
Health care aides	36
Senior general administrative personnel .	111
Other administrative (decision-making) personnel	726
Contractual personnel	57

Production and sale of pharmaceutical products

There is no national production. Pharmaceutical products are purchased and centrally stored by the State supply pharmacy, which comes under the control of the Ministry of Public Health; the products are distributed to the various health units in standardized quantities.

A State pharmacy was set up in 1970. This public commercial and industrial body has a social character and provides the general public with certain medicines and the usual special pharmaceutical products at reduced prices. It has its headquarters at Bangui, and has centres in the larger cities.

Health expenditure and costs

Medical consultations are free. Hospital treatment must be paid for in accordance with the categories laid down in the regulations now in force. All adults pay a subscription of 500 CFA francs a year (100 francs for schoolchildren and other children under the age of 15 years), in return for which they receive a health card allowing a discount on medicines. The funds thus collected are used to improve the health units. The cost of the health care services has not been calculated yet. The health budget for 1977 was 1 618 639 000 CFA francs, including running costs and capital expenditure as well as personnel costs. This represents 7.1% of the national budget.

7

Evaluation of the progress achieved between 1973 and 1977

In 1973 the maternal and child health activities were organized in Bangui and the social centres in the interior (in conjunction with the sanitation projects), including pre- and post-natal visits to homes. Since this date malaria chemoprophylaxis of women and children (the most vulnerable groups) has been efficiently organized, and an evaluation is underway.

The School and University Health Service in Bangui has extended its activities to the rest of the country: medical examinations, systematic educational visits, health control, school and field canteen services, and vaccinations.

In 1977 special attention was paid to the public health units and public health activities for rural health through a programme which consisted of replenishing materials, refurbishing existing health stations and building new ones, and extending the maternal and child health activities, the multiple antigen vaccination programme and the school health services in the major cities.

Trypanosomiasis cases at the end of 1977 numbered 157—53 detected in 1976 and 28 in 1977—compared with 404 in 1974. For the third consecutive year the number of leprosy patients cured was lower than the number of new cases; but these were 14 464 at the end of 1977, compared with 18 212 in 1974. Reorganization in the sectors where the disease has recurred, as well as changes in the health routine, are top priorities. There has been a substantial increase in treponemal diseases, particularly in the urban milieu and among schoolchildren.

An epidemiological map has been drawn up for onchocerciasis. Smallpox vaccination, which is no longer required in the Central African Republic, was given to 535 604 in 1976, and 155 762 in 1977. In 1976 the coverage of the yellow fever immunization programme was 9% for children between six months and five years of age, that of the measles immunization programme 6.37% for those aged between six months and two years. For BCG the coverage in the age group up to 20 years was 16.38%. Tuberculosis control is well in hand in Bangui, and progress has been made in the rest of the country.

Sanitation and environmental hygiene

Water supply is a top priority in rural zones. Due to the lack of underground water, and because of the difficulties involved in digging wells, the village populations take their water from stagnant pools. In the urban areas (Bangui, Bambari and Bouar), the National Water Service is responsible for water distribution.

Within the framework of the Water Decade (for which there is a national committee) a study is underway to determine national requirements. Sanitation is difficult, particularly in the towns, because the sewers and septic tanks which would enable soil pollution to be avoided are lacking.

Special services

Between 1973 and 1977, services for the social groups which to date had been least favoured were further increased. In view of the results already achieved, these activities will continue.

Outlook

Administrative measures for the next ten years include putting the public health code into effect, setting up a national health council, promoting improved health services management, improving health statistics, and establishing health programmes.

Training of personnel of all categories is to be developed at the Faculty of Medical Sciences, under construction.

The development of health services is to proceed, with the modernization of the health infrastructure, construction of a community hospital, strengthening of provincial units, gradual transformation of endemic disease sectors into integrated public health activity zones, and family health activities for the reduction of infant mortality under a UNFPA/WHO/UNICEF project. The fight against malaria and other parasitic diseases, and against venereal diseases, will continue with WHO assistance. The environmental hygiene and primary health care programmes will be developed. Screening and vaccinations within the framework of the extended vaccination programme are aimed to cover 60 000 children a year. A nutrition programme is to be drawn up (with educational and other activities from 1978). Guarantees are to be elaborated for the manufacture of essential pharmaceutical products. There will be participation in research through the National Laboratory of Public Health to be built in Bangui.

CHAD

Demographic and health statistics

The estimated population of Chad during the period 1973–1977 was as follows: 3 869 000 in 1973; 3 950 000 in 1974; 4 030 000 in 1975; 4 121 000 in 1976; and 4 215 000 in 1977.

The diseases most frequently notified during the same period were, in order of frequency: malaria, intestinal amoebiasis and other intestinal parasitic diseases, gastroenteritis, acute bronchopulmonary diseases, infectious hepatitis, measles, diseases of pregnancy and neonatal diseases, eye diseases, tetanus, tuberculosis, and vesical schistosomiasis.

Organization of health services

The health services come under the Ministry of Public Health, Labour and Social Affairs (the Ministry has held the Labour portfolio for almost two years now). The Ministry is assisted by the following technical departments: public health (with subdepartments for the major endemic diseases service and for sanitation); education and training of medical and paramedical personnel; administrative and financial affairs and equipment; the National School of Public Health and Social Service; and the National Supply Pharmacy.

The country is divided into 14 health *préfectures* and has the following health establishments: 7 hospitals (including 3 private hospitals), 19 medical centres, 20 infirmaries, 121 dispensaries, 8 major endemic disease centres, and 2 polyclinics.

Primary health care is provided by village health workers in certain *préfectures*.

Normally the staff of a hospital includes several physicians and nursing staff. On the other hand, because of the limited number of physicians, some medical centres have only one physician and some nurses; others, like the infirmaries and dispensaries (apart from the health centre of the public health demonstration area for training and research), are run entirely by State-registered nurses or staff with equivalent qualifications.

Personnel

The shortage of medical and qualified auxiliary personnel from which the country has been suffering began to improve during the period under review, as shown by the following table:

Year	Physi-cians	Pharma-cists	State-registered nurses	Mid-wives	Enrolled nurses
1973	17	—	73	14	314
1974	23	1	85	9	346
1975	29	3	85	17	386
1976	32	5	82	23	421
1977	42	7	82	26	451

Training establishments

The pace of training appears to be slow because Chad is dependent on training establishments abroad.

In 1965 the National School of Household Studies, the School of Hygiene and the National School of Nurses and Nurse/Midwives were merged to form the National School of Public Health and Social Service for the training of public health technicians, nurses and nurse/midwives, instructresses in household studies, social workers, and nursery nurses. It is planned to enlarge this School by opening sections for State-registered nurses, midwives and social workers.

The numbers of Chad nationals studying abroad in 1977 were as follows: medicine, 138; pharmacy, 17; midwifery, 20; nursing (State-registered), 15.

To make up for the shortage of medical staff, the country has recourse to bilateral technical cooperation. In 1973 15.3% of the total staff were nationals, and in 1977, 41.6%.

Health problems

A planning unit has now been set up in the Ministry and is compiling inventories of needs and engaging in programming. In addition to the customary curative and preventive activities,

Chad is developing rural medicine with primary health care and an expanded programme of immunization, The eradication of smallpox, which has been completed in Chad, is being consolidated by vaccination campaigns.

In 1977 the Ministry took part in the drafting of a four-year plan for 1978–1981; the health projects contained in the plan are directed to the following: malaria control; the control of amoebic and parasitic diseases in general; the national public health laboratory; the setting-up of a national maternal and child health service; the establishment of an ophthalmology institute; the expanded programme of immunization; the construction of the National School of Public

Health and Social Service; the improvement of the existing infrastructure; and the establishment of a pharmaceuticals manufacturing plant.

Resources for health work

The proportion of the total national budget devoted to health has increased constantly (3.8% in 1973, 4% in 1974, 5% in 1975, 7.3% in 1976, about 8% in 1977); international and bilateral cooperation, however, still make a substantial contribution to the resources for health activities.

EQUATORIAL GUINEA

Major health problems

Over the five-year period 1973–1977, the health profile has changed little. Against a background of endemic diseases (leprosy, trypanosomiasis, onchocerciasis, filariasis, yaws, venereal disease, intestinal parasites and nutritional diseases), special problems included difficulties in supplying drinking water to the town of Bata (Rio Muni province), and environmental hygiene problems. Two epidemics of measles were recorded in 1975 and 1976/77, with an exceptionally high mortality rate (above 50%).

Action taken

Health policy

The objectives of the National Health Plan are to promote health care by effectively reorganizing the administrative structure of public health services; to extend health coverage to the entire population; to train personnel; and to promote environmental hygiene by improving the supply of drinking water and continuing vector control.

Health legislation

Special legislation has not yet been drawn up.

Health planning and programming

The first stages of a public health programme were broached between 1970 and 1972 but could not be implemented for lack of personnel.

Organization of the health services

The health services were reorganized on the basis of the existing administrative divisions (provinces and districts); however, the infrastructure and equipment require total renovation.

Health care delivery

The country has 15 hospitals, of which two are provincial hospitals, with a total of 2800 beds; 13 district hospitals with a total of 670 beds; and 37 dispensaries and one leper colony, with accommodation for 107 persons.

Biomedical and operational research

None.

Education and training of personnel

Great difficulties have been encountered in training of health personnel; only auxiliary staff are trained at Bata.

Health resources

Health establishments (see "Health care delivery", above).

Health personnel

The country has a small number of doctors, nurses, and auxiliaries.

Manufacture and sale of pharmaceutical products

None.

Health expenditure

This is difficult to evaluate under present circumstances.

Evaluation of progress achieved between 1973 and 1977

Little progress has been made. The Malabo and Bata hospitals have been renovated. Antimeasles inoculations were given in 1977.

Outlook

It is intended to put the national health programme and an expanded immunization programme into operation.

ETHIOPIA[1]

Population and other statistics

Ethiopia, with an area of 1 221 900 km^2, has a population estimated at 29 300 000. The average population density is 24.0 inhabitants per km^2. About 90% of the total population live in rural areas. Other population data in 1976 were as follows:

Crude birth rate (per 1000 population)	44.7
General fertility rate (per 1000 women of child-bearing age)	188.0
Crude death rate (per 1000 population)	19.8
Infant mortality rate (per 1000 live births)	155.0
Child mortality rate (per 1000 population)	247.0
Natural increase (%)	24.9
Life expectancy at birth	43.7 years

Major health problems

The major health problems are communicable diseases, malnutrition, lack of basic sanitation and personal hygiene.

The leading 11 causes of morbidity diagnosed in 1976 were: venereal diseases (2 051 119), helminthiases (126 216), bacillary and amoebic dysentery (61 478), gastroenteritis (81 138), leprosy, all types (61 939), malaria (46 211), tuberculosis (33 954), schistosomiasis (21 801), trachoma (20 028), influenza (13 401), and filariases, including onchocerciasis (11 777).

Action taken

Health policy

Since the February 1974 Revolution, major events have included the declaration of the National Democratic Revolutionary Programme; the path to scientific socialism is clearly defined with the ultimate goal of establishing the People's Democratic Republic of Ethiopia. To achieve this, various proclamations and regulatory orders have been introduced. The broad masses are responsible for determining the ways and means of expanding the health services to be provided on the principles of self-reliance and democratic centralism. In line with this, the general policy of the Ministry of Health is oriented towards improving the health of the people living in the rural areas through the provision of health service units and through the

---

[1] Ethiopia, previously a member of the Eastern Mediterranean Region, was assigned to the African Region by resolution WHA30.35 adopted by the Thirtieth World Health Assembly on 18 May 1977.

participation of the people. Based on this general policy, the Ministry of Health has laid down its priorities as follows: prevention of diseases, with special attention to communicable diseases; expanding and upgrading basic health services; an integrated health service programme; maternal and child health care; training of health manpower; immunization; development of traditional medicine; development of an effective referral system.

Health legislation

Proclamation No. 91 of 1947 lays down general rules on public health, defining the powers and duties of the Ministry of Health. Pursuant to the authority vested in him by the above proclamation, the Minister of Health has issued legal notices revising regulations in various areas of health. These are the regulations for rabies control (1943), quarantine (1947), water (1950), food (1950), refuse disposal (1950), vaccination (1950), disposal of dead bodies (1950), venereal diseases (1950), communicable diseases (1950), municipal sanitation (1951), and pharmacy (1964).

Health planning and programming

The main functions of the Planning and Programming Bureau are to prepare plans and undertake research and consultative work. Its activities during the period under review included the preparation of capital investment projects for each year, with quarterly progress reports on the implementation of the projects; evaluation for each year of the plan period; collection of relevant data; contacting of international and bilateral agencies for assistance, and processing of the assistance; preparation of five-year plans; initiation of and participation in operational research; preparation of plans of operation for selected projects; and consultative and advisory tasks pertaining to planning and organization of health services.

Organization of health services

The Ministry of Health is the central health authority, responsible for overall planning, policy guidance, and supervision and administration. Under these departments there are 10 divisions. There are expert offices for planning and programming, auditing, legal questions, architecture and other aspects. The Ministry also has semiautonomous institutions for malaria

control, nutrition, central laboratory and research work, and pharmaceutical and medical supplies.

There are 14 regional health departments responsible for planning, implementing and administering health services in their respective regions within the framework of the health policy established by the Ministry of Health.

The general structure of the health services includes the health units of the peasants' and urban dwellers' associations at the "grass-roots" level; health stations of the conventional health services at the peripheral level; health centres and rural hospitals at the intermediate level; regional hospitals; and teaching and national referral hospitals. The referral system is being developed in line with the above structure.

Immunization

The following vaccinations were performed in 1976:

Smallpox	3 139 098
BCG	717 275
Yellow fever	468 413
Diphtheria/pertussis/tetanus	50 506
Poliomyelitis	46 133
Tetanus	17 905
Measles	11 601

Morbidity and mortality due to communicable diseases can be reduced effectively by immunizing the population. The expanded immunization programme which is in progress is intended to protect as many children as possible against smallpox, tuberculosis, measles, diphtheria, poliomyelitis, tetanus and pertussis. By 1977 the health services had reached only about 20% of the population. But with increased mobility of health workers and active participation of the community, it is hoped to cover about 50% of the total population by 1980.

Specialized projects and institutions

Special projects with national coverage include malaria control, the smallpox eradication programme, tuberculosis control and leprosy control projects. Those with limited coverage are for trachoma control and venereal diseases control.

Special institutions include the Central Laboratory and Research Institute, Ethiopian Nutrition Institute and the Drugs and Medical Supply Corporation.

It is to be noted that the existing special projects will be gradually integrated with the basic health services. The integration of malaria control services is already in progress.

Biomedical and health services research

Research is being conducted by the Central Laboratory and Research Institute (communicable diseases); the Ethiopian Nutrition Institute (nutritional diseases); the Ethiopian-Swedish Paediatric Clinic (maternal and child health and related nutritional problems); the Institute of Pathobiology (schistosomiasis and leishmaniasis); and the Armauer Hansen Research Institute (leprosy and leishmaniasis); the Addis Ababa University Medical Faculty staff carry out research in their respective fields. A committee has been established for research on traditional medicine with the cooperation of the Addis Ababa University Faculty of Pharmacy, and a subcommittee on health research has been created under the National Science and Technology Commission to coordinate support and encourage applied research.

Environmental sanitation

Environmental sanitation is one of the programmes for public health activities carried out at health institutions in general and in particular at health centres, including food hygiene, water supply protection, insect and animal pest control, and wastes disposal. The Environmental Health Division has sections for food and drinks inspection, water and wastes inspection, industrial health and general public health. A section for research and development was being organized in 1978. A national environmental control council was being established with the membership of officials of the Ministry of Health, the Ministry of Agriculture and Settlements, and the water resources authorities.

Health resources

Health establishments in 1977 included the following:[1]

Hospitals	84
Hospital beds	8 746
Health centres	106
Health stations	1 010

[1] Not including police and armed forces.

Health manpower resources and development

Medical and allied personnel and training facilities in 1977 were as follows:[2]

Physicians	396
Health officers	331
Pharmacists	79
Pharmacy attendants	93
Sanitarians	327
Nurses	1 488
Health assistants	4 397
Laboratory technicians	398
X-ray technicians	94
Allied health workers on special projects	2 172
Other auxiliary health personnel	113

There were two medical schools, one school of pharmacy, seven nursing schools, two schools for laboratory technicians, one for X-ray technicians, one for pharmacy attendants and eight for health assistants.

The Ministry of Health has drawn up a new curriculum for the training of different categories of health workers. The courses are made relevant to the actual health problems. The unduly long period of training has been shortened and the enrolment increased substantially. A study is being conducted on the possibilities for starting postgraduate medical training in the near future.

Health expenditure

In the fiscal year 1976/77 total government health expenditure was 83 892 302 birr, which is 5.75% of the total budget.

Production and sale of pharmaceuticals

The Ethiopian pharmaceutical manufacturing industry produces some of the commonly used drugs, but production can satisfy only 20% of the total needs. To combat shortages the development of the production centre for drugs, and traditional medicine, are given high priority.

A drug control division and drug policy are being developed. A medical commodities distribution system is being developed to distribute drugs, medical supplies and vaccines to all government health stations, health centres and hospitals promptly, at both headquarters and regional level.

[2] Not including police and armed forces.

Appraisal of progress made between 1973 and 1977

The following table illustrates the development of health facilities and resources during the period:

	Before 1973	Total	Increase (decrease) 1977	Increase (%)
Hospitals	85	84	1	0
Health centres	93	106	13	13.9
Health stations	649	1 010	361	55.6
Health manpower	6 447	7 603	1 156	17.9
Budget (in millions of birr)	51	83	32	62.7

The substantial increase in the number of health stations and health centres while the number of hospitals remained the same (the apparent decrease is due to the combination of two hospitals) indicates the shift from urban to rural and mass coverage. However the existing hospitals have been upgraded to serve as referral centres. As indicated earlier about 90% of the total population live in rural areas. The Ministry of Health believes that the basic health service programmes will not suffice alone to give effective health service to the masses, and the village health workers' programme, which has already been initiated, is designed to reach the masses at the peasants' and urban dwellers' association level. Each association will eventually have a health worker, selected from among the members, and the worker is to be given the necessary training, supplies and equipment. The associations will provide simple premises for treatment and supply, and support the health worker in meeting basic needs, including food and shelter.

Outlook

The goals of the Five-Year Rural Health Development Programme (1976–1980) are: to establish 500 new health stations, 50 health centres, and five rural hospitals, and to upgrade the existing ones; to strengthen the regional health departments, whose primary role is health administration and supervision, provision of diagnostic facilities and distribution of drugs and medical supplies; to establish four schools for health assistants, with a total output of 1200 health assistants; to upgrade two health centres in each region to serve as teaching centres for health assistants; and to establish peasants' and urban dwellers' association health units with village health workers.

GAMBIA

Major health and health-related problems

The prevalence of certain communicable diseases and malnutrition is of major importance in the Gambia. Those who are most afflicted with ill health are the 80% of the population living in rural areas, and it is the young children in these areas who bear the brunt in terms of sickness and death.

The incidence of diarrhoeal diseases, malaria, measles and respiratory infections is high, and tuberculosis, leprosy, chickenpox, and gonorrhoea are quite common. Ankylostomiasis, ascariasis, schistosomiasis, scabies, pertussis, amoebiasis, yaws, and tetanus are other common diseases.

The national infant mortality rate was estimated at 217 per 1000 live births in the 1973 census, though the rate for Banjul, the capital, is only about 60 per 1000 because of the easily accessible health facilities. About 45% of children die before they reach their fifth birthday, life expectancy at birth is 32 years for males and 34 years for females, the crude birth rate is 49 per 1000, the crude death rate 29, and the natural increase is 2%.

Environmental health conditions are unsatisfactory in both urban and rural areas, especially in the latter, where even the most basic needs are not met.

The lack of physicians and qualified health personnel and inadequacy of training facilities are major factors undermining all efforts to develop the health services, and the high wastage rate during and immediately after training is a serious obstacle to health manpower development.

The resources allocated to the health sector are quite insufficient to meet the enormous health needs of the country; it is therefore difficult to expand the health services, increase the coverage of the rural population, or develop the standard of services to a satisfactory level.

The quality and scope of services in nearly all existing rural health units are deficient because of lack of integration of services, inadequate supplies of drugs and medicines, unsatisfactory staff and insufficient supervision. Many communities in remote areas do not have basic health facilities within easy reach.

Lack of vehicles and of maintenance and repair facilities, combined with poor road conditions in some areas, is a big constraint on the development of an effective communication system between the rural health units, referral hospitals and the Ministry of Health.

Several weaknesses in the existing organization and procedures make it difficult to manage the health services efficiently and rationally. Health statistics and medical records are still rudimentary. The lack of trained personnel and other resources has prevented the establishment of regional health offices and urgently needed units for maternal and child health, rural health, epidemiological services, health planning, statistics and training.

Action taken

Health policy

The general policy is to protect the entire population from preventable diseases and untimely death and provide adequate facilities to treat the diseases that commonly occur in the community. The major emphasis in the five-year National Health Plan (1975–1980) has been on the consolidation of the existing health framework both to achieve a greater return for the funds made available and, in doing so, to reduce substantially the existing rural/urban imbalance.

Health planning and programming.

There is no health planning unit or programming officer in the Ministry of Health. A five-year national health plan has been prepared as part of the plan for economic and social development (1975–1980). The National Planning Committee continuously reviews the strategies and policies of the plan and the Development Review Committee monitors the implementation of the projects. Annual development plans are prepared on the bases of the five-year plan. In the Medical and Health Department a Maternal and Child Health Committee and a School Committee formulate plans for the development of maternal and child health, immunization and training activities and review the progress made.

A country health programming exercise was recently carried out with the collaboration of WHO to elaborate a programme of basic health services, particularly for the care of children and pregnant women.

Organization of health services

The Ministry of Health is headed by the Minister of Health, Labour and Social Welfare, who is responsible to the President. He is assisted by the Permanent Secretary who is in overall charge of the administrative machinery. The Director of Medical Services is the technical and professional head of the Medical and Health Department. He is assisted by one Medical Officer of Health and one Chief Nursing Officer. The hospitals, health centres and dispensaries are directly answerable to the Director, whereas the Medical Officer of Health is responsible for environmental health, the control of communicable diseases, and maternal and child health activities, including immunization programmes.

Biomedical and health services research

Research carried out by the Medical Research Council Laboratories at Fajara, jointly administered with the Government, covers many areas of interest, but is particularly concerned with malaria, including immunology. A malaria vaccine has been developed and is under trial, and studies have continued on the biology of *Plasmodium falciparum*, especially on the development of gametocytes.

Gambia is participating fully in WHO's Special Programme for Research and Training in Tropical Diseases; in this connexion a group visited the Medical Research Council in August 1977 with regard to the promotion of research activities.

Education and training of health manpower

During the period 1973–1977, 39 registered nurses (of a student intake of 79), 18 nurse midwives (of an intake of 32) and 35 public

15

health inspectors (of an intake of 57) graduated from the School of Nursing and Midwifery and the School of Public Health. A school for training community health nurses and another for training enrolled nurses started in 1976 and 1977 at Mansakonko and at the Royal Victoria Hospital respectively.

The following projects are being implemented to accelerate health manpower development:

(1) expansion of the school of nursing to facilitate increased intake, in-service training, and improved library facilities;

(2) expansion of the school of community health nurses to allow increased intake;

(3) establishment of a school at Bansang for the training of State-enrolled nurses;

(4) training of traditional birth attendants in order to improve the community effort towards self-help.

The training of physicians, senior officers and tutors is organized abroad through WHO fellowships, and scholarships offered by assisting governments or agencies. Laboratory technicians and assistants receive the first part of their training at the Royal Victoria Hospital, and scholarships are offered for completion of the course in the United Kingdom.

Health resources

Health establishments

There are 2 hospitals, 10 health centres, 18 dispensaries and 46 subdispensaries run by the Government, one hospital run by the Medical Research Council and another privately, and 12 clinics run by the missions,

Health manpower

In December 1976 there were 41 physicians (including 18 nationals), 5 dentists, 17 laboratory technicians and auxiliaries, 6 radiographers and X-ray technicians, 7 dental technicians and auxiliaries, 2 pharmacists, 192 registered nurses, 84 midwives, 123 nursing auxiliaries, 45 health inspectors, 21 leprosy workers and 7 tutors.

Production and sale of pharmaceuticals

There is no local production; all drugs and medicines are imported.

Health expenditure or cost of medical care

During the period 1972–1976 Gambia's recurrent budget increased by 101% and the gross domestic product by 96%, whereas the expenditure on health increased by only 75%. The total per capita health expenditure over the period 1972–1977 had a real growth rate of 4% per annum. The percentage of the total national budget devoted to health varied during the period from 7% to 9%, but salaries accounted for 60% of the health budget. During the same period the health sector's share of annual development expenditure fluctuated, averaging 5.6%.

Appraisal of progress made in the period 1973–1977

Despite the many problems that have had to be faced, considerable progress has been made in the health sector in recent years leading to a marked improvement in the delivery of health services.

Steady progress has been maintained in the implementation of the five-year national health plan. The country health programming report, elaborating the basic health services programme with particular emphasis on maternal and child health coverage, is now being studied by the Government.

The two hospitals—the Royal Victoria Hospital at Banjul, and the Bansang Hospital—are being continuously improved with the addition of new facilities and specialist services in order to increase their efficiency as referral hospitals. The newly built blood transfusion centre at the Royal Victoria Hospital is operating partially and the newly completed children's unit in the Bansang Hospital will soon start admitting patients. The total number of hospital beds rose from 613 in 1972 to 661 in 1976.

The Yorobawol health centre has been completed and plans are being made for it to start functioning. A new dispensary at Yundum airport and a polyclinic at Banjul have started operations and 12 subdispensaries built through community efforts have been added to the rural health units already in existence.

Government efforts to encourage communities to participate fully in health care activities are definitely yielding a good response. A laboratory building at Basse and a maternity ward at Kerewan are nearing completion as a result of community self-help.

The nucleus of a health statistics unit has been set up in the Ministry of Health, and some of the reporting forms have been revised following advice from WHO.

The quality of services in the rural health units has improved steadily as a result of increases in staff and new facilities, including improvements in the supply of drugs and medicines. The maternal and child health services have been intensified and are being gradually expanded; a pilot project has been operating in the Lower River Division since 1972, and the system for monitoring maternal and child health services has been improved.

Although a reasonable rural health infrastructure exists to provide for a considerable geographical coverage, the extent of actual coverage is difficult to determine precisely. About 80% of antenatal cases and 50% of children under five years of age attended the clinics as new cases in 1976, but deliveries taking place in institutions did not exceed 30% of the total number of deliveries.

The expanded programme on immunization receives priority and is an integral part of maternal and child health activities. Coverage has been expanded from year to year through assistance from WHO, UNICEF and the Government of the United Kingdom. The most remarkable achievement during the period has been the eradication of smallpox. Preliminary arrangements were completed for a mass BCG campaign to start in mid-1978, using vaccine and cold-chain equipment provided by UNICEF.

Leprosy control activities have been consistently maintained, and the number of registered cases has decreased substantially.

The prevalence of trypanosomiasis has declined to a negligible level, yellow fever is almost a disease of the past, and cholera has not occurred in epidemic form in recent years. Poliomyelitis is endemic, but the paralytic form is now rare. There is no evidence of onchocerciasis transmission.

The number of rural health units has been increased to 18, with the posting of more than one health inspector in those covering wider areas.

The Medical and Health Department has recently taken over responsibility for the cleansing services in Banjul; a masterplan for drainage and sewerage in Banjul and the Kombo St Mary area has been prepared for implementation in 1978 with financial assistance from the European Economic Community and the African Development Bank. A large-scale rural water supply project including the digging of wells is being implemented, and a pit latrine project has been initiated recently with the active support of the community. The mosquito control scheme started in Banjul has encountered difficult problems because of blocked drains.

A videotape experiment incorporating a health education component has proved successful.

Future goals

A health planning unit is to be established in the Ministry of Health, to start initially with a statistical officer and to be gradually strengthened as trained personnel becomes available. This will help improve data collection and compilation and planning capacity. It is planned to establish regional health offices at the divisional level, each in the charge of a trained medical officer; this will facilitate the effective administration and supervision of peripheral health units.

Plans are being made for the establishment of a central health education unit.

A few important units—for maternal and child health, basic health services, epidemiological services, training and nursing services—are to be established in the Medical and Health Department as a measure for strengthening the management capacity in the health services. A vector control unit is to be established with WHO assistance.

The existing health infrastructure network, in particular the basic health services, is to be selectively strengthened, and a fully integrated referral system within reasonable reach of the whole population is to be set up. A 50-bed hospital is to be established at Kaur to cater for the needs of the central area of the country. Five new health centres (one of which has been completed) and four new dispensaries (one of which is already functioning) are to be established during the current plan period. A master plan for modernizing Bansang Hospital is ready for implementation.

As a step towards the primary health care programme, community support—in terms both of financing and participation—is to be mobilized for both curative and preventive health measures. Health personnel, particularly those needed for the medium and lower levels, are to be trained in adequate numbers to meet the requirements of all the health services.

The health targets for 1985 may be described as follows: (1) to reduce wastage rates in training to 20% for females and 10% for males; (2) maternal and child health coverage for 85% of pregnant women and children under the age of 5 years; (3) the eradication or control of diseases against which effective vaccination is available; (4) a 30% reduction of morbidity and mortality caused by malaria, respiratory infections, diarrhoea, schistosomiasis, malnutrition, anaemia, and intestinal helminths; (5) the provision of facilities to improve environmental health.

GHANA

Major health problems

There are still too many avoidable deaths and diseases in Ghana. Life expectancy at birth is 47 years; the crude death rate is 20 per 1000 population; the infant mortality rate ranges from 63 per 1000 live births in the metropolitan area to 234 per 1000 live births in the remote Upper Region. The estimated annual number of deaths in children under 5 years is 120 000, and of these about 90 000 (or 75%) are deemed preventable. Among adults and older children about 80 000 deaths occur each year, and some 50% of these are avoidable.

It is estimated that 30% of the recorded deaths in Ghana are due to parasitic and other communicable diseases. Among children under 5 years old, 70% of deaths are caused by infections interacting with malnutrition.

The fast growth rate of the population, estimated at 2.7% to 3.0%, tends to outstrip the increase in food production. At the same time, inadequate arrangements for food distribution and some lingering beliefs, customs, habits, and practices regarding food utilization continue to undermine the nutritional status of the population. Malnutrition is common, aggravated during periods of adverse climate conditions and food scarcity.

The other major factors underlying the poor health status of the nation include:

— Inadequate health coverage. An estimated 70% of Ghanaians, mostly in the rural areas, do not have easy access to a hospital, health centre, health post, or other facility providing modern health care. Furthermore, the majority of the population in the rural areas live and work in small communities with poorly developed means of communication and transport.

— Misutilization and under-utilization of available resources. Many of the services provided in the past have not been focused on reducing effectively the main disease problems of the population. Furthermore, the involvement of the communities in starting and maintaining these services has so far been marginal.

— Poor environmental health conditions, especially with regard to water supply and wastes disposal, contribute to a high prevalence of communicable diseases, particularly the diarrhoeal diseases and other water-associated infections.

— Inadequate health resources aggravated by inflation and a rapid population increase.

Action taken

The magnitude and multitude of serious health problems in Ghana are such that the effort to attain better health for the population remains an uphill struggle, but the Government has continued its efforts to improve the national health service within the framework of the programme for overall social and economic development. In view of the inadequacy of available resources to meet existing and anticipated future health needs, a satisfactory level of health management is regarded as one of the important conditions for the advancement of the national health care system. During the period 1973–1977, therefore, one of the most significant steps taken in the health sector was the formulation of a five-year health plan, followed by the establishment of a planning unit in the Ministry of Health.

Development of health services

The current five-year health plan forms an integral component of the national plan for social and economic development, 1975–1980; the main emphasis is on the expansion of primary health care by increasing the number of health centres and health posts.

The main role of the National Health Planning Unit, set up in 1975 within the framework of the Ministry of Health, has been to modify the five-year health plan in order to implement a comprehensive and community-supported system of primary health care. The new primary health care system is designed to achieve two objectives: to increase health coverage in order to reach 80% of the rural population by 1990; and to ensure that the services provided deal with about 80% of the disease problems of the population.

The health care system is still characterized by a hierarchy of institutions managed on a strong regional structure. There was no major increase in the number of institutions during the five-year period. But the number of hospital beds available in the country increased from 8883 at the end of 1973 to 12 896 at the end of 1977 (approximately 45%). Some progress was also made towards expanding rural health coverage, the number of health centres and health posts having been increased by 11 from 107 to 118:

	1973	1978	% increase (decrease)
Teaching hospitals	1	1	—
Regional hospitals	8	8	—
District and other government hospitals	31	35	13
Mission hospitals	34	36	9
Other non-profit making hospitals . .	19	16	(15)
Other profit making hospitals	12	17	41
Health centres and health posts . . .	107	118	10
Total number of hospital beds	8 883	12 896	45

Control of diseases

Parasitic and other communicable diseases still constitute by far the largest disease problem in the country. But malnutrition is also prevalent, and the incidence of some noncommunicable diseases, notably hypertension, is already causing concern.

Biomedical and health services research was aimed at finding suitable methods for control of some of the main diseases—for example, research on methodology for the control of schistosomiasis in manmade lakes, and on local patterns of cardiovascular diseases, and feasibility studies for the implementation of the expanded programme of immunization.

The West and Central African subregion, which incorporates Ghana, was certified free of smallpox in 1976. Furthermore, the operational phase of the intercountry onchocerciasis control

programme in the Volta River basin area was started in 1975, with the support of several bilateral and multilateral aid agencies; the project area includes the Upper and Northern Regions of Ghana. The routine surveillance of a selected number of endemic and epidemic diseases was continued.

Promotion of environmental health

The improvement of environmental health conditions remains a formidable and expensive task, but the Government is determined to move forward in this field. To this end, large investments were put into water supply development throughout the country, and a considerable effort was also made for the provision of additional housing and the improvement of sewerage and drainage in cities.

The proportion of the population having access to public systems of water supply has increased steadily from 32.6% in 1970 to 38.2% in 1975, and 42.0% in 1977. But disparity between towns and rural areas has continued. In 1977 only 20% of the rural population had access to pipe-borne water systems or boreholes fitted with hand-operated pumps, whereas no less than 94% of the urban communities were served by house connexions or public standpipes.

The State Housing Corporation is the main government organization involved in house construction in towns throughout the country, while the Tema Development Corporation is responsible for the provision of housing in the port and industrial town of Tema. The output of the State Housing Corporation increased to 1264 housing units during 1972/73, 1528 units during 1973/74 and 1380 units during 1974/75—compared with an annual average of 500 housing units before 1972.

There was little progress in sewerage and drainage in towns, but plans were laid down to start sewerage and drainage projects in the two biggest towns outside the metropolitan area, namely Sekondi-Takoradi and Kumasi.

Health manpower development

The main problems in the field of health manpower are varying degrees of inadequacies in the numbers and quality of various categories of health personnel, and the absence of a national policy and plan for the development and utilization of health staff. Considerable

19

progress was made towards reducing these problems, and spectacular results were recorded in increasing the numbers of the various categories of health workers.

	1973	1976	% increase (decrease)
Physicians	789	1 011	28
Dental surgeons	33	60	82
Pharmacists	445	519	16
Nurses and midwives*	12 481	16 478	32
Laboratory staff*	520	449	(13)
Sanitarians*	870	852	(2)
Health centre superintendents	243	280	15

*Professionals and auxiliaries

A start was also made on drawing up a health manpower plan for Ghana.

General progress made between 1973 and 1977

Though unspectacular, the overall progress was steady. Considerable health resources were allocated and added to the health care system in terms of manpower and facilities. But there was also progress of an intangible nature: the political and medical leadership has begun to appreciate and support the development of primary health care, and thus to forego to some extent the traditional demand for a proliferation of hospitals.

All told, however, the increase in resources seems to have had but little impact on the health status of the population. It is estimated that some 130 000 Ghanaians, mostly women and children, are still dying each year from preventable causes. Furthermore, the fact that only one infection—smallpox—has been eradicated serves to underline what remains to be done in the field of communicable diseases.

The government health budget increased from 41 965 000 cedi in 1972/73 to approximately 128 414 000 cedi in 1976/77, an increase of 206%. However, inflation increased by about 204% during the same period, while the population was growing at a rate of about 3% per annum. The cost of running and maintaining hospitals and other health institutions keeps soaring, while the Government's ability to finance these services in the face of the current level of inflation and population growth has remained stationary or started to decline.

Despite the considerable efforts made for health development, little real progress has so far been achieved. It is clear that a new approach is required in order to improve both health coverage and the health status of the population.

Outlook for the future

The modest progress achieved can be ascribed to: a top-heavy health care delivery system with a noticeable lack of community involvement at the "grass-roots" level, and little or no coordination with other sectors, especially at the peripheral level; too much focus on the construction of facilities rather than the provision of appropriate services to deal with identified disease problems; emphasis on specialized hospital-based facilities and services for a small percentage of the population rather than on basic preventive services and health promotion for the majority.

The fact that these weaknesses have been recognized is in itself a hopeful sign for the future. Already the Government has taken steps to correct the situation: the National Health Planning Unit has been established with the object of formulating and implementing a new strategy for the delivery of health services—a primary health care system which permeates to the village level and is supported both by communities and by strong district health management teams. A start is to be made in 1978 on the implementation of the new system. Many obstacles are foreseen, but there seems to be no effective alternative strategy for reaching the goal of health for all within the next decade or two.

KENYA

Major health problems

The major health and health-related problems in Kenya are associated with child-bearing and child-rearing, communicable diseases, the effects of malnutrition, and hazards arising from poor environmental sanitation.

Action taken

Health policy

The Ministry of Health deploys health services through a network of provincial, district and subdistrict hospitals, and through health centres, subcentres and dispensaries. Additional support is provided by church organizations and nongovernmental health agencies, mainly for curative and maternity services.

Health legislation

The Public Health Act, revised in 1972, laid down by Act of Parliament the framework of the Ministry of Health, its Central Board of Health, and Department of Health. The Minister of Health administers in addition other Acts related to health, such as the Pharmacy and Poisons Act, the Dangerous Drugs Act, the Nurses, Midwives and Health Visitors Act.

Health planning and programming

In 1972 the Ministry of Health started to implement an integrated and comprehensive master plan for the development of basic rural health services, based on a network of health units, health teams, and family health services. Community participation and the cooperation of nongovernmental agencies continued to be promoted.

In 1974 the Ministry of Health, with the support of external aid, formulated an expanded and comprehensive five-year national family planning programme. Expanded activities in the fields of maternal and child health and family planning were the major features of the programme.

Organization of health services

The health structure is centralized and administered by the Ministry of Health in Nairobi. Each of the seven provinces is headed by a Provincial Medical Officer who is responsible for both curative and preventive services and is technically responsible to the Director of Medical Services in Nairobi.

Health-related services such as the provision of community water supplies and the control of waste water, air pollution and other environmental conditions have been organized by the Ministry of Water Development and the Ministry of Agriculture.

Biomedical and health services research

Biomedical and health services research that was undertaken until August 1977 under the aegis of the East African Community has been continued by the newly established National Medical Research Authority.

Education and training of health manpower

The University of Nairobi continued to provide graduate health manpower through the Faculty of Medicine and the Faculty of Engineering. In 1974 schools of dentistry and pharmacy were established and attached to the Faculty of Medicine. Postgraduate medical training programmes and a M.Sc. degree course in environmental health engineering were provided.

The training of auxiliary health personnel, particularly clinical officers (medical assistants), health educators, enrolled community nurses, public health technicians, and medical laboratory technicians, was also emphasized. The facilities of the Medical Training Centre in Nairobi were expanded in order to provide for increased intakes of these categories of trainees. Other health institutions continued to be used for training registered and enrolled nurses, nutrition and health education field workers and others.

Health establishments

At the end of 1977 there was a total of 80 hospitals (1 national, 7 provincial, 33 district, 24 sub-district, 8 for prisons, 2 for the armed forces, 2 psychiatric, 2 for leprosy, and 1 for infectious diseases), 191 health centres, 34 sub-health centres, 536 dispensaries, 17 mobile health units and 325 maternal and child health and family planning service delivery points. There were 11 941 government general beds, giving an average of 0.80 beds per 1000 population.

Health manpower

At the end of 1977 a total 10 270 health personnel were employed by the Ministry of Health. They included 600 physicians, 40 dentists, 50 pharmacists, 1070 clinical officers, 280 public health officers, 1320 registered nurses, 192 laboratory technologists, 230 pharmaceutical technologists, 196 physiotherapists/occupational/dental/orthopaedic technologists, 120 radiographers, 4250 enrolled nurses, 317 laboratory technicians, 113 radiographic film processors, 670 public health technicians, 230 nutrition field workers, 580 family planning field educators and 12 scientists (radiophysicists, parasitologists, biochemists and entomologists).

Production and sale of pharmaceuticals

Drug quality control services are still to be established. The Ministry of Health has, however, maintained adequate control of local production of pharmaceuticals, and considerable quantities of imported drugs conforming to international standards have been assured.

Health expenditure

The total capital expenditure allocated for health development in the 1974–1978 National Development Plan was K£ 28.5 million. This included K£ 6.5 million for rural health services; K£ 4.8 million for health training; K£ 1.8 million for public health services; and K£ 14.8 million for hospital development. In 1977 capital expenditure on health totalled K£ 7.7 million.

Appraisal of progress made between 1973 and 1977

Considerable progress was made in the health coverage of the population. Rural health facilities were increased from 603 to 761; 33 rural health training and demonstration centres were completed, or nearing completion; the number of government hospitals was increased from 75 to 80; and the total of general hospital beds was increased from 11 051 to 11 941.

At the end of 1977 the national family planning programme had successfully recruited 280 000 family planning acceptors through 325 maternal and child health and family planning service delivery points and 17 mobile units.

The total number of health personnel employed by the Ministry of Health increased from 6 952 to 10 270, with considerable increases in the number of physicians, dentists, pharmacists, clinical officers and registered nurses. A total increase of 48% was noted.

Since its inception in 1974 the Ministry of Water Development has taken measures to centralize activities in water supply, waste water disposal and water pollution control both in the rural and urban areas. By the end of 1977 community water supplies were available to an additional 500 000 people living in urban areas and rural centres.

Outlook

The Government's health goals, which have emphasized preventive programmes and health promotion while also ensuring curative services, concern essentially the strengthening and implementation of measures for prevention, control and eradication of communicable diseases; the expansion of diagnostic, therapeutic and rehabilitation services; and the promotion and development of biomedical and health services research. The greatest challenge has been that of bringing adequate facilities within reach of the rural population.

Under the National Health Development Plan, 1978–1983, it is proposed to increase all health establishments by 40% (the number of hospital beds would increase from 11 941 to 15 000, rural health facilities from 761 to 920, and delivery points for maternal and child health and family planning services from 325 to 700). Emphasis will continue to be given to the training of health manpower, particularly at the auxiliary levels; the targets set for 1983 are 1270 physicians, 160 dentists, 180 pharmacists, 1840 clinical officers, 390 public health officers, 2260 registered nurses, and corresponding increases in other categories of staff. With regard to environmental health, emphasis will be laid on housing and food sanitation. Targets include water quality improvements in 90 of the 270 community water supply schemes planned, 75 new waste disposal units, and 2950 additional latrines.

LIBERIA

Major health and health-related problems

In order to increase the contribution of the country's health programme to rural develop-

ment and improve the quality of life of the rural population, the Government has established the following health priorities:

(1) to develop permanent mechanisms and

structures for the continuous process of planning, implementation, evaluation and reformulation of the country's health development programme;

(2) to orientate manpower development towards meeting the needs of rural communities and train health personnel at all levels with special emphasis on the training of "frontline" health workers;

(3) to strengthen the health infrastructure and further develop integrated preventive and curative services with special attention to family health;

(4) to develop gradually, at the most peripheral level, primary health care activities based on community needs as an extension of the country's health care delivery system;

(5) to control communicable diseases with special emphasis on the prevention of measles, pertussis, tetanus, tuberculosis, diphtheria and smallpox;

(6) to improve environmental health and sanitation, including the provision of a safe water supply; and

(7) to increase laboratory support to communicable disease control.

Action taken

Health policy

The Ministry of Health and social Welfare aims further to strengthen and improve services throughout the country by implementing the following as speedily as possible with the resources available during the next five years: the development of logistics for rural health delivery, and small-scale construction projects; the provision of adequate medical equipment and services and the improvement of health facilities; stress on immediate preventive measures, including safe drinking-water, maternal and child health care, preventive dental and eye care, sanitation, and nutrition; primary health care, including training; an expanded immunization campaign; the development of strategic border town health care services and county hospital health services; county community welfare development programmes; the preparation of county health plans; the integration of non-governmental health services within the health care delivery services of the Ministry of Health and Social Welfare; improved health education; strengthening of the role of the Dogliotti Medical School and the John F. Kennedy Medical Center in health care delivery.

Health legislation

A New Public Health Law (Title 33 of the Liberian Code of Laws) was approved in July 1976. It covers the control of acute communicable diseases and conditions, environmental sanitation, health standards of public and private institutions, the regulation of drugs, the registration of births and deaths and the disposal of human remains, and the supervision of medical and allied health professions.

Health planning and programming

The National Socioeconomic Development Plan emphasizes the importance of the multisectoral approach to integrated rural development. An appropriate institutional machinery for the coordination and integration of sectoral programmes and activities at various levels is being set up. The Government has already taken two important decisions in this respect: the establishment of the National Planning Council, with a view to coordinating plans for all aspects of development; and the decentralization of the political and development administration to the county, which is the recognized unit for local development.

Planning within the framework of the county health care delivery system, based on the efforts of the National Health Plan to strengthen the existing health infrastructure, will continue. Community nursing programmes will form an integral part of the activities of the major county hospitals throughout the country. The expansion of the health care delivery system is currently geared towards reaching the population at the periphery and promoting primary health care. A data collection and information processing system is being gradually developed. In Cape Mount County the maternal and child health and family planning programme supported by UNFPA and WHO has fully utilized trained traditional birth attendants in promoting its integrated maternal and child health and family planning activities in several communities. Field health educators have been trained and are at present engaged in motivating the population to undertake simple sanitation measures. In Maryland County, with the cooperation of the Netherlands Government, a pilot project is being initiated to utilize village health workers in stimulating community involvement in health development.

Organization of health services

The Ministry of Health and Social Welfare, which was completely reorganized in 1974, consists of five bureaux—administration; planning, research, and development; curative or medical services; preventive services; and social welfare.

The Ministry is headed by the Minister assisted by two deputy ministers, one Special Assistant, one Assistant Minister, and directors heading the various bureaux. One of the two deputy ministers is also Chief Medical Officer and is in charge of technical matters, the other Deputy Minister is in charge of all administrative matters.

The Bureau of Planning, Research and Development develops short-range and long-range health plans. It is composed of four divisions: planning, health manpower development and training, vital and health statistics, and technical coordination. With the cooperation of USAID a three-year health management planning project was started in 1976, when a three-man planning team joined the bureau to assist in making an accurate appraisal of health needs and improve the planning capability of the Ministry.

The Bureau of Curative or Medical Services consists of four divisions dealing with nursing services; drugs and medical supplies; hospital and clinic inspection; and nongovernmental institutions. The Bureau is responsible for developing and implementing an effective health care system. It also handles official matters of all physicians and dentists employed by the Ministry. The divisions of hospital and clinic inspection, and drugs and medical supplies are headed by the Chief Pharmacist. The Chief Nursing Officer heads the nursing services.

The Bureau of Preventive Services consists of divisions of communicable disease control, environmental health and sanitation, and health education. It is responsible for implementing and administering environmental and sanitation services, health education, and the publication of informative programmes for preventive purposes.

The Bureau of Social Welfare is composed of divisions of family welfare, rehabilitation, and community welfare. Its functions are to ensure that adequate care is provided in homes and institutions for neglected and delinquent children; to organize community groups to combat the social problems confronting them; to organize foster care and adoption programmes; to promote legislation and programmes protecting children; to promote family planning as an integral part of family welfare; to encourage programmes for the prevention and control of juvenile delinquency; to promote family counselling and assistance, and research on family welfare.

Biomedical and health services research

The role of the Liberian Institute for Biomedical Research, established in 1975 as an autonomous government agency, is gaining increasing significance in the coordination of biomedical research activities undertaken with the collaboration of national and foreign institutes and agencies. These activities include the production and testing of a vaccine against hepatitis (in collaboration with USAID), surveys to determine the prevalence of Lassa fever and the production of immune globulin (in collaboration with Columbia University), the evaluation of therapeutic agents and insecticides for filariasis control (in collaboration with the Hamburg Tropical Institute in the Federal Republic of Germany), and research on resistance to antimalaria drugs (in collaboration with the Karolinska Institute in Sweden).

Education and training of health manpower

There are programmes for the training of medical and paramedical personnel in almost every county in the country; at present there are six training institutions, including a medical college. The John F. Kennedy Medical Center is at present engaged in a four-year programme on the training of specialists in particular aspects of surgery, paediatrics, internal medicine, obstetrics and gynaecology.

With the cooperation of UNICEF, the Family Welfare Division of the Ministry of Health and Social Welfare conducts four-month training programmes for traditional midwives at four training centres twice a year. UNICEF also assists the Ministry with refresher courses for traditional midwives and laboratory technicians. Refresher courses are also provided at all other institutions to help upgrade the standard of health workers.

Health resources

Health establishments

In 1977 there were in Liberia 32 hospitals (14 government, 10 concession, 6 mission and 2 private); 21 health centres (19 government, 1 concession and 1 mission); and 275 health posts or clinics (206 government, 7 concession, 30 mission and 32 private).

Health manpower

The following health personnel were employed in government hospitals and clinics in 1977: 28 surgeons, 49 general practitioners, 22 dentists, 379 State-registered nurses, 162 practical nurses, 19 nurse/anaesthetists, 16 dental technicians, 6 pharmacists, 164 assistant physicians, 174 certified midwives, 82 empirical midwives, 11 operating room technicians, 22 X-ray technicians, 84 laboratory technicians, 490 nurse aides, and 177 dressers.

Production and sale of pharmaceuticals

Liberia does not produce any pharmaceuticals; the Ministry of Health and Social Welfare, through its Division of Drugs and Medical Supplies, imports drugs for all government health institutions in the country. Concessionaires and private companies which are licensed are allowed to import drugs for their use, and pharmacies meeting the guidelines of the Pharmacy Board import approved drugs for sale.

Health expenditure

In 1976 the Government of Liberia changed its fiscal year from 1 January to 31 December of one year to 1 July to 30 June of the following year. Health expenditure in recent years was as follows: 1 January to 31 December 1975, US $8 566 982; 1 January to 30 June 1976, US $4 984 283; 1 July 1976 to 30 June 1977, US $11 820 911; and 1 July 1977 to 30 June 1978, US $16 889 013.

MADAGASCAR

Demographic and health statistics

At the latest census, carried out in 1974/75, the population was 7 568 577, 16.3% urban and 83.7% rural; 55.9% of the population were under the age of 20 years. The population density was 13 inhabitants per km². The average life expectancy at birth was 45 years; the fertility rate (for women between the ages of 15 and 49) was 20%; the birth rate was 41.85 per 1000 population, the crude mortality rate 20 per 1000, the annual population growth rate 2.1%, the infant mortality rate approximately 100 per 1000 live births, and the maternal mortality rate 1.27 per 1000 live births.

The communicable diseases most commonly reported in 1976 were: respiratory diseases (2 648 000 consultations) in particular acute bronchitis, and tuberculosis (incidence rate 1.4 per 1000, prevalence rate 1%); diarrhoeal and parasitic diseases (648 000 consultations), with a marked prevalence of helminthiasis in general and schistosomiasis in particular; children's infectious diseases—measles (188 863 cases) and pertussis (66 804 cases); malaria (average parasite rate 30%, clinical incidence 5%) (287 622 cases); leprosy (incidence rate 1 per 1000, prevalence rate 1%, number of patients under treatment, 36 000); sexually transmitted diseases—syphilis, gonococcal infections (prevalence rate 3%, number of cases reported annu-

ally, 62 000); plague (40 new cases); typhoid fever (682 cases) and paratyphoid (73 cases); poliomyelitis (10 cases); diphtheria (1459 cases); human rabies (six deaths).

In all, 72% of all consultations and 60% of deaths were due to communicable diseases, which tend to be concentrated in areas where there are malnutrition and poor environmental conditions, with the almost total absence of any environmental hygiene facilities (only 1.5% of homes have wells, 3% have waste pits and 6% have latrines, and 16% of the rural population have a piped drinking-water supply), and the low general level of health education in a population steeped in centuries-old tradition. Additional factors are the tropical storms to which the coastal areas are subject, and the paucity of human and financial resources for medicosanitary work.

Organization of public health services

The Ministry of Health was reorganized on 3 February 1976; its staff includes a Secretary General who assists the Minister and who has under him four services: finance, personnel, legislation and studies and planning, as well as the six provincial health services, which are further subdivided under 34 medical districts and municipal hygiene offices. As at December 1977, there were 836 public health units and

192 private health units with a total of 20 000 beds, or one to 432 inhabitants. There are 61 pharmacies and 752 medicine supply stores.

Hospital services

Health care is organized on a "hierarchical" basis with 723 units providing services from the periphery to the centre: first there are the units staffed by paramedical personnel (72%). At a higher level, there are 97 medical centres and 59 simple secondary hospitals run by doctors. Secondary medicosurgical hospitals, 10 in number, carry out routine surgical operations. The five main hospitals, each established in a provincial capital, provide specialized services and constitute regional reference centres for all laboratory tests. The general hospital in the capital provides a range of highly specialized services for referral at the national level. There are also 26 urban dispensaries, 11 mobile health teams, and eight municipal hygiene offices.

Health manpower resources and development

The following table shows health personnel in public service, including those abroad for training, by category as at 31 December 1976:

	Government services	Others	Training abroad	Total
Doctors[1]	568	39	57	664
Pharmacists[1] . . .	24	5	4	33
Dental surgeons . .	11	1	—	12
State-registered nurses	229	16	4	249
Nurses[1]	1 724	14	—	1 738
State-registered midwives	275	22	4	301
Midwives[1]	659	22	—	681
Other staff	1 157	5	3	1 165

[1] Including those qualified in Tananarive (diplôme de Tananarive).

Taking into account health manpower in private practice or private services, in 1976 there was on average one doctor to 10 800 inhabitants, one dentist to 89 000, one nurse to 3700, and one midwife to 8200. There is a great disparity in the geographical distribution of the personnel.

The methods of training health personnel were as follows in 1977:

Category and admission requirements	Duration of studies (years)	Number of schools	Number of students	Number of graduates
Doctors qualified in Tananarive (last intake), and in competitive examination . .	5	1*	44	44
State-qualified doctors	7	1	1 801	17
Dentists qualified in Tananarive	1.5	—	12	8

Category and admission requirements	Duration of studies (years)	Number of schools	Number of students	Number of graduates
Dental surgeons (baccalaureate) .	5	1†	150	None
State nurses (BEPC[1] and competitive examination) .	3	6	327	None
State midwives (BEPC[1] and competitive examination) .	3	6‡	87	None§

[1] Brevet d'études secondaires, premier cycle (secondary education, first level).
* Closed since 1977.
† Opened in 1977.
‡ Same school as for the female nurses.
§ No students of the State nursing school in 1977, but 40 from the old school in Tananarive.

Immunizations

The following vaccinations were carried out in 1977:

```
BCG . . . . . . . . . . . . . 104 457
Smallpox . . . . . . . . . . 339 465
Cholera   . . . . . . . . . .   3 043
DPT . . . . . . . . . . . . { 65 246 (third injection)
                            { 30 179 (booster)
TAB . . . . . . . . . . . . .   1 870
Yellow fever  . . . . . . . .   1 182
```

Specialized services

In 1977 there were 29 mother and child health units and six school health centres; the number of prenatal consultations in 1976 was 794 113; postnatal consultations, 179 962; marriage consultations, 1128; consultations for infants, 1 162 422; consultations for children aged 1–5 years, 1 721 107; consultations of school-age children, 457 048. Units of dental treatment number 91 453. There were also one children's hospital and dispensary, one hospital at Fenoarivo for pulmonary diseases including tuberculosis, 12 leper colonies, three antituberculosis dispensaries, one psychiatric hospital, one equipment centre, one professional reeducation centre, a Pasteur institute, one epidemiological centre, and one public health demonstration area.

Public health policy

The principle of decentralization gives priority to the control of communicable diseases and malnutrition, the promotion of preventive medicine, hygiene, health education and sanitation, and curative services. Thus, within the framework of the general health services, efforts are being made to improve the supply of medicaments; to encourage the active participation of remoter population groups in the construction and maintenance of rural health infrastructures (primary health centres); to strengthen the expanded immunization programme, antimalarial chemoprophylaxis and vector control; to develop a nutrition programme and a nutrition education programme (with nutritional rehabilitation centres for malnourished children); to extend basic sanitary measures (with initiation of the sanitation programme for 400 health units with the cooperation of UNDP and WHO); to set up mobile health teams attached to fixed centres; and to intensify staff training.

Health planning

By law No. 77–002 of 24 December 1977, planned development was adopted as the road to socialism. Health planning is an integral part of long-term socioeconomic development planning, with, in the first stage (1978–1984), the setting up of the structural and material bases for the development of socialism and in particular the necessary legislation and basic health machinery; a second phase of consolidation (1985–1992) of the socialist economy, involving the expansion of the social and cultural machinery; and a third for expansion and acceleration in several economic and social sectors and in particular the introduction of free medical care (1993–2000).

The plan for 1978–1980 will constitute the first medium-term plan: in order to attain the desired ratio of one doctor to 5000 inhabitants by the year 2000, 3320 doctors will be needed, an average of 110 doctors having to be trained

each year. Their training will be adapted to local conditions, with use of traditional medicines, preventive medicine and health education. As far as other health personnel is concerned, the needs to be met between 1978 and 1980 are as follows: 50 dentists, 50 pharmacists, 300 midwives, 500 nurses, and 1500 health assistants for the primary health care centres; 3000 additional hospital beds will be needed by 1980, as well as 50 new pharmacies and 700 drug supply units.

Medical and public health research

Scientific and technical research is carried out under the auspices of the Ministry for Higher Education and Scientific Research. This Ministry was created in 1976. In particular, the bodies entrusted with research in the field of traditional medicine and pharmacopoeias will formulate programmes of fundamental and applied research. There will be gradual institutionalization of traditional medicine and pharmacopoeias by the year 1980.

One manufacturing unit will be set up in each region for the production of medicaments in current use. Local resources in medicinal plants will be used to the fullest extent for such production.

The improvement of the methods used for gathering statistical data will provide a firmer basis for research.

Health budget

Public expenditure on health services in the period 1973–1977 was as follows (in millions of Malagasy francs):

	1973	1974	1975	1976	1977
Gross national product (GNP)	297 600	372 900	398 300	420 000	425 200*
State budget:					
Running costs	43 420	45 650	50 995	62 362	68 117
Investments	17 659	20 992	15 585	24 697	29 132
Total	61 079	66 642	66 580	87 059	97 249
Public expenditure on health:					
Running costs	4 922	5 115	6 038	7 490	7 872
Investments	334	654	390	470	672
Total	5 256	5 619	6 428	7 960	8 544
Share of State budget allotted to health services:					
Running costs	11.34%	11.20%	11.84%	12.01%	11.56%
Investments	1.89%	3.12%	2.50%	1.90%	2.31%
Total	8.67%	8.66%	9.65%	9.14%	8.79%
Health expenditure as a proportion of GNP	1.77%	1.55%	1.61%	1.90%	2.01%

*Provisional estimate

27

Evaluation of progress made between 1973 and 1977

It is difficult to make a quantified evaluation because of the radical changes that occurred in 1976 both in the political and administrative structures (decentralization) and in health policy. However, since 1976 the following steps have been taken in the promotion of public health: the adoption of primary health care as a general policy by the Ministry of Health; the organization of a body of health aides (under Decree No. 76–346 of 9 October 1976), the setting up of 33 centres for their training (under Decree No. 76–343 of 9 October 1976), and their recruitment and actual training; country health programming centred on communicable diseases control, maternal and child health, nutrition and health education; restructuring of the Ministry of Health through the reorganization of its services, and with decentralization; and creation of health brigades for the various decentralized units as a very important element in health programmes.

Outlook

Madagascar wishes to rely henceforth solely on its own resources and to cover its own needs in so far as the resources allow. This would imply the development in the next 10 years of local medicine that is efficient, cheap and suited to the circumstances. Thus, there will have to be a reduction in the sometimes superfluous drug imports, and promotion of national research. The fullest possible utilization of the country's resources in medicinal plants should also be fostered. This implies not only a reorganization of basic and in-service training but also the destruction of old structures and a profound change in attitudes so as to ensure that the whole population has equal access to health care. The health system is still unduly centred on therapeutic medicine and the emphasis should be shifted towards preventive medicine, with vaccination campaigns and sanitation schemes, through an intensive health and nutrition education campaign.

In order to make the best possible use of available hospital space, the facilities of public dispensaries, polyclinics and other peripheral health centres (including primary health care centres) should be exploited.

Public and private undertakings, as well as the decentralized public entities, will take an effective share of the expenditure on medicosanitary infrastructures so that progress can be made towards a system of freely available health services by means of a scheme of the social security type, which should also take care of the cost of supporting patients during the period of incapacity for work.

MALAWI

Major health and health-related problems

The following are of major public health importance in Malawi: malaria; schistosomiasis; diseases of childhood and infancy, including measles; gastroenteritis, respiratory infections and eye diseases; tuberculosis; leprosy; diarrhoeal diseases, including cholera; and malnutrition.

Although the real growth of the economy since independence has averaged about 7% per annum, and the standard of living has improved considerably, Malawi is still considered a relatively poor country.

Action taken

Health policy

The main aspects of the national health development policy are:

(1) the development of a comprehensive health care delivery scheme to cover the total population, through the establishment of the basic health services network;

(2) the prevention and control of communicable diseases through the establishment of an epidemiological surveillance system, the expanded programme of immunization, and

early case-finding and treatment; and (3) the training of personnel at all levels.

Health legislation

The currently valid health legislation consists of the Public Health Act 1948, the Mental Treatment Act 1962, the Dangerous Drugs Act 1956, the Pharmacy and Prisons Act 1942, the Medical Practitioners and Dentists Registration Act 1946, and the Nurses and Midwives Act 1968. According to the Government's request, a WHO consultant assisted in reviewing some of the existing health legislation in 1974 and 1975, and the Ministry of Health has taken steps to implement some of the recommendations made.

Health planning and programming

In 1971, at the request of the Government, a WHO team prepared a national health plan for the years 1973–1988. It included the development of basic health services and training programmes for all levels of staff. In addition, as a part of the plan, a "miniplan" was designed to improve child health services during the first five-year period (1973–1978), when the basic health services network had not yet been established. It has been realized during the implementation of the plan that it should be broken down into programmes and projects, with objectives and targets. A country health programming exercise is therefore being planned.

Organization of health services

One of the most significant achievements has been the eradication of smallpox. The disease had been endemic; 61 cases with 7 deaths were officially notified in 1968, and 65 cases with 4 deaths in 1969. Epidemiologists' reports, based on pockmark surveys, indicate that there were quite a few cases between 1969 and 1971. Maintenance vaccination and surveillance activities have been carried out during the past several years, and in March 1978 an international commission certified eradication.

For the prevention and control of common diseases among children under five, clinics have been established throughout the country. In 1977 there were 841 such clinics, both stationary and mobile, providing immunization, malaria cnemoprophylaxis, health education, nutrition services and various other forms of primary health care. Diarrhoeal diseases are quite common. Cholera has become a constant health problem since it was first introduced into Malawi in September 1973, and every effort is being made to control it. The Government has given continuous support to the control of chronic diseases such as leprosy, tuberculosis and schistosomiasis; during 1976, 269 446 children received BCG vaccination and 4453 were under treatment.

Some 70% of urban dwellers and 30% of the rural population had access to a water supply service in 1977. Remarkable progress has been made within the past few years in the provision of rural water supplies, particularly piped systems and protected shallow wells built on self-help schemes.

The training of health personnel at all levels has received higher priority. While certain types of professionals, such as physicians and engineers, are still trained abroad, there is now a wide range of training programmes in Malawi— for example, for registered and enrolled nurses, clinical officers, and medical assistants. The following training institutions were in existence in Malawi in 1977: 1 for registered nurse/midwives, 12 for enrolled nurse/midwives, 1 for clinical officers, 2 for medical assistants, 1 for health inspectors, 2 for laboratory assistants, 1 for health assistants, 1 for pharmacy assistants, and 1 for veterinary assistants.

Health resources

Health establishments. The health services are provided mainly by the Government and religious missions, which together make available over 9000 beds. Each district has a hospital which is the nucleus of the health services at the district level; central and general hospitals provide referral services. In 1977 there were 2 central hospitals, 1 general hospital, 21 district hospitals, 31 primary health centres, 385 health subcentres, 41 health posts, 5 leprosy hospitals, 1 mental hospital, and 8 urban health centres.

Health manpower. As the training programmes have been accelerated for the last ten years, there has been a steady increase in trained staff, particularly intermediate and auxiliary personnel, as follows:

	1965	1976
Physicians	84	106
Clinical officers/Medical assistants .	420	529
Dentists	3	11
Dental technicians	—	3
Dental assistants	—	28
Pharmacists	5	14
Pharmacy assistants	—	28
Veterinarians	—	25
Veterinary assistants	—	300
Registered nurse/midwives	1	547
Registered nurses	20	423
Enrolled nurses	16	1396
Enrolled midwives	112	1550
Laboratory technicians	2	22
Laboratory assistants	—	76
Radiographers	0	10
X-ray assistants	3	6
Health educators	0	2
Health inspectors	4	49
Health assistants	102	154
Nutritionists	—	1
Orthopaedic technicians	—	1
Occupational therapists	—	1
Health statistics technicians	—	5
Other auxiliaries	—	1159

Health expenditure. Government expenditure on health has steadily increased since independence, and the proportion of the total budget devoted to health has varied between 6.6% and 9.9%; the per capita government expenditure on health was slightly over 1.0 kwacha in 1977. More than 85% of the health budget is absorbed by the curative services.

Appraisal of progress and prospects

Development of comprehensive health care delivery system

Despite the strenuous efforts made to expand health services throughout the country and the establishment of a large number of hospitals, primary health centres, subcentres and under-five clinics, there are still many areas which are not covered. The Government therefore plans to continue with the development of a comprehensive health care delivery system, especially at the basic level, using the primary health care approach to meet the health needs of the rural communities.

Disease control and prevention

Whilst smallpox has been eradicated, there are still many diseases that need to be controlled. Higher priority must be given to the expanded programme of immunization against various communicable diseases of childhood, and to diseases such as malaria, schistosomiasis, tuberculosis, leprosy, diarrhoeal diseases and eye infections.

Health manpower development

The number of training institutions for health personnel has increased, and consequently larger numbers and more categories of health workers have been trained. Efforts will be intensified to expand and improve the training activities.

Improvement of environmental health

The situation regarding water supplies and general environmental sanitation has improved remarkably within the past few years. It is expected that by 1990 the whole urban and rural population will be provided with water supply services. Efforts will also be made to build more latrine facilities for the rural population and sewerage systems in urban areas.

MAURITIUS

Population and other statistics

At the last census, taken at the end of June 1972, the population of the island of Mauritius was 826 199. Mid-year estimates of the population and certain vital statistics for the years 1973 to 1977 are given on facing page.

Major health and health-related problems

Of the 6966 deaths registered in 1977, 2186 (31.4%) were due to diseases of the circulatory system, the main cause of death in Mauritius. In second place came diseases of the respiratory system, responsible for 897 deaths (12.9%) and

	1973	1974	1975	1976	1977
Mid-year population . .	834 781	845 755	856 516	867 885	881 761
Number of live births .	18 974	22 938	21 492	22 250	22 730
Birth rate (per 1000 population)	22.7	27.1	25.1	25.6	25.8
Number of deaths . . .	6 525	6 221	6 967	6 815	6 966
Death rate (per 1000 population)	7.8	7.4	8.1	7.9	7.9
Natural increase (%) . .	1.49	1.98	1.70	1.78	1.79
Number of infant deaths	1 201	1 045	1 046	900	1 023
Infant mortality rate (per 1000 live births)	63.3	45.6	48.6	40.4	45.0
Number of stillbirths . .	678	854	896	784	712
Stillbirth rate (per 1000 total births) . . .	34.5	35.9	41.7	35.2	31.3
Number of perinatal deaths*	1 111	1 272	1 335	1 199	1 162
Perinatal mortality rate (per 1000 total births)*	58.6	55.5	62.1	53.9	51.1
Number of deaths, 1–4 years	589	388	308	258	244
Death rate, 1–4 years (per 1000 population at risk)	7.5	5.1	4.1	3.3	3.1
Number of maternal deaths	29	31	24	25	38
Maternal mortality rate (per 1000 total births)	1.5	1.3	1.1	1.1	1.7

* Perinatal deaths include stillbirths and early neonatal deaths, i.e., deaths within the first week of life.

N.B. The above figures relate to the island of Mauritius. The estimated mid-year population of the State of Mauritius was 860 498 in 1973 and 909 169 in 1977.

in third place infective and parasitic diseases responsible for 496 deaths (7.1%), of which 382 were due to enteritis and other diarrhoeal diseases. It should be noted that there was a sharp decrease in the number of deaths due to infective and parasitic diseases over the period 1973 to 1977; in 1973 these had been responsible for 995 deaths (i.e., 15.2%). The number of deaths due to neoplasms fluctuated between 374 and 380 over the period 1973 to 1977. Other important causes of death for the year 1977 were accidents, poisonings and violence, with 431 deaths (6.2%), endocrine, nutritional and metabolic diseases with 368 deaths (5.3%), and certain causes of perinatal mortality, with 361 deaths (5.2%).

With regard to communicable diseases, the situation generally improved over the period 1973–1977. The number of cases of tuberculosis notified dropped steadily from 285 in 1973 to 191 in 1977. The downward trend in the number of cases of typhoid fever was halted in 1975 when there was an increase following the cyclone "Gervaise"; 17 cases were notified in

1977. Malaria, unlike typhoid fever, had not returned to normal after the effects of the cyclone by 1977, when the number of cases notified was 86 (64 indigenous), whereas in 1973 it had been only 13 (none indigenous). No case of poliomyelitis has been notified over the last decade, and only one case of diphtheria was notified in 1977. Although tetanus and pertussis are not notifiable in Mauritius, the available evidence suggests that, with regard to these two diseases also, vaccination programmes have been paying dividends. As to sexually transmitted diseases, the figures obtained for 1977 from the Social Hygiene Clinic set up in 1973 in Port Louis showed for the first time a decrease over the preceding year in the number of cases of gonorrhoea treated, and the number of cases of syphilis treated was the lowest since the opening of the clinic.

In the absence of specific legislation, the rapid expansion of industrialization during the 1970s presented potential health hazards in the form of environmental pollution and occupational diseases. Industrialization also brought in its wake several problems such as overcrowding in certain regions, and social diseases.

Piped water is available indoors to 27% of the population and to another 56% at less than 100 metres from their houses. However, the water distribution mains, which were laid in the 1880s, have undergone severe stress with the heavy road traffic and developed leakages which accounted for a loss of about 50% of water supplies from the system.

The sharp rise in the rate of natural increase in the population to about 2.9% yearly in the 1950s and early 1960s resulted in considerable strain on the country's social infrastructure despite the fact that the per capita gross national product increased from 1993 rupees in 1973 to 4735 rupees in 1977.

Health policy and planning

In its plans for the social and economic development of the country for the years 1971–1975 and 1975–1980, the Government laid down its health policy and strategy, which may be summarized as follows:

(1) implementation of a plan of action for a national family planning programme integrated within the maternal and child health services so as to bring down the gross reproduction rate to 1.12 by 1982–1987;

(2) development of the basic health services

through a network of health centres to provide the population with the following integrated services: maternal and child health, family planning, institutional midwifery, immunization, control of communicable diseases, nutrition and health education, environmental and occupational health, school health, dental health and general curative services. The health centre will also be responsible for primary health care delivery at the more peripheral level;

(3) improvement of the output of the trained health manpower required for development by expanding the training facilities; and

(4) consolidation and improvement of the preventive health services and hospital services through conversions and extensions and the provision of additional facilities.

Organization of health services

The Ministry of Health is responsible to the Central Government for the planning and implementation of measures to provide comprehensive free health services to the whole population except to those who are able and willing to pay.

The services comprise three levels of care: (1) domiciliary care, through home nursing as well as domiciliary midwifery; these services, however, are not available everywhere because of administrative constraints; (2) basic health care, through a network of dispensaries, family planning, maternal and child health clinics, dental clinics and health offices; (3) hospital care, through district, regional and specialized hospitals.

Health legislation

The health legislation, which needs to be consolidated and updated to face new situations, has been revised in areas where the need is most pressing.

Health manpower

The following table gives the situation as regards qualified health manpower as at 31 December 1977:

	Number			Population per health worker
	Public sector	Private sector	Total	
Doctors	280	96	376	2 418
Dentists	18	27	45	20 204
Pharmacists	8	48	56	16 235
Nurses/assistant nurses	1 249	90	1 339	679
Nurse midwives/ midwives	338	30	368	2 471

No training facilities are locally available for the training of doctors, dentists, occupational therapists and physiotherapists. Courses for the training of nurses, assistant nurses, midwives, radiographers and dispensers are run by the Ministry of Health, and courses in sanitary sciences, public health and works engineering, meat and other food and medical laboratory technology are available at the University of Mauritius.

Health establishments and hospital beds

In 1977 the State of Mauritius provided health care and services through the following establishments:

Public sector

	Number	Beds
District hospitals	3	321
Regional hospitals	4	1 430
Specialized hospitals	5	1 158
Medical institutions with beds	2	39
Dispensaries	48	—
Mobile dispensaries	5	—
Maternal and child health clinics	70*	—
Family planning clinics	85	—
Family planning supply centres	41	—
Mobile antenatal and family planning clinics	1	—
Dental clinics	9	—
Mobile dental clinics	2	—
Health offices	13	—

Private sector

	Number	Beds
Private clinics	6	176
Private non-profit establishments with beds	18	207
Pharmacies	48	—
Total number of beds		3 331

* Included in family planning clinics

The bed/population ratio was one to 272.

Production and sale of pharmaceuticals

There is only one pharmaceutical manufacturing firm which produces from imported ingredients some 100 items in the form of tablets, capsules, injectables, etc.—some 10% of the drug requirements. The total value of drugs imported as well as those manufactured locally amounted to over 40 million rupees in 1977.

Health expenditure

The recurrent expenditure of the Ministry of Health during the financial year 1976/77 was 116 million rupees (i.e. 9.2% of the national recurrent expenditure), and the capital health expenditure was 3 million rupees. The per capita expenditure on health was 130 rupees.

Achievements

A national family planning and maternal and child health programme was started in December 1972, with assistance from UNFPA, UNICEF and WHO. Most of the activities of the Family Planning Association have been integrated within the maternal and child health services of the Ministry of Health and the number of service points has been considerably

increased to meet the needs of the underserved population groups. Basic as well as primary health care has been widened through an increase in the number of centres. Thus, between 1973 and 1977 the number of maternal and child health clinics was increased from 53 to 70, the number of family planning centres from 91 to 127, and the number of dispensaries from 44 to 48.

With improved facilities and a substantial increase in health personnel, hospital waiting lists for operations and other interventions have been significantly shortened.

With regard to environmental health, good progress has been achieved in converting the conservancy system and the pit latrines into a water carriage system and water seal pit latrines.

More than 80% of schoolchildren and infants have been immunized against tuberculosis, diphtheria, tetanus, pertussis, poliomyelitis and smallpox.

The infant mortality rate, which averaged 62.4 per 1000 during the years 1968–1972, decreased to 48.6 per 1000 in the years 1973–1977, and the gross reproduction rate, which averaged 1.87 for the years 1968–1972, was brought down to 1.56 in 1973–1977 and was 1.49 in 1977. Life expectancy at birth, which was 58.7 years for males and 61.9 years for females during the period 1961–1963, increased to 60.7 years and 65.3 years respectively in the years 1971–1973.

SENEGAL

Major health and health-related problems

When the Fifth Plan for Economic and Social Development (1977–1981) was drawn up, the salient features of the health situation were as follows: in the face of real needs aggravated by the drought and increasing demands from society, the hospital capacity is low, the health personnel are poorly distributed and managed, the resources of the outlying health units are inadequate, and the facilities for communication and transfer of patients are still limited. Infant mortality is still very high, and the risk of epidemics is heightened by inadequate sanitation, both in the towns and in the villages; education of the public urging them to mobilize their own efforts

in the common struggle for health is still very rudimentary.

The following priorities have been laid down:
(1) to increase the management capacity of the health service by central restructuring so as to invigorate the planning process and ensure programming and supervision of health activities at all levels;
(2) to ensure the proper maintenance of the existing facilities;
(3) to develop the health sector by providing full coverage for 200 000 more inhabitants each year in accordance with the standards laid down for the extension of services, and primary health care;
(4) to develop human resources by adapting

training to meet better the needs of the country;

(5) to supplement this programme by individual campaigns (7 specific and well-defined projects).

Action taken

Health policy

Health policy focuses on the improvement of the health conditions of the worst-affected populations (in remote areas) or the least well-protected populations (in rural areas in general); the creation of suitable conditions for the rapid development of preventive and educational activities; and the intensification of research in priority areas (such as determination of optimum therapeutic procedures in inexpensive community medicine; availability of foodstuffs; factors responsible for the onset of killer diseases and forms of prophylaxis that can influence these factors).

Health legislation

Existing health legislation is being adapted to the development of the programme, and new legislation is being introduced where necessary. In particular water and environment codes are being prepared.

Health planning and programming

Efforts are being made to reinforce the planning process to make it continuous, and to standardize health programming; preparations were made for a country health programming exercise to be carried out in 1978. Four doctors received training in planning and 21 nurses and midwives were trained in planning and management at the centre for advanced nursing education.

Organization of health services

A programme of nutritional and health protection has been set up as part of a regional campaign for the Sahel countries under the auspices of the Permanent Inter-State Committee on Drought Control in the Sahel.

A number of changes are being made in the structure of the Ministry of Health; in particular, a parasite control service and a section for the control of sexually transmitted diseases and endemic treponematoses are being established.

The Fifth Plan specified that a primary health-care project should be set up in Sine Saloum Province (one of the country's eight provinces which contains 19.82% of the population and 12.17% of the land area). This was launched in September 1976 in a test area to study the various aspects of the programme, i.e., programming, implementation (including study of resources), evaluation and follow-up, and especially the possible nationwide application of the effective activities, whereby the entire project would be integrated into general development activities within the framework provided by the administrative reform.

While the "central restructuring" is still at the design stage, more dynamic and effective provincial structures have been introduced in the Sine Saloum test area, where a "Provincial think tank" is responsible for the programming and implementation of health activities. The following measures have been taken:

— The head of the "health post" (the basic health unit serving a "rural community") manages the health programme of the rural community.

— An extensive campaign is in progress to deal with the breakdown in supplies of medicinal preparations. The aim is to establish a standard stock of essential drugs and to decentralize procurement, putting it on a provincial and *département* basis. This is all the more necessary because of the "health huts" with their "village pharmacy"—in practice a box of basic drugs.

— The measles vaccination campaign covers about 80% of the susceptible population in the *département* of Cossas; the rural communities are contributing 820 000 CFA francs out of the total expenditure of 850 000 CFA francs for this project. It will serve as a model for extension of the single-vaccine campaign to the entire province in 1977 and 1978; the activities will subsequently be broadened to form an expanded programme of immunization.

— The setting-up of 74 rural maternity units, requested and constructed by the rural communities, will provide increased facilities for maternal and child health and for the improvement of the programme of nutritional and health protection.

— An integrated programme for the control of diarrhoeal diseases has been prepared.

— A special effort has been made with regard

to nosological statistics; a system which uses a daily collation table enables the head of each health post to send in his report on the last working day of the month. Use of this system is being extended.

Biomedical and health services research

Apart from the research being carried out by the University on traditional medicine and mental health, studies are being conducted in the Sine Saloum test area to find ways of improving the collection of statistics, overcoming shortages in stocks of medicinal products, and integrating the activities more fully by working together with the local communities.

Education and training of health manpower

Special attention is being given to the education and training of health manpower and, in particular, to the following aspects: the methodology of teaching, so as to improve the results of training; the planning and management capacity of staff at all levels; the extension of practical training courses to rural areas; and the training of specialist sanitation staff.

A school for dental auxiliaries is being established, and the school for public health technicians is being reorganized.

During the period under review three seminars on teaching methodology have been held in Dakar, and courses have been arranged at the centre for advanced nursing education, the Faculty of Medicine, the School of Midwifery, and the local training centres for heads of health posts in the provinces of Sine Saloum (61) and Cap Vert (32).

Between 1973 and 1975 the following personnel were trained: 32 doctors; 68 State-registered midwives; 145 State-registered nurses; 125 health technicians; 30 public health technicians; 21 trainees from the centre for advanced nursing education; 9 dentists; 23 dental auxiliaries; 70 community health agents for the maternity units and 32 for the health huts, all trained locally in the Sine Saloum test area.

Health resources

Health establishments

In 1976 there were 11 hospitals, 34 medical centres, 439 health posts, 74 maternity units, 60 maternal and child health centres, 7 sectors of the Major Endemic Diseases Service and 11 leprosaria, in both the public and private sectors. The mean bed/population ratio was one to 767; the individual ratios were one to 1321 for the hospitals, one to 2888 for the maternity units, and one to 4984 for other establishments. Under the administrative reform 74 rural maternity units (with 12 beds each) and 62 "health huts" (each with a box of essential drugs) are being constructed in the Sine Saloum test area through community efforts. Such units also exist in other provinces.

Health manpower

In 1976 there were 311 doctors (73 in the private sector and 163 foreigners, including 43 in the private sector), i.e., one doctor for 16 351 inhabitants; 90 pharmacists (67 in the private sector); 37 dentists (22 in the private sector); 380 midwives (21 in the private sector), i.e., one midwife for every 3295 women between the ages of 15 and 49; 2357 nurses (115 in the private sector); 228 public health technicians; 213 social workers; 1635 other technical personnel.

Health expenditure

In the financial year 1976/77 the health budget represented 7.32% of the total national budget; 62.5% of the health budget was spent on personnel, 34.5% on equipment and supplies (including 9.6% for drugs), and 3.0% on transfers of patients. For an estimated population of 5 114 000 inhabitants, this represented an annual expenditure of 1132 CFA francs per inhabitant. Although the proportion of the national budget devoted to health has been falling steadily since the end of the Third Plan (it was 9% in 1973), the annual expenditure per inhabitant has risen from 842.2 CFA francs to 1132 CFA francs. In addition, direct rebates amounting to 4000 million CFA francs have been made to communities (half for subsidized housing and half for the rural communities which have set aside 8% of this amount for health), and rural communities have participated in primary health care where such care is organized (in particular in the Sine Saloum province where each individual pays 50 CFA francs for the first consultation and 10 CFA francs for each subsequent consultation).

Appraisal of progress made between 1973 and 1977

Evaluation of the Fourth Plan (1973–1977) showed that health brought up the rear of the social sector, which itself was lagging behind the other development sectors. The health programming exercise carried out in 1978 should improve the preparation of health activities.

Outlook

The broad outline of the proposed goals for the next two years is as follows:

(1) updating of the health profiles of the provinces, on the basis of the health profiles of the *départements* in preparation for the country health programming exercise;

(2) as compared with 1977, a 50% increase in the number of women provided with assistance in childbirth, and a 25% increase in the number of consultations; and the development of a solution to the problem of shortages in drug supplies;

(3) implementation of an expanded programme of immunization, after solving the problem of the cold chain; the public will contribute financially to the campaign;

(4) evaluation of the activities of the centres for the programme of nutritional and health protection, so as to ensure more integrated participation in the "health-nutrition-water" programme of the Sahel countries;

(5) programming of health education activities to ensure the active cooperation of the public, in particular by making optimum use of local statistics and the communications support programme;

(6) completion of an inventory of existing wells and latrines in localities where there is a health unit, so as to draw up a more detailed plan of work for sanitation activities in 1979;

(7) evaluation of the programme for the training of community health agents, with reference to the activities of those already employed in the maternity units and health huts, with a view to improving that training;

(8) completion of a quantitative study to determine the real contribution of the communities to primary health care;

(9) as local activities are developed, the more widespread application of those that would be useful for the rest of the health services, after costing by the "Provincial think tank", supported where necessary by the central services.

UGANDA

Major health and health-related problems

During the three-year action programme which started in 1976 attempts are being made to improve health facilities and to alleviate the following problems:

— the high incidence of malnutrition, maternal and child morbidity and mortality rates due to preventable causes, specific diseases transmitted by vectors and animals (zoonoses), water shortage and pollution, unsatisfactory housing, and the problems of mentally sick and retarded persons;

— organizational and managerial problems like the lack of planning facilities within the Ministry of Health, the lack of national comprehensive laboratory services, insufficient training facilities, and inadequate coordination between the different ministries directly or indirectly concerned with public health;

— lack of manpower, transport, equipment, and maintenance facilities, and inadequate distribution.

Action taken

Health policy

Following the expiry in 1976 of the health policy contained in the third five-year development plan, a new three-year action programme is now in force. It contains proposals for economic and social development over the present three-year period, during which the Government will seek to reduce further the prevalence of diseases, improve the people's living conditions, extend health facilities to the rural areas, and encourage greater community participation in health action.

Health legislation

A venereal diseases decree was brought into force in September 1977, and food laws and regulations have been drafted.

Health planning and programming

Programme priorities in the health field were established following a workshop on country health programming held in April/May 1976. Arrangements are being made for the establishment of a health planning unit within the Ministry of Health.

Organization of health services

Serving under the Minister of Health is a Permanent Secretary who is also the Director of Medical Services, responsible for the supervision of health services and coordination with other ministries, agencies and institutions working in related fields. Together with the Deputy Director of Medical Services and the three Assistant Directors of Medical Services (for medical care, public health, and training, respectively) he is also responsible for the technical aspects of the administration of the health services.

The Assistant Director of Medical Services responsible for public health is assisted by two senior medical officers (responsible for disease control and maternal and child health), a public health veterinarian, a public health engineer, a health education supervisor, a chief health inspector and a biostatistician. The Chief Nursing Officer and her Deputy are responsible for the nursing services at the central level.

With WHO assistance, three new technical divisions have been established within the Ministry of Health, dealing with health laboratories, veterinary public health, and public health engineering.

Biomedical and health services research

The following five institutions are engaged in biomedical and health services research: the Uganda Virus Research Institute, in Entebbe; the Uganda Trypanosomiasis Research Organization, in Tororo; the Uganda Cancer Institute, in Kampala; the International Cancer Project of the International Agency for Research on Cancer in Arua; the Natural Chemotherapeutics Research Laboratory, in Kampala (traditional medicine).

Education and training of health manpower

About 100 Ugandan doctors graduate annually from the Makerere University Medical School, which also has facilities for postgraduate training in medicine, surgery, paediatrics, gynaecology and obstetrics, ophthalmology and pathology.

The Institute of Public Health, Makerere University, produces about 10 D.P.H. graduates annually. The approximate annual numbers of graduates from other training institutions are as follows: from the Institute of Public Health, Makerere University, 10; the Faculty of Veterinary Medicine, Makerere, 30; the Faculty of Medicine Technology, Makerere, 20; schools of Medical Assistants, 60; the School of Hygiene, 80; the Health Visitors' School, 20; the Medical Laboratory School, 60; the Public Health Dental Assistants' School, 20; nursing and midwifery schools, 500; the Assistant Health Visitors' School, 60.

Health resources

Health establishments

Category	Number	Number of beds
General hospitals	7	3 056
Rural hospitals	64	7 876
Psychiatric hospitals	1	957
Leprosaria	6	2 000
Health centres and dispensaries	350	6 273

During 1974 the total numbers of inpatients and outpatients treated at the various medical units were 742 960 and 6 378 420 respectively.

Health manpower

In 1975 there were 426 doctors, of whom 296 were employed by the Government. The doctor/population ratio was one to 27 000. Other health personnel included 558 medical assistants, 11 dental surgeons, 34 public health dental assistants, 14 pharmacists, 106 pharmaceutical assistants, 420 veterinarians, 387 professional midwives, 1592 enrolled midwives, 755 registered nurses, 1677 enrolled nurses, 18 physiotherapists, 63 laboratory technicians, 80 X-ray technicians, 170 health inspectors, 353 health assistants, 14 health educators, and 2 health statisticians.

Health expenditure

The budget for 1977/78 is estimated to amount to 4 024.4 million Uganda shillings, of which 268 million (or 6.6%) is allocated to the health sector. The development budget for the same fiscal year is estimated at 2 085.4 million shillings, of which 85.3 million (or 4.0%) is allocated to the health sector.

Appraisal of progress made between 1973 and 1977

The economy was placed in the hands of the Ugandans in 1972, and the five-year period under review has been mainly a transitional phase allocated to consolidating and strengthening the national economy and self-reliance. The three-year action programme now in force aims to rehabilitate the key sectors of the economy by eliminating the structural constraints that have adversely affected the production and distribution of goods and services, to lay a sound foundation for sustained and diversified future economic and social development.

Health services have been sustained during the transitional period largely thanks to technical assistance from the United Nations and other bilateral and multilateral sources. Despite difficulties, the BCG vaccination programme, which ended in December 1973, provided protection for 3.5 million persons below 15 years of age. The country has remained free of all quarantinable diseases, despite the threat of cholera from neighbouring countries.

Outlook

With the current upward economic trend it is envisaged that the health programmes formulated under the three-year action programme will run smoothly.

The main approaches will be through primary health care, the expanded programme of immunization, the training of personnel at all levels, and the improvement of environmental sanitation.

Five primary health care areas have been designated for feasibility studies to determine the best methods applicable to the local situation; all 38 districts of Uganda will have primary health care demonstration areas by 1983.

The Government plans to develop integrated disease control activities, including the strengthening of the central epidemiological and statistical units and the health laboratory and veterinary public health services. Top priority is to be given to the expanded programme of immunization, which is to be implemented with the assistance of WHO, UNICEF and the Government of Austria, and will cover the whole country by 1983.

With regard to health manpower development, efforts will continue not only to increase the number of personnel trained, but also to raise the standard of competence. Particular attention will be given to strengthening the teaching force, modifying curricula to bring them more into line with local conditions, and improving the contents of the various courses.

Poor sanitation and the lack of adequate and safe water supplies in rural areas are major contributory factors to the morbidity and mortality rates. With UNICEF and WHO assistance a programme for the improvement and protection of wells and springs on a country-wide basis is in hand, and a UNICEF-assisted project to provide 16 rural pipe-borne water supply schemes is also under way.

UNITED REPUBLIC OF CAMEROON

Population

The estimated population in the period under review was as follows: 1973, 6.3 million; 1974, 6.5 million; 1975, 7.2 million; 1976, 7.5 million. In 1977 a national census gave the population as 7 663 246.

The population structure by age group was as follows: 0–1 year, 3.5%; 1–4 years, 13.5%; 5–14 years, 26.4%; 15–54 years, 48.3%; 55 years and over, 8.3%. The population under 20 years of age numbered 3 782 310, according to field survey figures. The adjusted figures for male and female population were 3 754 990 and 3 908 256 respectively.

Major health problems

Communicable diseases

Trypanosomiasis. Foci of recrudescence are Bafia, Fontem, Wouri Estuary, Campo, Kousseri.

Figures for the Bafia focus are: 1973, 19 cases; 1975, 105 cases; 1976, 243 cases; 1977, 331 cases. Figures for the Fontem focus for the same years are: 256, 283, 359 and 464 respectively, with 325 cases in 1974.

Malaria prevalence is 100%.

Leprosy prevalence is 0.57%; in 1976 there were approximately 35 000 cases, in 1977, 40 000 cases.

Measles prevalence is 4%. In 1973 there were 28 976 cases, with 481 deaths and a case fatality rate of 2.2%; in 1974, 34 750 cases, with 700 deaths and a case fatality rate of 2%; in 1975, 16 311 cases with 495 deaths and a case fatality rate of 3%; and in 1977 (first six months), 9005 cases with 218 deaths.

Venereal diseases. Syphilis and especially gonococcal diseases are a problem; the average prevalence rate is of the order of 1.3%.

Cerebrospinal meningitis. In 1973 there were 1061 cases, with a case fatality rate of 6.9%; in 1974, 483 cases, with a case fatality rate of 7.5%; in 1975, 129 cases, with a case fatality rate of 14.7%; in 1976, 482 cases, with a case fatality rate of 6%; and in 1977, 558 cases, with a case fatality rate of 12.3%.

Measures taken

Health policy

Priority is given to preventive medicine, strengthening of maternal and child health activities, communicable disease control, and expanded programme of immunization; promotion of environmental health; and strengthening of community health education.

Health legislation

Draft laws governing the control of mental diseases and venereal diseases and draft decrees governing the practice of the health professions were elaborated.

Organization of health services

Special measures during the period included strengthening of health care structures in hospitals and rural areas, and implementation of primary health care.

Biomedical and health services research

Current activities include research in progress at the University Centre for Health Sciences, and prospects for participation in the Special Programme for Research and Training in Tropical Diseases are being developed.

Education and training of health manpower

These activities are being developed at the University Centre for Health Sciences at Yaoundé and in the various establishments under the supervision of the Ministry of Health.

Health resources

Health establishments

There are seven central hospitals and provincial referral hospitals, 40 *département* hospitals, 20 *arrondissement* hospitals, 300 health centres and dispensaries, 260 private health units run by religious bodies, and 64 private health units run by non-religious bodies.

Health manpower

Physicians numbered about 400 in 1977; dentists, 17, including three nationals; pharmacists, about 100; fully qualified nurses, about 700; auxiliary nurses, about 1000; various health technicians, about 100; and health auxiliaries, over 1000.

Production and sale of pharmaceuticals

There is no local pharmaceutical industry.

Health expenditure

The health budget—approximately US $4 per capita—was 6.7% of the national budget in the financial year 1972/73, 5% in 1975/76; and 4.9% in 1976/77.

Appraisal of progress made between 1973 and 1977

Communicable disease control

The main advances were the eradication of smallpox, marked regression in endemic leprosy, the promotion of an expanded programme of immunization, and strengthening of nationwide epidemiological surveillance.

Strengthening of health services

Valuable experience was gained with public health demonstration zones, improvement of the health infrastructure was achieved and community health education extended.

Health manpower development

Training of 116 national physicians and six types of health technicians was provided locally.

Promotion of environmental health

Progress included extension of piped drinking-water supplies in the main cities, water supplies for rural areas, and vector control.

Biomedical research

Research proceeded on the immunology of filariasis, and on parasitology. There was also participation in the Special Programme for Research and Training in Tropical Diseases.

Outlook

The main health objectives for the next 10 years are: (1) to develop the existing health infrastructure; (2) to intensify the control of the major endemic diseases and other communicable diseases, and in particular to improve and strengthen epidemiological surveillance and to promote an expanded programme of immunization; (3) to promote environmental health and the provision of drinking-water for rural communities; (4) to promote maternal and child health; (5) to protect the mental health of the community and the dental health of young people; (6) to promote the rehabilitation of the disabled; (7) to provide training in public health for all types of health personnel; and (8) to reduce regional inequalities and disparities.

UNITED REPUBLIC OF TANZANIA

(excluding Zanzibar and Pemba)

The United Republic of Tanzania, with a total area of 939 062 km² (including 53 483 km² of water), is located south of the Equator and is bordered by the Indian Ocean to the east, Kenya and Uganda to the north, Rwanda, Burundi and Zaire to the west, and Zambia, Malawi and Mozambique to the south. The climate is tropical but varies from hot and humid along the coastal belt and lowlands to moderate and cold in the mountainous belts. It is predominantly an agricultural country; the main exports are coffee, cotton, sisal, minerals, cashew nuts, tobacco and tea. It is categorized as one of the 25 poorest countries in the world; the per capita income was US $154 in 1976.

Demographic characteristics

The population's pyramidal structure, like that of any other developing country, has a broad base and narrows rapidly after the age of 15. The main characteristics of the population have developed as follows:

	1967	1976*
Crude birth rate (per 1000 population) . .	47.0	46.0
Crude death rate (per 1000 population) .	22.0	17.7
Rate of growth (%)	2.5	2.8
Infant mortality rate (per 1000 live births)	161	152
Life expectancy at birth	35	47
Population under 15 years (%)	44.4	47.4

* Interpolated from 1978 National Demographic Survey.

The large proportion of the child population under 15 years old causes a very high dependency ratio. The child-bearing population constitutes an equally high proportion (20.3%), making the size of the vulnerable group of population very large and creating great demands on the national health services.

Major health and health-related problems

Major causes of morbidity and mortality, as in most developing countries, are the communicable and parasitic diseases, which account for between 30% and 35% of all the diseases diagnosed at hospitals. Most of these diseases, which cause high morbidity and mortality in vulnerable groups, can be prevented by immunization and by environmental and personal hygiene. In all, poverty-linked diseases account for about three-quarters of all deaths. Malaria is the leading cause of hospital attendance and admission (accounting for between 10% and 15% of attendances).

Health policy and action taken

The broad national health policy is derived from the Arusha Declaration of 1967, which is the ideological basis for socioeconomic transformation. The broad objective of the policy was to extend health care facilities to the periphery in order to make services available to all citizens. Through the provision of a chain of dispensaries, rural health centres and district hospitals, the health service was to complement, support and promote the National Villagization Programme (*ujamaa* villages). Government was to assume responsibility for the operational costs of existing facilities and the establishment of new ones in order to provide free medical care to all. Under this policy, due emphasis was to be given to preventive and environmental health (in preference to sophisticated hospital-based care) relying mostly on inexpensive and modestly trained workers. In essence, the Government has as its goal the provision of a rationalized health care system, one that will be sensitive to the needs and aspirations of its population in terms of available resources, appropriate manpower and technology.

Health planning and programming

In 1971 the Biennial Conference of the National Union Party defined the strategies of the National Development Plan within the context of the Arusha Declaration. To this end, health, water and education were to be given national priority and emphasis was to be placed on the rapid development of the rural sector. A long-term plan up to 1980 was formulated. The broad objective of the plan was to set up an all-embracing rural health infrastructure comprising village health posts, rural dispensaries, rural health centres and rural district hospitals which would provide a solid foundation for curative and preventive services to the rural masses who form 90% of the population. The table below shows how targets set for 1980 are being met.

	1972	1977	Target
Rural dispensaries	1 494	2 088	2 200
Rural health centres	100	161	300
Hospitals	123	128	130
Medical officers	494	727	830
Assistant medical officers . . .	140	223	300
Medical assistants	335	930	1 200
Rural medical aides	578	1 393	2 800
Health auxiliaries	265	500	800
Maternal and child health aides	700	1 400	2 500
Nurse/midwives	3 259	5 658	6 000

The strategy and objectives of the third Five-Year Development Plan (1976-1981) are mainly derived from experience in the implementation of the first and second plans, which had sizable health components. The overall objective of the health component is to continue to implement former Party resolutions providing for basic health services to the rural areas. It will also re-emphasize the importance of community preventive health services.

The plan has four major sub-objectives:

(1) expansion and improvement of the rural health infrastructures, namely; village health posts, rural dispensaries and rural health centres, in order to cover more of the rural population and to improve the functional performance of existing facilities;
(2) limited expansion of the hospital services to cater for the growth of the population in order to attain the target of one hospital bed per 1000 population by 1980; improvement of the existing hospital facilities through the provision of modern diagnostic equipment and adequate and appropriately trained staff;
(3) more emphasis on prevention of communicable diseases;
(4) appropriate training of adequate rural health cadres for expanded rural health infrastructure.

Rural health services

The target is 2200 rural dispensaries (one per 6000 rural population) and 300 rural health centres (one per 50 000 rural population) by

1980, excluding population already served by other rural health facilities. More emphasis will be placed on community health services, especially the expanded immunization programme; maternal and child health services, including child-spacing programmes; outpatient services—with a view to screening patients for referral to hospitals; follow-up treatment of the patients referred from higher levels; environmental health activities, especially construction of pit latrines.

Hospital services

The target is to have one hospital providing free medical care in every administrative district, and one hospital bed per 1000 population per district, by the year 1980. Existing hospital services will be improved by the provision of X-ray units and modern diagnostic laboratory equipment.

In line with the policy of decentralization of psychiatric care, and in order to treat patients near their homes, regional psychiatric units and rehabilitation villages will be built in Kigoma, Mtwara, Bukoba, Morogoro, Shinyanga and Ruvuma regions by 1980.

Two existing hospitals (one each in the south-east and south-west of the country) will be upgraded to the level of consultant referral and teaching hospitals for those zones where there are at present no consultant services. A new consultant hospital is included in the plan for the new capital, Dodoma, drawn up by the Capital Development Authority.

Regional ophthalmic units will also be established during the plan period.

Preventive services

The main objective of the preventive services is to reduce morbidity and mortality caused by preventable communicable and other diseases. The following programmes will be implemented during this period:

Control of communicable diseases. The Epidemiological Unit will be strengthened in order to facilitate control of communicable diseases, including especially measles, diphtheria, tetanus, pertussis, poliomyelitis, tuberculosis, leprosy, malaria, typhoid, schistosomiasis, trypanosomiasis and cholera. The Unit will continue the maintenance phase of the smallpox eradication programme.

Expanded immunization programme. The target is to cover 90% of the eligible child population by 1980, immunizing them against tuberculosis, measles, poliomyelitis, tetanus, diphtheria, pertussis and smallpox. The existing and projected rural health infrastructure will be the operational base for the programme.

Maternal and child health services. The target is to cover 90% of the eligible population in order to reduce maternal and infant morbidity and mortality.

Environmental health services. The population will be encouraged, through health education, to build permanent houses, and build and use proper pit latrines; the availability of adequate and potable water supply will be assured.

Health training programmes. More emphasis will be placed on the training of rural health cadres in large numbers (the targets set for 1980 are given in the table in the section on "Health planning and programming" above).

A party resolution (Musoma, 1974) calls for all students to work for at least one year prior to their admission to undergraduate studies at the University. Their application must be supported by the local Party branch. In addition, deserving workers are given appropriate opportunities for advancement through career mobility; for example, a rural medical aide can ultimately become a fully fledged doctor, and a nursing assistant can become a fully fledged professional nurse/midwife.

The local Party hierarchy actively participates in the selection of rural cadre candidates in order to ensure their return to their respective villages.

Organization of health services

The Ministry of Health has the overall responsibility for regulating all health activities in the country. The Ministry is headed by a Cabinet-rank Minister, who is assisted by a Junior Minister (Parliamentary Secretary).

The Principal Secretary is the chief administrative executive of the Ministry, which has three functional components: (1) the Finance and Administration Section, which is responsible for the preparation of the Ministry's budget and financial control as well as carrying out all administrative duties, including supervision of the periphery; (2) the Planning Unit, which prepares medium- and long-range health plans and provides programme support through the production and utilization of relevant health information; and (3) the three Health Directorates. The Preventive Services Directorate supervises the implementation of planned preventive activities and organizes and undertakes disease surveys; the Manpower Development Directorate is responsible for reducing the shortage of medical and auxiliary staff by designing and implementing various health training programmes, including curriculum development; the Hospital Services Directorate improves the quality of care in hospitals by issuing proper guidelines and supervising the services.

Since decentralization of the administration in 1972 the Ministry of Health has been responsible for national health training programmes. It is also responsible for the consultant hospitals (with the exception of the Muhimbili Hospital, which was incorporated into a semipublic institution by Act of Parliament in September 1976) and for other special hospitals.

Education and training of health manpower

The strategy adopted for the improvement of health status includes the development of appropriate manpower to contribute *inter alia*, to the reduction of morbidity and mortality, especially those caused by communicable and preventable diseases. To this end, the Ministry has inventorized existing categories of personnel with specific, recognizable job descriptions and has restructured their training in order to relate educational requirement to the job that needs to be done, thus maximizing their effectiveness. The newly trained health personnel will be distributed equitably according to need and priorities of the service.

Health resources

Health establishments

Following the directive from the Party's Biennial Conference in September 1971, plans were made for the expansion of the rural health infrastructure, to be composed of village health posts, rural dispensaries and rural health centres (the progress made since 1972 and the targets for 1980 are shown in the table in the section on "Health planning and programming" above).

Health manpower (see previous section, and the table quoted above).

Financial resources

During 1977 the per capita health recurrent expenditure was 42.00 Tanzanian shillings per annum, constituting less than 3% of the gross domestic product, as follows: direct government expenditure, 34.5 shillings, voluntary agencies 4.5 shillings, semipublic and private sectors, 3.0 shillings. Considering current inflationary trends, this amount appears to be inadequate to meet the current needs of the health services. The constraint has promoted innovative approaches in health services design and implementation. The resulting strategy places great emphasis on the development of the rural health sector, training programmes for the development of complementary health manpower and preventive services. The need for such measures is emphasized by the fact that recurrent health expenditure has more than trebled over the past six years.

The following table shows the government recurrent health budget by type of activity for the financial years 1971/72–1977/78:

	1971/72 shillings (thousands)	%	1974/75 shillings (thousands)	%	1977/78 shillings (thousands)	%	% Change 1971/72– 1977/78
Administration	2 210	1.4	2 631.8	0.9	2 892.5	0.5	30.1
Hospital services	121 964	78.9	181 792.5	60.2	351 223.5*	65.5	188.0
Rural health centres	8 538	5.5	22 416.1	7.4	38.357.9	7.3	349.3
Rural dispensaries	8 300	5.4	35 328.8	11.7	59 690.9	11.1	619.2
Preventive services	5 965	3.9	37 499.7	12.4	47 098.2	8.8	689.6
Training and manpower	4 767	3.1	18 875.3	6.3	27 570.4	5.1	478.4
Medical production and supplies	2 776	1.8	3 338.2	1.1	9 370.7	1.7	237 6
Total	154 520	100.0	301 882.4	100.0	536 204.1	100.0	247.0

* Including 80 million shillings for Muhimbili Medical Centre, 50%. of which was for training of undergraduate doctors, pharmacists and postgraduate doctors. This has a distorting effect on the structure of expenditure.

	1971/72 shillings (thousands)	%	1974/75 shillings (thousands)	%	1977/78 shillings (thousands)	%
Hospital services*	2 280.2	52.0	8 860	12.2	23 454	19.6
Rural health centres and dispensaries	1 447.1	33.0	17 727	24.5	43 160	36.0
Preventive services	87.7	2.0	5 787	8.0	28 109	23.5
Training programmes . . .	570.0	13.0	39 635	54.8	23 999	20.0
Manufacturing and supplies	—	—	360	0.5	1 070	0.9
Total	4 385.0	100	72 369	100	119 792	100

* The falling percentage for this line item reflects the de-escalation of Government involvement in hospital construction.

Government capital health expenditure over the past six years reflects the drive towards the implementation of the rural health, training and preventive programmes.

The table above shows the structure of the capital health expenditure over the same period.

Appraisal of progress made between 1972 and 1977

The country's main objective in the field of health continues to be directed by broad policy guidelines, articulated in the Arusha Declaration of 1967 (the blueprint for national social and economic transformation). Within this context, rapid extension of the health infrastructure to the "grass-roots" level, together with the provision of adequate and appropriate manpower for the services, remains the supreme, specific objective.

The extent to which the country succeeded in meeting these objectives can be illustrated by the increase in the number of rural health centres, from 87 in 1971 to 161 in 1977 (excluding 60 under construction) and of rural dispensaries, from 1436 in 1971 to 2088 in 1977 (excluding 133 still under construction); the fact that nearly 60% of the eligible children were covered by the expanded immunization programme in 1977; and the tremendous increase in the intake capacity of the rural health cadre training centres since 1972, when expansion of training programmes was planned. For example, the intake capacity of the medical assistant training centre increased from 146 in 1972 to 272 in 1977 and the output increased from 48 in 1972 to 160 in 1977, the intake of rural medical aides increased from 146 in 1972 to 542 in 1977 and output increased from 40 in 1972 to 347 in 1977; and the intake of maternal and child health aides increased from 50 in 1972 to 611 in 1977 and output from 50 in 1972 to 440 in 1977.

The impact of these developmental efforts in terms of reduction of mortality as well as increase in life expectancy were to be more or less precisely known after the population census scheduled for August 1978, but the health status of the population as a whole could be said to have improved over the period under review.

Several problems have been encountered in the implementation of the health programmes. There have been considerable delays in the construction programmes. Rural health centres and rural dispensaries have not been properly completed on schedule, and the hardest hit programme is the health auxiliary school programme, which will not be completed as planned; as a result the targets for the production of health auxiliaries will not be met by 1980.

In some cases, developments in health outstripped those in other sectors. For example, adequate supervision of the health services provided at the periphery is greatly impeded by lack of transport and a poor communications network. In other instances, some of the activities of the other sectors are well in advance of those of the health sector. For example, provision of basic environmental infrastructure did not keep pace with the successful villagization programme, with the result that the emergence of focal epidemics was observed.

The situation is gradually being rectified, however, and the Party and the Government have reiterated the importance of keeping the environment clean and the need for building a pit latrine for every household.

The deficiency in the provision of mental health services has been articulated, as has the intention of rectifying this anomaly. A cohesive national mental health programme is being developed within the overall strategy of the development of national health services. WHO's collaboration had been requested for this endeavour.

National authorities are conscious of over-extension of services, and are therefore anxious to make the necessary adjustments to add quality to quantity. To this end it is envisaged that the decentralization policy of the Government will provide appropriate opportunities and incentives for holistic development on all fronts.

Outlook

No quantitative targets have been set for 1985 or 1990, but the overall objective will be to consolidate the rural health infrastructure by setting up village health posts in every village, improving the functional capacity of rural dispensaries and rural health centres and hospitals by the provision of trained health personnel, and improving the quality of care. The feasibility of institutionalizing traditional medicine will be explored. Emphasis will be on preventive services, improved environmental sanitation and improved housing.

UPPER VOLTA

Population and health statistics

In 1960 Upper Volta had 4 372 000 inhabitants. At an annual rate of 2% the population increased to 5 410 000 in 1972 and to 5 512 712 in 1975 (data from December 1975 census).

In 1975 the orders of magnitude must have been substantially the same as those based on the survey of 1960–1961; there may well have been a very slight increase in the birth rate and a drop in the mortality rate, producing an increase in the natural growth rate. The figures would then be as follows:

	Rate (per 1000)
Birth	50
Death	32
Infant mortality	189
Natural increase	18
Annual increase (1960–1970)	19.5
Annual increase (1970–1975)	21.3

Life expectancy at birth would thus be, in rural areas 32–33 years, and in urban areas 41–45 years.

The salient points arising out of these rates are: high infant mortality, especially during the post-neonatal period, which reflects the strong influence of an unfavourable environment during the first year of life; low life expectancy at birth, especially in rural areas; and a high rate of natural increase, offset by substantial emigration among young adults. Analysis of the age-specific and sex-specific mortality rates reveals excess female mortality during the reproductive period.

However, the annual rate of increase remains around 21 per 1000, which produces doubling of the population every 30 years.

Major health and health-related problems

The main public health problems confronting Upper Volta can be divided into three major groups:

— the high general morbidity rate, due in particular to the communicable diseases;
— nutritional deficiencies;
— problems of water supply and sanitation.

These problems are aggravated by the inadequacy of the health and social infrastructure.

The infectious and parasitic diseases undeniably occupy a dominant position among the causes of visits to health centres and of hospitalization.

Malaria is the probable leading cause of morbidity and an important cause of death. It is the third cause of mortality in children under one year of age, and clearly contributes to reducing the productivity of the working population. The entire country is malarious.

Measles is one of the leading causes of infant mortality. There seems to be a relationship between the previous nutritional status of the children and the severity of the diseases and the frequency and severity of ocular complications.

Schistosomiasis: the available reports are incomplete but indicate that the intermediate snail hosts of *Schistosoma haematobium* are widely distributed throughout the country.

Meningitis with its seasonal outbreaks, leprosy, tuberculosis, trypanosomiasis and intestinal parasitic diseases come next in importance, together with the worldwide diseases such as influenza, respiratory infections, digestive diseases, injuries, and the complications of pregnancy and childbirth.

Nutritional deficiencies are caused by the inadequacy of food production, problems of marketing and distribution, and the ignorance and low purchasing power of the population. Of children who are examined at dispensaries, 50% show varying degrees of undernutrition.

Quantitatively speaking, the number of calories available for each inhabitant is barely adequate or slightly below the requirements.

In general the quantitative consumption of protein seems adequate. The only aspect which presents problems is the quality.

Water supplies. There is a tremendous gap between the urban and rural areas. 12–17% of the population as a whole have reasonable access to water.

In 1976, 105 000 people out of a population of about 6 million, i.e., 1.75%, had running water in their homes and 72 000 inhabitants, or 1.1%, obtained their water supplies from stand-pipes. The remainder of the population obtained their water supplies either from masonry wells or traditional wells or from nearby ponds. Seven towns in Upper Volta have piped water supplies and there are five semi-urban centres with the rudiments of a water supply network.

As regards *sanitation*, the towns of Ouagadougou and Bobo-Dioulasso have net-works of open sewers and a service for the disposal of household wastes.

Action taken

Health policy

The aims are those laid down in the Five-Year Plan for 1972–1976:

— to implement and develop programmes for the control of communicable diseases;
— to develop the health services, particularly maternal and child health;
— to improve the material conditions for the practice of individual medical care;
— to provide training and further training for health personnel.

In order to achieve the worldwide objective of "health for all by the year 2000", Upper Volta will need to extend the structures concerned with the health of rural communities, to back them up with supervision that is adequate in both quantity and quality, and become self-reliant in the health field.

With this objective in mind, the broad lines of social and health policy are directed towards the taking-over of responsibility for health by the population itself. This involves the creation and strengthening of national institutions for the

training and further training of staff, the restructuring of existing health units and the provision of the necessary resources.

Health legislation

The Public Health Code was promulgated by Ordinance No. 70/68bis/PRES/MSP.P.AS dated 28 December 1970 and was published in the *Official Gazette of the Republic of Upper Volta,* No. 3, dated 21 January 1971.

Health planning and programming

Like the preceding two plans, the Five-Year Plan for 1977–1981 is intended as an outline. Nevertheless, a special feature of this plan is that it reflects the determination to exploit the economic potential for the benefit of the entire nation, within the country's borrowing capacity.

In the human resources sector (education, health and social affairs) the Government doubled its efforts between 1970 and 1977. Expenditure on teaching rose during that period from 1785 million to 4519 million CFA francs, while expenditure on health and social affairs rose from 854 million to 1690 million CFA francs.

Organization of health services

The Ministry of Public Health and Social Affairs was reorganized by Presidential Decree No. 74 of 31 July 1974 governing the functions and overall organization of the Ministry of Public Health and Social Affairs, and by Order No. 248 dated 25 June 1976 governing the functions of the various ministerial departments.

The Ministry consists of the Minister's Office and the Technical Services; the latter consist of the general Directorate of Public Health and Social Affairs, which coordinates five technical departments, each under the responsibility of a director: the Department of Health, the Department of Administration and Finance, the Department of Pharmaceutical Services, the Department of Social Affairs, and the Department of Professional Training and Courses.

The Department of Public Health is responsible for all activities concerned with health promotion, protection and treatment. It is responsible for the hospitals, for maternal and child health, for the sanitation services, for health education, for school health, for the nutrition services and for the laboratory services.

Since 1 January 1975, following the administrative restructuring of the country into 10 *départements*, each health sector corresponds to a *département*, and some of them have subsectors. Each of these health sectors is under the responsibility of a chief medical officer. The mobile units in operation are: the mobile ophthalmology group, three national immunization teams, 20 leprosy control teams with 125 treatment circuits, 16 Sahel mobile teams, and 28 mobile maternal and child health teams.

Biomedical and health services research

Biomedical research in Upper Volta is carried out by the Centre Muraz/OCCGE (Organization for Coordination and Cooperation in the Control of the Major Endemic Diseases), the Institute for Livestock Production and Veterinary Medicine in the Tropics, the Intercountry School for Rural Development Engineers, and the Inter-African Committee for Studies on Water Management.

Education and training of health manpower

In 1977 the facilities for health manpower training in Upper Volta were as shown in table below.

In October 1977 the training of midwives began at the National School of Public Health with 23 first-year students (core course shared with State-registered nurses and social workers).

The postgraduate training of specialist nurses (24 months' practical training) takes place in the Ouagadougou and Bobo-Dioulasso hospitals and in the Centre Muraz, in the following subjects: biology (2 State-registered nurses in 1977), pharmacy (2 enrolled nurses), chemistry (2 enrolled nurses), surgery (3 enrolled nurses), anaesthesia (4 enrolled nurses), and laboratory work (4 enrolled nurses).

In the academic year 1977–78, 438 students were being trained in the health professions abroad, as follows: physicians (203, plus 8 on specialist courses), pharmacists (70), dental surgeons and technicians (24), advanced nursing grades (13), public health nurses (2), specialist nurses (11), midwives (62), social workers (14), laboratory assistants (15), public health technicians (12), other technicians (4).

Health resources

Health establishments

The various types of fixed health units which form the backbone of the 10 health sectors in Upper Volta are as follows: 2 national hospitals—Ouagadougou (752 beds), and Bobo-Dioulasso (720 to 750 beds), 3 regional hospitals—Fada N'Gourma, Ouahigouya, and Gaoua, 11 medical centres, 28 *sous-préfecture* health centres, 37 *arrondissement* health centres, 119 dispensaries with maternity units, 135 dispensaries, 24 maternity units, and 48 specialist units, including sleeping sickness and leprosy hospitals.

The hospital bed capacity of Upper Volta (hospitals, medical centres, maternity units and health centres) is 3623 beds, one bed per 1680 inhabitants.

The specialized units in Upper Volta are: 9 tuberculosis centres, 13 sleeping sickness and leprosy hospitals, 2 school medical centres, 2 health education centres, 2 urban sanitation services, 16 maternal and child health centres, 4 ophthalmological dispensaries.

Health manpower

Local health manpower in Upper Volta in 1977 included: 42 physicians, 5 dental surgeons, 16 pharmacists, 3 nutritionists, 1 hospital administrator, 2 assistant hospital administrators, 2

	Duration of studies (years)	Number of schools (public)	Number of students 1976–77	Number of graduates 1977	Number of graduates 1973–1977
State-registered nurses (intermediate secondary school certificate with 5 years of secondary education and entrance examination)	3	1	123	35	169
Social workers and group educators (intermediate secondary school certificate with 5 years of secondary education and entrance examination)	3	1	37	8	38
Enrolled nurses (primary education, plus 3 years of secondary education and entrance examination)	2	1	114	44	116

hospital managers, health assistants, State-registered nurses, enrolled nurses, midwives, social workers, assistant social workers, group educators, auxiliary social workers, public health technicians, and special nurses for laboratory work, pharmacy, and radiology.

Production and sale of pharmaceuticals

There is no production of pharmaceuticals in Upper Volta. The infrastructure of the pharmaceutical services is as follows:

— Department of Pharmaceutical Services within the Ministry of Public Health and Social Affairs.
— Supply Pharmacy, responsible for supplies of medicinal preparations and equipment to health units.
— National Pharmacy, with two dispensing units run by pharmacists (one in Ouagadougou and one in Bobo-Dioulasso) and 17 sales depots in a number of towns in the provinces.

At present the health sectors can obtain supplies of medicinal preparations in two ways: central procurement through the Department of Public Health which handles all *Fonds d'Aide et de Coopération* orders by the conventional method (requests, calls for tender, processing of tenders and placing of orders—once the order has been received in Ouagadougou, the Department of Public Health distributes the medicinal preparations); or local procurement through orders placed by the sectors themselves or by independent health units. The orders made by the heads of health units are sent to the Supply Pharmacy for action. Often they are a response to urgent needs caused by a breakdown in normal supplies; by their very nature, therefore, they are a result of exceptional and unexpected circumstances. If the Supply Pharmacy has the required preparations available, it honours the orders by arranging a transfer to the health units together with an invoice for payment.

There are two private pharmacies in Ouagadougou, two in Bobo-Dioulasso and one at Gaoua, all run by pharmacists; there are also 63 private drug stores in the provinces.

Health expenditure

Health expenditure and costs of medical care in the period under review were as shown in table below (in thousands of CFA francs):

Outlook

Training of multidisciplinary health personnel needed for the development of health services in Upper Volta, particularly physicians, will be furthered by the setting-up of a University Centre for Health Sciences in Ouagadougou.

An expanded immunization programme is planned to achieve 100% vaccination coverage of the target population against measles, pertussis, tuberculosis, tetanus, poliomyelitis, diphtheria, smallpox, and yellow fever in the decade 1980–1990, using integrated fixed and mobile units.

The promotion of primary health care in the same period is planned to provide health coverage for the population by strengthening and adaptation of the existing health facilities, and setting up of new units, as follows: one primary health post per village, one health and social

	1972	1973	1974	1975	1976	1977
National budget	10 822 300	11 726 170	12 493 600	15 064 450	21 122 708	23 123 598
Personnel	6 087 850	6 659 805	7 085 585	7 877 819	11 036 630	13 212 362
Capital expenditure	945 725	960 537	997 919	1 302 234	3 065 519	1 872 952
Equipment	1 804 265	1 905 215	1 834 200	2 644 420	3 221 700	3 699 340
Health budget	814 555	904 079	937 079	1 165 562	1 224 430	1 690 142
Personnel	686 355	774 615	800 379	1 006 862	1 031 430	1 492 923
Capital expenditure	3 200	4 700	4 200	4 700	5 000	2 000
Equipment	115 000	115 000	133 300	154 000	188 000	195 219
(including medicaments)	(51 648)	(51 648)	(52 217)	(59 265)	(65 333)	(77 594)

Estimated per capita expenditure was as follows (in CFA francs):

	1972	1973	1974	1975	1976	1977
Health budget	150	164	166	203	209	283
Medicinal preparations	10	9	9	10	11	13

welfare centre for 15 000 to 20 000 inhabitants within a maximum radius of 20 km, one health centre per *arrondissement*, one medical centre per *sous-préfecture*, one hospital per *département*; and development of the national hospitals (Ouagadougou and Bobo-Dioulasso).

Appraisal of progress made between 1973 and 1977

The period 1973–1977 was characterized by a worsening in 1973 of the drought which had been in progress for several years; this upset the environmental balance, production and economy of Upper Volta, making increased external aid necessary.

The Ministry of Public Health and Social Affairs and the health sector were reorganized in 1974.

The National School of Public Health was inaugurated on 9 December 1977, with sections for State-registered nurses, State-registered midwives, social workers, and enrolled nurses.

Twenty-six nutritional rehabilitation centres were set up and are now operational.

Water supplies were improved by extension of water supply networks in Ouagadougou and Bobo-Dioulasso, and installation of piped water supplies from the Black Volta for the town of Koudougou, piped water supplies for seven semi-urban centres, construction of 4000 concreted wells in rural areas, and the drilling of several hundred bore-holes.

The admission requirements for training of health personnel were raised: in addition to the previous entrance qualifications (intermediate secondary school certificate and entrance examination), a further year of secondary studies has also been required since 1976 for nurses, midwives and social workers; for enrolled nurses, three years of secondary education are required in addition to the primary school leaving certificate and the entrance examination; The number of new students admitted for qualification as State-registered nurses increased from 40 to 78 in the period; those for qualification as enrolled nurses from 50 to 92.

In 1977 the section for State-registered midwives was set up within the new National School of Public Health. Previously they were all trained abroad. The course began with 23 students. Five midwives and 13 nurses received training as permanent teaching staff in the centres for advanced studies between 1973 and 1977.

In the field of communicable disease control, a BCG mass vaccination campaign was carried out for the age group 0–25 years south of the thirteenth parallel and for the age group 0–39 years north of the thirteenth parallel. The average coverage rate for this campaign is 85.8%, as confirmed by the survey and tuberculin tests performed during the study with a view to integrating the leprosy and tuberculosis control programmes from June 1975 to March 1977. The International Commission for the Certification of Smallpox Eradication in West Africa officially confirmed that smallpox had been eradicated from Upper Volta (23 March to 15 April 1976). The registered trypanosomiasis case rate fell from 0.02 in 1969 to 0.002 in 1975. The leprosy prevalence per 1000 inhabitants fell from 36.67 in 1965 to 20.8 in 1973 and 14.8 in 1976. The incidence per 1000 inhabitants fell during the same period from 2.55 to 0.4 and 0.36. No case of yellow fever has been reported since 1969. The activities of the Onchocerciasis Control Programme in the Volta Basin area have interrupted transmission of the disease throughout the country.

ZAMBIA

The national health policy for the decade formulated in 1972 by the President, when he declared that "by the end of the decade, health care will be free to all people and health institutions will be within easy reach of every Zambian", remains the cornerstone of national health policy. Already health care is free to all in Zambia. However, the drop in the price of copper has adversely affected the smooth implementation of the policy.

The objectives formulated on the basis of the President's declaration remain unchanged:

(1) to extend health services to the rural areas;
(2) to lay particular emphasis on prevention of disease and ill health;
(3) to expand facilities for training the personnel required to man the health services;
(4) to develop a basic structure through the

establishment of health centres throughout the country;
(5) to integrate the health services.

Decentralization is a national policy for all sectors of social and economic development.

Major health and health-related problems

According to statistics from health institutions, the commonest health problems are protein-energy malnutrition, malaria, pneumonia and other respiratory conditions, gastroenteritis, tuberculosis, and measles.

The 10 leading causes of hospitalization in 1975, affecting 203 164 out of a total of 385 846 inpatients (52.7%) were: accidents and injuries, 34 803 (9.0%), malaria, 33 491 (8.7%), disorders of pregnancy, delivery, puerperium, 25 708 (6.7%), gastritis, gastroenteritis and other diseases of the digestive system, 17 628 (4.6%), diseases of genitourinary system, 16 779 (4.3%), malnutrition and anaemia, 16 217 (4.2%), dysentery, enteritis and other diarrhoeal diseases, 15 400 (4.0%), pneumonia, 14 948 (3.9%), acute respiratory infections 14 158 (3.7%), measles, 14 032 (3.6%).

The 10 leading causes of mortality in hospital in 1975, which accounted for 10 480 of the total of 14 234 deaths (73.6%), were: disorders of newborn and perinatal period, 2625 (18.4%), malnutrition and anaemias, 1526 (10.7%), pneumonia, 1376 (9.7%), measles, 1128 (7.9%), gastritis, gastroenteritis and other diseases of the digestive system, 822 (5.8%), dysentery, enteritis and other diarrhoeal diseases, 628 (4.4%), diseases of the heart, 610 (4.3%), accidents and injuries, 601 (4.2%), malignant neoplasms and leukaemia, 595 (4.2%), tuberculosis, 569 (4.0%).

It is evident from the epidemiological pattern depicted above that most health problems are related to the environment. Large segments of the Zambian population still live in poor dwellings of mud and thatch, have no piped water and no proper refuse collection or disposal. Parasitism is an important cause of morbidity and reduced working efficiency. The people do not understand the nature of the diseases or their relationship to their environment.

The main indicators of the state of health of a nation are the morbidity and mortality rates (especially the infant and maternal mortality rates), and life expectancy. However, changes in these indicators usually take place very slowly. Moreover, it is difficult to apportion credit to the health services for any reduction in disease incidence rates, because such factors as nutrition, housing and earning capacity have an important impact on health. Nevertheless, improvements in disease rates and the utilization of health services remain important indicators of success, since they are measures of the overall welfare of the community.

Communicable disease prevention and control

The expanded programme of immunization—designed to reduce morbidity and mortality in childhood from diseases such as tuberculosis, tetanus, diphtheria, pertussis, measles and poliomyelitis—was started in 1976. Community participation is an important component of this programme, which is being actively pursued.

As a result of an immunization campaign initiated in 1965 and successfully implemented and maintained, there have been no indigenous cases of smallpox since 1968. The last imported case (from Zaire, through Kaputa) was in 1971; the fact that there were no secondary cases or general outbreak following this imported case is a measure of the real improvement of the health services of Zambia. In March 1978 Zambia was certified free from smallpox.

Although the extent of tuberculosis is not known accurately, it is clear that this disease constitutes a major public health problem. Provincial tuberculosis control teams were established in 1970, and vaccinations have been carried out at the rate of about 0.4 to 0.5 million per year. Case-finding has been extended and a tuberculosis register has been maintained since the establishment of a chest disease laboratory in 1973.

A campaign for the early detection of leprosy has been carried out in schools and communities. Treatment of patients has been improved to such an extent that a number of leprosaria have been closed.

Although cholera has spread since 1973 to neighbouring countries (Malawi, Mozambique, Kenya, Angola and the United Republic of Tanzania), there have so far been no cases in Zambia, largely thanks to the preventive measures undertaken by the health services.

Vaccinations against other communicable diseases have been introduced under the expanded programme of immunization. Since 1973 nearly a million children have been vaccinated against measles, nearly three million vaccinations have been performed against poliomyelitis, and about the same number against diphtheria, pertussis and tetanus. Since 1975 some localized cerebrospinal meningitis epidemics have occurred for the first time.

The immunization programme is being implemented through the maternal and child health services, which also carry out health education activities. In 1975 more than 40% of all children under five years old attended maternal and child health clinics at least once.

Health resources

Health establishments

In 1977 there were 81 hospitals and 688 health centres and subcentres, including government, mission, mine and industry facilities; the total number of beds and cots was approximately 20 000. This represents a big increase: between 1972 and 1976 seven new hospitals and 103 health centres were constructed, increasing the bed capacity by 3200. During the same period, in pursuance of the socialist and humanistic principles of the United National Independence Party, the private nursing homes run by the Zambia Medical Aid Society in Lusaka and the Copperbelt have been incorporated into the national health system.

With regard to the administration of health institutions, the most important step was the decentralization of the administration of district general hospitals and health centres with a view to making them more sensitive to the communities' needs. Since the abolition of medical fees in government-run hospitals in 1969, the Government has been committed to making available free health services to the Zambian population.

The ambulance service is almost nonexistent because of lack of vehicles and proper maintenance. There have been shortages of essential drugs from time to time because of foreign exchange and organizational problems. No new capital projects have been started since 1974, owing to lack of funds.

Health manpower

Although the lack of health manpower remains a critical constraint on the health services, the situation is improving gradually. More enrolled nurses and midwives, medical assistants and health assistants are being trained.

The approximate annual intake of the four schools for registered nurses is 260, that of the 17 schools for enrolled nurses, 500, and that of the nine midwifery schools, 200. If the present level of intake is maintained the number of nursing and midwifery personnel trained should be sufficient to staff health facilities adequately in the not-too-distant future. Of the 49 tutors teaching in the various nursing and midwifery schools in 1977, seven were Zambians; this situation would improve when the first group of tutors being trained at the postbasic nursing school qualified in 1978.

In 1977 there were 981 medical assistants and 313 health assistants, all nationals. The annual intake of trainees is approximately 70 for both medical assistants and health assistants. These two categories of health personnel are vital for the provision of primary health care, and it is expected that the intake will be increased as soon as the expansion of accommodation facilities is completed. Of the 27 teachers providing the courses for the medical and health assistants, 17 are nationals.

New nursing schools have been opened at Ndola Central Hospital, Kasama and Mansa, and midwifery schools at Ndola and Lusaka. The medical assistants' training school at Chainama has been expanded to increase the enrolment capacity from 117 to 320 students per year. Between 1973 and 1978 98 doctors graduated from the Medical School.

Research

In 1973 discussions were started between the Zambian Government and WHO on the establishment of a research centre at Ndola. In 1977 the laboratories were completed and an agreement was signed. The Tropical Diseases Research Centre will participate in the WHO Special Programme for Research and Training in Tropical Diseases.

The Pneumoconiosis Medical and Research Bureau has been incorporated into the Ministry of Health and now forms the nucleus of the expanded occupational health services.

Health legislation

The Medical and Allied Professions Act has been amended by Parliament to give due weight to Zambian qualifications and to include amongst registrable qualifications those in the paramedical field, such as laboratory technicians, health inspectors and radiographers. The aim of the Food and Drugs Act, enacted in 1972, is to ensure the quality and safety of food, the safety of cosmetics and the efficacy of drugs.

Appraisal of progress made between 1973 and 1977

On balance, the health services functioned satisfactorily, despite numerous problems related to staff shortages and lack of funds. The political will and leadership are there and, given the necessary inputs, the health sector could function even better. While there were many successes, there were also many failures—mainly related to the poor performance of the economy and the consequently reduced allocations to health. The lack of funds impaired all major activities; the expanded programme of immuni-

zation, for example, lacked funds for the purchase of the necessary vehicles, supplies and equipment.

Outlook

The Third National Development Plan aims to achieve an 80% coverage of expectant mothers and children through the maternal and child health services. The expanded programme of immunization aims to reach the same target with immunization against common communicable diseases.

All disease detection and control programmes, which will lay particular stress on tuberculosis, leprosy and malaria, will be accompanied by active health education and the establishment of a network of health institutions throughout the country. Primary health care, however, will remain the key strategy for health action.

REGION OF THE AMERICAS

ARGENTINA

Administration and organization

The main feature of the developments since 1974 has been the attempt efficiently to organize the health sector, making full use of the human, physical and financial resources of the State, social service, and private subsectors, since the level of care provided by them does not always reflect the effort and investment made.

As a result of the reorganization carried out in 1976, three subsecretariats and two general directorates were established: the new Subsecretariat of Individual Medical Services and Rehabilitation has as its primary responsibility the planning of medical care. It comprises national directorates of mental health, health establishments, dentistry and rehabilitation and a general directorate of health emergencies. The Subsecretariat of Collective Medical Services is responsible for the conduct of special health programmes such as those for the control of tuberculosis, Chagas' disease and sexually transmitted diseases. It comprises institutes concerned with the provision of services as well as institutes for research on health care maternal and child health, and environmental sanitation. It exercises authority over the national directorates of sanitation, health promotion and protection, maternal and child health, institutes and research. The Subsecretariat of Social Medicine and Health Supervision is responsible for the supervision of health personnel, of the preparation, registration and dispensing of drugs, and of the preparation and registration of foodstuffs, international trade and traffic. The national directorates of drugs, foodstuffs, medical examinations, frontiers and transportation are responsible to it. The General Directorate of Planning and Coordination and the General Directorate of Administration are also new.

Human resources

The following priorities have been designated by the Secretariat of State for Public Health: to ensure the harmonious development of the human resources that make up the health teams; to ensure their appropriate geographical distribution; and to determine the levels of professional personnel and of medical collaborators and to establish study plans in keeping with their professional responsibilities. A committee has been established for the planning of human resources, composed of officials of the Secretariat of State and the Ministry of Culture and Education. It is to make a comprehensive study of the training of human resources in the health area, and provision is made for the participation of health agencies that use such personnel, universities and scientific societies.

The planned course of action includes measures to establish a permanent information system; to prepare a manual on the classification of posts of public health personnel; to undertake activities designed to strengthen the establishment of a career service that includes all the human resources of the public subsector; to determine the human resources required for the execution of health programmes and to establish categories and levels on the basis of a clear classification; and to undertake studies that will make it possible to define and upgrade training institutions in accordance with national, regional and local needs.

Physical resources

The Secretariat of State for Public Health is responsible for studies and programmes, investments for new facilities, upgrading of installed capacity and regular maintenance.

Between 1974 and 1978 a trial was undertaken in the north-eastern region of Argentina of a methodological model for research in the rest of the regions and provinces of the country. Studies on each province and a first synthesis at the national level are available. When the national integrated health system was established, the information was used for the purpose of delimiting programme areas. Standards were prepared for the design of sectors and services, and documents on design, construction and equipment of medical care units, physical resources of health (architecture and equipment), and minimum requirements for the operation of various services of medical care units were produced.

Financial resources

The 1970s have seen major changes in the field of medical care; in a period of two years three laws were enacted which, although they did not originate in the Secretariat of State for Public Health, will have major consequences for the organization and financing of the health sector:

(1) Law No. 18 610 of 1970, in accordance with which each branch of industry must establish, if it does not already have one, a social service whose priority responsibility is to provide its members with medical care (financial contributions being made by both beneficiaries and employers). It established the National Institute of Social Services.

(2) Law No. 19 032 of 1971 similarly established, under a national institute, social services for retirees and pensioners financed by beneficiaries and employers, with a contribution from employed workers.

(3) Finally, in the same year, an institute of social services for rural and related activities was established. It is financed on a bipartite basis by beneficiaries and employers.

The traditional (public and private) financing pattern was thus modified by increased participation from the social services sector.

Medical care

Communicable diseases are still a major health problem in the country. The high mortality in certain areas (especially in the North and South) is in many cases due to diseases preventable by vaccination. Medical science has already developed the necessary technology for their control as well as highly efficient methods of protection. In recent years, communicable diseases have been, for all age groups, one of the 10 leading causes of death, accounting for approximately 5% of all deaths; they are the leading cause of death in children under 5 years of age (including diseases of the respiratory and digestive systems) and the second cause of death in the age group 5–14 years.

The Secretariat of State for Public Health is bent on improving the results achieved and on increasing surveillance and control activities in those areas in which mortality can be reduced with the resources available.

Rural health activities, initiated in 1969, were reduced during the first half of the quadrennium. Beginning in 1976, it was decided to assign them greater financial and technical support, and plans were made gradually to achieve coverage of more than 6 800 000 inhabitants. Accordingly in 1976, 500 000 inhabitants were covered; in 1977, 1 400 000 inhabitants were covered; and it is hoped to cover more than 2 million in 1978. Programmes are designed to provide health promotion and protection activities, rural basic sanitation, and medical and dental resources.

The activities are supervised by medical personnel and the nursing personnel of the hospital nearest the area. The activities are carried out by a multipurpose health agent who is a member of the community to be served and who is chosen by it. Once appropriately trained, this agent is capable of making a census of the population and of housing, cartography, referral of patients, referral of mothers and children for examinations under the maternal and child health programmes, vaccinations, first aid, distribution of milk, health and food and nutrition education, promotion of the family farm, sanitation, with emphasis on housing, water, excreta and refuse, elimination of insects, rodents and vectors, and collection of samples for disease studies.

Food and nutrition

Activities for improving food and nutrition consists of technical and financial support for the execution of provincial programmes of food and nutrition and medical care, using a multisectoral approach. Research in this area has been carried out through the National Institute of Nutrition, which conducts courses and is responsible for advice and supervision; and by a regional institute of nutrition sciences located in an area particularly affected by these problems which deals with the biological, production, and consumption aspects of foodstuffs.

Among the subjects dealt with during the period were the preparation of powdered meat for the enrichment of foodstuffs; growth and development studies; control of the distribution of iodized salt; use of non-traditional foodstuffs that are rich in protein and have a high biological value; and nutritional rehabilitation of preschool children. The Regional Institute of Nutrition of Northern Argentina has been very active in the areas of teaching, advisory services, nutrition education, research on such regional problems as endemic goitre in the Calchaquíes valleys, fluoridation of drinking water, research on the calcium metabolism of communities in the highlands, and determination of standards for haemoglobin and creatinine for the region.

Rehabilitation of the handicapped

The National Rehabilitation Service was established as a decentralized agency, the purpose of which was to speed up the development of a coherent national policy by preparing and implementing standards through its dependent units. It is being replaced by the National Rehabilitation Directorate, which comes under the authority of the Subsecretariat of Individual Medical Services and Rehabilitation. The specific objective of the programme is to achieve levels of care that meet the manifest demand for comprehensive physical, mental and socioeconomic rehabilitation of any disabled individual.

The most important activities undertaken in the years 1976–1978 were the initiation of an institute to provide mentally normal children suffering from motor disabilities with primary education and rehabilitation, another to provide care for persons suffering from severe motor disabilities who have serious environmental and socioeconomic problems, and a subprogramme for the purpose of establishing rehabilitation services in general hospitals for patients with acute conditions. The services have already been introduced into eight hospitals and are being introduced into 10 more. Further activities included sponsorship and participation in rehabilitation congresses held in Buenos Aires (in October 1976, the Argentine Rehabilitation Congress, and in October 1977 the VII Latin American Rehabilitation Congress); 450 fellowships were awarded during the period, and short-term consultantships and the services of a permanent consultant in orthotics and prosthetics were provided. Each year, national sports events were organized for disabled persons.

Environmental health

The development of environmental sanitation agencies since 1974 has been promoted by means of assistance agreements in the area of the planning of infrastructure services for water, drainage and solid waste for the urban and rural population. The objective is to prevent further deterioration in health due to the unsatisfactory quality and quantity of services, and to establish priority areas, achieve a gradual increase in coverage, and establish medium- and long-term targets.

A system was established for the control of drinking water in order to ensure the coverage of 70% of the population, and a scheme for the promotion and financing of basic sanitation facilities for the rural population was devised.

Efforts were made to organize the control of the water quality of water basins and to prevent deterioration. Measures were taken to establish a system for the control of air pollution in population centres with more than 500 000 inhabitants and in those places in which levels higher than those permitted by current standards may be reached. It was further planned to determine the principal forms of soil pollution in urban and rural areas and their relation to health, to investigate the degree of pollution at which the soil is subject to those risks and to establish the necessary standards for preventing deterioration.

Courses and seminars were held on urban cleansing, sanitary land fills, biological treatment of liquid effluents, rural basic sanitation, health radiophysics, water quality control, fluoridation, epidemiology and the environment, large-scale water systems, mining activity, and financing of sanitation.

Responsibilities for the preservation of water, soil and air resources, as well as for the regulation of the use of pesticides and other agricultural chemicals and the regulation of industrial activities that constitute hazards for human health, are shared with other sectors.

Health education

Since 1974 the health education sector has carried on its activities in accordance with a general policy designed to make the public aware of the value of health as an important individual and social good, and to encourage the acquisition of health habits conducive to further health promotion, protection, recovery and rehabilitation. These tasks were carried out by four principal working groups: research and standardization, personnel training, production and dissemination of media, and relations with provinces. Each of these groups had primary activities—those provided for in the programmes of the sector itself and relating chiefly to research and standardization—and support activities to health programmes, largely based on promotion using the media.

Legislation and standards

The standards and national legal provisions regulating the practice of medicine and its auxiliary branches, as well as the operation of establishments and premises in which medical care is provided, were fully enforced without difficulty during the period.

Efforts were made to ensure the further standardization and effectiveness of international agreements and regulations of which the country is a signatory; for example, those regulating air, sea, river and overland transport and the control of sanitation in the respective areas.

On the basis of the inalienable responsibility of the State for the technical control of drugs and foodstuffs, the corresponding standards were revised, and applied research in the area of pharmacology and food technology was undertaken. Improvements were introduced in the means for increasing the efficiency of the technical agencies of the Secretariat of State that will enable it to collaborate with and guide the pharmaceutical industry.

Foremost among the activities undertaken were the following: updating of the Argentine Food Code, composition of a national register of adverse effects of drugs and medicaments, updating of the law on drugs, updating of the "International Health Digest", and preparation of the National Therapeutical Formulary.

Argentina did not previously have any legislation governing and standardizing the use of human blood and its derivatives. Accordingly, a draft of a blood law was prepared which also establishes basic technical standards for ensuring its appropriate use and for protecting donors and recipients.

The constant progress of science makes it essential to update the National Pharmacopoeia; a new edition has been prepared and is at present in press.

The laws governing professional practice and drugs were also updated.

The National Institute of Pharmacology and Food Technology established standards for quality control that are essential for the supervision of medicinal products. Eight national standards have been prepared; 27 are being developed; and 30 already agreed upon are being planned. (For legislation on financing—see "Financial resources", above.)

Health policy and international cooperation

The principal objective of the policy of the Secretariat of State for Public Health at the international level is the affirmation at that level of the health policies established by the National Government. There is a coherent relationship between the health agreements that serve as a development instrument and the programmes being carried out in the country. Efforts are being made in particular to strengthen joint activities with neighbouring countries on concurrent health problems and to strengthen technical cooperation with all countries.

BAHAMAS

The Bahamas archipelago occupies an area of approximately 250 000 km^2 of the North Atlantic, extending from 80 km off the west coast of Florida at its nearest point to the mainland of the United States of America to 145 km from the northern coast of Haiti at its southernmost limits. It consists of over 700 islands and 2500 cays, with an area of 13 864 km^2, but only 15 of the former have a significant number of inhabitants. New Providence, the principal—though not the largest—island, is 34 km long by 11 km wide, and accommodates 116 000 of the mid-1977 estimated population of 211 000. The capital, Nassau, houses the seat of government, which is based on the British model, with a Governor General, Prime Minister, House of Assembly and a Senate. Tourism continues to be the most important factor in the economic life of the country, with 1.4 million visitors recorded in 1977. Although priority is being given to projects which will stimulate economic development, a comprehensive national development plan has not yet been presented to Parliament.

Organization of health services and health care delivery

In November 1977 the responsibilities of the erstwhile Ministry of Health were enlarged by the addition of those for national insurance to form the Ministry of Health and National Insurance, with a health and welfare budget in 1978 of $25.7 million, or 15.3% of the national recurrent budget, and representing a per capita expenditure of $113.92. With this budget, a three-tiered medical care service is provided by the three main hospitals—Prince Margaret Hospital (454 beds) and Sandilands Rehabilitation Centre (with 210 psychiatric and 150 geriatric beds) in New Providence and the Rand Memorial Hospital (50 beds) in Grand Bahama Island. In addition, primary care is provided at a total of 63 clinics in New Providence (7), Grand Bahama (6) and the other Family Islands communities (50). These are staffed by 16 medical practitioners and by 136 nurses and nurse-midwives, a number of the latter operating largely or wholly independently in the more remote localities.

Over the past four years, considerable effort has been devoted, with admirably satisfactory results, to the improvement of the physical facilities at the Princess Margaret Hospital in Nassau, where a first-rate new ambulatory care section was opened in July 1976 at a cost of $7.5 million. Work is in progress to adapt the original areas evacuated to provide improved clinical and administrative facilities which are to include a special baby care unit and increased accommodation for obstetrics and gynaecology. In addition, with the technical cooperation of UNDP and with PAHO as executing agency in part, efforts were also directed at improving the medical records system, laundry, food and maintenance services, the introduction of a cost accounting system and the development of supply management. A first extension of the laboratory was effected in 1974 and a second phase is nearing completion. The standards of performance were upgraded, so that in exercises in international quality control excellent ratings have been consistently recorded. During the period under review, new clinical services developed included neurosurgery, otolaryngology, and, with the voluntary assistance of visiting specialists, paediatric neurology and oncology.

At the periphery, two new clinics were established in New Providence and three in the Family Islands, where reliance continued to be placed on evacuation by sea or air in cases of emergency.

In the area of public health, the maternal and child health services were maintained, the school health services were extended to include further grades, an audiometric screening programme was introduced in 1975 and family life education was included in the health education activities.

Communicable diseases and immunization

The national immunization programme was extended in 1975 by inclusion of vaccination against measles for infants one year of age but 1976 and 1977 showed high prevalence of infection among children aged 2–3 years. Thus, overall prevalences among the age groups under-one-year and 1–4 years were 187 and 237 per 10 000 respectively. A serological survey of levels of immunity to poliomyelitis carried out in 1977 showed acceptable results in New Providence, but less satisfactory levels of protection in the Family Islands, due largely to shortcomings in the cold chain. Measures to improve this, and to administer one booster dose of vaccine to infants and schoolchildren in those areas, were underway when an isolated case of paralytic poliomyelitis was recorded in July 1978 in a vaccinated 6-year-old child in one of those islands. Appropriate local preventive measures were promptly instituted and no secondary cases were encountered.

The Bahamas has decided to participate in the WHO/PAHO sponsored Expanded Programme on Immunization; in the summer of 1978, immunization of young girls against rubella was also added to the national programme. The five leading communicable diseases reported in 1976 were influenza, 755.9 per 100 000 inhabitants; gonoccocal infections, 650.2; gastro-enteritis, 585.8; streptococcal throat (diagnosed clinically only), 579.2 and measles, 442.2. The striking increase in the prevalence of gonococcal infections and in syphilis has led to the first steps in developing a specialized unit for the sexually transmitted diseases.

With the collaboration and technical cooperation of the Caribbean Epidemiology Centre, three annual health service workshops have been organized since 1976 which have contributed to increased awareness of the need for strengthening epidemiological surveillance, principally of communicable diseases.

Manpower resources and development

The number of physicians remains at 7.8 per 10 000 inhabitants, but the number serving Grand Bahama and the Family Islands has increased from 14 in 1975 to 25 in 1978. There were 319 nurses per 100 000 inhabitants, with 18.5% of the total assigned to the community nursing services.

The number of dentists remains low, although in the health service they have increased from 0.16 per 100 000 inhabitants in 1974 to 1.9 in 1976. This has permitted the launching of regular circuits twice yearly in the Family Islands, but measures are now underway for augmenting this service by training dental auxiliaries who will increase the coverage and introduce elementary preventive activities in the programme.

For medical, and to a lesser extent for nursing staff, undue reliance continues to be placed largely on expatriate recruitment, particularly for lower and middle level categories, the relatively small number of returning national medical graduates having as immediate target appointment to the highest grades. The administrative services at the Ministry were strengthened by the appointment of a deputy chief medical officer, while those of the hospitals were upgraded by the assignment of four trained hospital administrators. With the technical cooperation of PAHO, some progress has been made also in improving the management services, but a great deal remains to be done in this sector if the most efficient and effective use of available resources is to be achieved. For purposes of planning, programming and evaluation of health services, a nucleus health information system is in the process of being established, but continued external support in this undertaking will be essential while national staff are groomed and trained to assume responsibility.

A postbasic training course in community nursing has operated each year since 1974, with a number of participants from other territories of the Commonwealth Caribbean. Specialized training in midwifery and psychiatric nursing were also introduced locally, while formal training was completed overseas by three registered nurses in psychiatry and one occupational therapist. Three university trained pharmacists also entered the service during the period under review. With the collaboration of the Royal Society for Health and the Bahamas Hotel Training College, a one-year training programme was successfully completed in Nassau for a first group of five health inspectors in 1977, and a second course was started in July 1978 with 12 candidates. For laboratory technologists, a three-year combined academic and service training programme commenced in 1977 with 15 students, in close association with the College of the Bahamas. For the more senior staff in the Department of Environmental Services, overseas training programmes in sanitary engineering and in environmental sanitation are being followed by an engineer and a senior health inspector. Finally, one of the two practising health educators entered a university training programme in 1978 under a PAHO fellowship.

Environmental health

Management of the environment is a priority activity for the Ministry. A modern environmental health act and regulations are in the final stages of enactment to provide the legal basis for coping with problems arising from urbanization and industrialization. Thus, in Grand Bahama, where an oil refinery and a modest chemical industry are already in operation, the hazards associated with these activities call for continuous monitoring. An important advance was made in 1978 when a modern solid waste shredding plant was installed in New Providence.

Health legislation

In addition to environmental health, activities in health legislation included enactment of the Medical Act, 1974 and the development of drafts covering an up-to-date Dental Act, a Private Hospitals Act and an Allied Health Professions Act. The need is, however, identified for updating the Health Services or Public Health Act and the introduction of modern legislation on abortion.

Appraisal of progress

These several activities have resulted in satisfactory improvements in some of the vital indices commonly used as a measure of progress in the health field, but others reflect the need for even further efforts. Thus there are as yet no more recent data on life expectancy than those of 1970: 60.4 years for males and 69.3 for females. In 1976, the crude death rate of 4.6 reflected the continued decline recorded since 1969, when it was 6.6. The crude birth rate has also maintained a steady decline, from 30.3 in 1969 to 25.6 in 1976, while the infant mortality rate has shown satisfactory improvement from 34.7 per 1 000 live births in 1975 to 24.8 in 1976; the neonatal mortality rate was 17.6 in the same year.

The principal causes of death in 1976 remained unchanged, with diseases of the heart (16.0%), malignant neoplasms (12.9%), cerebrovascular disease, pneumonia and cirrhosis of the liver jointly accounting for 45.9% of the total deaths reported. Alcoholism continues to be a major problem, responsible for 47.9% of male and 28.6% of female admissions to the Sandilands Rehabilitation Centre in 1977. An encouraging development in this area was the voluntary participation of the community in establishing a "halfway house" for the accommodation of 18 alcoholic patients motivated for rehabilitation.

Recognizing that the further extension of health service coverage will, of necessity, need to be based on the use of allied health personnel, studies are under way to introduce a training programme for nurse practitioners with the object of equipping them more fully for their tasks at the periphery. A further look is also being given to the practicability of introducing the category of health aide as a means of broadening the scope of health service delivered to the population.

BERMUDA

In addition to continuation of routine public health programmes, there were the following developments in the health field in the period under review:

(1) Increased surveillance of communicable diseases and visual presentation of notifications of these diseases by means of graphs.

(2) Increased checking of aircraft disinsection procedures and dissemination of information to airlines regarding the policy in Bermuda in relation to disinsection.

(3) Mosquito traps instituted at the airport to check the possible importation of *Aedes aegypti* mosquitos in view of the dengue outbreaks in the Caribbean (to date no *Aedes aegypti* have been found).

(4) Improved awareness among clinic doctors and nurses of the importance of the cold chain in relation to immunization procedures.

(5) Extended programmes of health education in schools, especially in regard to sexually transmitted diseases, family planning and family life.

(6) Development of the sexually transmitted diseases clinic by providing extra space and additional staff (this is still in the planning stage).

(7) Improved organization of family planning clinics in Hamilton, Somerset and St George, and the greater involvement of nurses in some gynaecological and family planning procedures.

(8) School medical inspections now take place at school entry and at school leaving only. The "Eleven Plus" medical examination has been scrapped in view of the low incidence of physical problems. Instead, more emphasis is placed on emotional and behavioural problems and on difficulties in learning, and to this end special referral clinics have been established on a weekly basis at each end of the Island.

(9) The introduction of vision testing of all schoolchildren on a yearly basis, or more frequently if necessary.

(10) The introduction of measles and rubella immunization as a routine procedure at child health clinics.

(11) The introduction of annual medical examinations for prison officers. The police already have an annual medical examination.

(12) Improved food handlers examination techniques supplemented by health education. Each food handler has an annual chest X-ray, and those working at the airport have annual or routine rectal swabs. Chefs, maîtres d'hôtel and heads of sections in the hotels and other establishments with catering services are made responsible for the personal hygiene of their

staff, and spot-checks are made at hotels and restaurants by a health inspector and a nurse from the Health Department.

(13) Control standards, both for the pollution of sea water and for potable water, have been established.

(14) The inauguration of a preventive dental programme for children, financed in a large measure by the Kellogg Foundation, using tropical and systemic fluoride.

(15) A renal dialysis unit has been established.

BOLIVIA

Status of health

Expectation of life. According to the preliminary results of the demographic survey made in 1975, expectation of life at birth is estimated at 48.2 years, representing an improvement of two years over previous estimates for 1974 based on projections of the 1950 census.

General mortality rate. The estimated general mortality rate based on the survey is 17.96%, showing a reduction of 1.44 over the estimates for 1974. The principal causal factors in the general mortality rate are diseases of the respiratory system and perinatal acute gastrointestinal disorders.

Infant, child and maternal mortality rates. In the survey the infant mortality rate was estimated at 174.7 per 1000 live births, an increase over the estimates for previous years (154.6 per 1000 live births in 1972 and 147.6 per 1000 births in 1974). The infant mortality rate is marked by the impact of respiratory, diarrhoeal, perinatal and other infectious diseases. The mortality rate for children of 1–4 years is 14.4 per 1000 of the population at risk. The maternal mortality rate is 48 per 1000 live births.

Morbidity rate. On the basis of hospital discharge data more than 80% of morbidity in children under one year old is attributable to gastrointestinal and respiratory diseases; in the 1–4 year age-group gastrointestinal and respiratory diseases continue to predominate, followed by accidents, assaults and diseases of the digestive system; in the 5–14 year age-group respiratory and gastrointestinal diseases, together with tuberculosis, predominate; over 15 years old the major cause of hospitalization is normal childbirth, followed by complications of pregnancy, diseases of the digestive system, accidents and assaults, to mention the four major factors.

The communicable diseases such as tuberculosis, measles, pertussis, tetanus and poliomyelitis, continue to represent one of the most important problems of public health in the country in respect of morbidity as well as of mortality, not only because of the scale of the harm they do but also because of the extreme vulnerability to them of age-groups under five years and their negative impact on the very young.

Communicable diseases and immunization

Of the deaths attributable to the 10 primary causes of mortality, 70% are the result of parasitic and infectious diseases. So far as morbidity is concerned, infectious diseases, both respiratory and gastrointestinal, account for the major share, of which a high proportion is preventable by specific immunization.

The control of these diseases is maintained through epidemiological surveillance, preventive medicine in the form of immunizations and environmental sanitation.

In 1977 epidemiological survillance services reported five epidemic outbreaks of pertussis in Oruro, Santa Cruz and Cochabamba, one outbreak of measles in Potosí, an outbreak of bubonic plague in the Department of La Paz and one of yellow fever in the same Department.

All these outbreaks were effectively controlled in their initial stages. The other communicable diseases, of which there have been no epidemic outbreaks, are also subject to epidemiological surveillance. In the case of malaria a total of 10 106 positive blood samples gave the following results: in Pando and Beni 3882 positive samples and in Tarija 3876, accounting together for 76.8% of the positive blood samples; the other samples were taken in various isolated localities in other departments. Insecticide spraying in 5732 localities with

83 955 dwellings followed, providing protection against malaria for 317 966 residents.

There were 594 deaths from tuberculosis in 1976, showing a mortality rate of 40.9, and 11 517 cases, giving a morbidity rate of 249.

In 1977, 106 992 poliomyelitis immunizations were carried out—50.1% of the programme target; DPT coverage was 33% with 59 858 immunizations, measles 73% (117 529 immunizations), and yellow fever 81.5% (88 866 immunizations).

An expanded immunization programme has been prepared; it is currently being reviewed. The financing of US $9 million by USAID over a period of five years will enable the entire communicable diseases programme to go forward, including the national malaria programme, which, as a result of analysis and evaluation, will be reorganized. A further phase is being planned in operations to control Chagas' disease following the current research phase and with similar financing.

Maternal and child health and nutrition

Maternal and child health. The high infant, child (1–4) and maternal mortality rates (see above) constitute a serious problem.

Women of childbearing age (15 to 49 years) constitute 23.9% of the population, and the fertility rate is high, estimated at 24.4 per 1000 women in 1975.

Deficient environmental and socioeconomic conditions and lack of effective coverage in treatment of pregnancy, childbirth and confinement are the factors conditioning the high maternal mortality rate recorded for 1971, with an estimated range of variation extending from 15 per 1000 live births in La Paz to 59.6 per 1000 live births in Riberalta. The problem is most serious in rural areas; a maternal mortality rate of 84 per 1000 live births was recorded in the rural area of La Paz in 1971. Abortions are, however, thought to have a significant bearing on the situation.

Action has been taken to organize and strengthen units operating at the regional level and some hospital health centres acting as local operational units, coordinating and integrating their activities with nutrition and immunization.

Nutrition. Undernutrition is common, especially among children under 15 years; protein-calorie deficiencies are especially serious, being present in some 15% of the population; nutritional anaemias are found in 50% of pregnant women, and goitre prevalence is about 75% in endemic areas.

Nutrition activities emphasize intersectoral coordination and are currently being expanded through mother's clubs, of which there are more than 800 providing health education in nutrition and arranging for the distribution of food. The clubs have achieved over 70% of their target and have more than 120 000 beneficiaries.

With the participation of other institutions and cooperative organizations encouragement has been given to the production and consumption of iodized salt.

Environmental sanitation and occupational health

Environmental health. In urban areas less than 50% of the population have potable water, and only some 27% have sewage disposal services.

In rural areas the water supply systems, covering 9% of the rural population, are uncertain, and only 5% have any form of sewage disposal system.

In 1977, 24 bored wells and 176 dug and driven wells were completed under the programme; 20 300 persons benefited from the construction of 6 water supply systems and 72 226 from the installation of 7832 latrines and 319 septic tanks.

An agreement on basic rural sanitation was signed for USAID financing of US $4.5 million. Operations under this agreement have begun with the identification of 13 rural localities for 1978 and 1979, with a view to installing water supply systems; communities are to participate actively.

The rural sanitation programme, with Canadian Government financing of US $1058 000, is fully operational.

Occupational health. The incidence of silicosis and tuberculosis in the mining sector in 1976 was 14.9%, compared with 22.4% in the early 1960s. The rate of accidents in the mining sector is 69 per million working hours.

The economic impact of accidents and occupational diseases in the mining sector, with a working population estimated at 65 000, has been analysed by the National Social Security Fund: its conclusions are that the direct and indirect costs of such accidents and diseases represent an annual loss of approximately US $4 million. Morbidity and mortality attributable to accidents at work doubled in 1965–1975 as a result of the absence of industrial safety and hygiene services in most workplaces. Morbidity from accidents at work in the manufacturing sector is 15.2%. Morbidity and mortality from pesticides are 1.23 and 0.60 per 1000 respectively.

Between 1976 and 1977 a programme of activities extended initial occupational health coverage to 20 172 workers in certain nationalized industries. An interministerial committee has been formed to examine and formulate policies of integrated action and is now fully operational.

Development of health services and medical care

The many public and private institutions that provide health services as their principal or collective function do not constitute a system that closely correlates and coordinates policies, action and activities. Their administrative procedures are different and independent of one another, forming an obstacle to inter-institutional cooperation. Each of the agencies has a structure organization based on specific legal instruments defining its nature, purposes, population, coverage and financing, so that they lack coherence and exhibit major disparities in financing and in the quality of services.

The widely dispersed population, their difficult accessibility and varied cultural patterns and socioeconomic levels make it necessary, in analysing the institutional coverage of services, to distinguish clearly between urban and rural services.

The provision of services through the formal health system, consisting of the Ministry of Social Welfare and Public Health, the Social Security agency and other agencies of the central Government, such as the Board of Social Action of the Office of the President of the Republic and other private institutions, is principally concentrated in urban areas with population centres of over 5000 inhabitants and supplies services of varying nature and complexity. Marginal areas of cities, with populations largely of rural origin, generally lack adequate services. Population centres of less than 5000 inhabitants receive little medical care—less than 0.4 health care visits per inhabitant per year—a situation due to a series of factors, including the following major ones:

— the distances involved and especially the transportation difficulties make it impossible to use available services in good time and under proper conditions;

— the tenuous financial resources of communities to some extent restrict their partici-

pation in programmes and activities that require community financial support; and

— low educational levels and traditional cultural patterns are a major obstacle to the understanding of health problems.

Nevertheless, the significant use made of health services in certain rural areas recently and the call for their introduction into others may be regarded as a positive major advance towards meeting the health needs of communities; in addition, internal migration, especially from rural areas to the periphery of cities and capitals of departments, has given an impetus to the more rapid identification of health needs and exerted pressure on authorities to meet them.

Activities in urban and rural establishments in 1977 showed progressive improvement in utilization of resources, and hospital discharges and medical consultations have shown average annual increases of 4.6% and 4% respectively over the past three years.

Administrative systems as a whole have been strengthened and developed with the participation of PAHO/WHO, USAID and UNICEF.

The regulatory and operational resources of nursing, health education and social services show a steady improvement.

Primary health care—national experiments. Since the 1960s the structure of the health services has incorporated integrated basic programmes undertaken, especially in rural areas, with the support of UNICEF for control of communicable diseases, maternal and child care, nutrition and environmental sanitation; community participation has been promoted and encouraged as a basic requirement of such programmes.

The Chuquisaca and Tarija projects are an early example of integrated action not confined to the health sector but extending to such intersectoral activities as agricultural education and the participation of the regional development corporations.

In the course of the present decade, within the broad outline of the policies, objectives and strategies of the National Health Plan, other projects have been organized and are being fully implemented, among them the Montero rural health project, the Ingavi project and the Concern project.

Montero rural health project started in April 1976 as a demonstration area for the expansion of health coverage into rural areas under the agreement between the Ministry of Social Welfare and Public Health, USAID, the Public Works Committee of Santa Cruz and the Methodist Church. The aim is the "design, implementation, evaluation and adaptation of a system of integrated health services in rural areas based on the criteria of regionalization and levels of complexity, with active community participation". Health services are to be provided according to five levels of complexity.

At the *first level* of minimal complexity, 40 communities of 30 to 120 families undertake health promotion and prevention activities and some basic health restoration activities under a health promoter, support being provided by a health committee supervised by one nursing auxiliary for 3 to 5 units of coverage.

At the *second level* (medium complexity) 3 communities, each of 120 to 200 families undertake health promotion, prevention and restoration activities under a nursing auxiliary who supervises 3 to 5 units of coverage in her basic health unit.

The *third level* is the most complex form of organization at the health area level, involving 4 health areas. Health prevention, promotion and restoration functions are performed and a referral centre is provided for patients in the various basic health units and units of coverage in the area. Both outpatient and hospitalization services are provided; the medical and paramedical staff of the hospital are responsible. At this level it is a grade II nursing auxiliary who performs the supervisory functions in the basic health units and units of coverage in the area and coordinates the activities of the health committees at various levels.

The *fourth level* is the highest local level of complexity in the Montero District, covering the treatment in Montero of cases from the city itself and of cases whose diagnosis or treatment cannot be handled in subdistrict hospitals. The services are provided by a general hospital, a paediatric hospital and a Montero rural project extension team. The activities include training for various levels of staff.

The *fifth level* is the highest level of technical capacity and equipment, providing for treatment of cases from the district and subdistrict levels, and involving planning, supervisory, evaluation and coordinating functions at the district and regional levels.

The *Ingavi project health unit* was formed by supreme decree of December 1975 to implement an integrated rural development project that seeks to raise the standard of living of a rural population in an area of approximately 800 km^2, located partly in the eastern region of the province of Ingavi and partly in the southern region of the province of Los Andes, both in the Department of La Paz, with the participation of various state agencies and with World Bank financing.

The objective, besides raising the living standard of the inhabitants of the project area, was to provide them with technical assistance and services in the fields of agriculture, education, health, housing and environmental improvements.

The *Concern rural health project* is being implemented in the Department of Pando in the north of the country to provide integrated health services under an agreement between the Ministry of Health and a private institution for assistance in the field of rural health located in San Diego, California (USA).

The objective is to extend the coverage of health services in the project area especially through primary health care, with the participation of other sectors. Financing was obtained under the community development agreement with USAID. The health component in the agreement provides for the expansion of services in depressed areas and is especially oriented to the needs of frontier areas. Financing of a further US $10 million through USAID was under negotiation—the sum to be used for the development of services in rural areas under a regional system with community participation, providing for a first basic level of primary health care.

Development of human resources

In 1977/78 the Bureau of Human Resources was organized and brought into service. Under the coordination and supervision of this unit four courses have been held for environmental sanitation technicians, 21 for nursing auxiliaries and three for officials and accountants in hospital units, a total of 757 persons having been trained. In addition, seminars and workshops for nursing and other auxiliary personnel have been held and have contributed to improvements in services. UNICEF, USAID and PAHO/WHO have participated significantly in the financing of these courses and seminars.

A project for the development and improvement of the School of Public Health has been prepared with the participation of the Inter-American Development Bank as part of the educational development plan formulated in association with the Ministry of Education.

CANADA

Population and other statistics

At the last census, taken in June 1976, the population of Canada was 22 992 604. Population estimates and other vital statistics for the period under review are given in the following table:

	1973	1974	1975	1976
Mean population	22 094 700	22 479 000	22 831 000	22 992 604
Number of live births	343 373	345 645	358 621	359 987
Birth rate (per 1000 population)	15.5	15.6	15.7	15.8
Number of deaths	164 039	166 794	166 365	167 009
Death rate (per 1000 population)	7.4	7.4	7.3	7.2
Natural increase (%)	0.81	0.80	0.84	0.88
Number of infant deaths	5 339	5 192	5 130	4 681
Infant mortality rate (per 1000 live births)	15.5	15.0	14.3	13.5
Number of deaths, 1–4 years	1 107	1 080	1 080	1 009
Death rate 1–4 years (per 1000 population at risk)	0.8	0.8	0.8	0.7
Number of maternal deaths	37	35	27	24
Maternal mortality rate (per 1000 live births)	0.1	0.1	0.1	0.1

Of the 167 009 deaths recorded in 1976, the main causes were: heart disease, including chronic rheumatic, ischaemic and other forms, and hypertensive disease (58 472), malignant neoplasms (36 467), cerebrovascular disease (15 964), accidents (11 251, including 5172 in motor vehicle accidents), pneumonia (5132), causes of perinatal mortality, including congenital anomalies, birth injury, difficult labour and other anoxic and hypoxic conditions (3780), bronchitis, emphysema and asthma (2958), diabetes mellitus (2945), suicide and self-inflicted injury (2935), and cirrhosis of the liver (2791).

Of the notifiable communicable diseases, the most frequently reported in 1977 were: gonorrhoea (51 233), scarlet fever and streptococcal sore throat (23 480), measles (8832), salmonella infections (4228), infectious hepatitis (4215), tuberculosis, all types (3197), syphilis, new cases (2998), rubella (2159), pertussis (1988), bacillary dysentery (1137).

Organization of the public health services

Responsibility for health matters is divided between the federal and the provincial govern-

ments. On the national level, the Department of National Health and Welfare is the principal federal agency in health matters. It is responsible for the overall promotion, preservation, and restoration of health, and for social security and social welfare. The Department acts in conjunction with other federal agencies and with provincial and local services. The provincial governments are directly responsible for the actual administration of health services.

The principal objective of the Department of National Health and Welfare is to maintain and improve the quality of life of the Canadian people. The Department aims to reduce the detrimental effects of environmental factors not within an individual's control and to encourage and assist the adoption of a way of life that enhances physical, mental and social well-being. Strategies for the attainment of these objectives include the development of national standards, the expansion of awareness and concern for health, economic and social problems, and the development of new or improved systems of delivery.

The branches of the Department of National Health and Welfare with responsibilities primarily for health matters are: health protection, medical services, health programmes, fitness and amateur sport, and long-range health planning. In addition, the Medical Research Council reports to Parliament through the Minister of National Health and Welfare.

The Health Protection Branch is responsible for developing an integrated programme to protect the public against unsafe foods, drugs, cosmetics, medical instruments and equipment, against harmful microbial agents and technological and social environments deleterious to health, against environmental pollutants and contaminants of all kinds, and against fraudulent drugs and devices. It is responsible for enforcing the Food and Drugs Act and Regulations, the Narcotic Control Act and Regulations, and the Radiation-Emitting Devices Act and Regulations. In addition, under the Hazardous Products Act and Regulations the Branch has joint responsibility with the Department of Consumer and Corporate Affairs for product safety.

The responsibilities of the Medical Services Branch include health care and public health services for Canadian Indians and Eskimos and all residents of the Yukon and Northwest Territories, as well as quarantine and immigration medical services, public service health, a national prosthetics service, and civil aviation medicine, disability assessment and emergency health services.

The purpose of the Fitness and Amateur Sport Branch is to encourage, promote, and develop fitness and amateur sport.

The Health Programs Branch exercises departmental responsibilities for promotion of health and well-being and the prevention of illness and disability and for assisting in the development and maintenance of appropriate health care services for all.

The Long Range Health Planning Branch is responsible for long-range (strategic) planning, and policy research.

Federal-provincial cooperation and collaboration are carried out through the conferences of ministers and of deputy ministers of health, and through federal-provincial advisory committees on institutional care services, community care services, health promotion and lifestyle, environmental and occupational health, and health manpower.

The responsibility for regulation of health care, operation of health insurance programmes and direct provision of some specialized services rests with the provincial governments; some health responsibilities are delegated to local authorities.

Provincial hospital insurance programmes, operating in all provinces and territories since 1961, cover 99% of the population. Under the Hospital Insurance and Diagnostic Services Act of 1957, the Federal Government provides financial assistance to the provinces towards the cost of providing hospital services to patients insured under these programmes.

Public medical care is provided under the Medical Care Act which was passed by Parliament in December 1966. By 1 April 1972 all provinces and territories had entered the federal programme. The plan must be universally available to all eligible residents on equal terms and conditions and must cover at least 95% of the total eligible provincial population (in fact the plans cover over 99% of those eligible). Comprehensive coverage must be provided for all medically required services rendered by a physician or surgeon.

Until April 1977, federal contributions to the provinces for hospital and medical care services were based on the cost of insured services incurred by the provinces, with the Federal Government reimbursing the provinces for approximately 50% of their expenditures. The Federal/Provincial Fiscal Arrangements and Established Programs Financing Act of 1977 modified the method of federal financing. Federal contributions now take the form of a transfer of fiscal concession and associated equalization to the provinces, in conjunction with equal per capita cash payments.

The Federal Government provides assistance to the provinces to improve and maintain the quality, supply, distribution, and productivity of all health manpower in Canada at a level that makes possible the delivery of effective and efficient total health services.

Institutional and ambulatory care for tuberculosis and mental illness is provided by agencies of the provincial departments responsible for health. Provincial programmes are giving increasing attention to preventive services. Programmes related to health problems such as cancer, alcoholism and drug addiction, venereal diseases, and dental health are being developed by provincial government agencies, often in cooperation with voluntary associations. A number of provincial programmes are also being directed to meet the needs of specific population groups, such as mothers and children, the aged, the needy, and those requiring rehabilitation care.

Public health or community health units are among the most decentralized. Some are also responsible for local health education, school health, and organized home care. Although local and regional involvement in health services has been concentrated on hospital planning and some aspects of public health, several provinces have inaugurated district and regional boards which participate in the coordination of all health-related services in their areas.

Hospital services

In 1977, there were 1389 hospitals in Canada providing 201 413 beds, equivalent to 8.7 beds per 1000 population. These beds were distributed as follows:

Category and number of hospitals		Number of beds
General hospitals	888	125 922
Allied special hospitals	371	39 289
Psychiatric hospitals	126	35 969
Tuberculosis hospitals	4	233

There has been a slight decline in the total number of hospitals and beds in recent years. In 1973 there were 1411 hospitals, with 212 650 beds. However, general and allied special facilities have remained fairly stable. In 1973 there were 913 general hospitals, with 125 253 beds, and 353 allied special hospitals with 28 604 beds. In contrast, psychiatric hospitals, while increasing slightly in number from 122 in 1973, have declined in bed capacity from the 41 821 reported in that year. Tuberculosis facilities have been reduced from the 7 hospitals with 542 beds in 1973. These changes reflect a greater emphasis on care for mental patients and those with tuberculosis in general hospitals and community based programmes.

Medical and allied personnel and training facilities

In 1976, Canada had 40 130 doctors, or one doctor for 578 inhabitants. Apart from such well-established professions as medicine, dentistry and nursing, definitions of occupations, mandates for practice, training, and regulation of health occupations vary considerably from province to province.

Trends during the past several years have included: increased specialization of function; establishment of a number of national associations of health personnel; a gradual shift in training of "auxiliary" personnel from on-the-job and hospital-based programmes to community colleges and other post-secondary institutions; developments in provincial certification and regulation of health occupations.

Communicable disease control and immunization services

Routine immunization commonly begins at two years of age. Administration is by physicians in private practice as well as through public health agencies. Programmes usually include diphtheria and tetanus toxoids, often combined with pertussis vaccine, some form of polio vaccine, measles vaccine and rubella vaccine. There are some variations in programmes between provinces, particularly with respect to use of live or inactivated polio vaccine, or a combination of these.

A national advisory committee on immunization has advised on schedules for infants and children, adapted to various approaches to polio vaccination. This committee also has suggested the type and dosage of influenza vaccine for each age group. This advice is given in anticipation of the strains of influenza which are likely to pose a threat in any given season.

With the increase in worldwide travel, health authorities are aware of the likelihood of introduction of parasitic and other diseases, many of which were previously unknown in this country. In addition, considerable interest is being generated in the epidemiology of diseases characteristic of the urban environment, and to recently identified problems, such as Legionnaires' disease.

Venereal diseases continue to be one of Canada's most serious communicable disease problems. The magnitude of the problem is greater than is apparent, in view of serious under-reporting of sexually transmitted diseases. However, there are indications that syphilis, which has shown a decline in incidence in recent years, is more adequately reported than gonorrhoea.

Control measures include routine premarital testing in some provinces, routine testing of prenatal patients, widespread public education measures, reporting of cases and contacts under provincial legislation, vigorous follow-up of contacts, and obligatory medical treatment provided under existing federal-provincial medical care plans. Innovative measures include mobile and street clinics, "hotline" telephone and radio services, improved reporting procedures, and confidential treatment of teenagers.

The majority of persons infected with active tuberculosis are now being treated as ambulatory patients. Free diagnostic services available through mobile and special clinics and routine hospital X-ray services help to control the disease, as does the availability of effective treatment methods. BCG vaccine is used on a limited scale.

Chronic and degenerative diseases

Although heart disease continues to represent a major cause of death, there has been a slight decline from the 1973 rate of 256 per 100 000. In that year the disease accounted for 4 129 000 days of care in general and allied special hospitals. In 1975, it accounted for 3 840 000 days. Among men aged 45 to 64, heart disease accounted for nearly 40% of all deaths in 1975, and the single diagnostic class, ischaemic heart disease, accounted for 9293 of the 25 367 deaths in this group.

As the second leading cause of death, cancer accounts for about one of every five deaths, most of them occurring in the middle and later years of life. The death rate from cancer was 147.7 per 100 000 population in 1973 as compared to 149.2 in 1975. The rate for females decreased from 132.8 in 1973 to 131.1 in 1975, and for males increased from 166.5 in 1973 to 167.4 in 1975.

"Statistics Canada" started a national cancer incidence reporting system in January 1969 in cooperation with the National Cancer Institute and the nine existing provincial tumour registries; a centralized registry has not yet been organized in Ontario. Participating provinces send a simple notification card with basic patient and diagnostic information for each new primary site of malignant neoplasm discovered.

Special provincial agencies for cancer control, usually in the health department or a special cancer institute, carry out cancer detection and research in cooperation with local public health services, physicians and the voluntary Canadian Cancer Society branches. Provincial cancer programmes operate both under the terms of provincial health insurance plans and under special supplementary services for cancer patients.

A Canadian renal failure register operated by "Statistics Canada" was started by and operates in cooperation with the Kidney Foundation of Canada. Its purpose is to register and follow all patients dependent on artificial kidney treatment (chronic peritoneal or hemodialysis) or who have received kidney transplants since January 1973.

There is no adequate estimate of the incidence of mental disorder. However in 1977 there were 129 397 admissions to psychiatric inpatient facilities. This figure represents a slight decline from the 132 001 admissions registered in 1975. There is increasing emphasis on treatment of the mentally ill in psychiatric units in general hospitals and in other community-based programmes.

In 1975, alcoholic psychosis and alcoholism accounted for 11 626 (19%) of the first admissions to inpatient psychiatric facilities. For the population 15 years of age and older, per capita consumption in litres of absolute alcohol increased from 8.55 in 1966/67 to 11.55 in 1975/76, a rise of 35.1%.

Patients with problems related to alcohol use are treated in hospitals, outpatient clinics, hostels, long-term residences or farms, and special facilities exist for the alcoholic offender. In each province, official and voluntary agencies carry out public education, treatment, rehabilitation and research.

Environmental and occupational health

In response to widespread concern about dangers to health and safety in the workplace, the Federal Government is establishing a new centre for occupational health and safety. This agency will promote the concept of a safe work environment and the enhancement of the physical and mental health of working people throughout the country.

Environmental health concerns are reflected in the work of federal and provincial health departments. A recent trend is the establishment of separate provincial departments or agencies to deal with environmental factors. Voluntary agencies and citizen action groups have stimulated many of the new approaches to environmental health. In the Department of National Health and Welfare the lead role is taken by the Environmental Health Directorate of the Health Protection Branch. The extent to which the effects of industrial pollution can reach the most remote areas is demonstrated by the Environmental Contaminants Program, which involves identification of pollutants and their sources throughout the country.

Progress in health services planning and development

In May 1974 the Minister of National Health and Welfare published a policy document, "A new perspective on the health of Canadians". This document marked the beginning of a new stage in Canadian health policies and programmes. Despite recent improvements in the organization of health care, the "new perspective" said that "there is little doubt that future improvements in the health of Canadians lie mainly in improving the environment, moderating self-imposed risks and adding to our knowledge of human biology". Five strategies were set out for pursuit of these improvements: health promotion, regulatory, health care efficiency, goal-setting, and research strategies; they are described below.

The period under review saw the development of a number of activities consistent with these strategies. Much of the initiative was taken by the Department of National Health and Welfare and other federal agencies. The commitment to pursue these strategies was further strengthened by a reorganization of the Department of National Health and Welfare.

Health promotion strategy

The Department of National Health and Welfare has recently brought together a number of health promotion programmes developed over many years. One major initiative is "Operation Lifestyle" which uses a variety of techniques to encourage Canadians to assume greater personal responsibility for health. Seven components are emphasized as of particular importance: alcohol, smoking, fitness, nutrition, drugs, stress and safety.

"Dialogue on Drinking", a national information programme sponsored by federal and provincial agencies, is aimed at establishing a social climate in which irresponsible drinking becomes less acceptable. It began in October 1976 and will continue to 1981.

The expanded federal role in fitness, sport and recreation included the creation of a Fitness and Amateur Sport Branch in the Department of National Health and Welfare.

Regulatory strategies

In recent years, consumer groups have increasingly drawn attention to the dangers of an industrialized and technologically-oriented society. Greater demands have been placed on the regulatory agencies at every level that are charged with protecting the population. At the federal level, much of the responsibility has been attached to the Health Protection Branch of the Department of National Health and Welfare.

Changing food technology requires means to ensure the safety of new types of ingredients and additives and packaging materials. A national system of reporting any foodborne outbreaks of disease has been established.

An interesting development is protection of the public against disorders related to lifestyle through regulation as well as through education and voluntary treatment. Regulations with respect to communicable diseases are well established; others, involving such matters as drug-related problems, are being formulated.

In February 1974, provincial ministers of health strongly endorsed adoption of legislation requiring the use of seat-belts in automobiles and lowering speed limits. Among the first provinces to enact such legislation were Ontario and Quebec.

Health care efficiency strategy

Throughout the past several years, federal and provincial health departments have shifted the emphasis from institutional care to new programmes to increase the efficiency of health care delivery.

The Federal/Provincial Fiscal Arrangements and Established Programs Financing Act of 1977 modified the method of federal financing and provided the provinces with increased flexibility in the development and administration of their health services, recognizing the greater emphasis in the provinces on preventive and community-based care. For example, developments in home care programmes, long-term care facilities and rehabilitation services have been of benefit to many of the elderly and disabled, or those suffering from chronic conditions, as care takes place more in the community and less in large institutions.

Most provinces have worked on innovative approaches to ambulatory care, establishing a variety of types of community health centres. In some cases, health and social services are being brought closer together.

Dental health programmes have made great strides. Apart from some oral surgery in hospital, most provincial health insurance programmes exclude dental care for adults. However, a number of provinces have introduced dental programmes for children.

Prescribed drugs, hearing aids, glasses, and various prosthetic and orthotic aids are provided to the elderly or to others in need, either free or at low cost, under various provincial programmes.

The Medical Services Branch of the Department of National Health and Welfare has been active in promoting the training of lay people in remote areas to assist in health education and in facilitating contacts between the population and those providing primary health care.

New technological developments have helped to close the gap between the type of health care available in urban areas and that in remote parts of the country. "Telemedicine" experiments have been conducted, several northern settlements receiving direct consultation on medical and surgical matters through television.

Goal-setting strategy

As health care in Canada represents such a complex pattern of federal and provincial responsibilities, consultation on all aspects of the subject is essential. Much of this consultation takes place through the federal provincial conferences of ministers and of deputy ministers of health, and thhough the advisory committees which report to them. It involves both resolution of immediate questions of common interest and medium- and longer-range directions for health policy and practice.

The emergent short- and medium-range issues include health problems related to lifestyles, native and Indian health, "telemedicine", and aging; small teams of experts identify manageable objectives, coordinate work both within and outside the Department of National Health and Welfare, and develop means for evaluating the results.

Medical and public health research

The majority of federal grants supporting biomedical research in universities and hospitals have been channelled through the Medical Research Council, which reports to Parliament through the Minister of National Health and Welfare. The funds provided by the Council represent about 43% of what is spent in Canada on health research. Of the Council's total expenditure of 56 720 000 Canadian dollars for dental, pharmaceutical and medical research in 1977/78, C\$45 470 000 were allocated for grants-in-aid, C\$10 280 000 for research scholarships and fellowships, and C\$970 000 for other research support and promotion. Expenditure for previous years totalled C\$43 713 000 in 1974/75, C\$47 434 000 in 1975/76 and C\$50 848 000 in 1976/77.

In 1973 the Department of National Health and Welfare combined the previous programmes for national health grants and public health research grants in a new National Health Research and Development Program. Funds are provided for applied and developmental research projects and related scientific activities conducted by universities, hospitals, health departments, and other non-profit health organizations, and for the training and career support of health research workers. Expenditure under the programme totalled about C\$10 690 000 in 1974/75, C\$9 061 000 in 1975/76, C\$8 128 000 in 1976/77 and C\$10 547 000 in 1977/78.

Projects include such areas as improving existing health services; testing the cost and effectiveness of new types of services, including home care for the elderly; identifying and measuring occupational health risks; tracing the spread of diseases; improving the understanding of mental health factors; assessing the efficacy of public health measures; and developing programmes for improving lifestyle.

Other programmes of the Department provide additional funds for specialized extramural research and conduct intramural studies.

Other federal departments and agencies carry out and support much health-related research. For example, the National Research Council is concerned with life sciences important to health. "Statistics Canada" collects and publishes a wide range of health statistics and has cooperated with the Department of National Health and Welfare on preparations for the 1978 Canada Health Survey.

Government health expenditure

The following table presents the pattern of change in total government health expenditure from 1972 to 1975. Figures are drawn from sources in "Statistics Canada" and the Department of National Health and Welfare. The consolidated expenditure is the total amount spent on health by all levels of government. A substantial portion of provincial costs are defrayed by the transfer and assignment of funds from the Federal Government. In order to avoid these sums being counted twice, total provincial spending is reduced by the amount of federal transfer payments in calculating the consolidated government expenditure.

Year	Total	Increase	Per capita
1972	C \$5 547 096 000	10.4%	C \$254
1973	C \$6 172 102 000	11.3%	C \$280
1974	C \$7 320 915 000	18.6%	C \$327
1975	C \$8 860 538 000	21.0%	C \$390

While this expenditure has increased substantially over the past several years, the proportion spent on health care has remained relatively stable in relation to gross national product (GNP) and total government expenditure, being respectively 5.3% and 13.4% in 1972, 5.0% and 12.9% in 1973, 5.1% and 12.4% in 1974, and 5.5% and 12.5% in 1975.

CAYMAN ISLANDS

The following improvements in health services were achieved in the period under review:

In the primary health care area there has been an increase in the number of doctors' visits to the outlying districts.

A full time practical nurse is now stationed in each of the major districts (East End, Bodden Town, West Bay).

Increases in the number of public health nurses has led to an increase in the number of home visits and teaching of families in the outlying districts, and the introduction of well baby clinics and antenatal clinics in West Bay and Bodden Town.

A referral system between hospital and district clinics (both inpatient and outpatient) has been introduced.

A family planning clinic has been opened.

The setting up of a clinic for handicapped children has led to the opening of a school for the handicapped and the initiation of a Genetics Programme. The schools and the maternal and child health clinic receive the services of a dental health educator.

The physical structures of clinics in West Bay and North Side have been completed.

A public health laboratory has been set up for the testing of water, etc. There have been improvements in disposal of garbage generally.

In the secondary care area there have been improvements in inpatient and outpatient hospital services, and the emergency service is now staffed 24 hours a day. Doctors are available for additional hours of service in general clinics and the hospital operating theatre.

Specialist paediatric, surgical, gynaecological and other medical clinics have been set up.

A maternity unit was set up separate from the general ward of the hospital.

Improvements have been made in the keeping of medical records.

Proper hospital sewage disposal and water purification systems were installed. A community social services unit was brought into operation.

General improvements included the physical structure of the dental clinic, and X-ray and laboratory services, giving, for example, greater sensitivity and wider range of X-ray pictures; periodic visits by a radiologist, and expansion of physical structure; periodic visits from an ear, nose and throat specialist; an auxiliary nurses training programme, under which 35 practical nurses were trained in order to meet nursing needs at that level in the hospital and the community; storage and control of drugs and supplies; provision of a physical therapy unit; appointment of school nurse for the High School; periodic visits of a plastic surgeon to the islands.

On Cayman Brac an increase in nursing staff was achieved, enabling the hospital to offer a 24-hour daily service, and the services of a resident anaesthetist and a dental auxiliary were made available, as well as a home for the aged and severely handicapped.

Personnel were trained in X-ray and laboratory technology, physical therapy, medical records keeping, hospital administration and administration of outpatient department emergency clinics, and management of the community social services unit.

CHILE

There is no doubt that the most noteworthy demographic development in Chile in recent years has been the decrease in births, a trend that began in 1964 after nearly 30 years during which the figures had remained stabilized at a very high level. The natural population growth has markedly declined, despite a sustained and significant drop in general mortality.

With the decrease in mortality occurring after 1930, which was not accompanied by a parallel

drop in births, the population growth accelerated and the total doubled by 1965—i.e., over a period of only 35 years. Some projections indicate that Chile will have a population between 15 and 16 million by the year 2000.

Another demographic factor worthy of note is the progressive and sharp relative decrease in the rural population. Nevertheless, in real figures the rural population has remained relatively stable since 1940.

General mortality, after remaining stable for more than 15 years at a figure of around 12 deaths per 1000 population, has declined, since 1964 to 6.9 per 1000 in 1977, the lowest in Chile's history.

Health problems

Causes of death

Chronic diseases and violence have come to predominate among causes of death: diseases of the circulatory system, malignant tumours and accidents, poisonings and violence were the causes of 29.7% of total deaths in 1963, 47.3% in 1977; while infectious and parasitic diseases, third in the list of causes in 1963, dropped to eighth place in 1977.

These changes in trends have made it necessary to introduce modifications in health programmes and the structure of the services.

Infant mortality. The decrease in infant mortality began in 1967, reaching its lowest point in 1977—47.0 per 1000 live births. The drop in absolute figures began as early as 1965, but this did not affect the rate until 1967, a phenomenon that is explained by the concomitant important decrease in the number of live births that also began in 1965. The observed decrease was 13.8% in the five-year period 1968–1972, and 27.9% in the five-year period 1973–1977.

Neonatal mortality remained stationary at a high rate until 1967, after which it fell to 20.9 per 1000 live births in 1977—a decrease of 40%.

Preschool child mortality. A close relationship has been noted between death rates in the 1–4 age group, and consumption of proteins, especially those of animal origin; FAO and WHO have utilized mortality in this age group as an indicator of the nutritional state of the population. Communicable diseases such as measles and pertussis are also important factors in the mortality of this age group, the seriousness of these diseases being closely related to the child's nutritional status and the communicable diseases often being the immediate cause of death in undernourished children.

Acute communicable diseases

The decline in death rates for acute communicable diseases that commenced at the end of the 1940s has continued, influenced, like the majority of other health conditions, by improvements in economic and social conditions, improved education, extension of health service coverage and, in the case in point, the availability of new and better antibiotics and especially the vaccination programme incorporated in the regular health activities.

The vaccination programme for diphtheria, pertussis and poliomyelitis has been intensified in recent years. The programme for measles started in 1964 continues. The results obtained by stepping up the poliomyelitis immunization programme are especially noteworthy. No case has been reported since 1975.

Mortality rates for typhoids and paratyphoids and, in general, the diarrhoeal diseases have remained high as a consequence of deficiencies in basic sanitation. Thanks to diagnosis and treatment, with timely hospitalization of patients, mortality from the salmonellas has been reduced to modest figures. However, consideration must be given to the high cost of such activities to the health services and to the community in general. Unification of the environmental sanitation services as a result of the recent creation of the National Sanitary Works Services will, it is expected, eventually make it possible to apply a more rational criterion to this serious problem.

Despite a declining trend tuberculosis continues to show the highest mortality rate among the communicable diseases.

Chagas' disease is endemic and occurs between the I and VII regions (18° to 35° South). There is no general information on its prevalence in the endemic zones and the only data available are those obtained in studies restricted to specific areas. In 1977, doctors reported 25 deaths from the disease.

At the same time as the decrease in the acute communicable diseases and tuberculosis, zoonoses of viral, bacteriological and parasitic origin have become more important as a result of their direct effects on human health as well as their indirect economic and nutritional impact through reduced livestock development.

Hydatidosis is the most important: in 1976 there were 820 human cases reported, with 48 deaths; 61 cases of bacterial carbuncle, with two deaths, and 37 cases of trichinosis, with 3 deaths, were reported in the same year.

When the rabies control programme was initiated, the disease was widely dispersed from the cities of Arica to the North and Osorno to the South (18°30' to 40°30' South), occurring in five-year cycles, with the canine species responsible for 86% of the cases.

At the present time the disease is restricted to isolated foci in the Metropolitan, VI and IX regions. Its cyclical recurrence has been interrupted and there have been no human cases in the past five years.

In recent years an increase in cases of reported venereal diseases (syphilis and gonorrhoea) has been noted, in part an actual increase as in most countries, and in part a result of the improvement in reporting of the diseases after better organization of the programme.

Noncommunicable diseases

Cardiovascular diseases have remained in first place among causes of death since 1968. In 1977 there were 3529 deaths from acute myocardial infarction; 2059 deaths from chronic ischaemic heart disease and 6842 from cerebrovascular accidents.

Some notion of the serious economic impact of cardiovascular diseases on the National Health Service may be obtained from the knowledge that 38 167 cardiovascular patients were hospitalized in 1973—6.1% of all hospitalizations for persons over one year of age (exclusive of obstetrical care).

Mortality rates for cancer tripled between 1918 and 1977, from 36.5 to 99.2 per 100 000 population. This increase reflects the increasing age of the population, and the gradual extension of the benefits of the social security system has resulted in increased access to health services and improved diagnosis, but there is also a real increase in incidence of the disease.

Each year 12 out of every 100 000 inhabitants are hospitalized for cancer, 4 out of 10 000 women die from cancer of the reproductive system, and 5 out of 10 000 men from cancer of the digestive tract.

The National Health Service studied the nutritional status of the population under 6 years of age coming under its control—81.1% of the total age group in 1977; 85.1% were normal; 11.9% showed signs of mild malnutrition and 3.0% moderate to advanced malnutrition. The greater number of eutrophics were found in the 0–5 months age group (90.4%), and the smaller number in the 12–23 months age group (81.5%). Calorie intake in the population was at a slightly (13.0%) lower level than recommended by FAO and WHO, and is being raised. The country is fulfilling protein consumption recommendations.

Environmental sanitation

In recent years the programme has been directed to solving the problem in the city of Santiago where a population of more than three million produces approximately 2000 tons of solid waste a day. The greatest risk is the lack of any satisfactory final disposal arrangements in places close to the population area.

In 1974, 74 366 food samples were analysed, 14.98% of them failing to meet standards. The corresponding figures for 1975, 1976 and 1977 were 75 658 and 13.70%, 93 266 and 12.22%, 108 049 and 12.57%, failure being due to microbic or chemical contamination or to organoleptic modifications.

The Metropolitan Region (Santiago), the largest demographic and industrial concentration in Chile, with its unfavourable geographic and meteorological situation, presents the most critical air pollution problem. A sampling network, complementing the Pan-American network, has been installed which measures daily averages of sulfur dioxide, nitrogen oxides and particulate matter in the air. There is also a fixed automatic station in the centre of Santiago that records concentrations of those pollutants and carbon monoxide and hydrocarbons. Results obtained in 1977 indicated that the highest air pollution indices were those for particulate matter and carbon monxide, which substantially and continuously exceeded the maximum values recommended by the international organizations.

Resources for health programmes

Health care establishments

On 31 December 1977 there were 37 758 hospital beds, 3.54 per 1000 population; 33 463 (88.6%) came under the Ministry of Health. All hospitals of the National Health Service, under the Ministry of Health, also provide ambulatory care through their outpatient clinics. The majority of hospitals in the remainder of the public sector and in the private sector also provide care for ambulatory patients.

There were also 277 clinics in operation, most of them in areas surrounding the large cities; but a substantial number provide care for the rural population.

There were 1080 health stations staffed by nurses, midwives or trained auxiliary personnel and located in rural areas, periodically visited by doctors and organized on a regional basis; that is, they are a part of the national health care system and report directly to the nearest hospital.

Financial resources

In 1969, public expenditures on health amounted to 5123 million pesos, or in terms of 1977 currency US $183 million. In 1977 these expenditures amounted to 9217 million pesos (US $330 million), an increase of 79.9%. These sums represent 2.05% of the gross domestic product for 1969, and 3.24% of that for 1977. Per capita public expenditures on health amounted to 557 pesos (US $19.9) in 1969 and 866 pesos (US $30.9) in 1977, an increase of 55.4%.

With specific reference to the Ministry of Health and its dependent agencies, the direct budgetary allotment increased from 2713 million pesos (US $97 million) in 1969 to 4364 million pesos (US $156 million) in 1978, an increase of 60.8%.

Human resources

There were 4340 doctors in service in 1961, or 5.5 per 10 000 population. In 1970 the number of practising physicians reached 6096, or 6.2 per 10 000 population. In 1977, despite the fact that the number of medical schools had increased to nine, and the number of graduates averages 500 a year, there were only 6516 practising physicians, the ratio remaining at 6.2 per 10 000 population. Stabilization of the doctor/population ratio is the result of migration occasioned by political events in recent years.

A programme initiated in 1956, offering general practitioners economic and professional advancement as incentives to voluntary residence in the rural areas is accepted by approximately 60% of graduates each year. Before inauguration of the programme there was one doctor for every 907 inhabitants in the province of Santiago (now the Metropolitan Region), and one doctor for every 3528 inhabitants in the remainder of the country. By 1970 the ratio was one to 1019 in Santiago and one to 2620 in the provinces; in 1978 it was one to 1240 in the Metropolitan Region and one to 1760 in the rest of the country.

There are three dental schools in the country. In 1968 there were 3250 active dentists in the country, or 3.4 per 10 000 inhabitants. Of this total 57.5% were employed in the public sector

in addition to their private practice, and 42.5% were engaged in exclusively private practice. In 1977 the number of active dentists reached 4300, or 4.0 per 10 000 inhabitants. This capacity is not being fully utilized, despite the fact that it falls far short of meeting the demand for dental care, while the conviction is expressed in many circles that some of the functions performed by dentists could be delegated to less specialized personnel, thereby allowing broader coverage of the population.

In 1977 there were 2350 chemists and pharmacists; it is estimated that 20% are employed in the public health sector, the remainder working in private industries and pharmacies. A sizable proportion of those in the public sector work in the clinical and bacteriological laboratories.

In Chile training for the nursing profession is at the university level. In 1977 there were 3201 nurses in Chile, or 3.0 per 10 000 inhabitants, 2337 of them working in the National Health Service. Some 46% of the nurses work in Santiago; 47% in cities of more than 20 000 population and 7% in localities with less than 20 000 population. The public sector employs 91.4% of the nurses.

Delegation of duties to personnel with less formal education is more frequent in this profession than in any other, in consequence of the compelling need. Vigorous efforts to make good the shortage of professional nurses have included increasing the number of nursing schools from 5 to 14. In 1977, 520 nurses graduated, a substantial increase compared to the five-year period 1969–1973, when the number of graduates averaged 297 a year.

Midwives are also trained at university level. In 1977 there were 2372 practising midwives, or 9.7 per 1000 live births, compared with 1442, or 5.3 per 1000 live births, in 1968. Distribution may be considered adequate, 36% working in Santiago, 54% in cities of more than 20 000 inhabitants and 10% in cities of less than 20 000 inhabitants.

The shortage of nurses has traditionally been made good by nursing auxiliaries without specialized training working alongside the doctors and nurses.

Since 1958, when nine-month courses were set up in the various regions of the country, some 19 775 nursing auxiliaries have been trained; it is estimated that some 800 auxiliaries without such training are still working in services under the Ministry, and they should be given such training in a year or two.

In the past, two professional groups were

created to cover the separate aspects of dietetics and nutrition. A single profession is being established with university-level training. In 1977 there were 672 nutritionists in the National Health Service. It is estimated that approximately the same number work in other public sectors and in the private sector.

There are now five university schools that train medical technicians for work not only in clinical laboratories but in all medical activities.

In December 1977 there were 617 workers employed by the National Health Service in environmental programmes. Of this total, 23 are sanitary engineers, 19 managing engineers, 3 doctors, 118 veterinarians and 4 biochemists.

One of the important duties of the National Health Service is that of safeguarding the environmental health of the entire country. These duties are discharged through the Department of Environmental Programmes and its several sections, including environmental sanitation and food control, and the Institute of Occupational Health.

COLOMBIA

Population and other statistics

The population increased from 23 million in 1974 to 24 million in 1978. This increase is smaller than the forecast made some years ago; the trend towards a lower mortality rate has been offset by a declining birth rate. The growth rate has indeed decreased considerably and the age structure is characterized by an increase in the proportion of older people in addition to the decrease in the proportion of young people, with higher life expectancy. In addition to the decrease in general mortality already mentioned, there has been a very slow decrease in infant mortality, for which the rate is still quite high, so that efforts in this sector are directed first and foremost to the care of lower age groups.

Health situation

Almost half the deaths result from 15 defined causes; diarrhoeal diseases continue to head the list as the main cause. However, a comparison of the present situation with the beginning of the decade reveals a decrease in the percentage of deaths caused by diarrhoea and enteritis from 9.4% to 7.9%; a reduction in the importance of diseases of the respiratory system, contrasting with the constant increase in heart and cerebrovascular diseases; an increase in the proportion of deaths from malignant tumours and accidents, and a reduction in malnutrition-related deaths.

Among compulsorily notifiable communicable diseases, the most evident increase has been in the incidence of malaria in new settlement areas. This can be attributed to technical difficulties such as the inaccessibility of these areas, the resignation of the community to its fringe position in society, the growing biological resistance of both the mosquito to insecticides and the parasite to drugs, the economic conditions in these areas and the changes in rainfall which have been favourable to the vector.

Since 40% of births take place in hospital, representing one-quarter of all hospitalizations, the hospital morbidity structure indicates that it might be advisable to introduce a system of maternal care according to the risks involved, thus filling available beds with high obstetrical risk confinement cases previously delivered at home under insanitary conditions. The availability of organized human, physical and financial resources through the national health system for the provision of services and the carrying out of environmental activities is another factor influencing the health situation of the population.

Health care delivery

The personal care programme has achieved very significant results to date. On 31 December 1977 Colombia had one physician for 1920 inhabitants; one dentist for 5541 inhabitants; one professional nurse for 7342 inhabitants and one certified auxiliary nurse for 1467 inhabitants. There are still imbalances in the availability of personnel, particularly in relation to dentists and professional nurses. In connexion with the geographical distribution and the population coverage for each category, the chronic problems of concentration in large urban centres and insufficient use of resources according to the complexity of the health problems are being considerably alleviated by the widespread use of auxiliary personnel, with strong emphasis on the system of delegating duties.

Between 1975 and 31 December 1977, primary health care services using nursing auxiliaries and rural extension workers were set up in 432 rural and urban fringe communities with a total of two million inhabitants. In 1978 the incorporation of 997 000 inhabitants of 152 rural areas and 393 000 inhabitants of urban fringe areas in the programme was planned, with sufficient technical and financial resources to make national health system services available for the first time to a total of four million inhabitants, or 37% of the nine million inhabitants who, at the beginning of the period under review, lacked the most basic health services. Sufficient well-equipped and well-managed health institutions of varying complexity, an adequate patient transport system and an appropriate communications network are indispensable to these strategies.

With regard to outpatient medical care in the health institutions, there was also a moderate increase, from 508 attendances per 1000 inhabitants in 1974 to 543 in 1977, and an increase in coverage from 27.8% to 30.4% of the population receiving benefits from the offical sector. In the priority groups—mothers and children—the coverage of pregnant women increased from 53.5% in 1974 to 80.5% in 1977; coverage of infants from 83.8% in 1974 to 87.8% in 1977; coverage of children aged 1–4 years from 31.3% in 1974 to 32.8% in 1977; coverage of children aged 5–14 years from 15.5% in 1974 to 19.7% in 1977.

The health sector participated actively in reorganizing compulsory social security, and the related health services played a major role in achieving national health system objectives. A Superintendency of Health Security was established to ensure the application of the health system's technical norms in providing medical care under social security arrangements.

With regard to the availability of hospital beds, 3966 beds were added during the period 1974–1977, with adequate organizational support and human and material resources. The total number of annual discharges per bed and the bed occupancy rate have both increased.

Health expenditure, costs and investment

The total financial resources of the official sector increased from 6598 million pesos to 11 186 million in the period 1975–1978, an increase of 69.5%. This substantial increase satisfactorily compensated for devaluation but did not allow the relative proportion of the total amount in the national budget to be maintained; this fell from 11.4% in 1974 to only 7.4% in 1978. The investment effort has been particularly outstanding. Between 1975 and 1978 alone, a sum of 9963.6 million pesos was guaranteed by the budget, together with direct contributions from the sectional health services. If to this are added the funds from the external credits allocated during the period, either already received or due to be received, for equipping hospitals and for water supplies and sewerage systems, a total of a little over 15 000 million pesos committed to and obtained for health investment is reached.

The resources available during the period 1975–1978 for the construction of new buildings for extension, renovation and other administrative contracts amounted to 1150 million pesos. Special priority has been given to investment in hospital equipment to ensure that the institutions of the national health system have the most up-to-date facilities available in modern medicine. For this reason, full support has been given to securing considerable external credits from the different countries producing this specialized equipment. Up to the middle of 1978, credits of more than 4500 million pesos had been obtained or were in the process of being secured.

Socioeconomic development and health planning

The basic objective of the socioeconomic and sectoral development plan for 1975–1978 was to achieve a rate of economic growth that would make possible the widespread creation of productive employment and would thus be of special benefit to the poorest 50% of Colombian society. The first part of the plan laid down general economic policies aimed essentially at promoting the rapid growth of labour-intensive activities. The second part detailed agricultural, industrial, export promotion and regional and urban development policies. The economic policies encourage integrated rural development and agricultural reform. The third part presented the basic social services, with programmes concentrated on the improvement of education, health and drinking-water services in the rural sector. The public expenditure programmes are based on the assumption that the most effective employment policy is to provide the work force with good education and good health in order to make it productive.

The central point of the social programmes is the national food and nutrition plan. Major emphasis is also given to the programme for the integration to services and community participation in urban fringe areas, aimed at improving the standard of living in these areas through rational use of their human potential and provision of the different public and communal social services offered by the State. The plan explicitly recognizes the close relationship between the various social problems in the fields of health, education and nutrition, justifying an overall approach to the problem in order to gain greater effectiveness in the allocation of resources and the achievement of the objectives proposed.

The national Government has identified the following health policies:

(1) increasing health service coverage, giving priority to the mother and the child as the most vulnerable population group;

(2) reducing the gap still separating rural and urban populations in matters of health protection services;

(3) reducing morbidity caused by infectious and parasitic diseases;

(4) making maximum use of existing hospital facilities so as to increase and improve services concerned with the recovery of health and supplying these institutions with human resources and other facilities indispensable to their operation;

(5) improving the training of auxiliary personnel so that the provision of more basic health services can be delegated to them, and providing adequate supervision to ensure the quality of these services;

(6) coordinating all the institutions for the improvement of health in order to avoid any duplication of effort or wastage of physical and human resources (new legislation has been drawn up for the formation of the national health system, which will facilitate the application of this policy); and

(7) integrating efforts in the health sector with those of other sectors so as to make a better contribution to social and economic development.

The following are some of the regulating mechanisms which have been developed to a considerable extent during the period under review:

— the legal norms forming the juridical basis of the national health system and regulating the fundamental aspects of its structure and operation; and the basic organization for its management (with definition of norms for the local or operating level), for the regional level (with administrative and operating responsibilities over several local levels), for the sectional level (with technical and administrative functions), and for the national level (with political and normative responsibilities);

— the systems for supervision and coordination which, taking as a basis the public or private origin of the health bodies and institutions, define their relations, establish the scope of the legal norms of the health system and define the limit of its responsibility;

— the subsystems responsible for planning, investment, information, supplies, personnel and research that lay down the specialized operational norms for those areas considered to be the most critical.

The health sector fulfils its responsibilities under the development plan by directing its efforts, first and foremost, to the widespread and rapid extension of primary and integral health service coverage, both to the people and to the environment of the rural and urban fringe populations, with the idea of channelling its efforts, where appropriate, through the national food and nutrition plan, the integrated rural development programme, and the programme for the integration of services and community participation in urban fringe areas.

Pharmaceutical production and costs

The adoption of a price policy satisfactory both to manufacturers and consumers, and the establishment of norms and mechanisms for production and quality control, have achieved results very much in line with initial expectations.

Environmental health

The programme for extended health coverage also includes activities in those environmental sectors which greatly influence the health status of persons living in fringe areas, that is, water supplies and waste disposal. The achievements of the two national organizations responsible for such operations have been outstanding: the National Health Institute for localities numbering 50 to 2500 inhabitants, and the National Institute for Municipal Development in larger localities. The work of the former is represented by the construction of 1386 water supply systems leading to an increase in coverage during the period 1974–1977 from 41.5% to 49% of the population by the programme. Total investment amounted to 688 million pesos, included a major contribution from the community of 70 million pesos. During the period, 178 rural sewerage systems were also constructed, achieving a 14% coverage at a cost of 80 million pesos, 8 million pesos being the contribution of the community.

The work carried out by the National Institute for Municipal Development covered 244 localities and cities, directly benefiting 3 594 000

inhabitants and leading to a change in coverage from 70% to 74% for water supplies and from 31% to 43% for sewerage systems.

Evaluation of progress between 1973 and 1978

The health level of the country's population, and in particular of the mothers and children, is showing definite improvement. The most important positive facts are the reduction in the relative importance of diarrhoeal diseases, enteritis and pneumonia as causes of death in the under-15-year age group, and the reduction in maternal mortality from traditional causes.

The incidence of gonococcal infections, measles, early syphilis, tuberculosis of the respiratory system, pertussis, typhoid, diphtheria, leprosy, viral encephalitis and human rabies also fell, while the incidence of malaria, meningococcal meningitis and acute poliomyelitis increased.

COSTA RICA

This study of the state of health of the country and of the existing health service system takes into consideration some goals of the National Health Plan, 1974–1980.

Population and other statistics

Life expectancy at birth summarizes the level of health of the country and permits periodical comparisons and measurements based on mortality and natality data. The value of this indicator in 1972 was 68.15 years, and the first and most general goal in the National Health Plan was to extend it to 71.08 years by 1980, a gain of 2.93 years (average annual gain 0.37 years). By 1976 a life expectancy at birth of 71.42 years had been achieved, a gain of 3.3 years in a period of four years, which thus surpassed both the expected gain for that year and the goal established for 1980. This increase in life expectancy is a consequence of the decline in mortality, especially in children under 10 years of age, whose mortality is very susceptible to the economic and social changes of a nation, in which improved health and medical progress and the expansion of coverage of public health programmes must play their part.

These demographic phenomena, which are very closely connected, produce substantial changes in the population, especially in its age structure.

Like many Latin American countries, the birth rate in the country has been high, but the general trend is towards a decline, to which are contributing such factors as the expansion of educational programmes and the supply of modern means of fertility control, changes in the outlook of women, and the migration of young women of childbearing age from the countryside to cities. During the last four years, the birth rate has remained virtually unchanged. In the period 1973–1975 there was an increase in the specific fertility rate for the population under 25 years. The age group 20–24 years made the largest contribution to the fertility rate, with a rate of 208 births per 1000 in 1975, followed by the age group 25–29 with a rate of 180 per 1000. On the basis of the age-specific fertility rates for 1975, the overall fertility rate in Costa Rica has been estimated at around 3.8 children per woman.

The mortality rate has declined 12%, from 5.2 to 4.6. Conspicuous in this general mortality rate are deaths in children under 5 years of age, not only because of the high number but also because of the causes of death. In 1976, more than 25% of total deaths were deaths in children under 5 years of age. It is to be noted that 25% of that mortality was due to infectious and parasitic diseases.

In 1976, diseases of the circulatory system and tumours accounted for 2882 deaths (31% of all deaths) and ranked as the two leading causes of death. The third leading cause was accidents, which was followed by diseases of the nervous system and prematurity.

Perinatal mortality or deaths occurring in connexion with delivery (deaths occurring in the first six days of life and late fetal deaths) also decreased appreciably during the period under review. In 1973 there were 26.9 perinatal deaths per 1000 births, but this rate fell to 24.5 in 1976, a reduction of 9% in that period.

In the period 1973–1976 there was a reduction of 26% in the infant mortality rate, which fell from 44.8 to 33.3 infant deaths per 1000 live births. This decrease is extremely important if it is borne in mind that the National Health Plan establishes as goal for the year 1980 an infant mortality rate of 38.08 per 1000 live births. The reduction in the infant mortality rate produced an 18% decline in the neonatal mortality while residual mortality declined 34%.

Communicable diseases

For morbidity data Costa Rica has three sources of information: a weekly report on communicable diseases, special surveys, and hospital discharges and outpatient consultations. In the period 1973–1976 certain diseases that can be prevented by vaccination were still an important cause of morbidity, in particular measles, pertussis and tuberculosis. Waterborne diseases have been declining, with the exception of viral hepatitis, the incidence of which increased in 1977.

In 1977 there was an 118% increase in gonorrhoea, a 62% increase in syphilis and a 313% increase in soft chancre. Venereal diseases occupy an important place in total notifiable diseases, and the population in the age group 15–44 years is the most affected.

Malnutrition

Since the national epidemiological surveillance system does not at present include the updated study on the nutritional status of the population, malnutrition is evaluated by means of surveys.

In 1976 a national survey was carried out. On that basis it was estimated that 57.4% of children under 5 years of age suffered from some degree of malnutrition, (43.7%, first degree; 12.2%, second degree; and 1.5%, third degree, according to the Gomez classification) and that 16.9% were below the normal height for their age or were stunted. The prevalence of iron deficiency amaemia was 16–20% and that of goitre, 18%. Vitamin A deficiency was found primarily in pre-school age children.

In 1977 another national survey was carried out. Its results showed that malnutrition in the children mentioned had been reduced to 53.2%, a decline of 7.3% (40.9%, first degree; 11.2%, second degree; 1.1%, third degree). The problem was more pronounced in rural areas, with a 58.6% malnutrition rate (44.0%, first degree; 13.3%, second degree; 1.3%, third degree) and less pronounced in the urban areas, with a 43.6% malnutrition rate (35.4%, first degree; 7.5%, second degree; and 0.7%, third degree).

Using weight/height standards instead of weight/age standards, the last mentioned survey showed that 37% of children under 5 years of age were underweight (weight was adequate in 53.2%, 8.4% were overweight, and in 1.4% weight was unknown), whereas when weight/age standards were used, 53.2% had been found underweight.

Because of the persistence of the problem of malnutrition in a majority of children, high priority has been given since 1975 to the food and nutrition programme. It has been completely reformulated and expanded, and many community institutions and organizations, as well as four ministries (those for health, education, agriculture and stockraising, and public works and transportation), are taking part in it.

Environment

Generally speaking, it may be said that environmental conditions are unsatisfactory and in some cases are deteriorating as a result of the rapid growth of the population, industrialization, urbanization, migration lack of regional and urban planning, increase in consumption, increase in waste and lack of efficient planning of natural resources. The risk of increased incidence of many diseases and disorders such as waterborne diseases, food poisoning, enteroparasitic diseases, occupational diseases, and deafness, is recognized.

In the decade 1963–1973 the number of houses rose from 231 153 to 330 857, an increase of 43.1%, but the population increased proportionately. The number of houses with sewer connexions rose from 30 420 to 49 044, an increase of 61.3%; the number of houses with septic tanks rose from 38 303 to 97 386, an increase of 154.3%; the number of houses with sanitary slab latrines rose from 43 959 to 90 489, an increase of 105.8%. There was a decrease of 58 957 (37.8%) in the number of houses without sanitary service. The percentage of unsatisfactory housing units fell from 34% to 13.5%, and the percentage of those with earth floors from 25.4% to 14.1%.

Between 1974 and 1977 a total of 65 000 latrines were distributed throughout the country, but it is estimated that only 25% of them were installed. Accordingly, future activities will be aimed primarily at educating the public and promoting installation of the latrines. Subsequently, between 40 000 and 50 000 additional latrines will be distributed and installed with a view to replacing those in poor condition and achieving the expected coverage.

Houses with connexions to the public water supply network increased from 140 363 in 1963 to 230 964 in 1973, an increase of 64.6%; those with connexions to private water supply systems from 17 604 to 27 885, an increase of 58.4%; and those with a well from 14 995 to 26 444, an increase of 76.4%.

Health service system and legislation

The existence of a large number of institutions and agencies responsible for health services in Costa Rica and the consequent duplication, omissions and lack of coordination led to the adoption of a policy of sectoral integration to cover the entire population with uniform comprehensive services.

Law No. 4750, enacted in March 1971, amended Article 3 of the Law establishing the Costa Rican Social Security Fund, and provided for universal health services to be established by stages, authorizing the institution to provide care for the needy, to cover occupational hazards and accidents, and to undertake programmes of preventive medicine. Law No. 5349,

enacted in September 1973, increased the material, human and financial resources of the Social Security Fund so as to enable it to extend its services to the entire population by means of a single comprehensive medical care service through the transfer of installed physical capacity and its sources of financing and the obligation to provide care for the insured and noninsured population. The execution of this programme gave rise to some conflict because trade union interests were affected, and at the present time the only public hospital which has not been transferred is the Doctor Carlos Luis Valverde Hospital in San Ramón. The law was supplemented by Law No. 5541, which regulates the status of the workers in the establishments transferred. This made it possible to expand the legal coverage of the Social Security Fund to approximately 82.8% of the population.

In October 1973 the General Health Law was enacted, defining a system for regulating the activities of individuals, enterprises, and the State in the field of health. In November 1973 the Organic Law of the Ministry of Health was enacted. It determines the structural and functional organization of the institutional services. Its execution also gave rise to conflict because the interests of many workers were affected. The General Directorates of Health and of Medico-Social Welfare were integrated into a single General Health Directorate. As a result, all the personnel have been covered by uniform labour regulations since November 1974. The services for statistics, transport, publications, personnel, supply, and—to a lesser extent—the accounting services, have been integrated.

Having delegated responsibility for medical care at higher levels to the Social Security Fund, the Ministry concentrated its efforts on complementary measures to develop:

(1) the rural health programme to provide basic care service infrastructure manned by auxiliary personnel in all rural areas lacking services. At the present time 251 health posts are in operation serving 650 000 inhabitants (95% of the rural population), and total coverage is expected to be achieved in 1979 through the creation of 25 more posts. In addition there are 42 health posts in the San Ramón area and 5 in the area covered by the Social Security Fund;

(2) the community health programme for the marginal urban areas to strengthen health centres for general medical care using auxiliary personnel to carry the services into

those communities. It at present provides services for 499 201 beneficiaries through 199 community health areas. It has been used in San Antonio de Nicoya, with five health posts operated by the Social Security Fund, and has been widely accepted and supported by the community; its use at higher levels of medical care is to be promoted.

The universal provision of social security, coupled with the strengthening and integration of the services at higher levels and the rapid development of basic comprehensive care, is supplemented by a process of increasing inter-institutional coordination, the purpose of which is unity of goals, policies and strategies and the creation of a national health service.

Administrative infrastructure

Among the main administrative constraints are the inadequate structural design; deficient inter-institutional coordination; lack of specific health laws; weakness of the mechanisms of the directing authority of the Ministry; unsatisfactory systems and methods of supervision; dichotomy, with communication barriers, between technical and administrative levels; unplanned allocation of resources; weakness in sectoral planning; insufficient participation of certain technical and administrative agencies in planning; insufficient integration of personnel, accounting and supply systems; and regional organizational weakness.

These constraints have been the subject of a programme of administrative development, which is being implemented primarily through specific projects that focus attention on the managerial process or on decision-making. They include the following:

Physical resources and productivity

The policy followed has been aimed at a better use of available resources to increase operational capacity, including modernization or repair of existing resources, and an extension of the infrastructure to the most deprived areas. With a reduction of 10% in the bed/population ratio it has been possible to maintain the annual discharge rate at the goal established for 1980, i.e., between 100 and 115 per 1000 inhabitants. The goal of 2.5 consultations per annum per inhabitant for 1980 has already been surpassed

(2.6 in 1976), the tendency being an increase of 0.1 per year.

Human resources

The number of physicians in practice increased from 908, or 5.2 per 10 000 inhabitants, in 1970 to 1483 (1309 registered and 174 undergoing social service) in 1977, giving a ratio of 7.2 per 10 000, thus surpassing the goal of 6.68 established in the National Health Plan for 1980. The improvement is primarily due to a substantial increase in admissions to and graduations from the Faculty of Medicine.

The number of dentists also increased from 246 registered with the Dental Association (1.4 per 10 000 inhabitants) in 1973 to 448 (2.2) in 1977, thus also surpassing the goal of 2 per 10 000 established for 1980 in the National Health Plan.

There was an increase from 796 nurses in service (4.3 per 10 000 inhabitants) in 1972 to 1112 (5.4) in 1977 (905 in Social Security Fund Service; 133 with the Ministry, and 74 with other institutions), thus surpassing the goal of 4.8–5.3 per 10 000 established in the National Health Plan for 1980. Between 1973 and 1976 a total of 439 nurses were trained, an annual average of 110.

The number of nursing auxiliaries rose from 3015 (15.9 per 10 000 inhabitants) in 1976, to 3436 (16.7) in 1977. Thus the goal of 16.1–17.8 per 10 000 for 1980 in the National Health Plan was reached. In the period 1973–1977 a total of 1576 nursing auxiliaries were trained, an annual average of 315.

The number of microbiologists in the public health subsector increased from 70 (0.4 per 10 000 inhabitants) in 1972, to 211 (1.0) in 1977. The goal established for 1980 in the National Health Plan of 0.6 per 10 000 in the public health subsector was thus surpassed.

The number of pharmacists in the public health subsector rose from 75 (0.4 per 10 000 inhabitants) in 1972, to 123 (0.6) in 1977; the goal for 1980 in the National Health Plan was reached.

Finally, the number of sanitary inspectors rose from 103 (0.6 per 10 000 inhabitants) in 1973 to 114 (ratio unchanged) in 1977. The 1980 goal is one to 10 000.

Financial resources

The health expenditures of the Ministry of Health, the sickness and maternity system of the

Social Security Fund and the Institute for Water Supply and Sewerage Systems increased by 37.8% between 1974 and 1975 and by 20.8% between 1975 and 1976, i.e., by 66.4% between 1974 and 1976. Health expenditures represented 5.6% of the gross domestic product in 1974, rising to 6.1% in the following two years. The result was that the annual health expenditure per capita increased from 384.72 Costa Rican colón (₡) in 1974 to ₡519.14 in 1975 and to ₡609.70 in 1976, an increase of 58.5%. The share of the Social Security Fund rose from 43.5% of the total in 1974 to 46.3% in 1975 and 51.7% in 1976. Concurrently, the relative share of the Ministry of Health fell from 43.2% in 1974 to 37.7% in 1975 and to 32.3% in 1976. This was primarily due to the rapid growth of the Social Security Fund and secondarily to the gradual transfer of hospitals from one institution to the other.

The relative share of Social Security was 48.0% in 1974, 47.6% in 1975, and 53.3% in 1976, whereas that of the Ministry of Health fell from 37.7% in 1974, to 31.9% in 1975, and to 28.6% in 1976. The income of the sector increased by 66.4% between 1974 and 1976, a figure equal to that of the increase in expenditure.

The unit cost of consultations rose from ₡28.88 in 1972 to ₡53.72 in 1976, an increase of 86.0%, and that of hospitalization from ₡111.22 in 1972 to ₡305.04 in 1976, an increase of 174.3%. These increases were due both to inflation and primarily to the increase in the quality of services with scientific and technological progress. Since the national economy cannot indefinitely finance increases in unit costs of such magnitude coupled with an increase in the services for meeting the increasing demand of a larger population, it is becoming necessary to streamline the use of resources in order to prevent possible negative effects on other sectors of the economy and thus to achieve the most balanced possible comprehensive development.

CUBA

During the period under review the progressive evolution of the health services has continued under the beneficial influence of the country's harmonious economic and social development and has itself in turn influenced this development favourably. Every day more people have easier access to health services, resulting in a simultaneous increase in the demand for better-quality care, particularly in view of scientific, technical and social progress. Due to a marked improvement in the standard of living and the provision of better and more widespread medical care, the morbidity picture has improved.

Organization of the health services

The principles of the system and its functions have remained unchanged. The only innovation to be noted is the recent incorporation of advanced training for physicians, stomatologists and nurses, giving the Ministry of Public Health full responsibility.

The new political and administrative division of the country, which came fully into force in 1977 with the creation of the "people's authorities" bodies, together with the new economic management and planning system, have necessitated an adaptation of the health system. The central administrative level now supervises and controls State and government policy with regard to health care of the population, and the 14 provincial levels and 169 municipal levels come under the provincial and municipal assemblies of the "people's authorities", respectively. The provincial and municipal levels are subject to dual supervision: in matters concerning standards and methodology they are subordinate to the central level, the Ministry of Public Health, and in administrative matters to the "people's authorities". The hierarchy of health care facilities has remained unchanged.

Health manpower resources and development

More than 7000 physicians graduated in Cuba between 1959 and 1974, and 5063 between 1974 and 1977, so that between 1959 and 1977 more than 12 000 physicians graduated. Work has continued on the improvement of programmes for specialists, and by 1978 there were 2745 resident students following specialized courses. In 1973 there was one stomatologist for approximately 4300 inhabitants and in 1977 there was one for 3590. An average of 5500 nurses and intermediate level technicians have graduated each year since 1974.

There has been further progress in the organization and quality of continuing education. As a general indicator, 13 397 courses for professional categories and intermediate level technicians were held in 1977, with a total of 121 958 participants.

Environmental health

The Ministry of Public Health fulfils an advisory function in environmental health, while the "people's authorities" are responsible for implementing activities. As far as atmospheric pollution is concerned, in 1974 it was indicated that the installation of a national sampling network and the introduction of preventive measures backed by appropriate sanitary legislation were envisaged; in 1977, 13 stations meeting PAHO standards were in operation in nine large cities and basic air quality indicators were being determined. There were also a considerable number of sampling stations for airborne particulates, hydrogen sulfide and nitrogen dioxide, and for corrosion, including that caused by sulfur dioxide. A new methodology has been introduced on a countrywide basis for the health supervision of very small localities, for projects for agricultural and social development, and for new communities having water supply and sewerage systems.

Health care delivery

In 1974 there were 336 polyclinics and one community teaching polyclinic in the experimental stage, while in 1977 there were 340 polyclinics, 60% of which had turned over to operate in accordance with the new community medicine system, and the community teaching polyclinic was fully operational.

In 1977 there were 42 842 hospital beds, giving a bed/population ration of 4.5 per 1000. The plan for the building of hospital units drawn up for the period 1976–1980, which is currently being implemented, provides for the establishment of 12 hospitals with some 6000 new beds.

As regards community participation, where in 1974 the social institutions gave extremely useful support to the health services, today the community truly participates, the users of the polyclinic taking an active part in the actual life of the unit and in the management board, making suggestions and criticisms for improvements in the provision of services.

Disease control

Priority is still being given to the national programme for the control of acute diarrhoeal diseases. Since 1968 these diseases have no longer figured among the five leading causes of general mortality. In 1974 the infant mortality rate was 2.9 per 1000 live births, and in 1977 it was 2.5. Typhoid fever is still endemic.

Acute diseases of the respiratory system still constituted an important cause of infant mortality during 1977 (3.7 per 1000 live births). There has been a decrease in the incidence of tuberculosis; in 1974 the rate was 15.4 per 100 000 inhabitants; in 1977 it was 13.1 per 100 000.

The incidence of syphilis decreased from 50.5 per 100 000 in 1974 to 39.3 in 1977. Partly as the result of a case-finding campaign, gonorrhoea has gradually increased, from 35.2 per 100 000 in 1974 to 85.9 in 1977.

In 1977 there was an epidemic of dengue fever, with 477 440 reported cases. Measures such as the large-scale education of the population and the control of the vector mosquito were taken which, following the identification of the species, and thanks to the advice received from PAHO, helped to solve the problem.

With the marked decrease in morbidity and mortality caused by communicable diseases, the noncommunicable diseases are coming more and more to the forefront.

Maternal and child health

With the help of new human and material resources, it was possible to bring down the maternal mortality rate from 5.6 per 1000 births in 1974 to 4.3 in 1977, and infant mortality from 29.3 per 1000 live births to 24.6.

Research

In 1973 a Research Directorate was created to complement the National Committee for Health Research, and in 1974 the National Council of Science and Technology was created. These form the basic structure, together with the system of existing or newly created institutes such as the Institute for Health Development. In 1977, 706 research projects were carried out, and 167 were completed, in the research and national health institutes.

Major developments in the period 1973–1977

The Nonaligned Countries Movement at its Fifth Summit Conference in Colombo in 1976,

and at the two meetings of health ministers and representatives of the nonaligned and other interested developing countries in Geneva in 1977 and 1978, took up the problem of health in member countries. A plan of action for health was approved, identifying areas in which they should build up a body of "know-how". The health ministers and representatives of the Movement agreed that the solutions found during the meetings should be oriented to coincide with the interests and suggestions of WHO, whose present slogan "Health for all by the year 2000" will become a reality only to the extent that health is provided to the hundreds of millions of people who make up the populations of developing countries—almost half the inhabitants of the planet.

DOMINICAN REPUBLIC

The Dominican Republic occupies the eastern two-thirds of the Island of Santo Domingo (also known as Hispaniola); its territory has a surface of 48 734 km^2 and its population as at July 1978 was estimated at 5 124 394, 47.5% below the age of 15 years. Some 50% of the population live in rural areas. The main objective of the health policy is to decentralize programmes and activities so as to ensure that, even in the most remote communities of the country, services and resources can respond to the most pressing health needs and that the necessary machinery is at hand to refer cases requiring specialized services to more highly developed centres.

Organization of health services

To that end, and in order to reorganize the national health system, the Government has been carrying out since 1973 a process of regionalization of the health services. The territory has been divided into six public health regions, each comprising a number of health areas corresponding to the various provinces which constitute the geographical subdivisions of the country; these are being provided with the necessary physical and material resources and personnel to enable them to function as self-sufficient units of decreasing complexity from the centre to the periphery.

In order to extend the coverage and expand the services provided to the rural population by the regular health services, a basic health services programme was implemented during the period 1974–1978, making use of local women health promoters from the communities to attend to the primary health needs of areas with less than 2000 inhabitants; 4000 women health promoters and 400 women assistant nurses were to be employed, all of them fully trained and duly supervised, in order to cover those sectors of the population which had no ready access to conventional health services.

In recent years a programme of administrative reform has been under way for a more rational use of available resources, adapting them to the needs of regionalization and to the new strategies.

Manpower development

Under a complementary training programme short- and long-term solutions are being sought for the problems caused by the shortage and inadequate distribution of health personnel.

The Department of Health had a total of 1203 doctors, 203 qualified nurses and 1970 assistant nurses on its staff in 1976; the numbers are increasing, although not at the desired rate. The hospital services of the Department of

Health have 7300 beds distributed over 91 hospital establishments.

There is increasing coordination of the training activities of the Department of Health with those of the universities.

Mortality and morbidity

In 1974 a survey was carried out for a general diagnosis of public health, aiming to provide a more accurate picture than was obtained with the information gathered through normal statistical channels, which is distorted by a high degree of under-registration. According to the data resulting from this survey, the general death rate stood at 14.7 per 1000 population, infant mortality was 103.8 per 1000 live births, and the mortality rate for the 1–4 year-old age group was 16.8 per 1000 population at risk. The mean life expectancy at birth was estimated at 55 years.

Communicable diseases

The rates recorded for 1976 showed that infectious and parasitic diseases constituted the main causes of death. Out of 25 125 deaths reported, 3456 were due to infectious or parasitic diseases (13.7%), the most important being enteritis and diarrhoeal diseases, with a death rate of 35 per 100 000 inhabitants; 184 deaths due to tetanus were reported, with maximum incidence in infants. Other important communicable diseases include poliomyelitis—which is endemic with occasional epidemic outbreaks (38 cases notified in 1977)—leprosy, tuberculosis and measles. An expanded immunization programme is being implemented in pursuance of the decisions of WHO/PAHO.

Malaria is well on the way to eradication; however, it is necessary to increase efforts for control and epidemiological vigilance.

Rabies is the most prevalent zoonosis; during the period 1962–1977, there were 76 deaths. In recent years, both diagnosis and immunoprophylactic treatment have been improved. Action continues to be intensified.

Family planning and nutrition

The Government has been developing an active family planning programme, which has been successful in that it has achieved a significant lowering of fertility rates. The birth rate, which in 1965 stood at 48 live births per 1000 population, fell to 35 per 1000 in 1975.

The nutritional status of the population constitutes one of the major medicosocial problems. In 1974 a nationwide survey carried out by the Department of Health revealed that 58% of children were suffering from protein-calorie malnutrition. A programme of nutrition information and promotion, and distribution of dietary supplements to small children, is being implemented and a nutrition coordination corps has been created to carry it out.

Environmental health

Existing waste disposal and other environmental facilities are deficient. In 1976 the dwellings of 60% of the urban population were connected to water mains, but barely 11% of the rural population had a drinking-water supply. There are also deficiencies in the facilities for the disposal of human waste.

Outlook

The new Government will spare no effort to raise health levels by carrying out priority activities and programmes in conformity with needs and with the resources available; in doing so, special emphasis will be placed on measures for the prevention of those diseases which constitute the main health problems.

Thus, a state of emergency has been declared in nine provinces bordering on Haiti because of the health conditions prevailing there; 150 rural clinics will be built, with housing facilities for the staff working there and with hospital beds for short-term patients or those awaiting more complex treatment.

A health committee will be set up in each sector or area covered by a rural clinic and will ensure that the population concerned is duly provided with health education facilities and is immunized, that the appropriate censuses are carried out and that the necessary basic health measures, such as provision of latrines, wells, and waste disposal facilities, are taken. The communities concerned will participate in the solution of their health problems.

ECUADOR

Basic information

The estimated population in mid-1977 was 7 556 000. According to the demographic indicators, 43% of the population was under 15 and 6.6% over 55 in 1977. The birth rate for 1975 was 31.3 per 1000.

Life expectancy at birth in 1974–1975 was 60.7 years. The general mortality rate was 7.8 per 1000 inhabitants in 1975. The infant mortality rate was 65.8 per 1000 live births, and the mortality rate for the 1–4 age group was 23.3 per 1000 inhabitants. Deaths from infectious and parasitic diseases accounted for 20% of total mortality in 1975.

The number of doctors, dentists and nurses per 10 000 inhabitants in 1977 was 6.17, 1.81 and 1.62, respectively. There were 1.9 hospital beds per 1000 inhabitants in 1974.

The environmental indicators show that, in 1977, 82% of the urban and 13% of the rural population had domestic potable water supply connexions. The proportion of the population covered by sewerage and sanitary excreta disposal systems was 6% in urban and 11% in rural areas.

The daily per capita calorie intake was 2070 in 1977.

According to the economic indicators, the per capita gross domestic product was 16 954 sucres (about US $678) in 1976.

The appropriation for the Ministry of Health was 9.6% of the national budget in 1977.

Institutional development

Two well defined stages of development of health institutions were closely linked to the policies of the five-year plan for the transformation and development of Ecuador (1973–1977): reorganization and planning; and development of the Ministry of Health. The following activities may be mentioned in connexion with the first stage (1972–1975):

Political and administrative reorganization, initiated by the issue of Decree No. 232 of 14 April 1972, which centralizes authority for the health service in the Ministry and dissolves the central and provincial welfare boards, their services being integrated with those of the Ministry. As a result, the Ministry is now the administering authority for 48% of all hospital beds (6271 beds).

—Formulation of the Five-Year Health Plan. This embodies the principle of total health, defined as action to "provide medical care from the cradle to the grave for both the healthy and the sick, wherever they may live...".

—The "Country Plan" for 1974–1977, with short- and medium-term programming based on the recommendations of the Special Meeting of Ministers of Health of the Americas held in Chile in October 1972.

—The second stage is accelerated growth and development of the Ministry. The following activities connected with this stage may be mentioned:

—Evaluation of the action taken prior to 1975 to build up the health infrastructure with a view to boosting such action so as to achieve the goals specified in the Country Plan. Thus, for the first time, an ambitious plan was formulated almost without parallel in the Americas as far as the volume and magnitude of the investment involved and the short period of time allowed for its execution were concerned.

—Formulation of a plan to extend coverage to the marginal rural areas, a plan which involves the establishment of 700 health posts, 300 of which were to be constructed during the first stage.

Operational development

Since the Ministry of Health was to begin its transformation and development activities by integrating such health agencies as the old social welfare boards, which had been completely inactive for more than 30 years, it was necessary to analyse the situation in those agencies with respect to: physical facilities, equipment, personnel, budget and administration so as to plan the changes and programme the activities which would provide a speedy solution to the enormous problems of delivery of services.

Health establishments and equipment

It was decided to encourage ambulatory treatment through health centres, subcentres and health posts; to increase the number of beds available for short stays in the gynaecological and obstetrical, paediatric and clinical and surgical emergency sections of the hospitals in the chief towns of cantons; to renovate all the hospitals in the chief provincial towns that were in a serious state of deterioration and carry out repairs and remodelling, as needed; and to improve the bed/population ratio. A mixed committee of national and international experts was established for this purpose. Under an agreement with PAHO, it undertook an analysis of the entire infrastructure and the preparation of designs for physical facilities, remodelling, and equipment. It was necessary also to look into the physical conditions in which the provincial health authorities were operating; many of them were located in premises that were unsuitable for the functions they were called upon to carry out in their respective communities.

The report prepared by the committee has borne fruit, for the country now has a comprehensive study on hospitals with different numbers of beds, accompanied by a list of equipment, coded for computer use, and information on organization, personnel, and financing. At the same time, a solution was found for the planning of the children's hospital under construction at Guyaquil, and the plans for the university hospital in the same city were completed, but it has not been possible to start construction because the land offered by the Guyaquil Town Council has not become available. In the hospitals of the chief towns of the provinces facilities are being reorganized, adapted, or newly built. The plan provided for all chief towns of cantons also to have modern, well-equipped functional units.

The activities carried on in the rural areas have been significant; it is hoped that when the project financed by the Inter-American Development Bank has been completed, most of the most urgent needs will have been fulfilled.

In addition to the planning and the construction of establishments, it has been possible to increase the number of staff, subject to budgetary limitations. In most of the hospitals for acute cases, the treatment rate has risen. Depending on their complexity, all the new hospitals that are opened have a standard ratio of 2 to 2.5 staff members per bed.

The delivery of health services has further been improved throughout the country by hospital reorganization and departmentalization, by development, in particular, of the departments of nursing, and by modernization of the food, dietetic, laundry and other services.

Financial resources

The health budget increased from 230 543 000 sucres, of which 145 833 000 sucres was the operational budget, 84 710 000 sucres capital, to 999 342 000 sucres in 1975 (903 425 000 sucres operational, 95 917 000 sucres capital), and 1 579 896 000 sucres in 1977 (1 255 294 sucres operational, 324 602 000 sucres capital).

This increase effectively reflects the priority assigned to the health sector by the Government. Whereas the Ministry's budget had previously been only 2.6% of the national budget, it rose to 9.6% in 1977. Internally, this was a budget increase of 593.4%, while the general budget increase was only 284.3%. If the increase in the gross domestic product is taken to be 167% over the same period, it is obvious that there has been a great deal of activity in the health sector, as a result of financing becoming available with the speed required by the circumstances; and whereas per capita expenditure was US $1.6 in 1964 for the whole of the health sector, it was US $8.52 in 1977 for the Ministry of Health alone.

Drugs

The Ministry has made a great and sustained effort to ensure that enough drugs are available to meet the demand. When the present Government came to power most drugs were imported, a few being manufactured in local plants. A national department fixed drug prices. The drugs were expensive and not available on demand; very few were to be found in the Ministry's establishments owing to budgetary stringency. A standard list of basic drugs was lacking.

The central body responsible for fixing drug prices was reorganized and provided with the staff necessary to keep up with the development of the pharmaceutical industry and to administer the programmes for supplying drugs to the Ministry's establishments.

International producers of pharmaceutical products were encouraged to install plant for the manufacture of their products so as to increase local production, promote the transfer of technology and increase the potential for scientific research in this field, while at the same time providing more employment for skilled local manpower.

A list of drugs was made that would serve as a national pharmacopoeia. Ecuador produces about 450 basic drugs required for every type of medical care, even the most complex, given in the health establishments of the Ministries of Health, Social Security, Welfare and the Armed Forces.

The drugs on the basic list of supplies for the Ministry's health establishments must now be purchased in Ecuador on the basis of competitive bidding among local manufacturers.

Those that, because of the complexity of their preparation, cannot be produced locally are imported directly by the Ministry and sold at cost price to health institutions and individuals through the provincial health authorities.

Increases in the prices of drugs are banned under Decree No. 29 of 25 February 1972.

Potable water and sewerage

The deficiency of potable water and sewerage facilities in urban and rural areas resulted from neglect over many decades, previous to the present Government; there was no definite policy to deal with the problem, and although many solutions were proposed, they were never successfully carried out. The policy of the Military Government in this field was based on the following strategic actions:

— Increasing and improving the technical, administrative and financial possibilities of the institution responsible for sanitary works by providing appropriate technical and financial support obtained through soft loans from the Inter-American Development Bank or funds from the oil resources.
— To determine priorities in urban areas which received community financial support through the municipalities and provincial councils.
– Establishing projects for the construction of potable water supply and sewerage systems for towns of up to 5000 inhabitants to be financed by reimbursable loans.
– Designing models of water supply units and programmes for the provision of water closets or latrines for rural areas, with non-reimbursable financing. The result of these activities from 1973 to 1977 was the execution of the following works:

	Completed	Under way	Total
Designs for water supply . .	174	197	371
Designs for sewerage systems	58	98	156
Construction of water supply systems	118	138	256
Construction of sewerage systems	20	58	78

In addition, 258 water supply units were constructed for a total population of 500 000 inhabitants, and 10 000 latrines and the same number of rural-type earth closets were installed.

A considerable number of water supply and sewerage projects were carried out between 1976 and 1977, thanks to the decisive action taken by the National Government to secure the necessary financing.

Control and improvement of the environment

The Sanitation Office is responsible, through the Division of Environmental Sanitation, for activities to control and improve the environment with a view to keeping the different ecosystems, and particularly air, soil and water, free from pollution. It has installed eight air pollution control stations in certain provinces under the Pan American programme, and has taken similar measures to determine the degree of pollution of surface-water sources preventable and controllable with the resources of modern technology. 43 stations for the control of solid wastes have been installed.

Health coverage

Maternal and child health protection has been one of the priority areas in the policy-making and administrative activities of the Ministry of Health. In the maternal and child health and family welfare programme included in the Country Plan, the goals to be achieved in 1973–1977 were specified.

The rate for "pre-natal control" reached in 1972 was 43.1%; the effectiveness of the services almost doubled in only four years, as by 1976 the protection rate was 81.3%. This is all the more noteworthy as the annual targets also increased. In absolute figures, the number of pregnant women examined rose from 26 005 in 1972 to 92 900 in 1977, an increase of 257%.

GUATEMALA

Major health and health-related problems

The diversity of economic and social conditions in the various regions of Guatemala means that different measures need to be applied to deal with the problems that hinder development. "Social poverty" manifests itself in a low level of education, poor housing and environmental conditions, malnutrition, ill health, and lack of social services for the majority of the rural population. It is estimated that the total population of Guatemala (at present 6 250 000) will have risen to about 9 300 000 by 1990 and to more than 12 million by the year 2000, and that at least 55% of the total population will be living in urban areas in 1990, most of them employed in the manufacturing and service industries.

Despite the Government's efforts and international financial and technical cooperation, living conditions continue to be deficient and progress towards a solution of this problem has been slow. Development of the health services has been hampered by a lack of financial and human resources, equipment and adequate administrative procedures.

Health policies and strategies

The 1975–1979 National Development Plan is a continuation of the effort begun in 1970 with adoption of the 1971–1975 Plan. Health policies have been concentrated mainly on increasing the health service coverage; environmental improvements; improvement of nutrition; and financing of the health services. To implement these policies and strategies, the Ministry of Public Health and Social Welfare has promoted basic programmes for planning and development of the health service system, disease control, administration of hospital care services, maternal and child health and family health, human resources development, food and nutrition, and environmental health. In all these programmes community participation is fostered, the basis of primary health care is reinforced, and the services are regionalized.

Health care delivery

With a view to achieving the objective of providing basic health services for the whole population, conveniently located and in a form acceptable to the people, emphasis is placed on primary health care, participation of the community, improvements in the efficiency of services, manpower development and coordination of the various sectors concerned with health.

Primary health care is based on the traditional systems accepted and practised in the communities, as well as on modern health technology. So far the programmes have been implemented mainly in rural areas, and certain adaptations in procedures and organization will be required for urban areas, where the influx of people from the rural areas is giving rise to serious economic and social problems.

The health care of the population, with emphasis on rural marginal groups and on mothers and children, was intensified in 1977 by efforts which, surmounting the losses inflicted by the earthquake of 1976, resulted in a volume of services that is larger than in any previous year and is still growing.

Since 1974, remodelling operations have been proceeding, and new plants and equipment have been built and installed in 38 hospitals of the Ministry of Public Health and Social Welfare. Plans for the next four years call for the construction of 10 new hospitals, three with 100 beds and seven with 30 beds each. The figures on hospital facilities and services are as follows:

	Beds	Discharges
1974	8 532	135 076
1975	8 410	228 752
1976	9 220	165 819
1977	8 846	160 992

The number of health centres has increased from 80 in 1973 to 159, and the number of health posts from 227 to 472.

The numbers of patients for which the Ministry of Public Health and Social Welfare provided services were 960 475 in 1974 (10.59% of the total population); 1 417 146 in 1975 (11.74%); 2 139 771 in 1976 (18.55%); and 3 256 261 in 1977 (26.57%).

The mass immunization campaigns are continuing and are being maintained at epidemiologically significant levels, with coverage of 80% of the population of children under two years old, who are immunized against poliomyelitis, pertussis, diphtheria, tetanus, measles, and (since 1977) tuberculosis. This means that half a million children are vaccinated each year.

All programmes have been accelerated, so that the population has access to the various levels of care; 3.5 million ambulatory patients were examined in 1977—twice the number examined in 1975. The Government has done everything possible to recover the ground lost in 1976 and to normalize health care delivery in the shortest possible time.

Manpower development

Intensive personnel training programmes suited to the actual situation of the country, particularly in the rural areas, have been continued. Of the total population, 64% live in 17 000 communities of less than 2000 inhabitants; the task of providing services is an arduous one, which is being accomplished through the efforts of the State with the participation of the community.

The administrative reform approved by the Government has resulted in a steady strengthening of the 24 health areas, enabling communities to participate in the system. Rural maternal and child care has been improved through the training of traditional midwives; programmes of epidemiological surveillance are carried out by malaria control volunteers, and patient referral is ensured through the training of health promoters, who have exerted a substantial impact on tuberculosis control and mass immunization campaigns, in which community participation is of major importance.

Environmental health

The policy as regards the environment has been concentrated mainly on:

(1) improving knowledge and obtaining a clear definition of the problem of environmental pollution, and promoting studies and research in this field;
(2) promoting specific activities such as the provision of drinking-water and the improvement of sewage disposal, housing and food control, efforts being made to achieve the maximum coverage of both the urban and rural environment;
(3) promoting an intensified campaign to increase public awareness of the importance of the environment for man and of the effects of

man's actions on the environment;
(4) encouraging all possible action aimed at preventing environmental pollution;
(5) coordinating efforts to utilize to the full the funds allocated to the various sectors involved.

Efforts are principally directed at basic sanitation. The national reconstruction programme is proceeding, and it can be said that 90% of the damage caused by the 1976 earthquake to latrines, water supplies and sewerage networks has been repaired.

Food and nutrition

A survey carried out in Guatemala in 1965 by the Institute of Nutrition of Central America and Panama (INCAP) and the Ministry of Public Health and Social Welfare confirmed the gravity and extent of the nutritional problem.

Specific objectives are to achieve adequate production and availability of food for the population; to increase demand and attain an adequate level of food consumption throughout the country, especially among the most needy sectors of the population; and to promote proper utilization of the food consumed.

The Ministry of Public Health and Social Welfare has pursued a national policy that continues to assign specific responsibilities to all the sectors concerned.

Financing of health services

Efforts are being made to rationalize the use of financial resources and to increase progressively the funds earmarked for the implementation of health programmes.

There is a chronic lack of resources, due to unequal distribution of the gross national product; the high and increasing costs of the health services (resulting mainly from unsound decisions); increasing expectations and demands on the part of the population; poor utilization of the resources available, owing to lack of coordination between institutions and the various sectors concerned with health; and the lack of the managerial competence necessary to ensure an optimal yield from those resources.

External financing and counterpart national budgetary appropriations have made it possible to start major infrastructural works. For example, a project for the extension of medical care, financed by a loan from the Inter-American Development Bank (IDB) is in progress for the construction of three 100-bed and two 50-bed hospitals, seven 30-bed health centres, 46 smaller health centres, 170 health posts, and four maintenance shops.

HONDURAS

Introduction

Honduras has an area of 112 088 km^2, divided into 18 departments with a total of 283 municipalities and about 18 000 hamlets, and a total population of 3 438 388. The capital city, Tegucigalpa, has about 350 000 inhabitants.

The reconstruction efforts to restore the areas hit by Hurricane Fifi and the execution of the National Development Plan, in conjunction with very favourable external factors, have made it possible in the past two years to overcome the recession the country suffered in 1974 and 1975, the average real growth for 1976 and 1977 being in excess of 6%.

Within the context of the National Development Plan, there has been a significant increase in the role played by the public sector in promoting development, as is evidenced by: high levels of real public investment, representing an average increase over the quadrennium of close to 25%; expansion of the services provided by the Government for agricultural extension, health and education; the granting of considerable amounts of credit and financial support to foster agriculture and livestock farming, forestry and industrial production; recovery of timber production, processing and marketing; the obtaining of greater domestic and external resources for financing development; and the establishment of governmental institutions or their reorganization to function effectively in the changing circumstances.

Under the National Development Plan the Ministry of Public Health has received considerable political and financial support, and was responsible in 1977 for about 11% of all public expenditure.

The health sector consists basically of the Ministry of Public Health and its infrastructure, the Honduran Social Security Institute, which covers about 4% of the total population, and the private subsector which offers services in the major population centres and is accessible only to those who can pay.

Main health problems and health policy

The main characteristics of the prevailing health situation are a high incidence of communicable diseases—including those which may be prevented by immunization—with a high mortality rate; lack of health facilities and direct medical attention; inadequate immunization coverage; and poor environmental conditions. There is a need for planning for the provision of infrastructures, equipment, human resources, supplies, and funds; programmed activities and objectives; regional planning, processes for the distribution of resources in accordance with needs, and administrative decentralization.

Hitherto only a small minority of the population has had access to the health services, which have been mainly oriented towards curative medicine; resources have been largely devoted to the provision of limited, high-cost services that have often been underutilized. Henceforth the emphasis is to be on preventive medicine and the development of primary health services covering the whole population, in particular in the rural areas, where 65% of the total population live. The extension of the primary health care services is to be based on the active participation of the population, taking into account traditional practices. Resources are to be particularly concentrated on nutrition, environmental health (including improvements in sewage and solid waste disposal, and water supplies); immunization; maternal and child health; health education; and the development of simplified methods of treating the more common diseases.

Action taken

Two fundamental strategies were adopted in this period: reorganization of the health services, and community participation in the health programmes. Support strategies concerned human resources development; development capabilities for both regulatory and executive administration (specifically the designing of instruments for administrative management, and measures for regionalization and administrative decentralization); determining of reference levels for care; investments; and the defining and integration of programmes.

Organization of health services

In implementation of the first strategy, the services were organized in a national health system, beginning with the restructuring of the Ministry of Public Health, and with the intention of incorporating the Social Security Institute. An appropriate internal organization was formulated, with a single Directorate-General of Health reporting directly to the Minister of Health.

Execution of the programmes at regional level has been entrusted to regional offices based on geographical area and population, with administrative decentralization. The offices have special resource programming and allocation and are staffed by specific programme personnel headed by a regional chief who reports to the Directorate-General of Health.

Health care delivery

For the provision of services in the National Health System two subsystems were defined, the institutional subsystem and the community subsystem, covering six levels of care. The community subsystem comprises the *first level* of care, which is provided by three volunteers: the health guardian, the trained empirical midwife and the health representative. The guardian is responsible for very simple medical care, information and patient referral; 907 guardians have been trained to date. The trained empirical midwife is responsible for care during pregnancy and childbirth, and for information and referral; there are 1519 such midwives. The health representative is responsible for community organization activities and for promoting environmental health; 1025 representatives have now been trained.

The institutional subsystem comprises the remaining five levels. *Level 2* covers a specific geographical area and population with a rudimentary establishment; the rural health centre staffed by a health auxiliary whose basic

responsibilities are to provide simplified medical care, to care for children and expectant mothers, assist the health guardian and local midwife, give information, refer patients and participate in community educational and promotional activities. The health promotion officer also works at this level, acting in cooperation with the health representative in organizing environmental sanitation and promoting environmental health.

Level 3 covers both the community and the rural health centres in a health sector based on a health centre with a doctor, who is backed by paramedical and administrative personnel and who possesses auxiliary diagnostic services (X-ray and laboratory services); the staff also provide information and refer patients.

Level 4 covers a health area with a rural hospital that provides support services to the health centres and rural health centres; it comprises general medical care and specialized care in paediatrics, gynaecology and obstetrics, medicine and surgery.

Level 5 covers a health region and is centred on a regional hospital, the key institution which supports the rest of the regional institutions and provides general medical care and specialized services.

Level 6 has as its representative establishment the teaching hospital offering medical care of the highest level of complexity in addition to its teaching, research and information activities, and receiving patients referred from all over the country.

Medical care has been strengthened by an increase in the number of establishments providing health services: the number of rural health centres has been doubled, eight regional emergency hospital centres and two regional hospitals are under construction, and the teaching hospital in Tegucigalpa is nearing completion.

During the period under review the number of hospital staff members per bed rose from 0.32 in 1974 to 0.97 in 1977 and the number of discharges increased by some 40%, largely as a result of the entry into service of the new hospitals. Institutional coverage of children under one year of age has been brought up to 60% and that of expectant mothers to 30%.

Health resources

Programming of human resource development has been initiated; in addition to the medical specialists in paediatrics and gynaecology and obstetrics, courses are under way for interns and surgeons who will enter service from 1981. Training programmes have been set up for auxiliary technicians in radiology, laboratory work, maintenance of equipment, nutrition and other specializations. Three training centres have been established for nursing and health auxiliaries which produce an average of 250 graduates a year. The refresher and continuing education courses for all health personnel have also been strengthened.

On the administrative side, the financial administration system (costs and estimates), information system, supplies administration system, and maintenance and other systems having already been put into operation.

The financing necessary for implementation of the National Health System as a whole has been furnished through a programme of investments directed primarily towards establishing an environmental sanitation infrastructure (for urban and rural water supply and septic tank and latrine construction), construction of health establishments, support for human resource development and development of appropriate administrative capability. Between 1974 and 1978 the Health Ministry's capital investments have increased fivefold.

Environmental health and disease control

In programming for the areas of direct service to the population, in addition to medical care, priority has been given to environmental sanitation, and specifically water supply and sewerage. In the first instance 44.9% of the population now has adequate drinking-water services and 27.6% has sewerage. As regards vector control, specifically that against *Anopheles* and *Aedes aegypti*, efforts were slackened somewhat, which resulted in rising malaria rates and a recent dengue epidemic. An intensive eradication campaign has accordingly been mounted. Food control activities have been considerably strengthened, extending to cover the whole country and to 90% of its establishments.

Epidemiological measures, especially immunization, have substantially reduced mortality rates from measles, poliomyelitis, tetanus, tuberculosis, diphtheria and pertussis. The immunization programme coverage is now between 56% and 75%. Total eradication of these diseases is still one of the chief goals.

MEXICO

Introduction

In accordance with the decisions embodied in the Ten Year Health Plan prepared by the Ministers of Health of the Americas in 1972, Mexico has assigned within its national development plans special importance to the role of the health sector as a primary factor in the economic and social development of the country.

A number of health programmes have been undertaken to deal with specific health problems and to meet the needs of the population. Of special importance during the years 1974–1977 were the programmes for the extension of health services; the prevention and control of communicable and noncommunicable diseases; maternal and child health and family planning; the prevention and control of environmental pollution; and health manpower training.

Despite the progress achieved, public health conditions in the country are strongly affected by demographic phenomena: in the period 1974–1977 the population increased by 11.1% from 58 117 709 to 64 594 402. The preponderance in this population of children under 15 years of age (29 849 073, or 46.21%) is reflected in the special public services that must be provided although the productive population is relatively small.

Extension of health services

A vast and gradual national plan is underway for the extension of health services, with health centres, health posts and hospitals, and for the rehabilitation and repair of existing facilities. In the period covered by this report 384 health posts, 94 rural health centres, 15 urban health centres and 15 urban hospitals were constructed.

In view of the dispersion of the population and the consequent low level of coverage a service manned by physicians was planned for areas with between 3000 and 5000 inhabitants and no access to regular health services.

Community medicine

Mobile units of one medical student, one dental student and one promoter provide communities with fewer than 500 inhabitants with primary care and health promotion services.

Communicable disease control and epidemiological surveillance

Infectious and parasitic diseases continued to be the leading cause of death during the period covered by this report.

Measles is a serious public health problem and causes an average of 9500 deaths per annum; 83% of the deaths are among children under 5 years of age. Control activities have been under way since 1973: children under 5 years of age living in communities with more than 500 inhabitants are vaccinated. Measles morbidity has been reduced by 80–95% compared with the average figures for the five years before 1973.

Pertussis causes an average of 4500 deaths per annum. A national vaccination programme started in 1974, and mortality began to fall; this trend continued in 1975 and 1976, and in the coming years it is expected to be reduced by 95% compared with the annual average of years since 1974.

Poliomyelitis, because of its medical importance and social consequences, is being controlled by means of intensive vaccination programmes initiated in 1972. There has been a sharp decline in its incidence, and although there have been a few outbreaks due to low vaccination coverage, the number of cases is steadily falling. In the period covered by this report the health services administered 24 627 335 doses of vaccine to children under 4 years of age in more than 14 000 communities.

Venereal diseases. Activities aimed at the early detection of cases, the diagnosis, treatment and follow-up of patients and the investigation of their contacts have been integrated into the regular activities of the competent units of the Department of Health and Welfare. The trend in these diseases is generally downwards although in recent years there has been an apparent increase in gonorrhoea believed to be due to better reporting.

Zoonoses. There are rabies control programmes in the 31 federal units and in the Federal District. They include such basic activities as vaccination and disposal of stray dogs, surveillance of dogs that have bitten people, laboratory diagnosis, early treatment of persons bitten, and health education.

The rabies control programme on the northern border of the country covers 12 cities. It is carried out with international funds and has succeeded in reducing the incidence of the disease. Rabies is no longer a problem of the canine population since in the period to which this report applies not a single case of human rabies was reported there. Only one outbreak of canine rabies occurred; that was in Ciudad Juarez, Chihuahua; it began in 1974 and was duly controlled. For the country as a whole a total of 13 950 cases of animal rabies were reported, as were 252 deaths due to rabies in human beings and 3 cases of postvaccinal neurological disorders following rabies treatment.

The national rabies control plan promoted and helped to finance the construction, equipment and operation of 6 veterinary antirabies centres. Together with the existing 8 centres, the 12 centres of the northern border programme and two in the Federal District, they are together serving a population of 16 500 000 inhabitants (1976).

Epidemiological surveillance of Venezulan equine encephalitis is continuing, and since outbreaks in 1972 no case of this disease has occurred. Special attention was paid to the clinical, epidemiological and laboratory investigation of all cases reported, which proved to be other nosological entities. No cases have been reported in horses.

Pinta, which was a serious public health problem in seven states of the Mexican Republic (Guerrero, Michoacan, Oaxaca, Chiapas, Mexico, Morelos and Puebla) has been controlled. By 1970 it was eradicated from the states of Puebla and Morelos; it is being eradicated in the state of Mexico and is the object of epidemiological surveillance in Michoacan, Guerrero, Oaxaca and Chiapas. Control activities, sustained in the previous four years, were increased in 1975 and 1976. The number of cases continued to decline; there were 248 in 1974, 112 in 1975, 99 in 1976 and 81 in 1977.

In order to appreciate the activities of the national pinta eradication campaign it is sufficient to compare the 115 000 cases identified at the beginning of the campaign and the 99 cases identified in 1976, a fall of more than 99%. It may therefore be said that pinta is no longer a public health problem in the country.

Leprosy control activities include case detection, diagnosis and classification, outpatient treatment, and personal, family and social group motivation to collaborate in the reporting of suspected cases of the disease; these activities are undertaken in 17 federal units and in the Federal District through 13 fixed dermatological centres and 12 mobile brigades. In 14 states where few cases occur epidemiological surveillance is maintained through reporting to health centres and to the headquarters of the coordinated services.

There were 14 882 leprosy patients on the active register in 1974, 14 775 in 1975, 15 002 in 1976, and 15 179 in 1977, a measure of the efficiency of case detection.

Onchocerciasis is an important public health problem in the states of Chiapas and Oaxaca. The prevalence of blindness, the most severe complication, is at present very low. There are at present 139 blind persons in the endemic areas, all over 38 years of age. All patients in the affected areas receive medical care, but the coverage of Simulium control activities is only 10%. The disease shows a downward trend, having fallen from 14.1% in 1973 to 11.7% in 1978 in the state of Chiapas and from 7.5% to 6.5% in the state of Oaxaca; these figures are 50% and 60% lower, respectively, than those recorded in 1972. The total number of registered patients in the two states was 14 416 in 1975.

Aedes aegypti *and epidemiological surveillance of yellow fever*

Systematic control activities and occasional checks continued in the Pacific, South-East and Gulf of Mexico areas, and surveillance was increased in the protection barrier area, with insecticide spraying in the communities in which the vector was detected. In 1975 and 1976, further reinfestations due to DDT-resistant *Aedes* were detected in the state of Quintana Roo; it was necessary to use malathion to control it. The remainder of the national territory is still free of *Aedes aegypti.*

The other diseases covered by the International Health Regulations have been eradicated in Mexico.

Accident prevention

In Mexico accidents are the fourth most frequent cause of death. The National Accident Prevention Council has promoted the teaching of the epidemiology and prevention of accidents in medical, nursing and social work schools. A number of publications on road safety, accidents in the home, organization of care in emergency situations and disasters was prepared, printed and distributed.

In 1975 the III Latin American Course on Toxicology was organized in Mexico, D.F. The National Information Centre on Poisonings has a continuous service providing information by telephone to physicians and the general public on emergency measures to deal with poisonings and on the emergency units open for treatment.

Programme for the detection of cervical and breast cancer

Cancer is an important public health problem, the fifth cause of death, and is following an upward trend, especially cervical cancer in women. Accordingly, standards and objectives for a programme for the early detection of cervical cancer were established in 1973. In 1974, programmes were organized in 9 federal units, and in 1975 in 22 units; all units now have such programmes. The country was divided into regions in order to ensure better distribution of treatment facilities.

Maternal and child health and family planning programme

The programme began in 1974 as part of the National Health Plan, 1974–1983, and all the institutions in the health sector participate. Beginning in 1975 provision was made for activities relating to statistical research, medical care, education and information. By 31 December 1976 there were 1826 family planning units. Physicians undergoing their social service work in health centres provide family planning services in addition to the usual functions.

In 100 urban health centres there are special personnel for family planning; in a further 219 the regular staff perform these functions. The services were used by 88% of the target population in 1974; by 75% in 1975; it is estimated that by 31 December 1976 there were a total of 632 679 users.

The General Directorate of Maternal and Child Health, in collaboration with the Research Institute, has carried out for the first time in Latin America an investigation of mental deficiencies and congenital metabolic disorders in children. Between 1975 and 1978 a total of 16 069 newborn babies had been studied in the hospitals of the Department of Health and Welfare.

Prevention and control of environmental pollution

The Government has created the juridical and administrative instruments for establishing the necessary infrastructure to control pollution: the Federal Law for the prevention and control of environmental pollution, and the regulations relating to the prevention and control of air pollution caused by emissions of smoke and dust. A subdepartment for the improvement of the environment has been set up within the Department of Health and Welfare.

Air pollution

A national inventory of fixed polluting sources (Air Pollution) was established. An analysis of the inventory showed that there were 787 441 establishments that were potential sources of pollution and determined that 71.04% of the total pollution due to smoke and dust was produced by 148 123 establishments and that the remaining 639 318 accounted for only 28.96% of the pollution. The goal accordingly established for 30 November 1976 was the control by that date of 65% of the atmospheric pollution caused by 72 048 significantly polluting establishments.

A system for the continuing surveillance of the pollution of the atmosphere in the large metroplitan areas of the country, and specifically in the cities of Mexico, Guadalajara and Monterrey, was designed and put into operation.

Water and soil pollution

The Department of Health and Welfare supports campaigns designed to reduce water pollu-tion under the responsibility of the Department of Water Resources.

Sewage is treated in 65 plants. In Mexico D.F. the water is reused for the irrigation of parks and gardens and, in the cities of Monclova, Saltillo, Monterrey and even in the Valley of Mexico, for industrial purposes.

The pollution of the soil caused by open dumps and by the unrestricted use of pesticides, fertilizers and detergents is a continuing cause of concern.

Noise

In accordance with the regulations for the prevention and control of noise, special commissions have been set up in the various cities of the Republic.

In order to ensure better enforcement of the provisions, a National Inventory of Noise Producing Sources has been set up.

Health manpower

During the years 1974–1977 the School of Public Health trained some 19 000 workers in different health fields. The number of training courses was increased from seven at the beginning of 1970 to 18 during recent years; 576 specialists in public health, hospital administration, industrial hygiene and safety, communicable diseases, health planning, family planning received training in public health.

Changes in organization and administration

Administrative reform. Since the end of 1976 the organization and planning of health activities have proceeded in accordance with the guidelines of the administrative reform undertaken by the executive branch of the Federal Government in several stages, from structural changes in the units of the public sector to new procedures for health care delivery.

Reorganization of the Department of Health and Welfare

In accordance with the administrative reform by the Federal Government, the structure of the Department of Health and Welfare has undergone the following changes:

(1) the Subdepartment of Planning was established and made responsible for regulating

97

and programming activities in the health field, the organization of units and the evaluation and supervision of programmes;

(2) the Subdepartment for Environmental Improvement was restructured to conduct activities for surveillance of sanitation, and control of air and water pollution, food contamination, toxic substances and noise;

(3) units were established for the supervision of medical education, for support of public health research and for the establishment of standards for basic medical care personnel and equipment;

(4) procedures were established for coordinated maternal and child health and family planning programmes; and

(5) a committee on administrative programming was established under the chairmanship of the Secretary of Health and Welfare, and was made responsible for promoting, studying and evaluating health programmes.

The Subdepartment of Welfare has introduced measures to increase services, with strategic programmes in priority areas, including the reorganization, establishment or improvement of services.

The General Directorate of Medical Care increased its budget by 445 million pesos and at the same time achieved a remarkable increase in all the medical care services, especially in outpatient care, family planning, detection of cancer and preventive care. It also achieved a substantial physical improvement in equipment, classrooms, and auditoriums as well as considerable progress in the teaching of nurses, nursing technicians, undergraduate interns and resident physicians. In the hospitals for which this Directorate is responsible there are a total of 4683 beds, the bed occupancy rate averaging 79.5%. The mortality rate was reduced by 0.3%.

The General Directorate of Social Welfare integrated its activities according to two main areas, operation and administration. In the first it improved the psychopaedagogical medical care sections, provided personnel training courses, established a family planning programme and a system for the supervision of feeding services in the establishments for which it was responsible. In the administrative area it established instruments for a manpower census, a study of the improvement of services, a continuing programme of conservation and maintenance, and a system of statistical control.

The 2408 units of the General Directorate of Maternal and Child Hea'th and Family Planning

and the services in 509 rural communities which were to number 3000 by mid-1978, made it possible to achieve the three-year goal established for that year. By 31 March 1978 there were more than a million users of services under the programme; consultations amounted to 1 553 941, of which 54% were in rural areas. Under the voluntary birth control programme 6635 surgical operations were performed, 36% of them in the Federal District.

The departments of teaching and communication, programming and evaluation, and national supervision have been reorganized to suit the new strategies of service delivery.

The goals fixed by the National Council on Population and Coordination of the National Plan were fulfilled to 112%.

The necessary infrastructure was established in the Subdepartment of Environmental Improvement to integrate activities with those of other government institutions. Establishments responsible for environmental pollution were graded for urgency of inspection visists, and improvement of human, technical and material resources was achieved.

A total of 106 502 establishments were inspected; 64.59% of the potential fixed sources of pollution were thus covered.

Earth probe, pilot probe and surface station subsystems were established for the collection, treatment, interpretation and evaluation of meteorological data, of which approximately 8 294 000 items were collected in the period 1950–1976. An automatic air pollution monitoring system consisting of 21 monitors was installed in the metropolitan area of Mexico City.

A manual and automatic system for the retrieval and treatment of information and interpretation and evaluation of results is operating. It started with the preparation of an inventory of food establishments; samples obtained from the inventory were in turn used to prepare, in cooperation with FAO, a national programme for the surveillance of chemical and biological contamination of foodstuffs.

Surveys have been made to investigate the contamination of household water supplies and its effects on the human body.

Studies were carried out to establish the maximum permissible levels of carboxihaemoglobin and lead in the human body.

Regulations for the prevention and control of noise were prepared and enacted.

Information on soil pollution from industrial sources was collected in order that the size of the problem could be determined and possible solutions defined. An inventory was made of a total of 79 458 establishments polluting the soil.

The use of the easily degradable organic fraction of solid waste to produce compost which can be used for the dressing of arable land was studied. A national inventory of solid waste was compiled as a basis for determining and evaluating control capacity in order to prepare preliminary draft regulations on soil pollution.

In order to measure the pollution of waste water, a model for the evaluation of the contaminating potential of the discharges of waste water from different industries is being set up. It covers the chemical analysis of the water, and the activity of the discharging establishment as well as its location.

NICARAGUA

Current health situation

The health situation is as follows: general mortality was estimated to be 16 per 1000 population in 1970 and 13.4 per 1000 in 1977 (the recorded rate is 8.2 per 1000). Estimated infant mortality continued to be 120 per 1000 live births (the recorded rate is 53.2 per 1000). Life expectancy for men rose from 48.8 years in 1970 to 54 in 1977; for women, it rose from 51.6 to 57 over the same period. The estimated birth rate rose from 46.8 per 1000 population in 1975 to 48 per 1000 in 1977. According to the survey carried out in collaboration with the Institute of Nutrition for Central America and Panama, 56% of the children under 5 years of age are suffering from some form of malnutrition.

A high percentage of the urban population has potable water and 76.9% have house connexions; on the other hand, only 43.3% of the rural population have any water supply at all. Only 35% of the urban population have a sanitary sewerage system for excreta disposal; about 60% use sanitary latrines.

The collection and disposal of solid wastes leave much to be desired. Bodies of water receiving drainage are often polluted; liquid excreta, industrial wastes, fertilizers, pesticides used in agriculture and other contaminants are often discharged directly into them.

The most common diseases are enteritis and parasitic diseases, the former being directly connected with unsatisfactory environmental sanitation and low-quality water supply. Other prevalent diseases are communicable diseases preventable by vaccination, respiratory diseases, diseases of malnutrition, tuberculosis and malaria.

The incidence of malaria, which used to be high owing to the vector's resistance to insecticides, has dropped as a result of a change in strategy; new techniques have been used in conjunction with the traditional methods, such as environmental sanitation by ditch-digging, draining of marshes and weeding of land.

New strategies are being used with mass BCG vaccinations also against tuberculosis, which used to cause high morbidity. The programme—which used to be a vertical one—has been integrated into the general services. Ambulatory treatment is given, hospitalization being reserved for special cases.

Morbidity and mortality from the above-mentioned causes are falling. Efforts have been made to improve the coverage of both the preventive and the curative health services. At the same time, there has been an improvement in institutional capacity and personnel training owing to the emphasis laid on primary health care, improved referral systems and community participation.

Constants efforts are being made to improve the health of the population through health education and community development, which are fundamental factors in the implementation of the different programmes.

Health care system

The different components are, in the public sector: the Ministry of Public Health, the National Welfare and Social Security Board, the local social welfare boards, the Nicaraguan Social Security Institute, and the medical department of the National Guard. There are other components from the private sector and religious groups. The infrastructure comprises 140 health centres, 40 hospitals, 8 polyclinics, 17 rural welfare units, 156 rural health posts, 102 family planning clinics, 16 nutrition education and treatment services, 15 community nutrition centres, and 15 suburban dispensaries in Managua run by the National Welfare and Social Security Board. Installed capacity will be increased over the three years starting in 1979 through programmes for the improvement of the rural health services, using a system of regionalization with various levels of care to be provided by 167 rural health posts. These will consolidate the health activities undertaken by the Government at the primary health level, where the bulk of the labour force is to be found as Nicaragua is essentially agricultural and the population therefore rural. The infrastructure also comprises two regional hospitals. A health plan is being implemented for Managua based on the concept of different levels of care, referral and regionalization. The Chontales Regional Hospital (200 beds), the El Rama Hospital (50 beds), the 14th of July Social Security Hospital (250 beds) and the teaching hospital of the National University (380 beds), have already been built.

Workers medical care is administered through the Nicaraguan Social Security Institute, which pays various benefits for sickness, disability, widowhood, old age and death, and work accidents. It covers 200 000 people, and the extension of social security to rural areas is under study.

Health policy

The aim of the Government's national health policy is to speed up the country's economic and social development. One of the goals of the Social Development Plan is to formulate dynamic health and social welfare programmes with nationwide coverage which will raise the standard of living, improving the health function, which in its turn, will have an impact on nearly all the economic objectives.

The resulting strategy and constituent reforms are focused on the urgent tasks of improving health in marginal social areas and providing primary health care. The aims are as follows:

(1) Coordination, integration and regionalization of the health services;
(2) extensions of the coverage of the health services, with emphasis on primary health care

and community participation;
(3) putting the national programming unit into operation;
(4) strengthening and restructuring programmes, with more emphasis on vaccination, epidemiological surveillance, maternal and child care and family welfare, and examining the efficacy and efficiency of administrative precedures;
(5) improving basic environmental sanitation in rural areas, with special emphasis on soil and water;
(6) developing a national food and nutrition policy;
(7) strengthening the training and improving the quality of manpower for health care by building up the Nicaraguan Institute of Health Manpower;
(8) improving the information system by establishing a National Health Statistics centre;
(9) extending social security coverage to rural areas and to the groups with the greatest social needs; and
(10) submitting the draft health code to the National Congress.

Principal activities

Maternal and child health and family welfare programme.

In accordance with the new policy and strategy laid down in the Health Plan, this programme was redefined to include pre- and post-natal care of the mother, integrated child care, family welfare activities and family planning; the Maternal and Child Health Division was restructured and reintegrated with the Family Welfare Division (Family Planning).

Seminars and workshops were organized for the study of norms, and the activities to be carried on in conjunction with the integrated maternal and child health programme of the National University were coordinated.

There is periodic inspection of the different health centres and other local health organizations. The programme has been in operation since 1968; it was originally financed by grants from USAID and counterpart funds provided by the Government, but the Government's share has gradually increased and it is now entirely Government-funded. The objective is to provide guidance for family life, improve family health conditions, help to propagate the idea of responsible paternity, provide educational medical attention for persons applying to the health services, and improve the health conditions of the family.

Advisory services have always been provided by USAID; at the present time there is one permanent adviser, and short-term advisers are also often available.

A national survey of traditional birth attendants was carried out. A project for the training of traditional birth attendants was recently put into operation and 800 midwives were trained.

Programme of medical care and mobile units for rural areas

This programme is aimed particularly at persons suffering from diseases which can be treated by ambulatory medical care, and assistance is given to those receiving care from health centres and health posts and the mobile welfare units. The mobile units provide simplified health care. Five of them are waterborne motor vehicles. The doctor visits the community once a week and the health posts are manned by inspectors and voluntary health workers or auxiliary nursing personnel.

The primary health care programmes, carried out in conjunction with the community development programme, include the rural community action programme, the programme to promote development with the accent on children and youth, the integrated medical programme of the Rigoberto Cabezas project, the programme for the villages in the north of the Chinandega Department, and the special programme for the Zumos of the Atlantic Coast, assisted by the Friends of Wisconsin.

The community development programme is being carried out in one region with the assistance of UNICEF and is aimed at making rural communities aware that they should help to solve their own problems. In the Rigoberto Cabezas project, medical care is given at the Hospital de Nueva Guinea, and ambulatory care is provided by mobile units and rural health workers in the 30 rural settlements of the Agrarian Institute of Nicaragua.

The aid programme of the Friends of Wisconsin is aimed at people in areas with a scattered population; the care is provided by trained health workers from the community itself.

Nutrition programme

Among a great variety of nutrition activities attention must be drawn to the organization of a technical committee on nutrition, a government body responsible for laying down national food and nutrition policy. A loan of US $3 million and a grant of US $500 000 have been approved by USAID.

The ministries and agencies connected with the production, consumption and utilization of foods will take part in defining the national policy on food and nutrition. This policy finds concrete expression in various projects, among which mention may be made of the epidemiological nutrition watch, the salt iodization programme, nutrition education by the mass media, provision of iron supplements for pregnant women, supplementary feeding of children, and manufacture of vegetable mixes from Nicaraguan products. Activities are focused on the rural population, particularly school-age children.

The programme of applied nutrition and the supplementary feeding programme were continued. The education and nutrition services were consolidated in 16 localities. An evaluation and control study was made of the radio-broadcast nutrition education programme, which is being carried out jointly by the Ministry of Public Health and USAID.

Communicable diseases

Special emphasis was laid on tuberculosis, sexually transmitted diseases, dermatological diseases—particularly leprosy—and leishmaniasis, yellow fever, rabies and malaria.

The dermatological hygiene section of the Ministry of Public health encourages activities connected with the control and ambulatory treatment of patients with leprosy and dermal leishmaniasis, among other dermatoses, the indicators for which show a progressive increase in new cases. Their spread has been limited by the detection and treatment of potentially communicable cases including clinical forms and suspected cases of leprosy. Nine cases of leprosy were confirmed in 1977 (5 lepromatous and 4 tuberculoid). Diagnostic guidelines and treatment schedules for leishmaniasis were given, in particular, to health personnel working in the areas of Jinotega, Matagalpa and Boaco, where the disease is endemic. Special treatment was given to members of the National Guard on short assignments in mountain areas. In 1977, 627 persons were treated. Enough of the specific preparation is available for the treatment of 4000 cases.

Efforts are being made to control *Aedes aegypti*, as some foci of yellow fever have been discovered despite constant fumigation. Persons entering Nicaragua from Colombia, and Nicaraguans returning from Colombia, have been given medical examinations since some cases of yellow fever occurred in Colombia.

Canine rabies attained epidemic proportions in 1977, when 282 dog's heads submitted for examination were found to be infected. There were also two cases of human rabies and one of reaction to the injections. The records show that 7288 prople were bitten; 2766 of them were treated and 41 380 doses of vaccine were administered. Fuenzalida-Palacio vaccine was used.

Immunization

Within the priorities laid down in the National Plan, the Expanded Programme on Immunization adopted by WHO is being followed, with mass programmes extending coverage of the rural and peri-urban sector. In the latter, advantage is taken of the social and political structures known as *antones*, with the cooperation of public and private institutions, and permanent vaccination services are provided through the regular health system.

Epidemiological surveillance

There has been a notable improvement over the last years in the telegraphic notification of diseases likely to produce epidemics. As a result of the improvement in notification, a monthly epidemiological bulletin has been produced which indicates the measures to be taken with respect to diseases classified as dangerous; local

health services are thus kept constantly informed. A training course in epidemiology was organized in which 17 nurses participated.

Epidemiological surveys of encephalitis, poliomyelitis and malaria have been carried out.

Environmental sanitation

The environmental sanitation programme was intensively applied in rural areas, while in the cities there was continued improvement of public water supply, excreta disposal, garbage collection, market and slaughterhouse hygiene and health inspections of housing and food; the services were extended to the outskirts of the urban communities.

The rural basic sanitation programme is aimed to provide potable water by means of simple water channels, wells and windmills, to install sanitary latrines and improve garbage and waste water disposal. Before these measures were taken efforts were made to educate the community to adopt specific norms of behaviour which would help to solve its problems; a community self-help system was set up for the operation of the programme.

Sanitary improvements were planned for 890 rural communities with populations of between 50 and 800. Loans of US $5 million from USAID and US $3 million from the World Bank are being provided and under agreements signed by these agencies with the Government. With the loan from the World Bank it is planned to cover some 550 communities with populations of between 50 and 800 inhabitants in three regions over the four years 1978–1981. With the loan from USAID it was planned to cover about 340 communities with populations of between 50 and 800 in the other three regions over the four years 1977–1980.

PANAMA

General health programmes

In 1973 the Government decided gradually to integrate the institutions responsible for health care so as to avoid duplication of effort and waste of resources and to increase capacity in order to meet the growing demand for more and better services. By 1978, only one of the country's nine provinces remained to be integrated—

the province of Panama. Integration has involved great expansion of the capacity of the health system in order to cover a larger population and extend the health services to rural areas. Personnel from the communities have been trained and given the major role in integration.

The priorities established in the social sphere govern the health services, including maternal and child care—preventive and curative care—with facilities for the referral of patients from one level to another so as to ensure that the best health resources in the system are available to the population, and with a measure of regional autonomy. Resources for ambulatory care have made it possible to carry out 1270 examinations per 1000 inhabitants, and the hospitals have achieved 23.7 discharges per bed per year, with fluctuations between the extremes of 43.9 in the province of Herrera and 17.5 in Panama. In every area, efforts have been made to increase installed capacity. In view of the steady rise in operational costs, administrative improvements are being introduced to ensure more effective use of the resources, together with in-service training programmes in hospital administration and the critical area of hospital and equipment maintenance.

Family health

When reorganizing its administrative structure, the Ministry of Health established the Family Health Office in January 1975 with the aim of promoting action for family health, combining programmes for adult health, maternal and child health, mental health, dental health and nursing. Each programme continues with its own special activities, and joint action is coordinated at the central level, through planning and programming meetings, analysis of the results achieved and the difficulties encountered in the execution of the programme and evaluation of their impact, and teaching and supervisory activities at the local level.

The structure of the Family Health Office is repeated in the regions of Azuero, Colon, Chiriqui and Veraguas. In the other provinces the directors of health services are selecting members of their staff to set up such offices.

Maternal and child health

In 1977 the target population was 65.4%, comprising 42.4% of the population who were under 15 years old (0–1 year, 3.0%; 1–4 years, 12.3%; 5–14 years, 26.6%) and the female population of reproductive age (15–44 years), representing 22.0% of the population.

The greatest demand for consultations is for childhood diseases, and these absorb a large proportion of the resources: for a total of 724 200 children under 15 years old, 882 406 examinations for these diseases were made in 1977 (1.2 examinations per child); 1 065 504 examinations had been programmed, so that 83% of the target was met. Such consultations increased between 1972 and 1977 by about 68.3%, an average annual increase of 13.7%. Hospital care for this group in 1977 was 13.5% higher than in 1972, and the examination/discharge ratio, which was 22 to one in 1972, rose to 32 to one in 1977. The result of these efforts was a substantial improvement in such indicators as infant mortality, premature births, and—especially—late births. The improvement can be attributed to vaccinations and the drop in the morbidity and mortality rates for diseases preventable by vaccination. Better care at delivery made it possible to carry out early checks of the newborn. In-service training courses on the care of vulnerable children, care in paediatric clinics, and other related subjects continued.

Clinics provided professional care for 76.6% of deliveries in 1977, giving a health service coverage 12.3% higher than in 1972.

With the extension of community health services the prenatal clinics were able to double the number of examinations between 1972 and 1977, the increase in the last year being 14% or more, but only 25% of the women returned for after-care in 1977. This may be due to the educational efforts for planning that are being made for pregnancy right through to birth. In 1977/78, 9285 women (41% of them under 25) attended family planning clinics. Four courses on family planning and sex education were held, some of them for adolescents.

Adult health programme

The 'adult health' programme establishes norms for the health services for the population over 15 years old (58.5% of the total population), which continues to grow as in the period 1974–1978, when the health of adults improved, as is shown by the drop in the general death rate and in the death rates for specific age groups and diseases, especially diarrhoeal diseases and pneumonia. Degenerative and violent causes of death continue to replace infectious diseases as a primary cause of death after the enormous efforts to combat communicable diseases made ·by the Ministry of Health.

As the morbidity data in hospitals only cover cases admitted and do not include outpatients, no definite trend can be detected for the period 1974–1978. Nevertheless, the principal reasons for hospitalization corroborate the observation regarding the causes of deaths; there were a high proportion of degenerative disease cases and injuries due to violence. Another striking fact is the number of abortions, which continues to be high despite the availability of contraceptives.

The number of hospital beds available for adults increased from 1974 to 1978 throughout the country; the increase was greatest in the provinces the health services of which were integrated during that period. The figures for the use of hospital beds do not show any definite trend but they indicate under-utilization. Medical consultations continued to increase at an average annual rate of 21.5% during the period; the ratio of one consultation per inhabitant per year was exceeded in 1976. The figures for hospital discharges have been somewhat erratic, probably owing to problems with the recording of the statistics. There was no change in the ratio of five discharges per 100 medical consultations from 1974 to 1977.

Immunization did not achieve wide coverage, generally speaking. This is a matter for concern, except in the case of smallpox vaccination, which is being discontinued because the disease has practically disappeared, and BCG vaccination, which has become virtually unnecessary for adults owing to the routine vaccination of newborn children. Although there were mass vaccinations against measles in the vulnerable groups of indigenous adult population, the coverage is not adequate. However, no objective evaluation of the vaccinations that have been performed can be made until the immunological status of the population is known from the results of the forthcoming serological survey. Antitetanus injections only achieved 10%–20% of the desired coverage, but coverage is increasing by 85% to 100% a year. Owing to a small outbreak in 1974, protection against yellow fever reached the impressive figure of 53.6%. The levels of coverage dropped sharply after 1974, however, and fell below the 10% a year required to keep the population protected.

Environmental health

Rural potable water supply. Thanks to several decades' experience the deliberate policy of the Revolutionary Government in making communities real agents of change, 53.2% of the rural population, some 826 000 persons, or 50.2% of the total population, were supplied with potable water by 31 December 1974, compared with only 18.8% of the rural population between 1900 and 1960. The most spectacular progress was made in the 1970s: the percentage rose to 63.8% between 1974 and 1977. Only 1% of the rural population was served by in-house connexions in 1960 and 6.9% in 1970. The proportion rose to 21.1% in 1974 and to 23.9% in 1977. The substantial improvement is due to a sustained programme of construction of water mains, with financing that became available in 1970, and a programme of rural wells, which was adequately financed in 1955. Financing has been secured for the construction of 150 additional water mains, which will be built in 1979 and 1980.

Environmental sanitation. With regard to sanitary excreta disposal, the number of latrines constructed from 1974 to 1978 totaled 32 670 and benefited a population of 163 350. There are now sanitary latrines for 22.3% of the urban and 74.2% of the rural population, representing 47.3% of the total population. A campaign is continuing to connect all houses to the sewer system in communities that have such a system. As to the collection, transport and final disposal of solid wastes, advisory services have been made available to all the responsible *municipios* and institutions. During the period 31 incinerators were constructed, mainly in communities with populations of less than 2000. Technical advice is being provided for the improvement of Panama City's solid wastes disposal system, which has been the source of serious problems in the surrounding areas for many years.

A campaign of construction and clearance of drainage channels to reduce mosquito breeding grounds and systematic campaigns to control rats have been less effective than they might have been owing to lack of cooperation on the part of the public in keeping empty patios and vacant lots clean, and to lack of garbage cans or other arrangements to ensure an efficient urban cleaning system.

Food inspection, because of its importance at the urban level, has been entrusted to a special section. There is regular inspection of establishments for food preparation and distribution and, through the health centres, stricter control has been exercised over food handlers, for whom special training courses have been organized; 4301 were trained during the period and 55 479 health certificates were issued.

PARAGUAY

Eradication or control of diseases

Malaria eradication

In 1972 a committee of technical specialists of the malaria eradication service and international experts made an evaluation of the programme, confirmed the successes achieved and urged the Government to allocate the funds needed to maintain the programme's priority in its health plans. This priority activity in fact continued without interruption, sufficient funds having been made available as and when required for specific programme aspects. Eleven of the country's 19 departments, covering 74% of the national area and containing 48.5% of the population, were transferred from the attack to the consolidation phase in 1973, leaving 25.95% of the area with 34.9% of the population in the attack phase.

In December 1976, following a new evaluation made by Paraguayan and PAHO/WHO experts, it was decided to transfer the Misiones, Central and Neembucú departments in the Eastern Region and the entire Chaco or Western Region from the consolidation to the maintenance phase. Concepción, San Pedro, Cordilleras, Guairá, Caazapá, Itaipú and Paraguari departments have been moved into the consolidation phase. Caaguazú, Alto Paraná, Amambay and Canendiyú departments, i.e., all the departments bordering on Brazil, have been left in the attack phase.

The following table shows the areas and population figures for the different programme phases as of December 1977:

Distribution	Area (km^2)	%	Population	%
National total	406 752	100	2 804 703	100
Non-malarious area	200	0.05	458 744	16.4
Maintenance phase	271 010	66.4	631 288	22.5
Consolidation phase	80 749	19.6	1 238 497	44.1
Attack phase	54 793	13.5	476 174	17.0

Chagas' disease control

A geographical reconnaissance and housing census was carried out in Caraguatay district, Cordilleras department, to ascertain, among other things, the percentage of triatomid-infested dwellings. As part of a programme to control Chagas' disease, the malaria eradication service is negotiating with German and Japanese insecticide manufacturers with a view to implementing a pilot plan with their products. Negotiations are also under way with the Japanese Government to obtain technical and financial assistance for the campaign. Contacts are being maintained with Argentina and Brazil regarding the Chagas' disease programmes. Under its staff training programme, staff members of the malaria eradication service have been given fellowships for specialized studies in Chagas' disease control in Brazil and Venezuela.

Yellow fever control and Aedes aegypti eradication

Paraguay started its Aedes aegypti eradication campaign in 1948. Aedes aegypti was last found in Asunción in March 1954. Subsequent searches produced no finds, and the urban yellow fever vector was declared eradicated in Paraguay in July 1957 and has remained so since. The malaria eradication service is responsible for Aedes aegypti surveillance. The number of localities where surveillance was carried on was reduced in 1961, but a special watch is still kept at Asunción international airport where all aircraft that have called at countries still infested are inspected for mature insects. No Aedes aegypti have ever been found during any of these checks. In view of reinfestation in neighbouring countries, new epidemiological surveillance strategies are being considered.

The jungle yellow fever epidemic which occurred in various countries in 1974 reached Amambay department, adjacent to Brazil, in northeast Paraguay. Appropriate epidemiological measures were taken to prevent it from spreading into the rest of the country. A total of 143 433 persons were vaccinated, particularly in the area of the joint Brazilian-Paraguayan hydroelectric project at Itaipú.

There is no dengue.

Tuberculosis

The mortality rate for tuberculosis is dropping fast, as has been particularly evident since 1974. In 1973 it was 22.2 per 100 000 inhabitants and in 1977, 13.6. The Ministry's efforts in standardizing treatments using new drugs and in early case detection have unquestionably contributed to this important achievement. Morbidity has also declined appreciably, from 124.9 per 100 000 inhabitants in 1973 to 69.2 in 1977. An active vaccination programme has been under way since 1954.

Numbers of BCG vaccinations since 1974 were as follows:

1974	121 012
1975	78 957
1976	113 346
1977	115 606
	428 921

By 1977 a total of 1 559 739 doses of vaccine had been administered.

Diseases preventable by vaccination

Considerable progress has been made with the vaccination programme, though the dispersal of much of the population over rural areas causes certain problems. It is nevertheless expected that the target for the decade will be met. The programme to extend service coverage to the rural areas by the strategy of primary care and community participation will help toward this goal. Paraguay is free of smallpox.

Poliomyelitis. The vaccination programme for the 1–4 year age group has not been entirely satisfactory. The number of vaccinations given in the period 1974–1977 was 279 055. The average yearly number of cases was 60. The number of vaccinations was doubled in 1977 and a further doubling was planned for 1978.

Pertussis, tetanus, diphtheria. Five deaths from pertussis were notified in 1977, and the average for the period was 14 cases per year. The mortality rate target of 1.0 per 100 000 inhabitants proposed for the decade was bettered by 1975, when it was 0.7; it was 0.3 in 1977.

The tetanus mortality rate fell to 6.2 per 100 000 inhabitants in 1977 from 15.7 in 1968, but is still above the target for the decade. The deaths from tetanus particularly concerned new-born babies delivered in rural areas by lay or practical midwives. The plan to extend health service coverage to the rural areas, with new personnel for the health posts, and the strategy of primary care and community participation, will help to bring down the tetanus mortality rate.

There were only four deaths from diphtheria

among children under one year of age in the period 1974–1978, an average of seven deaths a year for all ages.

Morbidity dropped to 0.7 in 1976, a very promising figure since the target for the decade is 0.1 per 100 000 inhabitants. At the beginning of the decade the rate was 6.3 per 100 000.

Meningococcal meningitis. There were an average of 86 cases a year in Paraguay between 1974 and 1978. Most of them involved type C meningococci to begin with, but type A appeared later; they did not show resistance to sulfa drugs. There were 133 cases in 1975, the greater part of them confined to a particular population group. Total deaths numbered 58 (16% of cases).

Cancer

The National Cancer Institute inaugurated new facilities during the period. Statistics show that cancer, like traffic accidents, is regrettably looming steadily larger among causes of death. The Institute is also a teaching centre, and it serves as a focal point for the efforts of the Ministry of Public Health and Social Welfare, insurance institutions, private charities, the Paraguayan Anti-Cancer League and numerous private bodies.

Environmental health

Water supply

In 1974 the National Environmental Health Service, established by Law 369/72, had running water systems operating in six towns of the interior of the country (Piribebuy, Villeta, Artigas, Rosario, Villa Alegre and Choré), while similar systems were in an advanced stage of construction in 13 more towns; studies had been started for another seven. Preliminary feasibility studies had started in nine other localities.

Of all deaths among children under one year old 18.1% are caused by diarrhoea, and the percentage rises to 28% if the 1–4 year age group is included. The utmost importance is attached to the water supply programme. By 1975, running water supply systems were functioning in 12 of 40 towns programmed to have them installed during the period 1975–1977.

The National Environmental Health Service is responsible for drinking-water supply to the rural areas and to urban centres with under

4000 inhabitants. The projects are carried out with the full participation of the communities concerned, from feasibility study to completion of the project and administration of the system; each community designates members to operate the system. The total cost of the systems in operation to date was 43 292 499 guaraníes, of which ₲12 017 270 was contributed by the Ministry of Public Health and Social Welfare, ₲23 210 074 by the communities and ₲8 065 155 in the form of loans from the Ministry (a revolving fund was especially established for the purpose in the Sanitation Service).

As of 31 December 1977, there were 18 water supply systems in operation and a further 16 in various stages of construction, 13 of which were to be completed in the course of 1978. By the end of 1977, ₲135 million had been invested, 50% of this sum being contributed by the beneficiary communities.

Numerous courses have been held for voluntary sanitation auxiliaries, sanitation board members and system administrators. Seminars have also been held on programming and evaluation.

Stores have been built and workshops and other facilities set up at a cost of ₲14 million. Improvements have been made to the central office premises, and housing and offices have been built to form local headquarters in settlement areas (Choré, Minga Guazú and Juan León Mallorquín), which include workshops and supply depots.

The Government increased the Environmental Health Service's budget by 540% between 1972 and 1977. In December 1977, a loan of US $6 million was obtained from the World Bank to help finance a project costing US $11 million. A further loan of DM4 million from a German institution will also be used for water supply.

Environmental pollution

An ambitious environmental pollution control programme has been launched. Water resources pollution control, with primary emphasis on industrial wastes, is being carried out in the basin of Lake Ypacarai, and on the Paraguay River where it flows through the capital.

Air pollution control has been begun in Asunción and consideration is being given to setting up two measurement stations as part of the Pan American system. Control of soil pollution is based on a programme to promote

national urban refuse collection. The personnel necessary for starting the activities have been trained with PAHO/WHO technical assistance. The programme is the responsibility of the Paraguayan Organization for Intermunicipal Cooperation and the Municipal Development Institute, the latter being the financing agency for the municipal sector.

Food hygiene programme

Food hygiene inspection activities are being carried out in 54 municipalities and in Asunción. These cover 1700 stores and shops selling foodstuffs and 106 food-processing industries, and are thus of considerable epidemiological significance.

Occupational hygiene and safety

Equipment, instruments and training for specialized personnel have been provided for this important programme, which is proceeding in 1238 industrial undertakings in Asunción and 93 in other parts of the country.

Health services

The efforts designed to strengthen the national health system were continued throughout the period 1974–1977. The coordination between the components of the system is very promising. All the functional aspects of the regionalized health services system have been reexamined and brought into line with the pertinent standards.

Health services at varying levels of complexity of care have been offered since the First Five-Year Health Plan, 1958–1962. The country is divided into nine health regions, each of which is subdivided into a certain number of programme areas. During the period 1974–1978, very positive progress was made towards strengthening the entire system. The salaries of doctors, nurses and midwives were increased, with additional payments throughout the rural areas and further incentives for those working in the more distant and border areas. Health services were developed in the north settlement axis.

At the primary level the executing agency is the health post, with trained personnel, serving population groups of fewer than 2000 persons, the emphasis being on communicable diseases, mother and child care and family welfare, rural basic sanitation, community organization and development, first aid, volunteer training and other standardized activities such as vaccination, health education and the keeping of statistics. At the next, "basic" level the executing agency is the health centre, located in the chief towns of municipalities (there are 171 in the country) and departments (19). The centres serve towns of over 2000 and possess hospital facilities, the number of beds depending on the size of the town and its area of influence. Integral services are provided for health promotion, curative treatment and disease prevention. At the "complementary" level regional health centres with a minimum of 50 beds and higher-qualified medical and paramedical staff represent the highest level of the regionalized health services.

Services involving special diagnostic equipment are centralized in specific institutions because of their cost and complexity and the specialized staff required.

The sum of 197 071 727 guaraníes was spent on expanding, remodelling and re-equipping existing health centres and posts in the interior of the country and establishing new ones. The Ministry's budget was increased by 105.13% between 1973 and 1978, from ₲526 714 112 to ₲080 457 117.

In strengthening the health services, attention was paid to manpower, improving the regionalized health services system, and various seminars and courses were held to improve the administration of the health services.

Health manpower development

A survey of human resources in health was carried out, in conjunction with the first national seminar on human resources for health, sponsored by a core group for development research in education and health. During the seminar an in-depth analysis was made of the survey findings, which underlined the need for training of intermediate-level auxiliary technical personnel and review of the curricula followed in the teaching of medicine.

The plan for training auxiliary personnel in order to extend coverage led to the establishment of three schools: one for nursing auxiliaries for the health posts, one for obstetrical auxiliaries and one for obstetricians. Courses for dental technicians, anaesthetists, laboratory staff and statisticians were added at the Vocational Training School, and private institutions were encouraged to provide the training needed by pharmacists and other technical personnel in the health field.

The unequal distribution of professional medical and paramedical personnnel between Asunción and the rest of the country led to a policy of creating positions and providing extra pay for personnel to work in the rural areas. Long and short courses, seminars and fellowships were allocated preferentially to personnel operating in the interior of the country. Provision is also made for establishing intermediate staff training institutions in the rural areas.

Courses in public health and planning held during the period 1974–1977 are currently being evaluated.

National health planning

A National Health Plan for 1976–1980 was drawn up. This plan falls within the framework of the National Development Plan and serves as the vehicle for implementation of the national health policy, laying down general and specific goals and the means that will be used to attain them.

One of the general goals is extension of the coverage of the health services to the entire population, the plans for which were presented at the Fourth Special Meeting of Ministers of Health of the Americas and are now being implemented.

The project to extend health service coverage using the primary care strategy with community participation will be implemented in three regions to which priority has been assigned as they contain 40.1% of the country's population. The pertinent studies have been completed and the project will be started in 1979: 87 health posts and 10 health centres will be built and equipped, and additional equipment will be installed in two regional health centres. The important element is the utilization of a type of community worker, the volunteer health worker, who when properly trained and integrated in the institutional health system will provide highly beneficial assistance to the scattered rural population which cannot be served by the regular health services.

In the subsequent stages of the Plan, it is proposed to increase the installed capacity of the health establishments by some 52%. This increase will be greater for the primary level (66%). The complete Plan will call for

₲560 406 200, equivalent to US $28 415 922, of which US $14 million will be for the Environmental Health Service and US $14 415 922 for the programme to extend coverage of the services.

Health legislation

The highlights were completion of the drafting of the Sanitary Code, which is now before Congress, and the instituting of medical insurance for State employees.

Maternal and child health and family welfare

In 1975 the health policy with regard to care for the family as a unit was propounded in which the mother-child combination plays a major role. Standards for care during pregnancy, birth and the time immediately thereafter, and for nursing mothers, have been updated. The preliminary draft of the Minor's Code has been completed and an agreement had been signed with the National University for the retraining in mother and child care of doctors from the interior of the country, which has proved an unquestionable success.

The family protection services are integrated with the general health services, being financed through an agreement concluded with USAID.

The infant mortality rate for 1976 was 86.5 per 1000 live births. Neonatal mortality fell from 40.0 in 1973 to 35.1 in 1976. The downward trend has persisted throughout the decade. Maternal mortality, which was 5.6 per 1000 live births in 1970, fell to 4.8 in 1977. About 50% of hospital admissions are on account of pregnancy and its complications, which indicates the scale of the demand for care for mothers. Of all first consultations in 1976, 42.2% were in respect of children under five.

Nutrition

Various surveys have been made, one of them, in 1977, on "critical areas of the population". A survey conducted in 27 localities and involving 4078 persons showed that, with an average of 3098 calories per capita and a protein consumption of 87.1 grams, the Paraguayan people were among the best fed in the Hemisphere. Food availability is adequate. The protein consumed is primarily of animal origin. The survey, made in a population in which malnutrition was to be expected, showed that children under 5 years old were in fact suffering from a degree of undernourishment, but that the number of serious cases was negligible.

The prevalence of endemic goitre is very close to the target of 12% for the decade; in relation to the last decade there has been spectacular progress in the eradication programme. The Government is formulating a national nutrition policy.

Rural development

During the period 1974–1977, the first integrated rural development project was carried out with World Bank assistance in the area of the Juan León Mallorquin and General Stroessner repatriation schemes (Caaguazú, Alto Paraná), coordinated by the National Social Progress Council. This project provided rural dwellers with land, granted credit to medium and small farmers, furnished technical advisory services, schools, roads and health services, training and nutrition education, and is considered a full success.

In 1977 the Government signed the second Itapúa integrated rural development project which, like the first, provides for credit to farmers, technical advisory services, roads, schools and health centres and posts. Execution of this project is now fully under way. The project will use rural health promotion personnel on an experimental basis, with advisory services from Colombia's Rural Development Institute.

A special study was made during the period 1974–1977 of the Itaipú hydro-electric scheme area; the Ministry of Public Health has been providing for the normal progress of this immense undertaking since 1975.

Health and social welfare

In addition to assistance to the aged in homes and to children in kindergartens, foster homes and children's institutions, the work in this sphere has been extended to deal more intensively with young people through camps, job-finding, social surveys, psychosocial consultations and prevention and treatment of drug addiction.

PERU

Introduction

The policy which inspired two successive biennial plans in the health sector, those of 1975–1976 and 1977–1978, respectively, follows the key note struck by the Armed Forces Government which, in 1970, entered on a "second phase". The basic orientation of Government policy continued to be the gradual transfer of political and economic power to a free, democratic and organized society. Agrarian reform and transfer of land ownership has been almost completed, and the task is now to make the peasant able to exploit the land more rationally and satisfactorily. Educational reform continues to advance in accord with the original plans, preparing the citizen for work and development. A national social security pension scheme has been created, unifying social benefits for clerical and manual workers; the medical care system for all workers protected by social security is also about to be unified.

The health cooperation with other countries in the Region, which inspired the Hipolito Unanue Agreement, is continuing.

Health planning

The Sectoral Health Planning Office operates as a Directorate General in the headquarters of the Ministry of Health. It forms part of the national planning system whose central body is the National Planning Institute. During the four-year period biennial plans for 1975–1976 and 1977–1978 were drawn up, distinguishing problems of the sector and assessment of the health situation; sectoral policy for the two-year period; and programming for the first year of the two biennials (1975 and 1977), considering objectives, goals, activities and health sector investments.

Ministry of Health Investment Programme

During the last two-year period in particular the Programme was marked by restrictions which increased still more in 1978—the "year of austerity"—owing to the development of a serious and prolonged stage of fiscal penury which is a reflection of the world economic crisis; the construction and equipping of 25 fifty-bed rural hospitals and the remodelling of another three, which would have given a total of 1400 beds, had to be interrupted when contractors failed to fulfil their contractual commitments. The construction of several hospitals was left incomplete and in some cases had hardly been started. Nevertheless, measures are being taken to ensure continuance of this work so as to satisfy the demands of the communities.

Health legislation

Regulations on water and food safety and waste treatment in national and international transport and regulations for the utilization of inorganic products recoverable from waste have been approved.

An urban sanitation plan has been drawn up and is in the study and coordination phase. It would be applied by the municipalities, mainly in order to ensure better disposal of solid wastes which, particularly in Lima, constitute a very serious problem.

Communicable diseases control

Results are being achieved which can be considered satisfactory as regards keeping communicable diseases incidence low, thanks to widespread use of immunization prodecures. Nevertheless, the incidence of metoxenous diseases such as malaria, bartohellosis (Carrion's disease) and yellow fever, has been slightly increasing, with a few epidemic outbreaks. Jungle yellow fever is a cause of serious concern, since the budgetary provisions for case detection work, domestic spraying and immunization of those at risk are inadequate.

Since smallpox has been completely eradicated vaccination is no longer compulsory; only those travelling to a zone threatened by smallpox are vaccinated, or those coming from one and who left it less than 14 days before the risk developed. Furthermore, the smallpox strains in the National Institutes of Health are about to be destroyed.

An annex has been built to the Rimac Hospital (Hospital area No. 1) for the isolation and care of infectious and contagious disease patients, in particular leprosy cases (the patients from the old Guia Hospital have been transferred there since the latter hospital was demolished).

The number of malaria cases has risen alarmingly recently (insecticides are no longer provided by UNICEF). Nevertheless, in accordance with the present decentralization policy, resources available to the National Malaria Service are being transferred to the health regions. This has been done as regards the Chiclayo malaria zone, which has been transferred to the northwestern health region, and also the Tarma malaria zone, which has been transferred to the middle central health region.

The modern concept is spreading that tuberculosis control should be based on bacteriological examination of the sputum, to an increasing extent abandoning chest X-rays, which were less specific and much more expensive. The reintroduction of the antituberculosis stamp is being arranged so as to provide social assistance funds for tuberculosis patients and enable the tuberculostatic drugs they require to be purchased.

Activities of the National Institutes of Health

The construction of the new building to accommodate the National Institutes of Health is continuing. Training is also proceeding by means of fellowships for study abroad, and technical personnel are receiving in-service training in the Institutes for more extensive and responsible tasks.

In addition to the present production of the vaccines in most common use, i.e., vaccines against pertussis, diphtheria, typhoid and rabies, a few other preventive and therapeutic sera are being prepared.

Efforts have continued to extend the activities of the Institute of Occupational Health to a larger proportion of the population working in the manufacturing and mining industries. As regards atmospheric pollution, evaluation studies are being made, chiefly on the fumes emanating from refining plants at the mines.

National food and nutrition programmes

Mainly with the cooperation of the World Food Programme and USAID, the following programmes are being continued and have slightly increased their coverage: the school food programme, the programme for nutritional assistance to mothers and preschool children, the programme for nutritional assistance in hospitals, and the people's nutrition programme.

Biological and Drug Control Centre

This department of the National Institutes of Health has the task of controlling products of the pharmaceutical industry. However, its scope and capacity are still insufficient for exercising control which would give absolute certainty of the suitability of pharmaceuticals. In particular, it is necessary for control and analysis to go further than merely ensuring the accuracy of the composition of these products, and to investigate their clinical effects.

Health care delivery

The services of the Ministry of Health establishments showed a moderate increase during the years 1974–1977, related to change in availability of resources. In 1977 there was an increase of 30.7% in hospital beds as compared with 1974. The hospital bed discharge rate improved over the period from 21.7 to 23.3 per bed. The average stay also improved, from 11.5 to 10.6 days; on the other hand, the bed occupation rate fell from 68.1% to 67.4%.

Physician consultations fell from 3.8 per hour in 1973 to 2.9 in 1977. The coverage for the programme population is 66.8%, with 0.47 consultations per inhabitant per year.

Other activities, such as home visits and dental care, followed the same pattern as the hospitalization and medical consultation activities.

The peripheral services for direct care have not changed recently as concerns organization, functions and programmes, except for the creation of a multisectoral decentralized body to which all the separately administered health establishments and services of the Eastern Health Region responsible to the Ministry of Health have become directly attached. It has its own resources, to which have also been transferred the budgetary resources of all sectors with jurisdiction in the department, including those of the Eastern Health Region.

Health manpower

In 1977, of a total of 10 514 physicians in the whole country, the greatest percentage was in the

Lima Metropolitan Health Region (70.8%), and the smallest in the Eastern Central and Southern Altiplano regions (0.5% and 0.6% respectively). Similarly, the rates show that Lima has the highest proportion of physicians to population (15.8 per 10 000 inhabitants) and the Southern Altiplano the lowest (0.7 per 10 000). The Ministry of Health employs 30.9% of all the physicians in the country.

The greatest percentage (47.4%) of all personnel working in the peripheral services of the Ministry of Health are in Metropolitan Lima, while the percentages are very small in the Middle South (4%), in the South Altiplano (2.8%) and in the Eastern Central Region (only 2.1%).

Health expenditure

In 1977 the Ministry of Health expended a total of 11 591 996 000 soles on running costs and investment programmes (not including projects of local interest organized by different departments). Of that sum, running costs amounted to 9 651 480 000 soles, shared between national and regional programmes. As regards regional programmes, the greatest expenditure was in the Lima Metropolitan Region, amounting to 35.6% of the total, while the percentage for the Eastern Central Region was only 1.5%.

The per capita running costs for the population covered by the Ministry of Health programmes in 1977 was 871 soles at the national level. The greatest per capita expenditure was in the Lima Metropolitan Health Region, namely 1123 soles, and the smallest in the North-western Health Region, namely 246 soles.

Environmental sanitation

In environmental sanitation, provision of services in 1974 increased by 22.1% over the previous year, and in 1975 the figure was higher; in 1976 and 1977 there was a slight decrease.

SURINAME

Suriname, an independent republic since 1975, is situated on the north-east coast of the South American Continent, between French Guiana, Brazil and Guyana. It has a surface area of approximately 163 000 km^2, with a tropical rain forest climate and an average temperature of 26 degrees centigrade. Health conditions in general are considered to be good, which the following information supports:

	1974	1975	1976	1977
Mean population . . .	387 525	383 644	365 113	376 297
Live births	11 809	10 031	11 176	—
Birth rate (per 1000 population) . . .	30.5	26.1	30.6	—
Deaths	2 406	2 670	2 593	
Death rate (per 1000 population) . . .	6.3	7.0	7.1	—
Natural increase (%) . .	2.4	1.9	2.4	—
Infant deaths	450	481	417	—
Infant mortality rate	38.1	48.0	37.3	—
Deaths, 1–4 years . . .	164	139	73	—
Maternal mortality rate	—		—	—

Population and other statistics

At the last census, taken in January 1972, the population of Suriname was 384 900. Preceding independence in 1975 massive emigration to the Netherlands took place. Population data and other vital statistics for the period under review are given in the adjoining table.

Since 1972 the statistical information system has worked under great difficulties because of a serious lack of qualified manpower. As a consequence, health statistics are mostly unavailable or inaccurate.

Health care policy

In 1976 the Ministry of Health submitted a National Health Care Plan for Suriname 1976–1980, which was approved by the Cabinet of Ministers in March 1977. In structure the plan is generally in conformity with the Ten Years' Health Plan for the Americas. Major features of the plan include a programme of services providing for a medical care system the policy of which aims at a systematic extension and improvement of primary care, a national health insurance scheme with obligatory participation of all citizens is expected to be operational by January 1979 and the establishment of a new environmental sanitation division. Another feature of the plan is the development of infrastructure, and measures include the current reorganization of the Ministry of Health, its main responsibilities being legislation, setting and surveillance of norms, general policy making, with delegation of direct health care delivery; establishment of a council for social security, to determine general policy for the National Health Insurance Scheme; and provision for a national medicare foundation. The Executing Agency for the National Health Insurance Scheme has been established.

Major causes of death

The most frequently stated causes of death (1974–1976) are listed in the following table:

Cause	Number of deaths		
	1974	1975	1976
Diseases of the circulatory system (cardiovascular disease	513	599	652
Symptoms and ill-defined conditions (including senility)	208	181	238
Diseases of the respiratory system . . .	172	175	189
Malignant neoplasms	153	193	146
Causes of perinatal morbidity and mortality	139	189	226
Infectious and parasitic diseases	108	57	97

Principal public health problems

Malaria continues to pose a serious threat to the inhabitants of the interior. The following table illustrates the extent of the problem in terms of the frequency distribution of malaria cases.

Area	Population	Slides examined		Positive cases	
		1976	1977	1976	1977
Non-malarious	153 960	1 520	1 297	26	21
In maintenance phase	190 280	13 457	2 324	10	6
In consolidation phase	45 788	18 917	16 059	39	16
In attack phase	31 530	45 670	47 821	462	950
Total	421 558	79 564	67 501	537	993

Schistosomiasis, although still a major problem in the coastal rural area, has effectively been controlled through systematic search for parasitic carriers and specific treatment. In most parts of the infected areas the rate of prevalance has been reduced remarkably. The rate of incidence remains the same. Evaluation (through PAHO consultants) of the control programme indicated that a relatively high percentage (20–30%) of the milder infections pass undetected.

Gastroenteritis apparently remains a health hazard in early childhood although the magnitude of the problem cannot be accurately assessed.

Control programmes for *leprosy and sexually-transmitted diseases* are highly centralized within the Dermatology Service of the Ministry of Health. After the closure of the last leprosarium in 1972, case detection and treatment procedures of leprosy have improved. Both programmes appear to operate quite satisfactorily, although the control of sexually-transmitted diseases is experiencing difficulties similar to those found elsewhere.

Infectious and parasitic diseases still remain on the list of major causes of death. For this reason a national immunization programme was started in January 1976. The part of this programme aiming at the school population is reaching 95%, while efforts to reach the pre-school child have not been as complete and successful as was hoped (less than 40%). The latter is symptomatic of the insufficient infrastructure of the maternal and child health programme.

Resources

Hospital services

In 1975 the total number of hospitals and establishments for inpatient care was 16, providing 2044 beds. Of these institutions eight with a total capacity of 1538 beds, were government-owned. The ratio was 5.3 beds per 1000 population.

The urban/rural distribution of beds showed a bed/population ratio of 6.7 and 2.4 respectively per 1000 population. Ambulatory care is provided through outpatient departments of hospitals, health centres and medical aid posts.

Medical and allied personnel and training facilities

The following table lists the number of all health professionals and the ratio to the population of 1975:

Category	Total	Per 10 000 population
Physicians	194	5.1
Dentists	18	0.5
Midwives	73	1.9
Nurses	480	12.5
Practical nurses	277	7.2
Nursing aides, auxiliaries, etc.	334	8.7
Pharmacists	15	0.4
Pharmaceutical technicians	83	—
Sanitary engineer	1	—
Sanitary inspectors	7	—
Dieticians	5	—

Approximately 20 physicians graduate annually from the Faculty of Medicine of the University of Suriname.

Nurses are trained in one public and two private schools offering a basic course of three and a half years. In the last five years 25 staff nurses, 5 community health nurses and 20 tutors have been trained in postbasic courses.

A training course for dental auxiliaries is producing middle-level technicians for comprehensive oral health care for the young.

National budget for health care

The total budgetary expenditure of the Ministry of Health increased between 1972 and 1976 by 65%, from US $9 857 777 to US $16 278 888. The expenditure on health as a percentage of the total national budget decreased from 9.83% to 7.23%. The per capita government expenditure on health for 1976 was US $45, compared with US $46 in 1972.

Besides the regular budget expenditure a considerable amount was spent in capital investment on construction, equipment and transport facilities. The funds were granted by the Ministry of Finance out of a special fund raised through an extra levy on bauxite exports. In addition, funds from the Dutch Development Aid were made available for construction activities.

National development plans affecting the health sector

Since the Republic of Suriname became an independent sovereign State in 1975, a national development plan has been formulated of which the main overall goals are increased economic growth, increased employment opportunities, and improved living conditions of the total population.

To achieve a balanced spread of social and economic activities, geographical areas were designated to which most of the development efforts are directed. A major project among these plans is the large-scale development of the thinly populated area of western Suriname.

Industrial and agricultural activities in this and other almost virgin ecosystems, combined with mass migration of the labour force, will certainly pose major environmental and other health problems. Although coordinated national planning is still not a routinely practised procedure, attempts are continuously being made to bring together experts of the various sectors and disciplines to guide development plans and activities. In this respect the Ministry of Health has been involved in an ecological survey of the western Suriname area. Cooperation also exists between the Ministries of Health and Development and/or companies active in the area, to promote and protect the health of their labourers.

A PAHO/WHO executed project, financed by UNDP, is also active to assist in furthering the national objectives in agriculture, particularly in the area of home production of protein, through increasing the national herds of livestock.

The water supply programme is being carried out following the specifications of a report on a study made by PAHO/WHO under the auspices of UNDP from 1969 to 1973. The report contains proposals for the satisfaction of needs up to the year 2001.

The Government is endeavouring to supply drinking-water to at least 80% of the rural population by 1981, through the building of new treatment plants and distribution systems and the extension of existing installations.

It is estimated that the programme will cost approximately US $17 million for new construction and another US $8.5 million for improvements and expansion for the decade 1971–1980.

The Suriname Water Company will finance improvements and expansion in the Paramaribo, New Nickerie and Albina areas.

The goals for 1981 are the following:

| | Estimated population | Population served (%) | | |
		House construction	Easy access	Total
Urban	280 000	95	5	100
Rural	270 000	50	32	82
Total	550 000	73	18	91

UNITED STATES OF AMERICA

The Government is committed to assuring access of all citizens to the best quality health care it can afford. Attainment of this goal is being pursued by every federal agency concerned with health care. During recent years particular attention has been focused on access to health services, prevention of ill-health, development of knowledge and regulatory activity. In addition, a growing awareness on the part of consumers is being fostered so that they may assume more responsibility for their own health, and learn how to use the health care system more appropriately.

Health status indicators

Mortality

In general there has been a steady decline in mortality rates since 1972 for every age and racial group of the population, both male and female. The decline in infant mortality from 18.5 per 1000 live births in 1972 to 14.0 in 1977 (provisional figure) was particularly marked; such a 25% drop over a five-year period was unusual compared with the past half-century. There is evidence that the rate of decline in birthweight-specific neonatal mortality has been approximately equal for each birthweight group over 1000 grams. Since past declines had been primarily in the birthweight group over 2500 grams the recent rapid decline in mortality for low birthweight infants is particularly noteworthy.

The decline in overall adult mortality rates reflects declines in a wide variety of cause-specific rates. Nearly half the deaths are attributed to cardiovascular causes. Mortality rates for hypertensive and rheumatic heart disease and cerebrovascular diseases continued the decline that started several decades ago. Mortality rates from ischaemic heart disease, which began to decline during the late 1960s, continued to decline during the period 1973–1977. Malignant neoplasms constituted the only frequent cause which did not show a decline during the period. Declines in age-specific mortality rates for each of the age groups under 65 years were offset by increases in older age groups. Mortality rates for cancers of certain sites have been declining while cancers of other sites, particularly lung cancer, have been increasing.

Morbidity

There is little evidence of a general decline in morbidity rates comparable to the decline in mortality. The chronic degenerative diseases are the primary cause of disability. Prevention programmes for such diseases are receiving major emphasis.

Communicable disease patterns

Veneral diseases. Incidence of gonorrhoea, the most frequently reported communicable disease, levelled off, and showed a slight decline during the period, reversing a trend of over 15 years of continued increases. Penicillin-resistant strains of gonorrhoea, first recognized in 1976, were detected in several outbreaks. All were contained, and so far no endemic foci have been established.

A long-standing trend of increasing incidence of primary and secondary syphilis was also reversed in the period by a decline which first became apparent late in 1973.

Tuberculosis. The case rate for 1977 was 14.2 per 100 000 population (30 148 cases is the provisional figure), compared to a rate of 15.9 in 1975, a reduction of 10.7%. The number of cases reported in 1975 had shown an increase as a result of classification changes introduced in January of that year. Similarly, tuberculosis mortality continued to decline, with 3130 deaths reported in 1976, the lowest number ever recorded.

Influenza. The recurring struggle to prevent excess morbidity and mortality from influenza epidemics was punctuated by the appearance of a new strain, A/New Jersey/76, early in 1976. Isolated seven years after the previous large scale influenza epidemic, A/New Jersey/76 represented a major antigenic shift of the kind seen when widespread epidemics threaten. A massive immunization programme to prevent the potential epidemic resulted in the vaccination of 48.1 million persons, but was halted after some of those vaccinated developed nervous complications.

Legionnaires' disease. In 1976 there was an outbreak of an initially mysterious disease which caused pneumonia among 180 persons who had attended a convention in Philadelphia. There were nine deaths. Investigations led to the discovery of a previously unrecognized agent, Legionnaires' bacterium. Further study revealed this agent to have been the cause of unexplained epidemics a decade earlier, and a continuing cause of sporadic infections throughout the United States and in Europe.

Dengue and malaria. In mid-1977 an epidemic of dengue types 1, 2, and 3 began in Puerto Rico; it had attacked an estimated 10% of the island's population by the end of that year. Although the number of cases of imported malaria among armed forces personnel continued to decline, malaria imported by civilians showed a three-fold increase between 1972 and 1977.

Access to health care

The major portion of health care services is provided by the private sector. However, the Federal Government provides direct health care services to some groups specifically designated by federal statute, and reimburses with federal funds many services provided by the public, semipublic and private sectors. The Federal Government has as a major objective the improvement of access to health care for the underserved and special population groups and the curbing of the rapid rate of increase of health care costs. In 1965, 5.9% of the gross national product was spent on health care. In 1977 the percentage was 8.8.

Health care financing and planning

In June 1977 the Health Care Financing Administration was created, bringing the disparate health care financing mechanisms of the Department of Health, Education, and Welfare (especially Medicare and Medicaid, which provide health care coverage for 50 million people) under a single cost control agency, which was also given responsibility for basic quality control and for preventing fraud and abuse. It faces a major challenge after the escalation of health costs in the past ten years. Innovations to increase efficiency in management and reduce "red tape" have already been instituted. Regulations providing that the services reimbursed from federal funds must meet certain criteria have become a major element in planning reimbursement strategies. The Health Care Financing Administration recognizes the right to equal

access to care throughout the nation, with a special responsibility to the elderly and the poor.

Another initiative is the community-based health planning programme. Established by the National Health Planning and Resources Development Act (Public Law 93–641), which came into force in January 1975, it covers health services, manpower and facilities. It was evident that a national health planning policy was required which could provide for the development of resources, especially medical facilities and new technology, and assist in setting priorities for federal programmes and investments. The massive infusion of federal funds into the existing system in the 1960s with no cost containment incentives—indeed, with a number of inflationary elements—contributed to the increase, yet failed to produce an adequate distribution of health resources. Cost increases and technological advances, the changing age distribution of the population—the growth in the number of elderly with their higher service needs—and the shift from predominance of acute and infectious conditions to chronic health problems, have spotlighted a need for, and triggered widespread interest in improved health planning and resources distribution. Public Law 93–641 was intended to provide the structure and the support for effective health planning and a more systematic development of resources, especially new technology. A number of features were designed specifically to avert an insuperable health care crisis.

Public Law 93–641 made two amendments to the Public Health Service Act, Titles XV and XVI. Title XV required the Secretary of Health, Education, and Welfare to issue guidelines, by regulation, concerning national health planning policy. The guidelines include standards for the supply, distribution and organization of health resources; and a statement of national health planning goals expressed in quantitative terms to the extent possible. Title XV also provides for the creation of a National Council on Health Planning and Development, composed of 15 members broadly representative of health consumers, providers, planning agencies and other qualified persons. The Council advises the Secretary on the guidelines, the implementation and administration of the programme, and the implications of new medical technology for the organization, delivery and equitable distribution of health care services. Under Title XV, Congress authorized a network of planning agencies, known as health systems agencies, each responsible for a health service area of between

500 000 and 3 million residents, with at least one centre for the provision of highly specialized services. Title XVI establishes an organizational framework for financial assistance to various modernization and construction projects for medical facilities.

Health care delivery

The federal health sector provides the full range of preventive and curative health services to American Indians and Alaska natives directly through the Indian Health Service, with emphasis on the effective use of paramedical personnel and indigenous workers. Several types of auxiliary have been trained. The "*community health medic program*" trains Indian people as physician's assistants, stressing community medicine and work in remote areas under telephone or radio supervision by physicians. Health services in the small isolated villages of Alaska are provided by trained "*community health aides*", village residents who receive initial training of approximately 12 weeks, with subsequent periodical advanced training courses. They provide primary health services to village residents under radio supervision by physicians in field hospitals. To provide more effective links between the health care delivery system and Indian communities, local Indian people are used as "*community health representatives*". Employed under contractual arrangements with tribal organizations as liaison workers, they provide translation services, transport patients, assist in health education and preventive programmes, and carry out a number of health-related tasks determined by the local communities.

To increase community involvement in planning and carrying out their health care programmes, Indian health boards have been established at all levels—community, state and national. These health boards have vastly increased the sense of participation by local populations in determining the nature of their health programmes and in setting local health care priorities.

To combat the many environmental health problems confronting Indians and Alaska natives in their homes and communities, the Indian Health Service expanded its environmental health staff by 54% between 1973 and 1977. Starting in 1961, safe water and adequate means of waste disposal were made available to approximately 100 000 homes, of which nearly half were new and improved housing units constructed under other federal programmes. These efforts contributed significantly to the 69% decrease in the Indian infant death rate since 1955 and in the 89% decrease in the death rate for gastoenteritis during the same period.

The Federal Government also provides direct health care to the Coast Guard and the Bureau of Prisons, as well as occupational health services for federal employees.

Medical support to the underserved

A new strategy makes use of community health centre and migrant health centre programme funds and utilizes National Health Service Corps personnel to develop primary health care delivery capacity in areas of greatest need. The strategy integrates and makes the best use of available health resources by developing primary care systems for one or several counties or communities in both urban and rural areas identified as having critical health manpower shortages or severe lack of medical services. The strategy was tested in 1975 and 1976 through the "rural health initiative" and "health underserved rural area" programmes, and found to be very effective; an urban initiative has been developed to meet needs in inner city areas.

Health care for mothers and children, particularly preventive services and early diagnosis, has been recognized as having high potential for reducing premature death, preventing disability, and cutting health care costs. A "child health initiative" has been developed to improve the health of mothers and children, as well as to promote their physical and emotional development.

Specialized services

Emergency medical services. Since 1974 the Public Health Service has been administering a grant programme for the development of comprehensive emergency medical service systems.

Mental health. The number of residents in state and county mental hospitals fell from 475 200 in 1965 to 191 300 in 1975, a decrease of 60%. The sex composition has changed; generally the men have outnumbered the women in the past decade. But in both, schizophrenia was diagnosed for almost 50% of residents of each sex.

The trend observed since the dramatic turning point in the early 1970s continued, with patients being seen and cared for by the community mental health system. It is estimated that more than 6.7 million people have been reached by the mental health care system. The report of the President's Commission on Mental Health issued in April 1978 indicates that close to 15% of the population needs some form of mental health services, and focused on the underserved, i.e., children, adolescents, the elderly, racial and ethnic minorites, the poor, and migrant farm workers.

Approximately 88% of research on mental health and behavioural sciences is federally supported; private sources fund about 4% and state governments 8%. During the period 1967–1977 there was a steady decline in support, but the 1978 research budget has been restored to US \$135 million.

Since 1973 the National Center for the Prevention and Control of Rape and the Center for Studies of the Mental Health of the Aging have been established, with research and training as the primary focus. Efforts continued in the areas of mental health of children, crime and delinquency, and minority mental health problems.

Alcoholism. The 1970s have seen the development of a nationwide alcoholism treatment service delivery system. There has been a significant movement in recent years towards the accrediting of treatment facilities and the accrediting and training of alcoholism counsellors. More than 250 alcoholism treatment facilities have met the standards of the Joint Commission on Accreditation of Hospitals and have been accredited. Through its Career Teacher Program, the Federal Government has provided support to one-third of the nation's medical schools to provide training for physicians working with alcoholics.

Past efforts at alcoholism prevention, which concentrated primarily on the individual, have met with very limited success. A new approach is being formulated on the public health model which, rather than concentrating on the individual, or host, involves host, agent and environment.

Drug abuse. Since 1973 the drug abuse problem has shown a tendency towards stability, with several important variations. Most significant of these are the decrease in the use of heroin and the increased use of marihuana, cocaine, and phencyclidine. One of the most important developments was the creation of the National Institute of Drug Abuse in September 1974. It has become the leading authority in drug abuse

prevention. Since 1976, the federal role has been to stimulate treatment of drug abuse and then to stabilize the support, with the states and third parties taking over the larger part of the costs. Relying exclusively on professionals for treatment programmes has been found to be both unworkable and extremely expensive. Using some auxiliaries has lowered costs, raised effectiveness and relevance, and made it possible to run modern treatment programmes.

Biomedical research

During the years 1974–1977, the National Institutes of Health (NIH), in addition to their categorical research objectives, placed special emphasis on the following areas: arteriosclerosis, hypertension, and lung disease; identification of harmful man-made agents in the environment; diseases and other special problems of the elderly; diabetes mellitus; arthritis and related musculoskeletal disease; protection of human subjects of biomedical and behavioural research; population research and family planning; epilepsy and Huntington's chorea.

The Research on Aging Act of 1974 established a National Institute on Aging (NIH's eleventh institute). The obvious need for tangible and immediate improvement in the quality of life for the aging population was reflected in a shift in the emphasis in research from its exclusive disease orientation to a broader inquiry into normal physiological changes with age, the behavioural constitution of the aged, and the social, cultural, and economic environment in which people grow old.

The Sudden Infant Death Syndrome Act of 1974 authorized specific and general research on the sudden infant death syndrome through the National Institute of Child Health and Human Development.

Legislation in 1975 extended and amended research on family planning and population questions. Title X of the Public Health Service Act became the sole instrument governing the extramural, collaborative, and intramural research of the Department of Health, Education and Welfare in "biomedical, contraceptive development, behavioural and program implementation fields related to family and population". In addition, three temporary national commissions were created for the control of epilepsy, Huntington's chorea, and digestive diseases.

The Health Research and Health Services Amendments of 1976 extended authorization and amended provisions governing the programme of the National Heart and Lung Institute, placed increased emphasis on blood-related research and changed the Institute's name to the National Heart, Lung and Blood Institute.

(See also under "Mental Health", above).

Special prevention initiatives

The National Consumer Health Information and Health Promotion Act (Public Law 94–317) was adopted in June 1976, providing broad authority for the support of such activities as research and demonstrations to identify environmental, occupational, social, and behavioural factors affecting health, and the determination of those educational and preventive measures that can be implemented to improve health as it is affected by such factors. The legislation also established the Office of Health Information and Health Promotion in the Office of the Assistant Secretary for Health with, as its principal activities, participation in policy development, supervision and coordination of activities of the Public Health Services and the Department of Health, Education and Welfare in disease prevention and health promotion, identification of needs and development of resources to meet them, changes in current federal policies and governmental and nongovernmental programmes, and dissemination of health information to the public. These functions are performed in collaboration with the Public Health Service agencies, other components of the Department, other federal agencies, and the private sector. The National Clearinghouse for Health Information was to be established by January 1979 under this legislation.

In 1977 the federal health agencies began special efforts in several specific areas of prevention, including childhood immunization and prevention of adolescent pregnancy, smoking, and sexually transmitted diseases. The goals of the "immunization initiative", which began in April 1977, are two-fold: to raise immunization levels for vaccine-preventable diseases (measles, mumps, rubella, poliomyelitis, diphtheria, tetanus, and pertussis) for children under 15 years of age from present levels of 50–80% to at least 90% by October 1979; and to establish a permanent system to assure comprehensive immunization services to the three million children born each year.

Disease prevention and health promotion activities throughout the Department of Health, Education, and Welfare totalled some US $1 819 000 million for the fiscal year 1977, divided among activities related to the improvement of the environment, activities related to the enhancement of lifestyle, and the delivery of preventive services to various population groups.

The Departmental Prevention Task Force has identified 12 targets for development of strategies in disease prevention and health promotion: to reduce the incidence of chronic disease (cardiovascular, neoplastic, respiratory, diabetes mellitus, arthritis, etc.), communicable diseases, traumatic injuries and deaths (homicide, poisoning, motor-vehicle accidents, etc.), mental retardation and congenital defects, morbidity and mortality associated with pregnancy and the neonatal period, dental disease, diseases related to vision and hearing, emotional disorders, and abuse of narcotic, psychotropic and other substances; and to enhance development of children and adolescents and general physical and emotional well-being.

Health data development

In addition to the design and maintenance of national data collection systems, conduct of research in statistical and survey methodology, and cooperation with other agencies at home and abroad in order to increase the availability and usefulness of health data, new activities have been initiated or existing programmes expanded in the following areas:

(1) a nationally representative medical care expenditure survey to provide accurate data on utilization, expenditures, and sources of payment for medical care in the United States; and
(2) a national survey of family growth designed primarily to produce data on factors influencing trends and differentials in fertility and family planning practices.

Health manpower

Many of the health manpower incentives begun in the early 1970s, such as the improvement of the distribution of health staff according to geographical considerations and specialities, with particular emphasis on primary care, have been continued and strengthened.

In an effort to alleviate the severe maldistribution of physician services, the Federal Government implemented several programmes to increase the number of physicians for family medicine and other aspects of primary care.

Emphasis is being given to demonstration projects which may eventually become national models or prototypes in primary care instruction programmes for doctors both before and after graduation.

Qualifications for health personnel

The development and application of systems of licensing, certification or registration of medical personnel received increasing attention. The updating of the Licensure Information System, containing a computerized compilation of state statues and regulations governing qualifications for 35 health occupations in the 50 states, the District of Columbia, Puerto Rico, and the Virgin Islands, was completed in 1976. In 1977, 65 major health-related agencies established the National Commission for Health Certifying Agencies. The Commission will establish national standards for certifying bodies. The National Commission on Certification of Physician's Assistants was established in 1975. More than half the states require certification by the Commission.

Trends in medical education

In 1977 there were 22 accredited schools of veterinary medicine. Curriculum changes included the addition or expansion of courses in herd management, preventive medicine, public health, environmental health, and human health and nutrition.

A major attempt was begun to affiliate schools of paediatric medicine—currently independent institutions—with academic health centres, and broaden the clinical curricula in general medicine to involve the paediatrician in the evaluation of the patient as well as to recognize systemic diseases as they relate to conditions of the lower extremities.

There have been changes in the content of curricula and location of training in optometry, with new emphasis on courses in related aspects of nutrition and behavioural and sociological factors.

There has been a strong shift in emphasis in the curriculum for pharmacy from the physical sciences to the biological sciences—from drug production to patient orientation. Compliance with instructions of medication of chronic patients, especially among the elderly, was the subject of closer study. An interdisciplinary health care team concept was incorporated into many programmes of clinical pharmacy.

The Nurse Training Act of 1975 (Public Law 94–63), which extended nurse training authorities to 1978, revised capitation provisions, added new purposes to special projects authority, and added new authorities for advanced nurse training and nurse-practitioner training programmes. Stimulated by federal support, the overall quality of nurse-practitioner programmes dramatically improved in the period 1973–1977 and their number rose.

An important development in this period was the establishment in 1976, when it was noted that foreign-trained nurses had had difficulty in becoming licensed, of the independent, non-profit Commission on Graduates of Foreign Nursing Schools, with functions similar to those of the Educational Commission for Foreign Medical Graduates.

During the years 1973–1977, a variety of programmes were implemented to develop dental manpower for high quality services to encourage practice in remote and underserved areas by residency training in general dental practice; and to provide information about requirements for dental manpower and services. A new residency programme to train graduates in general dental practice began under Public Law 94–484.

Significant progress was made in training personnel for more than one discipline (e.g., X-ray and medical laboratory techniques), in order to meet the needs of small rural health care facilities, and in developing intensive weekend instruction programmes in advanced health and allied skills.

Large numbers of military-trained technicians in health and allied professions entered the civilian health care delivery system from 1974 to 1977. Operation "Military experience directed into health careers" placed some 5000 veterans annually; estimates are that another 5000 annually found placement through their own efforts. The positive cost/benefit factor was significant.

Regulatory activities

Food and drugs

In 1974 the Food and Drug Administration produced the "regulatory letter", a formal notice to a specific person or firm, charging specific violations of the law, setting a date for corrective action, and advising the parties that court proceedings will be started if the violations are not corrected. The purpose is to secure compliance and consumer protection in the shortest possible time and with the least expenditure.

Promoting quality control at the plant level has become the primary goal of regulations. New techniques of inspection, sampling, and analysis have been introduced, and many explanatory regulations and guidelines developed. "Hazard analysis and critical control point inspection", for example, is a preventive programme aimed at identifying those points in a food establishment where safety problems are likely to occur, and evaluating the control procedures at these points.

In 1977 a programme to provide for the periodic review of all food additives in order to ensure that they are safe according to up-to-date standards was initiated.

In January 1977 regulations were issued establishing procedures which assure the quality of generic drugs, so that drug products with the same active ingredients produce the same levels in the body for therapeutic action.

Enforcement of the first federal regulatory standard ever set for medical and dental X-ray units began in 1974. The standard directly affects over 130 million people each year who have one or more X-rays (65% of the population). The Diagnostic X-ray Standard will reduce two major causes of unnecessary X-ray exposure: the practice of using a beam larger than needed, and the need for retakes.

Medical Device Amendments to the Federal Food, Drug, and Cosmetic Act were enacted in 1976. Under the new legislation, the Food and Drug Administration has national responsibility for the regulation of medical devices intended for human use.

In 1977 manufactures of estrogen drugs were ordered to provide a lay-language brochure to women who have had the female hormone prescribed for relief of menopausal symptoms or after menopause. The brochure warns women that higher doses and longer treatment produce a greater risk of uterine cancer.

In the same year the first vaccine against pneumococcal pneumonia was licensed. Despite the wide use of antibiotics, pneumonia today is the fifth leading cause of death, killing an estimated 25 000 of the population annually. The vaccine protects against the type of pneumonia which accounts for a major portion of these and is effective in at least 80% of those who receive

it. Also in 1977, the Food and Drug administration issued the first license for hepatitis B immune globulin, an effective treatment for low-dose exposure such as might occur through accidents involving infected needles, splashing, or pipetting.

In spring 1976 the Food and Drug Administration expanded its efforts to regulate the nation's safety testing industry. The objective of this programme is to increase bioresearch surveillance and take necessary corrective action (1) in nonclinical toxicology laboratories, in order to test the safety of new products on animals and determine their status relative to proposed "good laboratory practices"; (2) among clinical investigators performing efficacy tests on regulated products using human subjects in order to relate them to proposed regulations on "Obligations of sponsors and monitors of clinical investigations"; (3) in institutional review committees designed to assure that the rights and welfare of institutionalized human subjects of clinical investigations are adequately protected; and (4) through cyclic review of food additives, initiated in 1977, to ensure that all food additives are re-evaluated for safety using the most up-to-date information available.

In 1977 a task force was appointed to study the effectiveness of antibiotics in animal feeds and to determine whether these uses are safe for animals and humans.

Environmental health

Since its establishment as an independent regulatory agency in 1970 the Environmental Protection Agency has been working towards ensuring coordinated and effective action to protect the national and international environment. During the period 1973–1977 most of the relevant legislation was amended and the Agency has been granted new and increased authority by Congress through enactment of the Safe Drinking Water Act of 1974; amendment of the Federal Insecticide, Fungicide, and Rodenticide Act in 1975; enactment of the Resource Conservation and Recovery Act of 1976; enactment of the Toxic Substances Control Act of 1976; amendment of the Federal Water Pollution Control Act in 1977; amendment of the National Clean Air Act in 1977; and amendment of the Marine Protection, Research, and Sanctuaries Act in 1977.

In 1977 the Agency's first comprehensive national plan for reducing noise was announced.

VENEZUELA

Population estimates and some indicators of the level of health

Estimated population was 11 517 827 on 1 July 1974 and 12 736 686 in 1977. A recent study by the Directorate-General of Statistics underscores that by the mid-1980s the country will have a population of around 14 million, about 80% concentrated in the urban sector.

Life expectancy at birth has increased owing to the decline in mortality, especially infant mortality, since 1974 with improved health and medical care conditions in the country. The infant mortality rate was 53.8 per 1000 live births in 1973 but had fallen by 16% to 44.5 in 1976. The birth rate continued to drop, from 37.6 per 1000 in 1974 to 36.5 per 1000 in 1977. Mortality among infants aged 1–4 is still falling, while maternal mortality has remained almost constant.

	1974	1975	1976	1977
Estimated population (in millions)	11.63	11.99	12.36	12.74
Life expectancy at birth	—	67	—	—
Birth rate (per 1000 population)	37.6	35.8	36.8	—
General mortality (per 1000 population)	6.5	6.0	6.2	—
Deaths over 50 years of age (percentage of general mortality)	44	45	—	—
Infant mortality (per 1000 live births)	46.0	44.7	44.5	—
Infant deaths (percentage of general mortality)	27	26	—	—

There have been fewer cases of tuberculosis and typhus. No smallpox cases were recorded.

Heart disease is still the major cause of death, with an increasing mortality rate. Accidents of all types take second place, with a more or less stable rate, cancer third, with an increasing rate in the first three years of the study; pneumonia, fifth in 1974, 1975 and 1976, dropped to sixth place in 1977, its position being taken by enteritis and other diarrhoeal diseases. Diabetes mellitus, twelfth in 1974, rose to tenth in 1975 and 1976 and ninth in 1977. Tuberculosis was thirteenth in 1974 and twelfth in 1975, 1976 and 1977. Measles fell from fifteenth place in 1974 to twenty-third.

Organization of health services

The *National Health Council* was established by Decree No. 276 of 22 July 1974 for the purpose of advising the Government on the "formulation of health, welfare and social security policy".

The Council consists of the Minister of Health and Social Welfare, who is its Chairman, the presidents of the Venezuelan Social Security Institute, the National Academy of Medicine, the Venezuelan Medical Federation and the Venezuelan Public Health Association, representatives of the Venezuelan Association of Schools of Medicine, and seven members who may be freely appointed and dismissed by the President of the Republic.

The Council meets every 15 days, considers documents forwarded to it and keeps itself informed by means of summaries prepared for the purpose from the epidemiological bulletins and other publications and opinions in the public health sphere.

The Council prepares reports and recommendations and adopts guidelines for the solution of national health problems. It has established norms and bases for the activities and programmes in the health sector.

In implementation of the recommendations of the Fifth National Public Health Congress, the President of the Republic established the *Coordinated National Health Service* by Decree No. 1841 of 19 October 1976, in order to unify the health services by means of coordinated action at the central and regional levels by all the national, state and municipal institutions with a view to obtaining comprehensive and efficient medical care for the entire population.

The Medical Care Services were increased significantly during the four-year period: from 347 hospitals in 1973 the number rose to 440, with an increase of 5157 in the number of beds, from 34 530 in 1973 to 39 687. The bed population ratio remained the same owing to the parallel increase in population. The average stay in hospital was eight days. The number of health centres increased from 37 to 76 as a result of construction and remodelling of municipal hospitals and rural clinics; the remodelled hospitals provide not only recovery services but also services designed actively to promote and protect health. The number of rural clinics rose from

501 to 529. Around the regional hospitals in the major cities nine suburban outpatient centres were established where, besides medical care, instruction in health promotion and protection and environmental sanitation is provided. In 1977 there were 2167 rural dispensaries, 938 of which were engaged in the "simplified medicine" programme.

The Advisory Council to the *Maternal and Child Division* was formed by ministerial resolution at the beginning of 1974. Its Chairman is the Chief of the Division, the other members being the President of the Venezuelan Paediatric Society and 12 other persons closely connected with maternal and child health.

In 1973 there were 389 paediatric centres in the country; in 1977 there were 526. Diagnostic studies for the first stage of the premature birth prevention programme sponsored by the Latin American Centre for Perinatology (through PAHO), the Maternal and Child Division and health commissions, are being carried out in certain maternity hospitals in Caracas, Maracaibo, Valencia, Maracay, Mérida and Cumana. The Maternal and Child Division has cooperated actively in the programming of the Coordinated National Health Service.

Communicable diseases

Diseases preventable by immunization

Over the four-year period 1974–1977 all rates used as indicators in formulating the ten-year plan displayed a downward trend. By 1977 the diphtheria morbidity rate was 0.4 per 100 000—less than half the target rate of 1.0 per 100 000; the pertussis mortality rate (1.1) was almost on target (1.0). The poliomyelitis morbidity rate coincided with the target of 0.1 per 100 000, while the mortality rates for tetanus (1.1) and measles (2.8) were still well above the targets of 0.5 and 1.0, respectively.

Rabies is still a problem although only 19 cases in humans were recorded—a reduction of 37% compared with the number of known cases in the preceding quinquennium (1970–1973). Canine rabies, accounting for 84% of the cases diagnosed, is still the chief problem. The number of canine and feline cases in the period 1974–1977 was 1757, a 12.9% increase over the total for 1970–1973, which was 1556.

Annual regional courses in Spanish on epidemiological surveillance and control of communicable diseases, sponsored by WHO/PAHO, have been held since 1972.

A total of 64 epidemiologists were trained, 27 of whom were Venezuelan physicians.

Malaria

By 1961 malaria had been eradicated in 430 920 km^2 of the 600 000 km^2 forming the originally malarious area; 407 975 km^2 were recorded as malaria-free by WHO—the largest malaria-free area achieved anywhere in America. The area still infected, that adjoining Colombia and Brazil, is currently in the attack phase; it measures 139 946 km^2 and has a population of 565 761. The situation improved in the period 1974–1977 owing to changes in the attack procedures and stepping up of spraying cycle frequencies in some areas; employment of other measures such as use of drugs in mass programmes in communities where there had been an annual incidence of 50 or 100 cases per 1000 inhabitants in the preceding quarter; and insecticide "fogging" in selected areas.

Chagas' disease

The main vector of Chagas' disease—*Rhodnius prolixus*—is common throughout the country. Of the total of 691 municipalities, 531(76.8%) are infested. The area infested by *R. prolixus* totals 628 295 km^2 and had an estimated population of 8 573 170 in 1977.

Diseases transmitted by Aeges aegypti

As of 1966, responsibility for the *Aedes aegypti* eradication programme started in 1947 was transferred from the Sanitary Engineering Division of the Ministry of Health and Social Welfare to the Division of Rural Endemic Diseases. Sanitary controls of land and waterways have in the past four years detected 195 vehicles harbouring *A. aegypti* bound for the area free of the vector. Sanitary education activities were carried out in the working area by personnel properly trained and supervised by qualified sanitary inspectors. With the reorientation of the programme for control instead of eradication, a series of nationwide campaigns have been carried out which, while they have not eradicated *A. aegypti*, will guarantee its control and make urban transmission of jungle yellow fever unlikely.

Noncommunicable diseases

In the period 1974–1977 heart and cerebrovascular diseases maintained the same ranking as in the preceding quadrennium (1969–1973), first and seventh respectively among causes of death. Cardiovascular diseases continued to increase in significance as causes of death. In 1974 heart disease caused 8906 deaths, giving a mortality rate of 76.6 per 100 000, while cerebrovascular diseases were the cause of 3504 deaths, giving a mortality rate of 30.1 per 100 000. In the 25–44 years age group, heart disease was the third cause of death and cerebrovascular disease the seventh. Between 45 and 64 years and 65 and 74 years heart disease was the leading cause and cerebrovascular diseases the third. Among persons over 75 heart disease was again the leading cause of death and cerebrovascular diseases the second.

In 1974 there were 9223 discharges of heart patients from hospitals and health centres of the Ministry of Health and Social Welfare.

Environmental health

Occupational health and safety

An occupational health programme covering 25% of the economically active population employed in manufacturing and 4.6% of the population employed in all economic activities is being carried out by the Ministry of Labour, the Ministry of Health and Social Welfare and the Venezuelan Social Security Institute. Because of growing industrial development and the limited manpower allocated to the programme, the coverage did not increase in the period 1974–1977. In the Ministry of Health and Social Welfare, however, the personnel has been increased, especially in the last two years, by the addition of 5 engineers, 7 physicians, 3 pharmacists, 8 inspectors, 4 radiological technicians, 1 chemist and 3 nurses; this personnel is being trained in the field with a view to expanding the coverage of the programme. In 1977 a working group was formed by the three competent bodies to report to the National Technical Committee of the Coordinated National Health Service, charged with drawing up a plan for coordination in matters of industrial hygiene and safety. The working group completed its assignment in 1978 and

submitted a coordination plan designed to prevent duplication of functions and dispersal of resources. A draft version of an Organic Law on Working Conditions and Environment has been prepared and will shortly be submitted to Congress for its approval.

Radiation protection

Venezuela has approximately 3500 sets of X-ray equipment for diagnostic purposes, and 8000–10 000 staff of the Ministry of Health and Social Welfare, the Venezuelan Social Security Institute and private clinics are exposed to ionizing radiation in the course of their work. In the period 1974–1977, and especially in the first two years, radiation protection control suffered badly from loss of staff; in 1974 there were one physician and one inspector, in 1975 just the one physician. In 1976 a team of one engineer and four technicians was formed, a chemist and an engineer's assistant were added in 1977, and the work was incorporated into the occupational health programme. There were 233 inspections in medical institutions (as against 33 in 1974), 106 studies and investigations (as against 43), and equipment calibration has been reintroduced; however, the dosimetry laboratory has not yet been set up. The competent section in the Division of Control of the Quality of the Environment has checked 9 X-ray units, 17 cobalt 60 units and one cesium 137 unit used in radiotherapy in medical institutions of the Ministry of Health and Social Welfare, covering a total staff of 72 exposed to ionizing radiation, and has inspected 540 dental X-ray units with a total staff of 615 in the Caracas metropolitan area.

Environmental pollution

During the period 1974–1977 basic changes were made in the structure for the atmospheric pollution control programme. As of 1975, following the determination of needs in earlier years, specific control activities were started under the programme, which is operated by the Ministry of Health and Social Welfare, while the evaluation activities were transferred to the atmospheric pollution research programme, also under that Ministry; from 1977 programmes of the Ministry of the Environment were also incorporated. The activities included: setting up of a specific structure with specially trained personnel; selection of potentially polluting regions and areas, and compilation of an inventory of emission sources; review of 110 plans for industrial facilities and waste incinerators, ensuring inclusion of adequate controls at the planning stage and preventing the addition of new emission sources; inspection of 1500 fixed pollution sources, especially in dust-emitting industries, and taking of the necessary corrective measures; participation in a programme to relocate polluting industries established in Caracas; preparation of a manual of procedures; checking of 100 complaints about sources of pollution.

Water supply

The Ministry of Health and Social Welfare is responsible for the construction of water supply systems for towns with fewer than 5000 inhabitants, and, as of 21 October 1975, for localities with fewer than 1000 inhabitants (Presidential Directive No. 17).

Since 1974 the rural water supply programme has received unequivocal support from the National Executive, which has ensured the availability of funds for intensifying the installation of new systems and reconditioning existing systems. The population served by the rural water supply programme numbers 523 916 in over 800 localities, and estimated investment is 189 760 bolívares.

Housing

Under Presidential Directive No. 17 of 21 October 1975, the rural housing programme aims at localities with fewer than 1000 inhabitants. According to Ministry of Development census data, 2 444 826 persons live in these localities; the projection of growth for 1980 sets the figure at 2 732 673. The ratio of occupants per occupied dwelling works out at 5.88 in the urban areas and 6.04 in the rural areas. A high proportion of rural dwellings have one room, and the serious consequences of crowding for the physical and mental health of the occupants are obvious.

The programme seeks to provide dwellings with an entrance porch, three rooms (separate accommodation for parents, girls and boys), a living-cum-dining room, bathroom, and a back porch with washing facilities.

Construction of such housing alone cannot constitute sanitary living conditions; it must be combined with education for greater life expectancy and true social well-being. This aim is pursued through the different educational activities of the sanitary extension personnel.

The Ministry of Health and Social Welfare is responsible for the programme administrative expenses, and the Agricultural and Livestock Credit Institute for capital expenditure. In the period 1974–1977 a total of 40 904 dwellings were built for a population of 245 420 at an approximate cost of 341 315 000 bolívares.

SOUTH-EAST ASIA REGION

BANGLADESH

Population and other statistics

At the last census, taken in March 1974, the population of Bangladesh was 76.2 million. Population estimates and some other vital statistics for the year 1977 are given in the following table:

Mean estimated population	82 700 000
Number of live births	3 890 000
Birth rate (per 1000 population)	45
Number of deaths	1 570 000
Death rate (per 1000 population)	17
Natural increase (%)	2.8
Number of infant deaths	540 000
Infant mortality rate (per 1000 live births)	over 140

The communicable diseases most frequently notified in 1977 were: diarrhoea diseases (496 000), malaria, new cases (28 855), leprosy (27 352; new cases, 1162), tuberculosis, all forms (24 723), cholera (10 461), pertussis (5109), typhoid and paratyphoid fevers (5073), diphtheria (507), poliomyelitis (85).

Organization of health, population control and family planning services

The responsibility for the health services and population control and family planning rests with the Ministry of Health and Population Control, which has a Health Division and Population Control and Family Planning Division. The Presidential Adviser in charge of Health and Population Control is assisted by a Secretary, with joint secretaries, deputy secretaries and section officers for each division separately.

For the purposes of government administration, Bangladesh is hierarchically divided into four divisions, 19 districts, 62 subdivisions and 422 *thanas*. The smallest administrative area, the *thana*, has a population of about 200 000. The administration of the Health Division services follows the hierarchical arrangements of these geographical units. Directorates of health services are responsible for the levels of division and below.

The Health Division is organized into four directorates: the Directorate of Health Services (Preventive), the Directorate of Health Services (Curative), the Directorate of Nursing Services, and the Directorate of Drug Administration.

Each *thana* has a health centre or "*thana-health-complex*" with a 31-bed hospital, includ-ing six maternity beds, and one, two or three qualified doctors. The *thana* health centre may be a dispensary under the charge of a qualified doctor. Each subdivision has a small hospital with 50 to 100 beds; and each district has either a teaching or a non-teaching hospital with 100 to 150 beds. The larger general and specialized hospitals are in the major towns.

There are about 10 900 family welfare workers working in the rural areas, each responsible for preventive, promotive and simple curative care in about six villages. In a *thana* there would be about 25 family welfare workers, one sanitary inspector, one health inspector and six assistant health inspectors working under a *thana* health administrator (a qualified doctor).

The Population Control and Family Planning Division is organized into six directorates under the charge of a Director General. These services have the highest Government priority. Each directorate is headed by a Director. Two officers are posted in each district—one responsible for general administration and another for technical administration and supervision. Similarly, in each *thana* there is provision for a family planning officer and a medical officer. There are three maternity hospitals (120 beds) and 93 maternity and child health centres (492 beds) attached to the Family Planning Directorate. Most of the hospitals under the Health Division also have a family planning and maternal and child health component.

Hospital services

In 1977 Bangladesh had 133 government hospitals providing 12 631 beds, to which over 300 000 patients were admitted. The bed/population ratio was thus 1.7 per 10 000. These and other health establishments, not including special hospitals for communicable and noncommunicable diseases (see below), were as follows:

	Number of hospitals	No. of beds
General hospital[1] . . .	109	10 721
Specialized hospitals and clinics	24	1 910
Rural health centres . .	289	2 690
Rural dispensaries . . .	1 920	—
School health clinics . .	25	—

[1] Including those for transport workers (railways), prisons and the police.

129

Facilities for ambulatory treatment were available in 1977 at 130 hospital outpatient departments and 2324 dispensaries.

Medical and allied personnel and training facilities

In 1977, 5191 doctors, 1271 qualified nurses (1238 senior and 33 junior) and 1180 nursing attendants were in government service. The total number of compounders in government service during the year was 2143. Bangladesh has three postgraduate medical institutes, eight medical colleges, four schools for medical assistants, 18 training institutes for nurses, one postgraduate nursing college and two institutions for auxiliary medical staff.

In addition, in-service training is provided at the Institute of Epidemiology, Disease Control and Research, the Institute of Public Health Laboratory Services, the National Institute of Preventive and Social Medicine, and the Institute of Public Health Nutrition and various other institutions. Training in population control and family planning is given in the National Institute for Population Research and Training for senior government staff, and in 11 other institutes for junior administrative staff.

The following table shows the numbers of doctors, nurses, midwives and lady health visitors trained in 1975 and 1976 compared with the total for the period 1970–1974.

	Doctors	Nurses	Midwives	Lady health visitors
1970–1974	460.8	117.2	141.2	38.6
1975	581	145	171	56
1976	630	341	87	22

The Government has undertaken health manpower development programmes in the context of socioeconomic development and has accorded top priority to rural development in order to improve the living conditions of the rural people, using the *thana*-health-complex scheme, which incorporates the primary health care concept and principles. Further, the Government, recognizing the importance of efficient administration for development efforts, has emphasized the need for improvement in managerial capacities at all levels, and proper utilization of the available resources. The training and utilization of unqualified medical practitioners and untrained midwives in the delivery of health services are being considered in this context.

The main features of the programmes of reorientation of medical education and development of appropriate and adequate medical manpower are thus the development of auxiliary manpower for the *thana*-health-complex scheme, because sufficient physicians could not be trained and mobilized for the rural areas, and the reorientation of undergraduate medical education towards community needs.

The following auxiliary medical personnel were trained in the period 1972–1976:

Sanitary inspectors	130
Laboratory technicians	52
Dental technicians	12
Radiographers	31
Radio technicians	2
Physiotherapist	1
Blood bank technicians	2
Pharmacists	53
Compounders	900
Microscopists[1]	650
Family planning assistants	4 288
Family welfare workers	10 999

[1] Trained for *thana*-health-complex laboratory work.

Communicable disease control

The incidence of malaria was reduced to a minimum during 1970. The massive migration which followed the 1971 war, and other factors, precipitated a recrudescence of the disease. Nearly 20% of the population live in malaria high risk areas, compared with less than 10% in 1971. DDT spraying and drug prophylaxis are being carried out in these areas.

In 1974 a plan was implemented for the eradication of smallpox. By October 1975 the country was free from smallpox. After a two-year period of intensive surveillance it was certified free from smallpox in December 1977 by an international commission.

The control of tuberculosis is based on BCG vaccination, case-finding and treatment. The BCG vaccination programme was launched in 1976 and 6.8 million eligible children (defined as previously unvaccinated children under 15 years) were vaccinated by December 1977. By 1980 the total of 37.7 million eligible children are to be vaccinated. Facilities for the treatment of tuberculosis are available in 13 hospitals (1000 beds) and in 44 tuberculosis clinics. There were also three leprosy hospitals with 130 beds, and five other infectious disease hospitals, with 180 beds.

Noncommunicable diseases

Facilities for the treatment of patients with chronic diseases and for rehabilitation are limited. In 1977, treatment of cancer cases by radiotherapy was available in five hospitals, of which three had hospital beds for cancer patients. All major hospitals have cardiology services. The only mental disease hospital has 428 beds and provides inpatient treatment only; ambulatory care and limited inpatient care are given in teaching hospitals. An institute of endocrinology is being established by the Diabetic Association, with government assistance. There is an eye bank with facilities for corneal grafting.

Maternal and child health

In 1977, 93 centres were engaged in maternal and child health care; 106 126 pregnant women, 22 537 infants and 115 505 children aged 1–5 years attended these centres. Domiciliary care was given to 1558 pregnant women, 6263 infants and 16 291 children up to five years old. A total of 11 684 deliveries were conducted in institutions.

Country health programming

The first exercise was carried out in 1973 as a trial run by WHO of newly conceived procedures. It was limited in scope because the national five-year plan had already been formulated. The second exercise was conducted in 1977 by the Government with WHO support in anticipation of the next five-year plan, 1980-1985. With the guidance of a steering committee comprised of senior officials from the Government, a working group prepared 10 health programmes which were presented in a document approved by the Government in September 1977: primary health care, static health care, communicable diseases control, environmental health, manpower development, management control, supply and maintenance, drug production and control, population control, and interministerial coordination.

Factors influencing the development of health plans

The rural population, comprising 92% of the total population, is very much underserved by qualified health manpower. The shortage of doctors and nurses, aggravated by emigration to the Middle East countries and unwillingness to work in the rural areas, has prompted the Government to begin training medical assistants and to search for alternative approaches to bring primary health care to everyone in the rural areas. There is a high demand for health services in the rural areas, mostly because of a high incidence of communicable diseases. This demand is now met mostly by indigenous and unqualified allopathic practitioners.

The extreme poverty and very low level of living of the general population are serious impediments to participation in community development activities. The growth of rural development schemes is being stimulated by the Government, including the promotion of community participation in rural health services. Women are encouraged to emerge from their *purdah* pattern of social life to support community development efforts and take part in family planning activities.

The high maternal and infant mortality rates, the high incidence of water-related diseases and the underutilization of the health services (especially by women and children) are expressions of the poverty of the rural population, their age-old ways with water, defecation habits and other customs, the shortage of safe water, the conservative attitudes of the women and traditional ideas about the causation of illness.

Population growth is recognized as a major obstacle to development. High national priority is given to population control; a National Council for Population Control has been constituted and certain health services for maternal and child care are administered by the Population Control Division of the Ministry of Health and Population Control.

Geography and climate have shaped the economic structure and philosophy of the people. Rivers and water dominate their lives. Poverty, ignorance and illiteracy, associated with age-old patterns for the use of water, determine the high incidence of water-related diseases. One fifth of the country is inundated during the monsoon each year. This creates annual national crises when valuable national resources, including scarce health resources, have to be diverted. For several months each year, large parts of the country are accessible only by boat.

Road and railway transport and access to health centres are difficult and time-consuming.

There are six regional radio stations, and the total circulation of Bengali daily newspapers amounted to only about 250 000 in 1977. Health education through the mass media does not easily reach the rural population, especially the women. Direct contacts by basic health workers and group educational activities at the village level are essential.

Production, importation and sale of drugs

There are over 160 pharmaceutical laboratories licensed to manufacture specified kinds of medicines. Of these, 28 are large or medium-sized and the rest are small. During 1976 the local firms manufactured nearly 80% of the drugs consumed in the country. The total drug consumption was about US$ 50 million in the same year.

Only items registered by the Ministry of Health may be imported, subject to the import policy published by the Government. Drugs and medicines for the public sector are procured by the Central Medical Stores.

As a result of studies by WHO, UNICEF and the Government, a tentative list of 31 essential drugs has been drawn up for primary health care. The Government Pharmaceutical Unit in Dacca has been producing seven basic items—acetylsalicylic acid, phenacetin and caffeine (APC), sulfadiazine, sulfadimidine, phthalylsulfadiazol, antacid, spirits of chloroform and iodine tincture. Plans are under way for the phased expansion of the Unit to produce more of the 31 essential drugs.

BURMA

Major health and health-related problems

Country health programming, initiated in January 1976, identified 51 major health problems which were arranged according to their priority ranking, singly or by subgroups (having similar etiology or responding to available technologies, for example) as follows: malaria; pulmonary tuberculosis; gastrointestinal diseases; nutritional diseases; maternal and perinatal conditions; leprosy; zoonoses; accidents; communicable diseases preventable by immunization; snake bite; cardiovascular diseases, nephritis, cirrhosis of liver, peptic ulcer; mosquito-borne diseases; neoplasms; respiratory infections; trachoma; mental diseases; dental diseases; venereal diseases; noninfectious eye diseases; skin disorders.

Action taken

Health policy

The framework of the national health planning process is the 20-year national plan for economic development, which was drawn up in accordance with the policy guidelines laid down by the Central Committee of the Burma Socialist Programme Party. The main objectives of the

health sector policy are:

(1) to raise the health standards of the working people and to provide efficient treatment for all diseases;
(2) to promote simultaneous improvement of both preventive and curative health services, with higher priority for prevention;
(3) to narrow the gap between rural and urban areas in the availability of health care services;
(4) to achieve progressive improvement in health care facilities with more cooperation from the public; and
(5) to extend and improve social services, including those for health, apace with economic progress.

Health legislation

The following instruments have been promulgated and the Department of Health is responsible for their enforcement: Public Health Law, 1972, the Dental Act, and acts governing nurses and midwives registration, registration of private nursing homes, dangerous drugs, epidemic diseases, food and drugs, ghee (cooking butter) adulteration, leprosy, and vaccination.

Other acts that contain components related to

health, but the responsibility for the enforcement of which lies with ministries other than the Ministry of Health, concern animal pests, merchant shipping, aircraft, city of Rangoon Municipal affairs, other municipal matters, cantonments, ports, rural self-government, railways, towns, and villages.

Health planning and programming

The introduction of country health programming was preceded by two health planning courses for senior staff of the Department of Health and a two-week country health programming workshop for the Directors-General of Health, Medical Education and Medical Research.

Country health programming was undertaken according to WHO guidelines, and programme descriptions were completed in June 1976 when programme proposals were submitted to the Minister of Health for approval. The following service and support projects were formulated and documented in detail by January 1977, and approval in principle by the Cabinet was obtained in July 1977:

Service projects. (1) primary health care and basic health services; (2) environmental sanitation; (3) expanded programme of immunization; (4) family health care; (5) vector-borne diseases control; (6) medical care.

Support projects. (1) health information service; (2) laboratory support services; (3) staff and procedure development; (4) supplies, maintenance and repair; (5) production and quality control of biologicals and pharmaceuticals; (6) health practices research.

The country health programme covers a five-year period from 1977/78 to 1981/82. The first year was devoted to preparatory activities such as training of health auxiliaries and community health volunteers and procurement of supplies and equipment. Implementation commenced on 1 April 1978 and will run concurrently with the third four-year economic development plan. Country health planning has been coordinated with other development sectors, and the 147 townships earmarked for the implementation of the primary health care and family health projects are also the focal points for the planning and implementation of educational and social welfare services, and water supply programmes. Development programmes in different sectors, thus coordinated and synchronized, are expected to reinforce and complement each other.

Organization of health services

Health care is administered from the central Department of Health in the Ministry of Health through 14 state or divisional health directorates to the township or rural health services at the periphery. The Department of Health is headed by a Director-General who is responsible for the overall planning and administration of the health services. He is assisted by five directors for: medical care; public health; disease control; planning, administration, finance and training; and laboratory services. At the peripheral level the township health officer assists in public health work. A station medical officer heads the station health unit which is attached to a station hospital (an upgraded rural health centre). Maternal and child health care is provided by centres in townships and urban areas, and rural health centres deliver health care for rural areas, all of which come under the administrative and technical supervision of the township medical officer.

The health care system therefore covers three broad categories, medical care, public health and disease control. These are supported by laboratory services, the health statistics section (health information), the nutrition project, and the Bureau of Health Education. Certain sections of the Department of Health which deserve mention are those for occupational health and environmental sanitation in the Public Health Division, social security medical services and medicosocial work in the Medical Care Division, and port health in the Disease Control Division. The indigenous medicine services are also affiliated to the Department of Health.

Biomedical and health services research

Research activities are coordinated by the Department of Medical Research. Current projects are either part of the activities of the Department or of WHO-sponsored programmes (intercountry projects of the Regional Office for South-East Asia or the Special Programme for Research and Training in Tropical Diseases).

Education and training of health manpower

A promising and, it is hoped, significant result of country health programming has been the emergence of new categories of community health volunteers, namely the community health worker and the auxiliary midwife. A total of 5280 of the former and 3200 of the latter are scheduled to be trained for work under the supervision of the peripheral basic health service staff by 1981/82. Training of basic health staff as well as personnel of the special disease control programmes to function as multipurpose health workers and reinforce the rural health staff is also necessary, so that a severe strain will be imposed on the training component of the "staff and procedure development" project. Since 1973 preliminary steps have been taken for the establishment of a health manpower development project, and some studies of type and duration of training, registration and employment, as well as discontinuation are in progress. Reliable data are needed and a health information system may be a useful rallying point for these efforts.

The Department of Health and the Department of Medical Education are jointly responsible for health manpower production in the country. The former trains all paramedical personnel for health services delivery. The latter undertakes undergraduate training for the medical degree, training of dental surgeons and auxiliaries such as dental nurses and technologists, and postgraduate training for specialities. The Department of Health has 16 midwifery schools turning out about 500 midwives per year, one school for lady health visitors, producing 55 visitors per year, one health assistant training school producing 500 public health supervisors per year, one paramedical institute training a total of about 50 radiographers, physiotherapists, medical technologists and pharmacists per year, one postgraduate nursing school training nurses in certain specialities (about 150 a year), one indigenous medical school training about 50 indigenous medical practitioners per year, two compounder training centres producing about 30 compounders per year, and one laboratory training centre training 65 laboratory technicians per year. The Department of Medical Education has three medical institutes which together turn out about 500 physicians per year, one dental institute training 50 dental surgeons, 10 technicians and 20 dental nurses per year, diploma courses, and 11 mastership courses.

The above training programmes are well subscribed, which augurs well for the health planning processes in both the short and the long term.

Health resources

Health establishments

There were 436 civil hospitals in the country at the end of 1975, providing approximately 26 000 inpatient beds. A comparison between 1964 and 1974 shows, however, an inordinate increase in the hospital services work load of 130%–170%, compared to an increase of only about 50% in capacity in terms of institutions and beds. Public health services are delivered through rural and urban health centres, maternity and child health centres and school health services. Rural health centres provide ambulatory health care to the rural population. There were 1077 such centres at the end of 1977 and 169 rural station hospitals had been established each with one doctor, two nurses, one compounder and four lay workers. Some 60 doctors have now been posted to head health teams in rural health centres. Urban health centres are mainly situated in large cities such as Rangoon and Mandalay. There are 54 such centres providing general medical, paediatric and dental care, maternal and child health services, school health care, health education, nutrition counselling, immunization against and control of communicable diseases and supervision of environmental sanitation measures. In addition to services already mentioned, maternal and child health care is provided by 285 centres functioning in smaller towns, each under the management of midwives and lady health visitors. As yet there are only 49 school health teams, most of which are in towns and cities. In the townships without a team, the township medical officers with the assistance of maternal and child health staff provide school health services, whereas in the rural areas, rural health centre staff meet this need. The urban and maternal and child health centres and school health services have a total of 180 medical officers, 466 intermediate-level multipurpose health workers/supervisors, and 1399 other multipurpose health workers. The ratio of health personnel to the population covered by these three services (excluding hospital staff) is one to 3086.

Special disease control programmes exist for the control of the 5 major diseases, malaria, tuberculosis, leprosy, trachoma and filariasis. Smaller units undertake control of epidemics, venereal diseases, dengue haemorrhagic fever, etc. In 1975, staff involved in these programmes numbered 2124 for malaria, 937 for tuberculosis, 907 for leprosy, 527 for trachoma, 75

	1973	1974	1975	1976	1977
Physicians	4 280	4 909	5 550	5 700	6 153
Medical assistants:					
Health assistants	1 389	926	990	990	1 414
Public health supervisors (grade I)	—	—	71	84	179
Multipurpose health auxiliaries:					
Public health supervisors (grade II)	—	—	30	50	255
Dentists/dental surgeons:					
High (university) level	103	149	195	244	283
Middle (non-university) level	319	319	319	319	319
Dental operating auxiliaries:					
School dental nurses	—	10	29	48	58
Non-operating dental auxiliaries:					
Dental technicians	—	28	40	60	60
Pharmacists/chemists	54	68	68	68	72
Professional midwives (including lady					
health visitors)	10 442	10 872	11 403	11 792	12 440
Professional nurses	3 989	4 518	4 816	5 035	6 070
Nursing and midwifery aides:					
Nursing aides	238	238	238	238	238
Physiotherapists	60	84	87	90	90
Medical laboratory technicians (grade I)	168	213	280	306	306
Assistant medical laboratory					
technicians (grade II)	267	308	371	403	403
Sanitary engineers	46	46	46	46	46
Medical radiological technicians:					
X-ray technicians (grade I)	133	167	171	171	171
Assistant medical radiological technicians:					
X-ray technicians (grade II)	—	—	—	51	65

for filariasis and 336 for venereal diseases, giving a total of 4906.

Only about 10% of the rural population (about 6000 out of 65 000 villages) have direct access to basic health services and in the urban areas, in spite of expansion of hospital and other services, demands are still not met, particularly for preventive health measures.

Health manpower

The numbers of various categories of health personnel in the period 1973–1977 are shown in the table above.

Production and sale of pharmaceuticals

The Burma Pharmaceutical Industry is the sole producer of all drugs and medicines, including tablets, galenicals, sterile products and biologicals in Burma. It works under the supervision of the Pharmaceutical Industries Corporation in the Ministry of Industries and its products are distributed through the Trade Corporation. The expanded programme of immunization and the primary health care/basic health services and family health care projects will largely depend upon sufficient local production of vaccines and drugs for their success and, together with all other consumer demands, will probably entail a doubling of pharmaceutical production.

Health expenditure

The increases in current and capital government expenditure and in contributions from other sources in the period 1973–1977 are given in the following table.

Type of expenditure	1973	1974	1975	1976	1977
	Kyat	Kyat	Kyat	Kyat	Kyat
Current	153 860 218	165 711 800	171 395 130	185 997 680	210 539 290
Capital	9 901 612	8 723 772	6 659 040	7 506 557	11 476 650
Contributions from other sources	2 827 568	1 129 764	1 513 338	2 145 570	2 211 560
Total	166 589 398	175 565 336	179 567 508	195 649 807	224 227 500

Appraisal of progress between 1973 and 1977

The most significant achievement in the period under review was the introduction of the country health programming processs in 1976, which established the first of a continuum of health planning cycles based on sound principles and a practical systems-approach methodology. The highest priority of the resulting People's Health Programmes, operative since 1 April 1978, is the provision of comprehensive health care to the unserved or underserved rural population.

Outlook

It is hoped that the following objectives will be achieved by 1982:

(a) Malaria: a 25% reduction in annual parasite incidence from 0.57 to 0.43 per 1000 population; a 25% reduction in slide postivity rate from 4.25% to 3.2%; and a 25% reduction in case fatality rate from 1.6% to 1.2%.

(b) Gastrointestinal infections: a 25% reduction from 109 to 87.2 cases per 1000 hospital admissions;

(c) Dengue haemorrhagic fever: a 25% reduction in morbidity from 55.2 to 41.4 per 100 000 population under 15 years of age; and a 25% reduction in case fatality rate from 4.1% to 3.1%.

(d) Filariasis: a 25% reduction in persons with microfilaraemia from 4% to 3%;

(e) Plague: a 25% reduction in incidence rate from 3.7 per 100 000 population endemic areas;

(f) Maternal mortality: a 40% reduction from 1.7 to 1.02 per 100 live births;

(g) Iron deficiency anaemia among pregnant women: a 10% reduction from 60% to 54%;

(h) Infant mortality: a 27% reduction from 56 to 41 per 1000 live births;

(i) Leprosy: a 25% reduction in infective cases from 3 to 2.25 per 1000 population;

(j) Diphtheria: a 75% reduction in annual incidence from 2000 to 500 per 100 000 children aged 0–4 years;

(k) Pertussis: a 62% reduction in annual incidence from 4000 to 1500 per 100 000 children aged 0–4 years;

(l) Tetanus neonatorum: a 60% reduction from 5 to 2 per 1000 live births; adult tetanus: a 26% reduction from 9.53 to 7 per 1000 hospital admissions;

(m) Poliomyelitis: a 80% reduction in annual incidence from 500 to 100 per 100 000 children aged 0–4 years;

(n) Tuberculosis: a reduction in the annual risk of infection from 1.66% to 1%.

INDONESIA

Major health and health related problems

The health situation is characterized by a high infant mortality and a high incidence of and mortality due to communicable diseases. Environmental sanitation is unavailable to the greater part of the population, and the utilization of health services, especially in the rural areas, is low. Low levels of nutrition, in addition to infectious diseases, are a major contributing cause to infant and child mortality, while the low utilization of health services adds to the difficulties of control of communicable diseases, especially those preventable through immunization.

In 1976 the infant mortality rate was estimated to be about 110 per 1000 live births. Diarrhoeal diseases, including cholera, are a major cause of morbidity and mortality. The incidence of tuberculosis is about 150 per 100 000 per year, and malaria is a further serious cause of morbidity and mortality, especially in rural areas outside the islands of Java and Bali. The childhood diseases diphtheria, pertussis and tetanus neonatorum also account for a heavy death toll. Dengue haemorrhagic fever, a fairly new disease in Indonesia, appears to be spreading and is beginning to affect the rural areas. Leprosy remains a problem in certain areas, with a conservative estimate of prevalence of 80 per 100 000 population. There is a high incidence of eye and skin infections. Helminthic infections are highly prevalent and aggravate nutritional problems. The prevalence of anaemia is high, especially among children and pregnant women. Endemic areas for goitre include an estimated 12 million of the population. The prevalence of vitamin A deficiency was found to be 1.5–13%, and it is estimated that 60–70% of cases of blindness in children are caused by this deficiency. Dental and periodontal diseases and conditions affect three quarters of the population. Accidents are mainly a problem in urban areas but appear to be increasing with development, as are sexually transmitted and mental diseases.

By the middle of 1976, it was estimated that only 33% of the urban population and 6% of the rural population had access to safe water. Satisfactory sanitary disposal was available to 17% of the urban population and to 20% of the rural population. The low level of sanitation is presumably responsible for a number of the problems mentioned above, such as diarrhoeal diseases, helminthic infections and eye and skin conditions.

The average bed occupancy rate in hospitals is about 50%, with around 25% of all admissions relating to maternity. About 7% of all deliveries are in hospitals, with another 25% under the supervision of the health services at home or in maternity clinics. Attendance of pregnant women and children at maternity and child health centres is quite low.

Action taken

The main health policy, adopted for the Second Five-Year Development Plan, 1974/75–1978/79, was:

(1) to give a high priority to physical expansion of health services to the underserved areas and to development centres;
(2) to emphasize the services providing health care to the young and to the productive age groups;
(3) to emphasize ambulatory health care; and
(4) to assign a higher priority to preventive measures.

The major health legislation enacted during the period under a review affected the deployment of medical personnel to rural areas, providing for a compulsory period of rural service following graduation.

In 1975 the Ministry of Health was reorganized with the establishment of a Bureau of Planning under the Secretary-General, with clear responsibilities for the formulation of medium- and short-term plans. Planning cells, functionally related to the bureau, were also established in each directorate-general and each Province.

A health centre programme was formulated in 1975, detailing the functions and activities of health centres with emphasis on the extension of services. A health centre manual was developed to guide the health centres in the implementation of their work. A system is being developed for the referral of patients between health centres and hospitals and between hospitals of different type. Pilot schemes are in operation for primary health care and for village health insurance.

Health services research and development continued to expand during the period under review. After completion of a morbidity and mortality survey based on households, major research was carried out on disabilities, hypertension, nutrition, insecticide and pesticide hazards to man and the designing and testing of a health management information system.

An increase in the number of medical graduates was achieved during the period. There are over 400 schools and academies producing all types of paramedical personnel including nurses, midwives and their teachers, laboratory technicians, X-ray and dental technicians, sanitarians, physiotherapists, and nutritionists; a number of nursing and midwifery schools have been adapted to train community health nurses. A large number of traditional birth attendants have also been trained.

Health resources

At the end of 1977 there were about 4000 functioning health centres, approximately 12 000 polyclinics, including those in the health centres and sub-centres, 7000 maternal and child health centres, and 1000 units such as eye, mental health, maternity and tuberculosis clinics. There were also 1200 hospitals with 85 000 beds; half of them were general hospitals and those accounted for three quarters of the beds.

The health manpower available at the end of 1977 is estimated to include 10 000 doctors, 2000 dentists, 1400 pharmacists, 45 000 nurses, 17 000 midwives, and 5000 sanitarians. Varying proportions of these work in the public sector, from 35% for pharmacists to about 70% for sanitarians.

A large proportion of the pharmaceuticals used in the country is produced locally, and practically all the vaccine requirements at present can be met by local production.

Health expenditure by central government in 1976 accounted for 1.7% of total expenditure. Total government expenditure per capita for the same year was estimated at 1111 rupiah, and private expenditure per capita was estimated at 555 rupiah, giving a total of 1666 rupiah.

Progress made

During the period under review, Indonesia was declared smallpox-free (in 1974) and yaws was virtually eliminated, except for a few endemic foci. Malaria incidence was reduced in Java and Bali from 400 per 100 000 population in 1973 to 111 per 100 000 in 1976. However, the incidence remains at about 10% in the population of other islands. Some 18 million children were given BCG vaccination in the period 1974–1977 and 57 000 tuberculosis patients were placed under treatment. The fatality rate due to cholera was reduced from 16% in 1972 to 4.5% in 1977.

During the period 1974–1977 the following water schemes were completed: 448 piped systems; 1110 rain water collections; 400 spring protections; 109 artesian wells; and 40 319 hand-operated pumps installed. In addition 632 656 family or household latrines were built.

In family planning the number of new acceptors increased from 57 000 in 1969–1970 to 10.7 million at the end of 1977. In Java and Bali 28% of eligible couples are current users, in the other islands 8.2%.

The number of health centres increased from 2343 in 1974 to over 4000 at the end of 1977, so that each subdistrict has at least one health centre, while larger subdistricts have a health centre per 30 000 population. The number of doctors assigned to health centres increased from 10–15 per year in the period prior to 1973 to 500–600 per year at present. Even with the very much larger number of health centres the proportion of centres with a doctor increased from 20% in 1973 to over 50% at the end of 1977. The number of medical graduates increased from 500–600 per year before 1973 to 750 in 1977, and is expected to stabilize at around 1200 per year from 1978.

Goals for the future

The overall goal is to create better opportunities for each member of the population to obtain the highest level of health. The specific goals in the medium-term future are:

(1) the reduction of morbidity and mortality due to communicable diseases to the lowest levels that can be achieved by an appropriate technology;
(2) the improvement of the nutritional status of the people and the elimination of deficiency problems;
(3) the improvement of the environment, sanitation and protection from pollution;
(4) the extension of the coverage and utilization of health services and improvement in the quality of services;
(5) an increase in the community awareness about healthy living and its participation in services aimed at improvement of their health status; and
(6) the development of family welfare.

MALDIVES

Population and other statistics

At the last census, on 1 January 1978, the population of Maldives was 143 046. Of this number 29 555 live in the only urban settlement of Malé. The following are the vital statistics available:

	1974	1975	1976	1977
Mean population . . .	128 697	131 469	135 308	139 868
Growth rate (%)	2.15	2.92	3.37	2.87
Death rate (per 1000 population)	17.3	10.5	11.6	11.8
Birth rate (per 1000 population)	38.9	39.8	45.3	40.5
Infant mortality (per 1000 live births)	136.5	88.9	106.2	120.7

Organization of health service

The Ministry of Health is responsible for the planning and implementation of health services and is also the executive authority. It has besides the administrative staff at the Ministry, divisions for public health and control of communicable diseases, the Government Hospital, the Water and Sanitation Authority, and the Allied Health Services Training Centre.

The Government Hospital has a bed capacity of 40. There are 21 health centres in the atolls, manned by community health workers, which mainly afford only basic health care.

Medical and allied personnel and training facilities

Available health manpower comprises the following:

Doctors	8
Nurses	8
Nurse aids	27
Other auxiliary health workers[1] .	54
Domiciliary workers	23
Civil engineering technicians . .	2
Mechanical engineer	1
Laboratory technicians	3
Radiographers	2
Dental mechanic	1
Traditional midwives	173
Practitioners of traditional medicine	155
Sanitary inspector	1

[1] Community health workers and health assistants.

The training of allied health personnel is carried out at the Allied Health Services Training. Centre in Malé, where an 18-month course is conducted to train community health workers. In addition, a one-year course for nurse aides and a six-month course for traditional midwives is conducted. Plans are under way to train a new category—family health workers—at this Centre, for the delivery of very basic health care in the areas of immunization, nutrition, health education, follow-up activities delegated by the tuberculosis, leprosy, filariasis, and malaria control programmes, and general environmental health.

Communicable disease control and immunization services

Tuberculosis, leprosy, filariasis and malaria are the major communicable diseases and there are national programmes to combat them.

Waterborne diseases have lately been given high priority, as together they form the greatest cause of morbidity. The recent epidemic of gastro-enteritis and chloera (in March to May 1978) was clearly aggravated by the lack of safe potable water. In January 1976 a programme for the detection and treatment of tuberculosis and leprosy was launched; it is scheduled to cover the total population by the end of 1979. A malaria control programme is also being carried out, with increasing success from year to year.

The following numbers of cases of major diseases were reported for the period 1974–1977:

	1974	1975	1976	1977
Tuberculosis	159	173	184	139
Leprosy	277	211	180	186
Malaria	2 251	1 105	580	260
Filariasis	661	272	324	269

Environmental health

There is neither a piped water supply system nor a sewerage system in any part of the country. However, studies were conducted in 1974 with UNDP assistance on the provision of both these services, and the project is still awaiting funds. Water is mainly drawn from the large number of shallow open wells, and from rain catchment. A programme for the chlorination of wells throughout the country is currently in operation. Control of pollution of the underground water supply is a major problem, especially in the urban district of Malé. No comprehensive programme has been drawn up for this purpose as yet.

It is estimated that in 1977, 56.2% of the population had access to chlorinated drinking water, and after the epidemic of cholera in March–May 1978 chlorination has been introduced and accepted on a very much larger scale. Rain water catchment tanks are also being provided to the rural population, and in 1977 the percentage having access to this type of drinking water was 8%.

Government health expenditure.

Total government health expenditure for 1974, 1975, 1976, and 1977 was 1 277 904.96, 1 260 936.78, 1 264 170.01 and 1 486 529.74 Maldive rupees respectively.

MONGOLIA

Action taken

Health policy

During the period 1973–1977 efforts were directed towards the attainment of the health objectives established by the Sixteenth and Seventeenth Congresses of the Mongolian People's Revolutionary Party. Important decisions made by the Politbureau of the Central Committee of the Party in 1973 specified in detail requirements in the public health system: improvement in health organization and management; expansion and intensification of all preventive activities; modernization of medical care; and strengthening of health services, supplies and equipment. The basic principles of the socialist health system were further strengthened and health protection and promotion has become the concern of the whole nation.

Health legislation

A Health Act was passed on 27 June 1977 and came into force on 1 January 1978. Much of the existing health legislation has been adjusted to the requirements of the new Act.

Health planning and programming

There has been a substantial improvement in health management, planning and statistics and the health data processing system has been modernized. Cooperation with WHO in this field will be expanded. A number of standards and norms have been reappraised. Measures have been taken for more effective use of financial resources. Some positive results have been achieved in the field of health economics. National seminars have been conducted with WHO assistance.

Organization of health services

Traditionally, attention has been paid to rural health care. New rural health centres with feldshers or physicians have been organized and existing ones have been improved, so that basic health services have been extended to cover the population in the most remote parts of the country. At the same time *intersomon* (inter-district) hospitals have been strengthened, the mobile medical care system has been expanded and emergency care services upgraded. A national conference of primary health care was organized in 1977. The development of specialized medical care services in the centre and in the *aimaks* (provinces) covering about 30 specialities, has been accelerated. The WHO fellowship programme has been very useful in this venture.

Special attention has been given to sanitary-epidemiological services, and the volume of preventive sanitary work has been doubled. Nevertheless, rapid urbanization has led to the development of sanitation problems that did not exist 20 to 30 years ago. Measures have been taken to improve the work environment and to prevent environmental pollution. With WHO cooperation, the causes of air pollution in Ulan Bator have been studied. Efforts have been made to persuade nonmedical state authorities to include in their plans more provisions for health protection activities.

The public health laboratory services have been expanded and strengthened, with the assistance of WHO, UNICEF, and UNDP.

The national programme of communicable disease control has achieved, with WHO, UNICEF, and UNDP support, good results: poliomyelitis and diphtheria have been virtually eliminated; pertussis morbidity rates have been sharply reduced; and meningococcal meningitis has been reduced. Mass campaigns, organized jointly with the national verterinary service, have been undertaken to immunize sheep and goats against brucellosis using Rev. 1 vaccine produced locally.

Coverage of the population with comprehensive dispensary care has been expanded. The physician-district principle as a basic prerequisite for successful dispensarization is being introduced into the medical care system. The present objective is to staff clinics and policlinics with good physicians, to increase outpatient services and to strengthen the professional ties between hospital, policlinic and physician-district.

The occupational health services are being reassessed and the number of factory physician-districts increased.

In the field of oral health the objective has been to increase the number of staff and to direct their efforts towards prevention of oral disease.

Most of the *aimaks* have mobile medical care units. In 1975 they visited more than 70 *somons* and treated more than 110 000 patients.

Much has been done in the field of maternal and child health The joint activities of many state, cooperative, and public organizations and the central Commission of the National Children's Fund have produced good results, with useful contributions from WHO and UNICEF. The institute of Maternal and Child Health was established in 1977.

Research

Research activities, mainly of an applied nature, have covered aspects of cardiovascular diseases, nutrition, communicable diseases, organization of health services and maternal and child health. Some fundamental research projects have also been undertaken. Research in traditional medical technology looks promising.

Education and training of health manpower

The health manpower potential of the country has been further increased and the level of competence of medical staff has been raised. In collaboration with WHO and UNDP, measures have been undertaken to improve the education of all categories of health workers and ensure their proper utilization. The State Medical Institute, Ulan Bator, has moved into new premises. Nursing education has been improved. The training of physicians has been extended by one year. In 1973–1974 an assessment of the work of all the staff with higher and middle-grade education was completed, and it has contributed to increased competence and professional responsibility.

Health resources

Health establishments

The health services infrastructure covers the whole country. The aim during 1973–1977 was the further development of specialized health care and expansion of qualified care of the rural population. By the end of 1977 the total number of hospital beds was 15 749 (101.4 beds per 10 000 population). There were 34 large general hospitals, 30 specialized hospitals, 20 paediatric hospitals, 49 *intersomon* hospitals, 279 *somon* physician health centres, 1070 feldsher health units, 52 policlinics, 26 *sanepid* stations, 29 emergency care stations, and 84 milk kitchens. During the Fifth Five-Year Plan (1971–1975) 200 million tughriks were spent on the construction of health establishments and purchasing of equipment. An ambitious programme in this field was developed. The Union of Soviet Socialist Republics, which has assisted the country in recent years, has constructed a number of new hospitals, health centres and other health establishments.

Health manpower

By the end of 1977 there were 3184 doctors (20.5 physicians per 10 000 population) and 11 235 workers with middle-grade education (feldshers, midwives, nurses, laboratory technicians, dental technicians, X-ray technicians, etc.; 72.2 per 10 000 population). The present aim is to improve utilization of these human resources and to establish an optimum balance between basic, qualified and specialized medical care.

Production and sale of pharmaceuticals

The country exports medicinal plants and produces blood preparations, gammaglobulin, vitamins and other preparations from local raw materials. There are plans to expand the cultivation of medicinal plants, and to produce biologicals and medicaments utilizing animal materials and microbiological techniques. Cooperation with WHO, FAO, and UNIDO in this field is needed.

Budget

In 1977, 258.2 million tughriks were spent on health care. This is equivalent to 168 tughriks per head.

Appraisal

During the period under review the resources of the national health service increased. Expansion of coverage has resulted in a positive change in health indices. In 1977 an average of 8.3 doctor's visits per person were recorded. Attendance by 98% of all pregnant women was recorded and 98.7% of all deliveries took place in maternity homes. Infant and maternal mortality rates have decreased. Good results have been registered in communicable diseases control.

Future goals

The objectives for the next 10 years include: further strengthening of preventive services; greater efforts by health and other authorities; more effective use of health resources; expansion of qualified and specialized care coverage of the rural population; further reduction of morbidity and mortality rates; and health promotion among the active population.

SRI LANKA

Sri Lanka has a land area of 65610 km^2 and a population estimated at 13.73 million in 1976. Population estimates and some other vital statistics are given in the following table.

	1973	1974	1975	1976
Estimated mid-year population (in thousands) . . .	13 091	13 284	13 514	13 730
Crude birth rate (per 1000 population)	28.0	27.5	27.7	27.6
Crude death rate (per 1000 population)	7.7	9.0	8.5	8.0
Natural increase (per 1000 population)	20.3	18.5	19.2	19.6
Maternal mortality rate (per 1000 live births)	1.2	1.0	—	—
Infant mortality rate (per 1000 live births)	46.3	51.2	51.5*	—
Neonatal mortality rate (per 1000 live births)	29.9	29.1	—	—

* Estimate

Life expectancy in 1971 was 65.6 years; 64.2 years for men and 67.1 years for women. The literacy rate in 1971 was 78.5%; 85.6% for men and 70.9% for women.

Organization of health services

The people of Sri Lanka enjoy free national health services. Responsibility for the delivery of health care lies with the Ministry of Health, which is headed by the Minister of Health, assisted by the Deputy Minister of Health. Government policy decisions are implemented through the Health Secretariat headed by the Secretary for Health, who has at his disposal an Additional Secretary, a Senior Assistant Secretary, the technical services of the Director of Health Services, 5 deputy directors (Medical Services, Public Health Services, Laboratory Services, Administration, and Planning) and their assistant directors; the operation centre is in Colombo. The Island is divided into 16 health divisions, each headed by a Superintendent of Health Services; there is, in addition, a Superintendent for the Colombo Group of Hospitals. For administrative purposes the services may be considered as preventive and curative; however, in practice, the two operate in close cooperation. The Superintendent of Health Services implements regional health services with the assistance of the medical superintendents in charge of provincial hospitals, the district medical officers and the medical officers of health.

The curative service is implemented through the Colombo group of 11 hospitals, 13 special hospitals, 9 provincial hospitals, 15 base hospitals, 109 district hospitals, 106 peripheral units, 85 rural hospitals, 26 maternity homes and 350 central dispensaries, (92 establishments act as both central dispensaries and maternity homes). The General Hospital, Colombo and most of the provincial hospitals have all specialities whilst the base hospitals provide a more limited care. It is estimated that the Government provides 60% of health care services, the private sector 40%.

For the purpose of delivery of community health care, the Health Divisions are divided into 102 health areas, each headed by a medical officer of health assisted by public health inspectors, public health nurses and public health midwives.

There are specialized campaigns against malaria, tuberculosis, venereal disease, filariaisis and leprosy, each administered by a Superintendent. These campaigns are closely coordinated with the overall system of medical care.

The Department of Ayurveda (traditional system of medicine) is also administered by the Ministry of Health and is headed by the Commissioner of Ayurveda. There are five ayurvedic hospitals and three ayurvedic dispensaries manned by ayurvedic doctors.

The Ayurvedic Drug Corporation imports, exports and manufactures ayurvedic drugs for the Government and private sectors. There are approximately 10 000 ayurvedic registered practitioners in the private sector.

The State Pharmaceutical Corporation, which is reponsible for the import and distribution of most drugs, has been transferred from the Ministry of Industries to the Ministry of Health.

Policy

The aims of the Government have been to raise the health status of the population and to provide a satisfactory health care delivery system to meet the needs and demands of the people. In order to achieve this, it has been necessary:

(1) to promote coordination and/or integration at all levels including the ayurvedic or indigenous system of medicine, with special emphasis on control of malaria, provision of safe drinking-water, disposal of waste, family health services and primary health care including nutrition and health education:

(2) to provide closer cooperation between teaching institutions and national health administration;

(3) to reorient the training pattern of health personnel on the basis of the country's health problems;

(4) to reorganize and utilize existing resources and strengthen where necessary with additional resources; and

(5) to provide incentives for health personnel, taking into consideration the problem of brain drain, and to determine alternative strategies to provide better health care.

Health problems

The increase in population has increased the demand for health care services, and the situation has been further aggravated by limited financial, manpower and material resources, while the rising cost of living, urbanization, natural disasters and low per capita income brought malnutrition and endemic diseases to complete a vicious circle. The incidence of malaria, venereal diseases, gastrointestinal diseases, leprosy and heart disease have been on the increase in the past few years.

However, a large portion of morbidity and mortality can be attributed to inadequacies in prevention.

Hospital care services

There has been a gradual expansion of the hospitals services in the past 5 years. Efforts have been directed towards strengthening the health services in the periphery, since the rural population comprises about 80% of the total population. Specialist services have also been strengthened. The total number of medical officers in service was 2120 in 1971 and 2168 in 1976. Despite an average annual intake of around 220, the effective increase was only 48 new doctors, owing to the large number of resignations, of graduates sent abroad on specialized training, and retirements and deaths.

In addition to the shortage of trained personnel there is a shortage of electromedical and other equipment. A heavy work-load, old equipment, and lack of vital spare parts and maintenance has led to the frequent breakdown of the diagnostic service.

There has also been a shortage of ambulances and other vehicles; 75% of the vehicles are over 10 years old and in an unsatisfactory state.

A significant step taken during the period was the decision to reestablish the training of assistant medical practitioners, which had been suspended for some years. A training programme was started in 1974. These officers are being posted to smaller medical institutions at the periphery.

Health education activities were stepped up in all hospitals. A number of family health clinics were established and sterilization programmes were expanded.

The exodus of doctors to developed countries remains unabated. Shortages of assistant medical practitioners, nurses and paramedical staff have continued, hindering the development of hospital services.

Public health services

Environmental sanitation activities have been intensified. The construction of latrines has been increased. The Water Supply Board has taken steps to supply safe drinking-water and help in the provision of sewerage facilities. The sum allocated annually for latrine construction in the period 1970–1974 was 400 000 rupees, in 1975 it was increased to 3 000 000 rupees and the subsidy for each latrine was increased from 25 to 75 rupees.

Family health. The number of acceptors of

family planning methods has increased appreciably. The growing demand for female sterilization cannot be met owing to shortages of anaesthetists, operation theatre time, beds and equipment. Remedial measures have been taken as
far as possible to overcome these constraints. It
is encouraging to note that the population
growth rate dropped from 2.24% in 1971 to
1.96% in 1976.

Health education has been given a very high
priority in view of its importance in all public
health programmes. Regular training programmes and seminars have been conducted and
action has been taken to promote community
participation in public health programmes. In
order to mobilize rural leadership, over 6 000
volunteers have been trained to undertake
health education in project areas. In 1973 a
school health education programme for teachers
was started on a provincial basis. Action has
been taken to establish more school dental
clinics in remote areas where facilities are lacking at present.

Communicable diseases

Quarantine activities have been continued. An
outbreak of Eltor cholera in 1973 was brought
under control, but there has been an outbreak of
dysentery caused by a new strain of *Shigella
dysentariae*, and measures have been taken to
improve environmental sanitation with the
limited resources available. *Rodent control* measures have been intensified in the port area. A
programme has been drawn up, in collaboration
with WHO, for effective eradication of rabies.

Malaria continues to be a major public health
problem. Because of the development of resistance to DDT by the known vector, *Anopheles
culicifacies*, a crash programme to spray malathion has been undertaken. In affected areas, the
cooperation of village volunteers has been obtained to intensify the health education drive.
Steps have been taken to get aid from donor
agencies for malaria eradication.

The *filariasis* incidence rate fell from 0.5% in
1972 to 0.4% in 1976. In the Colombo municipal region it is 0.40–0.46%. The Colombo
municipality has been covered by vector control
activities to combat filariasis and a threatened
outbreak of dengue and dengue haemorrhagic
fever of epidemic proportions.

Venereal diseases continue to be a problem.
Factors contributing to their increase include

urbanization, tourism and the rapid socioeconomic changes of the recent past. Steps
have been taken to intensify the programme by
way of treatment, and investigation and follow
up of contacts and defaulters from treatment.

Leprosy has increased, probably as a result of
more intensified case-finding chiefly in the
school age group. Case detection, treatment and
follow-up of defaulters from treatment are
methods used to combat the disease.

	Malaria Number of cases microscopically positive	Tuberculosis Total number of cases	Leprosy Total number of cases	Venereal disease Total number of cases
1973	277 713	5 970	7 491	10 593
1974	314 448	6 074	7 860	16 385
1975	400 777	7 324	8 518	19 548
1976	—	6 823	8 995	19 285
1977	—	—	9 510	—

Above figures are from government medical institutions only.

Health manpower development

During the period 1973–1977 training programmes at the Institute of Hygiene, Kalutara
were organized for public health personnel and
medical officers prior to their appointment as
medical officers of health to respective stations.
There has also been a number of refresher
courses for public health inspectors, nurses and
midwives. A project has been formulated to
expand this Institute and raise it to international
standard with the collaboration of WHO.

The Medical Research Institute is involved in
research in epidemiology, nutrition, production
of vaccine and diagnosis. Because of the increase in workload resulting from the epidemics
of cholera and gastrointestinal diseases, a large
intake of laboratory technicians commenced in
1975, and more doctors have been sent for
specialization.

During the period of review, three additional
departments of physical medicine and rehabilitation have been established in the provinces.
These were in the charge of qualified physicians
and supported by a regular output of 15–20
physiotherapists per year. A rehabilitation hospital to provide inpatient care for 300 patients
has been started, and will provide a complete
rehabilitation programme for the disabled. This
relieves the Colombo group of hospitals and
provides a training centre for many categories of
health workers.

There are four provincial prosthetic and orthopaedic workshops in addition to the main workshop in Colombo. A number of technicians have been sent abroad for training by WHO and the World Rehabilitation Fund.

Drugs, vaccines and blood transfusion services

The State Pharmaceutical Corporation was established in 1972 under the control of the Ministry of Industries and in 1977 was transferred to the Ministry of Health. It imports and supplies drugs to all government medical institutions through 14 divisional drug stores. It also supplies drugs to private retail traders, private practitioners and hospitals. A quality control laboratory established in 1971, with expertise and equipment from Japan, started functioning in 1972. The laboratory ensures the conformity of drugs to prescribed standards. It has undertaken analysis on behalf of the Ministry of Health, the State Pharmaceutical Corporation and private manufacturers. Analysis of samples increased from 192 in 1972 to 686 in 1975 and is steadily increasing. The supply of drugs to the institutions has been unsatisfactory owing to lack of transport and inadequate financial provision. Divisional drug stores have therefore been established and a committee has been set up to report on the need for rationalizing purchase, reducing costs, and improving estimations for and distribution of drugs.

The National Blood Transfusion Service is responsible for collection, storage and distribution of blood. Its activities cover all major hospitals and surgical centres in the Island. Annual collection averages about 41 000 pints (23 300 litres) of blood and nearly 75% is from unpaid donors.

Medical and radiological equipment

A programme was drawn up in 1975 to order more equipment for the replacement of old units and for extension of services. An additional cobalt radiotherapy unit was installed in 1975 and a further unit is being set up at the Teaching Hospital, Kandy.

Health planning and programming

The Five-Year Plan for the Health Sector 1972–1976 was drawn up as part of the overall development plan of the country in a conscious and deliberate attempt to introduce changes in the economic and social wellbeing of the people. However, the progressive implementation of the plan has been hampered by the world food shortage, the rising cost of food, the widespread drought in the country, the fuel crisis and consequent increase in prices of drugs and surgical items, and the brain drain. New proposals have been formulated annually for capital investment and there are annual plans for the effective implementation of the Five-Year Plan. A revised Five-Year Plan 1975–1979 was drawn up in 1975. The Planning Unit of the Ministry of Health works closely with the Planning Ministry in formulating the annual implementation programmes for all projects and programmes. Progress review reports are received quarterly for evaluation of set targets. Statistical data have been collected and processed periodically. A health manpower study consisting of 11 substudies was carried out with the collaboration of WHO, and the report was submitted in 1973. The Planning Unit was concerned in examining the requirements of professional personnel of the health services and projected the requirements for a five-year period.

THAILAND

Major health and health-related problems

The major problems can be summarized as follows: the population growth rate; maternal and child health (complications of pregnancy, iron deficiency anaemia, the high rate of prematurity, the high infant mortality rate, and malnutrition); the high incidence of preventable communicable diseases (pertussis, diphtheria, tetanus neonatorum, tuberculosis); poor environmental sanitation, favouring water- and foodborne diseases; vectorborne diseases (malaria and dengue haemorrhagic fever); leprosy, respiratory infections and skin diseases; mental health, and particularly drug abuse; and accidents.

145

Health policy

The Government is working to provide preventive, promotive, curative, and rehabilitative health services in an integrated fashion, emphasizing services to the rural population, who are severely underserved. Rural health service facilities are being expanded to cover all local administrative units (*tambon*). In the meantime, the efficiency of the health service delivery system is to be improved through the concerted efforts of related sectors, government agencies, and the general public. More administrative authority and responsibility are to be delegated to provincial health administrations in order better to utilize the available resources for the fulfilment of health needs.

Specific guidelines are also being developed, aimed at providing free medical care to the low-income group, increasing the number and capability of health personnel, encouraging public participation, preventing and controlling drug addiction, and improving the nutritional status of the population.

Health planning and programming

The Fourth Five-Year Plan came into operation in October 1976. WHO and other organizations of the United Nations system, and bilateral cooperation agencies, were closely associated in the preparation of the Plan, which is based on country health programming and project formulation. The main emphasis was laid on the improvement of the health of the rural population, especially at the village level (*muban*). The health goals are:

(1) reduction of population growth by providing effective birth control measures and adequate coverage of the target group;
(2) prevention of loss of life and improvement of mother and child care by an organized programme to provide maternal and child health services through public and private institutions;
(3) improvement of the nutritional status of the population and prevention of the dire consequences of nutritional deficiencies in the vulnerable groups, by making available those nutrients which are essential to growth and development, providing nutritional information to mothers, organizing institutional care for preschool children, and eliminating certain

nutritional problems through specialized programmes;
(4) effective control and eradication of communicable diseases through the development of effective surveillance networks and increased utilization of general health service infrastructures and public health laboratories, as well as specialized programmes to cope with certain communicable disease problems;
(5) protection of the population against environmental health hazards through the development of rural and urban water supply schemes and safe excreta and refuse disposal system and through constant monitoring of environmental pollution—and specifically, water pollution control; and protection of the population against food contamination by improvement of food handling procedures;
(6) better medical care for the population, improving the efficiency and effectiveness of medical care services rendered by hospitals and health centres and introducing a national health insurance scheme to provide free care for the poor;
(7) effective use of the health infrastructure to provide integrated health services, and extension of health units, together with the training and development of health manpower to provide increased coverage of the rural population with better health services;
(8) creation of a corps of volunteers and "communicators" at village level to form an extension of the health worker's services, so as to provide better coverage of the population by essential health services;
(9) strengthening of national health planning and management, and improvement of the related health information system;
(10) encouragement of the national production of essential raw materials for the pharmaceutical industry to provide economical drugs and medicines and to ensure national self-sufficiency; and strengthening of the quality control of drugs and biologicals;
(11) maximum coordination and cooperation among various governmental and nongovernmental agencies in order to make possible the effective solution of problems of health and health manpower development.

Organization of health services

Health services are provided by both the private and public sectors. The ratio of average per capita expenditure on health in the private and public sectors has been about three to one. The private sector concentrates on curative medicine, particularly in Bangkok and the 126 municipalities (*amphoe muang*), and the dissemination of information and provision of services in family planning. The health services of the public sector are concentrated in the provincial areas. Metropolitan Bangkok has a separate public health administration and heavy concentration of both governmental and private sector health facilities and manpower. There is a great disparity in the scope and quality of medical services available with the disproportion heavily in favour of the capital.

Extending over the entire country, and underlying both the public and private medical care systems, there is a variegated network of traditional medical practitioners and traditional health practices integrated into the traditional Thai cultural patterns, and this network serves directly or indirectly about half the population for the treatment of its symptomatic problems. The reliance on self-medication and traditional practitioners is especially predominant in rural areas where other health services are either not available or not accepted, or cannot be afforded. The provincial health care services have been designed by the Ministry of Public Health to deal as efficiently as possible with a large rural population using the small number of health facilities manned by trained staff.

About 85% of the population live in rural areas outside Bangkok and the municipalities. The health service coverage in the rural areas is inadequate. According to current government policy, there should be a district hospital with at least 10 beds and one medical doctor in each rural district outside Bangkok and municipalities. Each administrative unit should be provided with a health centre, staffed by one midwife and one junior sanitarian. There should be a midwifery clinic with one midwife for a cluster of villages with at least 2000 population.

In addition to their generally low coverage, the rural health facilities are only used by a small proportion of sick people (estimated at 17% in 1970).

In order to solve this problem as well as to encourage community participation, a number of projects have been undertaken to support general health services or tackle specific problems from central or local levels.

The primary health care scheme developed through country health programming and project formulation is now in the implementation phase. The main aim is to develop primary health care all over the country in a coordinated manner, using past experience and encouraging all initiatives in order to maintain spontaneity of effort and particularly to emphasize intersectoral coordination.

Biomedical and health services research

The Medical Science Branch, which is one of the ten scientific branches of the National Research Council, promotes research on national medical and health problems; supports qualified scientists working on approved research projects through research grants; and finances institutional research in the form of contractual services for medical or public health research required by government agencies or organizations.

Medical research is conducted both in the universities and in the Ministry of Public Health. In accordance with the policy of the Medical Research Committee the emphasis in medical and health research is on infectious diseases, malnutrition, diseases caused by polluted natural or man-made environments, family planning, medical and other biological data on Thai populations (genetics, physiology, anatomy), mental health problems, including drug addiction, and medical and health service practice.

Education and training of health manpower

Since it seems unlikely that sufficient physicians can be trained and placed in rural areas, there has been a movement away from conventional training of physicians and nurses towards the training of primary health care workers. The training of middle-level health workers such as practical nurses, sanitarians, and midwives will also be expanded. The skills and information of the traditional health practitioners will be improved in the hope of making them more effective.

The training of executive and middle-level administrators, managers, and health planners is being promoted in order to improve the operational efficiency of the health system.

Health resources

Health establishments

In 1976 there were 60 590 hospital beds, giving a ratio of 13.1 per 10 000 population. There is a heavy concentration of both governmental and private sector health facilities in Metropolitan Bangkok. In 1974, Metropolitan Bangkok, with a population of about 4.3 million, had 34 government hospitals, with a total of 13 000 beds, while the other 70 provinces, with a total population of about 36 million, had only 97 government hospitals, with about 22 000 beds in all. Bangkok also had 39 private hospitals having more than 25 beds, compared with only 24 such establishments in the rest of the country.

At the end of 1976 there were 255 district hospitals, medical and health centres, 3500 health centres, and 1450 midwifery clinics.

Health manpower

The physician/population ratio is approximately one to 1000 in Bangkok, one to 30 000 in smaller municipalities and one to 150 000 in the rural area. In 1975 the total number of physicians was estimated to be about 5000, of whom 1800 were in the Ministry of Public Health, 2200 in universities and the Ministry of Defence, 600 in city and state enterprises, and only 400 in private practice. In the same year there were 12 653 nurses.

Production and sale of pharmaceuticals

Thailand produces the following vaccines: smallpox, tetanus toxoid, diphtheria/tetanus,

diphtheria/pertussis/tetanus, cholera, typhoid, rabies and BCG.

Health expenditure

In 1976 the total government expenditure on health was 3855.58 million baht. This represented 6.15% of total government expenditure, or 88.49 baht per capita. At the same time the private expenditure on health was estimated to be 10 082 million baht, or 231.39 bhat per capita.

Outlook

Targets have been established for the coming decade to reduce the incidence of important diseases to between 20% and 60% of present levels. In the area of environmental sanitation the aim is to provide safe water to 50% of the urban and 25% of the rural population, and to provide for excreta and refuse disposal for 75% and 50% of the urban and rural population respectively.

Targets for immunizations are 15 million persons for diphtheria/pertussis/tetanus vaccination and 8 million for BCG vaccination.

The health coverage target for the rural population has been set at 30%. The targets for antenatal care and safe delivery are set at 50% of pregnancies and postnatal care at 68% of deliveries.

EUROPEAN REGION

ALBANIA

Basic population data

At the end of 1977 the population was 2 513 600, with a density of 87.4 per km². The birth rate is high and the population predominantly young. The natural increase rate is 21.6 per 1000. In 1976 the birth rate was 28.7 per 1000, the death rate 7.1 per 1000, and the expectation of life was 69 years.

Administrative organization of the health services

Public health is organized on a preventive basis and medical care is available free of charge at all times to the entire population. The health service is provided by a wide network of institutions covering even the most remote areas of the country, and includes highly specialized, specialized and general services. The health service, established on the basis of morbidity studies and examination of the specific characteristics of the area, takes the form of hospital, outpatient and home care. The compulsory notification and treatment of communicable and occupational diseases is performed by a system of dispensaries and specialized health institutions. A salary during any period of disability and an old age pension on retirement are guaranteed.

Albania is divided into 26 districts (*rrethe*). The Ministry on Health is responsible for health administration, including research, training and medical care. In each district the health services are controlled by the district health departments, the directorate of public health and epidemiology in each district and the relevant consultative councils composed of specialists and heads of the different services.

Medical care is organized on a district basis, and includes preventive and curative care. The services are provided through the directorate of public health and epidemiology, the outpatient clinics, the outpatient services at work centres, the agricultural cooperatives and, in the towns and villages, through the hospitals.

In rural areas the basic health service unit for a group of villages is the health centre, where medical care is provided by the physician, the paediatrician, the stomatologist, the pharmacist and the respective auxiliary personnel. These centres have all the necessary technical facilities. In each village there is an outpatient service providing medical care, a maternal and child welfare service, and a maternity unit with several beds and the necessary personnel to provide mother and child with the care required. Alongside these facilities, in the country (in areas with a certain number of inhabitants), area hospitals are set up which occupy a higher technical level in the health service. In these hospitals care is provided by pathologists, one- or sometimes two-paediatricians, a stomatologist, a pharmacist and the necessary auxiliary personnel. These hospitals also have a biochemical and clinical laboratory, a dental laboratory, a radiology unit and other specialized services.

In the towns, medical care is provided in outpatient clinics, outpatient services in work centres, hospitals in small towns, and specialized hospitals in district centres. The specialized hospitals have departments for cardiology, cardiosurgery, neurology, neurosurgery, psychiatry, nephrology, urology, endocrinology, haematology, gastroenterology and allergology. Similar departments are also organized, as required, in all districts, with facilities for the examination and treatment of patients. The emergency service is organized to provide rapid medical assistance in every health centre at any time.

In Tirana the Institute of Oncology offers wide assistance in the prophylaxis and treatment of neoplasms.

At the end of 1976 there were 806 hospital establishments with a total of 16 683 beds, giving a bed/population ratio of 7 per 1000 (146 of these were hospitals with a total of 11 087 beds, representing a bed/population ratio of 4.5 per 1000). There were also 89 outpatient clinics and dispensaries, 17 outpatient clinics providing specialized care, 26 tuberculosis dispensaries, 51 stomatology clinics, 635 stomatology units in rural areas, work centres and schools, 68 dental laboratories in the towns and 80 in the villages, and 160 pharmacies in the towns and 264 in rural areas, with 220 pharmaceutical units in the villages.

Side by side with these institutions there is a large network of rest homes for the protection and promotion of the health of children and workers. These homes have 7960 places and are open throughout the year. There are also homes for the old and the handicapped.

Preventive services

The principal task of these services is the prevention and control of communicable diseases. The preventive services are controlled by the Ministry of Health, which has set up a large network of institutions like the Institute of Public Health and Epidemiology and the directorates of public health and epidemiology in the 26 districts. These institutions have a number of advanced- and intermediate-level personnel and the necessary equipment for bacteriological screening, chemical analyses and the study of the problems of pollution and environmental protection.

Activities to control tuberculosis are directed by the Tuberculosis Institute. Attention is focused mainly on the vaccination of newborn babies and X-ray examination of the population—mine workers and other groups at risk. As a result of these measures the disease is no great threat at present. BCG vaccine is prepared by the Institute of Public Health and Epidemiology and meets the country's requirements.

Special attention is given to the screening and control of communicable gastrointestinal diseases and to viral diseases. As a result of the continued strengthening of laboratory services, preventive screening has increased ten-fold since 1970. Dispensaries for the treatment of these diseases have been set up, attached to the outpatient clinics in the main villages, and the vaccination of children and population groups most exposed to these diseases has been increased.

Mass vaccination campaigns against smallpox, measles, diphtheria and pertussis, tetanus, tuberculosis and poliomyelitis are carried out and special groups are also vaccinated, for example, against cholera and yellow fever. The vaccinations are compulsory and free of charge to the entire population. These measures have been very successful in the prevention of communicable diseases, so that for several years there have been no cases of measles or diphtheria and only very rare cases of poliomyelitis, tetanus and pertussis. Louse-borne typhus, malaria, trachoma and syphilis have disappeared completely over the last few years. Other venereal diseases and drug and alcohol abuse present no problems.

Eighteen different vaccines, including those against tetanus, diphtheria and pertussis, measles, smallpox, cholera, plague, typhoid fever and rabies, are prepared in the country.

Environmental protection is provided by a decree for the protection of the air, water and soil, under the responsibility of the Ministry of Health. The problem is followed up and studied from a technical and scientific point of view by the respective department of the Institute of Public Health and Epidemiology and by the 26 directorates of public health and epidemiology in the districts, assisted by the laboratories where the various analyses are carried out to detect the causes of chemical and other pollution. There are no pollution problems caused by industry, which is new and developing. Nevertheless, the problem is carefully followed by the health authorities.

The Ministry of Health has a division responsible for the school health and each district has a school health department directed by the physician or assistant physician in charge of studies on the physical development of children, public health students in schools, and related questions.

Special attention is devoted to occupational health and the prevention of of occupational diseases. The Ministry of Health has a division of occupational health directed by a physician. Occupational health departments have also been set up in the 26 districts, directed by physicians specializing in public health, assisted by the occupational health laboratories. The Institute of Public Health and Epidemiology also has a department concerned with these problems. In connexion with the prevention of occupational diseases, studies are carried out in production centres, mines and other work sites on the risks of infection by dust, and in industry on noise level and other relevant factors. An outpatient medical care service has been set up in each work centre for the health protection of workers. This service is directed by physicians or assistant physicians who are responsible not only for investigating occupational morbidity in the centres, but also for the prevention and control of occupational diseases. Specialized blocks have been incorporated in the central hospitals to treat occupational disease cases.

Maternal and child health

Particular care is given to maternal and child protection. Prenatal advisory centres are available and usually operate on the same premises as gynaecological clinics in the towns and in rural areas. Likewise, in many of the large work centres there are advisory units for women which offer not only a pregnancy testing service but also act as gynaecological clinics.

According to the law in force, from the time

of conception and throughout pregnancy, women are excluded from heavy work and night shifts. They are entitled to 35 paid days leave before and 49 days after confinement. Nursing mothers may leave work every three hours to feed their children.

There are centres in every town district and every village where physicians and nurse/midwives examine children aged 0–3 years. Pregnant women and small children receive a free vitamin supply; vitamins A and D are given on a regular basis for rickets prophylaxis. The obstetric and gynaecological and maternity hospitals have blocks for newborn babies with a paediatrician in charge. Special institutions have been created for the children of sick parents and also for mentally handicapped children. All children from birth to the age of 14 years are visited and treated by paediatricians.

In the field of oral health regular dental care is provided to children and young people. Sodium fluoride tablets are used for the prevention of decay.

At the end of 1976 the country had 2552 crèches, with 49 810 beds, 765 obstetric/gynaecological and maternity hospitals with 3896 beds, and six paediatric hospitals with 1200 beds.

Health education centres are open in every district and are equipped to educate the people in protection against communicable and occupational diseases.

Research

There are a number of scientific medical institutions controlled by the Ministry of Health and financed by the State: the Institute of Public Health and Epidemiology, the Institute of Community Medicine, the Tuberculosis Institute, the Institute for Paediatric Studies and Research, the Central Laboratory for the Control of Drugs and the Cancer Centre.

Health manpower development

The Ministry of Health is responsible for programming the country's requirements in health personnel. This programming is based on the five-year plans for the development of the country and on the needs of the health service.

At the end of 1976 Albania had the following health personnel:

Physicians	2 641
Stomatologists	637
Pharmacists	532
Veterinarians	823
Medical physicists	3
Other scientific specialists or professional personnel	95
Midwives	993
Nurse/midwives	4 185
Qualified nurses	2 863
Assistant/auxiliary nurses (intermediate level)	3 938
Nursing assistants (basic level)	1 478
Dental auxiliaries	608
Pharmacy auxiliaries	725
Physiotherapists/kinesitherapists	80
Medical laboratory technicians	410
Medical radiology technicians	115

The doctor/population ratio is one physician or stomatologist to 767 inhabitants.

Advanced health personnel—physicians, stomatologists, dentists and pharmacists—are trained at the Tirana University Medical Faculty. Physicians are trained for five years, stomatologists for four years and pharmacists for three years according to a programme drawn up by the Ministry of Health and the Ministry of Education and Culture. At the end of this programme all personnel undergo one year's in-service training, after which they take the final examination and are qualified. On qualifying they are at the disposal of the Ministry of Health which indicates their work place and field of work and authorizes them to practise. All physicians, after qualifying, specialize for three years as general physicians in the university clinics. They then have the opportunity to take further specialization courses, in accordance with the demand, in specific fields. The duration and content of these specialization programmes are subject to approval by the Ministry of Health. All specialists must attend a post-university training course every three to five years.

Secondary medical schools provide a four-year course of training for intermediate-level personnel being trained as nurse/midwives, dental auxiliaries and pharmaceutical auxiliaries. Laboratory technicians receive one year's training in a general or professional secondary school. The State pays the entire cost of training personnel and the students receive study grants and are accommodated in student hostels.

Finance

The budget of the Ministry of Health, which covers all expenditure relating to health care and protection but does not include social security, amounted to 392 213 000 leks in 1977.

153

AUSTRIA

General background

Austria has nine independent federal provinces which are divided into administrative districts. In all, 97.1% of the population are covered by social insurance schemes which reimburse fees for medical care of any kind provided by doctors under contract, by the health centres set up under the insurance schemes, and by hospitals. Care for people who are not insured is paid for by the local social welfare office.

There are a large number of internationally recognized mineral springs and health resorts.

Country health situation

The general health situation is satisfactory. In recent years no case of any disease coming under the International Health Regulations has occurred, and there has been no major outbreak of notifiable diseases. Mass immunization against poliomyelitis was carried out and there has been no new case within the last few years, illustrating the success of the oral immunization programme. The Ministry defrays also the costs of vaccination against tuberculosis, smallpox, diphtheria, tetanus and pertussis.

In the field of mental health an important task is to control excessive alcohol consumption. An annual Alcohol Campaign Week is held to bring home to the public the harmful effects of alcohol consumption. The health departments of the larger towns and district authorities have advice centres for the mentally ill.

Great efforts were made in the field of family health. Since the introduction of the mother-and-child health card (*Mutter-Kind-Pass*) in 1974, providing for various preventive health examinations for the pregnant woman and the newborn and growing child, infant mortality has been reduced by 30%. There are preventive health examinations for all healthy people from 19 years of age onwards; they are free of charge, the costs being defrayed by the social insurance schemes.

In recent years the principal causes of death have been heart diseases, malignant neoplasms, accidents and pneumonia. The following table shows the distribution by age group in 1975 (the total at 31 December 1975 was 96 041):

	Heart diseases	Malignant neoplasms	Accidents	Pneumonia
Below 1 year .	8	11	60	86
1–4 years . . .	5	33	124	29
5–14 years . . .	14	69	246	16
15–44 years . .	480	740	1 643	81
45–64 years . .	4 299	4 860	923	265
65–74 years . .	9 582	6 781	831	727
75 years and over . .	18 992	6 514	1 631	2 247

The most frequently notified diseases are influenza (266 892 cases in 1974), gonococcal infections (11 051 in 1976), scarlet fever (6563 in 1976), tuberculosis (2506 cases in 1976), and infectious hepatitis (1940 in 1976).

Administrative organization of the health services

The Federal Ministry of Health and Environmental Protection is the supreme health authority. It is responsible for the central administration, for formulating health policy, the drafting of essential laws and general directives and the technical supervision of health services and training. Owing to the Federal Constitution of the Austrian State and the very extensive autonomy enjoyed by the nine provinces (*Länder*), the Federal Ministry does not exercise direct power over the local health services, which are exclusively the responsibility of the provinces. The provincial governments are competent to issue regulations and to take executive measures as well as measures of an economic nature.

The governor of each province is responsible for implementing the directives of the Federal Ministry of Health and Environmental Protection. He is assisted by a health advisory council and has under his authority a senior health officer who, supported by various specialists, exercises executive powers over the province's health services.

The local authorities at the lowest administrative level come under the governors of the provinces. Each of these district authorities has a health officer and centres for maternal and child health, tuberculosis, school dental services and general health examinations. There are also centres for mental health, and care of the elderly and disabled. All these institutions are open to the general public. The district health authorities supervise the implementation by the small communes of federal or provincial measures. Each commune is obliged by law to engage a medical officer, but several communes may join togethe1 for the purpose. It is the duty of the medical officer to assist the mayor by advising on local health activities.

In the organizational structure of the health services there have been no major changes since 1973.

Main health laws and regulations since 1973

Laws

Federal Law of 20 March 1973 revising the Federal Law on Nursing, Medical Laboratory Technicians and Medical Aides.

Federal Law of 3 July 1973 revising the Law on Pharmacies.

Federal Law of 3 July 1973 on Indemnity for Damages caused by Vaccinations.

Federal Law of 4 July 1973 revising the Law on Tuberculosis.

Federal Law of 5 February 1974 revising the Law on Control and Extirpation of Zoonoses.

Federal Law of 5 February 1974 revising the Law on Tuberculosis.

Federal Law of 3 May 1974 revising the Law on Hospitals.

Federal Law of 26 June 1974 on an Austrian Contribution to the UN Environment Programme.

Federal Law of 12 July 1974 revising the Law on Physicians.

Federal Law of 7 November 1974 revising the Law on Epidemics 1950.

Federal Law on Food, Products to be Consumed, Admixtures, Cosmetics and Commodities.

Federal Law of 4 July 1975 revising the Law on Physicians.

Federal Law of 4 July 1975 revising the Law on Nursing, Medical Laboratory Technicians and Medical Aides.

Federal Law on Plasmapheresis.

Federal Law of 6 May 1976 on Hygiene in Bathing Places and Saunas.

Federal Law of 14 December 1977 revising the Law on Hospitals.

Regulations

Regulation of 30 August 1973 on Drugs on Prescription.

Regulation of 26 October 1973 on Training and Examination in General and Paediatric Nursing in the second, third and fourth year of training.

Regulation of 18 December 1973 on Training of General Practitioners and Specialists.

Regulation of 20 June 1974 on Training and Examination of Medical Laboratory Technicians.

Regulation of 9 January 1975 revising the Regulation on Smallpox Vaccination.

Regulation of 29 November 1974 on Training and Examination of Psychiatric Nurses.

Regulation of 13 June 1975 revising the Regulation on Training and Examination of Medical Aides.

Regulation 23 September 1975 revising the Regulation of Training of General Practitioners and Specialists.

Regulation of 17 May 1976 on Maximum of Residues of Substances used as Pesticides in or on Foodstuffs of Vegetable or Animal Origin.

Regulation of 29 June 1977 on Training and Examination of Supervisors for the implementation of the Law of Foodstuffs 1975.

Regulation of 31 October 1977 on the Admixture of Substances Preventing Oxidization to Foodstuffs.

Health plan

A Plan of Health and Environmental Protection has been prepared by the Federal Ministry of Health and Environmental Protection.

Health planning and management support services and programmes

In order to assist the Federal Ministry in the planning of health care and development of health services the Federal Institute for Public Health was established by virtue of the Federal Act of 25 January 1973. This Institute has the following tasks: preparation of methods for obtaining the data which are important for the health of the population, and collection, analysis and processing of such data; documentation; studies and research activities and provision of information on health services research; preparation for the planning of health services, in particular the organization of medical care, including hospital care, preventive medicine, social medicine and environmental hygiene; organization of education and postgraduate training for public health service personnel.

Curative and preventive services and programmes

Hospital services

There were 325 hospitals with a total of 84 856 beds in 1976, distributed as follows:

	Number	Beds
General hospitals	134	48 974
Paediatric hospitals	6	1 285
Tuberculosis hospitals for patients 4–14 years of age	3	274
Other tuberculosis hospitals	12	2 952
Surgical orthopaedic hospitals for accident and other urgent cases . . .	15	2 328
Chronic diseases hospitals	25	3 487
Maternity hospitals	20	156
Hospitals for obstetrics and gynaecology	3	681
Hospitals for psychiatry and neurology	16	12 794
Army hospitals	7	498
Clinic for alcohol addicts	1	184
Prison hospitals	9	446
Other special hospitals and clinics	19	2 196
Convalescent homes	15	1 021
Sanatoria	35	2 403
Sick bays in old people's homes	5	5 177

The Federal Ministry of Health and Environmental Protection is responsible on behalf of the Federal Government for the health supervision of the hospitals. Under the Federal Constitution the Government is responsible for the main legislation and health supervision relating to hospitals, while the enactment of regulations and executive and economic matters are the responsibility of the provincial governments. Public and private hospitals, as well as the independent outpatient health clinics, come under the hospital legislation. No hospital may be set up or may operate without a licence from the provincial government. A hospital can be awarded public status only if it is a nonprofit-making institution and conforms to the provisions of the Hospitals Act. It must be open to everyone, have the same rate of charges for equivalent services, and may set aside no more than one-fifth of its beds for patients who pay higher rates. A public hospital may be administered and managed by the Federal Government, a provincial government, local commune, a public body, foundation or public fund, or by any other body which has legal status. A professionally qualified doctor is in charge of the medical and auxiliary services and an administrator is entrusted with responsibility for administrative and economic matters.

The Federal Ministry of Health and Environmental Protection has prepared a Hospital Plan in two parts, for acute care, and for long-term and special care, in accordance with the second revision of the Hospitals Act (1974), specifying principles governing hospital establishment and minimum requirements to be applied in a regionalized plan for the whole country. Three general types of public hospitals are provided for: standard hospitals, special hospitals and central hospitals.

Outpatient services

Health care is available for the population from free practising doctors, who for the most part have contracts with the various health insurance schemes. More than 97% of the population are covered by health insurance. Each insured person can at any time freely choose a doctor who has a contract with the health insurance agency.

Outpatient care is available in the outpatient services of the various clinics or hospital departments. For insured persons there are also the many outpatient centres of various social insurance schemes.

Mobile nursing services visit the homes of incapacitated patients; special services for the elderly, for the chronically ill and the disabled are also available.

On 1 January 1977 there were 303 independent outpatient centres including 84 dental units, 75 diagnostic laboratories, 325 Red Cross units with ambulances and in some cases with physicians, and 834 outpatient departments operated by hospitals.

Special services and programmes

Environmental health

An essential part in general public health is played by the six federal public health laboratories. The main task of these laboratories is to conduct bacteriological and serological investigations; a virus laboratory and a department for radiology and air hygiene, mobile facilities for bacteriological and virological water tests, and radiological, civil defence and air pollution measurements are attached. A network of special measuring centres has been established to check environmental radioactivity. An advisory commission for radiation protection has been established in the Ministry of Health and Environmental Protection.

In the field of air pollution and civil defence the federal public health laboratories maintain close contact with other institutions and services. The Federal Ministry for Agriculture and Forestry, in close cooperation with the Federal Ministry of Health and Environmental Protection, is responsible for control of drinking-water and surface waters. In the field of drinking-water supply and sewage disposal the Ministry's work consists mainly in supplying expert advice regarding the authorization of new facilities. The disposal of solid and liquid wastes is a matter of increasing importance. Where industrial hazards are concerned the Ministry delegates public health officers to inspect the premises of any persons living in the neighbourhood of industrial plants who consider that their health is endangered.

Industrial hygiene and occupational health are the responsibility of the Federal Ministry for Social Affairs.

Communicable diseases

These, as stated above, do not constitute a serious problem.

Maternal and child health

Services are provided by the district authorities at 3064 centres, including 948 mobile units. Considerable purchases have been made in order to improve the technical equipment of the obstetric and infant care departments of the hospitals. The care for pregnant women will be improved by measures including publicity work. Expectant mothers have to undergo the preventive medical examinations to qualify for payment of the national child allowance, the evidence of such examinations having been entered on the "mother-and-child health card".

School health

All schoolchildren are under the supervision of a physician, but there are no special school health service units. Examination sheets have been prepared by the Ministry taking into account the latest methods of approach with the aim of collecting data for statistical evaluation as a basis for health programmes for children and young persons.

Health care for the elderly

Disabled persons and patients suffering from chronic and long-lasting diseases are given care in special institutions.

Mental health

An important task is the control of excessive alcohol consumption and drug abuse. It is planned to modernize the provisions governing detention of mental cases. A legal basis for mandatory admission of persons who are otherwise seriously afflicted with personality disorders (alcoholics or drug addicts) to an institution for therapy has already been elaborated. Emergency centres for suicide prevention have been set up.

Early diagnosis

Basic programmes for cancer, diabetes and cardiovascular complaints have been introduced.

Accident prevention and control

Several research studies were initiated and financed by the Ministry of Health and Environmental Protection. The Ministry has issued an "emergency card" with name, address and relevant health data for the owner (blood group, vaccinations, diabetes and other diseases, allergies, etc.).

Dental health

Protection is provided through educational and preventive programmes. Dental treatment of children and prophylactic dental examinations are carried out by school dental services. Caries prevention by fluorides is supported and financed by the Ministry of Health and Environmental Protection.

Pharmaceuticals

The inspectors of the Federal Institute for Chemical and Pharmaceutical Testing supervise the pharmacies and are responsible for controlling pharmaceutical specialities. The Ministry leaves control of the drug trade and of observance of the regulations in pharmacies, the pharmaceutical industry and the whole-sale trade to the local authorities, whose public health officers inspect the establishments concerned in collaboration with a special official of the Federal Chemical and Pharmaceutical Control Laboratory. The distribution of drugs to the consumer is reserved for the pharmacies.

The Federal Ministry of Health and Environmental Protection is responsible for the general control of foodstuffs, beverages, cosmetics, and substances used in food. At the intermediate level this control is carried out by the health authorities of the provinces.

Health education

The same Ministry, in conjunction with the Austrian Public Health Association, places emphasis on the dangers of smoking, overeating, alcoholism and drug abuse, and on accident prevention.

Biomedical and health services research

Medical research is carried out at the university hospitals in Vienna, Graz and Innsbruck and a great number of institutes such as the Austrian Institute for Cancer Research and the research institutes for rheumatic diseases. Generally basic research is in the hands of the Ministry for Science and Research. The Ministry of Health and Environmental Protection supports research only in those fields for which it is responsible. The Federal Institute for Public Health, founded in 1973, deals chiefly with public health information and research studies.

Health manpower development

Manpower planning and projection of requirements

The Federal Ministry of Health and Environmental Protection is responsible for health manpower planning. A study of demand for medical practitioners, which deals with forecasting, supply and planning, was initiated and financed by the Ministry. The Ministry promotes the establishment of general practitioner's practices.

Health manpower training

The Federal Ministry of Science and Research is responsible for the university training of physicians, pharmacists and veterinarians. The Federal Ministry of Health and Environmental Protection is responsible for the practical postgraduate training of physicians and the training of other health workers, including nurses, medical technicians, health assistants and midwives. The Federal Ministry for Education and Culture is responsible for the first year of training in general and paediatric nursing. The training of physicians lasts 5 years with an additional 3 years for general practitioners, 6 years for specialists and 2 years for dentists; an additional 3 years of training in several sub-specialities for specialists is provided. The training of pharmacists and veterinarians lasts 5 years, general and paediatric nurses 4 years, psychiatric nurses 3 years, medical technicians between 2.5 and 3 years and midwives 2 years. In 1977 there were the following medical training establishments:

School or faculty	Number
Medicine and pharmacy	3
Veterinary medicine	1
General and paediatric nursing etc. . . .	57
Psychiatric nursing	9
Physiotherapists	5
Laboratory technicians	6
X-ray technicians	7
Dieticians	5
Occupational therapists and ergotherapists	2
Logopaedic-phoniatric-audiometric therapists	3
Orthoptists	2
Medical-technical auxiliaries	10
Midwifery	6
Health assistants (courses)	202

Cost and financing of health services

Financing of health care

In 1976 the part of the budget of the Ministry of Health and Environmental Protection allocated to public health amounted to 436 729 000 Schillings.

Social security scheme for sickness and health insurance

In 1976, 7 293 000 persons (97.1% of the population) were covered by social insurance. In 1976 the expenditure of the social insurances for sickness, old-age and accident insurance amounted to 102 384 000 Schillings (14.1% of the gross domestic product).

BELGIUM

General background

Belgium is bounded by the Netherlands, the Federal Republic of Germany, Luxembourg and France, with a western coastline on the North Sea. Its area is 30 513 km². On January 1977 the population was 9 823 302 or 321.1 per km². The capital city, Brussels, has a population of just over one million.

In 1975 the birth and death rates were both 12.3 per 1000. In the same year the infant mortality rate was 16.1 per 1000 births. Life expectancy during the period 1968–1972 was about 71 years. The main causes of death recorded in 1975 and 1976 were : cardiovascular diseases, malignant tumours, cerebrovascular diseases, accidents, poisonings and violence.

The principal diseases notified in 1976 were : turberculosis, gonococcal infections, infectious hepatitis, scarlet fever, salmonella infections. The apparent increase in the number of cases of tuberculosis disease as compared to previous years is due only to a better understanding of the disease.

Practically the whole, if not the whole of the population is insured against sickness (National Institute of Sickness and Disability Insurance).

Administrative organization of the health services

The Ministry of Public Health and of the Environment is responsible, broadly speaking, for environmental health and the promotion, protection and improvement of public health.

Other ministerial departments are, however, responsible for various aspects of health: sickness and disability insurance is, as stated above, the responsibility of the National Institute of Sickness and Disability Insurance, which comes under the Ministry of Social Insurance; occupational safety, hygiene and health are dealt with by the Ministry of Employment and Labour; preventive and curative services for the military, by the Ministry of National Defence; preventive and curative services for prisoners and minors placed in youth welfare centres, by the Ministry of Justice; health and domestic animals, by the Ministry of Agriculture; university training for medical professions (medicine, dentistry, pharmacy, and veterinary medicine), by the Ministry of National Education and Culture; while the Ministries of Public Health and of National Education are jointly responsible for paramedical training.

Internal organization of the Ministry of Public Health

The central administration of this Ministry is made up of a Secretary-General's office, to which the Institute of Hygiene and Epidemiology, which will be dealt with later, is attached, and several general directorates, the chief of which are responsible for public hygiene, social health, medical establishments and assistance. The General Directorate of Public Hygiene comprises technical inspection services for nuisances, foodstuffs, meat, pharmacy, and sanitary engineering, and the health assistance service for the civil population.

The laboratories come under the Secretary-General's office. In Brussels they are grouped together in the Institute of Hygiene and Epidemiology, which includes departments of microbiology, virology, environment and pharmaco-toxicology. This Institute carries out varied and important work in the field of environmental control, the prevention of communicable diseases, vaccine and serum control, and is responsible for the preparation of smallpox vaccine. It also carries out important research in the sanitary field. Laboratories under the control of the Institute of Hygiene and Epidemiology are established in some provinces and act as hygiene laboratories, other laboratories performing the same work come under the control of the provincial administrations.

The majority of hygiene services are organized at regional level. In each province there are one or two hygiene inspectors and inspectors of foodstuffs, meat and pharmacy. Other services are also decentralized: health protection of schoolchildren and of civil servants and inspection of welfare services. However the services responsible for medical establishments and for sanitary engineering (water distribution and treatment) are centralized, but this does not prevent the responsible technicians from working in the provinces when necessary.

This organization, described here only schematically, has superseded that which existed in earlier times and which has not altogether disappeared (see below). The French law of 16/24 August 1790 and the Belgian common law established communal autonomy in matters of hygiene. The Ministry of Public Health plays the double role of a subsidizing organization and of controller for the communes and the inter-communal organizations. It performs the same function with respect to medicosocial organizations such as the National Children's Organization, the National Organization for Protection against Tuberculosis, and the National Organization for Cancer Control.

Organization of health services

The practice of medicine, dentistry, pharmacy and veterinary medicine is free in Belgium, provided that practitioners are in possession of the appropriate diplomas and are entered in the professional register (there is no such registry for dentistry).

Insured persons can choose their doctor, dentist or pharmacist among those having signed agreements with the National Institute of Sickness and Disability Insurance, which also govern the rates for reimbursement of medical expenses by insurance organizations. The same free choice is available where hospitals are concerned, on the condition that these establishments are approved by the Ministry of Public Health and of the Environment. This approval is subject to the observation of architectural standards, standards of general organization and those specific to each service. Hospital establishments must moreover be integrated in a set plan, organized at national and regional level.

The hospitals and clinics are controlled either by public social aid centres, which have replaced the public welfare committees, or by private organizations (mutual aid societies, religious communities, etc.), or by the universities. Technical and financial control of these establishments is exercised by the Ministry of Public Health. In 1976 there were 50 706 beds in hospitals and general clinics, and 25 636 beds in psychiatric establishments, giving a total of 76 342 beds.

Organization of preventive services

L'Oeuvre nationale de l'Enfance, a body set up under the Act of 5 September 1919, is responsible for maternal and child health and organizes pre- and postnatal clinics for infants and children of preschool age, permanent and temporary homes for mentally deficient children, and holiday homes and camps. Health protection of schoolchildren is the responsibility of school medical inspection centres and teams approved and subsidized by the Ministry of Public Health. The service is closely concerned with tuberculosis prevention and screening in the young.

The Ministry of Public Health is responsible for medical sports control and lays down the rules for sports which are obviously dangerous such as boxing, the participation of minors in cycle races, etc. The taking of drugs during sports competitions is strictly forbidden.

Health protection of workers is the responsibility of factory and interfactory medical services, which are controlled by the Ministry of Employment and Labour.

The military, who undergo strict medical examination before enrolment, are the responsibility of the Inter-Forces Medical Service under the Ministry of National Defence.

Institutions for health promotion and protection

There were the following specialized institutions as at 31 December 1977:

Clinics for the prevention of tuberculosis	92
Centres for cancer control	10
Venereal disease clinics	22
Mental health clinics	49
Pre-natal clinics	246
Infant welfare clinics	1 172
Infant welfare home-visiting services	603
Clinics for children, 3 to 6 years	658
Crèches	236
Day nurseries	22
Maternity homes	15
Child home-care services	10
Beds for mentally deficient children	4 145

Environmental health

As mentioned earlier, the French law of 16/24 August 1790 and the Belgian common law established communal autonomy in the field of hygiene. Making use of this autonomy, local authorities have founded a great variety of services: water supply, drainage, water treatment plants and physical education establishments such as stadiums, swimming pools, etc. Moreover, since 1901, each commune has been required by law to establish a meat inspection service, as confirmed by the law of 5 September 1952.

However, the increasingly technical nature of

sanitary measures necessitates resources, both in specialized personnel and supplies, largely beyond the capacities of individual communes. The 1907 and 1922 laws gave permission to the communes to join forces as a means overcoming the deficiencies. Intercommunal societies for water supply and treatment and for refuse disposal, intercommunal laboratories for the control of foodstuffs and other similar establishments were thus founded.

As a further result of the increasing specialization of techniques required, the State has instituted inspection services in the fields of foodstuffs, meat, medicines and sanitary engineering, carried out by specialists having the necessary university qualifications, who collaborate with highly qualified laboratories (the Institute of Hygiene and Epidemiology, provincial university and private laboratories). A high degree of specialization is obviously characteristic of the most recent problems of environmental health: atmospheric pollution, pollution from ionizing radiations, contamination of foodstuffs, problems resulting from the use of pesticides, etc. Here again, and for the same reasons as before, the technical services of the State supersede those of the local authorities.

Other organizations which have been founded have made an efficient and coordinated contribution to the improvement of the environment; for example, a national society for housing and low-cost accommodation, established in 1919, which is now called the National Society for Housing, and a national society for small proprietors, now called the National Society for Proprietors. These two societies support the construction of healthy homes, available to families of modest income. A national society for water supply, established in 1913, must also be mentioned in this context, having been responsible for rousing the regions from their inertia in this regard and for the installation, particularly in rural areas, of an ever-widening water supply network. The law of 26 March 1971 founded the "Sociétés de Bassin", with a view to ensuring the methodical treatment of industrial and urban water supplies upstream and downstream.

The transfer of certain central government responsibilities to the regions in accordance with article 107 (d) of the revised Belgian Constitution (see below) will not change the procedure, which force of circumstances makes inevitable, by which higher and better equipped authorities than those at regional level intervene in the field of sanitation.

Public health information and research

Services in the Ministry of Public Health and of the Environment are responsible, among other things, for a general studies service, which is building up impressive records and publishes annually a list of bibliographical references; an information processing centre, which edits a public health yearbook of statistics, and a medical establishment administration, which carries out an annual census of hospitals and clinics; while the Institute of Hygiene and Epidemiology and the Centre for Population and Family Studies carry out a wide variety of important research projects.

In other ministerial departments, the role of the National Institute of Veterinary Research in the field of animal health is comparable to that of the Institute of Hygiene and Epidemiology in the field of human health.

The Royal Medical Academy of Belgium and the Royal Flemish Academy of Public Health of Belgium receive the work of Belgian researchers and give rewards for the best work. The academies act together to advise the Government.

Various laboratories controlled by the regional administrative authorities, among which the Institut Pasteur at Brabant merits first mention, make an important contribution to knowledge in the field of communicable diseases.

The same applies to those laboratories attached to the chairs of hygiene and social medicine in the universities. Belgium has four schools of public health which come under the separate universities of Brussels and Louvain. The Universities of Ghent and Liège award a scientific public health diploma. Furthermore, the Institute of Tropical Medicine in Antwerp makes an important contribution to knowledge in the field of tropical bacteriology, virology, parasitology, epidemiology and pathology.

The National Fund for Scientific Research provides material assistance to researchers working in scientific establishments and under the jurisdiction of committees of morphological medical sciences, physiological medical sciences, bacteriology, pathology of communicable diseases and hygiene, clinical sciences, pharmacy and veterinary medicine. A fund for research in the medical sciences, founded by the National Fund, by agreement with the Ministry of Public Health, is financed from the Ministry's budget and provides subsidies to individual researchers or groups of researchers with a view to undertaking wide-scale research.

Finally, the contribution of the private sector, particularly of the pharmaceutical industry, to the progress made in studying the composition, biological action, side effects and dosage of drugs must not be forgotten.

Principal public health problems

Belgium is in the process of establishing a new internal structure which will give more autonomy to the regions and to the cultural communities which make up the country. This reform will lead inevitably to the transfer of certain central government responsibilities to the new regional or communal entities, which are not yet fully organized. Care must be taken that such development does not disturb the unity of jurisprudence and technical activity required in a country with a limited area, a dense population, and a high rate of population movement.

The main public health problems in Belgium are specifically those which inevitably arise in a densely populated, highly industrialized country. These problems are discussed very thoroughly and the discussions are not limited to technical considerations but include, for example:

(1) the country's drinking-water and industrial water supply and the construction of storage dams;
(2) the treatment of waste water, both industrial and household, which should be carried out by societies established in the different river basins;
(3) problems resulting from ionizing radiations and the operation of nuclear power stations;
(4) problems resulting from atmospheric pollution.

Other problems are equally serious, even if they have not been brought to the attention of the public so insistently. For example:

(1) the constant increase in health expenditure (see below);
(2) other financial problems, particularly concerning the continued deficit of the sickness and disability insurance and the hospitals;
(3) the action to be taken with regard to smallpox vaccination in view of the almost total eradication of smallpox announced by WHO;
(4) the spread of rabies in the eastern provinces of Belgium is also an important epidemiological problem;
(5) finally, recent epidemics of meningococcal and streptococcal infections have prompted widespread work, both in the field and in the laboratory, and have led to the detailing of those preventive measures to be taken against these dangerous diseases.

Health expenditure

Since 1973 health expenditure has been subject to very close methodical controls, and proves to be increasing rapidly. It should perhaps be noted, in this context, that the methods of investigation used during the past five years greatly improved on those methods previously used. It is clear that the problem goes beyond the framework of the Ministry of Public Health budget. A whole range of factors are involved and have, as a whole, been the subject of annual systematic examination since 1973. Health expenditure is analysed as follows (see the table below):

(1) by source or origin, expenses being grouped according to whether they are the responsibility of (a) the National Institute of Sickness and Disability Insurance; (b) the different ministerial departments; (c) the regions; (d) the communes; or (e) the semi-public and private sector.
(2) according to destination. The following

	Curative	Preventive	Environ-mental	Occupa-tional health	Social health	Education	Research	Support services	Totals
			(in millions of Belgian francs)						
National Institute of Sickness and Disability Insurance	107 321.0				44 310.2				151 541.2
Government	15 327.4	6 958.9	17 992.7	6 403.2	19 438.0	238.1	2 747.4	1 517.4	70 623.1
Regions	743.5	743.5	1 083.0			30.5	153.8		2 754.3
Communes	5 580.4	5 006.5	26 063.5						36 650.4
Semi-public and private sector	42 800.0	27 868.8	69 379.1	8 755.8			1 500.6		150 304.3
Totals	171 628.3	40 577.7	114 518.3	15 159.0	63 748.2	268.6	4 401.8	1 517.4	411 873.3

expenditures are calculated separately: (*a*) curative medical services; (*b*) general and preventive medical services; (*c*) environmental health; (*d*) occupational health; (*e*) medicosocial assistance; (*f*) medical and paramedical education; (*g*) scientific research in fields related to public health; (*h*) a variety of expenses of a logistic nature, classified as "support" services.

Health expenditure amounts, in all, to about 4% of the gross national product.

BULGARIA

Background information

The country is divided into 28 administrative districts (*okrugs*); this includes the capital Sofia, which has the status of an independent district. The districts are subdivided into urban and rural communes.

In 1976 the population was 8 785 763, an increase of 54 329 or 0.6% over 1975. The area was 110 928 km^2, giving a population density of 79.20 per km^2. The age distribution of population was 22.3% under 14 years, 66.5% in the age group 15–64, 7.8% between 65 and 74, and 3.4% aged 75 years and over.

In 1976 the birth rate was 16.5 per 1000 population, the death rate 10.1 per 1000, the infant mortality rate 23.5 per 1000 live births, and the natural increase 6.4%. In the period 1973–1975 the death rate constantly rose (from 9.45 per 1000 population in 1973 to 10.31 per 1000 in 1975), but in 1976 it fell to 10.05 per 1000.

For the period 1974–1976 life expectancy was 71.3 (68.7 for males and 73.9 for females).

Mortality

Over half of all deaths were caused by circulatory diseases (51.8% in 1973 and 53.5% in 1976); the proportion of deaths from neoplasms was also high (15.1% and 14.1% respectively), respiratory diseases accounted for 11.4% and 11.0% respectively, and accidents, poisoning and violence for 5.7% in both years.

Infant mortality fell from 26.15 per 1000 live births in 1973 to 23.05 per 1000 in 1975, although an increase was evident in 1976 (23.46 per 1000).

The most common cause of death in infants was pneumonia (993 per 100 000 population at risk in 1973 and 875 per 100 000 in 1976), followed by birth injury and difficult labour (344 per 100 000 and 275 per 100 000 respectively), other anoxic and hypoxic conditions (295 and 268 per 100 000 respectively) and congenital anomalies (151 and 159 per 100 000 respectively).

Morbidity

Two methods are used to assess the health status of the population—specialized scientific research and routine statistics. Only data on morbidity and mortality obtained from routine statistics have been used in this review. For the period 1973–1976 the incidence of diseases notified at public health establishments varied between 888.7 and 950.8 per 1000. In children under 14 years of age morbidity varied between 1065.6 and 1151.2 per 1000 and in adults (15 years and over) between 818.2 and 901 per 1000.

A slight improvement can be noted in the pattern of morbidity in the period; the categories of disease maintained their order of incidence. Respiratory diseases were the most common, followed by diseases of the nervous system and sensory organs, circulatory diseases and diseases of the digestive system.

In the period 1973–1976 influenza was the most common communicable disease, with epidemic peaks of 1981 per 100 000 in 1974, 6742 in 1975 and 3059 in 1976. Some droplet spread infections have also remained at a relatively high level of incidence, such as rubella (505 per 100 000 in 1974), chickenpox (474 per 100 000 in 1975) and mumps (401 per 100 000 in 1975) although they declined in 1976.

Incidence of active tuberculosis continued to decline, from 609 per 100 000 in 1973 to

47.7 in 1976, and prevalence likewise fell from 307.6 in 1973 to 240.0 in 1976.

A marked downward tendency was also noted in the incidence of the following diseases: scarlet fever (from 155 per 100 000 in 1973 to 69 in 1976), measles (from 563 to 192), dysentery (from 199 to 97), infectious hepatitis (from 125 to 116) and pertussis (from 9 to 1.6). The remaining communicable diseases showed an exceptionally low incidence (less than 0.5 per 100 000) and are therefore of little significance.

Incidence of malignant neoplasms has remained at an almost constant level (217.2 per 100 000 in 1973 and 217.3 in 1976), but prevalence rose by 119 per 100 000 (from 994 in 1973 to 1113 in 1976).

Incidence in the various localities registered little change in the period 1973–1976, while there was a tendency in all localities for prevalence to increase, the most notable increase occurring in cancer of the mammary glands, the cervix uterus and the skin.

Organization of the health services

The health services are organized and directed by the Ministry of Health, which has the following subdivisions: the teaching and research complex of the Medical Academy, the planning and information unit, the administrative and executive unit, control unit, services unit and the main computer centre. These basic subsections incorporate boards whose chief functions include forecasting, planning, and economic and efficiency study of public health and medical services for the community; social security and the development of collectives; sanitation and epidemics control; and organization and control of medical service.

At the regional level public health is directed by the national health and social security board in the provincial people's council. According to the size of population and the number of public health establishments and medical personnel in a given administrative unit (*okrug*) the board is subdivided into three sections. The board is headed by a director who is a specialist in social hygiene and public health administration. An executive committee of the provincial people's council appoints the director with the approval of the Ministry of Health.

Health planning

Plans for the development of public health are drawn up in conjunction with the national economic plans, which are prepared in consultation with the various other ministries and are coordinated by the National Planning Committee. The public health plans thus form part of the five-year national economic plan. The indices for the five-year plan are provided each year by the annual national health plan, which aims, as far as is practically possible, to meet the needs of the community as regards medical care.

The chief goals of the public health plan for the coming years are as follows: the further improvement of the structure of the public health services network in accordance with the changing needs of the community; increased efficiency of the medical services; reduction of certain variations in the medical care provided in different provinces.

Curative and preventive services and programmes

Inpatient care

In 1976 there were 185 hospitals, of which 143 were general hospitals and 42 were specialized hospitals (including the hospital complex of the Medical Academy). There are departments in general hospitals for children, obstetrical and gynaecological patients, and for contagious and infectious disease patients.

The large majority (76%) of hospital beds are concentrated in the provincial, district, urban and factory hospitals and the hospital complex of the Medical Academy. The total number of beds in hospitals and outpatient establishments was 75 022 in 1976. There were 18 133 beds in sanatoria and health resort establishments. Thus the total number of beds in hospitals and sanatoria was 93 155, or 10.6 beds per 1000 inhabitants.

Outpatient care

The overall number of independent outpatient establishments and polyclinics in 1976 was 3620, of which 2065 were feldsher points, 156 rural health centres, 950 rural district health centres, and 37 rural polyclinics. An important part of outpatient care is provided by polyclinics attached to rural, district, provincial and factory hospitals and the hospital complex of the Medical Academy.

Outpatient medical care is run on a local district basis, with the local district doctor acting as the basic link in the outpatient polyclinic establishment and serving a set number of people resident in a given territory or grouped according to industries. There are therapeutic, occupational, paediatric and gynaecological and midwifery sections. The team working in the local doctor's district comprises middle-grade auxiliary medical workers such as feldshers, midwives and nurses.

Outpatient care is thus provided at the local level by the services of the local doctor's district, at the district level by the district hospital, at the provincial level by the provincial hospital, and at the regional, interregional and republic level by the regional, interregional, Medical Academy and specialized hospitals.

There are 64 specialized dispensaries which carry out a number of interregional functions, for example, in pneumophthisiology, oncology, dermatovenereology and psychoneurology, and which provide specialized care accordingly. Highly specialized care in some narrowly specialized fields is also provided by the institutes and clinics of the Medical Academy including an oncological institute, an endocrinological, geriatric and gerontological institute, an institute for cardiovascular diseases, a paediatric institute, a neurological institute, an institute for psychiatry and neurosurgery, an institute for midwifery and gynaecology, an institute for haematology and blood transfusion, an otorhinolaryngological and ophthalmological institute, and an institute for health resort therapy and physiotherapy.

Maternal and child health

Supervision of children and expectant mothers is carried out in women's and children's clinics. There were 2655 women's, children's and maternal and child clinics in 1976. Employed women are entitled to periods of paid leave for pregnancy, birth and infant care—10 months for the first child, 12 months for the second and 14 months for the third. When the period of paid leave has expired, mothers are entitled to unpaid leave until the child reaches the age of three years. There were 74 945 crèches in 1977 providing, in all, 17 places per 100 children up to the age of three years. Medical care of children under 14 is organized in paediatric districts, with one doctor per 1000 children. School doctors each look after an average of 2000 to 2200 children. There are 50 health schools and sanatoria for chronically sick children.

Medical care of adults and the elderly

In addition to the socialist system of public health care, providing medical care at all levels to adults and elderly people, there are special experimental gerontological clinics in the hospitals of some provincial towns. All provincial hospitals have departments for convalescence and prolonged treatment, in which those suffering from chronic diseases represent a large proportion of the patients.

Oral health care and the control of dental caries

Planned treatment of dental caries is the basic principle of the dental care service. Treatment and preventive inspection includes: organized collective examinations for children from three to seven years of age, schoolchildren, expectant mothers, people receiving treatment for chronic diseases, and people working in environments harmful to health. The rest of the community receives dental care on request.

First aid services

The first aid system comprises independent first aid and emergency care stations in Sofia, Plovdiv, Narna and Pleven, departments of first aid and emergency medical care in provincial hospitals, and first aid sections in district hospitals. The independent stations have specialized teams for cardiology, neurology, surgery, midwifery and gynaecology, toxicology and intensive care, and others forms of specialized and highly specialized medical care.

With a view to increasing medical efficacy as regards road traffic accident injuries, efforts have been made to improve and expand the activities of the specialized and nonspecialized teams working in the independent first aid stations, the first aid departments of the regional hospitals and the first aid units of district hospitals. Mobile medical teams have been set up which patrol the main roads at peak hours in an attempt to increase the speed with which medical care is administered to accident victims.

Public health programmes

Public health programmes are drawn up on the basis of governmental laws for the protection of the environment and the improvement of medical service. Special programmes have already been implemented to raise the standard of health education; control cardiovascular diseases; protect and improve mental health; update medical technology and education and the public health system; develop preventive health care, hygiene and epidemiology, outpatient polyclinic care, maternal and child care (by

1980), dental care (by 1980), inpatient care, the occupational health service and medical services associated with physical culture, sport and tourism; control of malignant neoplasms and gastroenteritic diseases and Salmonella (in the period 1972 to 1975); develop sanatoria and health resorts; and promote the observance of a balanced diet.

Biomedical and health services research

With a view to the structural integration of the departmental research institutes and medical faculties, a single complex has been created within the Medical Academy, where 10 200 students are trained for scientific and academic research in medical treatment, organization and methods.

The scientific community of the Medical Academy is currently working on seven coordinated interdepartmental programmes including protection of the environment, improvement of foodstuffs, and population dynamics.

Health manpower development

The Ministry of Health is doing all in its power to take on, train, qualify and place senior and auxiliary medical personnel. Enrolment at institutions for higher and auxiliary medical education is also controlled by the Ministry of Health after close scrutiny of the needs of all provinces and with the consent of the State planning authorities.

The breakdown of the staff engaged in the public health service on 31 December 1976 was as follows:

	Number	Number per 10 000 population
Physicians	19 312	21.98
Stomatologists	3 901	4.44
Pharmacists	3 146	3.58
Feldshers	5 760	6.56
Midwives	7 518	8.56
Nurses	37 182	42.32
Laboratory assistants (clinical and X-ray technicians)	6 037	6.87
Dental technicians	1 962	2.23
Assistant pharmacists	4 092	4.66
Other auxiliary medical personnel	2 652	3.02
Junior medical personnel	34 299	39.04
Other personnel	43 247	49.22

Cost and financing of health services

The health services are financed from the national budget. Total expenditure on public health (current expenditure and expenditure on capital investment) represented 6.17% of the national budget in 1976.

The average cost per day of one bed in a provincial hospital is 10.86 leva.

CZECHOSLOVAKIA

Population and other statistics

In 1976 the population was approximately 14 974 000, the birth rate was 19.2, the death rate 11.4 and the natural increase 7.8 per 1000. Infant mortality was 20.8 per 1000 live births. The expectation of life at birth has been constantly around 70 years in recent times (about 67.0 for men and about 73.6 for women). If a male lives till 50, he may hope to live to 72.1 years on average, if he lives to 60, he may hope to live to 74.7. A woman in her fifties may hope to live to 76.9 years, and if she attains 60 years, to 78.4.

The major causes of death in 1976 were diseases of the circulation, malignant neoplasms, diseases of the respiratory organs, accidents, and diseases of the digestive tract. The most frequently reported communicable diseases in 1976 were measles, diphtheria, infectious hepatitis, dysentery and gonorrhoea. Incapacity for work was about 4% on average.

In 1976 Czechoslovakia had a total of 232 general hospitals with 114 260 beds; 25 hospitals for tuberculosis patients (6551 beds); 34 psychiatric hospitals (16 795 beds); 79 other specialized hospitals; and 15 highly specialized inpatient treatment institutions. In all, there were 147 534 hospital beds, approximately 10 beds per 1000 population. In addition to this there were 3198 places in sanatoria and 32 484 places in resort establishments.

Administrative organization of the health services

Health care in Czechoslovakia is planned and provided by the State as an integral part of its economic and cultural structure. From the legal standpoint, health matters are regulated by the Federal Assembly, the Czech National Council and the Slovak National Council. A federal ministry of health has not yet been established and a uniform policy for the whole State is ensured by the mutual cooperation of the Ministries of Health of both national republics, which deal with the most important matters concerned with health protection. They are assisted in doing so by the ministerial academic councils, by research institutes, by institutes of advanced medical and pharmaceutical studies and by similar institutes for middle-grade personnel, medical statistics and health education. Help and advice are also supplied by specialists of all kinds, together with consultative groups. Members of the academic councils and the chief specialists are drawn from among leading scientists.

The Ministry of Health in each of the two republics is the supreme health service body, dealing with the organization and detailed supervision and control of preventive and curative services, directing scientific research, providing advanced training for medical personnel, taking charge of the medical industry and medical supplies, and being responsible for the medical sector as a whole.

The management of health services is decentralized. At regional and district levels, health comes under the management of regional and district national committees, which are elected bodies. The decision-making and supervisory bodies under the national committees are the health and social security commissions, mainly consisting of elected members. The executive agency responsible at regional level for implementing the decisions of the national committees and executing more specialized directives and orders of the Ministries of Health is the department of health of each regional national committee; at the district level this is either the Department of Health and Social Security or else an independent health department.

A specific feature of Czechoslovakia's health system is provided by the national health institutes. Medical institutions subordinate to the regional national committees are grouped in association with one another through the regional national health institutes which bring highly specialized services together. They include a hospital and type III polyclinic, a regional hygiene station, specialized treatment institutions, a regional school for the health professions and, where necessary, other regional institutions. Their task is to organize and provide the community with specialized services not available at district level, to make arrangements for advanced training for medical personnel, pharmacists and other medical workers, and also to play a part in the management of public health at regional level.

The district national committees are responsible for medical institutions grouped together in district national health institutes. These incorporate a hospital with type II and type I polyclinics, district sanitary stations, an intermediate school for the health professions, pharmacies and other establishments.

Assistance during illness, and social security, are provided by the State for all those in employment and for members or their families. The agency responsible for hospital insurance is the Central Council of Trade Unions with its various bodies; the agency for social security is the federal Ministry of Labour and Social Security, both national Ministries of Labour and Social Security, the institution for pensions insurance and the national committee.

Health legislation

The basic legislation on health is a law of 1966 on the protection of the health of the nation, and all the amendments to it. A new regulation promulgated in 1974 by the Czech and Slovak Ministries of Health concerned the network of medical establishments, which included in its provisions the integration of hospitals and polyclinics into larger-scale units, more effective use of equipment and staff, and improvements in the processes of diagnosis and treatment.

A new draft regulation relating to medical personnel and other health workers is currently being prepared which defines the different categories and specialities of medical personnel and the advanced education they must receive after completion of their specialized training. Part of this new regulation already in force requires district physicians to have gained special experience in general medicine or general practice.

Health planning and programmes

The Fifteenth Party Congress held in 1975 laid down the health policy to be followed during the period 1976–1980 and put forward the following objectives. First, a further improvement in the quality of medical care through the area and factory medical sectors; greater attention to the health of employees in industry and large-scale agricultural units; continued accent on the preventive aspects of medical care with proper coverage of the entire population through the *dispanser* (outpatient centre) system; and integration and modernization of the system of medical institutions and services to suit present trends in specialization, economics, demography and town planning.

The federal public health programmes have been drawn up on the basis of an analysis of current trends in morbidity, invalidity, and mortality among the population in order to solve the most important medical and socioeconomic problems of society. The programme in *maternal and child health care* consists in the main of a range of measures for providing the younger generation with a healthy background, for reducing morbidity and mortality among the newborn, and for achieving harmonious later development of children.

The programme for *care of the chronically ill and the elderly* consists of a range of medical and social measures providing sufficient hospital and sanatorium beds for the chronically ill, the establishment of convalescent homes for the sick and an increase in nursing staff at medical health centres to provide home care of the chronically sick and the elderly.

The *cardiovascular diseases control* programme is aimed at more thorough prevention and effective tracing, diagnosis, treatment and rehabilitation of patients.

The *oncological diseases control* programme involves interrelated measures, mostly devoted to the primary prevention of malignant tumours, and includes prophylactic screening to identify precancerous states and the early stages of malignant tumour growth.

The *virus diseases* control programme has as its object a further gradual reduction in viral diseases of the respiratory system, in which the focus of attention is on preventive, therapeutic and organizational activities aimed at reducing their incidence.

Other health projects are being developed for the period up to 1990 and in some matters to the year 2000.

Research institutes in the area of health care assist in developing programmes for health protection, health planning and health administration; among them the Institute of Social Medicine and Health Administration plays an important part, particularly in medical services planning and administration and in the establishment of programmes and computerized management systems. The Institute for Medical Statistics is developing, for the national Ministries of Health of both the Czech and the Slovak Republics, statistical surveys on the performance of outpatient and inpatient establishments, on the network of medical establishments, on the numbers of medical and other health personnel, and on the health status of the population and its mobility.

Curative and preventive services

Medical establishments providing curative and preventive services, the sanitation and hygiene service, and the pharmaceutical service form an integrated countrywide system in which all medical care is provided free of charge. A close network of medical care establishments has been developed, and no distinction is made between the rural and urban populations as regards the provision of medical care. There are 25.96 practising physicians per 10 000 population, or one to 385 inhabitants (in the Czech Republic 377, in Slovakia 404).

There are three types of hospital: type I provides prevention and treatment facilities for a catchment area of 50 000 population. It provides inpatient treatment for patients with short-term illnesses without complications, giving them complete treatment until they recover, and carrying out emergency hospital services. It also provides, when necessary, transport to hospitals of higher categories. Type I hospitals must have departments of internal medicine and surgery and may have departments of gynaecology and obstetrics, and of paediatrics. There were 115 hospitals of this type in Czechoslovakia in 1976.

Type II provides specialized care of kinds that type I establishments are not in a position to provide, for catchment areas of up to 200 000 population. This type of hospital normally has 13 departments; there are 75 of these hospitals in the country.

Type III provides, in catchment areas of approximately a million population, the specialized care that is not handled by hospitals and polyclinics of type I or II. There must be a minimum number of 17 departments in a hospital of this type, which normally has about 1500–1700 beds. There are 27 type III hospitals in Czechoslovakia.

The basic unit in the medical care system in Czechoslovakia is the district medical post (which can be either in a geographical district or attached to an industrial undertaking) administratively linked to the hospital and polyclinic, for which it provides detached outpatient facilities.

At 31 December 1976 there were 4339 geographical medical districts, with 1875 district medical posts, including 370 polyclinics. A district post provides services for one or more districts, in villages or on the outskirts of towns, and has a district physician (on average one for 3500 inhabitants), a district paediatrician (one for 1300 children), a gynaecologist (one for 9000 women), and a dentist (one for 2500 inhabitants). A factory medical post has a factory doctor (one for 1150–1800 workers, depending on the category) and provides specialized services according to the nature of the undertaking and the composition of the work force. In addition there are nurses (paediatric, obstetrical, and sometimes dental) and dental assistants, whose task it is to assist the physicians in their work. The district services recently gained a new category of health worker, visiting nurses (about 0.5 per administrative district), responsible for the care of the chronically ill.

There are 2.55 physicians per 1000 population in the outpatient curative and preventive services; and 1.58 health workers of the intermediate category for each physician practising in the outpatient care system.

Specialized services and programmes

Environmental health. It is incumbent on responsible organizations and individuals to ensure basic sanitation and hygiene. Organizations are supervised by the hygiene service. For the public, basic hygiene is administered by the national committees through special agencies, and voluntary work is organized to improve the environment.

The Constitution makes provision for measures to prevent pollution of the environment, promote the health of the population and foster the development of its physical and mental capacities. The public health authorities are involved in the effort to develop a healthy environment. The terms of reference include the establishment of standards and principles of health and hygiene for use in connexion with regional planning, new building developments at district and town level, and the architecture of buildings, together with continuing hygiene supervision and measures to deal with identifiable defects. Separate government agencies provide supervision and control of technical measures for the control of air and water pollution.

Occupational health. The health and hygiene service's activities to ensure healthy working conditions necessarily have a bearing on national economic planning, as technical development, industrial planning and the introduction of new machinery affect the healthy working environment. There is continuous surveillance, and the chief physician has a supervisory role at national level.

Prevention and control of communicable diseases is based on special legislation determining the methods to be employed in prophylaxis, the duties of the citizen, the tasks of the hygiene service, the obligations of medical and other health workers, and the activities required of different organizations and agencies. This legislation makes provision for inoculations; for screening activities by health professionals; for measures regarding carriers of disease-causing pathogens; for quarantine disinfection and rodent control; for screening, diagnosis and treatment; for measures to combat foci of infection; for the reporting and investigation of communicable diseases; for activities to prevent the spread of hospital infections; for principles governing material containing disease-causing pathogens, and protection against the importation of communicable diseases from abroad.

Laboratory services are an integral part of the hospital and polyclinic system's "common diagnostic and therapeutic components", including departments of clinical biochemistry, blood transfusion, haematology, allergy and clinical immunology, and laboratories or departments for investigations concerning the respiratory system and the circulation. The sanitation and hygiene service laboratories provide facilities for general and community hygiene, occupational and food safety, and occupational health including microbiology at places of work.

In addition to the maternal and child health care programme described above, *protection of children* of school age is provided as part of general school care and by hygiene and epidemiological service. Regular preventive examinations of all children are carried out, and services for sick children and children with innate hereditary or developmental disabilities are provided by the outpatient services.

Health care of the elderly forms part of the public health programme for the care of the chronically ill and the elderly (see above).

Accident prevention and control. Active involvement in the work of the governmental committee for road safety has produced a series of measures which are being systematically implemented.

Emergency and relief services are organized on a 24-hour basis, providing medical care where life is endangered, and are directly linked by a central control system to the appropriate hospital department of anaesthesiology and resuscitation, and sometimes to the intensive care unit of individual hospital departments.

Pharmaceutical production is centred upon a national institution under the direct control of the Czech Ministry of Health. Pharmacies are an integral part of the national medical associations; and most drugs can be obtained with a doctor's prescription, a small number being sold freely.

Health education is provided by special departments of the medical associations, headed by doctors.

Biomedical and health services research

Biomedical research is directed by the departments of both national Ministries and is constantly controlled and monitored by the science councils. It focuses on problems of health and epidemiology and clinically-related medical research, little different from those in other industrially developed European countries: social problems affecting human, industrial and environmental relations; viral and cardiovascular diseases; malignant neoplasms; mental health; care of the young; problems associated with tissue and organ transplantation; and diseases of the locomotive system. In the Czech Socialist Republic, medical and biomedical research is organized as part of the State plan of applied and basic research. As regards applied research, 25 projects are being tackled under the direction of both Ministries with the medical and pharmaceutical faculties of the two republics. Basic research is directed by the appropriate institutes of the Czech and Slovak academies of science, and with the participation of health research institutes.

Doctors have a six-year course of studies (five years for stomatologists) in eight medical faculties providing training in the specialities of general medicine, paediatrics, stomatology, hygiene and epidemiology. Pharmacists have a five-year period of training in two faculties. Postgraduate training of doctors and pharmacists is given at two postgraduate institutes in Prague and Bratislava. Medium-level health personnel are trained at 76 schools forming part of the regional medical associations, and studies last four years. Students who have completed secondary education may take a two-year supplementary medical school course. Health personnel of lower grades receive their training as health workers, dental laboratory technicians and tutors in a two-year medical school course.

Financing of health services

In 1976 the total national budget amounted to 290 071 million korunas, of which 18 656 million korunas were expended on the health services. Per capita expenditure on health was 1250.59 korunas.

DENMARK

Basic country data

At the last census, taken in 1976, the population of Denmark was 5 079 879, divided by age group, as follows: 0–14 years, 1 132 496; 15–64 years, 3 250 835; 65–74 years, 433 849; 75 years and over, 262 699. The birth rate was 12.9, the death rate 10.6 per 1000 population. Expectation of life at birth for men was 71.1 years, for women 76.8 years.

After the Second World War Denmark underwent industrialization and urbanization; 4 million of the population of 5 million live in cities and suburbs. Travelling distances are short and communications good. The country is divided into 14 counties of approximately 350 000 inhabitants and 277 municipalities of 20 000–30 000 inhabitants.

Organization of the public health services

At the national level, almost all the major ministries are concerned with some aspects of the public health services, but the Ministry of the Interior is generally considered the supreme health authority, as it administers medical and nonmedical personnel, hospitals, legislation on pharmaceutical substances, on epidemics, on vaccinations and quarantine, as well as maternal and child health and certain other domains.

The State Serum Institute and various other laboratories also come under the Ministry of the Interior. The Ministry of Social Affairs is responsible for the health insurance scheme, care of the old, the mentally deficient and the physically disabled, and vocational rehabilitation. Other ministries dealing with health questions in their respective fields are the Ministry for the Environment, the Ministry of Education, the Ministry of Agriculture, the Ministry of Housing, the Ministry of Justice and the Ministry of Labour.

At the local level the elected bodies, primarily the local governments, have a general responsibility to provide and operate sufficient facilities for inpatient care. They are also responsible for control services. Other local bodies are responsible for environmental sanitation, food hygiene and housing. The national Government, however, exerts a strong influence even in those matters which are formally left to be dealt with by local bodies; 16% of local government expenses for health and medical care are defrayed by the national Government.

With a view to coordinating the activities of the various agencies concerned with health matters, the national Government has a central agency, the National Health Service, which—besides certain executive functions in the administration of health services—has an advisory and supervisory role with respect to the various health functions of government departments as well as those of the local authorities. Its executive functions include the licensing of medical personnel and the control of the production, import and sale of drugs, in particular the regulation of the sale of narcotics. It is also responsible for the collection and publication of medical statistics. The staff of the National Health Service consists mainly of members of the medical, pharmaceutical, nursing and administrative professions. The Director-General of the Service is a physician.

Primary health care and changes in the provision of health services

Responsibility for the planning and supervision of the health services is shared by the counties and the municipalities. The counties are responsible for the institutionalized health services (i.e., hospitals), the municipalities for the primary health care system. In or about 1970, reforms resulted in a decentralization of the responsibility for the health services from the State level to local authorities.

The comprehensive health care system in a county leaves only very specialized functions, such as neurosurgery, radiotherapy and kidney transplantation, to the State, and some neighbouring counties share specialized services.

Up to April 1973 the primary health care services were mainly organized and financed on the basis of compulsory local health insurance, subsidized and controlled by the State. The Public Health Security Act of June 1971 which came into force in April 1973 assigns the administration of health security to the county boroughs and to the municipalities of Copenhagen and Frederiksberg.

Health security is paid by the county boroughs and 35% of the amount is refunded by the State. The contributions of the citizens are paid through income tax. All Danish citizens and foreigners with residence in Denmark are automatically entitled to the benefits of the Public Health Security Act.

Since 1 April 1976 all patients, regardless of their income, may choose once a year to be placed either in health insurance group 1 or health insurance group 2. Patients in group 1 have free medical attention by the general practitioner. Patients in health insurance group 2 have free choice of general practitioner as well as free choice of specialist without being referred by their general practitioner. As of April 1976 there were 87% in group 1 and 12% in group 2. The patients in group 2 have to pay that part of the medical fees —somewhat higher than the charge for group 1 patients—that exceeds the amount paid by the public health insurance for a similar service to a group 1 patient. Hospital treatment is free of charge for both groups of patients.

Until 1970 more than 100 municipalities were immediately responsible for the hospital services for somatic conditions. The Hospitals Act of 14 June 1974 increased State supervision, particularly with regard to planning of hospitals. The day-to-day running of hospitals is, however, the responsibility of 14 county boroughs and of the municipalities of Copenhagen and Frederiksberg. As of 1 April 1976 mental hospitals with affiliated nursing homes were placed administratively under the county boroughs in which they are situated.

The Daily Cash Benefit (Sickness or Maternity) Act came into force in April 1973. The daily cash benefit is payable to a person who, on medical grounds, is unable to carry out his usual or similar work. In some cases, however, the benefit is payable also in the event of partial incapacity for work. The Act provides for a compulsory as well as a voluntary insurance scheme. Persons working as employees are ensured daily cash benefits on a compulsory basis from the first day of absence. Other persons qualifying for daily cash benefit are eligible for the benefit after five weeks' illness from the first day of absence, and may join a voluntary scheme covering the first five weeks' illness. Persons carrying out domestic work may be ensured the benefit on the voluntary basis only. The benefit for a week cannot exceed 90% of the average weekly earnings of the beneficiary.

The health insurance services also pay part of the costs of medicaments if they are included in a list issued by the Minister of Social Affairs.

Health legislation

Acts and government orders during the period 1973–1977 included the following:

—Act No. 350 of 13 June 1973 on *induced abortion* grants any woman residing in Denmark the right to termination of her pregnancy provided that the operation is performed before the end of the twelfth week of pregnancy.

—Act No. 332 of 19 June on *compensation for nuclear damages* introduces a liability for damages of the owner of nuclear plants and the State in case of an accident in the plant.

—Act No. 661 of 23 December 1975 on *occupational environment* states the duty of the employer to see to it that safety and health conditions at work are fully adequate. The

Minister of Labour is authorized to fix regulations regarding industrial health care service.

—Act No. 327 of 26 June 1975 on *medicines* states that any use of medicines within Danish territory is dependent on an authorization from the National Health Service, which controls and gives directions for the activities thus authorized.

—Act No. 52 of 20 February 1976 introduces the *free choice* of individuals to be placed in either *health insurance group 1 or 2*.

—Government Order No. 88 of 2 March 1976 grants patients in Denmark access to *free, highly specialized medical treatment abroad* provided that certain conditions are fulfilled.

Curative and preventive services

In 1976 there were 121 somatic hospitals and 16 psychiatric hospitals, totalling 44 390 beds. A few hospitals are owned by the State. The hospital services cover physical and mental diseases and include diagnosis and treatment. They are mainly directed towards hospitalized patients, but are increasingly also ambulatory in order to relieve hospital bed capacity. They give diagnostic assistance to general practitioners through well established laboratory and X-ray services, and provide training centres for hospital and primary health care personnel. Hospital prophylactic services include cancer screening and lung clinics.

Health personnel

Approximately 130 000 persons were employed in 1974, i.e., about 5.7% of the total manpower, part-time staff being counted as equivalent to approximately 105 000 full-time staff; 75% are employed in hospitals, the rest being divided between the primary health care sector's four main groups: medical practice, dental practice, pharmacies and external services (public health nursing, home nursing, and midwife services).

(1) *Personnel in hospital services*:

Doctors	5 510
Nurses	16 590
Other ward, examination and treating department personnel	33 710
Personnel of assisting departments	25 440
Total	81 250

(2) *Personnel in other services:*

General practitioners	2 740
(a) in general practice	2 450
(b) in rest of health sector	290
Specialists	450
Public health nurses	1 050
Midwives	500
Home nurses	2 300
Dentists	3 540
Physiotherapists	1 070
Pharmacists	1 450
Chiropodists	600
Others	10 400
Total	24 100

General practitioners

In 1977 there were 2740 general practitioners— one to about 2000 inhabitants— fairly evenly distributed, the density being slightly higher in the major cities. More than 50% work in group practices of two to seven doctors.

Every citizen of 16 years of age or over has the right to choose a general practitioner living within 10 km of his residence and to receive medical attention and health examinations and inoculations free of charge. The practitioner has access to laboratory assistance and X-ray examination services (e.g., in district hospitals), can call on public health nurses, home nurses, and local social service, and can refer the patient to specialist consultants and hospitals.

In preventive medicine the practitioner gives health examinations in pregnancy and the postpartum period, and to preschool children, and advice on contraceptive techniques and sexual questions.

By agreement between the Danish Medical Association and the County Councils Association practitioners in the Copenhagen area are paid an annual fee per listed patient, others a basic fee per patient plus a fee for specific listed services. Both are responsible for their own practice, daily running costs and pension.

A further agreement between the County Councils Association and the Danish Medical Association provides the criteria for general practice: three years postgraduate clinical training, and 120 hours of a postgraduate university course in clinical disciplines and social medicine.

Public health nurses (health visitors)

Municipalities are obliged by law to employ public health nurses (two to three years' practical training after three years' nursing education,

followed by a one-year postgraduate course at university level). The ratio is one to 8000 inhabitants if the nurse is only occupied with children of the preschool age, one to 5000 if the school-age children are included. The first visit is made early in the postpartum period, and in the first year after birth regular visits are made according to the family's needs, subsequently concentrating on families at risk. Problem patients are referred to the general practitioner and may receive the direct assistance of the local social services.

Midwives

The midwife is a civil servant, working with general practitioners and public health nurses when the baby is born at home (less than 10% of all deliveries). A midwives' school at the University Hospital of Copenhagen gives a three-year training course.

Home nurses

The municipalities are obliged to employ home nurses—the ratio being one to 4000–5000 in urban areas, one to 2500–3000 in rural districts—to meet the need for nursing in the home after medical treatment, and to help relieve nursing homes for the chronically ill and the elderly.

Home nurses, who cooperate with the general practitioners, hospital nursing staff, and local social and health services, are registered nurses, mostly with no formal postgraduate education but with several years of clinical training in hospitals and other institutions.

School physicians and nurses

The school health service is a preventive activity to be regarded as a continuation of the preventive pre-school health examinations. The municipalities are obliged to offer five examinations by a school physician during the nine years of compulsory schooling. The number of examinations has recently been reduced to allow greater surveillance of children at risk from social, psychological or somatic conditions.

The school physicians (most of them local general practitioners on part-time service after a two-week course) are assisted by school health nurses (public health nurses, half of them also in part-time service).

Dentists

The dentists work to prevent caries and periodontitis as well as providing examination and treatment services; 2000 of the 3540 dentists work independently under an agreement between the Dentists Association, the County Councils Association and Copenhagen municipality, on a fee-for-service basis. For the adult population (over 16 years) treatment and some preventive activities are partly free of charge. The citizen's choice of dentist is completely free. Many municipalities provide dental care for the children in the compulsory school age group— some 600 000 children were covered by this arrangement in 1978. Elsewhere the municipality and the dentists have an agreement which provides for dental care free of charge to the same age group. In some municipalities this service has been extended to cover adults up to 20 years of age. Dental hygienists—a new profession—are increasingly occupied in prevention.

Dentists' training lasts five years, with a further year's subordinate service before full registration.

Physiotherapists

Physiotherapists mainly treat patients referred by the general practitioner. They work independently (with some exceptions in the Copenhagen area) according to a contract between the Danish Physiotherapists Association and the County Councils Association on a fee-for-service basis. The patients pay one-third of the total cost for physiotherapy and the county pays the rest. Many municipalities employ physiotherapists in nursing homes and homes for the elderly, for example, but also in an advisory capacity to the social service, or when, for example, a patient's institutionalization might be postponed.

Occupational therapists

This category does not practise privately. The training lasts three years in schools founded by the State.

The elderly and the handicapped

Care for the elderly and the physically or mentally handicapped is provided by the primary social and health care team at the municipal level—especially by the home nurses, but also by the general practitioners. The aim is to help them to stay in their homes as long as possible.

Medicines

Part of the cost of prescribed medicines of certain categories is paid direct by the county to the pharmacy (75% or 50% or nothing, according to necessity, efficiency and price). Patients with severe chronic diseases and disabilities, low income, old-age or disability pension can obtain medicines free of charge through the municipalities' social and health services.

Transport

The same categories of patient obtain free transport for medical treatment by a general practitioner or specialist. Ambulance transport in case of an emergency or acute illness certified by a physician is paid by the counties.

Biomedical and health services research

The Danish Medical Research Council gave high priority to clinical pharmacology, teratology and research in primary health care and societal factors and diseases in the period 1973–1977.

In the same period the Danish Hospital Institute was established, and the former Tuberculosis Index became an Institute for Clinical Epidemiology.

Health services research has been strengthened, with increased priority to primary health care research. The Institute of Social Medicine, the Institute of General Medicine, and the Danish National Institute of Social Research have been expanded.

Costs and financing of health services

During the fiscal year 1973/74 total health expenditure, including nursing homes, was 12 892 million Danish kroner. Of this amount 3322 million concerned the primary health care services; 7120 million concerned hospital services and 2450 million the working and construction of nursing homes. The working expenses of the hospital services was approximately 6200 million kroner in 1973/74.

The primary health care services are financed

by the counties (general practitioners, dentists, medicines, surgical treatment), by the municipalities (home nursing, public health nursing, school medical officers, vaccinations) and by the State (50% refund of the municipalities' expenditure on home nursing and public health nursing). To this should be added the part of the expenses paid by the patients themselves, especially those for medicines, medical care and specialist services.

The counties pay the hospital service expenses. However, the State still runs the two highly specialized hospitals, Rigshospitalet (the Copenhagen University Hospital) and the Finsen Institute. The fact that the counties and municipalities pay the major part of the expenditure for the hospital services should not, however, be taken to imply that it is covered by municipal taxation.

General subsidies to counties and municipalities were introduced in order that the repeal of the system of reimbursements and transfers should be offset by a corresponding increase of the State contribution. For 1976/77 it is estimated that approximately 35% of the countries' expenses will be covered in this way.

FINLAND

Population and other statistics

Owing to marked emigration to Sweden and the other Scandinavian countries, population growth has been very slow—from 4 591 842 in 1966 to 4 730 837 in 1976. In 1976 the birth rate was 14.1, the death rate 9.5; life expectancy at birth was 67.5 for males and 76.1 for females (at the age of 65 years, life expectancy was 77.0 for males and 80.7 for females). In very recent years the male mortality has been showing a tendency to improve. In the period 1960–1970 the life expectancy of males at 40 years of age was 69.4 years but in 1976 the comparable figure was 70.5 years (in the 1960s no such progress could be shown); for females the corresponding figures are 75.8 and 77.7 years. The share of the older classes in the age-distribution is not at present exceptionally high but a continuous growth is noticeable:

	1966	1976
0–14 years	1 213 037	1 017 056
15–64 years	2 997 456	3 189 507
65–74 years	267 474	360 952
75 years and over	113 875	163 322

Health situation

A rather positive picture emerges if infant mortality (9.6 per 1000 live births in 1976) and infectious diseases are used as indicators. There have in recent years been no epidemics of typhoid, and a few minimal epidemics of paratyphoid and dysentery, but numerous small epidemics of other salmonelloses. The improved hygienic conditions are also reflected in the small number of infectious hepatitis cases (in 1956, 7212 cases of this disease were notified, in 1966, 363 and in 1976, only 79). The last case of trachoma was found in 1957, of diphtheria in 1965, of poliomyelitis in 1961. In 1973 and 1974 there was an epidemic of meningococcal meningitis in which some 70 persons died. Syphilis is not a severe problem; gonorrhoea is relatively common, but there are signs that it is decreasing. Numerous cases of tuberculosis are found yearly (3194 in 1976), almost all in persons aged 40 years or more. The risk of infection, at present about one per thousand, is diminishing by about 10% yearly, thanks also to very thorough BCG vaccination measures. The last case of tubercular meningitis in children was found in 1966.

Diseases of the circulatory system are an especially severe problem; in the years 1972–1974 the mortality due to diseases of heart and blood circulation was 655 per 100 000 males aged 35–64 years. This was about 51% of the total mortality. The number of accidents has also been markedly higher than in the neighbouring countries, and comparisons of rates for pulmonary cancer have been very unfavourable for Finland in recent years. The trend has however been toward improvement for all these conditions.

Chronically ill patients receive drugs free of charge. In 1976 about 12% of the population used this service, the rate varying between 17% in an economically less developed province and 10% at the opposite end of the scale.

It can be concluded that the health situation is not as good as in other Nordic countries but is comparable with other so-called developed nations. In recent years a favourable development was noticeable in problem areas like heart diseases, accidents and lung cancer.

Organization of the health services

Health service and medical care are seen as obligations of society and rights of the citizen. Traditionally, and under the present legislation, the communes have responsibility for organizing the services, smaller communes forming services jointly. Health administration is regionalized. The communes have an elected council with proportional representation and they have financial autonomy and the right to levy tax. With some exceptions, the rural and urban communes have the same rights and responsibilities. The main costs are divided between the local and central authorities. The central Government subsidizes the commune.

The executive powers and the responsibility for health care are to a great extent decentralized, but supervision and direction are largely centralized. The central Government licenses physicians and other key personnel as well as institutions like hospitals, supervises the use of tax money, and encourages the communes with subsidies, usually 50%. If the services are not properly organized the central administration can resort to economic sanctions.

Health services are mainly paid from taxes, with a small direct payment by the patients. National health insurance covers all citizens but is quite separate from the provision of hospital services, preventive and other services. It partly compensates private physicians' fees, travel services, cost of drugs used at home, and maternity and other costs.

Health laws and regulations

The Primary Health Act 1972 made possible a complete reorganization of primary care with the help of health centres, and introduced new health planning. The Mental Health Act 1977 was to be applied from 1 January 1978.

Health plan and country health programming

Formal planning, with appropriate programme budgeting, has been systematically applied in the health field since 1972. A plan covers five calendar years and is updated yearly. The first such plan concentrated on personnel and financing, and contained statements about methods and processes. The local authorities' plans developed within this framework are approved by the National Board of Health. The most recent plan, published on 2 May 1978, covers the years 1979–1983. Its two parts concern primary care and hospital services. Some sectors, including environmental health, private services and health insurance are not included in the formal plan.

The manpower register and hospital discharge reporting system are examples of support services constituting data banks geared to the health management and planning process.

Curative and preventive services

General considerations

The public sector is predominant in both preventive and curative services. Infectious disease services and those for maternal and child health and vaccination, for example, are organized by local authorities and given completely free of charge to everybody. The private services in these fields are very minimal. There are some private hospitals in the country, most of them owned by nonprofit organizations. Together they account for about 4.3% of the hospital bed capacity of the country. There is a considerable amount of private practice, mainly on a part-time basis, subsidized by national health insurance. It is estimated that in 1976 there were 4.9 million consultations (31%) in the private and 10.7 million (69%) in the public sector. The private sector has laboratories and diagnostic services but relies mainly on public hospitals.

The country is divided into five university hospital regions and 21 hospital districts for specialist care. If the university hospitals, which are combined regional and teaching hospitals, are excluded, the number of general hospital beds per 1000 population varies regionally between 3.4 and 5.4. The changing population structure and ongoing construction will diminish these differences. The health centres have beds, which also compensate such differences.

	Number	Population covered	Number of beds
General hospitals			
University hospitals	5	945 000	7 116
Central hospitals	16	145 000	6 383
Intermediate hospitals etc.	23	60 000	3 347
Local hospitals (including health centres with beds)	172	25 000	12 105
Private hospitals	51		3 150
State hospital	1		308
Paediatric hospital	1		170
Mental hospitals			
State mental hospitals	2		585
Central mental hospitals	22	215 000	10 483
Other mental hospitals	47	90 000	8 798
Tuberculosis hospitals			
Central sanatoria and tuberculosis departments of general central hospitals	18	260 000	2 296
Other tuberculosis hospitals	2	385 000	112
Other hospitals or special institutions	356		16 513

Hospital services

There are five categories of public hospitals. Besides general hospitals, mental hospitals, tuberculosis hospitals (sanatoria) and the hospitals of special institutions (such as the army and prisons) there are beds in most health centres for acute cases, minor illnesses, aftercare and observation, but also for chronically ill patients.

All hospital physicians are salaried. The working week is 37 hours. Private practice outside working hours is authorized. There are some semiprivate beds in most hospitals.

In principal the patient pays for "board" during the hospital stay. In 1978 the all-inclusive charges were the equivalent of US $3.4–4.1 in general hospitals, US $3.4 in mental hospitals and health centre hospital departments. No charges are made in tuberculosis hospitals.

Shown above are hospital bed statistics for December 1976.

Other medical care establishments

The primary health care services were organized in 1972, when a special act on primary health care came into force, bringing the previously sectorial elements into a comprehensive system under the local authority. It is intended to facilitate continuous planned development. The health centre is primarily the unit for primary care serving 10 000 or more of the population. The system now covers the whole country, with 218 health centres.

Besides general practice, maternal and child health services, school health, dentistry for children, and physiotherapy, most centres have some beds for chronic diseases cases; laboratory and X-ray services would not be justifiable for ambulatory care alone.

In addition to hospitals the following institutions gave medical care in 1976:

	Number	Population covered
Health centres	218	20 000
Tuberculosis dispensaries	46	100 000
Mental health centres	86	50 000
Rheumatic disease dispensaries	19	
Private ambulatory care institutions	638	
Private practitioners' surgeries (mainly part-time)	2 000	

All hospitals have an outpatient polyclinic. In intermediate hospitals it serves both for specialist consultations and for inpatient admissions. The physicians of hospital departments usually also serve in the polyclinic. Specialized dispensaries are a part of tuberculosis and mental health services. The dispensaries for tuberculosis usually serve about 100 000 people and mental health dispensaries 50 000.

There have been some difficulties in ensuring cooperation between primary care, specialist outpatient care and hospital services under the same local authorities, due mainly to prevailing attitudes and to some extent to shortages of personnel.

Environmental health

In 1976 about 67% of the population was living in households connected to piped water supplies and about 60% in households connected to sewerage systems. There are health inspections of water systems; some 40 000 samples are tested in laboratories annually and about 15% of the samples are found unfit for human use—mostly those from private wells.

Air pollution has so far been local; the control

measures cover areas where the problems are worst. Single measurements are giving way to continuous measurements, most of them made in the more populated southern coastal area. The noise measurements made in urban areas are taken into account in zoning and housing programmes; the environmental health authorities check plans with a view to noise prevention. Water pollution control measures are the responsibility of the National Water Board. The National Board of Health has issued microbiological, physical and chemical quality standards for household water. Inspections are made to determine how these standards are met. There are also public health standards for public beaches, swimming baths and camping grounds.

Communicable disease prevention and control

The communicable disease situation has been rather stable in recent years. Meningitis cases were so numerous in 1975 that an immunization programme was carried out to bring the disease under control. Sexually transmitted diseases continue at a rather high level—though the number of gonorrhoea cases is slowly falling. The number of syphilis cases is rising.

Child and school health services carry out immunization programmes. The adult population receives certain vaccinations; for example, rubella vaccination is given to mothers after delivery at the hospital of delivery, and poliomyelitis vaccine boosters are given to men in the army.

Noncommunicable disease prevention and control

The National Board of Health has set up task forces to draft plans for the care of specific diseases. Mental health, circulatory diseases, rheumatic diseases and diabetes are already the subject of a prevention and care programme, and others are under consideration.

The national plan for organizing the primary services includes development of preventive measures for mental health, with closer cooperation between mental health services and the primary and social services.

In 1977 the Office of Health Education was formally established at the National Board of Health. It has so far created antismoking and nutrition programmes.

Health laboratory services

There is a central government-owned Public Health Laboratory with seven regional laboratories to serve the health centres, hospitals and private practitioners. Main functions are prevention of contagious diseases, microbiological, immunobiological and chemical examinations, vaccine production, evaluative scientific research and quality control. The central laboratory has bacteriological, immunobiological, virological and production services and, since 1976, also an epidemiological research unit.

Maternal and child health

The objective is for expectant mothers to visit the health centre once a month during the first 8 months of pregnancy and once a week during the last month, with a check-up 5–12 weeks after delivery. This objective has almost been reached. There is also a preparatory programme; every mother receives an infant and child care kit.

Infants aged two weeks are checked in the health centre for handicaps, malformations and illnesses, and are included in the vaccination programme (see above). About 1.6 million examinations are made annually at the health centres.

School and university health services

Schoolchildren are covered by the services of the health centre in the district in which the school is situated. The services include both the health of the 800 000 pupils and the health aspects of the school facilities. Physicians examine some 500 000 schoolchildren annually, and well over a million visits are made to the school nurses during the year. Chronic conditions have been found in nearly 3% of pupils annually in recent years.

Student health services are organized by the Student Health Foundation, which maintains a health centre in 15 communities for 75 000 enrolled students.

Occupational health

Of the 2.2 million employees, only half are covered by organized occupational health services, while 200 000 receive the services organized by health centres mainly for small enterprises. Municipalities and communes provide occupational · health services to their employees—smaller communes are served by the health centres.

A government proposal to extend the specialized services to all employees and self-employed persons was to become effective on 1 January 1979. Employers would be made responsible for organizing the services for their employees and health insurance would reimburse 60% of the costs.

Health care of the elderly

Statistics indicate that population growth is strongest in the oldest age groups. Demand for services have been so great that in spite of noticeable increase in both inpatient and outpatient services, with special attention to the elderly, the health centres still have plans to enlarge them during the present five-year planning period and even beyond. For the next five years, 400 new beds will be provided annually in health centres, and beds will be transferred from the homes of the aged to the health centres, which will be staffed accordingly.

Accident prevention

Despite great interest in accident prevention, there is no formal comprehensive programme. However, several special groups are active in this sphere.

The health centres work to prevent home accidents in general and accidents involving children in particular, the Traffic Safety Board to prevent traffic accidents, and the occupational health authorities to diminish health hazards at work. The Institute of Occupational Health has important research and teaching activities, and the occupational health services in the health centres rely heavily on this Institute to teach the professionals needed for their development.

Emergency and relief services

Under the Primary Health Act 1972, health centres organize their own transport and ambulance services or make the necessary arrangements with a public or private agency. The majority of such services are provided by privately owned vehicles, the health centres providing only about 10% of the transport services with their own vehicles. In 1976 there were altogether 570 vehicles, of which the health centres owned 61 and other communal agencies (mostly fire departments) 127. Current national health plans include provision for a maximum of 50 additional vehicles yearly for the health centres.

When transport is not provided by a health centre, health insurance will refund the costs, except for a patient fee which in 1977 was equivalent to US $ 0.50.

Oral health

In 1976 the dental health services provided by the health centres free of charge covered all children under 17 years of age. Health centres also provided dental services to the 245 000 adult patients in 1976, but the majority are treated by private dentists. There is no refund from the health insurance for dental services.

Of 1 245 000 children under 17 years of age in 1976, 64% were examined in the health centres and 68% of those examined needed dental care. Plans include measures to raise the age limit to 18, to provide dental care free of charge to expectant mothers and to increase the dental services for the adult population in the health centres, where the charges are lower than those of private dentists.

Drug monitoring

The number of licensed pharmaceuticals has been slowly decreasing; there were 3702 in 1976. Finland has a monitoring system for adverse reactions and is a participant in the WHO international monitoring system. The register received 530 reports from physicians in 1976. The National Board of Health has a register of congenital malformations which also serve for the monitoring of adverse reactions to drugs. The quality control of pharmaceuticals is effected by the Medicines Control Laboratory.

Health education

Health education, traditionally a part of maternal and child health and school health services, is to cover the whole population through the primary services at health centres. In order to coordinate these activities and issue guidelines for hospitals and health centres, the National Board of Health now has a health education office, which has produced recommendations for antismoking activities and nutritional education. Health centres have organized group health education sessions on family planning, mental health, physical exercise, and nutrition.

Health information services

These form an integral part of the health care system. Data are collected at the local level, processed and included in the plans, which are sent to central authorities for approval. The central authorities in turn process regional and national data for the use of the local and district authorities.

Biomedical and health services research

Much of the research is done at local and regional level and is subsidized, like other health activities. In each of the five medical colleges there is a department of public health, whose tasks include research. The Academy of Sciences actively supports research and has appointed a commission to plan health service research. The National Board of Health's department for planning and evaluation does some research, and about one million Finnish marks are distributed in grants for research and development. Numerous associations and foundations also support research.

The value of medical research was estimated at 73 million Finnish marks or 0.07% of gross domestic product in 1975.

Health manpower development

Health manpower development is the responsibility of the educational authorities, with health authority consultation. The licensing authority is the National Board of Health, which has computerized registers for all relevant personnel categories. Basic medical education takes six to seven years and the specialization about four years. There are State-controlled examinations for clinical specialties. Specialties number about 50% of total physicians. There is no organized further education for physicians.

Health manpower development figures for 1976 were as follows:

	Students	Graduates	Institutions
Physicians	3 561	460	5
Dentists	1 004	134	4
Pharmacists	663	144	3
Nurses (basic)	4 023	1 509	27
Practical nurses	2 255	2 249	26
Psychiatric attendants	474	343	10
Laboratory technicians	870	260	7
Radiographers	370	113	4
Dental technicians	89	11	1
Opticians	191	22	2
Physiotherapists	796	240	7
Children's nurses	395	463	9
Dental assistants	487	463	7
Massagists	257	331	10

Cost and financing of health care

The costs of health care provided by the local authority (commune, municipality) are partly refunded by the central Government. The mean level of subsidies is about 50%; they are weighted on the basis of the income level of the commune from 39% for the wealthiest to 70% for the poorest.

Of the total current health expenditure of 7201 million Finnish marks (6.6% of gross domestic product) in 1976, central and local government accounted for 4666 million, sickness insurance 923 million, and net private expenditure 1612 million.

Of total capital health expenditure of 477 million Finnish marks, central Government accounted for 275 million, local government for 202 million.

Current health expenditure by type of services was as follows: inpatient care, 3788 million Finnish marks, outpatient care, 3271 million, environmental health, 119 million, other services, 23 million, totalling 7201 million.

The inpatient cost per day averaged 194 marks in hospitals and 179 in health centres in 1976.

Appraisal of changes and major action taken (1973–1977)

The health trends are positive; the differences in health status between Finland and other Nordic countries are diminishing. Problems such as tuberculosis control seem to be susceptible of solution within a reasonable time.

The active development of primary care under special legislation is a major development. The health centre concept is very well suited to the country's circumstances. Another major achievement is the introduction of programme budgeting and appropriate planning. The health manpower shortage seems to have been remedied. There is no very marked change in the volume of health service research, but its importance is more generally recognized.

FRANCE

Basic population data

On 1 January 1977 the population of France was 52 701 975, with a density of 96.8 inhabitants per km^2. Paris and suburbs had over 9 million inhabitants.

The birth rate in 1976 was 13.6 and the death rate 10.5 per 1000 population, compared with 16.9 and 10.6 per in 1972. Life expectancy was 69.0 years for men in 1976 compared with 68.8 in 1972; for women it was 76.9 in 1976 compared with 76.1 in 1972.

Health situation

The only overall evaluation of the state of health of the nation is that afforded from the negative viewpoint of mortality and morbidity. All deaths must be certified by a medical doctor and then declared. In 1975 there were approximately 560 000 deaths, corresponding to a mortality rate of 10.7 per 1000 inhabitants. There is no continuous registration of illnesses and no overall index of morbidity, such as incidence or prevalence of diseases. Available data is based on annual statistics or *ad hoc* surveys, which, while they do not permit the exact frequency of occurrence of the various diseases to be determined, provide interesting information on the distribution of different forms of pathology. Diseases of the circulatory system stand out as a high priority area. In addition, the importance of tumours also emerges clearly in view of the number of deaths and long-term illnesses which result, and indicates the vast number of therapeutic measures which are required.

The major causes of death are diseases of the circulatory system, tumours, accidents, poisoning and injuries, and symptoms and ill-defined conditions. But the ranking varies according to age, sex and social and professional position.

Accidents, in terms of both human lives and impact on the economy, are the leading cause of hospital morbidity. The majority of information sources place respiratory and digestive conditions amongst the five most prominent ailments; however, the sources differ over the exact ranking. In addition, the high proportion of mental disorders within overall morbidity—particularly in the case of long-term conditions—must be noted. Finally, musculoskeletal diseases and dental and muscular diseases constitute another of the most important causes of morbidity.

Administrative organization of the health services

Responsibility for public health lies with the Minister of Health and the Family, who is assisted by a Secretary of State.

The organization of services is integrated within the framework of the country's existing administrative divisions. In 1977, after a series of conclusive experiments, an important decree completed the unification of all the services responsible for state public health and social services, as well as others with similar aims. This was achieved ' by merging—at the regional level—the Social Security system, the Regional Social and Health Action Service and the General Health Inspectorate, and it coincided with the re-establishment—at the government level—of the Ministry of Health and the Family.

The reform has three objectives:

(1) greater cohesion between the various state services and the application of an overall health policy (this concerns the external health and social health services, as well as the other services previously separate from the Social Security system, and permits two very different advisory administrations to be merged in a single organization);

(2) administrative reform in each of the areas of activity affected by the merger, by re-establishing, through the new structure, unequivocal unity of command for the regional and the departmental director (they alone are responsible, and report to the Prefect on the functioning of their services);

(3) re-establishment of the balance between the various territorial levels of hierarchy, with greater consistency in the directives prepared by the central administration, and systematic participation of the various services in the determination of ministerial policy. The regions thus became the supporting structure in planning as well as in economic and social development.

Organization of medical care

Since January 1978 the various forms of health insurance have covered 100% of the population. In respect of the principles of the medical charter (free choice by the patient of his doctor, freedom of prescription, payment for services rendered and respect of medical confidentiality), an insurance system based on reimbursement has been adopted. With the exception of hospitalization costs—which are paid directly by the insurance company (whether for public or private institutions)—the patient is reimbursed for all or part of the doctor's fees and of the cost of medicaments. Generally the patients share represents 20% of the total costs. Medical care is provided by general practitioners or specialists in private practice, either individually or—as is increasingly the case—in groups, in public or in private hospitals, and in a small number of medical dispensaries created and run by the communities, mutual insurance companies, labour organizations and nonprofit associations.

Hospitals and similar establishments are classified according to the range of technical services they can offer, the type of patients they treat, and their organizational structure. A distinction is made between hospitals for acute illnesses, institutions for convalescence, cure, rehabilitation, or mental disease treatment of medium duration, long-stay hospitals and, finally, local hospitals. In 1975 there were 892 state hospitals (430 000 beds), 2574 private hospitals (172 000 beds), 55 state tuberculosis hospitals (9200 beds), and 114 mental hospitals (106 000 beds). This gives a total of 717 000 beds, slightly less than 14 beds per 1000 inhabitants.

Organization of preventive medicine

In the area of health the Seventh Plan gave priority to preventive measures, to which both planning and decision-making bodies were specially adapted, while substantial financial means were made available for the purpose.

The new orientation essentially aims at education and information of the public, and training of medicosocial staff and teachers.

Education and information efforts concentrate on those risk factors which have wide-ranging consequences, such as tobacco and alcohol, which are clearly implicated in cardiovascular disease and cancer.

Prevention of diseases attributable to environmental factors is one of the Ministry of Health's primordial tasks. This mission is carried out in conjunction with the other relevant ministerial departments such as the Department of Agriculture in the case of nutrition, the Department of the Environment in the case of pollution and the Department of Equipment in the case of housing.

The development of health consequences of the presence of pollutants in various areas of the environment requires that research be carried out. The latter is aimed at determining the short-, medium- and especially the long-range effects, on the human organism, of exposure to small concentrations of pollutants in the environment. Within this context, meteorological and medical data are being studied.

The network of 17 poison control centres installed in hospital centres, in conjunction with the emergency medical aid services, as well as the hospitals' own clinical toxicology services, permit poisoning emergencies to be dealt with.

Surveillance of sanitary conditions in the environment aims to monitor qualitative changes, facilitate epidemiological studies, set up early warnings systems and supervise the enforcement of existing regulations.

The Minister of Health and the Family is providing assistance within the framework of the European Economic Community in drafting international regulations concerning environmental hygiene, and at the national level collaborates with the Ministry of the Environment, which has a coordinating mission in this area. The regulations deal with drinking-water, water for recreational activities, water treatment, housing, and chemical and other products. Regulations concerning the use of asbestos are being drafted under the direction of the Ministry of Health and the Family.

Responsibility for communicable diseases control is situated at the community level, and particularly at the level of the *départements*. The following vaccinations are mandatory for children: smallpox, tetanus, diphtheria, poliomyelitis and tuberculosis. These, as well as typhoid and paratyphoid vaccinations, are also compulsory for certain professional groups such as hospital personnel. Each *département* has a public health laboratory, which generally also serves as a water testing laboratory.

The Ministry of Health is drafting health regulations related to procreation, and to the surveillance of young children; the question of custody is a primary concern of social welfare services related to preventive measures.

A number of public bodies complement the work of private practitioners in a certain number of specialized areas, notably in the case of tuberculosis, venereal diseases, psychiatry and maternal and child health.

Tuberculosis cases are decreasing in frequency as well as in seriousness. This is confirmed by study of the specific mortality and morbidity rates. Thus, in 1975, tuberculosis mortality (all forms and ages) was 0.05 per 1000 inhabitants— or 0.05% of deaths from all causes. In 1976, according to the data provided by compulsory notification, morbidity was 37 per 100 000 population. Tuberculosis control as a whole is now the responsibility of a specialized hospital service. This service operates through multidisciplinary teams in dispensaries in geographical sectors.

As of 1 January 1977, the control of sexually transmitted diseases was organized around the 411 special dispensaries or sections of general dispensaries, and 145 units in penal institutions.

The organization in sectors of psychiatric services for adults, children and adolescents is progressing. Specialized psychiatric hospitals are giving way to psychiatric services located in general hospitals, permitting the patient to be treated closer to the home surroundings.

Maternal and child care includes compulsory premarital examinations of both parties. Examinations during pregnancy, and close surveillance of the newborn and of infants, are aimed at early identification of possible handicaps and, later, at monitoring physical and mental development. Demographic policy has led to the inclusion in legislation on social security and social assistance of important measures favouring the family.

The school health service assures the medical surveillance of children enrolled in the preschool, elementary and secondary school systems, as well as of their teachers (only preventive medicine for students in higher education comes under the Ministry of Education).

Cancer control outside the private medical sector and hospital system comprises 26 specialized centres for advanced consultations. In 100 cities which do not have such centres a particular effort is made in the area of the prevention of cancers associated with alcohol and tobacco and in early detection and treatment of cancer of the uterus.

Cardiovascular disease epidemiological research centres work in cooperation with neighbouring countries and with WHO. They have identified the risk factors in this area and their respective importance.

An increase in drug addiction has made it necessary to organize specific treatment and prevention units linked to provide a therapeutic chain where the drug addict can find a form of care adapted to each phase of his treatment.

A large antitobacco campaign was launched in 1975. This includes legislative measures such as almost complete banning of advertising for tobacco and limiting of smoking in certain public areas, as well as educational measures such as an information campaign concerning the effects of smoking on health and the introduction of information on the dangers of smoking into medical school syllabuses and secondary school programmes.

Organization of biomedical research

Biomedical research is carried out partly by the National Institute of Health and Medical Research, the Pasteur Institutes and the Radium Institute, under the Ministry for Health and Social Security, and partly by universities and the National Centre for Scientific Research, under the Ministry for Universities. The Ministry for Industry, Commerce and Crafts is also involved through the Commission for Atomic Energy and the National Centre for Space Studies, as is the Ministry for Agriculture through the National Institute for Agronomic Research, and the General Delegation for Scientific and Technical Research through concerted action on basic credits for research.

The desire to define a coherent national research policy despite the diversity of institutions competing to attain common goals has led to the definition of a functional overall research commitment, designed according to a set of goals and subject to interministerial coordination—a responsibility assumed in 1974 by the Ministry of Industry and Research, transferred in April 1977 to the Prime Minister and delegated to his Secretary of State for Research, who has authority over the General Delegate for Scientific and Technical Research.

A committee for the coordination of biomedical research was set up in 1967, composed of representatives of ministerial departments and interested groups and presided by the General Delegate for Scientific and Technical Research, under the jurisdiction of the Minister for Research.

Definition of biomedical research policy and priorities

The priority accorded to biomedical research in the Sixth Plan and constantly reinforced in research budgets from 1971 to 1975 was confirmed once again in the Seventh Plan for Economic and Social Development (1976–1980).

The objective can be defined as the identification of priority areas to be strongly promoted within a programme of priority action for the "development of the national scientific potential" correlated with steady support for less crucial sectors. First, three basic disciplines essential to the efficiency of finalized research in the life sciences are to be developed: basic and applied immunology; basic and applied microbology; and physicochemical and biochemical research on molecular interactions.

Priority areas in finalized programmes include: the brain, mental health and behaviour; the reproductive processes, genetics, perinatal and normal and pathological development; and medication and molecular and clinical pathology.

Finally, in order to ensure a better quality of life, research must be reinforced in disease prevention, public health and health economics.

Financing of biomedical research

In 1976 the total public funds for biomedical research were estimated at 1800 million francs, of which just over 700 million represents spending on research by universities in the form of teaching grants and 1070 million in research grants subject to the interministerial procedure governing the overall research commitment, divided as follows: 392 million francs administered by the Ministry for Health (345 million for the National Institute for Health and Medical Research and the associated central service for protection against ionizing radiation; 47 million for other relevant bodies under the aegis of the Ministry for Health), and 549 million administered by the Ministry for Universities (471 million for the National Centre of Scientific Research and 78 million for specific university

research grants), the remaining 129 million being administered through budgetary allocations for biomedical research to bodies dependent on other Ministries (41 million of this goes to work financed by research funds of the General Delegation for Scientific and Technical Research).

Total credits for biomedical research under the overall research commitment were increased during the Sixth Plan from 581 million francs in 1971 to 936 million in 1975 (an average annual growth rate of 13%), then to 1070 million in 1976.

Numbers and training of health personnel

As of 1 January 1976 there were 80 954 physicians in active service (one to 650 inhabitants). Other health personnel included:

Dentists	26 326
Pharmacists	19 352
Midwives	9 227
Nurses	203 106
Masseurs, kinesitherapists	30 281
Speech therapists	5 413
Orthopaedists	775
Hearing-aid technicians	1 011
Chiropodists	6 252

Cost and financing of the health services

Health spending in the period 1974–1977 can be broken down as shown below (in millions of francs).

Major developments in the period 1974–1978

Public health

Preventive health measures have been reinforced by: development of health education (especially campaigns against smoking and on nutrition for infants and pregnant women); continuation of the perinatal programme; reorganization and reinforcement of the external services

	1974		1975		1976		1977	
Hospital care	33 776	(42.2%)	44 326	(44.3%)	55 762	(47 6%)	65 057	(49. %)
Outpatient and home care	25 171	(31.4%)	30 641	(30.7%)	35 061	(29.9%)	38 799	(29. %)
Medical supplies	20 543	(25.7%)	34 312	(24.3%)	25 481	(21.8%)	26 363	(20. %)
Transport of patients	590	(0.7%)	717	(0.7%)	826	(0.7%)	940	(0. %)
Total	80 080		99 996		117 130		131 159	

of the Ministry of Health and the Family. Health protection has taken the form of different measures such as legal provisions to avoid excessive medical radiation and to modify prenatal examinations. For better family health care, legislative and regulatory provisions have been introduced on voluntary interruption of pregnancies and family planning, within the framework of a family policy intended to give greater responsibility to individuals and couples.

Hospitals

The provisions of the Hospital Law (1970) have been applied during the last few years. These include participation of private establishments in public service and the use of health cards to determine the number of beds and the major items of equipment necessary to cover the needs of the population.

Pharmaceuticals

Two noteworthy laws, on veterinary pharmacy (29 May 1975) and on cosmetics (10 July 1975), were passed, and a new policy on medication has been defined and applied to give stricter control of medical advertising, a closer check on tests, more severe standards for including drug costs in social security reimbursements, new

ways of fixing prices, which now have an important influence on the direction of the pharmaceutical industry, and a reorganization of the drug monitoring service.

Social security

Measures included generalization of social security by a law of 2 January 1978, better dental coverage, substantial increase in minimum old-age and retirement pensions, and improvement of family allowances.

Social welfare

Important advances were the directive of 30 June 1975 on handicapped persons, and the numerous applied texts (44 decrees were published), the law of 30 June 1975 on social and medicosocial institutions, and the two priority actions included in the Seventh Plan, one concerning care of the elderly, the other the family.

Research

Priority for research in the Seventh Plan, aimed at reinforcing the scientific potential of the country, has meant substantial credits for medical research as well as better-organized working facilities.

GERMAN DEMOCRATIC REPUBLIC

General background

The German Democratic Republic is a socialist country. There are 15 counties—including Berlin—divided into 219 districts. Of the national income, 95% is contributed by the public sector, 1% by the semipublic sector and 4% by the private sector. Industry is the leading economic sector, and there is a high degree of industrialization of agriculture. Of the population, 74% live in communities of more than 2000 inhabitants; 25% live in cities with more than 100 000 inhabitants. The population on 31 December 1976 was 16 767 030, which, for an area of 108 179 km^2, gives a population density

of 155 inhabitants per km^2. Population in the age group 0–14 years numbered 3 491 258, those of 15–64 years, 10 545 840, those of 65–74 years, 1 757 012 and those of 75 and over, 972 920.

Two world wars have produced an unfavourable age and sex structure, the former characterized by a large proportion of old people, which is also due to high life expectancy; 16% of the population are 65 years of age or over.

The population decreased by 2.3 per 1000 in 1976, the birth rate being 11.6 per 1000, the death rate 13.0 per 1000.

Male life expectancy at birth is 68.82, at 65 years it is 80.88; female life expectancy is 74.42 (89.25).

	1973	1974	1975	1976
Mean population	16 979 620	16 924 737	16 850 125	16 786 057
Number of live births	180 336	179.127	181 798	195 483
Birth rate (per 1000 population)	10.6	10.6	10.8	11.6
Number of deaths	231 960	229 062	240 389	233 733
Death rate (per 1000 population)	13.7	13.5	14.3	13.9
Natural increase (%)	−3.0	−3.0	−3.5	−2.3
Number of infant deaths	2 806	2 844	2 885	2 727
Infant mortality rate (per 1000 live births)	15.6	15.9	15.9	14.0
Number of deaths, 1–14 years	1 682	1 512	1 592	1 413
Death rate, 1–14 years (per 1000 population at risk)	0.5	0.4	0.5	0.4
Number of maternal deaths	49	42	39	38
Maternal mortality rate (per 1000 live births)	0.3	0.2	0.2	0.2

Country health situation

Population and some other statistics for the period under review are shown above.

Of the 233 733 deaths recorded in 1976, the main causes were—diseases of arteries, arterioles and capillaries, 51 519 (30.7 per 10 000 population), ischaemic heart disease and other forms of heart disease, 43 434 (25.9), malignant neoplasms, 37 165 (22.1), hypertensive disease, 19 224 (11.5), bronchitis, emphysema and asthma, 9816 (5.8).

The communicable diseases most frequently notified in 1976 were—feverish infection of the respiratory tract (3791.9 per 10 000 population), mumps (35.0), scarlet fever (19.9), infectious hepatitis (3.8), and viral influenza (3.7).

Administrative organization of the health services

Health authorities

The health service is administered by the Government. Social welfare services are integrated into the national health service. Basic health policy decisions are made by the Ministry of Health at the highest administrative level if not taken by the People's Chamber (parliament) or the Council of Ministers. In accordance with the political and administrative structure, there are health and social welfare departments both in county councils (intermediate administrative level) and in district councils (lower administrative level). The departments are headed by the county or district health officer, who is elected by the "people's representation," at the respective level, from its own ranks. He is advised by medical specialists. The health and social welfare departments of the county and district councils are under the technical control and supervision of the technical department of the higher level and under the political and administrative control and supervision of the "people's representation" of the same level and its council. At the central, county and district level there are governmental sanitary inspectorates, which are responsible for management and supervision in the fields of protection against infection, of environmental health and food and nutritional hygiene.

Health laws and regulations

A great number of laws and provisions essential to the further development of the health and social welfare services were promulgated in the period under review. The following provisions are of particular importance:

Joint decision of the Politburo of the Central Committee of the Socialist Unity Party, the Council of Ministers and the National Executive of the Confederation of Free German Trade Unions, on further measures for the implementation of the social policy programme adopted by the Eighth Party Congress (25 September 1973);

Order of 18 December 1973 on expert medical appraisals;

Law of 19 December 1973 on trade in narcotic drugs (Narcotic Drugs Law);

Order No. 1 of 23 May 1974 on the advanced training of physicians and dentists (Medical Specialists and Dental Specialists Rules);

Order No. 2 of 23 May 1974 on the advanced training of physicians and dentists (sub-specialization of medical and dental specialists);

Ordinance of 14 November 1974 on the workers' and salaried employees' insurance system;

Order of 19 June 1974 on medical examinations to determine the fitness of workers;

Order of 29 November 1974 on the formation of retail prices and the application procedure for prices of medicaments and similar products;

International Health Regulations (1969) adopted by the Twenty-second World Health Assembly, 1969, as amended by the Twenty-sixth World Health Assembly, 1973;

Civil Code of 19 June 1975, and Introductory Law of 19 June 1975 for the Civil Code;

Ordinance of 4 July 1975 on the performance of organ transplantations;

Order of 21 August 1975 on the recognition of the qualifications of nurses and other middle-level health personnel by the professional schools for medical personnel;

Ordinance of 11 December 1975 on the State Sanitary Inspectorate;

Ordinance of 22 April 1976 on preschool educational establishments;

Curriculum for the study of medicine, April 1976;

Curriculum for the study of dentistry, May 1976;

Order of 13 January 1977 on the registration of physicians (Registration of Physicians Rules);

Order of 13 January 1977 on the registration of dentists (Registration of Dentists Rules);

Order of 13 January 1977 on the registration of pharmacists (Registration of Pharmacists Rules);

Labour Code of the German Democratic Republic of 16 June 1977;

Order of 14 October 1976 on the Pharmacopoeia of the German Democratic Republic;

Law of 7 April 1977 on trade in poisons (Poisons Law);

Ordinance of 29 July 1976 on further improvements in social assistance to the seriously and very seriously handicapped;

Notification of 24 September 1976 of adoption of the amendments to Articles 34 and 55 of the Constitution of the World Health Organization adopted by the Twenty-sixth World Health Assembly on 22 May 1973.

Health plan and country health programming

The plans for health and social services are part of the overall national economic plans, close coordination being maintained between the planning process for health and social services and that of other sectors. Planning is carried out at the national level and at the county, district, municipal and community levels, and by the health establishments. Long-term plans cover a period of 15–20 years, medium-term plans a five-year period and short-term plans cover one year. Long-term planning identifies demands in the health and social welfare fields and establishes priorities to meet these demands. The main objectives are the improvement of the health status and further increases in life expectancy.

The prime task under the present five-year plan for the development of the national economy in the period 1976–1980 is the further raising of the material and cultural living standards of the people on the basis of rapid growth in socialist production, scientific and technological progress and labour productivity. Accordingly, the focus is on enhancing the quality and effectiveness of medical and social care, especially through concentration on key medical research tasks and the planned translation of research findings into medical practice, and on the prevention, early detection and early treatment of widespread disease; extension of surgical specialties; the construction of new, and modernization of existing, outpatient and inpatient establishments; increased admissions to professional schools for nurses; and more places in crèches, and in homes and nursing homes for the elderly. Particular attention is given to construction and modernization work on the Charité (teaching hospital), Berlin, and the completion of the construction of hospitals and polyclinics in other counties.

Curative and preventive services and programmes

Outpatient and inpatient care is provided as primary or specialized care according to the number of medical specialties and the degree of specialization of the diagnostic and therapeutic establishment. Inpatient primary care is provided by local and district hospitals. Specialized inpatient services are available at larger district and at county hospitals as well as at university clinics. Some highly specialized inpatient establishments are under the direct control of the Ministry of Health.

The area covered by a hospital for inpatient primary care is divided into several territorial units for outpatient primary care. There are also the polyclinics with six or more specialities for outpatient care and outpatient units with two to six specialities. Because of the State character of the health service, the proportion of the private sector is small; 18% of dentists and 4% of physicians work in their own private practices. Differences between rural and urban medical care have been largely eliminated.

Hospital services

In 1976 there were a total of 571 hospitals with 180 466 beds (107.5 per 10 000 population), distributed as follows:

	Number	Beds
State hospitals under central management	123	19 503
State hospitals under local management	359	147 966
Confessional hospitals	81	12 541
Private hospitals	8	456

The total number of treatments was 2 342 810 (1395.7 per 10 000 population), the number of patients treated was 13 per bed. In all there were 49 887 627 hospital-patient-days. The number of physicians at hospitals was 10 566.

Medical care was also provided at the following establishments outside hospitals (as on 31 December 1976):

Polyclinics	422
Polyclinics at places of work	112
Medium-sized outpatient units	641
Outpatient units at places of work	306
Small outpatient units	1 058
State surgeries	1 622
State dental surgeries	998
Working consulting rooms	2 084

Physicians working in outpatient facilities numbered 16 997, or one to 988 inhabitants, in 1976. Visiting nurses numbered 5146. Consultations in State outpatient facilities totalled 147 167 700. Dentists working in outpatient facilities numbered 8108, or one to 2070 inhabitants. Consultations in State dental outpatient facilities totalled 25 271 488.

Special services and programmes

The tasks of the State Sanitary Inspectorate comprise protection against infections, including the prevention and control of communicable diseases, vaccination and the manufacture of vaccines and other immunizing agents; disinfection; sterilization; control of pests constituting a hazard to health; transportation of the sick; communal hygiene, including the residential environment, public construction, and town and communal planning; recreation, and holidays for children and young people; use of clothing material; measures to preserve the quality of the soil, the air, and water; noise, collection, disposal and recycling of manufacturing and consumer wastes; food and nutritional hygiene, including surveillance of trade in foodstuffs and consumer goods; establishment of a health-promoting diet; public catering; protection against contaminants and poisons; and disposal of the dead.

As a result of comprehensive preventive measures and of general improvements in living conditions, communicable diseases have lost their former importance. In 1976 communicable diseases—excluding tuberculosis—caused a mere 0.22% of all deaths. There has been no case of poliomyelitis since 1962, of diphtheria since 1974 and of tetanus in children since 1974. These achievements and the reduced morbidity from pertussis and measles are attributable to the consistent implementation of the Government's vaccination programme, which provides compulsory vaccinations against smallpox, poliomyelitis, tuberculosis, diphtheria, tetanus, measles, and pertussis.

Because of high life expectancy, the chronic and degenerative diseases more frequent in higher age groups are of great public health significance. There are phased programmes for the control and treatment of certain chronic diseases; they were designed to ensure adequate care in accordance with local conditions, and are in differing stages of implementation. Those against diabetes, malignant neoplasms, mental disorders, cardiovascular diseases, chronic renal diseases, chronic pulmonary diseases and rheumatic diseases are under way.

Expectant mothers receive attention in prenatal units, of which there were 892 in 1976. The activities of these units are closely coordinated with those of inpatient obstetric establishments. Effort for early coverage and attendance have resulted in 87% of all expectant mothers' consulting the prenatal units and receiving specialized care before the end of the sixteenth week of pregnancy.

Child health centres exist for infants and young children up to three years of age in crèches. In 1976, crèches accommodated 570 per 1000 children aged 0–3 years. Compulsory vaccinations are administered in the centres. Children and young people between 3 and 18 years of age receive health care in the establishments of the Youth Health Service, where compulsory examinations and vaccinations are performed. Almost all preschool children undergo school fitness examinations 18 and 6 months prior to school admission; specialized care is organized where necessary. Mass examinations are carried out for schoolchildren at three different ages, as well as for school-leavers. Early vocational guidance is given to physically or mentally handicapped school-leavers.

The rehabilitation of handicapped persons is the responsibility of all medical sectors. Numerous legal provisions cover school education and vocational and social rehabilitation for the handicapped. Establishments include special schools and workshops.

There are more than 105 000 places in more than 1200 homes and nursing homes for the elderly. In the residential quarters, the People's Solidarity Organization provides additional assistance in the form of household help and meals for elderly people living alone and in need.

The exclusively State-run factory health service performs specific tasks in the field of occupational health. It also provides primary medical care for employees and to some degree for local inhabitants.

There is a unified system of emergency medical services. The Rapid Medical Aid Service provides medical care to injured persons and those with an acute illness, on the spot and during transportation, until their admission to an inpatient care establishment. The service has divisions for urgent medical aid and urgent home visiting. The former is a mobile specialized medical care service, while the latter is a mobile primary care service.

The Medicaments Law of 1964 stipulates that only such medicaments may be marketed as have proven their efficiency and safety, and the use of which is necessary for the preservation and promotion of health. Trade in medicaments is subject to permanent government supervision. Drugs and chemicals for laboratory and clinical diagnosis, like medicaments, are subject to compulsory notification and standardization, irrespective of whether or not they are intended for direct application in human medicine.

Health education is considered a duty to society. The centre of health education is the Public Health Museum in Dresden. Numerous organizations—in particular, the German Red Cross of the German Democratic Republic—are actively involved in health education.

Biomedical and health services research

Medical research is carried out at three different levels of priority:

– research assignments under the State plan, in cardiovascular diseases, tumours, protection against infections, occupational health, medical diagnostics and medical aspects of environmental protection;
– research assignments, under the central plan of the Ministry of Health, on a total of 19 task complexes including perinatology, human genetics, diabetes mellitus, health protection of children and young people, and gerontology;
– research assignments under the responsibility of research institutions such as medical institutes at university level.

Research associations and research teams have been established combining interdisciplinary research capacities from different public sectors, with a view to fulfilling the above-mentioned medical research commitments. They work according to joint research programmes under the supervision and control of the Ministry of Health, which is advised by a Council for Medical Science.

Health manpower development

Health and social welfare manpower development and planning are part of governmental manpower planning and, as such, of national economic planning. In accordance with the administrative organization of the health service, planning is carried out at the respective level. Training and further training is part of the fully integrated socialist education system. The study of medicine and dentistry takes place at six universities and three medical academies, that of pharmacy at two universities. Highly qualified teaching staff for professional schools for medical personnel are trained at the Humboldt University of Berlin. One year of premedical training in nursing is compulsory before entering the six-year course in medicine or the five-year course in dentistry. Graduates of these courses are awarded the diploma in medicine or dentistry. The diploma is required for State registration as a physician, dentist or pharmacist and for courses leading to the two doctoral levels A (doctor of medicine) and B (doctor of medical sciences). Undergraduate studies are followed by compulsory specialization in one of 32 branches of medicine and three in dentistry; this specialization takes four to five years of on-the-job training under the guidance of supervisors of advanced training. Subspecialization is provided additionally in such fields as cardiology/-angiology, diabetology, traumatology, and gastroenterology.

The continued postgraduate training of medical and dental specialists is the responsibility of the Academy of Postgraduate Medical Training and of a countrywide system of clinics offering postgraduate courses. Important contributions to the advanced and postgraduate training of medical personnel are made by the medical societies, which every year organize congresses and symposia.

A total of 60 professional schools for medical personnel provide three-year courses of studies in 17 different branches to nurses, children's nurses, midwives, dental nurses, crèche instructors, physiotherapists, medical laboratory technicians and other categories. The professional schools admit trainees having completed the tenth grade of comprehensive schooling.

Pharmaceutical engineers, medical preparators and other specific categories are trained at corresponding professional schools, correspondence courses of between three years six months and four years being available for most categories. Most of those trained at the professional schools may undergo further training in a speciality after two years of practical work. For example, nurses may become operating-theatre nurses, skilled nurses for anaesthesia and intensive therapy, or skilled nurses for psychiatry and neurology.

The training of skilled health and social welfare workers, such as masseurs, dieteticians, pharmacy specialists, and orthopaedic mechanics, takes two to three years.

In 1976 the establishments of the State health and social welfare system employed 429 613 workers and salaried employees of whom 32 097 were physicians (including those in private surgeries), 8108 dentists (including those in private surgeries) and 3498 pharmacists. The number of undergraduates in 1976 was 7020 in medicine, 2992 in dentistry and 437 in pharmacy.

Cost and financing of health services

Allocations for medical care, including the cost of medicaments, remedies and appliances defrayed by social security schemes, amounted to about 5% of the national income in 1976. An average of 305 marks per capita was made available from the national budget, not including social security. The real costs are, however, higher, because the firms, cooperative societies and other establishments make available considerable financial means for health protection.

All treatment, and preventive and rehabilitation measures by the medical and social welfare services, are free of charge. In addition, cash benefits such as sick pay and household money, disability and accident pensions, pregnancy and maternity allowances, financial aid for mothers of sick children, are paid. The cost of health and social welfare services is defrayed by the State and the social insurance schemes. All those gainfully employed contribute 10% of their wages, but no more than 60 marks per month, to the compulsory sickness and pensions insurance scheme.

Major developments in the period 1973–1977

There was a marked improvement in the health status of the population. Major achievements include significant reductions in infant and perinatal mortality, the repression of communicable diseases and improvements in the early detection and early treatment of certain diseases. Essential headway was made in occupational health.

Important changes were introduced into the training and further training of health and social welfare manpower. New regulations for medical undergraduate studies, postgraduate courses and professional schools for medical personnel were in large measure completed.

GERMANY, FEDERAL REPUBLIC OF

General background

The Federal Republic of Germany is a Federal State consisting of *Länder*, which include both city and territorial states. The *Länder* have their own national status, but are integrated in the Federal Republic. They have their own right to legislate and also participate in Federal legislation in the *Bundesrat*. They similarly implement not only their own laws but also Federal laws; and health and social legislation, in particular, typifies the federative state principle.

Geographically and climatically, the country's situation in central Europe gives rise to no special problems as far as health care is concerned.

The regional distribution of the population is marked by heavy concentrations in certain areas. In 1976 some 35% of the population were living in areas with over 100 000 inhabitants, some 45% – i.e., almost 28 million people—in conglomerations which covered approximately 7% of the total area of the country. In areas with particularly high concentrations of population (e.g., the Ruhr, the Rhine-Main area), density levels reach over 2000 inhabitants per km^2; in sparsely populated rural areas the density level is frequently less than 100 inhabitants per km^2.

In 1976 the social budget, which represented the sum total of the social services provided by the State institutions, public corporations and employers, amounted to 356 900 million marks; compared with the gross national product of 11 135 100 million marks this represented a proportion equal to 31.4% for social services (in 1960 it was 20%). Almost 40% of the social budget is spent on the care of the elderly and dependants, 30% on health and 15% on assistance to families. Social expenditure makes up one third of the public budget funds of the Federal Republic and its *Länder*, and is financed from contributions of insured persons and employers.

Country health situation

General

Changes in the health situation in recent years have been determined basically by the following factors: the infections and deficiency diseases of the past have been replaced by the diseases of "civilization" in an industrial society, mainly cardiovascular diseases, cancer and mental diseases. The manifold health consequences of changes in the natural and social environment cannot yet be fully assessed, but the conditions of professional and working life are not in keeping with the requirements of health.

To date, comprehensive surveys of the health status of the total population have not been conducted. However, a system of spot checks (microcensus) are made in selected households. In 1976 they showed that the most frequent diseases were those of the respiratory organs (23%), the circulatory system (22%) and of locomotion (13%). Some 5% of the population sampled suffered from mental disorders, and 1.3% were diabetic, while 7.2% had been injured in accidents.

Notifiable diseases

Certain infectious diseases are subject to compulsory notification, and for especially dangerous infectious diseases there is also an obligation to report suspected cases. The most frequent notifiable diseases in 1975 were as follows (cases per 100 000 population): gonorrhoea, 96.7; infectious enteritis, 48; scarlet fever, 43.5; and infectious hepatitis, 33.8. For most other diseases the figure was under one per 100 000.

Mortality by selected causes of death

Whereas in 1927 infectious diseases, including tuberculosis and pneumonia, were the most frequent cause of death, resulting in about 20% of

191

the total mortality, and the share of cardiac, vascular and circulatory diseases (about 15%), malignant neoplasms (about 12%) and so-called unnatural causes of death (about 5%) made up approximately one-half of the total mortality, today cardiovascular and circulatory diseases rank in first place, accounting for 46% of the total mortality; malignant neoplasms, with 20%, are the second most frequent cause of death; and unnatural causes represent 6%. Thus these three groups alone account for 72% of the total mortality. Infectious diseases, including tuberculosis and pneumonia, account for only 4% of total mortality.

Maternal and infant mortality

In the past few decades maternal mortality has fallen; in 1977 it still amounted to 34 per 100 000 live births. Infant mortality, at 15 per 1000 live births in 1977, reached its lowest point, mortality among male infants being about one-third higher than among females, and that among illegitimate infants more than 50% higher than among infants born in wedlock.

Hospital patients

In 1976 some 10 700 000 patients received inpatient treatment, 87.5% of these in hospitals for acute cases and 12.5% in special hospitals. The number of patient days totalled 219 600 000, a drop of 1% compared with the previous year. The average duration of hospital stay fell in 1976 by 0.7 days to 21.5 days; in hospitals for acute cases it fell from 16.7 to 16.3 days; and in special hospitals it rose from 60.8 to 61.2 days.

Administrative organization of the health services

The delineation of responsibilities between the Federal Republic and the *Länder* also holds good for the distribution of functions in the health service. In the area of social insurance, to which large parts of health care also belong, individual citizens also have substantial autonomy.

At both Federal and *Land* levels, competence is divided among various ministries, but their areas of responsibility differ from *Land* to *Land*. At the Federal level, questions pertaining to health are dealt with by the Federal Ministry for Youth, Family Affairs and Health (human and veterinary medicine, the professions, medicaments, pharmacy, foodstuffs and consumer protection); by the Federal Ministry of Labour and Social Affairs (social insurance, medical care under the sickness insurance system, hospitals, rehabilitation, labour protection); by the Federal Ministry of the Interior (environmental protection) and by the Federal Ministry of Research and Technology (research). The Federal Republic has no comprehensive right of legislation as far as health matters are concerned, but it has a limited role in relation to measures against infectious diseases and diseases which constitute a public danger; to the health professions; drugs and medicaments; narcotics; toxic substances; foodstuffs and other consumer items; social insurance and labour protection; financial support of hospitals; and public welfare.

Insofar as the Federal Republic has not been given or does not exercise jurisdiction, responsibility for legislation lies with the *Länder*, which also directly implement Federal laws. Coordination of activities is achieved by means of the Conference of Health Ministers, the Working Group of Medical Administrators, and a number of working groups of the Federal Republic and the *Länder*. Both the Federal Republic and the *Länder* have advisory bodies, such as the Federal Health Board and the health boards of the *Länder*.

Health laws and ordinances

The most important laws and ordinances since 1973 include those on hospital finances (1972); the Federal ordinance relating to nursing personnel; the law on the further development of health insurance (1976); the law on the containment of health insurance costs (1977); the Federal law on protection against emissions (1974); the law on detergents (1975); the ordinance on drinking-water (1975); the total reform of the law relating to foodstuffs (1974); the reform of the law relating to medicaments, and the law on rehabilitation (1974); the law relating to the severely disabled (1974); the law on work safety (1975); the ordinance on places of work (1975); and the radiology ordinance (1973).

Health plan and health programming in the Länder

There is no comprehensive national health plan, nor are there comprehensive plans in the *Länder*. Special programmes are drawn up according to needs in individual problem areas.

Curative and preventive services and programmes

The system of health care is a mixture of public and private services. Outpatient care is almost exclusively in the hands of physicians in independent practice, whereas inpatient care is provided by the hospitals. The State public health service performs functions in the field of health protection and assistance.

Planning is designed to secure an equitable distribution of health care resources, but in practice, and particularly in the field of outpatient care, there are differences in regional distribution. This results in lower densities of physicians in certain rural areas and particularly in areas on the edge of cities. Furthermore, there is a shortage of medical practitioners for general practice.

Hospital services

At the end of 1976 there were 118.3 hospital beds per 10 000 population, but with substantial differences among the various *Länder* with regard to bed density. The highest bed density is in a city state (178.1 per 10 000), while bed density in territorial states ranges from 124.5 to 104.9 per 10 000. The average level of bed utilization in 1976 was 82.6%.

Outpatient care

Outpatient medical care and services are provided for the population by the panel doctors' and panel dentists' associations, which bring together physicians and dentists who are in independent practice. As a rule, the services are provided in individual practices or in new forms of community and group practices.

At the end of 1976, some 56 969 of the 122 075 physicians practising in the Federal Republic were in private practices; and of the total of 33 858 practising dentists, 30 139 were in private practices. Of the 56 255 specialists physicians, 52.2% were engaged in outpatient care.

The principle for general medical care is that there should be one medical practitioner for 2400 inhabitants. Similarly, the need for specialist physicians of various kinds is based on the following numbers of population per specialist: ophthalmologist, 24 500; surgeon, 47 500; gynaecologist, 16 000, specialist in internal medicine, 10 000; paediatrician, 25 000;

neurologist, 50 000; and orthopaedist, 37 000. These figures largely correspond to the present ratio of specialist doctors to population at the Federal level.

Staff in nonmedical professions usually participate in outpatient care in the capacity of employees of a physician in private practice. The current development of a network of social care centres for nursing, care and counselling functions that are outside the scope of medical treatment, has resulted in such activities being carried out to an increasing degree autonomously, especially by nursing staff and social workers.

Public health service

In 1976 some 4068 physicians and 1814 dentists were engaged full-time in public health work; and there were 2603 social workers. The public health service does not participate in direct medical care.

Special services and programmes

Under the system of health care in the Federal Republic, with the extensive catalogue of functions of the statutory health insurance system, the number of special services and programmes is limited and the pattern of these functions cannot easily be compared with similar services and programmes in other countries. In addition to those already described, the following services should be mentioned:

The emergency environment programme of 1970 and other environment programmes are executed in part by other ministries or by authorities set up specifically for the purpose. The programmes are concerned not only with the prevention of hazards, but are intended to deal actively with all factors related to water, air, soil, noise, traffic and urban construction.

The prevention and control of infectious diseases is the province of the public health service, and at present there are no special programmes in this field. Maternal and child care is provided within the public health service, by private physicians, by hospitals and by independent associations. It covers family planning and family care, pregnancy counselling and preventive examinations, health assistance for the newborn and infants, and examinations of children aged 2–5 years.

School health care is a responsibility of the public health service. It includes periodic examinations, consultations with school doctors, and health welfare measures.

Occupational health is the subject of a programme which includes all measures necessary for correct organization of work from the point of view of health and places and conditions of work. The prevention and control of accidents come under this heading. Implementation of the programme is the responsibility of the works medical service, the public health service and the statutory accident insurance bodies in particular.

In addition to health care of the elderly within the framework of general health care, various measures are implemented by the Federal authorities and the *Länder* which are also relevant to health. For instance, help is given to senior citizens to maintain their independence for as long as possible, and to residents of special homes to maintain their ability to play an active part in the life of the community.

Emergency and auxiliary services are the responsibility of the *Länder*, most of which have organized 24-hour emergency services and coordinated the various emergency organizations and the fire service.

In the field of dental health, special reference should be made to child dental care, which is again the responsibility of the *Länder* and is oriented towards prevention.

The production, marketing, distribution and control of drugs is governed by the Drugs Act. Drugs may be marketed only when they have been tested by an acceptance procedure as to qualify, efficacy and safety. A stage-by-stage plan and the pooling of information on the monitoring, collection and evaluation of adverse reactions ensure that essential measures can be taken promptly in response to such reactions.

Health education is conducted by the Federal and *Länder* health authorities, schools and independent associations, and is coordinated by the Federal Centre for Health Education. The main aspects of its work are campaigns against drug and alcohol abuse, smoking, unsatisfactory nutrition and lack of exercise, and family planning advice.

Biomedical and health services research

Biomedical and health services research is not controlled centrally but is conducted by universities, clinics, major research institutions and health authorities of the Federal Republic and the *Länder*, by the Max Planck Association, and by private research institutions, partly on a nonprofit basis, and also by the research institutions of industry. This broad spectrum of participating institutions is promoted in varying forms by the Federal Republic, the *Länder* and other public or private bodies.

In 1976 the Federal authorities spent a total of 430 400 000 marks to promote research and development in the health field, and in 1978 the Federal Government prepared a general programme for research and technology in the service of health and an action programme to improve coordination and to suggest priorities in health research.

Health manpower development

There is minimal ministerial responsibility for health manpower planning. In order to determine needs, forecasts are prepared at regular intervals by the Federal authorities and by the *Länder* and others involved. The information obtained from these forecasts is evaluated in connexion with the development of medical faculties and universities and other relevant educational institutions.

Competence for admission to the medical and allied professions lies with the Federal authorities, which also control training given at the appropriate faculties of universities, schools for specialist professions, clinics, hospitals and other health service institutions. In 1976 there were 28 medical faculties with 9629 persons commencing their studies. These included students in general medical faculties (8285) and faculties of dental medicine (1344). In addition there were faculties of veterinary medicine (674 students), and pharmaceutical faculties (1835 students). There were, in 1975, also 1765 schools for health workers, including 944 public and 821 private schools. By far the largest number of pupils (52 473) were being trained for the nursing profession.

In 1976 some 5559 licences to practise were issued to physicians and 1171 to dentists. In 1965 there was one physician to 691 inhabitants; there was one to 564 in 1976. Between 1965 and 1976 the number of specialist physicians increased by 54% and the number of nonspecialist physicians by 34%. The number of physicians practising in hospitals has also increased steadily over the past few years and has more than doubled since 1960. Likewise, there was a steady increase in the number of nursing staff in hospitals, from 110 570 in 1960 to 247 642 in 1976.

Costs and financing of health services

The health care system in the Federal Republic is financed by various bodies – State, statutory health insurance system, private health insurance schemes and other systems such as social assistance—and the total expenditure is not known. However, since over 90% of the population are members of the statutory health insurance system, the figures for expenditure in this give the most reliable idea of cost trends.

In 1973 and 1974 the increase in such expenditure (20%) was particularly rapid; in 1976 the rate of increase fell to 9% and, in 1977, to below 5%. In 1976 the total expenditure of the statutory health insurance system amounted to some 70 000 million marks, which is equal to almost 6% of the gross national product.

Hospital expenditure rose from 6000 million to over 19 000 million marks between 1970 and 1976. In 1975 the growth rates of 20%–35% were almost halved to around 15%, and in 1976 and 1977 the rates fell even lower. In 1976 expenditure totalled 191 256 million marks. Per capita expenditure per hospital day by the statutory health insurance system was about 145 marks.

On average, expenditure for outpatient treatment by physicians has risen by 17% annually since 1970, but by 1976 the rate of increase had fallen to around 6%. Total expenditure in 1976 amounted to 11 924 million marks.

Expenditure on drugs, dressings, medicines and aids obtained from pharmacies increased for several years at a constantly high rate (15%–20%). In 1976 the rate of increase fell to 8%, and in 1977 to 1%. Total expenditure in 1976 was 9642 million marks.

About 8% of the population have complete insurance coverage outside the statutory health insurance system, predominantly under private insurance schemes.

The statutory health insurance system is characterized by the principle of payment in kind, as distinct from the cost reimbursement principle which governs private health insurance schemes. The insured person or his family claim medical services, drugs or hospital care, but the health insurance system does not subsequently reimburse his costs, but concludes agreements with the providers of the services concerning their delivery, extent and nature.

Major developments in the period 1973–1977

Under the hospital finances law of 1972, and the corresponding hospital laws of the *Länder* and the Federal ordinance relating to nursing personnel of 1973, new instruments were created for increasing the economic stability of hospitals, controlling demand for and supply of hospital services, optimizing working procedures and throwing greater light on cost-effective factors. On the basis of the experience gained during the period under review, the hospital finances law is at present being amended with a view to improving the possibilities for intervention, control and planning.

The law on the further development of health (1976) created the necessary instruments for planning and for the distribution of panel doctors' services according to demand. Another development was the law on the containment of sickness insurance costs (1977).

High priority has been given to environmental policies, and within the context of the environment programme of 1971 the following legislative measures were implemented; by the Federal Law on protection against emissions (1974), the law relating to air purity and noise control was substantially revised and brought up to date. In order to improve the level of purity of waters, a law on detergents was passed in 1975, the water economy law was amended and quality requirements for drinking-water valid for the entire Federal Republic were embodied in an ordinance on drinking-water (1975).

A law on environmental statistics (1974) provides for the regular collection of ecological, economic and financial data.

A Federal law on dangerous substances, aimed at reducing hazards to man from toxic and other harmful substances, is in preparation.

The rapid development of industrial production of foodstuffs, the use of new technologies and procedures in preparation, processing and packaging, and changes in consumer habits call for intensified protection of the consumer's health. The total reform of the law relating to foodstuffs (1974) thoroughly revised and updated regulations in this field. Several episodes involving drugs have demonstrated the need for greater drug safety, and the law on the amendment of the drugs act (1976) ensures a high degree of drug safety.

The humanization of the world of work, aimed at creating a better working milieu, has become a main feature of social and health policy. The necessary foundations for this were laid in a series of laws and ordinances: the work safety law of 1973, the ordinance on work places (1975), and the radiology ordinance of 1973.

The conditions for the successful reintroduction of disabled persons into work and society have been improved by statutory regulations, construction and development of rehabilitation institutions and a number of other measures. Particularly noteworthy are the rehabilitation adjustment law, the law relating to the severely disabled (1974), and the development of a network of modern rehabilitation institutions which are aimed at permitting a return to working life immediately after restoration to health.

A Federal Government programme to promote research and development in the service of health has the aim of intensifying function-oriented research and practical development in the field of health. The highlights of this programme are: research to improve preventive measures; the development and testing of methods of early detection; the development and validation of concepts relating to diagnosis, treatment and rehabilitation; and research aimed at improving health policy control mechanisms and the planning of the health care structure.

The basis for a reform of medical training has been created with the new ordinance relating to the licensing of physicians (1970). Medical training now comprises university studies of six years, which include practical training in a hospital establishment. The aim of the 1970 reform is to achieve a rationalized form of training that relates both to the practice and to the patient.

In other health professions, too, developments are being constantly checked and training systems adapted to bring them into line with the requirements of a modern health service. This is also the aim of the new law on nursing and midwifery.

GREECE

Background information

The mainland of Greece is a peninsula jutting out from the south of the Balkans into the Mediterranean; it is deeply indented by long sea inlets and is surrounded by many islands. The total area of the country, including the islands, is 131 990 km^2.

At the last census (1971) the population was 8 768 671 (66.43 persons per km^2), of whom more than 2 500 000 lived in the agglomeration of Athens and Piraeus.

In 1975 the birth rate and the death rate were 15.7 and 8.9 per 1000 population, respectively; the natural increase was 0.81%. The infant mortality rate was 24.0 per 1000 live births. In the same year, the expectation of life at birth was 71.6 years for males and 76.0 years for females. The principal causes of death were: heart diseases (14 356 deaths), malignant neoplasms (14 066 deaths), cerebrovascular diseases (13 278 deaths), accidents (3830 deaths) and pneumonia (3010 deaths). The most frequent communicable diseases are those peculiar to early childhood: pertussis, rubella, mumps and chickenpox. Mention should also be made of influenza, tuberculosis, infectious hepatitis, brucellosis, typhoid fever and bacillary dysentery.

Social security (sickness, old age and disability funds) has become established in Greece during the past 40 years. The most important body in this field is the Social Security Institution, which comes under the Ministry of Social Services and covers a large number of workers and employees. In addition, there are 73 sickness insurance funds.

Administrative organization of the health services

The Ministry of Social Services, which was reorganized between 1968 and 1975, is responsible for public health and the organization of medical care, social welfare and social security.

The central administration comprises, under the Minister, two under-secretaries of state, a general secretariat, three directorates-general (for health, social welfare and social security) and various general services. The Minister and the Directors-General are assisted by a National Health Council and a dozen advisory boards and special committees.

The Athens School of Public Health and the National Drug Control Laboratory come under the Directorate-General of Health.

At the regional level, there are 15 health divisions and 15 social welfare divisions, as well as 40 health sections and 40 social welfare sections. All these services constitute the external services of the three Directorates-General.

At the local level, there are 1420 rural dispensaries (chiefly in mountainous areas) and 126 health centres which, under the direct control of the above services, provide medical and pharmaceutical care for the local population.

Organization of medical care

Doctors are free to practise privately. Hospital care is provided by private doctors, by local authorities, by social security schemes and by voluntary bodies, including the Red Cross. Such care is available free of charge to the rural population.

The legal status of hospitals (both general and specialized) may be classed as follows: State hospitals, voluntary hospitals and private clinics are subject to State licence and control; in the rural areas, "health stations" serve a population of at least 5000 and have 6 to 15 beds for urgent cases and deliveries.

In 1975 there were 722 hospital establishments with a total of 57 791 beds (6.6 beds per 1000 population). They consisted of: 129 public hospitals (26 665 beds), including 94 general hospitals (13 721 beds) and 35 specialized hospitals (12 926 beds); 26 hospitals controlled by private institutions (7254 beds), including 12 general hospitals (2637 beds) and 14 specialized hospitals (4617 beds); 441 private clinics (22 919 beds); and 126 public health stations (953 beds).

The specialized hospitals and clinics included 57 psychiatric establishments (12 919 beds).

Organization of preventive services

The Ministry of Social Services is responsible for health, and for social and technical measures for water supply, environmental sanitation and housing improvement.

Because funds are limited, water-supply work has been restricted; nevertheless, 85% of the population is served by efficient water-supply systems. The chlorination of drinking-water is compulsory in all localities with more than 1000 inhabitants. The drinking-water of the Athens area is subject to systematic quality control.

Communicable disease control is the responsibility of the Ministry of Social Services but is delegated to the local services. It includes the compulsory notification of cases, epidemiological surveys, the isolation and treatment of patients, vaccination and disinfection. Special laboratory examinations are carried out by the microbiology laboratory of the Athens School of Public health, the Central Public Health Laboratory and the hygiene laboratory of the University of Salonika.

Tuberculosis control is organized by the Ministry in conjunction with the private research institutes for thoracic diseases in Athens and Salonika. Twenty-nine special dispensaries and 12 sanatoria throughout the country are engaged in this work, in collaboration with the health divisions and sections and health stations. Mobile units are used for performing BCG vaccination, which has been compulsory since 1960. The vocational rehabilitation and social reintegration of former tuberculosis patients are carried out by four of the biggest sanatoria in the country.

Antimalarial activities have been carried out successfully, the number of cases in 1977 not exceeding 45 (all imported from Africa). In collaboration with WHO, special programmes are being conducted to prevent the importation of new cases from Turkey.

Typhoid fever is still widespread (424 cases in 1977), but is decreasing as a result of improved health measures.

Measures to promote the welfare of the mother and of the child (up to the age of 14 years) are mainly the responsibility of the National Institute of Social Welfare and Relief and are financed by the State.

The provisions governing the isolation and treatment of mental patients date from 1973 (Act No. 104 of 1973). Legislation on preventive work and aftercare is very incomplete. A programme for reorganizing mental health care is under consideration.

There are three Cancer Institutes (in Athens, Piraeus and Salonika) with a total of 851 beds. The establishment of a national cancer control service, the organization of cancer control committees in each district and the setting up of cancer dispensaries in some general hospitals are envisaged.

Public health information and research

The Athens Public Health Laboratory carries out control of water, milk and other foodstuffs, produces vaccines and does research work. The hygiene and microbiology laboratories of the universities of Athens and Salonika, the Pasteur Institute of Greece and the veterinary service's microbiology laboratory also produce sera and vaccines and carry out research.

Supply and training of health personnel

In 1977 there were 17 500 physicians (i.e., one to 472 inhabitants), 7000 dentists (i.e., one to 1181 inhabitants), 3200 midwives, 1400 veterinarians, and 15 500 nurses (including 5500 with diplomas).

More than 50% of the physicians practise in Athens, Piraeus and environs, while 25% practise in other large towns. In order to remedy this unequal distribution, an Act passed in 1968 required young doctors to practise for at least one year outside the Athens and Salonika areas, in health stations or in rural dispensaries.

Physicians are trained at two faculties of medicine, in Athens and Salonika. Studies last six years and a specialist degree requires a further three to six years' study. Public health doctors must undertake a year's postgraduate training at the School of Public Health in Athens. There are 12 schools of nursing, three of which also provide training for public health nurses.

Financing of health services

Social security expenditure in 1976 totalled approximately 9655 million drachmas. Allocation from the national budget to public health institutions and to the health and insurance councils amounted to 2845 million drachmas, while expenditure on medical treatment for members of the Civil Service was 2367 million

drachmas, giving a total of 14 867 million drachmas.

Environmental health

Administrative organization of environmental health protection services. The Division of Environmental Health, which forms part of the Directorate-General of Health, is responsible at the central level for environmental health. Its main objectives are pollution control and environmental sanitation through the adoption of legal, administrative and technical measures. The criterion for these measures is the protection and promotion of public health.

The health divisions and sections are responsible, at the local level, for environmental pollution control with a view to the protection and promotion of public health.

Since 1973 the Ministry of Social Services has issued and amended health regulations relating to drinking-water, the disposal of wastes and waste-water, swimming-pools, cemeteries, and banning the use of fuels with a high fuel-oil content in order to reduce air pollution.

Treatment and prevention services and programmes. In June 1976 the National Council for Planning and the Environment was set up under the Ministry of Coordination. This is a high-level coordinating and supervisory body which is aimed at environmental protection at the national level.

The Ministries of Social Services, Industry and Energy, Communications, the Merchant Marine and Agriculture are responsible for implementing related plans in their respective fields.

Education of health personnel. The School of Public Health, Athens, is in charge of the education of public health physicians. Centres of higher technical education are responsible for the education of public health inspectors. So far, Greece has no establishment for training sanitary engineers. It is proposed to introduce special courses for sanitary engineers at the School of Public Health, Athens.

Health service expenditure and finances. During the period 1973–1977, under the "minor sanitation work" programme of the Ministry of Social Services, 165 million drachmas were allocated for water-supply work, 136 million drachmas for sewerage work, and 19 million drachmas for miscellaneous sanitation work. Under the public investments programme, water-supply work was carried out to the value of 6800 million drachmas, sewerage work to the value of 900 million drachmas and other work to the value of 134 million drachmas. The Greek Government devoted 72.5 million drachmas to the programme for environmental pollution control in the metropolitan area of Athens, while US $700 000 was allocated to this programme by WHO within the framework of the United Nations Development Programme.

HUNGARY

General background

The population was 10 672 000 at the end of 1977. The population density is 115 per km². Of the overall population, 19.6% live in the capital, 32.4% in towns, and 48% in rural areas. The percentage of urban population increased from 48.6% in 1972 to 52% in 1977. One city (Budapest) has more than a million inhabitants; and there are five towns with populations over 100 000.

The country is an agricultural one, with a medium level of industrial development; and the agriculture is largely industrialized. In 1976, 20% of the active wage earners worked in agriculture and forestry. National per capita income has risen steadily, from 28 925 forints in 1971 to 41 362 in 1976.

Average life expectancy at birth in 1974 was 66.5 years for males and 72.4 years for females.

Administration of health and other services is the responsibility of the Executive Committees of the 19 county and one metropolitan (Budapest) councils, each of which has its own budget.

Administrative organization of the health services

In 1950 the Ministry of Health replaced the former Ministry of Public Welfare. The Council of Ministers governs the health services through the Minister of Health, who is the highest authority in health matters and is responsible for the provision of health care to the entire population except for members of the armed forces. Within the framework of the Ministry of Health there is a Health Scientific Council—a consultative board that expresses professional opinions and puts forward proposals, the members being prominent representatives of the medical disciplines.

Duties and tasks in the health sphere include the development of public health and the prevention of infectious diseases and epidemics; provision of preventive and curative health services; provision of drugs; health education; administrative measures connected with spas and health resorts, as well as with the investigation and utilization of mineral waters and medicinal waters; education and training of health personnel, including specialist and postgraduate training; creation, maintenance and development of health organizations; provision of medical supplies and prosthetic aids; preparation of health organizations for dealing with major emergencies.

The Ministry of Health carries out its tasks in cooperation with a network of national health institutes and special county institutions. It supervises, advises, and controls the institutions under its professional authority, being directly responsible for more than 40 national health institutes. The regional health administration system is responsible for 77.5% of the hospital beds and for outpatient services, public health epidemiology, and maternal and child health.

A health information system is directed by the Central Statistical Office as an integral part of the national information system.

Insurance

Since 1950 it has been the task of the national health service to provide health care for insured active wage earners and their dependants, within the framework of a system of social insurance managed by the trades unions. Expenditure on social insurance and the national health service is incorporated in the national budget; the contributions of the employers are included, employees contributing only towards their pensions. In 1976, 25% of social insurance expenditure went towards health care.

Health legislation

The period 1973–1977 covers the last three years of the fourth economic plan and the first two years of the fifth. The Health Act, which came into force in 1972, has had a decisive influence on health policy. It lays stress on preventive measures, the creation of more favourable environmental conditions, the provision of free medical and inpatient care, the uniform administration and management of the national health service, and cooperation between institutions. It attaches special importance to social involvement and to the promotion of medical scientific development.

A Council of Ministers' resolution, published in 1973, provides for measures to ensure access by women to safe methods and devices for birth control and to build up a national system of health counselling for women and families. By raising the child care benefits, which may be drawn for three years, the opportunities for working women to bring up and educate their children were increased. Increased family allowances have improved the financial status of large families and provided for parents caring for sick children.

After extensive preparatory work a unified preventive and curative service was initiated in 1976. In 1977 a new system of drug purchase was introduced in order to simplify the distribution of drugs, dressings, and prosthetic devices. The choice of drugs on sale without prescription was expanded, and the price of drugs (with and without prescription), dressings, and prosthetic aids was established at about 15% of the former retail price. This should lead to a substantial decrease in the doctors' workload.

The health plan and national health programmes

As has been noted, the period 1973–1977 includes the final phase of the Fourth Five-Year Plan and the first two years of the Fifth. The previous plans had been characterized by rapid increases in the number of health and medical services and in health manpower (especially doctors), as well as a decentralized build-up of basic health institutions. To provide universally accessible primary medical services, an institutional system had to be set up. During the Fourth Five-Year Plan the development of a system of county, district, and municipal hospitals was completed and the further development and re-

construction of multi-profile county hospitals and certain national institutes was started. By 1977 certain new types of services had become available such as haemodialysis units and intensive care departments, and the cardiac surgery centres had been strengthened.

The Fifth and subsequent plans aim at the gradual provision of continued, systematic care for the entire population and the prevention of disease and disability through the public health and epidemiological services.

Curative and preventive service and programmes

The preventive and curative service is guided, within the framework of the national health service, by 33 national institutes, under the direct control of the Ministry of Health. The primary aim is to ensure that each patient is treated where the requisite professional knowledge, skills and equipment for dealing with his or her specific condition are available. By means of planned and compulsory division of labour, the professional activities of the health care delivery system—from the primary health care level through the municipal, country and regional levels up to the national institutes—are coordinated to this end. This was one of the most significant developments in the period under review.

Hospital services

In Hungary, inpatient services are provided by the clinics of the medical schools, the national institutes, the general hospitals, the metropolitan-regional, county, metropolitan-district, and municipal hospitals, special hospitals and sanatoria, maternity homes, aftercare hospitals for chronic patients, and specialized spas and climatotherapeutic institutions.

There are also institutions that are partly preventive and curative and partly social, such as homes for patients with chronic diseases (including tuberculosis and mental illness) and homes for mentally or physically handicapped children.

The number of beds in inpatient institutions and maternity homes increased from 86 517 (83.1 per 10 000 population) in 1972 to 92 358 (87.0) in 1976. In the same years, discharges from these establishments numbered 1 851 377 and 1 913 453, days of inpatient care 27 374 784 and 27 961 404, and the average duration of stay 14.8 and 14.6 days, respectively.

Primary health care

The number of district health centres increased from 3898 in 1972 to 4101 in 1976, district paediatric centres from 722 to 932; The number of inhabitants per district health and district paediatric centre increased in the same period from 2111 to 2250 the number of factories with industrial health services from 1312 to 1655, and the number of doctors providing occupational health care from 1544 to 1862.

The district paediatric services are organized mainly in towns and cities, where they have taken over the provision of health care for the child population. The district paediatrician usually has one assistant in addition to maternal and child health nurses.

The industrial health service examines employees for job fitness, offers expert advice, organizes and directs first aid in the factories, and participates in the treatment, continuing care and appraisal of the working capacity of employees. It studies their health status and promotes healthy conditions of work and the elimination of conditions detrimental to health. It is also involved in the rehabilitation of the handicapped.

Specialist services

The significant improvement in the tuberculosis situation made it possible for the tuberculosis control services to extend their activities to the provision of care for nontuberculous chronic lung diseases, firstly organizing the fight against lung cancer; more than 50% of lung cancer cases are detected at a relatively early stage of X-ray screening, which improves the chances of successful operation.

The National Institute of Oncology manages the cancer diagnostic and therapeutic services provided by 69 regional and seven independent hospital oncological dispensaries and by 93 specialist outpatient services. There is compulsory notification, and the primary and specialist care institutions of the dispensaries carry out extensive continuing care and control. Nearly 600 000 screenings were carried out in the female population 30–69 years old, and the examination of nearly 150 000 cervical smears contributed to the early detection of tumours.

Psychiatric care is administered by the National Institute of Neurology and Psychiatry. There are 80 neuropsychiatric dispensaries and specialist outpatient services, most of them organized during the period under review. There are almost 11 000 beds, of which 2300 were provided in the period 1972–1976. In 1976 the number of patients on the register and receiving continued care was almost 110 000. The development of mental health care and modernization of the facilities are programmed for the present decade.

The Fifth Five-Year Plan provides for the development of a new campaign against alcoholism, further developing the national dispensary system, and with more intensive continued care and treatment for alcoholics.

Care for dental and oral diseases is administered by the Central Institute of Stomatology of the Metropolitan Council, which fulfils the tasks of a national institute. The outpatient facilities of the Institute provide dental and oral treatment, dental prosthetic treatment, child dental services, and orthodontic and dental X-ray services.

Accident and emergency services are controlled by the National Institute of Traumatology. The Institute participates in the provision of care for the injured, who are treated at emergency outpatient or inpatient facilities, develops new methods, offers professional guidance and expert opinion, and carries out postgraduate training and supervisory duties. The inpatient institutions handle about 110 000 victims of accidents a year, half of them in general surgery departments.

Industrial and road traffic accidents are notifiable to the Central Statistical Office. In 1976 almost 120 000 persons suffered industrial accidents and 24 000 were injured in a total of 19 000 traffic accidents. As compared to 1972 the incidence of industrial accidents decreased by 10%, that of fatal industrial accidents by almost 20%. The numbers of road traffic accidents and of fatalities were almost the same as in 1972.

Protection of mothers, infants, children and young people

Under the leadership of the chief medical specialists of the county hospitals, maternal, infant and child health activities have been integrated. Under the overall guidance of the Ministry of Health and the professional authority of the National Institute of Infant and Child Health, as well as the National Institute of Obstetrics, a system has been created which exercises leadership and control over both in- and outpatient services and employs methods of prevention on a large scale. This was a significant achievement during the period under review, and the new population policy heralded by the governmental resolution of 1973 was built on it. In order to improve demographic and reproductive indices the following objectives, guiding principles and programmes were adopted: general acceptance of the ideal of two or three children per family, thus ensuring constancy of the population; deliberate family planning, ensuring that the child should be born at the proper time and under adequate conditions; prevention of undesired pregnancies by means of modern methods of contraception, reducing the number of induced abortions; elevation of the professional and technical levels of pregnancy care and management of parturition, resulting in a decrease in premature births and providing adequate treatment for unhealthy neonates; increased efficiency of continued health care for infants and children in order to ensure adequate development, and, in cooperation with the organs of education, the shaping of health attitudes; improvement of the health care for young people, helping the choice of trade or profession and satisfying the needs both of the individual and of society.

Health education and dissemination of health information

These are the responsibilities of the National Institute of Health Education of the Ministry of Health. It has the continuous task of disseminating health information to the population from childhood to old age and of participating in their education for healthy living. There are also special campaigns utilizing the mass media.

Biomedical and health services research

Research is carried out at the medical universities and at other academic and national institutions. Scientific investigations also take place in the in- and outpatient institutions.

During the current five-year plan period, of 534 research projects in the 12 main research fields, 393 (73.6%) were of portfolio level. Every research proposal is screened by various scientific committees. Almost 40% of the investigations are biomedical and the most important ones are studies of cardiovascular and neoplastic diseases. Research is also going on in the fields of human genetics, immunology, neuroendocrinology, metabolic diseases and replacement of organs and tissues.

The principal aim of research into biologically active compounds and vaccines is to ensure that, within the framework of international cooperation, Hungary takes part in the solution of problems of drug research and in the provision of better medicaments and vaccines.

The development and use of computer technology in medical research and in the organization, planning and management of health services include investigations in automatic evaluation of electrocardiograms, in diagnosis, and in certain areas of clinical epidemiology. Studies concerning automatic analysis of biological signs have been begun. The development of a uniform health information system is continuing.

In the period of research which began in 1976 attention is being focused upon the interactions and relationships between the health status of the population and environmental factors—social, biological, physical and chemical.

Research into perinatal mortality aims to reduce the mortality rate, to prevent premature birth, to ensure healthy development in infants, and to study the regulation of vital processes and the physiology and pathology of fetal and neonatal life.

In the field of transplantation research efforts are being made to gain insight into the complex immune background of transplantation procedures.

Health administration research is supplying new data concerning changes in the morbidity of the population, furnishing the basis for the national comprehensive morbidity study which started in 1978.

In the field of research into the etiology, pathology and therapy of tumours, intensive investigations are going on to elucidate potential carcinogenic effects of chemicals in the environment. Significant efforts are being made into the cytostatic treatment for neoplastic diseases.

In the pathology and management of injuries, research aims to improve treatment and preserve working abilities more effectively. Useful results have been achieved in the field of surgical suture materials.

In human genetics research, extensive cytogenetic studies have been conducted through the differential staining of chromosomes. Further efforts are being made to expand the use of perinatal genetic diagnostic methods; and more extensive screening for congenital metabolic diseases is also planned.

Health research accounted for 244 million forints in the 1976 budget for scientific institutes and projects—10% more than in 1975.

Health manpower development

The highest level of health manpower education and training is provided at the four medical universities, in one postgraduate school of medicine (which has university status) and at the Health College operating within the framework of the latter. The number of training institutes in the four medical universities decreased by two, to 73; the number of clinics and university hospitals remained unchanged at 67.

Medium-level health training is full-time. It was provided in 1976 in 49 special health schools (four-year courses) and in 22 special health schools (three-year courses), as well as in in-service courses. The special high school qualifies general nurses and assistants in 23 specialities; other special qualifications may be obtained by attending 10-month, in-service training courses. The number of students was approximately 12 000 in 1977. Graduates of the special health school qualify for employment in 12 specialities; other qualifications may be obtained by attending 10-month, in-service special courses. In 1977 there were nearly 5000 students.

The duration of the in-service training courses is two years. Nurses, midwives, paediatric nurses, laboratory assistants, X-ray assistants, special assistants, pharmacy assistants, social home nurses and maternal and child health nurses receive medium-level training.

In addition to the medium-level training there is also basic training lasting six months for autopsy room aides, health wardens, disinfectors, ambulance attendants, operating theatre and other aides.

Postgraduate training for doctors and pharmacists every three to five years is compulsory. In 1976, 5500 doctors and 900 pharmacists attended postgraduate training courses.

Drug supply

Most drugs (85%) are supplied by the national pharmaceutical industry, the remaining 15% being imported. Drugs can be sold only after systematic investigation and official registration, followed by issue by the Ministry of Health of a permit for marketing. Drugs are on sale exclusively in pharmacies. The National Institute of Pharmacology exercises official control and issues the registration certificates. In the process of manufacturing drugs there is also internal quality control extending to every batch of products.

The National Institute of Pharmacology supplies regular information on drugs and pharmaceutical products to doctors and pharmacists. The continuity of drug supply is the responsibility of the wholesale company, which is directly subordinate to the Ministry of Health. Drug supply in the field is ensured by the county pharmacy centres supervised by the county council health administrative authorities. In 1976 there were 1402 pharmacies (one to 7578 inhabitants). In larger hospitals there are institutional pharmacies, the number of which was 65 at the end of 1976. Some 800 doctors in villages far from a pharmacy have a drug dispensary.

Costs and financing of health services

Expenditure on the health services is included in the national estimates, but does not include allocations for investments.

The health and social budgetary provisions in the period under review were as follows (in millions of forints):

	1972	1973	1974	1975	1976
National income	325 300	360 000	377 000	402 000	441 000
Health and social expenditure*	10 598	11 517	12 482	13 878	14 724
Share of national income	3.26%	3.20%	3.32%	3.47%	3.34%
Increase of health and social expenditure over previous year	10.0%	8.7%	8.4%	11.1%	6.1%

* Including costs of maintenance of health and social institutions run by the Ministry of Health, central and county-operated institutions, training of doctors, health college training, health scientific research, as well as reconstruction of institutions, but not the 85% budgetary support for druq purchases by the population and other social insurance costs.

Health expenditure in 1976 was distributed as follows (in millions of forints):

	Amount	Percentage
Preventive and curative services	7 592	51.5
Maternal and child health	1 428	9.7
Universities, clinics	917	6.2
Public health epidemiology (together with the central institutes)	321	2.2
Social homes	791	5.4
Other responsibilities (including reconstruction)	3 675 (1 127)	25.0 (7.7)
Total	14 724	100

ICELAND

General background

Iceland is the most sparsely populated country in Europe. About half of the population lives in or near the capital, Reykjavik, the remainder in communities along the coastline. Although the economy is fundamentally based on fishing and farming, there has been rapid movement of the labour force out of primary and into secondary and tertiary economic sectors. Iceland enjoys a relatively high standard of living. Unemployment has been less than in most other countries. As in other welfare states there exists a comprehensive social security system, covering pensions, health, employment injuries, family allowances, and unemployment.

Country health situation

During this century Icelanders have experienced a remarkable improvement in general health as well as in economic conditions. Life expectancy in recent years has risen to 71 and 77 years respectively for males and females. In 1976 the infant mortality rate was 7.7 per 1000 live births—the lowest figure as yet on record—and the crude death rate has for some time remained stationary at approximately 7 per 1000.

Common infectious diseases like diphtheria, scarlet fever, measles and influenza, which often caused high mortality, and typhoid fever, no longer cause any great concern.

The chief causes of death in 1976 were heart diseases, malignant neoplasms, cerebrovascular diseases, accidents and pneumonia. The communicable diseases most frequently notified in 1976 were influenza, pertussis, scarlet fever, measles and meningococcal infections.

Administrative organization of the health services

Under the new law on health services—passed in 1973 and revised in 1978—relating to the reorganization of the health services, responsibility for hospitals is transferred to the communities and emphasis is laid on group medicine practised in health centres as opposed to private practice. Under this law the Ministry of Health and Social Security remains the central body responsible for health matters. The Director-General of Public Health, a physician, is the Government's chief adviser on all matters concerning medical service and public health. He is the disciplinary head of the medical and paramedical professions.

The country is now divided into eight health regions, each with one acting health centre doctor as a chief medical officer. Each region is divided, in turn, into areas and districts based on health centres. These combine all preventive and curative outpatient services and are intended to provide the services of general practitioners, specialists, midwives, public health nurses, dentists, physiotherapists, social workers, and other health personnel.

Every administrative community is required

204

to have a sanitary board, the members of which are elected by the local council. Sanitary inspectors are employed in the towns and larger villages. The sanitary boards are responsible for such matters as environmental sanitation, food control and the supervision of public amenities as laid down in public health regulations and bylaws. In carrying out their functions the boards are guided and supervised by the appropriate health centre or district physician and by the National Institute of Environmental Health.

Curative and preventive services and programmes

Curative and preventive services are provided by health institutions and—outside hospitals— by health centres, general practitioners, specialists, independent societies, sanitary boards and institutions such as the National Institute of Environmental Health.

In 1977 there were 35 hospitals in the country, with a total of 3261 beds, or 14.7 beds per 1000 inhabitants, including 24 general hospitals with 1973 beds, of which six, with 1417 beds, have specialized departments. Beds in other institutions number 454.

Primary health and outpatient services are usually provided by health centres, except in the Reykjavik area, where they are mostly provided by general practitioners, specialists and hospital staff.

Independent societies play an active role in the health services. Cancer detection services are operated by the Icelandic Cancer Society. Routine health examinations for heart diseases come under the auspices of the National Association for the Prevention of Heart Diseases.

Biomedical and health services research

Medical and health services research is being carried out in various institutions and laboratories in the University of Iceland, the National Institute of Environmental Health, the Office of the Director-General of Public Health, hospital laboratories and public health laboratories.

The Ministry of Health and Social Security influences research policy by providing subsidies and financing institutions and activities.

Health manpower development

From 1965 to 1975, manpower in health services as a proportion of the total working population increased from 3.0–3.2% to 6.2–6.8%; it is still rising rapidly. The manpower needed in primary health care has been estimated at 130 doctors and 110 nurses; at present 65 doctors and 40 nurses are working in this part of the health services. In addition there are about 30 independent general practitioners and 25 nurses in mother and child clinics which operate under the former legislation. There is as yet no manpower plan for the hospital services.

University training for physicians, dentists, physiotherapists, pharmacists and nurses is given in Reykjavik, the duration of the course of studies being the same as in other Scandinavian countries. Specialist training is mostly obtained in the Scandinavian countries, Great Britain and North America.

Cost and financing of health services

The cost of the health services has increased from 3% of the gross national product (GNP) in 1950 to about 7% in 1975. Hospital costs increase even faster than primary health care and were in 1977 about 75% of the total cost of the health services.

In 1976 health expenditure was estimated at 18 205 million kronur, or 7.1% of GNP.

Changes and major activities between 1973 and 1977

Health statistics show the health status of the population to be improving. For instance, the perinatal mortality rate fell to 9.3 per 1000 live births in 1976 and the mortality from heart diseases seems to be decreasing.

One of the major changes in health policy during the decade involves more emphasis on primary health care. According to this policy many health centres are being established and the activities on primary level are being reorganized.

Training for physiotherapists and pharmaceutical assistants has been provided in Reykjavik since 1973.

IRELAND

Organization of the health services

The legal basis for the health services is contained in the acts passed by the National Parliament, and the actions of all the other organs of administration must conform to those acts. In general those governing the provision of the health services (and notably the Health Acts of 1947, 1953 and 1970) do not lay down in detail how the services will operate but leave this to be specified in regulations by the Minister for Health, in guidelines and directives issued by his Department, and in the decisions of the health boards and other executive agencies.

Most of the powers given to the Minister for Health relate to the making of statutory regulations and orders and to the general supervision of the activities of the health boards and other executive agencies in the provision of health services. All statutory powers are vested in the Minister.

The functions of the Department of Health include the preparation, effective carrying-out and coordination of measures conducive to the health of the people, and in particular measures for the prevention and cure of disease; the treatment and care of persons suffering from physical defects or mental illnesses; the regulation and control of the training and registration of personnel for health services; control over the appointment and conditions of service of appropriate health officers; the initiation and direction of research; provisions to ensure that impure or contaminated food is not marketed and that adequate nutritive standards obtain in essential foodstuffs; the control of proprietary medical and toilet preparations; the registration of births, deaths and marriages; and the collection, preparation, publication and dissemination of information and statistics relating to health.

As from April 1971 eight regional health boards were established in accordance with the provisions of the Health Act (1970) to take over the administration of the health services from the then existing health authorities, which numbered 26. Prior to this change, counties were the administrative units for health services. The health boards comprise larger and more effective units, a number of counties in each region being grouped for this purpose. There are also a considerable number of executive agencies apart from the health boards. They include the Blood Transfusion Board, the Rehabilitation Board, the Medico-Social Research Board and the Drugs Advisory Board.

A special body, the Hospitals Council, was established under the Health Act (1970) to share with the Minister, his Department, the health boards and the voluntary hospitals the function of controlling and coordinating the hospital services. It was set up in recognition of the fact that many of the hospitals, including most of the important teaching hospitals, were in the hands of voluntary bodies and it was necessary to involve these, and the medical consultants, in the general planning and control of the hospital services. It has wide advisory functions. At least half of the 23 members of the Council must be registered medical practitioners engaged in a consultant capacity in the provision of hospital services.

Besides various other specialized advisory bodies, there is a general statutory body, the National Health Council, to advise over the whole field of health care. Most of the advisory bodies have strong professional representation and at least half the members of the National Health Council must be nominated by the medical and ancillary professions.

Each health board has the statutory obligation to make health services available. The availability of free hospital services in a public ward has now been extended to the entire population. Private hospital services are available under a voluntary health insurance scheme. A free general practitioner service, based on payment by health boards of a fee per item of service to the doctor, is provided for up to 40% of the population. The essential feature of this service is that the eligible person is offered a choice of doctor. This is a complete departure from the principle of the dispensary system under which one doctor was appointed for a defined area to provide the service. For the rest of the population the cost of general practitioner care is alleviated under a scheme whereby the cost of prescribed drugs and medical requisites are subsidized. Drugs for a number of long-term ailments and conditions are available without charge.

Hospitals

The Irish general hospital system is organized on a dual basis. Some of the hospitals are owned and operated by health boards and the others (generally referred to as voluntary hospitals) are owned and operated by lay boards or by religious orders. The voluntary hospitals are almost entirely confined to the city areas and particularly to Dublin. Separate hospitals cater for special categories of patients such as psychiatric, orthopaedic, cancer, sanatoria and infectious diseases cases. There are homes for the elderly, and the development of geriatric services includes rehabilitation and institutional care, with the emphasis on domiciliary care being provided by health board and voluntary organizations.

Hospitals, both health board and voluntary, now depend on public funds for all but a relatively small proportion of their income. With the exception of a small number of private hospitals, the voluntary hospitals participate in the provision of services for those entitled to them under the Health Acts and are paid certain fixed capitation rates by the health boards. The majority of the voluntary hospitals are general teaching hospitals associated with at least one of the medical schools.

The main feature of the health board hospital system is the county hospital, of which there is one in most counties. It provides a general medical, surgical and maternity service for the area. These generally have about 200 beds, and the consultant staff is comprised of surgeons, physicians and obstetrician-gynaecologists, with the services of radiologists and an anaesthetist and supporting resident medical staff. There are regional hospitals (500–600 beds) or other large general hospitals in the main centres of population. These hospitals have the full range of consultant staff and provide a comprehensive specialized service. With the changes in the administrative structure for the health services under the Health Act (1970) and the setting up of the Hospitals Council and regional boards, steps have been taken towards the integration and reorganization of the hospital services based on the development of regional and larger hospitals.

Another feature of the health board hospital service is the district hospital. There is one or more in each county. All are small institutions and they generally range in size from 20 to 40 beds; some district hospitals are larger. They have the services of a general practitioner who is the medical officer to the hospital, and the service given is limited to medical and maternity cases requiring non-specialized care.

The main services for the mentally ill are based on the 23 health board psychiatric hospitals, which contain over 15 000 beds. There are

15 private mental hospitals or homes providing in all 1500 beds. Clinics have been set up in each health board area which provide psychiatric outpatient facilities, and supportive community services are provided by trained teams of psychiatric personnel (including nurses and social workers). There is an ever-increasing emphasis on outpatient services, community nursing services, social work services, short-term psychiatric units attached to general hospitals, hostel accommodation and rehabilitation.

Health boards do not provide special institutions for the care and treatment of mentally handicapped persons, but make arrangements for the admission of such persons to residential centres (hospitals, homes and schools) conducted by voluntary bodies, mainly religious.

Health manpower

The medical, dental and nursing professions are controlled by special registration bodies such as the Medical Council, the Dental Board and the Nursing Board, and so also are a number of the auxiliary and ancillary professions. The registration bodies have the duty of ensuring that the standards of training and knowledge required at the examinations held by the medical, dental and nursing schools are adequate. The new Medical Council set up under the Medical Registration Act (1978) will be an enlarged body, and, in addition to its functions in relation to control of standards of undergraduate training, registration and discipline, it will be responsible for control of standards of postgraduate education and training and will be empowered to introduce medical specialist registration, which is a feature of Member States of the European Economic Community.

There are five medical schools, one at each of the constituent colleges of the National University at Dublin, Cork and Galway, at the University of Dublin (Trinity College) and at the Royal College of Surgeons, Dublin. The bodies granting degrees in dentistry are the National University of Ireland, the University of Dublin (Trinity College) and the Royal College of Surgeons, Dublin. There are some 80 recognized schools for the training of nurses at hospitals throughout the country.

The Council of the Pharmaceutical Society of Ireland is the governing body for pharmaceutical chemists. Their training is a combination of theoretical and practical instruction with apprenticeship under a member of the Society.

The courses of study are taken at University College, Dublin and Trinity College, in association with the Society's College of Pharmacy, Dublin.

The Opticians Board, Dublin, arranges for the training and registration of opticians (ophthalmic and dispensing) and for supervision of the practice of the profession.

In addition to the above professional categories for which there is statutory registration, there are many other important groups contributing to the services. These include such medical auxiliaries as physiotherapists, radiographers, chiropodists, dieticians and laboratory technicians and other groups such as health inspectors and those working in social fields concerned with health services. Also, there is the corps of administrative staff with supporting functional and clerical staffs involved in the day-to-day administration and operation of the health and hospital services.

Prevention and welfare

Communicable diseases

The advances made over the past decade in regard to the more significant infectious diseases continue to be maintained. The incidence of tuberculosis has shown a marked decline. The number of newly-discovered cases is falling each year, and eradication of the disease from the community now seems an attainable goal. The position in regard to other diseases is equally encouraging. Few, if any, cases of poliomyelitis, diphtheria or typhoid now occur. Vaccination and immunization schemes are operated by health boards. Prophylactic compaigns have concentrated on diphtheria immunization, BCG vaccination against tuberculosis, poliomyelitis immunization and, more recently, immunization against rubella. Hospital treatment for tuberculosis and other communicable diseases is free to all.

Measures for preventive health and community protection include the payment of maintenance allowances to persons undergoing treatment for infectious diseases, and allowances may also be paid to carriers of the diseases. Primarily the scheme is applicable to those with tuberculosis, but it covers also persons suffering from poliomyelitis, diphtheria, typhoid, paratyphoid, typhus, dysentery, salmonella infections, scarlet fever and streptococcal sore throat.

Food and drug control

As part of their duties in controlling the spread of infectious diseases, health boards have functions in supervising the hygiene of food supplies. They have also functions in relation to the quality and safety of food and drugs for the general wellbeing of the public. Hygiene in the manufacture, preparation, sale and serving of food is governed by regulations. The sale and distribution of poisons and dangerous drugs are subject to a number of statutory controls. There are specific provisions in relation to dangerous narcotic drugs and, more recently, a number of regulations have been brought in to restrict the sale of several drugs and medicines so that they may not be issued except on prescription. The Drugs Advisory Board was established in 1966 to provide a service to monitor newly introduced medicinal products as to their safety for human use. The Board is also responsible for collecting and disseminating information on side-effects and reactions associated with drugs already in use, and for furnishing advice on precautions and restrictions in the marketing and use of such drugs.

Fluoridation of water supplies for oral health

A noteworthy development in recent years in preventive services was the fluoridation of water supplies to prevent dental decay. A statutory obligation is placed on health boards to arrange for the fluoridation of piped public water supplies in their areas, the amount of fluorine added not to exceed one part per million. The local sanitary authorities operating the water supplies are obliged to cooperate as agents of the health boards in fluoridation. The scheme was commenced in the Dublin area in 1964 and has been extended to most of the piped water supply schemes in the country. In areas not served by piped supplies or where the piped schemes are small, schemes have been brought in for applying fluoride by means of regular mouth-rinsing by the children under suitable supervision. Results of studies show a marked reduction in the incidence of caries after the introduction of fluoridation.

Environmental health

The Department of the Environment has overall responsibility for environmental services, including water supplies and sewage disposal, which are operated at local level by sanitary authorities.

Early diagnosis of disease

Health boards have authority to operate schemes for conducting tests to screen the population, or susceptible groups, for preclinical signs or symptoms of disease.

School health

A Child Welfare Clinic Service and School Health Examination Service are in operation. Health boards are obliged to make available a child welfare clinic service for all schoolchildren under six years of age. The service, which is free of charge, is primarily preventive, its main purpose being to provide advice, to discover defects at an early stage and to secure, as far as possible, treatment for them and, in general, to try to raise the standard of health of preschool children. Health boards are also obliged to provide an examination service free of charge for pupils of national schools and, in certain circumstances, for pupils of other schools providing elementary education; health boards arrange with the school authorities for the periodic attendance of a doctor to examine pupils and for any nursing services required. They may also arrange for the attendance of a dentist.

Increasing attention is being given to the social services aspect of community health care with the setting-up of the regional health boards, which will have responsibility for coordinating the non-institutional services and will stimulate greater awareness among the public generally of the need for organized voluntary service.

Other social and welfare services for health

Welfare services associated with the health services include maintenance allowances to physically and mentally disabled persons, rehabilitation programmes, financial assistance and home helps for the aged, maintenance and care of orphans and children who are deserted by their parents, and contributions to voluntary bodies providing similar services. Increasing attention is being given to the social services aspect of community health care, and to stimulating greater awareness among the public of the need for organized voluntary service; to this end a National Social Service Council representing a cross section of voluntary and statutory interests in social work has been set up.

The preventive services include the provision of the necessary facilities and measures to prevent the spread of specified diseases in compliance with the International Health Regulations.

Occupational health is the responsibility of the Ministry of Labour, which has a staff of inspectors to enforce the relevant legislation.

Research

The Medical Research Council organizes and carries out research in medicine, financing it mainly from funds made available by the Minister. The Council has nine members—eight nominees of the Universities and other medical licensing bodies and a chairman appointed by the Minister. The Council's primary concern is with basic research on the causes of and cures for diseases, and most of its funds go towards grants for projects in these fields. It has not been part of the Council's function to conduct widespread projects on morbidity or on the operation of health services.

To extend work on morbidity, the Medico-Social Research Board was established in 1965. Its functions are to organize and administer surveys and statistical research in relation to the incidence of human diseases, injuries, deformities and defects, and the operation of the health services. The Board has 12 members who are appointed by the Minister. The Board is also concerned in a study, under the aegis of WHO, on the incidence of ischaemic heart disease, involving the establishment of a register of cases. The Board has also been concerned in work on the incidence of alcoholism and drug abuse.

Research facilities and laboratory services are provided by the constituent colleges of the National University at Dublin, Cork and Galway by the University of Dublin at Trinity College and by the Royal College of Surgeons, also at Dublin. Health boards have their own laboratories.

Health education

Improved measures have been introduced to inform and educate the public more effectively in matters of health and in the principles of hygiene and health preservation. A central institution, the Health Education Bureau, was established in 1975 to coordinate and develop health education nationally. The Bureau is responsible for formulating integrated health education programmes in accordance with agreed national priorities and in cooperation with the statutory and voluntary bodies engaged in the area of preventive health.

Planning

The Department of Health and the health boards are involved in planning on the basis of programmes designed to achieve defined objectives. The three overall programmes adopted by the boards are for community care (including primary health care), general hospital care, and special hospital care; the focus is on positive and preventive health measures—for example, health care for target groups, such as children, old people, persons suffering from mental illness or physical or mental handicap—and on hospital specialities such as medicine, surgery, and obstetrics. The aim is to define desirable standards for the whole spectrum of health services, to develop plans to bring existing services up to these standards, and to establish an order of priorities taking account of the resources available to meet them.

The management structure for the health boards reflects the three overall programmes referred to. Thus, under the chief executive officer of each health board there are programme managers and functional officers (finance, personnel, planning and evaluation),

who comprise the management team. In all health board areas there is a programme manager for community care and a community care team under a medical director. In the larger areas there are separate programme managers for general hospital care and for special hospital care, while in the areas of the smaller boards the same person manages both programme areas.

When fully developed, the programmes will facilitate the development of good management techniques and secure economy and effectiveness in the operation of existing health services and their development to meet future needs.

Cost and financing of the health services

The total cost of the health services for the financial year 1977 was 315 267 000 Irish pounds. This represents 6.28% of the gross national product. The National Exchequer met 94.5% of the non-capital expenditure on health services.

Capital expenditure by health boards and by voluntary hospitals is met by grants from the National Exchequer supplemented by grants from the Hospital Sweepstakes Funds and loans made available by the State. The capital expenditure for 1977 on the building of hospitals amounted to 16 million Irish pounds of which 13.5 million was provided by the State by way of grants, two million from loans by the State and 500 000 from the Hospitals Trust Funds.

ITALY

Health situation

There are no great variations in the health situation as compared with the period before 1972. The population, which was 54 137 000 in 1971 according to the census, rose to 56 014 000 by 1976. Mortality from infectious diseases continues to decrease, while that from chronic and degenerative diseases is increasing. This trend is obviously linked with the increase in life expectancy and, consequently, with the increase in absolute terms of the prevalence of the diseases of middle and old age. There is therefore reason to believe that these are the

major problems of the health services, which should be given the means to provide appropriate prevention and treatment. As they are long-term diseases, provisions are needed to provide social as well as health care.

Another priority problem is that posed by the prevention and control of pollution, especially industrial pollution. Responsibilities in this field are shared by various ministries other than the Ministry of Health, especially the Ministries for Industry and Labour, and administrations at various levels. Legislative provisions for improving and coordinating controls and action in this field are being adopted.

Administrative organization of health services

The decentralization of health functions to the regions has proceeded in expectation of the setting up of the National Health Service. There are 20 regions with populations that vary from 100 000 to a maximum of 8 million. Regions are empowered to legislate in health matters within the framework of the Constitution and the general laws of the State. Through funds supplied by the State, they finance preventive services, school health services, immunizations, and the training of auxiliary and ancillary personnel. In addition, they are responsible for the implementation of the Regional Hospitals Plan. Hospitals are financed through a National Hospital Fund, which is shared by the regions in accordance with special and local requirements.

The health service reform provides that the health services are administered directly by the region according to various planned models. Generally speaking, there are, under each regional health department, boards of health, hospitals and outpatient services. There are also provincial health and diagnostic laboratories. Local health units, with their management committees, health councils, and service directorates, come under the regional health council.

Hospitals

Hospitals are autonomous public bodies administered by boards comprising representatives of the regional and communal authorities, who are appointed in proportional representation of their political parties within administrations. There are regional general and specialist hospitals, provincial hospitals and area hospitals.

The regional hospital covers a population of at least one million. It provides highly specialized services and always includes a general medicine department, a general surgery department, a laboratory for clinical and chemical analysis, a radiology department and an anaesthesiology department.

The provincial hospital comprises separate departments for general medicine, general surgery, obstetrics and gynaecology, paediatrics and orthopaedics. In addition, it includes a laboratory; radiology, anaesthesiology, and morbid anatomy units, and a pharmacy; and departments—or wards or units—for infectious diseases, geriatrics and long-stay conditions, neurology, otorhino-laryngology, urology, dermatology and dentistry.

The area hospital includes separate medicine and surgery departments, and paediatrics and obstetrics and gynaecology wards. Linked to them are a radiology unit and a laboratory for clinical and chemical analysis. Some also include an orthopaedics ward.

Health personnel

The Directorate-General for Hospitals and Social Services of the Ministry of Health is responsible for management of health personnel with regard to the appraisal of their services and the qualifications required for carrying out their work in hospitals and other health establishments.

In recent years the need has been felt for planning, at university level, the admission of students to the faculties of medicine in order to avoid training an excessive number of doctors and to adapt required levels to those of the European Economic Community.

Italian universities are directly responsible for the education of doctors and specialists, and diplomas are awarded exclusively by them.

Health workers are trained in special schools which are under the jurisdiction of the regional, provincial and area hospitals and which award diplomas for the various categories (professional nurses, non-specialist and auxiliary health workers).

The administration of education of medical personnel is the State's responsibility, but it is integrated in forecasts and implementation measures developed by the individual regions in order to train staff well-adapted to meet local requirements.

The number of doctors on 31 December 1977 was 139 167. The majority of physicians have specialist qualifications and practise either as general practitioners or as specialists. The number of hospital physicians was 49 700 and the number of private physicians 75 874.

Legislation following the recent reform provides for free practice of doctors who are not employed full-time by hospital and other public establishments, with agreements making available regionalized health care to all citizens. Provision is made to enable such doctors to practise after working hours and outside the framework of their contractual agreements with their employers.

Health expenditure

Official estimates of health expenditure expressed as a percentage of gross national product are as follows: 3.2% in 1966, 4.3% in 1971, 5.7% in 1974, 5.2% in 1975, and 4.9% in 1976.

The greatest increase in health expenditure is seen to have occurred in the years between 1971 and 1974; it decreased slightly in the following years.

The greater part of health expenditure is financed from funds collected by the health insurance organizations. These include contributions of the employers and the employees in respect of health and disability insurance. The largest item of expenditure is hospital services, followed closely by drug supplies. Between 1975 and 1976 the increase in general expenditure amounted to 22%.

Mention should be made of the fact that the various legislative measures approved between 1974 and 1977 tend to provide that the National Health Service should replace the health insurance organizations for health costs. This is an important innovation, if it is considered that 90% of the population receive health care provided by the various health insurance organizations, which are of various types and provide assistance to various groups of employees. With the setting-up of the National Health Service, they will disappear, health care being provided and managed directly by the regions. It is a unique process of simplification and rationalization.

As far as production costs are concerned, drugs are next in importance. The cost of health is a topical question, and expenditure on drugs is not only a matter of health management; other factors are involved, and it is difficult to distinguish which are the most important. However, with the gradual merging of the various health insurance organizations into one regional system of health care, it is expected that drug expenditure will decrease owing to the introduction of a principle by which the insured person pays a sum that varies according to the importance and the production costs of the drug.

LUXEMBOURG

Administrative organization of the health services

Health activities are the responsibility of the Ministry of Public Health, which is often simultaneously in charge of other ministerial departments. In view of the country's small size, the health administration is not elaborate. The Directorate of Public Health at the Ministry is both a central administration and an executive body, since there is no degree of decentralization in the country's public health services. The Director of Public Health is assisted by three medical health inspectors and a deputy medical inspector, three pharmaceutical health inspectors and a sanitary engineer. (A general law on the Directorate of Public Health is in preparation.)

While general public health is the responsibility of the State, much of the social health work is carried out by semi-official and private bodies under the supervision of the Ministry.

Organization of medical care

Almost all the population is covered by a number of health insurance schemes under which the insured person pays a share of the costs.

The private practice of medicine is general, and the patient pays his fees direct to the doctor, subsequently receiving a reimbursement.

The country does not have general dispensaries or health centres; there are only the private doctors' surgeries and hospitals with outpatient departments. In 1977 there were 29 public and private establishments, comprising 21 general hospitals, 2 maternity homes, 1 children's hospital and 4 other institutions. These establishments had a total of 2781 beds for acute cases, or 7.7 per 1000 population. (The 2 sanatoria for tuberculosis patients have been assigned new functions.) There are 8 miscellaneous institutions with 1833 beds.

Organization of preventive services

More than 98% of the inhabitants have a public mains water supply. The State is endeavouring to improve waste-water purification, which is of a satisfactory standard in the towns but it still inadequate in certain rural areas. An air pollution control network has been in operation since 1972.

Foodstuffs are subject to adequate and well-organized control measures.

Compulsory immunization against smallpox was abolished by the law of 14 February 1977. Immunization against poliomyelitis, diphtheria, tetanus and pertussis is practised on a very wide scale. Immunization against rubella is offered to girls and young women who are found to be receptive.

The law of 20 June 1977 concerns the health surveillance of pregnant women and young children. Within the framework of the school health service, private doctors who receive their fees from the State carry out regular examinations of school-age children.

Tuberculosis control is based on tuberculosis dispensaries and a mobile X-ray service.

Mental disease prevention services are being developed with the establishment of a mental health dispensary (there will probably be two more at a later date).

The Factory Inspectorate has a factory medical inspector, while certain factories have factory doctors under the joint supervision of the Factory Inspectorate and the Inspectorate of Health.

Public health information and research

The Directorate of Public Health has a health statistics service. It receives technical advice from a Central Council of Hygiene and a Medical Council.

The Institute of Hygiene and Public Health, which is subordinate to the Directorate of Public Health, is chiefly a public health and biological analysis laboratory, and does not carry out public health research work at the present time.

Supply and training of health personnel

In 1971 there were 410 doctors for 357 000 population (1.14 per 1000 inhabitants), 98 dental practitioners (0.27 per 1000 inhabitants), 130 practising pharmacists, 36 practising midwives, 1000 nurses and 337 nursing assistants.

Apart from the first-year studies in medicine, dentistry and pharmacy, there is no university medical course, and the requisite education must be obtained abroad. Similarly, qualified hospital nurses receive any additional training abroad. Nurses, on the other hand, are trained in the Grand Duchy.

MALTA

General background

The Republic of Malta consists of the main islands of Malta and Gozo and of other smaller islands only one of which, Comino, has some 15 to 20 residents. The 1976 census gives a total population of about 305 000, while the population estimate for the end 1977 is 309 000; Malta accounts for 90%, Gozo for the remaining 10%. With a total land area of 316 km², the average density is about 978 inhabitants per km². Population growth is of the order of 1% per year, with variations due to migration. In the last three years the previous trend of net emigration has been reversed, and yearly net immigration exceeds 1000 persons.

Owing to the small size of the islands and the concentration of population, there is no official distinction between urban and rural areas. Those living in scattered farmhouses in the countryside represent not more than 10% of the total.

The 1977 per capita gross national product was estimated at 765 million Maltese pounds and the annual increase over the past three years has averaged 20%. The gainfully employed population represents about 37% of the total. Income is fairly evenly distributed. The average family numbers between four and five persons. There has been steady progress in the manufacturing sector and the tourist industry. The overall activity of the tourist sector accounted for about 8% of the gross domestic product.

Country health situation

Marked overall progress has been achieved over the last 30 years in the field of communicable diseases as the result of preventive measures applied by the Department of Health, including prevention of importation of disease, improvement in hygiene, eduction, better social standards, immunization and other measures. Various diseases such as diphtheria, poliomyelitis, and trachoma have been eradicated. No case of diseases subject to the International Health Regulations has been recorded for several years. There has been a considerable reduction in the incidence of other diseases, including brucellosis, typhoid fever and pertussis. Tuberculosis is another disease against which marked progress has been achieved with a record low figure of 20 cases of pulmonary tuberculosis in 1977. International travel threatens new hazards. Long-stay visitors, especially from countries where tuberculosis is still prevalent and where drug resistance is a problem, have to be screened with a view to preventing importation of the disease, especially the resistant forms.

Mortality from communicable diseases is insignificant. They have been replaced by ischaemic heart disease, malignant neoplasms, cerebrovascular and other vascular diseases as a major cause of morbidity and mortality. Diabetes mellitus with its complications persists as one of the priority diseases, providing ample scope for research locally on account of its high prevalence.

The findings of a preliminary study of the nutritional status of the islanders in 1970 suggest that diabetes mellitus occurred in 15% of males and 16% of females over the age of 45 years. Other findings suggest that 20% of males and 15% of females over 45 had hypertension.

There is growing awareness of the multitude and multiplicity of the problems posed by an aging population not only in the medical but also in the economic and social fields. Demographic trends and projections indicate that about 12.5% of the population are 60 years of age or older.

Although the traditional problems of the environment are being satisfactorily controlled, new problems are emerging as a result of the inevitable conflict between economic and technological requirements and the necessity of maintaining optimal environmental standards. As in many other European countries, the economic viability depends to a large extent on the continued development of industrial, agricultural and tourist potential, all of which, unless controlled, could contribute to the degradation of the environment. It is, therefore, the basis of Malta's strategy to develop these sources of economic growth in such a way that they result in the minimum possible environmental damage.

Administrative organization of the health services

Health authorities

Under the Minister of Health and Environment (since 1976 the environment has been the responsibility of the Minister responsible for public health), the implementation of health policy is the responsibility of the Chief Government Medical Officer who is assisted by the principal medical officers and senior medical officers in the planning, running and control of the community health and environmental services, as well as the hospital services. There are various statutory bodies responsible for advising the Minister on health-related matters. The Council of Health has the legal responsibility of advising on all health matters, including certain legislative measures affecting the public health. Under the Ministry a new board has been established which advises the Minister on environmental matters. Another statutory board, the Clean Air Board, has powers in matters of air pollution.

At the periphery, the community care and hospital services are under the charge of the medical officers of health and medical superintendents, who are responsible for their day-to-day administration.

The size of the island makes subdivision under local authorities unnecessary.

The Minister of Welfare, Labour and Culture is responsible for all matters affecting social security.

Coordination with and support from other sectors—whether environmental, educational, agricultural or social services—is ensured at central level, especially in so far as government sectors are concerned. This cooperative effort has been made possible through the formulation of a national development plan which embraces the various sectors.

Health laws and regulations

The main health legislation since 1973 concerned food control, mental health and drugs control. The Food, Drugs and Drinking-water Act which was enacted in 1972 was complemented by various regulations which updated the food laws and allowed the repeal of previous legislation.

The Mental Health Act (1976) governs the admission of patients to psychiatric hospitals, and the provision of treatment facilities and other mental health services. It also makes provisions for the treatment of persons convicted for certain drug abuses.

The Drugs Control Regulations (1976) are aimed at the control of psychotropic substances in accordance with the 1971 United Nations Convention. They include very strict controls on amphetamines, methaqualone, phenmetrazine and methlyphenidate, for which a medical practitioner requires prior approval from the Chief Medical Officer before prescribing.

Other laws strengthened the control on emission of fumes from motor vehicles and banned smoking from places of entertainment and public transport buses. There are also special controls on tattooing.

Health plan and country health programming

The present health plan is part of the Development Plan, 1973–1980, for all sectors, and is aimed at the strengthening of hospital services; the provision of certain hospital facilities not previously available; the strengthening of environmental services; and the fullest possible development of health care services in the community. The plan is being carried out through a massive capital investment programme entailing the building of new premises, the adaptation and modernization of buildings, the procurement of equipment and an intensive programme for staff training both in Malta and, where this is not possible, overseas.

The plan envisages the provision to the whole population, irrespective of means, of a free community service, a free general practitioner service and a free hospital service through the introduction of a national health scheme.

Curative and preventive services

Hospital services

The government hospitals provide a comprehensive service to the whole population. Nominal charges are made except to those entitled to free hospital treatment either because they are in a lower income group, or—irrespective of their means—because they are long-stay patients.

St. Luke's Hospital provides a comprehensive range of inpatient and outpatient services for acute conditions. A smaller but very modern hospital on the island of Gozo also offers a high

standard of such care. The total bed complement in government hospitals is just over 3300, but under the capital investment programme a projected total complement of approximately 3600 beds was to be reached by 1979. There are approximately 260 further beds in private hospitals.

Primary medical and nursing care services

In addition to the environmental and personal health services, the Department of Health offers to the lower income group the following free community-orientated services:

primary medical care by community medical officers who hold clinics at government dispensaries and pay home visits to patients in their area who are entitled to this service;

primary nursing care, including home visits by day or night for care, advice and treatment as prescribed by the general practitioner; community nursing care at primary and peripheral clinics, domiciliary midwifery service comprising antenatal visits, home deliveries and postnatal care; domiciliary care of housebound elderly and disabled persons.

Primary care medical service for patients other than those in the lower income group is provided entirely from the private sector; it is estimated that approximately 120 doctors are working in general practice. Primary nursing care services for patients other than those in the lower income groups are available through private nursing organizations on a fee-for-service basis, either directly or through general practitioners.

Special services and programmes

Basic sanitation. Well over 90% of habitations are connected to the public sewers, which discharge far out at sea. There has in recent years been a major drive by the Ministry of Works to extend the public sewers with a view to abolishing the remaining cesspits on the islands. About 99% of households have a chlorinated piped water supply. Day-to-day administration is the responsibility of the Waterworks Department.

Environmental pollution control. Public cleansing services are provided by the Department of Health (under the Ministry of Health and Environment). In addition to daily cleaning of streets, there is daily house-to-house refuse collection (excepting Sundays). Air pollution is the responsibility of the Clean Air Board, and day-to-day control is one of the functions of its health inspectors.

Communicable diseases prevention and control. Communicable diseases have for several years ceased to be a major problem in Malta. Smallpox, diphtheria, poliomyelitis and cholera have not occurred for several years. Other diseases are markedly on the decline. There were 10 cases of typhoid, 10 cases of brucellosis and 20 cases of pulmonary tuberculosis in 1977.

Routine immunization is offered free of charge in the clinics run by the Department of Health against smallpox, diphtheria, tetanus, pertussis, poliomyelitis, tuberculosis and influenza. Immunization of girls against rubella was introduced in 1977. The Port Health Services' medical officers and health inspectors control importation of disease.

Health laboratory services. Analysts and bacteriologists are employed at the Public Health Laboratory, whose main function is the control of food, water and drugs as well as the checking of pathological specimens in cases of infectious disease. There is regular monitoring of food and water supplies. The assistance of reference laboratories abroad is sought in certain viral investigations.

Maternal and child health. Apart from services provided in the government hospitals, the Department of health runs regular clinics in the towns and villages.

School health. School medical officers and nurses care for the health of schoolchildren with routine medical examinations, immunization, advice on hygiene, and treatment.

Occupational health. In addition to medical officers with qualifications or experience in industrial health, the Department of Health has recently obtained the services of an Occupational Hygiene Officer. A fresh survey is being carried out of all local industries, and modern industrial health legislation is planned. The Occupational Hygiene unit of the Department provides free advice to industry, and notifies the Commissioner of Police prior to the licensing of all trades and industries—which is a legal requirement.

Health care of the elderly. It is the policy of the Government to ensure that the increasing proportion of the population who are elderly are given, as a social right, all necessary sustenance, help and other forms of assistance to enable them to live a full life. A broad-based plan of action is under way to implement this policy. In the health care and welfare fields, the health authorities are providing free medicines, a free domiciliary nursing service and a free home-help service to those living at home who cannot afford to pay for these services themselves; moreover, additional and better facilities are being made available in hospitals for elderly long-stay patients who require medical, nursing and other care. An expert on aging has recently visited Malta to advise the Government on the further development of the services for the care of the elderly.

Noncommunicable disease prevention and control. The passing of the Mental Health Act in 1976 was aimed at improving the mental health services. It is the aim of the Department of Health to provide specially trained staff, including psychiatric nurses and social workers, to work in this field.

Cancer is notifiable, and a cancer register is kept. The use of substances known to be carcinogenic is under strict control.

Oral health. In addition to treatment facilities in hospitals, special care is given to schoolchildren, for whom there is a free school dental clinic. Periodontal disease is a major problem, and steps are being taken to train dental hygienists locally.

Health education. Full use is made of the mass media. Health education forms an integral part of the duties of all paramedical staff.

Biomedical and health services research

Research is carried out in various divisions of the Department of Health in collaboration with the University of Malta. Recently a research committee has been set up by the Government to coordinate research. It is chaired by the Dean of the Faculty of Science of the University.

Health manpower development

The Ministry of Health is responsible for health manpower planning. The development plan for health takes into account the manpower requirements for present and predicted future needs in the light of the expansion of the health services. The original manpower projections are reviewed regularly.

There is local training of undergraduates in medicine, pharmacy and dentistry; the graduates are referred abroad for their further training.

The Department of Health's programme for the training of paramedical personnel has been strengthened in recent years, where possible locally, in the following disciplines: radiography, physiotherapy, medical laboratory technology, nursing, midwifery, speech therapy and the health inspectorate services. There are other paramedical personnel for whom training is not available locally and for whom a programme of training abroad is in operation.

Costs and financing of the health services

Total health expenditure for the financial year from 1 April 1976 to 31 March 1977 was 8 290 781 Maltese pounds. Recurrent expenditure was 7 058 948 pounds, and the amount spent on capital items was 1 231 833 pounds. These amounts represented 11.39% and 3.86%, respectively, of total government expenditure.

Recurrent expenditure divided by major services was as follows:

	Maltese pounds	
Hospitals	5 169 967	(73.24%)
Centre administration	492 067	(6.97%)
Community care services	175 349	(2.48%)
Others (including environmental and preventive services)	1 221 565	(17.31%)

Social security scheme for sickness and health insurance

The National Insurance Act provides for sickness benefits and pensions on a contributory basis, and for free treatment in government hospitals of persons injured at work.

The National Assistance Act provides for free treatment in government hospitals for those who do not have sufficient means, who are suffering from a notifiable infectious disease, who require treatment for cancer or who suffer from diseases of special scientific interest.

The National Assistance Act also provides for free medicines for those who do not have sufficient means or who suffer from tuberculosis or from certain chronic diseases.

MONACO

General background

The Principality consists of a highly urbanized community of 25 000, located in a particularly healthy region on the north coast of the Mediterranean. The standard of living is high. Sanitary conditions are satisfactory, medical personnel are plentiful, epidemics do not present a problem. Thus, for the present at least, the authorities have no major difficulties to contend with.

Population statistics

In 1976 the population was 25 029 in an area of about 1.75 km², giving a population density of 14 500 per km². The population by age group was as follows: 0–14 years, 3169; 15–64 years, 15 881; 65–74 years, 3398; 75 and over, 2581. The average annual population increase is 1%.

There were 452 births in 1976, giving a birth rate of 18 per 1000, and 497 deaths (19.8 per 1000). It may incidentally be noted that of the 524 deaths which occurred in 1977, more than 25% were of people aged over 85.

Country health situation

There are no very serious health problems, and the number and quality of the physicians are wholly satisfactory. It would perhaps be advisable to develop certain preventive medical services, such as maternal and child health care.

Administrative organization of the health services

Under the authority of H.S.H. the Sovereign Prince, government is exercised by a Minister of

State and three governmental counsellors (for finance, public works and the interior). Public health is included among the responsibilities of the Counsellor for the Interior. Specialized services are under the authority of the Director of Health and Social Affairs, who is assisted by a physician and four pharmacy inspectors, as well as by a Consultative Committee for Public Health.

Sanitation, cleanliness of housing and food shops, for example, fall within the jurisdiction of the Mayor, who acts under the supervision of the Minister of State.

Social security

Only salaried workers benefit from social insurance covering sickness, disability, death, accidents at work and certain benefits for dependants. However, salaried workers and self-employed alike (tradesmen, craftsmen, professionals, etc.) belong to pension funds which pay benefits on retirement.

Those providing care (physicians, surgeons, dentists, medical auxiliaries) are paid directly by the patients, who are subsequently reimbursed (wholly or partly). However, those who benefit from free medical care do not have to make any payment in advance; for services to this category of patients, physicians, surgeons, dentists, etc., are paid directly by the social security institutions.

The Social Services Equalization Fund, which is independent but under government control, pays benefits in case of sickness, maternity, disability or death, to salaried workers; An independent pension fund pays retirement pensions to salaried workers; another, for the self-employed, pays retirement pensions to its members; occupational accidents are covered by private insurance companies.

All these insurance systems are self-financed, with no government participation.

Health laws and regulations

Legislation has been passed since 1973 on practice of the profession of midwife; exclusion from school of children suffering from contagious diseases; vaccination techniques; qualifications of physicians, and use of human blood.

In addition, the Principality has approved the protocol amending the Single Convention on Narcotic Drugs and acceded to the Convention on Psychotropic Substances.

Discussions are in progress on bills concerning medicine, dentistry, pharmacy, the auxiliary medical professions, and pathology and biomedical laboratories.

Health plan and country health programming

The Government's main objectives are: enlargement and modernization of the Centre Hospitalier and improvement of preventive services (occupational health, vaccinations, maternal and child health, sports medicine).

Curative and preventive services and programmes

There have been practically no changes since 1973 in the organization and functioning of the preventive and curative services. There is a general hospital with a clinic and two preventive medicine departments, the Occupational Health Office, and the school and sports health inspection service.

Hospital services and medical care

The Principality has a general hospital, the Centre Hospitalier Princesse Grace, with an outpatient department.

The Centre Hospitalier is an independent public institution run by an Administrative Council, whose major decisions are subject to government guidance. The whole population of Monaco, together with that of adjacent French communes, can use the Centre Hospitalier. In addition, the population can attend two clinics which perform simple medical procedures (injections, for example) and provide minor treatment, and 41 physicians and 24 nurses practise in the town and are thus at the service of the population.

Special services and programmes

Basic sanitation is the responsibility of a para-administrative service which took over from the Monaco Sanitation Company. Household waste collection as well as road sweeping and washing are carried out every day without exception.

The Principality has only a little industry which, for the most part, can be classified as "clean". Water and air pollution do not present a particular threat. However, laws have been passed prohibiting all activities which pollute either water or the air. The technical services of the Government make the necessary checks.

Communicable disease prevention and control present no particular problem in Monaco.

A plan for the organization of a government service to be responsible for maternal and child health is still under discussion; at present it is the responsibility of family doctors.

There is a school health service employing two full-time specialists who conduct annual health check-ups among the 5000 children attending schools in Monaco.

There is an Occupational Health Office which is a private institution under government supervision. It employs five full-time specialists, who perform health check-ups for all employees in the Principality (about 17 000) at least once a year.

A geriatric department is now open at the Centre Hospitalier for patients with illnesses related to old age. There is also an old people's home for able-bodied old people. A physician attached to the home carries out regular health check-ups.

There is an emergency department at the Centre Hospitalier where the injured and sick are admitted at any time of the day or night. For very serious cases, emergency transport is arranged to the large hospitals in Nice or Marseilles.

The two school health physicians are assisted by dental inspectors, who do an annual dental check-up for all schoolchildren.

Biomedical and health services research

There is no health research establishment as such in Monaco.

Health manpower development

Manpower planning and projection of requirements are the responsibility of the Govern-

ment, and in particular the Department of the Interior, assisted by the Directorate of Health and Social Affairs.

Only two categories of health personnel are trained in Monaco: nurses, in an official school; nursing aides, at the Centre Hospitalier.

Authorizations for the private practice of a health profession are granted by the Government.

Cost and financing of health services

Total government expenditures in 1976 were as follows:

	French francs
Operations	274 035 580.74
Equipment	190 385 547.48
Total:	464 421 547.48
Operating cost of the health services	780 554.89
Operating cost of the sanitation service	7 394 513.81
State subsidy for equipping the Centre Hospitalier	1 332 164.20
Social security payments (excluding retirement pensions) to government employees	10 000 209.57

The unit daily cost of hospital care was 591.70 francs for surgery services, 439.00 francs for services rendered by physicians, 1 049.00 francs for reanimation services, 209.90 francs for chronic diseases services, and 148.60 francs for convalescent treatment services.

Appraisal of developments between 1973 and 1977

The health of the population has remained excellent. A school dental service for all schoolchildren has been established, a vaccination centre opened, and an annex for patients with chronic diseases inaugurated at the Centre Hospitalier.

MOROCCO

Background information

The area of the country is some 650 000 km². It is subject to a number of factors making the climate different from that of other Mediterranean countries. To the north of the Atlas rainfall

is fairly abundant, while to the south water running off the mountains towards the desert is only partly recovered by oasis agriculture. The overpopulated settled zones give way to a region with a scattered nomad population.

In 1977 the population of Morocco numbered

18 247 000. The birth rate and death rate were respectively 46 and 17 per 1000 population.

Administrative organization of the health services

Responsibility for public health is borne by the Ministry of Health, which consists of the Minister's Office, the Council of Health and the Inspectorate General (both of them directly responsible to the Minister), and the central administration and its external services. The central administration consists of the General Secretariat, the Directorate of Technical Affairs and the Directorate of Administrative Affairs. Under the control of the Minister, the General Secretariat organizes and coordinates all the different branches of the Ministry and ensures compliance with the decisions of the Minister.

The Directorate of Technical Affairs is in charge of programming and evaluation for the prevention of disease and care of the sick, and for improving the level of community health. It includes the Division of Epidemiology, the Division of Infrastructure and the Division of Population. The same Directorate also comprises the National Institute of Hygiene, the Central Pharmaceutical Service, the National Laboratory for Drugs Control, the National Blood Transfusion and Haematology Centre and the Environmental Hygiene Service. The Directorate of Administrative Affairs consists of the Division of Personnel and Budget, the Division of Supplies and Equipment, and the Division of General Affairs. Finally, there is the Department of Data Processing, which is attached to the General Secretariat.

In the field, there are 36 provinces or *préfectures* whose task it is to represent the Ministry of Public Health throughout the area for which they are responsible. The chief medical officers of the provinces or *préfectures* ensure implementation of health policy and the execution of the Minister's decisions. They are responsible for organizing, supervising and coordinating services in their separate districts. Each of them is assisted by an executive officer for administrative affairs and three assistants: a Chief Medical Officer for Ambulatory Services, a Chief Medical Officer for Hospitals, and a Chief Medical Officer for Laboratories. There are also provincial technical boards made up of medical specialists, sanitary engineers and statisticians.

Organization of medical care

Health programmes are put into effect through the different health areas. The health area is directed by a medical officer and has 45 000–75 000 inhabitants. Each area has a health centre for general and specialized medicine staffed by one or more physicians. The health area is divided into sectors of some 15 000 inhabitants, each one having a dispensary, in which health auxiliaries provide health care, carry out vaccinations, and promote maternal and child health, environmental sanitation and health education. In 1975 there were 105 urban health centres, 128 rural centres, and 219 urban and 654 rural dispensaries.

The hospital network is divided administratively into national university hospital centres, regional hospital centres, provincial hospital centres and zonal hospitals. In the past 15 years an effort has been made to increase the number and capacity of the hospitals, to improve their facilities and to increase their efficiency.

In 1977 the country had 29 848 hospital beds and 2051 beds attached to rural health centres.

Organization of preventive services

The control of communicable diseases is the responsibility of specialized technical services for malaria, tuberculosis, eye diseases and other specific diseases, which supervise the implementation of the programme by the provincial services under the responsibility of the Directorate of Technical Affairs. Child health care is integrated with the basic health services at every level, from the area dispensaries upwards.

For environmental health matters, the central sanitation service is represented at the provincial and prefectural level by the municipal offices of hygiene. These employ polyvalent engineers, who will gradually be replaced by specialist sanitary engineers as the latter are trained.

Occupational medicine comes under the Ministry of Labour, but medical treatment of workers and their families is provided by the public health services, whose resources are also used for detecting and preventing occupational diseases.

Health manpower development

In 1977 there were 856 public health physicians, or one to 21 341 inhabitants, in addition to private practitioners and medical officers in the armed forces. There are about 64 pharmacists and 33 dentists working in the public health field, excluding the much larger numbers of private pharmacists and dentists.

A major effort has been made to train doctors within the country. Every year since 1965 the Faculty of Medicine at Rabat has produced 100 doctors, and it will soon be training 150 annually. A second faculty of medicine has been set up at Casablanca which gives grounds for hoping that in the next few years a greater number of Moroccan medical personnel will emerge to occupy public health posts and satisfy the needs of the public and private sectors.

By 1977 Morocco had trained since independence 200 senior nursing staff, more than 2250 State nurses and 9057 registered auxiliaries. There are 26 schools for registration, 12 technicians' training schools and one senior staff training school. At the same time, correspondence courses enable the most gifted to take the competitive examinations for entry to the schools preparing candidates for the State diplomas.

Public health research

The National Public Health Laboratory is made up of a group of specialized laboratories for bacteriology, parasitology, toxicology, etc. The Drugs Control Laboratory is attached to it for technical purposes.

There is also a National Blood Transfusion Centre which supervises the provincial centres.

Financing of the health services

In 1977 the public health budget amounted to 406 869 179 dirhams for operational expenditure and 195 460 000 dirhams for investments. This represents 4.5% and 1.6% respectively of the national budget, and is equal to about 33 dirhams per inhabitant.

NETHERLANDS

Background information

The Netherlands has an area of 41 160 km^2. In 1976 its population was 13 734 000 (409 inhabitants per km^2). The capital, Amsterdam, had a population of 975 500, but the largest city is Rotterdam, which had 1 022 700 inhabitants. In the same year the birth rate and the death rate (per 1000) were respectively 12.9 and 8.3, giving a natural increase of 0.46%. The infant mortality rate and the maternal mortality rate were respectively 10.5 and 0.11 per 1000 live births in 1975. The expectation of life (1975) was 77.6 years for females. The main causes of death in 1975, in order of incidence, were heart diseases, malignant neoplasms, cerebrovascular diseases, bronchitis and accidents. In 1975 the communicable diseases most frequently notified were salmonellosis (6452 cases), scarlet fever (1422), rubella (1325) and infectious hepatitis (1183).

Administrative organization of the health services

The responsibility for national public health rests with the Minister of Health and Environmental Protection, who is assisted by a Secretary of State, a Secretary-General, and three directors-general (for public health, for environmental hygiene and for the National Institute of Public Health). A number of advisory boards give scientific and practical advice to the Minister. Technical advice is given by the six chief medical officers in charge of the State supervision of public health, who deal respectively with public health and medical inspection, mental health, pharmaceutical problems, foodstuffs, environmental hygiene, veterinary health and the Licensing Act provisions. The supervisory board thus comprised will shortly be integrated within the Ministry.

At the provincial level, the regional medical officers are concerned with the same problems as the chief medical officers, their tasks being centred more closely on control and inspection. Provincial councils of health, which were established in 1956, are responsible for coordinating the health work of the local authorities and the voluntary organizations. Under recent hospital legislation they play an advisory role in hospital planning.

Local authorities are closely concerned with health care and have a good deal of executive responsibility. In small communities the local authority for health matters is the mayor, while in large municipalities there is a local medical and health service.

Much work in the field of health is carried out by private nonprofit-making bodies, which play an important role in the Netherlands health services.

Organization of medical care

All persons in paid employment and earning less than a fixed amount (in 1977, 33 650 guilders, or US $13 575) are compulsorily insured. This affects about 51% of the population. The insurance covers services provided by the general practitioner (either at his surgery or at the patient's home), the specialist and the obstetrician, drugs, one year's hospital nursing, and treatment in a sanatorium. A special scheme provides for long-term care in mental hospitals and other institutions for mental and other conditions. Dental care, with certain restrictions, is also covered. Since 1960 health care may be provided for more than one year. In general, private insurance schemes provide the same benefits, except for general practitioner care. There are special schemes for old people and independent workers.

In 1976 the bed capacity in health care institutions was 99 786 (7.2 beds per 1000 inhabitants), 74 116 of them in general and special hospitals, including teaching hospitals, 25 670 in mental hospitals. In addition there were 27 426 beds in homes for the mentally retarded, 42 522 in nursing homes, 2436 in institutes for the deaf and the blind, 988 in medical homes for children, and 1133 in medical day nurseries. There was thus a total of 174 290 beds.

These figures do not include homes for the elderly without sickbay (137 250 beds in 1976), orphanages, and other similar non-medical establishments.

Mental health care is the special responsibility of the Minister and the Chief Medical Officer for Mental Health; the latter is assisted by full-time regional psychiatrists. The procedure for voluntary admission of patients to psychiatric institutions is similar to that for general hospitals. For compulsory institutionalization a legal authorization is required. New legal provisions are under preparation. Furthermore, mental patients are being cared for to an increasing extent in psychiatric departments of general hospitals.

Special clinics have been set up to provide care for patients with tuberculosis (five special departments in general hospitals with a total of 200 beds), and special clinics are available for cancer and rheumatism patients.

Certain other specialized services have been developed and reorganized in recent years. Geriatric services have been established in some areas, where special departments have been organized to administer them. The central registration of cancer cases is carried out by the national cancer control organization. The national blood transfusion laboratory has been considerably developed, especially in the field of research.

The Cross Associations (referred to below in connexion with preventive services) have organized home nursing services, which employ 3720 nurses and have 1670 branches with 3 000 000 members who pay an annual subscription. These associations also receive subsidies from the central and local government authorities.

Organization of preventive services

Environmental sanitation is mainly the responsibility of the local authorities, but examination of drinking-water and air pollution control (for which there is a national automatic monitoring system) are carried out by the National Institute of Public Health. Nearly the whole population has drinking-water, and over 89.5% of the population had sewage disposal services in 1975.

With a few exceptions, the local authorities are also responsible for providing preventive services, often with the assistance of voluntary organizations. In fact, since the end of the nineteenth century the voluntary bodies known as the Cross Associations (religious and lay bodies) have played a leading part in preventive medicine. In small municipalities they run health centres, advisory bureaux and centres for the issue of medical equipment for use in the home. Previously emphasis was laid on maternal and child welfare and the care of tuberculosis patients, but nowadays their activities also include mental health, the care of rheumatism and cancer patients and the care of the elderly.

The maternal and child health services resulting from the above collaboration were provided in 1975 by 90 maternity welfare centres, 2990 infant welfare clinics and 2862 child health clinics. The infant mortality rate, which is one of the lowest in the world, testifies to the efficiency of these services.

The school health service, the costs of which are shared by the State, the provinces and the municipalities, consists of 143 school health centres which cover nearly all schoolchildren. Its functions are purely preventive.

About 95% of all children are immunized against diphtheria, tetanus, pertussis and poliomyelitis, and the girls also against rubella. Immunization against measles starter later and has covered 80%. Immunization against small-pox is no longer obligatory, consequently the state of immunity is much lower.

Dental care to schoolchildren was provided by 115 dental services in 1976.

As a result of the increase in the number of social psychiatrists and other psychiatric personnel, it has been found possible to extend district and local psychiatric services, which have as their object both the follow-up of discharged patients and the prevention of mental illness, to the whole country.

Occupational health in general is controlled by the Government, but services in this field are organized by the individual enterprises. As the number of doctors who have received special training increases, so the occupational health services develop in scope.

Some years ago a new development started with the setting up of regional consultation agencies for health education. At the moment a committee for national planning in health education is preparing a new structure for health education at national and regional levels.

Public health information and research

There have been considerable advances in medical and public health research. This is carried out at the Netherlands Institute of Public health and Hygiene, Bilthoven, in 17 regional public health laboratories, in municipal food hygiene laboratories, in universities and teaching hospitals, in private research centres and in the laboratories of institutes and agencies of the Netherlands Central Organization for Applied Scientific Research. In 1971 this Organization set up a Health Research Council, presided over by the Secretary-General of the Ministry of Health.

The Ministry of health influences research policy by providing subsidies and financing government research centres and activities such as those of the National Institute of Public Health and Hygiene, and also through the Health Research Council, which establishes priorities and guides research activities.

Supply and training of health personnel

In 1975 the Netherlands had 22 913 active physicians (of whom 4962 were general practitioners), or one per 760 inhabitants; 4688 active dentists; 1257 pharmacists (of whom 919 were independent pharmacists); 880 midwives; 4350 public health nurses; 72 100 hospital nurses (including 34 700 student nurses); 2980 hospital laboratory and radiology personnel; and 4789 physiotherapists (of whom 2687 were working as independent physiotherapists, 872 in general hospitals, and 1230 in other health institutions).

Medical training is given in eight medical faculties (five State, one municipal, one Protestant and one Catholic). Education in the clinical disciplines is given at teaching hospitals and "affiliated" hospitals, both private and public. These hospitals, which include some special hospitals (18), are also used for postgraduate training.

In 1975, the training of (registered) nurses took place in 188 general hospitals. There were 21 schools for nurses that were quite separate from any hospital. Assistant nurses (enrolled nurses) were trained in 29 general hospitals, 11 special hospitals, 16 mental hospitals, 261 nursing homes and 46 schools for enrolled nurses.

Physiotherapists receive their education in 20 schools of physiotherapy. The Technical University of Delft offers a one-year course in sanitary engineering.

Financing of health services

In 1976 expenditure on health reached 20 000 million guilders (8.5% of GNP), of which 10 075 million were from compulsory or voluntary social security schemes. This was equal to 732 guilders (US $300) per head of population.

NORWAY

Population and other statistics

At the last census, taken in 1976, the population of Norway was 4 026 152. Population estimates and some other vital statistics for the period 1973–1976 are given in the table below.

Of the 40 216 deaths recorded in 1976, the main causes were: chronic rheumatic heart disease, hypertensive disease, ischaemic heart disease, other forms of heart diseases (13 078), neoplasms (8413), cerebrovascular disease (5710), pneumonia (2865), ill-defined conditions (1963), accidents (1917), bronchitis, emphysema and asthma (634), diabetes mellitus (279), congenital anomalies (250), cirrhosis of liver (219), suicides (433), homicides (30).

The communicable diseases notified most frequently in 1976 were: hepatitis (471), typhoid fever (5), paratyphoid fever (13), other salmonella infections (308), dysentery (bacillary and amoebic) (75), meningococcal infections (321), meningitis (376), ornithosis (45), malaria (56), staphylococcal infections of newborn (258), other infectious disease (1383), infection following vaccinations (59).

The communicable disease cases in 1976 reported by the National Institute of Public Health can be summarized as follows: influenza (196 086), streptococcal infections (49 952), mononucleosis (2877), measles (not vaccinated) (2534), measles (vaccinated) (670), rubella (4180), mumps (22 394), pertussis (1094), acute gastroenteritis (56 367), scabies (32 017), pediculosis (3590), gonorrhoea (over 18 years of age) (13 013), gonorrhoea (under 18 years of age) (1143), syphilis (280), other venereal diseases (128).

Organization of the public health services

The Ministry of Social Affairs has overall responsibility for both the health and social services. In the health sector, executive action is taken by the National Directorate of Health Services, headed by a medical administrator, the Director-General of Health. The Directorate is divided into 10 divisions, dealing respectively with local health services, finance and employment, social medicine, psychiatry, hygiene, nursing services, pharmacy, dentistry, hospitals and planning.

Norway is divided into 19 provinces, one of which is the capital city, Oslo. The provincial public health officers represent the National Directorate of Health Services at provincial level; their main duty is to superintend the health services within the province and to supervise the implementation of the laws and regulations on medicine and sanitation. They also supervise the activities of all local public health officers, and oversee all health personnel working within the area; and they head provincial committees, which assess the benefits from the rehabilitation and disability insurance scheme.

According to the Norwegian Health Law of 1860 every commune has a board of health chaired by the local public health officer. In the rural areas and the towns, the public health officer is both a general practitioner and a health

	1973	1974	1975	1976
Mean population	3 960 613	3 985 258	4 007 313	4 026 152
Number of live births	61 208	59 603	56 345	53 474
Birth rate (per 1000 population)	15.5	15.0	14.1	13.3
Number of deaths	39 958	39 464	40 061	40 216
Death rate (per 1000 population)	10.1	9.9	10.0	10.0
Natural increase (%)	0.63	0.62	0.49	0.45
Number of infant deaths	730	622	625	561
Infant mortality rate (per 1000 live births)	11.9	10.4	11.1	10.5
Number of deaths (1–4 years)	187	18	162	165
Death rate 1–4 years (per 1000 population at risk) boys/girls	0.84/0.58	0.86/0.56	0.78/0.50	0.80/0.54
Number of maternal deaths	2	4	4	7
Maternal mortality rate (per 1000 births)	0.03	0.07	0.07	0.13

administrator. In the cities he is a full time health administrator. The main duties of the local health board are: environmental health, communicable diseases control, family health, school health, mental health, health education.

Changes in the provision of health services

Since January 1971 the country has had an integrated, coordinated social insurance system covering the whole population. The most important conditions covered by the national insurance scheme are: medical care, including hospital care, physiotherapy, certain dental services, family planning, sickness benefit limited to 90% of the income, rehabilitation benefit, permanent disability benefit for 50% working capacity, occupational accidents and diseases, unemployment benefit, old-age or retirement pensions, benefits awarded to widows and children under 18 years in case of death and loss of breadwinner, maternity benefits, benefits to unmarried mothers, child allowances, war injuries. The scheme is financed by a special premium paid in addition to the ordinary taxes, and by contributions from employers, municipalities and the State.

Primary medical care is given either by the local public health officer (the district doctor) or by private practitioners. An increasing part of the specialist care is given in hospital outpatient departments.

From 1 January 1975 a revised reporting system for infectious diseases was introduced. The administration of the reporting system is carried out by the National Institute of Public Health. Individual (nominative) and summary reports are submitted weekly by physicians. The system gives special up-to-date information to all doctors in the country and has proved very efficient.

Hospital services

In 1976 Norway had 189 hospitals and inpatient establishment with 31 550 beds, equivalent to 7.2 beds per 1000 population. In addition there were 568 somatic nursing homes (including nursing homes for special diseases) and somatic nursing departments in combined old-age and nursing homes, with 22 708 beds, 127 psychiatric nursing homes, with 4480 beds, and 118 establishments for the mentally deficient, with 583 beds.

The distribution of the 190 hospitals by number of beds, number of patients admitted and number of patient days in 1976 was as follows:

Category	Number	Number of beds	Number of patients admitted	Number of patient days
General and local hospitals	87	20 204	525 017	5 839 615
Maternity and cottage hospitals	61	1 263	11 646	415 916
Tuberculosis hospitals	4	214	1 040	63 271
Mental hospitals	20	7 835	10 513	2 576 798
Orthopaedic hospitals	4	401	5 852	116 076
Hospitals for rheumatic diseases	5	479	3 521	139 328
Cancer hospital	1	353	8 157	110 248
Hospital for epileptics	1	164	397	40 944
Rehabilitation hospitals	5	589	3 071	197 586
Other specialized hospital	1	48	185	10 020
Total	189	31 550	569 399	9 509 782

The majority of hospitals are governmental, and central or local government or National Insurance covers all expenses. All hospital care is free. According to the Hospital Act, ambulatory care is regarded as part of the hospital activities. Ambulatory specialist care is often given both by specialists outside the institutions and by doctors in inpatient establishments as an integral part of their services. The volume of ambulatory care has grown rapidly with the reorganization and expansion of the hospital services under the Act.

Communicable disease control and immunization services

After the introduction of oral vaccine, poliomyelitis cases fell from an annual average of 728 in the period 1951–1955 to zero during the period under review; the majority of the population and more than 90% of the children have been immunized. Tuberculosis morbidity and mortality still continue to decrease. Young adults have been a special target group for the BCG vaccination programme. A central register was established in 1962. Since 1969 the case-finding programme carried out by the National Mass Radiography Service has concentrated on high-risk groups selected according to an analysis it made of the register. Particular attention is given to the care of tuberculosis patients with additional problems, such as mental illness, mental subnormality or alcoholism.

For drug-resistant cases of pulmonary tuberculosis a centralized project has been established. The lesser-known second-line drugs can only be obtained through the pharmacy of the Oslo University Hospital and are available to sanatoria and lung disease departments only. Information about new drugs and guidelines for their use are distributed to these institutions by the Health Services of Norway. The policy has been to ensure that antituberculous drugs are prescribed by specialists well acquainted with the efficacy and the side effects of these drugs.

The incidence of gonorrhoea has increased rapidly, from 1866 cases in 1955 to 14 156 cases in 1976. The annual number of syphilis cases is decreasing; there were only 280 in 1976. The immunization scheme for children includes vaccination against smallpox (cancelled from 1976), diphtheria, pertussis, tetanus, poliomyelitis, measles and tuberculosis. All girls of 13–15 years of age are offered vaccination against rubella.

As an indication of the immunization programme, the National Institute of Public Health produced or delivered the following amounts of vaccines in 1977:

Poliomyelitis, oral	456 710 doses
Smallpox (40 095 persons were actually vaccinated	117 777 doses
Diphtheria, pertussis and tetanus	182 315 ml
Diphtheria and tetanus	126 085 ml
BCG	270 000 doses
Typhoid	32 175 ml
Typhoid and paratyphoid A + B	2 000 ml
Measles	52 009 doses
Diphtheria	—
Cholera	76 025 ml
Tetanus	37 625 ml
Yellow fever	about 10 000 doses
Pertussis	500 ml
Rubella	2 017 doses
Influenza	103 640 doses
Meningoccus (A + C)	17 doses

Specialized units

In 1976 there were 1368 centres for maternal and child health care. As a rule, prenatal care is provided by the general practitioner. In 1976,

99.6% of deliveries were in medical establishments. At least 95% of children under 1 year of age receive medical care services. According to law, the local board of health in each municipality is responsible for the school health services which cover the total population. The school dental service is organized and financed by the municipalities. It offers dental treatment free to schoolchildren, as decided by each municipality. The public dental service is organized and financed by the county. It offers free dental care to children aged 3–17 years and treatment at 50%–reduced fees to regular attenders aged 18–20 years. The Government refunds 60% of the fee paid by the county. In 1977 dental care was given to approximately 630 000 children.

In 1977, 3072 industrial establishments provided medical and health services for about 425 000 workers; 48 doctors worked full-time and 688 part-time in the occupational health services.

Other specialized units include 1 tuberculosis hospital, 3 venereal diseases policlinics and 3 public health laboratories, including that of the National Institute of Public Health.

Medical and allied personnel and training facilities

At the end of 1976 Norway had:

Medical doctors	7 630*
Dentists	3 930
Veterinarians	916
Pharmacists	1 553 (1975)
Nurses	20 485
Assistant nurses	10 082
Physiotherapists	3 148

In the school year 1976/1977 the arrangements for training of professional and auxiliary health personnel were as follows (provisional figures from the Central Bureau of Statistics):

Category	Duration of study (years)	Number of schools	Number of new students 1976/77	Number of graduates 1976/77
Doctors	6–6.5	4	441	281
Dentists	5	2	132	119
Pharmacists	5	1	38	40
Veterinarians	5.5–6	1	39	38
Dental auxiliaries	2	2	24	17
Laboratory assistants	2	9	88	149
Physiotherapists	2	2	147	130
Radiographers	2.5	3	33	62
Medical secretaries	1	3	61	58
Nurses	3	29	1 929	1 465
Assistant nurses	1	52	2 819	2 467
Midwives	1	2	90	82

* One doctor to 529 inhabitants.

Environmental sanitation

In 1972 Norway had a total of 1 075 145 dwelling units, of which 997 594, or approximately 93%, were provided with piped water. The urban population living in houses connected to public sewerage systems totalled 1.5 million, while 2 230 000 inhabitants living in rural areas had adequate sewerage disposal systems, such as pit privies or septic tanks.

Major public health problems

The most important public health problems in Norway are ischaemic heart disease, cancer, cerebrovascular diseases, traffic accidents and environmental pollution.

Social and economic developments of significance for the health situation

A law on hospital planning, coordination and financing came into force in 1970. The provinces are given the full responsibility for the planning, construction and running of hospitals and most other somatic health establishments. The planning and extension of health establishments and their activities are supervised by the Director-General of Health Services, in accordance with directives given by the Government. The costs of running these establishments are paid by the National Insurance Scheme and the owner, mainly the province.

Medical and public health research

Medical and public health research are carried out in research institutions, hospitals, universities and by groups of individual doctors in the primary health service. Norway has no coordinated research programme. The three research councils, the Norwegian Research Council for Science and the Humanities, the Agricultural Research Council and the Royal Council for Scientific and Industrial Research, spend about 20% of the total research budget.

Government health expenditure

In 1976 total general government health expenditure amounted to 12 336 million kroner of which 9354 million kroner went on care and treatment in institutions. The expenses covered by the central Government and the National Insurance scheme amounted to 8497 million kroner and included the following items:

	Kroner (millions)
Treatment in somatic institutions	4 558
Psychiatric institutions	906
Mentally retarded and epileptics	507
Care for the physically handicapped	99
Medical treatment, drugs, etc	2 045
Dental treatment	146
Preventive and general public health services . .	113
Education and training of health personnel . . .	71
Other	51

POLAND

Basic information

The Polish People's Republic covers an area of 312 627 km^2 and has a population of 34.9 million. The average density of population is about 110.7 per km^2. Poland is administratively divided into 49 voivodships (provinces), including three large cities treated as separate units. Each voivodship is divided into cities and communities; there are 808 cities and 2138 communities. The capital, Warsaw, has over 1.5 million inhabitants. Some 55% of the population live in urban areas. The birth rate is 19.1%, the death rate, 9%, so that the annual rate of population increase is 10.1%.

The proportions of various age groups in the population are as follows:

0–14 years	8 312 000 (23.9%)
15–64 years	23 040 000 (66.1%)
65–74 years	2 371 000 (6.8%)
75 and over	1 122 000 (3.2%)

As far as the employment structure is concerned, over 38% of the working population is employed in building and industry and 29% in other spheres of the national economy. Over 540 000 are employed in various institutions concerned with health care, medical sciences and social welfare (3.1% of the working population).

National income in 1975 was 1 261 400 million zlotys, taking as the basis prices that had been stable since 1971. The average yearly increase in national income in the years 1971–1975 was 9.8%. In the year 1977 the share of health and social welfare expenditure in the State budget was 8.2%, and per capita expenditure was 1802 zlotys.

Health situation

The main health problems are cardiovascular diseases, diseases of the respiratory tract and alimentary system, cancer and mental diseases and diseases of the nervous system. Accidents, especially those that occur at home, in public places and on roads are also among the main causes of death. The average death rate, 8.9 per 1000 population, is one of the lowest in the world. During the last 25 years the death rate in the reproductive age groups fell by three-quarters.

The death rates for cardiovascular diseases and malignant tumours have increased; 44% of deaths are caused by cardiovascular diseases and 23% by cancer. Accidents, traumas and poisonings are also increasing and in 1976 caused 8% of deaths. The death rate for infectious diseases and respiratory tract diseases fell significantly (1.7 and 5.4 per 10 000 respectively). Out of the total of 670 000 deliveries there were only 95 maternal deaths caused by complications. The speed with which the rather high infant death rate is decreasing is one of the most rapid in Europe. In 1976 it was 23.8 per 1000 live births but it still remains higher than the European average.

Enormous progress has been made in tuberculosis control. The number of new cases decreased to 24 700 in 1976, the most significant decrease being observed among children and adolescents.

After the increase in venereal diseases in the 1960s there is at present a marked decrease (from 22.4 per 10 000 population in 1970 to 12.7 in 1976).

Among cardiovascular diseases the predominant place is taken by arterial hypertension, together with coronary diseases occurring alone or combined with heart failure. Further increases in morbidity, mortality and disability from this disease have to be noted.

There was also an increase in morbidity from malignant tumours, from 171.5 per 100 000 in 1970 to 184 in 1976. The majority of the neoplastic diseases are cancers of the alimentary tract, genital organs and respiratory passages.

The morbidity from mental diseases and diseases of the nervous system is at present between 450 and 500 per 1000 000, an increase in neuroses being offset by a decrease in acute psychoses.

The health status of the industrial workers does not differ very significantly from that of the rest of the population. The professional diseases do not create a major problem either from the point of view of general health or from the epidemiological point of view.

The average health status of children and adolescents does not differ significantly from that in other countries with similar standards of living. The improvement and acceleration of physical and mental development is observable in terms of adolescents' greater height and general psychomotor development than those of preceding generations. The health survey of six-year-olds in 1975–1977 showed 75% of them to have normal physical and mental development. The only problems encountered frequently in children are sight and hearing defects, and dental caries and malocclusion.

Organization of health care and social services

Administrative organization

The Ministry of Health and Social Welfare, headed by the Minister, is responsible for specifying needs, issuing the organizational and legislative regulations and directives for the activities of the health care system, as well as planning and shaping staff policy. The Minister supervises the training of medical personnel, the research activities of the institutes, and drugs and equipment supply. He is advised by the Board of the Ministry and the Scientific Council.

At the local level the health care and social welfare problems are dealt with by the local councils as the representatives of the state authorities. The local councils are, at the first level of community self-government, followed by city district, town and voivodship councils. On those levels health problems are dealt with by the subcommittees on health, social affairs and environment protection, which initiate and control the activities of local administration bodies.

Each local (voivodship, town, district or community) council is headed by an executive director representing the state administration and responsible to the level above for health and social services. The advisory body to the executive is the health and social welfare division of the local council. The head of this division is chief medical officer of the area, appointed by the head of the local council with the agreement of the Minister of Health. The chief medical officer of the area is competent to make decisions pertaining to the health problems on behalf of the local administrative authorities.

Both the organization and the activities of the social welfare system have been shaped by social and economic and demographic changes in the last 30 years. The Constitution guarantees the right of every citizen in need to State aid. The main aim of the social welfare services is to help those disabled and elderly persons who are unable to care for themselves. The activities follow two directions: community aid (financial support, home services, etc.) and a system of institutions (homes for the elderly, nursing homes for the chronically sick and disabled, the blind, retarded children, etc.). Another form of welfare institution, day care centres for retired people, was started recently.

The majority of social service workers are voluntary unpaid workers. In 1976 there were 57 000 of them. The social welfare development policy is directed towards increasing the number of qualified social workers so that every primary health care unit, both urban and rural, can employ one. An important role is played by such organizations as the Polish Red Cross and the Polish Committee for Social Welfare.

Health and social welfare institutions

In the years 1973–1975 some significant changes in the organization and structure of the institutions subjected to the Minister of Health and Social Welfare were made. The hospitals, outpatient clinics, ambulance units, nurseries and homes for the elderly which had hitherto been separate entities were integrated into centres under one board of directors. Social services were included in the scope of activities of the centres. These changes allowed for better use of the material and financial resources, made

the services of the staff more effective, and enabled the administrative units to employ more modern methods of management and financing. The effects were seen in the team work of the units, which made preventive, therapeutic and rehabilitative care more widely available. Continuity of health care has been ensured and the activities pertaining to the individual and the environment have been unified.

At present the structure of the integrated health care centres comprise: local centres which serve 30 000–150 000 inhabitants; industrial health centres in areas where heavy industrial plants are concentrated; students' health centres and voivodship health centres, including voivodship hospitals and specialized centres for inhabitants of one or several voivodships (three to five voivodships form a region). There are also independent voivodship specialized hospitals, teaching hospitals and hospitals belonging to the research institutions. All these institutions work in close cooperation with sanatoria, health resorts, and homes for the elderly, chronically sick, disabled or retarded.

The local centre consists of several units which provide primary health care for inhabitants, for employees, and for children. A local health centre consists of a hospital and specialized outpatient clinics as well as an emergency service employing several ambulance units. Besides these there are nurseries, crèches, homes and day care centres for the elderly, all of which are branches of the health centre.

In urban areas health care for the inhabitants of a given area is provided by district outpatient clinics. The scope of services of such clinics include general practice, internal medicine, paediatrics, obstetrics and gynaecology, dental care and environmental social welfare services. They provide preventive care, therapy and rehabilitation services as well as filling the role of social welfare centres.

The voivodship health centre provides additional specialist services and may serve as a consultation or reference unit for patients who cannot be treated in local centres. Besides its hospital function it supervises the activities of the local centres, controls specialist services in the region and organizes postgraduate training for medical personnel. It also comprises highly specialized outpatient clinics, an emergency service and social welfare centre.

Specialized centres such as neoplastic disease centres, psychiatric care centres and lung diseases centres complement the integrated local and voivodship hospitals.

Health care delivery system

All matters connected with health care are the responsibility of the State, which also bears the basic expenses for the establishment and management of health and social welfare institutions.

Every inhabitant has the right to full medical care and assistance without distinction between so-called public health and the health of the individual. All authorities have to consider as part of their activities the requirements of health care protection.

The fact that the State has ensured the right to full health care, health protection and medical assistance is best expressed by their inclusion in national socioeconomic plans, with the establishment of the executive authority in the form of the Ministry of Health and Social Welfare to administer the uniform, comprehensive system of health care and social welfare.

Over 99% of the population is covered by the national insurance system, which ensures the preventive, therapeutic and rehabilitative services free of charge to everyone. The right to medical services includes outpatient care, both primary and specialist, inpatient care (hospitalization) as well as emergency (first aid and ambulance) services. The patient pays 30% of the actual price of drugs, the rest being covered by the State. Some categories of patient receive drugs free of charge.

The activities pertaining to preventive care, therapy, and rehabilitation as well as social welfare are conducted by State health service institutions under the Ministry, local and voivodship institutions subjected directly to the chief medical officer of the voivodship, and central or regional institutions supervised directly by the Minister. Some of the health care institutions are subjected to other ministries, but the Minister of Health and Social Welfare and voivodship authorities have the right to influence and coordinate their activities. Parallel to the national health service institutions there are medical cooperatives; private practice is a marginal form of service.

Health care is based on the results of research in the medical sciences. Secondary and higher medical schools and academies provide the highly qualified professional staff and ensure their continuous education and specialization, as well as the upgrading of medical workers of all levels.

The health care and social welfare system is based on long-term planning according to the needs and demands of the population, scientific and technological progress and social and economic conditions. The long-term development programme for the years 1975–1990 has been approved by the Government; more specific health plans are included in five-year and yearly national social and economic development plans. Programmes for the development of health services are also elaborated at voivodship level.

The marked improvement in the epidemiological situation is exemplified by the decrease in morbidity from diarrhoeal diseases from 31.8 to 10.4 per 100 000 inhabitants and in food poisoning from 330 to 129.6 per 100 000, between 1973 and 1977.

A slight increase in life expectancy was observed; in 1976 it reached 66.9 for men and 74.6 for women, a not very significant increase, owing to gradual aging of the population.

The system of continuous postgraduate education has been further developed, as have the system of specialist supervision by research institutes, and undergraduate training. The salaries scheme for employees of health service institutions changed. New regulations concerning the employment of medical staff aiming at full use of staff according to needs, have been put into force. Rehabilitation has been integrated with therapy, including professional rehabilitation of the disabled and their reintegration in society.

Primary health care

Primary health care is provided by general practitioners, paediatricians and stomatologists and gynaecologists employed in local outpatient units or clinics, occupational health clinics and village health centres. It is closely linked with social welfare—in every medical clinic there is an environmental social welfare unit. The team, consisting of a general practitioner, a nurse and a social worker, covers the 3000–5000 people in a region. Another team, consisting of a paediatrician and several nurses, takes care of children and adolescents. A third, consisting of a gynaecologist and a midwife, ensures that all pregnant women and those who suffer from diseases of the genital organs receive special care. An additional team of stomatologists and prosthetic surgeons provides preventive, therapeutic and prosthetic dental services.

Health care in the work-place is also part of primary care, covering over 6.3 million industrial workers, including transport and building industries.

Particular attention has been paid to mother and child care. Over 92% of all deliveries take place in hospitals and 100% take place under the supervision of a qualified physician or a midwife. The system of care includes periodical tests and examinations in pregnancy and after delivery. Health care is the most important activity in the care of children and adolescents, starting with examinations of the newborn and continuing with tests at 2, 4, 6, 10, 14, and 18 years of age, covering over 90% of the population in these age groups. School clinics have been established in nearly all schools, and in over 80% of school clinics there are a physician and a dentist.

Immunization against infectious diseases is compulsory, and 41 million immunizations were performed in 1976.

All children receive preventive treatment against scabies, and the majority against caries; fluoride compounds are given to individuals for special treatment purposes, and drinking-water is fluoridated.

Specialized services

Specialist care complementing primary health care is organized at the local level, and highly specialized services are provided at the voivodship, regional and country levels.

Comprehensive first aid services for accidents and sudden illness are available at community and at voivodship level. Over 4000 mobile teams give first aid *in situ* or at the patient's home. When necessary there is air transport.

There was rapid development in reanimation, intensive therapy, cardiac diagnosis and surgery, external dialysis, kidney transplantation, stereotactic operations in neurosurgery, and endoprosthetic vascular surgery, during the period under review.

Health resources

Institutions

Between 1945 and the early 1970s the number of hospital beds (sanatoria included)

doubled and those in psychiatric hospitals even trebled. The number of places in homes for the elderly, the disabled and the chronically ill also increased considerably. The most rapid increase was in the years 1971–1977, when hospital beds increased by 28 800 to equal the European average. The places in nurseries increased by 25 700 and village health centres by 815. With the marked decrease in tuberculosis morbidity some beds that had been occupied by tuberculosis patients could be transferred for other purposes.

Many hospitals, outpatient clinics and social welfare homes have been modernized.

Manpower

The numbers of qualified medical personnel have increased many-fold since the 1950s. All the objectives that were set in the long-term programme for the development of health care and social welfare services have been achieved. The next long-term programme sets the number of physicians per 10 000 inhabitants at 20 for the year 1990, and the number of pharmacists and dentists should reach 5.6 per 10 000; 220 000 nurses and midwives will be required, to give 59 per 10 000 population and three nurses to one physician. Intermediate medical personnel should reach 24 per 10 000 by the year 1990, giving a total of about 86 000— mainly laboratory assistants and technicians.

The constant progress in science and technology, and the need for continuously raising the level of health care services, forces health service personnel to continue their training in postgraduate studies which are organized by the centre for postgraduate medical education (for all high-school graduates wishing to obtain first and second-degree specializations as physicians, dentists, pharmacists and some other categories) and the centre for post-diploma training of intermediate medical staff. Medical academies and voivodship centres for postgraduate training also conduct such courses. Some 70% of physicians are first- or second-degree specialists.

PORTUGAL

During the period 1970–1976 the population increased by 12.2%, owing largely to an influx from the ex-colonies after their accession to independence. This amounted to an average

annual population increase of 2%.

The 0–14 year age group constituted 28.8% of the population in 1970, 27.9% in 1975. The corresponding figures for the other age groups were; 15–64 years, 61.9% and 62.2%; 65–74 years, 6.3% and 6.8%; 75 years and over, 3.0% and 3.1%, respectively.

The birth rate was 20.8% in 1975 (20.8% in 1970). The overall mortality rate was 10.4% (10.8%), the infant mortality rate 38.9% of all live births (58.0%); the maternal mortality rate 0.43% (0.73%). Life expectancy at birth was 65.2 years for men and 72.4 for women in 1975 (65.3 and 71.0 respectively in 1970), while at age 65, life expectancy was 12.4 years for men and 14.9 for women (12.9 and 15.3 respectively in 1970).

For administrative purposes, Portugal is divided into provinces, districts, communities and parishes. The organization of health services mirrors this structure, but new health regions and districts are proposed by the Health Research and Planning Office, taking into account the maximum population and geographical area which can practicably be served. The present communities will be maintained as districts.

Administrative structure of the health services

Health authorities

The Ministry of Social Affairs at present comprises two Secretariats of State, one for Social Security and the other for Health. There is, in addition to the Secretariat General (responsible for coordination and technical and administrative support), a Research and Planning Office; a National Institute of Health (responsible for scientific investigation, the central reference laboratory and the organization of specialized education in some related fields, such as nursing and laboratory staff, health inspectors and agents); a National School of Public Health (responsible for postgraduate education in public health, industrial medicine and hospital administration); an Institute of Tropical Medicine and Hygiene (responsible for education, research and information on tropical medicine and public health overseas); and health services inspectorates (responsible for supervising the application of laws and regulations by the health services and establishments and providing administrative and legal support to them).

There are also a Directorate General of Health (charged with ensuring that basic medical and sanitary coverage is provided, particularly in disease prevention and health promotion); four medicosocial institutes to provide technical support (to be integrated with the above Directorate General); a Directorate General of Hospitals (the National Blood Institute comes under the control of this body); a Central Commission of Medicosocial Services (which services cover social security provisions for general and specialized treatment of pensioners and their families within a single treatment network; three inter-hospital commissions for coordination in the northern, central and southern zones; and four coordination inspectorates (one for Lisbon) to represent the general directorates and central institutes in the central and regional bodies for economic planning.

An "Administration of Health Services" has recently been created at the district level, charged with promoting their functional integration with the support of the health services commissions in each community. It consists of representatives from the Secretariat of State for Health, from the district and municipal civilian authorities and from the public (the latter are designated by the labours unions and by the individual health services authorities). Decentralization is expected to be based on it once the National Health Service is put into operation.

Health legislation and regulations

A public debate was under way during the period under review on the manner of enactment of the National Health Service law, which, sanctioned by Article 64 of the Constitution, will profoundly alter the entire health sector, from the basic premises to the relationship between the National Health Service and the private medical sector. It will also profoundly alter the central and peripheral administrative organization through a new system of funding.

Since 1973 the laws and regulations affecting the health sector had been specific; since promulgation of the Constitution in 1976, they have been directed to the solution of pressing problems, but already within the framework of a National Health Service—that is, coverage of the entire population by one existing health scheme (present coverage is 98% of the population) and rapid integration of the various schemes into a single uniform entity. Establishment of the basis for the Service will of course be followed by a period of intensive legislative activity.

Health planning and programming

Programming is dominated by the major objective set in Article 14 of the Constitution: progressive establishment of a free, universal, comprehensive national health service—which would represent a form of state guarantee of each citizen's right to health protection.

There is no need to refer to the current plan already under way, or to its programme. A new plan covers the period 1979–1984.

Health manpower planning

Manpower planning will be required with the establishment of the National Health Service. The expected reorganization of the Secretariat of State for Health is to determine responsibilities for planning.

Doctors

Undergraduate training of doctors falls under the aegis of the Ministry of Education and Culture (there are two faculties in Lisbon, two in Porto and one in Coimbra). Postgraduate and specialized training is provided by health services under the auspices of the Secretariat of State for Health. Candidates wishing to qualify as public health doctors must attend courses at the National School of Health.

Dentists

Two dental schools were set up in 1977, one in Lisbon and one in Porto. Both are under the direction of the Ministry for Education and Culture.

Nurses

In 1977 the curriculum for nursing aides was eliminated. Aides with the required experience can become third level nurses, who then can take a course for promotion. New graduates begin at the second level. There are three types of nursing career: (1) hospital care nursing candidates must have completed the general curriculum at one of 18 public and five private schools (there is an additional course in nursing administration, given by the Public Nursing School for Teaching and Administration); (2) the curriculum for public health nursing is taught at one public school (qualified nurses may take postgraduate courses in public health at the same school); (3) nurses who have completed the general secondary school curriculum are qualified to teach (an additional, higher course in teaching is offered by the School for Teaching and Administration).

Specialized postgraduate courses are offered in the following subjects: obstetrics, rehabilitation, and mental health and psychiatry.

The National Institute for Health is responsible for the orientation, coordination and funding of nursing education.

Pharmacists

Pharmacists receive their degree from the School of Pharmacy, which is under the auspices of the Ministry of Education and Culture.

Senior laboratory technicians

A course is offered by schools under the Ministry of Education and Culture. Students may progress through five further levels, some qualify directly for advanced levels. Those with doctorates or senior posts at a university or at the National School for Public Health, or with exceptional research qualifications, may enter directly at the higher levels.

Auxiliary technicians in allied services for diagnosis and therapy

Until December 1977 two separate career possibilities existed, one for therapists—physiotherapists, kinesitherapists, and orthophonists—certified by a public school under the Centre for Rehabilitative Medicine in Alcoitao, the other for auxiliaries trained in specific fields such as radiology in centres in a few general hospitals. Regulatory Decree No. 87 of 30 December 1977 established a single category "auxiliary technician in allied services for diagnosis and therapy" covering cardiographers dieticians, ergotherapists, physiotherapists, neurophysiographists, optometrists, orthophonists, orthopticians, laboratory assistants, prostheticians, radiographers and radiotherapeutic assistants.

Hospital administrators

A course in hospital administration is given by the National School for Public Health for candidates holding degrees in economics, finance, law, medicine, pharmacy or social and political science.

Sanitary engineers

A course is offered to those with basic training in engineering by the New University of Lisbon under the aegis of the Ministry of Education and Culture.

Public health technicians and auxiliary sanitary technicians

Training is provided by the National Institute for Health.

Financing health care

It has been noted that the budget for health in the public sector increased from 3699 million escudos in 1970 to 15 800 million in 1975, representing respectively 2.1% and 4.2% of gross domestic product at market prices. No figures are available for the private sector.

Current health expenditure

No financial information in the required form is available. However, figures for spending in the public sector and the semipublic sector, i.e. non-profit-making bodies not belonging to the State (the Medico-Social Insurance Service and the Service for Assistance to Civil Servants) in 1970 and 1975 are given in the following table (in millions of escudos):[1]

	Central administration	Local administration	Medico-Social Insurance Service	Total
1970	1 365 (36.9%)	63 (1.7%)	2 271 (61.4%)	3 699
1975	4 706 (29.8%)	38 (0.2%)	11 064 (70.0%)	15 808

---

[1] Gross domestic product at market prices in 1975 was equivalent to US $14.620000, representing US $1547 per capita (at current prices and rate of exchange). The average annual increase at constant prices for the period 1970–1975 was 4.7%.

[2] This figure is probably too high because of duplicate enrolments.

In 1975, daily rates at the five main general hospitals varied from 581.36 to 868.96 escudos, an average of 742.57 escudos.

Social security

Medicosocial programmes cover 9 474 183 inhabitants or 97.7% of the total population.[2] It can be said that the goal of providing insurance coverage for the entire Portuguese population has been attained.

Risks and expenses covered by the programme include the following:

(1) subsidies for illness, maternity or temporary incapacity;

(2) outpatient assistance by preventive medicine units of the Medico-Social Services: consultations, nursing care, diagnostic services and home visiting, including child birth care. (Patients pay a token fee. For some specialized or diagnostic services patients may be referred to public or private hospitals with which the Service has established fee agreements);

(3) the Services have fee agreements with the Directorate General of Hospitals covering hospitalization in general hospitals and maternity clinics.

Similar agreements have been made for hospitalization in other specialized hospitals with the Portuguese Cancer Institute, the Antituberculosis Service and the Institute for Psychiatric Assistance;

(4) under an agreement with the Association of Pharmacists the Services subsidize sales of medicine, paying 25% or 40% of the sales price depending on whether it is of Portuguese or foreign origin;

(5) Services participate in the cost of prostheses; patients are reimbursed for the entire costs of transport.

Publications

The latest work of interest deals with diagnosis and development strategies for the health sector. This report was published by the Research and Planning Office of the Secretariat of State for Health and was used for medium-range government planning.

ROMANIA

Background information

The country has an area of 237 500 km². On 31 December 1977 the population was 21 764 000 (91.6 inhabitants per km²).

In the three decades since the Second World War, Romania has become an industrial country in which only one-third of the working population are now engaged in agriculture; over 82% of the national income is derived from non-agricultural branches of the national economy. At the same time, remarkable achievements have also been scored in agriculture, as a result of substantial investments in this sector in recent decades. The production of grain cereals has more than doubled since 1938, and it has been possible to achieve an almost fourfold increase in meat production compared with 1950, while milk production has more than doubled.

The income represented by the remuneration of workers' and peasants' labour, social insurance pensions, State allowances for children and other payments, has increased considerably. The number of persons sent to balneoclimatological stations and children's camps exceeded two million in 1977.

The technical facilities and services enjoyed by communities have increased—the drinking-water network has grown fourfold, and the volume of drinking-water supplies eleven-fold. More than a million dwellings will have been built during the period 1976–1980.

Important laws have been passed for improvement of the environment and control of pollution of the air, water, soil and subsoil. Another important activity is the systematic surveillance of towns and villages for a balanced distribution of manpower.

Health status

Demographic aspects

Between the two censuses on 15 March 1966 and 5 January 1977 the population increased by 2 454 360, the average annual rate of increase being 1.1%.

Vital statistics for the past five years show the following trends:

	1973	1974	1975	1976	1977
	(Rates per 1000 population)				
Live births	18.2	20.3	19.7	19.5	19.6
Deaths	9.8	9.1	9.3	9.6	9.6
Natural increase	8.4	11.2	10.4	9.9	9.9
Marriages	8.2	8.3	8.9	9.1	9.2
Divorces	0.7	0.9	1.6	1.7	1.2
	(rates per 1000 live births)				
Stillborn	11.1	11.2	10.3	10.0	9.8
Infant deaths	38.1	35.0	34.7	31.4	31.2

The fertility rate provides a picture of the trend in live births; the fertility rate (per 1000 women aged 15–49 years) was 70.4 in 1973, 79.3 in 1974, 77.5 in 1975, 77.3 in 1976 and 77.5 in 1977.

The main causes of death in 1976 were diseases of the circulatory system (510.2 per 100 000), respiratory diseases (148.3 per 100 000), malignant neoplasms (131.3 per 100 000) and accidents (58.9 per 100 000). Mortality remains higher in males (9.9 per 1000) than in females (9.2 per 1000); 80.7% of all deaths occur in people aged over 50 years. Infant mortality is declining, the main causes in 1977 being respiratory diseases (14.4 per 1000), perinatal causes (6.4 per 1000) and congenital disorders (4.1 per 1000).

Morbidity characteristics

The main characteristics of morbidity during the period 1973–1977 were as follows:

	1973	1974	1975	1976	1977
	(rates per 1000 population)				
Tuberculosis (cases admitted for treatment)	141.9	119.5	110.0	93.6	82.3
including:					
new cases	129.1	108.2	99.0	83.4	73.4
readmitted cases	12.8	11.3	11.0	10.2	8.9
Syphilis	31.5	29.5	24.4	17.8	15.2
including:					
recent cases	26.5	25.5	21.2	15.6	13.6
Viral hepatitis	329.5	269.7	256.5	207.2	264.8
Dysentery	128.8	120.1	130.6	103.9	108.5
Diphtheria	0.01	0.02	0.04	—	—
Poliomyelitis	0.04	0.05	0.15	0.07	—
Typhoid fever	1.38	1.96	0.97	0.87	0.6
Cerebrospinal meningitis	1.3	1.0	0.90	0.99	1.11
Scarlet fever	75.8	87.3	82.0	90.9	103.0
Tetanus	0.36	0.27	0.23	0.24	0.21
Measles	598.0	582.4	558.7	531.1	573.7
Pertussis	109.6	69.3	61.2	72.8	62.2
Chickenpox	359.7	353.5	397.0	367.0	326.5

A number of diseases are disappearing as a result of immunization; namely, diphtheria, poliomyelitis, tetanus and typhoid fever. Although still high, morbidity from tuberculosis and veneral diseases is steadily declining. There is high morbidity from viral hepatitis, measles and chickenpox.

Mortality from infectious diseases (not including tuberculosis) fell from 19.2 per 100 000 in 1970 to 7.2 per 100 000 in 1976; that from tuberculosis has fallen from 18.5 to 5.6 per 100 000 during the same period.

Organization of health services

Romania is divided into 40 districts (the Municipality of Bucharest having a special status within the framework of administrative organization of the territory), with 236 towns (including 47 municipalities) and 2706 communes. Responsibility for all activities in the field of health, including medical education and research, lies with the Ministry of Health. The Supreme Health Council, a State body subordinate to the Supreme Council for Economic and Social Development, draws up the general lines and main targets for development of health activities and monitors their implementation.

In each district and in the Municipality of Bucharest there is a health directorate, a local organ of the State administration, which is subordinate both to the executive committee of the district People's Council and that of the Municipality of Bucharest, and to the Ministry of Health. The district health directorates and the health directorate of the Municipality of Bucharest ensure the coordination, organization, implementation and control of all health care activities carried out by all the health units located within the territory of the district of the Municipality.

Health legislation

Among the most important laws and regulations on public health passed since 1973, forming the basis of the organization and activities of health units, the following should be mentioned:

—Decree No. 296 (1976), amended by Decree No. 398 (1977), concerning the establishment of standards for health units, together with an order of the Minister of Health on units and technical norms in certain fields of medical care;

—Law No. 9 (1973) on the protection of the environment;

—Law No. 61 (1974) on protection against ionizing radiation in connexion with the development of activities in the nuclear field, together with an Order of the Minister of Health No. 274 (1974) on the establishment of standards for the health protection of the population against radioactive contamination and ionizing radiation;

—Order of the Minister of Health No. 9 (1974) establishing health standards relating to the production, preparation, sale and transport of foodstuffs and beverages;

— Order of the Minister of Health No. 131 (1977) on the establishment of the functions of health units, the duties of health personnel, and technical standards for tuberculosis prevention and control.

A draft law on health protection has been drawn up and submitted to the competent bodies for approval.

Health planning

The activities of the health units are based on the targets and tasks set in the current five-year plan (1976–1980) and in the programme for the improvement of medical care.

In some priority areas of health protection plans and programmes have been prepared, including programmes for the prevention and control of diseases that constitute major public health problems, especially cardiovascular diseases and cancer.

Curative and preventive services and programmes

The State provides free medical care for the entire population according to the principles of integration of preventive, curative and rehabilitative activities. The division of the territory into zones, each with health units and personnel corresponding to the number of inhabitants and to the medical care needs of all categories of the population, ensures the operation of a basic health network which meets all medical care requirements in a given area.

The central unit is the area hospital; the hierarchical organization of the system depends upon the hospital-polyclinic unit, to which the dispensaries are subordinate. All health activities are integrated in that of the area hospital, specific tasks being assigned to each level according to the level of service. General medical care, as the first level, is provided by the medical dispensary or joint dispensary (depending on population density) located in each commune or district. The dispensary has four to eight physicians working on a shift basis throughout the day. In workplaces and schools the dispensaries are organized according to the number of workers or pupils.

General outpatient care is oriented towards prevention and active surveillance with a view to the early detection of diseases in the preclinical stage and the application of measures embodied in the health programmes.

Specialist outpatient care is provided by the area hospital through polyclinic consultation centres whose functions include that of technical control of the dispensaries in the area.

Polyclinics forming part of the hospitals share their complex technical services and specialized personnel, which contributes to the quality of medical work in outpatient care and broadens the experience of serving staff.

Area hospitals are organized according to three categories depending on their functions and coverage: hospitals with at least 120 beds serving an area of 30 000 inhabitants; hospitals with at least 250 beds, located in a town or municipality which is not the principal town for the district, organized for health care for approximately 100 000 inhabitants; and hospitals with at least 700 beds, located in the principal town of the district and in large municipalities, and possessing all or almost all specialist services. In addition there are area hospitals, located in university centres and in other large urban centres and covering several districts, with a wide range of specialist services; and the single-speciality hospitals for psychiatry, plastic surgery, paediatrics, convalescence, etc.

Specialized services

An important part in the development of disease prevention is played by the district sanitary-epidemiological centres and the hygiene and epidemiology laboratories under the area hospital structure. The former carry out research on causes of disease and factors affecting the health of the population, monitor environmental hygiene and implement and check measures for the prevention and control of infectious, occupational and widely prevalent diseases, acting as a State health inspectorate.

Important activities have been carried out to ensure protection of air, soil, water, and foodstuffs, the prevention of poisoning by, for example, pesticides, and the implementation of measures to ensure proper hygiene conditions in places of work and to eliminate risk factors.

In the field of infectious disease control the range of vaccines and biological products has been widened and health measures have been taken to eliminate factors involved in the transmission of such diseases.

Special attention is devoted to maternal and child health, particularly the medical surveillance of pregnant women, obstetrical care, active surveillance of children's health, the promotion of children's physical and mental health, the early detection of diseases, and prompt treatment. Measures include pregnancy and maternity leave and a reduced work programme for mothers of young children.

Measures have been taken to improve conditions of work and education of young people, including the development of physical training and sport among the young.

Prevention and control of chronic noncommunicable diseases are based on organized screening of high-risk groups, adequate treatment, continuous monitoring and rapid medical intervention. Since the latter is an all-important factor in the treatment of accident victims, special measures include the provision of rapid transport vehicles equipped with resuscitation apparatus, the judicious location of resuscitation units or intensive care units in medicosurgical services, and the supply of adequate medical equipment and specialized teams.

Health education of the population is the subject of a plan drawn up by the Supreme Council of Health. It includes tasks for all State bodies and institutions, and measures aimed at the entire population and at specific population groups.

Biomedical and health services research

The Ministry of Health, through the Academy of Medical Sciences, organizes, directs and controls all scientific medical activity, ensuring the coordination of all research capabilities. The

Academy is responsible to the Ministry for the execution and practical application of scientific medical research. It coordinates scientific medical research independently, regardless of the originating unit.

Medical research is integrated with medical education and medical care; the Ministry of Health is concerned to link the work of research institutes and groups with the specific problems of medical care units in the interests of the practical application of biomedical and health services research.

The subjects of research include pollution of water, air, soil and food; the effect of working conditions on health status and the performance of the human organism; rational nutrition; the prevention and control of cardiovascular diseases, cancer, neurological and mental diseases, occupational diseases, rheumatic diseases, and endocrinal metabolic diseases; dental care and the prevention of dental caries; the physiology and pathology of human reproduction; the development and physical and psychoneurological health of children and young people; optimization of maternal and child health care, and of other forms of medical care in relation to social and economic phenomena; the acquisition and assimilation of new drugs; and the development of appliances and apparatus for medical use.

Health manpower

Responsibility for the planning of training for higher-level and nursing personnel lies with the Ministry of Health, which submits the teaching plan to the Ministry of Education, whose principal function is to ensure the training of specialists in all fields. The education plan for health personnel is an integral part of the economic development plan.

Medical education units, the faculties of general medicine, stomatology and pharmacy and health colleges are administratively and functionally subordinated to the Ministry of Education and the Ministry of Health. These teaching units are financed from the State budget.

In 1977 there were 12 faculties of general medicine and stomatology and 4 faculties of pharmacy in 6 university centres.

Those who have completed studies in the faculties of general medicine (six years), stomatology and pharmacy (five years), are entitled to practise as soon as they obtain the diploma of physician or pharmacist. Postgraduate

professional education of physicians and pharmacists is organized at the central level in the six medical university centres, and at the local level in the principal towns of districts, through practical training, courses and individual programmes. The law provides that each specialist shall follow some form of postgraduate training every five years.

Nursing personnel, who are at present trained only in vocational schools, the studies lasting four years, are entitled to exercise their profession upon completion of their studies, after a 12-month period of practical work. At the present time, there are 29 vocational schools in as many localities, distributed evenly throughout the country.

In 1977 there were 35 889 physicians, including 6541 dentists; 5625 pharmacists and 125 749 nursing staff; 19 597 persons were studying at the faculties of medicine and pharmacy and 6299 at vocational schools.

Financing of the health services

Health services are financed by the State. The amount set aside for this purpose in 1976 was 11 182 million lei (or 521 lei per capita), 50.6% of this sum being spent on hospitals and 31.7% on outpatient services.

Major developments in the period 1973–1977

Since 1973 the health status of the population has steadily improved; this is reflected in the favourable development of the main indices: the expectation of life in 1976 was 70 years, the infant mortality rate had fallen to 31.4%; there had been a considerable reduction in infectious diseases, although certain infectious diseases of viral origin and chronic noncommunicable diseases remained at a high level.

In the field of scientific research knowledge of certain disease risk factors and of factors conducive to the maintenance of health, and methods of diagnosis, treatment and rehabilitation, have improved, contributing to the establishment of various health activities on a scientific basis. Medical research has also contributed to an improvement and diversification in the production of sera, vaccines and other biological products, especially blood derivatives, and to the introduction of new therapeutic drugs.

SWEDEN

Basic country data

With only 8 236 179 inhabitants on 31 December 1976, Sweden has one of the lowest population densities in Europe. Nearly 90% live in the southern half—the density varies from 231 per km² in Stockholm county to 30–45 in some central counties and only 3–4 in the vast northern counties covering almost half of the total land area. Since a reform in 1974 reducing the number of municipalities from 850 to 277, the exact migration from rural to urban areas is not recorded. In 1975, 82.7% of the population was living in localities; 37% in the 20 largest cities. The population by age group was as follows in 1976:

0–14 years	1 695 030
15–64 years	5 267 295
65–74 years	794 402
75–years and over	479 452

Some other population data for the period under review are given below.

	1973	1976
Mean population	8 136 774	8 222 310
Live births per 1000 population	13.48	11.96
Deaths	10.52	11.03
Excess of births	2.96	0.93
Emigrants	4.96	3.10
Immigrants	3.62	5.53
Population increase	1.49	3.34
Infant deaths per 1000 live births	9.9	8.3

The tendency is towards fewer births and an increase in the elderly population (9.9% were aged 70 or over in 1975). In the 3.1 million households the average number of persons is 2.7; 7% of the population are immigrants, two-thirds of them from the Nordic countries.

Mean expectation of life at birth in 1975 was 72.07 years for men, 77.65 for women. At the age of 65 it was 14.04 years for men, 17.16 years for women.

The gross domestic product at market prices in 1975 was 286 717 million kronor. The number of gainfully employed in 1975 totalled about 4.1 million—34% in industry, 18% in trade, transport and communications, 41% in other services and only 7% in agriculture, forestry and fishing. The normal working week is 40 hours and the average hourly wage for a male industrial worker as of spring 1976 amounted to 27.13 kronor. Unemployment in August 1977 was 2.1% of the labour force.

Country health situation

Communicable diseases. Owing to incomplete reporting systems the range of communicable diseases is hard to assess. Tuberculosis, however, is no longer a public health problem, and there have only been two reported cases of poliomyelitis in the past 10 years.

Certain communicable diseases are the subject of central notification in accordance with current health laws, the major ones being, in 1976, acute gonorrhoea (26 394 cases), scarlet fever (6651), salmonella (2190), and infectious hepatitis (1016).

Diseases and conditions diagnosed in inpatient care. In a recent study covering one region the following were the 10 most frequent causes of hospitalization: circulatory diseases, malignant tumours, injuries and poisoning, diseases of the central nervous system, respiratory diseases, diseases of the musculoskeletal system, others (such as abdominal pain), diseases of the urogenital organs, and mental disturbances.

The most important causes of death in 1976 were diseases of the circulatory systems, neoplasms, accidents, poisoning and violence, diseases of the respiratory systems and diseases of the digestive system.

Hospital admissions per 100 000 inhabitants in 1975 were: for somatic acute care (non-surgical) (6191), psychiatric care (1583), surgical specialities (8832), others (997).

Long-term care for somatic conditions was the cause of admission of 72 per 1000 inhabitants over 74 years of age.

Physician consultations per 1000 population numbered 2721 in 1975 (excluding private practitioners, who accounted for 6.25% in 1976); 48% were given by physicians outside hospitals. Consultations in district care with doctors and nurses, and for maternal and child care numbered 1194 per 1000 population.

Home care visits were paid to 36 565 patients in 1975 (45 visits per 1000 inhabitants aged 70 years or more).

National health insurance statistics show that in 1976 cases receiving sickness benefits numbered 7 001 800; the majority of subjects (more than two million) were aged 20–29 years. The average duration of sickness per person was 23.2 days (compared with 14 days in 1966); the benefit per registered highest number of days were for persons aged 50–59 years. Main causes are colds, diseases of the joints and back, and mental disturbances. Cases needing hospital treatment totalled 12.5%. Most hospitalization was for circulatory diseases and tumours. Disability pensions were paid to 296 646 and handicap benefits to 25 365 persons, main causes being diseases of the joints and the back, circulatory diseases and mental disturbances. Occupational injuries number 145 836. The expenditure per registered employee was 2398 kronor in sickness cash benefit, 308 in parental insurances, 204 for physicians consultations, 181 for dental care, 64 for hospital care, and 31 for aids to the handicapped.

Care of the elderly. Those aged 67 years or more numbered 1 090 150 of a total population of 8 236 179 - and this population group has the biggest impact on the health situation. In 1975 the 13.4% of the population aged 65 years or more received 37% of the acute somatic care, 82% of the long-term care, and 38% of the psychiatric care.

Alcoholism is a serious health problem. Many factors indicate a hidden addiction to alcohol in about 300 000 inhabitants, resulting in sick-leave from work, and early retirement on pensions.

Administrative organization of the health services

Health authorities

The responsibility for health lies with the county councils, currently numbering 26, each with about 250 000 inhabitants. Legislation provides that the county councils organize medical services (physical and psychiatric treatment in both inpatient and outpatient care) for all county residents. All hospitals and health centres are administered by the county councils, with only a few exceptions.

The two spheres of influence of the State are;

the Ministry of Health and Social Affairs, which draws up general plans for the operation of health and medical care services (the Committee for National Health Planning, connected to the Ministry, coordinates planning and designates physicians); and the National Board of Health and Welfare, which has supervisory functions over both public and private medical care.

Besides the county councils the following authorities contribute in different fields of health care: the municipalities are obliged to provide general public health care, which implies the prevention and elimination of sanitary inconveniences and the continuous improvement of hygienic standards; the county medical officer advises municipalities and other organizations on matters regarding public health; and the county veterinarian, domestic science adviser, public assistance consultant, child care consultant, and temperance officer share the responsibility for public health in a broad context.

National health insurance

National public health insurance, 15% of which is financed by State grants and 85% by employers' contributions, is compulsory for all residents aged 16 years or over and guarantees protection from loss of income through illness, injury or disability. The social insurance is financed by employers' contributions, State grants and grants from the municipality. The central administration is the National Social Insurance Board, and there are 26 local social insurance offices.

Health laws and regulations

Health services. The Abortion Act (1975) specifies that abortion is free on demand up to the end of the eighteenth week of pregnancy; before the twelfth week the woman need consult only a doctor, after that she must also see a counsellor. The woman may be refused an abortion only if it will mean a risk to her life or health. After the eighteenth week the approval of the National Board of Health and Welfare is required.

The Sterilization Act (1975) emphasizes the right of any man or woman aged 25 years or over to choose sterilization as a means of birth control; those aged 18–24 years require the approval of the National Board of Health and Welfare, and this is granted only for genetic reasons, or—in women—for medical reasons.

Insurance. The dental insurance legislation (1974) applies to all residents aged 17 years or more (those under 17 have free dental care from the National Dental Service).

The patient insurance legislation (1976) provides compensation to patients in case of unforeseen injuries resulting from medical treatment at a public institution.

The partial pension scheme legislation (1976) permits any employee, on reaching the age of 60, to reduce his or her working hours and combine part-time work with a partial pension.

The occupational injuries insurance legislation (1977) provides compulsory insurance for all employees against injuries and disease incurred during work and on the way to or from work as well as against harmful influence on health suffered during work.

The parenthood benefit legislation (1977) gives parents 90 days leave to be taken up to the time when the child completes the first year at school.

Occupational safety. The Workers' Protection Act (1974), has been replaced by the Working Environment Act (1978), based on the principle that both the employee and the employer shall cooperate for a safer environment, while the employer bears the main responsibility. Local safety committees are compulsory at any place of work with 50 or more employees.

Traffic safety. Legislation provides the compulsory use of safety belts by drivers and passengers in the front seat of motor vehicles (1975); of helmets by motorcycle drivers and passengers (1976); of day warning lights on motor vehicles (1977), and of helmets by "moped" drivers (1978).

Environment protection. The Act on Products Hazardous to Man and the Environment (1973) stipulates that products which may conceivably harm people or the environment are to be handled with special care. A licensing system regulates the use and sale of certain products. Furthermore, a number of new regulations have been passed, such as the Act on the Declaration of Noxious Wastes (1976), the Car Exhaust Ordinance (1976), the Act on Sulfurous Fuel (1976),

the Act on Measures against Pollution of Water by Boats in the Baltic Sea (1976) and the Ordinance on International Road Transport of Hazardous Goods (1974).

Health plan and country health programming

In 1975 the National Board of Health and Welfare published a programme of principles, "The Swedish Health Services in the 1980s", which encompasses a period of 10–15 years. The philosophy behind the programme is based on the principle of equal access for all according to the need for medical care, the principle of the health "offensive", and the view of man as a psychosocial unit. The aims are an increase in primary care facilities and preventive measures and of resources for long-term care, improved care of the patient in health centres, and integration with other social services.

A structural model for public health services has been elaborated with three components which are not institutions but functions:

(1) primary care for the population in a limited district, comprising all treatment and health services provided outside hospitals and central nursing homes (the number of posts for district medical officers to increase by about 8% annually, and the resources for home care for chronic diseases and postoperative conditions, and for day care, to be extended).
(2) county care for patients with life-endangering conditions or diseases requiring special staff and technical resources: and
(3) regional care for patients requiring highly-skilled specialists and special equipment.

Among health planning and management support services and programmes mention has already been made of the Committee for National Health.

Planning. The Federation of Swedish County Councils brings together all principals of health and medical services, and, with the National Board of Health and Welfare, makes annual predictions for one year and five year periods. A National Institute for Planning and Rationalization of Health and Welfare Services is operated by the Government and the Federation of Swedish County Councils.

Curative and preventive services and programmes

Hospital services

There were the following hospital establishments in 1975:

	Number	Beds
Regional hospitals	8	14 175
County hospitals	26	28 168
County annex hospitals	93	30 223
Mental hospitals	19	15 362
Cottage hospitals and nursing homes for somatic conditions	323*	26 813
Mental nursing homes	242**	8 887
Special hospitals for the mentally retarded	6	1 468
Residential homes for the mentally retarded	153	11 297
Total	880	136 393

*Including 53 private institutions.
**Including 154 private institutions.

Regional hospitals represent nearly all medical specialities, have about 1200–2300 beds, and have combined duties in research, training and education; the population covered varies between 0.6 million and 1.6 million. County hospitals have 15–20 specialized wards, have a high degree of preparedness and provide medical service for primary care, covering a population of 200 000–300 000. County annex hospitals represent the specialities of internal medicine, general surgery, anaesthesiology and radiology, the population covered varies between 60 000 and 90 000.

All except two regional hospitals run by the State and two private hospitals are administered by the county councils.

Until recently medical care had been very hospital-oriented. The hospital beds were distributed as follows according to type of care: 19 769 beds (or 2.4 per 1000 inhabitants) for acute non-surgical care for somatic conditions, 38 498 beds (or 4.7 per 1000 inhabitants) for long-term care for somatic conditions, 32 741 beds (or 4.0 per 1000 inhabitants) for psychiatric care, 22 264 beds (or 2.7 per 1000 inhabitants) for surgical specialities.

The special facilities generally include both in- and outpatient facilities. The number of outpatient consultations is relatively low—about 2.7 visits per inhabitant a year; of these, 50% are to physicians at hospitals, 30% to general practitioners and specialists at health centres, and 20% to private practitioners.

Medical care outside hospitals

The public health districts are subdivided into primary care districts with 10 000–50 000 inhabitants. Every district has one or more health centres. In 1975 there were 680 health centres, 1877 district medical officers' posts and 2050 district nurses.

Home care and domestic help

In 1975, 36 565 persons (or 45 per 1000) aged 70 years or over were assisted by home care personnel or by relatives receiving an allowance to provide such care; 328 553 persons received home help services from 74 692 home-care aides and 3192 domestic help assistants in 1976.

Special services and programmes

Basic sanitation and environmental pollution control. Laws and regulations are issued by the Ministry of Health and Social Affairs. The chief responsibility for environmental matters is vested in the Ministry of Agriculture. The National Environment Protection Board is the central administrative agency in the ecological sphere. At the regional level the county administrations have a number of tasks in the prevention of water and air pollution, and public health, and are responsible for regional planning. At the local level current regulations are inforced by the municipalities and inspections are made by the public health inspector.

Communicable diseases prevention and control

The child welfare centres carry out an immunization programme, including smallpox, tetanus, diphtheria and pertussis, poliomyelitis, measles and mumps. Vaccinations are given to practically all children. In the school health system the programme is reinforced by, for example, rubella immunization for girls. Vaccinations are also given during military service. Special immunization programmes, adapted to the actual risks, are provided for certain groups of personnel, such as nursing personnel, sanitation workers, persons handling infectious material and persons frequently travelling abroad.

The responsible authority at the county level is the county administration through the county medical officer.

Health laboratory services. The National Bacteriological Laboratory is an independent government authority performing diagnostic examinations of samples, pharmaceutical preparations, food, water or other materials; seeking uniformity and safety in diagnostic examinations; providing bacteriological preparations; supervising epidemic and communicable disease control, and carrying out research in connexion with these tasks.

Maternal and child health. At the 652 maternity centres distributed all over the country doctors and nurses with special training provide prenatal and postnatal maternal care and counselling on contraception. More than 90% of all expectant mothers are registered at maternity centres and make an average of 12 visits per pregnancy. All births take place in hospital maternity wards. Psychoprophylactic courses led by community midwives are well attended.

There were 1341 child welfare centres in 1974 providing over 99% coverage of all infants and 70% coverage of preschool children with mainly preventive services for vaccinations, nutritional education, advice on child-rearing and mental hygiene, and monitoring of physical and mental abnormalities.

All newborn children are reported to the centre that they will attend about 10 times a year as infants, three times as one-year-olds and twice a year thereafter. The child health nurse also makes home calls. At the general health examination of four-year-olds, sight, hearing, speech, teeth, nutrition, physical development and behaviour are checked.

For children with various types of physical and mental handicaps there are comprehensive therapeutic activities and a number of specialized institutions such as those for cerebral palsy cases, the deaf and the blind. Continuous efforts are made to integrate handicapped children into society and the regular school system.

The chief medical officer for child health is consultant for child health in the county; district child health medical officers' posts are increasing in number. In rural areas the district nurse is in charge of child health.

School health. The health of comprehensive school pupils is checked four times. In secondary school health checks start in the first (lowest) form and are made every second year. The school doctor, nurse, psychologist and social worker form a team for comprehensive care of the individual pupil. In recent years counselling on sex and human relations has become part of the general health education activities, and in some school districts school gynaecologist posts have been established.

Occupational health. Access to and the influence of local trade unions on occupational health care are regulated by agreements between the central trade union organizations and the Employers' Confederation. In 1977 occupational health care was provided in all companies with 1000 employees or more and for many State, county council and municipal employees through special staff medical officers or 190 centres for occupational health; 1.7 million out of the total 4.5 million employees had access to such health care.

The authority on matters regarding occupational health is the National Board of Occupational Safety and Health. The subordinate local bodies are the district agencies of the Industrial Safety Inspectorate. Departments of occupational medicine have been established in regional hospitals.

Health care of the elderly. Municipalities are obliged to provide the required housing facilities for the elderly. Old people may receive at home the assistance of home care aides or domestic help, medical care from the district nurse or from a relative, who receives a public allowance for such care.

Day centres are attached to most large old people's homes and offer various activities and medical and social services. There were in 1977 also about 8000 municipal "service houses", containing private apartments with special service facilities. There are special transport services available.

Care of old people unable to live on their own is provided in long-term hospitals. There are 20.3 beds per 1000 inhabitants aged 70 years or over; homes for old people, or nursing homes, with 8.3 beds per 1000 inhabitants in this category; facilities for acute somatic conditions, with 4.5 beds per 1000; and geriatric wards for psychiatric cases, with 5.8 beds per 1000.

The increasing proportion of the elderly in the population has overburdened specialities such as orthopaedics, oncology and internal medicine. There are insufficient beds for long-term care, and 10%–30% of the patients in some hospital wards are waiting to be transferred. About one-third of all pharmaceutical preparations sold are consumed by the 20% of the population aged 65 years or over.

Noncommunicable disease prevention and control. Prevention aims at the avoidance of premature death, sick-leave and premature pensions and, among young people, accidents, especially traffic accidents. For the age-group 45–69 there are special measures against cardiovascular diseases and tumours and, among the risk factors affecting cerebrovascular diseases and ischaemic cardiac diseases, particularly smoking and hypertonia. There are also national health education programmes on diet and exercise.

Special programmes for the prevention of tumours have as their object extensive anti-smoking campaigns to reduce lung cancer and local breast cancer screening research projects, while cancer of the uterine cervix is the subject of routine screening by vaginal cytology examinations of women aged 20–49 years. For the coordination of preventive and curative measures special oncological centres are being established in the seven medical regions.

Mental health care of preschool children is provided in the child welfare centres, of schoolchildren by the school psychologist, and of adults by the mental hospitals and psychiatric departments in hospitals, where there are services for regular consultations, day-care and inpatient care. The general trend in mental health care is towards decentralization and increased outpatient care in the primary care system. Rehabilitation efforts are being inforced, and the establishment of boarding homes as an alternative to conventional inpatient care is becoming more frequent.

Accident prevention and control. The Swedish Road Safety Office coordinates traffic safety efforts throughout the country. A local voluntary traffic safety committee, with both public and private representatives, coordinates traffic safety projects in most municipalities. Traffic education is given to both preschool children and to schoolchildren (about 20 school hours a year).

The Swedish Life-Saving Society and Swimming Association work for the elimination of drowning accidents and for safety during all activities on, in and near water.

The Joint Committee for the Prevention of Childhood Accidents is formed of representatives of a large number of public authorities, professional associations, voluntary associations and insurance companies. It collects and analyses all childhood accidents. It also disseminates information to all parents, through the child welfare centres and other bodies.

Emergency and relief services. Plans at national, regional and local level are worked out by special medical disaster committees to meet the need for extraordinary measure in case of severe chemical accidents, epidemics, explosions, fires, poisoning (air, water, food), natural disasters (landslides, floods, storms), radioactive radiation, or traffic accidents.

At the national level the Medical Disaster Commission under the National Board of Health and Welfare has a coordinating role, giving advice to medical authorities at regional and local level and stimulating the planning, information, education and training of medical, administrative and voluntary personnel. In accordance with a master plan from the Commission each county council and each hospital has a medical disaster plan worked out by a special committee. Under the hospital disaster plans doctors and nurses can rapidly be sent out to the disaster area to examine the injured and to give first aid treatment.

Oral health. The total number of practising dentists was 7394 in 1976, 50% in private practice, 41% employed by the National Dental Service; 6% were both private practitioners and worked for the Service, and 3% were teachers or research staff at the odontological faculties. The county councils are responsible for the dental care of children and adolescents. Private dentists cover 80%–85% of the dental care of adults and the remaining 15%–20% are covered by the National Dental Service.

Pharmaceuticals. The Swedish pharmaceutical industry accounts for about 40% of the domestic drug sales. The Association of the Swedish Pharmaceutical Industry represents 18 Swedish drug marketing companies. The Association of Representatives of Foreign Pharmaceutical Industries represents about 50 foreign companies.

Drugs have to be registered with the National Board of Health and Welfare before they can be marketed. All serious and fatal adverse drug reactions as well as new and unexpected adverse reactions have to be reported.

Drug sales in 1976 amounted to 2467 million kronor (the consumption per inhabitant in 1975 was 268 kronor) with the highest figures for drugs used in cases of circulatory disturbances (18.1%), for the treatment of infections (10.0%), psychopharmaceutical preparations (8.5%), cough and cold preparations (6.1%), hormone preparations (5.6%). Sales of drugs accounted for 9.4% of the total costs for health and medical care in 1975 (0.76% of the gross domestic product).

Health education. The Committee on Health Education within the National Board of Health and Welfare plans, directs and coordinates activities and initiates regional and local measures. Most counties have a local committee consisting of the county medical officer, representatives of the county council, the municipalities, schools, sports organizations, domestic science advisers and voluntary organizations. At the municipal level activities are carried out by various administrations.

In 1977 Parliament launched a new policy to combat alcoholism. The central responsibility rests with the National Board of Health and Welfare. The main target group is adolescents. A ten-year programme on diet and exercise, launched in 1971, aims at reducing the consumption of fat and sugar and increasing the consumption of root crops, vegetables and grain products, and at encouraging regular exercise. A 25-year programme was launched in 1973 in order to create a society opposed to smoking. All tobacco products are now provided with warning texts. Planned parenthood work emphasizes knowledge of human relations and contraceptives instead of abortion, through education in schools, adult education organizations and material directed to the general public. Other programmes deal with such subjects as dental health, communicable diseases, and the training of health educators.

Mental retardation. The National Board of Health and Welfare (for medical care) and the National Board of Education (for education and training) are the responsible authorities, while the county councils are obliged to provide education, care and housing facilities in accordance with the principles of integration in the community, decentralization of treatment, small-group therapy and normalization.

Special institutions in 1975, included 606 day nurseries, 12 663 special schools, and 3464 establishments for sheltered employment, covering a total of 16 738 persons. Domestic assistance was also given to 4807 persons or 57 per 100 000 inhabitants. Special accommodation was provided in 9805 nursing homes, 1453 special hospitals, 2190 student hostels, and 1979 boarding homes, covering a total of 15 427 persons.

Biomedical and health services research

There is close cooperation between clinical and preclinical research, resulting in constant reorientation of research activities to meet the current health and medical policies. Of the total international medical research work, 1% to 2% derives from Sweden. Basic research is concentrated in the six teaching hospitals with preclinical institutions related to the medical faculties of the universities. Clinical research is mainly done at the teaching hospitals and big county hospitals, while applied research is also performed at other levels.

The initiator and adviser for financing is the Medical Research Council, which distributes annually about 80 million kronor. The costs of research and development correspond to 4.5% of total costs for the public health services.

Health manpower development

The medical personnel active in 1975 included:

Physicians	14 050
Nurses, nurse/midwives	48 380
Midwives	630
Sanitary inspectors	820
Physiotherapists	4 030
Occupational therapists*	1 810
Social workers etc.*	1 620
Assistant nurses	13 700
Psychologists	700
Aides, orderlies etc.*	54 400
Mental nursing personnel	14 200
Dentists	7 060
Dental technicians**	2 700
Dental hygienists	150
Dental chairside assistants**	8 400
Pharmacists	740
Pharmaceutical assistants	3 100
Technical personnel in pharmacies	6 380

* In hospitals for somatic conditions.
** Estimate.

Manpower planning and projection of requirements

Through a reform in 1977 all universities and colleges are included in a nationwide regional organization under the Ministry of Education. The responsibility for the training of health personnel lies with this Ministry, while the actual planning and realization of the set goals are shared between the National Board of Education (for comprehensive and secondary school education) and the National Board of Universities and Colleges (for higher education).

Health manpower training

In 1977 the total intake of students in the 34 nursing schools was 10 314. All nurses are either registered or have defined competence (assistant nurses). After basic education there are possibilities for specialization in one or two terms of postbasic education. Nursing may be taken at 120 secondary schools with a wide variety of courses. Main alternatives are health and medical services, geriatrics, psychiatric nursing, child and youth welfare and child nursing. In 1977 the intake to the first alternative was 5402, and that for child and youth welfare 2200.

Occupational therapists are trained at nine schools and physiotherapists at three schools.

The number of people employed in health and medical care has doubled in the last 10 years, but although it now totals 250 000–300 000 there is a considerable shortage of personnel. In 1977, 4.2% of all nursing posts at hospitals were vacant. The intake of students for all kinds of nursing is being increased by about 3% annually.

Medical education

There are six medical faculties at universities with affiliated university hospitals, which are also regional hospitals. The intake of medical students in 1976 was 1246. All have the opportunity of receiving hospital posts after the 5.5-year undergraduate study course, first as interns (general service period of 21 months) for the licence to practise, and then as residents in order to obtain the general practice or specialist certificate (4–5 years specialist training). Medical education is organized by the Medical Education Board of the University, which is separate from and independent of the Medical Faculty Board, which handles questions concerning research and research education. Postgraduate education of physicians is supervised by the National Board of Health and Welfare. There are no programmes for continuous education, but further education for physicians with specialist qualifications is provided through courses arranged by the specialist organizations.

Five-year programmes laid down by the Ministry of Health and Social Affairs, and revised annually, for the allocation of new posts and of posts for specialist training, are the instruments for adjusting the supply of physicians to the fields given priority in current health policy, i.e. general practice, psychiatry and long-term medicine (including rehabilitation). Nearly half of the new positions in 1977 were allocated to outpatient care. The intake of students is being increased in order to fill the present shortage of physicians. The number of graduates (registered as physicians) will rise from 1101 in 1977 to 1144 in 1980, an annual increase of about 5.4%.

Costs and financing of health services

The costs of health and medical care are covered by the revenue of the county councils. The share of the gross domestic product allocated to health and medical care at market prices in 1975 was 24 213 million kronor or 8.4%. Government final consumption, at current prices, for health expenditure was 17 319 million kronor, or 24.2%, and for social insurance and social security, 9663 million or 13.5%.

Private final consumption, at current prices, for medical care and health expenses was 5251 million kronor or 3.5% of the total consumption expenditure.

An analysis of current health expenditure shows that the costs for health services in 1975 included 15 275 734 000 kronor for hospital care (1861 per inhabitant), 1 909 095 000 for health and medical care outside hospitals, and dental care (233 per inhabitant), 1 576 287 000 for care of the mentally retarded (192 per inhabitant), and 958 952 000 for social assistance (116 per inhabitant).

SWITZERLAND

General background

Switzerland's area is 41 293 km², about one third of which is uninhabitable. At the end of 1976 its population was estimated at 6 346 000, giving a density of 153.7 persons per km². Berne, the capital, had 148 600 inhabitants. In 1976 the birth rate and the death rate were respectively 11.7 and 9 per 1000 population, the natural increase therefore being 0.27%. The infant mortality rate was 10.7 per 1000 live births. Life expectancy for the period 1968–1973 was 70.3 years for males and 76.2 years for females.

Country health situation

The main public health problems are the same in Switzerland as in most other industrialized countries: the increasing numbers of older people, environmental pollution, and illnesses resulting from excessive comfort and insufficient physical activity (obesity, metabolic disorders, cardiovascular diseases, alcoholism, abuse of tobacco, etc.). In 1976 the main causes of death, in descending order of frequency, were diseases of the circulatory system, malignant tumours and accidents.

Administrative organization of the health services

That the 22 cantons of the Confederation preserve a large degree of autonomy is particularly evident in the field of health. Certain public health matters come within the competence of the Confederation, in particular those relating to international obligations, those that call for close coordination and those concerning surveillance of communicable diseases, control of foodstuffs and the sale of toxic substances, protection against ionizing radiation, development of the pharmacopoeia, control of narcotics, environmental protection, insurance against sickness, accidents and invalidity, and new problems as they arise. The federal laws are applied either by the appropriate bodies of the Confederation or by the cantonal authorities. In addition, a number of intercantonal agreements have been concluded for the purpose of resolving problems which come within the competence of the cantons but for which joint cooperation was necessary, such as drug control and social welfare.

The Department of the Interior of the Federal Government is responsible for the health services at the federal level, the relevant activities being carried out by the Federal Public Health Service and the Federal Offices of Social Insurance, Statistics, and Environmental Protection.

The cantonal health services, while not having a uniform organization, nevertheless have some features in common. The cantonal health administration is attached to one of the departments with cantonal executive authority, the Council of State, and comprises the various administrative and technical services necessary for the supervision and organization of hospitals, medical practice and the nursing professions, and for the control of foodstuffs and environmental hygiene. It has a cantonal medical officer and a cantonal veterinary officer and, sometimes, a dental practitioner, a pharmacist and one or more cantonal chemists. There are also medical officers in the districts, where they are responsible for several communes, and in the large towns.

The communes form the local health authority and the larger communes have organized their health services on the same lines as those of the cantons.

The three levels of public health functions (federal, cantonal and communal) make it very difficult to initiate a medium- or long-term health plan. However, sound development is assured by several bodies responsible for coordination, the most important being the Conference of Cantonal Directors of Health Affairs, as well as by semi-official or private bodies such as the Swiss Institute of Hospitals, the Swiss Association of Hospitals, the Swiss Red Cross, and the Swiss Academy of Medical Sciences, which are in constant contact with the public authorities.

Curative and preventive services and programmes

Insurance against sickness is optional except in certain cantons, where it is compulsory for some categories of people. However, nearly 95% of the population are insured under recognized insurance schemes supervised by the Federal Office of Social Insurance and which, in order to be recognized, must fulfil certain minimum requirements laid down by the law on sickness and accident insurance.

Industrial workers and craftsmen are compulsorily insured against occupational accidents.

Old-age and survivors' invalidity insurance is provided by compulsory national schemes financed to an extent of about four-fifths by the contributions of employees, employers and self-employed workers and benefiting all women over the age of 62, all men over the age of 65 as well as widows, orphans and the disabled. Contributions, which are calculated as a percentage of income, are not, however, considered as a tax.

Medical practice is private, and includes the services available to those covered under insurance schemes, in which case a fixed scale of charges applies. Only medical officers and most hospital doctors receive salaries. There are virtually no health centres and the number of group practices is gradually increasing.

The average density of physicians in private practice is one practitioner for 992 people, varying from one for 587 in some urban areas to one for 1767 in mountain areas. General practitioners work mostly in medium and small communities and in the country, while the majority of specialists (68% of the physicians in private practice) are in the towns. However, the work of many specialists, particularly in the country, but also to a lesser degree in the towns, goes beyond the bounds of their speciality and resembles that of the general practitioners. In spite of these differences in distribution, access to specialists is satisfactorily ensured for the population as a whole thanks to the density and quality of communications facilities.

Hospital services

Most of the hospitals are public institutions, run by the cantons or the communes. Polyclinics, generally providing specialized services, are attached to the large hospitals and provide treatment free of charge.

Medical care outside hospitals

In some cantons, home treatment of the chronically ill and the aged is highly developed and well organized by the authorities. In others, it is developing with the help of public health nurses, often belonging to voluntary bodies. There is close cooperation between physicians and health personnel in giving the treatment. In renovating urban areas or constructing new buildings, an effort is made to provide conditions enabling the aged to remain in contact with the environment they know.

Special services and programmes

In all, 98.8% of the dwellings are connected to the water-supply system, but isolated dwellings (1.2%) are supplied from pure water springs.

The great majority of the population are served by drainage systems and about 60% by water treatment plants. The construction of new pipelines will link 75–80% of the population to existing treatment plants. Also, 87 new plants are under construction and 70 projects are ready to be launched. These arrangements are the responsibility of the cantonal and communal authorities, under federal legislation.

Communicable disease prevention and control, based on a federal law and carried out by the cantons, is receiving renewed interest in the field of gastrointestinal diseases due to the modern methods of distributing foodstuffs. Immunization against poliomyelitis has resulted in the disappearance of the disease. Constant efforts in epidemiological surveillance are reducing the number of cases of tuberculosis; public campaigns are regularly organized for radiological screening of tuberculosis. Most other communicable diseases are virtually no longer a public health problem, with the exception of sexually transmitted diseases, which are slightly on the increase. Maternal and child health services, with more than 700 clinics, are available to the population as a whole. School health services are provided for all children of compulsory school age. Apart from school dental services, which are provided for the majority of schoolchildren, using mobile dental units in isolated areas, dental care is carried out on a private individual basis.

Emergency care is provided by ambulance services under the police authorities or hospitals, or organized on a private basis and also, in the case of assistance high in the mountains, very urgent transport or transport over fairly long distances, by the Swiss Air Rescue Guard.

The sale of drugs and medical equipment is regulated by the Intercantonal Office for the Control of Drugs whose decisions are applied by the cantonal authorities.

Biomedical and health services research

Population and health statistics are prepared by the Federal Office of Statistics in conjunction with the statistics offices in the larger cantons.

Technical expertise to meet the needs of the Federal Public Health Service is provided by some 15 federal commissions, the five university institutes of social and preventive medicine and other public health bodies.

Medical research is carried out chiefly in the

university institutes and the large hospitals, and is financed both by the cantons and by the Confederation (National Scientific Research Fund). The National Scientific Research Fund finances applied research in social and preventive medicine, conducted mainly in the institutes of social and preventive medicine. National research programmes concerned with health economics, cardiovascular diseases and the social problems of old age and adolescence have been started. A special grant has been made for basic cancer research and for the coordination of clinical cancer research. The large pharmaceutical companies conduct studies themselves and finance others in the universities.

Health manpower development

Physicians are trained at five medical schools under a federal programme adapted to modern educational methods and using new examination methods.

Nurses are trained in three years and nursing assistants in 18 months, in accordance with a programme drawn up by the Swiss Red Cross and in schools recognized by that body. There are 36 schools for general nurses, 23 for mental health nurses, 11 for maternal and child health nurses, and 35 for nursing assistants. Nursing supervisors of various levels are trained in the Red Cross colleges of nursing at Zurich and Lausanne. Other courses for supervisors are provided by the Swiss Association of Hospitals.

Midwives undergo three years of training in obstetrical clinics. The other categories of technical staff are trained at specialized institutes.

Authorization to practise a medical profession is granted by the responsible canton. Physicians holding a federal diploma, given to Swiss citizens only, are automatically authorized to practise in the canton where they file a request. A few cantons also have the right, under their own legislation, to grant the authorization to practise on their territory to physicians who do not have a federal diploma.

Cost and financing of health services – social security

Four-fifths of the amount paid out in sickness insurance benefits is provided by those insured (insurance premiums, costs), the balance by the public authorities (federal, cantonal, communal) and to some extent also by the employers.

In 1976, the expenditure of sickness insurance schemes amounted to 4500 million francs. The expenditure on the compulsory accident insurance, covering about 50% of workers, amounted to 1400 million francs. Private sickness and accident insurance companies spent nearly 800 million francs.

In 1976, with a gross national product of 141 000 million francs, consumer expenditure on health amounted to 8700 million francs and the expenditure of the public authorities (federal, cantonal and communal) to 4000 million francs for social insurance, plus 4000 million for public health and 2000 million for environmental health. Old-age and survivors' benefits (about 9000 million francs) are not included in these figures.

TURKEY

Background information

The Republic of Turkey covers 756 000 km^2 of the Anatolian peninsula in Asia and 24 000 km^2 of the Thracian peninsula in Europe. It is, both geographically and historically, a link between East and West. This influences the entire fabric of life.

In 1976 the population was estimated to be 41 million, with a density of 52 per km^2; 57% of the population lives in rural areas. The country is divided into 67 provinces (il), which themselves are divided into districts (ilçe). According to the 1975 census there are 36 cities with populations over 100 000, Istanbul being the most populated, with 2 550 000 inhabitants. There is a high rate of urbanization. The ratio of urban to rural population increased from 26.3% in 1960 to over 40% in 1975. Industry is developing rapidly, but the economy of the country is still largely based on agriculture.

Country health situation

Major health problems are related to infectious and parasitic diseases. Malnutrition, reaching up to 40% prevalence in some parts of the country, aggravates the problems. Recently, diseases caused by environmental pollution and other effects of industrialization have shown an increase. Diseases of old age such as malignant neoplasms and vascular lesions affecting the central nervous system, are also increasing. In 1976 the five main causes of death in principal towns of the provinces and districts, in order of incidence, were: heart diseases; pneumonia; senility without mention of psychosis; ill-defined and unknown causes; malignant neoplasms; and gastritis, duodenitis, enteritis and colitis except diarrhoea of newborn. In 1976 the communicable diseases most frequently notified were measles, infectious hepatitis, pertussis, meningococcal infections and bacillary dysentery.

Malaria, which fell to 1000 cases in 1970, started to become a problem again with 37 000 cases in 1976.

Some 36 infectious diseases are notifiable. Unfortunately there is underreporting of infectious diseases, as well as of deaths and births, owing to the lack of manpower and to communication difficulties.

Administrative organization of health services

The organization of health services follows the same pattern as that of the administrative system. At the central level the Ministry of Health and Welfare is responsible for health policy and health services. The Minister of health is assisted by an under-secretary of state who heads the health administration; the latter has four deputies, and under these are the general directors.

At local level, each of the 67 provinces has a provincial director of health appointed by the Ministry of Health, who is subject to the administrative authority of the Governor and the technical authority of the Minister. He is responsible for both preventive and curative health services as the highest health official in the province. In each of the 591 districts a physician appointed by the Ministry leads a team of health workers, advises the district administrator on matters of public health and carries out preventive and curative work as well as forensic medicine.

At municipal level, health administration is mainly concerned with hygiene and environmental health services. There are doctors in large municipalities who are appointed by the Ministry of Health and paid from the municipal budget. The administrative framework of the government-supported health service suffers from fragmentation. Various ministries and official agencies such as the workers' insurance scheme have their own systems of medical care and different salary scales, creating problems of standardization, coordination and recruitment.

New laws on full-time employment of health personnel and on environmental sanitation are to be discussed in the Parliament in the near future.

The third five-year development plan ended in 1977. Because of recent government changes the fourth five-year plan has not yet been prepared, but the 1978 programme of the Government was published. Priorities for the health sector in 1978 were set out as follows:

(1) an environmental health coordination committee at ministerial level to combat air pollution and other environmental health hazards;

(2) a health insurance scheme to provide health care to the needy;

(3) a balanced distribution of health personnel and resources as well as a more effective service;

(4) more thorough control of nutritional substances and pharmaceutical products. The national pharmaceutical industry was to be developed to provide cheap medicaments.

(5) health manpower was to be increased through more efficient and faster manpower development methods as well as incentives for government service.

Curative and preventive services and programmes

The Government of Turkey, through an act of Parliament, is committed to a programme of socialized (nationalized) health services to rural areas and to development of both preventive and curative services. Starting with the first five-year plan in 1963, the socialized health services have been developed to cover 32 provinces out of 67, mainly those in Eastern Turkey, where the need for health services is greatest. The rest of the country is expected to be covered by 1982. So far, 1139 health units and 4276 sub-units have been put into operation.

The services, which include primary health care, environmental sanitation, control of communicable diseases, immunization, health education, maternal and child health care and family planning, are free of charge.

Each health unit serves a population of 7500 and is staffed full-time by a team consisting of a physician (not entitled to private practice), a public health nurse, a sanitary technician and a midwife. Attached to a health unit there are three or four "subunits" which serve 2500 population and are staffed by a midwife. Care is taken to provide a free, equal and integrated service even to the outermost periphery. Ambulatory and home care are stressed and priority is given to preventive services.

The peripheral units are supplemented by hospitals of 50 beds per 50 000 population. There are larger hospitals (200 to 500 beds) in each provincial centre. The public health activities of the units are supported by the public health departments of the provincial health directorate; they include health education, maternal and child health care, malaria eradication and public health laboratories.

In the other parts of the country, while the curative services are organized in a similar manner the public health activities are carried out by the old system of nonintegrated, vertical services delivered by a physician, an environmental sanitation technician stationed in the district centre, and several midwives in the villages.

In the socialized and nonsocialized sectors of the country private doctors (41% of the total) are allowed to practise alongside State-employed doctors.

Both government and privately employed doctors tend to concentrate in large towns; 70% of all doctors live in the three largest cities (Istanbul, Ankara and Izmir). Other categories of health personnel are more evenly distributed.

Categories of hospitals and their bed capacity are as follows; 679 general hospitals with 60 118 beds, 37 maternity hospitals with 3806 beds, 9 mental hospitals with 6425 beds and 57 other specialized hospitals with 12 840 beds, making a total of 782 hospitals with 83 189 beds, of which 588 hospitals with 51 207 beds are government hospitals. The total number of hospital beds represents a rate of 19.7 per 10 000 inhabitants.

Services are planned and administered centrally at the Ministry of Health and Social Welfare through respective departments headed by general directors. The local health authorities are responsible for the preventive services at provincial, district, municipal and village levels. Data gathered from the periphery are analysed, evaluated and published at the Ministry by the Department of Health Statistics and Propaganda, which is also responsible for health education throughout the country.

The Department of Public Health is the most important department of the Ministry. It is responsible for communicable disease prevention and control, environmental health services (including pollution control), nutritional services, public health laboratories (41) and enterobacterial laboratory units (142). At the periphery, services are organized and coordinated through the provincial director of health.

Although single-purpose programmes such as the tuberculosis control programmes (253 dispensaries, 38 mobile X-ray teams), trachoma control programmes (41 dispensaries, 70 treatment units), venereal diseases and leprosy programmes are still considered important, recently more emphasis has been placed upon controlling bacterial and viral enteric infections and malaria through peripheral health units integrated with other services.

Road traffic accidents and environmental pollution, especially in large towns, are recognized as recent problem areas and are being combated through coordinated efforts of several responsible ministries.

Apart from the previously mentioned 1139 health units and 4276 sub-units, maternal and child health and family planning services are available at 167 centres and 808 posts.

Occupational health is the responsibility of the Ministry of Labour, working in conjunction with the Ministry of Health through regional directors and inspectors of labour, whose task is to examine work-places. Preventive mental and oral health services and the services for the care of the elderly are as yet insufficient.

The National Institute of Public Health, with its four regional branches, provides vaccines and serums, and acts as a central reference and control laboratory for the other 41 public health laboratories and 142 laboratory units.

Biomedical and health services research

Medical research is carried out mainly in the various medical faculties. Public health research is done chiefly by the National School of Public

Health, which is also an advisory body to the Ministry of Health. Research in the field of community medicine is undertaken by the community medicine departments of medical faculties.

Funds allocated to research, particularly public health research, are rather low. Health service research priorities are determined by the Ministry of Health and the National School of Public Health.

Health manpower development

The shortage of health personnel, mainly physicians, for public health work has not been made good. The problem of their concentration in large urban centres aggravates this deficiency in the rural areas. Qualitative shortcomings are a bigger consideration, however, and more difficult to remedy.

In 1977 Turkey had the following resources in health manpower, excluding military personnel: 23 769 physicians (5.6 per 10 000 inhabitants), 5954 dentists (1.4), 10 572 pharmacists (2.5), 2607 veterinarians, 15 394 midwives (3.7), 13 193 nurses (3.1), 9543 health officers (2.3), 7275 nursing aids as well as 1839 technicians in medical laboratory service, radiology and environmental health.

Physicians are trained in the 15 faculties of medicine (1976). Faculties of pharmacy and of dentistry (8) also exist.

Auxiliary health personnel receive their training mostly at the professional schools under the Ministry of Health, as well as at faculties of medicine and other institutions. For nurses there are four-year courses at 38 public health colleges. There are also three higher schools of

nursing which offer a four-year nursing course at university level. Midwives undergo four years of training at six health colleges. Rural midwives are trained in 19 health schools. Since October 1976 the duration of training in health schools has been increased from three to five years (rural midwives are accepted by the schools after five years of primary schooling). Four special colleges of health train male public health workers, while laboratory and X-ray technicians are educated at two colleges. There is also a college for environmental health technicians.

The National School of Public Health in Ankara provides postgraduate education in public health and arranges in-service training courses for practising medical staff.

Cost and financing of health care

The 1976 budget for the Ministry of Health and Social Welfare amounted to 5000 million liras (US $200 million). This represented 3.53% of the State budget and was less than the previous year's allotment. The figure does not include funds listed under the hospital expenditures of other ministries and institutions. About 60% of the expenses were for personnel and 20% for services; 43.7% of the budget was allocated to the Department of Curative Services.

Social insurance institutions provide health services for nearly two million insured workers and their dependants. Government employees— about a million—and their families are also insured. Recently a new insurance scheme for three million self-employed has also started. All these schemes lack preventive services and are partly financed by the employer.

UNION OF SOVIET SOCIALIST REPUBLICS

General situation

In January 1977 the population was estimated to be 257 800 000, of whom 159 600 000 lived in towns and 98 200 000 in rural areas. Population and some other demographic indices for the period under review are as follows:

	1973	1974	1975	1976
Population (in millions)	248.6	250.9	253.3	255.5
Birth rate (per 10000 population)	17.6	18.0	18.1	18.4
Death rate (per 1000 population)	8.7	8.7	9.3	9.5
Natural increase (per 1000 population)	8.9	9.3	8.8	8.9

In 1976, morbidity (per 100 000 population) from various communicable diseases was estimated to be as follows: scarlet fever, 149.4; measles, 125.0; pertussis, 12.9; tetanus, 0.2; diphtheria, 0.07; acute poliomyelitis, 0.04.

Health status

Public health is run on a socialist system of national socioeconomic and medical measures for the protection and promotion of public health, the prevention and reduction of morbidity and mortality, the provision of healthy living and working conditions, the maintenance of a high capacity for work and the prolongation of life.

Measures for the protection of public health are aimed at improving its organization, extending the system of hospitals and polyclinics, raising the standard of medical care, increasing the production of medical equipment and highly effective drugs, developing medical science and increasing control of the most dangerous diseases.

Health services are divided into two groups; those for prevention and treatment of diseases, and those for health and epidemiology. The principal treatment and preventive establishments providing the most extensively used type of medical care are polyclinics and outpatient units, which operate on a district or territorial basis. Considerable strides have been made in extending the network and the capacity of these establishments and in providing medical personnel to staff them. In 1976, a total of 35 700 such establishments recorded 2400 million visits to doctors (or 9.4 per capita of the population), as against 2000 million in 1972. From 1971 to 1975, the development of polyclinic care had continued through the construction of large independent polyclinics or polyclinics combined with hospitals (designed for 800 to 1200 visits per shift).

The chief trend in the development of urban polyclinic establishments in recent years has been the widespread introduction of specialities. Citizens now receive qualified medical care not only in the principal specialities (therapy, surgery, traumatology, neurology, ophthalmology, otolaryngology, and stomatology), but in many narrower specialities (rheumatic heart disease, gastroenterology, pulmonology, endocrinology, oncology, allergology, urology, proctology etc.).

Local district medical services are being systematically strengthened and local doctors' districts reorganized into smaller units. In 1982 there is expected to be, on average, a local district doctor or therapist for every 2000 adults (and one for every 1700 by 1985).

The activities of preventive care and treatment establishments are constantly being expanded; in 1976 more than 107 million individuals underwent preventive screening. The *dispanser* method, which is a synthesis of curative and preventive care, has become the most important type of health care. The number of patients receiving prophylactic medical examinations increased by a factor of 1.4 over a period of five years to reach an estimated 36 700 000 in 1976. There are three main trends in the development of *dispanser* services: the number of diseases covered is increasing; the quota of health subjects undergoing prophylactic medical examinations is rising; and the use of such services for various examinations is becoming more widespread.

The system of inpatient medical care is being developed principally by the construction of large, modern, multipurpose specialized hospitals on a standard design. Between 1970 and 1976 the total number of beds increased by 413 000, and at the end of 1976 the public health services had 3 076 000 hospital beds— 119.3 beds per 10 000 population, as against 109.2 in 1970. More than 56 million people annually receive treatment in inpatient establishments, and more than 70% of the budget allocation is expended on maintenance and treatment of patients.

The increased number of beds, the construction of large hospitals, the reconstruction and strengthening of existing establishments and their provision with highly effective medical instruments and equipment, together with the centralization of curative, diagnostic and auxiliary services have made it possible to organize all-union, interrepublican, republican, interregional, regional and municipal centres of various types. The all-union centres are particularly important, especially those for cardiological and cancer research.

An efficient first aid and emergency care service has been developed. The main establishments providing this service are first aid stations, staffed by specialists and equipped with special health transport. Between 1970 and 1975 the number of first aid and emergency medical care stations and departments rose by a factor of 1.2 and the number of people treated by a factor of

1.4. In 1975 alone first aid and emergency medical care stations provided emergency medical care to more than 71 million patients and accident victims. In 1976 first aid and emergency medical care stations numbered 4051.

A new type of establishment is the emergency care hospital combined with first aid station. There are currently 73 such hospitals with 40 400 beds, making it possible to expand the development of specialized teams in first aid centres and thereby increase the facilities for treatment and diagnosis of patients and accident victims *in situ* and on the way to hospital.

Preventive care and treatment for industrial workers is provided by a special network of health establishments in industrial undertakings and also by medical establishments forming part of the territorial network, such as polyclinics, hospitals, *dispanser* services, and also by the extensive network of clinical hospitals and medical and research institutes. It is a feature of the organization of the occupational health service that preventive care and treatment is provided to workers separately for each industry. The health centre, which is a complex medical establishment, embracing a polyclinic, a hospital and factory consultation rooms run by doctors and feldshers, is the basic link in the occupational health system. The development of large health centres in industrial enterprises, improvements in the organization of their work, cooperation with the territorial health services, and the extension and strengthening of workshop units, have had a beneficial effect upon workers' health and brought about a reduction in morbidity.

The medical care system for rural communities is organized according to levels. The first is the rural doctor's district comprising a combination of medical establishments: rural district hospitals, feldsher-midwife centres, feldsher consultation rooms, collective farm maternity homes and institutions for the education of children. The second level is that of the *rayon*, and the third that of the *oblast*. The central *rayon* hospital provides specialized qualified medical care to rural communities, administers the health services of the *rayon*, and the activities of the local district hospitals, directing patients to them for cure and consultation by specialist physicians and analysing the results of the work of the local district hospitals.

A visiting service exists to provide specialized medical care to rural communities in *oblast* hospitals and other *oblast* treatment and prevention establishments. Through this service, visits by

specialist physicians are organized to *rayon* hospitals where they hold clinics, undertake medical investigation of the population and gain first-hand knowledge of primary medical care in the rural area.

The national system for the protection of the health of children, which is codified in the basic health legislation, embodies the idea that all should have access to free, highly qualified preventive medical care. A large number of medical personnel are involved in child health protection: the number of paediatricians was 99 500 in 1976 (3.9 per 10 000 population). The system of paediatric care comprises three closely interlinked elements: polyclinic, hospital and sanatorium. Outpatient polyclinic establishments, of which there are more than 12 000, occupy the leading place in this system.

Children's polyclinics are health centres for the supervision of the physical and mental development of children, promotion of the proper way of life, physical education, nutrition and the raising of strong, healthy children.

Children receive continuous preventive screening from birth up to the age of 14 years, and this allows for home nursing and constant supervision of their state of health. Long before the birth, the local district paediatrician and nursing sister visit the expectant mother at home, and provide the necessary advice. After leaving the maternity home, the child is visited at home by both the paediatrician and the nurse; in the first year the child either attends the doctor's surgery or is visited by the doctor at home a minimum of 14 times.

A system of general education and organization of medical care for children in preschool centres has been introduced. More than 12 million children attend such centres, and in the summer months seasonal centres open in addition where five million children are looked after. More than 10 million children take an annual holiday in "Pioneer" (scout) camps.

Great importance is attached to the development of curative and preventive care for women. Midwifery and gynaecological care is provided by a wide network of women's outpatient units, feldsher and feldsher-midwife posts. There are currently more than 10 000 women's outpatient units providing curative, preventive and social care for expectant mothers and gynaecological patients, controlling abortions and dealing with sex eduction.

The salient feature of current activities in women's outpatient units is the development of specialized care. Central consultation clinics have an important role to play in this, providing specialized care for women giving birth prematurely or having immunological complications in pregnancy, expectant mothers with external genital diseases, gynaecological patients suffering from infertility, endocrine abnormalities, etc. There has been rapid development in services for the prophylaxis and early detection of hereditary diseases and the prognosis of hereditary or congenital pathology.

An important means of raising the quality of medical care for expectant mothers and gynaecological patients is the development of inpatient obstetric and gynaecological care. Specialized establishments or departments exist now for expectant mothers with obstetric and external genital pathology.

Improvements are being made year by year in Soviet legislation guaranteeing health care and proper living and working conditions for the expectant and breastfeeding mothers, and mothers with children aged up to one year.

Administrative organization of the health services

Health authorities

Public health services are part of a national system governed by an Executive Committee of national deputies who are the chief administrators of health care.

The central departmental administrative authority for all health matters in the Union as a whole, and representing the State, is the Union-Republic authority, the Ministry of Health of the USSR. The work of the Ministry of Health is directed by the Council of Ministers, the Minister of Health being a member of the Government and nominated by the Supreme Soviet.

The health authorities are normally subordinate to two administrative bodies. The Ministry of Health of the Union Republic falls within the competence of the Council of Ministers of the Union Republic as regards matters of general scope and, for matters of departmental reference, it comes under the Ministry of Health of the USSR. The ministries of health in the autonomous republics, and the *oblast, kraj* and municipal health departments, are subordinate to the corresponding authorities with general reference and to the Ministry of the Union Republic. *Rayon* health departments fall within the competence of the *rayon* councils of national deputies and their executive committees, and

also the higher departments of the public health authorities. The principle of twofold administration ensures that both national interests and local characteristics are taken into account.

The Ministry of Health of the USSR has a board consisting of the Minister (chairman) and members who deputize for him should the need arise, and other senior staff of the Ministry. The composition of the board is approved by the Council of Ministers on the recommendation of the Minister of Health.

Authorities with national power in local areas are the councils of national deputies in *krajs, oblasts,* districts, *rayons,* towns and villages, which administer public health both independently and through the executive and managerial authorities under a council. Within the executive and managerial apparatus there are branch health departments (boards) to see to it that the rights and responsibilities of area councils of national deputies are observed and fulfilled.

Social insurance is run on a national basis from static funds. All workers and employees receive social insurance completely free of charge. Funds for social insurance are part of the national budget, passed by annual session of the Supreme Soviet. In all its forms social insurance covers all workers without exception and is compulsory. Social security costs are met out of funds allocated annually from the national budget for this purpose.

Individual types of welfare and social services provided by social security include: personal pensions, benefits to the aged and to single mothers, monthly assistance to the elderly and incapacitated, resettlement benefits etc.

Social security matters in the autonomous and union republics are directed by the republic ministries of social security and locally by the *kraj, oblast,* municipal and *rayon* councils of national deputies through the departments of social security of the corresponding executive committees.

Treatment services and programmes

The control of cardiovascular diseases has become a matter of great national importance. Particular attention is devoted not only to the treatment of cardiovascular diseases but also to their prevention, in which prophylactic screening, continuously available hospital services and treatment in sanatoria or health resorts play an important part. The total number of places in sanatoria for rheumatic heart disease patients at the end of the Ninth Five-Year Plan (1971–1975) was 60 000.

The control of malignant neoplasms is also considered very important. Cancer consultation centres and departments in polyclinics and cancer dispensary departments in hospitals are the chief elements in the network of cancer services. At the beginning of 1976 there were 250 cancer dispensaries and 3193 cancer dispensary departments and consultation centres. The *dispanser* method in oncology provides supervision of patients. At the end of 1975 there were some 1 856 400 patients and individuals recovering from malignant tumours registered at cancer dispensaries. In 1975, 50 600 beds were occupied by cancer patients. There are 16 specialized cancer research institutes and five radiology institutes. A cancer research centre with a large experimental section and a clinic with 1000 beds is being constructed.

Health planning

The health service, like all other aspects of the building of socialism, is based on planned principles and forms part of the national economy. Health planning is both annual and long-term. The health section of the Tenth Five-Year Economic Plan, 1976–1980, envisages the implementation of measures for developing prevention and prophylactic screening, increasing the amount of medical care available, raising the standard and developing specialized types of medical care, expanding the diagnostic and curative work of outpatient polyclinic establishments, removing the disparities between medical care in urban and rural areas, raising the standard of training received by medical personnel, and developing and improving the financial and technical basis of the public health service.

Research in medicine and public health

In the research development plan for 1976–1980 sums have been allocated for research in medicine and public health from the national budget which was approved by the Academy of Medical Sciences and the Ministry of Health of the USSR in 1975. In the period under review research projects to study the health status of the population were carried out, making it possible to determine the state and level of physical development of the population as a whole; to improve the quality and efficacy of treatment, diagnosis and preventive care in urban and rural areas; to determine the administrative form and volume of care to be provided by expanding preventive screening to cover the whole population; to improve techniques of current and long-term planning; and to determine the level of public health development in the long term.

Important research is being carried out in the various fields of clinical medicine, in biomedical problems, health and hygiene. A great deal of research is being carried out on the prevention of cardiovascular diseases, cancer and accidents, and on the treatment and rehabilitation of patients.

In 1977, 105 institutes (including 75 medical institutes and institutes of advanced medical studies, and 25 research institutes and universities) participated in research on social hygiene and the administration of public health services.

Health manpower development

Numbers of medical personnel are one of the most important indicators of the level of development of the public health service and the provision of qualified medical care. At the beginning of 1977, the total number of doctors in the USSR was 864 600, or 33.5 per 10 000 population.

The training of doctors takes place at 78 medical institutes, 5 pharmaceutical institutes and 9 medical faculties of universities in the various regions.

Auxiliary health personnel have a large role to play in the public health service, and numbered 2 585 800 at the beginning of 1977, or 100.3 per 10 000 population.

The training of auxiliary health personnel takes place at training institutes in auxiliary health for the various specialities.

According to forecasts for the next planning period, future manpower requirements from higher and auxiliary health education institutes and research institutes for public health establishments will be 38.2 doctors and 129 auxiliary health personnel per 10 000 population.[1]

---

[1] Venediktov, D. D. *International public health problems* (1977) Moscow.

Financing of health services

The principal source of financing is the national budget. Costs for the public health services and physical culture in the national budget amounted to 9300 million roubles in 1970 and 11 500 million roubles in 1975. In 1976, expenditure on public health and physical culture came to 11 853 million roubles, or 5.2% of the national budget. Of this sum, 644 million roubles went on capital investments. Expenditure on maintenance of curative establishments was 10 358 million roubles and on preventive establishments 488 million roubles.

Outlay on public health and physical culture (inclusive of capital investments) is also drawn from the resources of national, cooperative, trade union and other public enterprises and organizations and from collective farms.

Taking all these expenses into account, expenditure on public health and physical culture amounted to 15 thousand million roubles in 1976 (14 600 million in 1975 and 11 800 million in 1970) which represents some 4% of the gross national product.

These figures do not include research, training of medical personnel and payment of public health administrative authorities.

Major developments in the period 1973–1977

In recent years measures have been implemented to develop specialized types of medical care, to strengthen the medical services, to centralize certain services, and to develop the phased treatment of patients with acute pathological conditions. This period has seen the emergence of large, multipurpose, specialized treatment centres, first aid hospitals, all-Union and republic centres for various types of medicine and health care, and rehabilitation centres. Within the medical services, resuscitation and intensive care units, convalescence and rehabilitation units have been set up. An automated, computer-operated system is being introduced into preventive care training establishments. Great attention has been given to the development of disease prevention, and the expansion and extension of the *dispanser* method of health care; to this end the network of establishments of the *dispanser* type, sanatoria and preventive clinics, women's consultation clinics, has been extended, local doctors' districts have been divided up into smaller units, and the quota of the population served by *dispanser* services has been increased.

UNITED KINGDOM OF GREAT BRITAIN AND NORTHERN IRELAND

General background

The United Kingdom consists of four countries—England, Wales, Scotland and Northern Ireland, each with some degree of automony which is reflected in differing arrangements for health service administration—and occupies the greater part of the British Isles. The economy is based largely on industry, commerce and allied services and the population is overwhelmingly urban. Mortality and morbidity rates tend to be higher in the urban than in the surburban or rural areas.

Country health situation

Population estimates and some other vital statistics for England and Wales for the period under review are as follows:

	1973	1974	1975	1976
Population	49 153 800	49 158 900	49 157 100	49 142 400
Number of live births	675 953	639 885	603 445	584 270
Birth rate (per 1000 population)	13.8	13.0	12.3	11.9
Number of deaths	587 478	585 292	582 841	598 516
Death rate (per 1000 population)	12.0	11.9	11.9	12.2
Natural increase/decrease (%)	+0.18	+0.11	+0.04	−0.03
Number of infant deaths	11 407	10 459	9 488	8 334
Infant mortality rate (per 1000 live births)	16.9	16.3	15.7	14.3
Number of deaths, 1–4 years	2 099	1 922	1 699	1 469
Death rate, 1–4 years (per 1000 population at risk)	0.69	0.65	0.60	0.55
Number of maternal deaths	88	81	77	78
Maternal mortality rate (per 1000 live births)	0.13	0.13	0.13	0.13

One half of all deaths in 1976 are ascribed to circulatory disorders, of which the main components are ischaemic heart disease (26%) and cerebrovascular disease (13%). One-fifth of all deaths are caused by some form of cancer, of which the commonest is cancer of the trachea, bronchus and lung (6%). The third largest group of deaths are those attributed to respiratory disease, of which the various forms of pneumonia (9%) and bronchitis, emphysema and asthma (4%) are the main components.

In the same year the most frequently notified communicable diseases were: measles (55 498 cases), tuberculosis, all forms (10 098), scarlet fever (9712), dysentery, all forms (6217), infectious hepatitis (5954), pertussis (3907), acute meningitis (1896), malaria (1162) and typhoid and paratyphoid fevers (240). There were 9051 cases of food poisoning.

Administrative organization of the health services

The main feature of the new organization in England since 1974 is the unified control of the health services at three levels—central department, regional health authority and area health authority. The Secretary of State for Social Services remains accountable to Parliament not only for the broad development of health services in England but also for their detailed functioning. However, differences in the need for health services and in the existing level of provision call for local variety and flexibility in their management and a degree of local knowledge which a central government department could not possess. Responsibility for managing the health services is delegated, therefore, as much as possible to local bodies, but in such a way that the Secretary of State remains fully accountable to Parliament for their operation. For this reason regional and area health authorities are accountable to the Secretary of State for the performance of the functions delegated to them, and he has powers to direct them in the functions which they may exercise on his behalf and in the manner in which they carry out these functions.

The Department of Health and Social Security is headed by the Secretary of State for Social Services, aided in his health service responsibilities by a Minister of State and two Parliamentary Under-Secretaries of State.

In Scotland the powers and duties of the Secretary of State for Scotland are exercised by 15 health boards and the Common Services Agency, which supplies those services that can be provided more effectively on an all-Scotland basis. Independent practitioners are in contract with health boards and joint ophthalmic committees, not with family practitioner committees. Since 1974 the powers and duties of the Secretary of State for Wales have been exercised on his behalf by eight area health authorities directly accountable to him; as in England, each has a family practitioner committee. A Welsh Health Technical Service Organization, responsible for certain technical functions, is also directly accountable to him.

Health laws and regulations

The two main statutes governing the service in England and Wales, the National Health Service Act 1946, and the Reorganization Act 1973, which provided powers for the 1974 reorganization, have been consolidated in the National Health Service Act 1977. This provides for a Central Health Services Council to advise the Secretary of State for Social Services and the Secretary of State for Wales on general matters relating to the provision of services under the Acts, and for standing advisory committees to advise both the Secretaries of State and the Central Council on specified matters. The Scottish Health Service Planning Council and its National Consultative Committees perform a similar function in Scotland. The National Health Service (Scotland) Acts of 1947 and 1972 govern the services in Scotland.

The Secretary of State has wide general powers to provide health services, and specific duties to provide the services. The duties are qualified by the phrase "to such extent as he considers necessary to meet all reasonable requirements". The services listed include hospital and other accommodation; medical, dental, nursing and ambulance services; facilities for the care of expectant and nursing mothers and young children; facilities for the prevention of illness; other facilities required for the diagnosis and treatment of illness; and facilities for family planning. Similar provision exists for Scotland.

A further important piece of legislation is the Health Services Act of 1976, under which the 4400 or so private beds in National Health Service hospitals are being phased out. However, in certain circumstances, patients needing specialized treatment may still be treated privately in National Health Service hospitals. The first 1000 beds have been phased out by the Government and the remainder are being dealt with by an independent Health Services Board.

Health plan and country health programming

Prevention

In 1976 the Government published "Prevention and health: everybody's business", the introductory paper to a series of discussion papers, the first being "Reducing the risk: safer pregnancy and childbirth", and the second, "Occupational health services". Other topics to be covered over the next three or four years will include nutrition, alcoholism and heart disease. The first report of the Expenditure Committee of the House of Commons on Preventive Medicine has reaffirmed the importance of prevention and in response to it the Government will issue a White Paper. One of the main aims of the new initiative on prevention is to encourage individual members of the public to accept greater responsibility for their own health. Here local health committees have an important contribution to make.

Some services are predominantly concerned with prevention; for example, health education, the health visiting services, immunization, genetic counselling, antenatal care and screening for fetal abnormalities, fluoridation and chiropody. But most health services have a preventive role where they are concerned, for example, with early detection and treatment of disease. Prevention forms an important part of the day-to-day activity of most of those working in the health and personal social services. The primary health care team has the essential role of giving specific advice to individuals on how to remain healthy; and of forestalling admission to hospital or residential care by warning against the development of unhealthy habits or detecting early signs of disease.

Community care

The publication quoted above emphasized the importance of adjusting the balance of care to provide greater support in the community; the term "community" covers a whole range of provisions, including community hospitals, hostels, day hospitals, residential homes, day centres and domiciliary support. The term "community care" embraces primary health care and all the above services, whether provided by health authorities, local authorities, independent contractors, voluntary bodies, community self-help or family and friends.

The adjustment in the balance of care will be gradual and slow. Progress will vary depending on economic constraints, local choice and differences in the existing levels of provision. Where the pace is slow the hospital service should continue to make adequate provision.

Curative and preventive services and programmes

Practically all residents in Britain use the National Health Service. The majority are registered as patients of a family doctor and only a very small number have a family doctor whom they consult privately on a fee-paying basis. All family practitioners are free to treat private patients in their own surgeries. Doctors practising at health centres can obtain permission to use the facilities for private work provided that there is no disadvantage for National Health Service patients.

A National Health Service family doctor may refer a patient for private consultation or private treatment as an inpatient. Some people prefer to pay for private consultation and treatment provided largely by consultants whose main work is in the National Health Service. Private treatment takes place in hospitals and nursing homes outside the National Health Service or in National Health Service hospitals authorized to treat private patients.

Among the major users of private medicine are subscribers to provident schemes which make limited payments for private health care in return for annual subscriptions. Some middle-grade or senior staff of firms are covered by group schemes operated by their employers. Some of the provident schemes have private hospitals and these are being expanded as private pay beds are phased out from National Health Service hospitals.

Other people treated privately are those coming to Britain for medical treatment because of the high prestige of British medicine.

Supply of health facilities in the United Kingdom is variable; the methods used to distribute financial resources to the National Health Service have, since its inception, tended to reflect the historic basis for the supply of health service resources and by responding comparatively slowly and marginally to changes in demography and morbidity have also tended to perpetuate the historic situation.

Hospital services

Hospitals provide the specialist elements of health care which are beyond the scope of primary care services. Hospital services include all the main specialities besides general medicine and surgery and their various branches: obstetrics and gynaecology, paediatrics, psychiatry, geriatric medicine, mental handicap, accident and emergency services and others; and the clinical support services (radiology, pathology, etc.). Services may be provided on an inpatient (both long- and short-stay), outpatient, or day-patient basis according to the type and severity of illness concerned. Hospital clinical services are supported by a wide range of "hotel" services such as catering, domestic and laundry services; and the maintenance of hospital buildings, grounds and equipment is also a significant call on resources.

In accordance with professional practice access to specialist services is normally obtained through the patient's family doctor or general dental practitioner. However, admission to mental handicap hospitals is often in consultation with the social services department of the local authority. There are about 6 million episodes of inpatient treatment and about 9 million new hospital outpatients each year; there are also some 9.5 million new attendances each year at accident and emergency departments.

Medical care outside hospitals

The general medical service. The family doctor—an independent practitioner with a contract to provide services with the family practitioner committee—practising alone or in partnership or in group practice, is often the patient's first point of contact with the National Health Service. He is concerned with all types of illness—physical and mental—which cause his patients to seek assistance, and he acts as a link between them and other parts of the service. Everyone aged 16 years and over may choose his own doctor (parents or guardians normally choose for children under 16 years) and a doctor is free to decide whether to accept a person on his list as a patient. However he is obliged to give necessary treatment to any person applying to him for treatment who is not on the list of another doctor or who needs treatment in an emergency. Of the total population 97% is registered on the National Health Service lists of family doctors.

A family doctor is expected to give his patients all necessary and appropriate services within the sphere of general practice. He can give them maternity services, either entirely or in cooperation with a hospital obstetric department; and he can give women patients free family planning guidance and supplies. An additional fee is payable for maternity and certain family planning services. If a second opinion is required from a specialist in a particular field, the general practitioner may refer his patient to the specialist, usually at a hospital—though in suitable circumstances he can ask a specialist to visit the patient at home. However, certain X-rays and pathological tests are in some places available directly to the family doctor. Except in accidents and in other limited circumstances patients have access to hospital treatment only through their family doctor. Family doctors are remunerated through a combination of allowances, capitation fees and fees for item of service.

Primary health care teams. The role in the primary health care service played by health visitors, district nurses and midwives is being increasingly enhanced by the integration of these employees of the area health authority into primary health care teams, where they work in partnership with general practitioners. In a few areas the multidisciplinary team extends to include dentists, chiropodists and local authority employed social workers. Where such integration has taken place, it is possible to coordinate the care of individual patients and to develop educative and preventive services. The first step towards the formation of primary health care teams is the attachment of health visitors and district nurses to general practices, which means that they work with the patients on the list of those practices. In 1973, 79% of health visitors and 77% of district nurses in England were so attached; about 17% of general practitioners now practise from health centres designed to accommodate the full primary care team, and many others work from premises adapted or purposely built for team work. The concept of the integrated team remains an objective rather than a fully developed aspect of the National Health Service.

The general dental service. Like family doctors, general dental practitioners are independent practitioners under contract to provide or arrange to provide for their patients all the treatment needed to ensure a reasonable standard of dental efficiency and oral health. Any registered dentist may enter into contract with any family practitioner committee to provide general dental services. Dentists do not have lists of patients in the way that family doctors do—a patient is free to seek treatment from any dentist, just as any dentist is free to accept or refuse any patient. General dental practitioners are remunerated by the family practitioner committee mainly by fees for item of service.

The approval of the Dental Estimates Board must be obtained before a dentist may proceed with certain types of treatment. The Dental Estimates Board and the Scottish Dental Estimates Board were established, respectively, under the National Health Service Acts of 1946 and 1947 to approve all estimates for treatment submitted by dentists and to authorize payment for the treatment they approve. Patients pay statutory charges direct to the dentist. As with other health service charges there are exemptions from charges for certain groups.

Special services and programmes

Basic sanitation. In England and Wales the appointed water authorities and in Scotland the regional and islands councils are responsible for water supply and sewerage.

Environmental pollution control. The control of outbreaks of infectious diseases, food safety, control of air pollution and noise, working conditions in offices, investigation of unfit housing, clean water and refuse collection and disposal are the responsibility of the local government authorities, each of which has a chief environmental health officer. Advice is given on the medical aspects of environmental health by administrative doctors employed by the health authorities; in England and Wales they are district community physicians known as Medical Officers for Environmental Health, and have dual responsibilities to both authorities. Their responsibilities usually concern notifiable disease and food poisoning; medical advice on water supply and sewerage (see above) and immunization services.

Communicable disease prevention and control. The health authorities have general responsibility for the prevention of diseases and cooperate with the local authority environmental health services in controlling outbreaks of infectious disease and food poisoning.

Immunization. The area health authorities and health boards carry out planned programmes of immunization against diphtheria, tetanus, pertussis, poliomyelitis, measles, tuberculosis, and—for females only—rubella. This protection is given free of charge in family doctors' surgeries, health centres, child health centres, or at school. Although immunization is voluntary, the Government and the health authorities encourage people to obtain protection from these diseases. Health control is also applied at points of entry into Britain in order to prevent the spread of certain infectious diseases which may have been contracted.

Health laboratory services. The Public Health Laboratory Service is a Government-financed service run by a board appointed by the Secretary of State for Social Services and the Secretary of State for Wales. Its main function is to monitor microbial diseases. Diagnostic services are provided for hospitals, family doctors and environmental health officers in 54 regional and area laboratories. Specialist diagnosis is given in 16 reference laboratories which investigate suspected outbreaks of infection and are involved in the surveillance of the prevalence of certain types of microbe and those with antibiotic resistance.

Maternal and child health. Services for mothers and children include maternity facilities in hospital, child health centres, school health services, help for handicapped children, and hospital and specialist services for children.

School health. Area health authorities (health boards in Scotland and health and social services boards in Northern Ireland) are responsible for the medical and dental inspection and treatment of schoolchildren. School medical inspections are normally carried out on school premises by doctors with special knowledge and experience of conditions likely to interfere with normal learning. The purpose of the inspections is to identify as early as possible any departure from normal, to ensure that proper advice and treatment are being obtained, and to advise the education authority, the school, the parents and the pupil of any health problem which might require special consideration during school life.

Occupational health. Occupational health services seek to prevent disease and accidents in place of work. Legislation sets out certain standards concerning health, safety and amenity in factories and offices. Inspectorates enforce the legislation. Many employers maintain medical and nursing services for their employees, although not required to do so by law.

Health care of the elderly. Since the need for medical attention increases with age, over half of hospital beds in England (excluding maternity and psychiatry) are occupied by people aged 65 and over. Special departments of geriatric medicine are becoming more common, and priority is being given to their establishment in all district general hospitals. Elderly patients are also referred to other hospital departments.

A greater part of a family doctor's time is taken up with the needs of older patients and, in recognition of this, he receives higher capitation fees for those patients on his list who are 65–74 years of age and those aged 75 and over. The district nurse also makes home visits to assess nursing needs and to provide care, including treatment prescribed by the family doctor. The tasks of the nurse include teaching relatives to undertake care and helping patients towards self care. Nursing aids and chiropody services are normally available free of charge, following professional assessment of need.

Noncommunicable disease prevention and control. Recent years have seen an increase in the emphasis placed on preventive services in the National Health Service. The publication of "Prevention and health: everybody's business", quoted above, was part of a growing awareness of the importance of prevention both in the health services and in other relevant fields such as education for healthy living in schools and ensuring a safer environment both at home and at work.

Mental health. Treatment for mental disorder is provided as part of the National Health Service. Patients can consult their family doctor, have domiciliary visits and receive specialist advice at hospital outpatient clinics as they would for any other illness. The vast majority of patients are treated voluntarily; in 1974, for instance, some 169 307 of the 194 082 admissions to National Health Service psychiatric hospitals were informal.

Accident prevention and control. The Health and Safety at Work Act 1974 is designed to cover everyone at work and to further the protection of the general public against industrial hazards. The Act provides for securing the health, safety and welfare of people at work; protecting other people against risks to health or safety arising from the activity of people at work; controlling the keeping and use of dangerous substances and preventing their unlawful acquisition, possession and use; and controlling the emission into the atmosphere of noxious or offensive substances.

The legislation is administered by the Health and Safety Commission and the Health and Safety Executive. The basic obligations laid down in the Act are supported by ministerial powers to make regulations dealing with a wide range of health and safety matters. Regulations will be supplemented, where appropriate, by codes of practice approved by the Commission.

Guidance is also issued at all levels on the prevention of accidents in the home.

Emergency and relief services. Most hospitals have specialized accident and emergency departments. Moreover, a blood transfusion service, a pathological laboratory service and an ambulance service are at the disposal of every hospital. The blood transfusion service relies completely on voluntary blood donors and has more than 1.5 million donors on its panels. It is administered by regional health authorities in England, the Common Services Agency in Scotland, the South Glamorgan Area Health Authority in Wales and the Eastern Health and Social Services Board in Northern Ireland. There are 20 regional transfusion centres—13 in England, 5 in Scotland and one each in Wales and Northern Ireland. Where necessary on medical grounds, free transport by ambulance is provided between home and hospital. In some areas the ambulance service is augmented by volunteers using their own cars. In Scotland an air ambulance service is available in the more remote mainland and island areas.

Oral health. Patients seeking National Health Service dental treatment are entitled to receive all treatment necessary to make them dentally fit. Dentists may also take private as well as National Health Service patients (see also the section on the general dental service, above). A major problem in this field is dental decay for which fluoridation of water supplies is a safe preventive measure. The Government is encouraging water authorities to increase the percentage of the population receiving fluoridated water. The vast majority of area health authorities have decided to fluoridate.

Health technology. The central Government health departments are responsible for ensuring that the National Health Service receives supplies of the right kind and quality. Over 500 million pounds is spent annually on equipment and supplies. The Department of Health and Social Security has been designated as the "sponsoring department" for the medical and pharmaceutical industries, a function exercised on a United Kingdom basis on behalf of all the central Government health departments.

Strict controls are maintained over the manufacture and distribution of medicines and the marketing of new medicinal products. The Medicines Act 1968 covers all aspects of the control of medicine for human and veterinary use, except prices, and narcotics are also controlled through the Medicines Commission.

Health education. Health education is a fundamental part of the preventive services. The main bodies concerned are health authorities, local authorities, the Health Education Council and the Scottish Health Education Unit. Most health professionals are frequently involved in health education. Much is done in the course of contacts that doctors, dentists, health visitors, midwives, nurses and pharmacists have with their patients. In addition group health education is often undertaken, for example, with expectant mothers and parents of young children and in antismoking, cervical cytology and obesity clinics.

Other services and programmes. There are many other publicly funded health services in Britain involving, amongst others, ophthalmic services, pharmaceutical services, abortion (not Northern Ireland), family planning aids, and special services for the handicapped and disabled. Publicly funded health programmes include medical research and the discouragement of cigarette-smoking.

Biomedical and health services research

England and Wales

The Office of the Chief Scientist advises the Department of Health and Social Security and the Welsh Office on the organization and promotion of research and development in support of the services for which the Secretary of State

for Social Services is responsible. These bodies have established a number of research liaison groups comprising administrative and professional officers from the relevant policy divisions and the Chief Scientist's organization. Their purpose is to define for their areas long- and short-term research requirements and priorities, and to secure the promotion, supervision and application of research and development to meet them.

Commissions for research are arranged by the Department's research management organization and the research is carried out by a variety of external research units including a number of teams under long-term support arrangements. Clinical and biomedical research is funded mainly by the Medical Research Council; in 1975/76 over 7 million pounds was expected thus to be spent, accounting for more than 30% of the total research expenditure. Arrangements are being developed for the participation by health departments in England, Wales and Scotland with the Medical Research Council in the formulation and development of policies over the whole field of biomedical research, and for improved coordination of commissions more directly relevant to National Health Service priorities and objectives.

Scotland

In Scotland, the Chief Scientist of Scottish Home and Health Department is supported by a separate structure. He is advised by the Chief Scientist Committee, whose membership includes a wide range of academic specialists in medicine and allied fields and the chief professional officers of the Department, and whose chief function is to advise on the main objectives of research and development in relation to the National Health Service in Scotland and the broad needs of its components. The Committee is in turn supported by four committees of a more specialist nature which are concerned with specific proposals for biomedical, health services, computer and equipment research and development, respectively. Close links are maintained at official level with both Department of Health and Social Security and Medical Research Council and there is a representative of the Council on the Chief Scientist Committee and on the Biomedical Research Committee. In addition, both Departments are represented by chief officers on the Council and also by scientific nominees on the research boards set up by

Council, thus enabling them to make positive contributions (in line with their contribution of funds) to Council policy. In 1975/76 the Scottish Home and Health Department contribution was expected to total just over one million pounds.

Costs and financing of health services

Sources of finance

The National Health Service in Great Britain derives its income almost entirely from public funds. Revenue from National Health Service contributions paid by employers and employees represents about 8% of the cost of the service. About 2.5% comes from charges for certain services including prescriptions, dental and optical treatment and private beds in National Health Service hospitals.

Relationship to other public expenditure programmes

The total sum spent on the National Health Service is determined by the Government following the annual survey of public expenditure which brings together estimates for the following four years of the cost of all programmes and relates them to prospective resources. The health and personal social services programme is the third largest, coming after social security and education and ahead of defence and housing.

Planned public expenditure on health services, 1976/77

The results of the latest survey have been published in the White Paper on Public Expen-

diture to 1979/80, and show that current expenditure on health services is planned to grow, in real terms, at an average annual rate of 1.8% over the period from 1976/77 to 1979/80, although public expenditure as a whole (excluding debt interest) will be roughly stable. Within the total amount, current expenditure on hospitals and community health services is expected to increase at 1.4% a year and that on the family practitioner services (general medical practitioners, dentists, opticians and chemists) by 3.3% a year. Capital expenditure will however fall. The details at 1975 survey prices are as shown in the table at foot of page.

The National Health Service resources, measured in real terms, have roughly doubled since its foundation in 1948. The share of gross national product spent on the service has also risen substantially. In 1949 the proportion of gross national product (at factor cost) taken up by the service was 4.0%, whereas in 1974/75 it had reached 5.4%. The proportion of total public expenditure (excluding debt interest) allocated to the service has remained fairly constant since 1951, ranging between 8% and 10%.

Charges to National Health Service patients

As indicated above, receipts from charges to patients play a comparatively minor role in the financing of the National Health Service. It was estimated that receipts in 1975/76 in Great Britain would amount to approximately 106 million pounds, as follows:

	pounds
Prescriptions	27 600 000
Dental	35 800 000
Ophthalmic	20 300 000
Hospital services	22 700 000

	1976/77	1977/78	1978/79	1979/80
		(in millions of pounds)		
Capital				
Hospitals and community health services	328.5	299.7	299	298
Family practitioner services	0.3	0.3	—	—
Other health services	7.9	10.6	11	10
Central and miscellaneous services	1.7	1.7	1	1
Total capital	388.4	312.3	311	309
Current				
Hospitals and community health services	3 126.4	3 174.9	3 216	3 259
Family practitioner services	849.9	884.2	911	938
Other health services	75.8	77.6	79	81
Central and miscellaneous services	113.6	114.5	113	112
Total current	4 165.7	4 251.2	4 319	4 390
Total	4 504.1	4 563.5	4 630	4 699

There are exemptions from prescription and dental and ophthalmic charges for people in various categories such as those in receipt of supplementary benefits, children and those on low income. Charges for private beds are determined annually to reflect the average cost of inpatient services in the type of hospital and accommodation provided.

Appraisal of developments in the period 1973–1977

Despite limited resources, progress was being made towards the achievement of the fundamental purposes of reorganization. The process of securing a more even geographical distribution of services was being carried further, and extra resources were being directed towards the priority services. Hospital services were being rationalized and the community services were being strengthened.

On 1 April 1974, the planned reorganization of the National Health Service was put into effect. With the exception of the postgraduate hospitals, the health services, of which the school health service now formed a part, were brought together under the management of area health authorities who were required to set up the family practitioner committees to administer the contracts of general practitioners, dentists, pharmacists and opticians. The same Act which reorganized the Service also appointed a Health Service Commissioner to investigate complaints against health authorities.

It became possible to plan and organize the services of each district on a comprehensive basis. This was the task of the multidisciplinary teams at each level of the Service. The vehicle was to be the new planning system. Priorities were to be identified through widespread discussion inside and outside the Service. The aim was to delegate more responsibility to health authorities without undermining the Secretary of State's accountability to Parliament for the money spent on the Service. The key to this was an objective basis for allocating money to health authorities.

There was now a common budget at each level of the Service. All nurses, both in hospitals and in the community, were responsible to the District Nursing Officer. Attachments of nursing staff could be discussed with the family practitioner committee, on which the area health

authorities were strongly represented. Representatives of the hospital medical staff and of the general practitioners played a full part in district management, and professional advisory committees were established at each level of the Service. A unified administration had been created.

The new authorities were set up by August 1973 and appointed their officers in readiness for the takeover. The transfer of responsibility took place remarkably smoothly, but it inevitably took time for new working relationships to be established and for all concerned to become accustomed to new ways of working. The new regional health authorities had to establish community health councils for each district to represent the interests of users.

Acrimony resulted from the Government's decision to phase pay beds out of the National Health Service, changing the arrangements made under the 1946 Act by which hospitals could set aside private wards for patients willing to pay the full cost of their accommodation and treatment.

The rapid expansion of health centres continued after reorganization. Between the end of 1973 and the end of 1976, the number of doctors working in health centres increased by about 40%. By the last year there were 789 health centres in operation. Under an Act passed in late 1976, doctors entering general practice in the National Health Service could be required to have vocational training.

In 1974 the new Government decided that the family planning service should be free. From July 1975, free family planning services for women were also provided by general practitioners.

In 1975 a comprehensive long-term programme to improve the quality of services for the mentally ill was set out in a White Paper. The core of the programme was a shift in care and treatment services into local communities.

Reorganization had brought the different parts of the health services under common management at the local level, but the key social services which could reduce the need for health services were the responsibility of the local authorities. To encourage collaboration, health and local authorities were advised to set up joint care planning teams to consider the needs of various groups such as the elderly, for both health and social services care.

The unification of the Health Service made it possible to introduce a more rational basis for allocating money to regions and from regions to areas and districts. A working party was set up in 1975 (the Resource Allocation Working Party) to recommend how allocations should be made to regions, areas and districts. A substantial move towards target allocations recommended by the working party was made in 1976/77—the last year in which special allocations were made to regions for the running costs of new buildings. The system brought special help to the deprived regions. A similar system was adopted in Wales and Scotland.

YUGOSLAVIA

The Socialist Federal Republic of Yugoslavia is a federal state consisting of the Social Republics of Bosnia and Herzegovina, Croatia, Macedonia, Montenegro, Serbia and Slovenia and the Socialist Autonomous Provinces of Vojvodina and Kosovo which are constituent parts of the Socialist Republic of Serbia.

The right of every citizen to health care is gauranteed by the Constitution. Workers have the right to health and other care and personal security at work. In accordance with the law and self-management agreements, workers have an established right for themselves to health care and other rights in case of illness, decrease of working ability, pregnancy, and for their dependants.

According to the Constitution, federal laws regulate questions of the protection of the population against communicable diseases representing a threat to the country as a whole, the control of the manufacture and trade in pharmaceutical products and poisons, the production of and trade in narcotics and psychotropic substances and the trade in and transport of radioactive and other dangerous materials. The socialist republics and socialist autonomous provinces determine by their laws the basic rights of all citizens in the field of health care. The broader aspects of rights to health care are determined by workers themselves within their self-managing communities.

The rights to health care determined by laws and self-management agreements, are realized by workers in self-managing communities on health care. Health institutions which, according to the Constitution, are organizations of a special social interest, provide health care to all citizens.

Population and other statistics

Yugoslavia covers a surface of 255 804 km^2 and by the middle of 1977 it had a population of 21 767 000 inhabitants, that is 85 inhabitants per km^2. During the whole postwar period there has been an intensive and dynamic economic and social development. Concurrently with the socioeconomic development, the living and working conditions of the population have also improved, and this in turn has had its impact on the demographic changes in the population. The birth rate decreased over most of the period but for several years it remained around 18.0 per 1000 inhabitants. The death rate has remained stationary, while infant mortality continues to decrease.

	1974	1975	1976	1977
Birth rate per 1000 population	18.1	18.2	18.1	17.1
Death rate per 1000 population	8.4	8.7	8.5	8.4
Infant mortality rate per 1000 live births	40.9	39.7	37.1	35.2
Natural increase	0.97	0.95	0.96	0.93

Indices of demographic movement differ greatly from republic to republic, as well as within regions of the republics. Thus the birth rate varies from 14.2 to 35.3; death rate from 5.9 to 10.5; infant mortality rate from 19.3 to 69.8; natural increase from 0.38 to 2.86. In 1972, the average life-span for men was 65.4 years and for women 70.3.

The housing conditions are constantly improving. The number of flats with piped water supply, bathrooms and central heating has increased markedly.

The number of people in employment is also increasing, the annual rate of increase being about 4.5%. Concurrently with this trend, there is a constant decrease of the rural population which at present comprises only 33% of the total population of the country.

Health status of the population

Mortality and morbidity data now have most of the characteristics of developed countries.

The following are the death rates per 100 000 population for various diseases and other causes in 1971 and 1975:

	1971	1975
Cardiovascular diseases	286	359
Neoplasms	101	116.3
Pulmonary diseases	51	64.3
Accidents	66	60.1
Infectious and parasitic diseases	32	24
Tuberculosis	17	12
Ill-defined diseases	241	147.2
Other causes	93	96

The percentage of deaths between 1971 and 1975 due to cardiovascular diseases increased from 32.9% to 41.5%, while those due to neoplasms increased from 11.6% to 13.4%.

Communicable diseases are subject to obligatory notification. The total number notified in 1976 was 170 590 cases with 2 970 deaths. The most frequently reported were the dysenteries (37 860), measles (31 487), hepatitis (28 257), tuberculosis (19 358 new cases), toxic infections (13 240), pertussis (6 706), and viral meningitis (3 697).

In outpatient institutions, the number of attendances continues to increase. Thus, in 1976, there were 76.4 million attendances at general practice and specialist service centres, 5.1 million at maternal health care centres, 10.7 million at child health care centres, 7.6 million at centres concerned with the health care of female children, and 14 million at occupational medicine units.

In addition, almost a million systematic medical examinations of schoolchildren were performed.

In hospitals, 2 368 620 patients were treated with a total number of 42 087 387 hospital days, with an average duration of treatment of 17.7 days for both general and special hospitals; for general hospitals alone it was 14.9 days.

The prevalence of tuberculosis continues to decrease. In 1976, there were 78 847 registered cases, 48 882 males and 29 967 females. There was the following age distribution: 0–4 years 655 cases, 5–9 years 1233 cases, 10–14 years 1301 cases, 15–19 years 2815 cases and over 20 years 72 847 cases. That is, 92.4% of the diseased patients were over 20 years of age.

The changes in the health status of the population in the last few years reflect the decrease of acute communicable and parasitic diseases, the gradual increase of chronic diseases, particularly cardiovascular and chronic pulmonary diseases and malignant neoplasms. The numbers of accidents and cases of mental disease are also increasing.

Health legislation

The new Constitution of the Socialist Federal Republic of Yugoslavia enacted in 1974 has opened a very important era in the development of socioeconomic relations in the field of health.

By the Constitution and the related legislation, a new socioeconomic status of all workers in associated labour organizations has been determined, with the workers in the health field forming a constituent part of the total associated labour and social organizations.

The republics and provinces determine through their own legislative procedure the basic principles in the field of health, including health care, its organization, training of health manpower, organization and functioning of self-managing communities of health interests. Users of health care and health workers associate themselves in these self-managing communities. Assemblies of self-managing communities of health interests are established on the delegate principle. An assembly is composed of two councils: the Council of Users and the Council of Providers of Health Care. In the Assembly of self-managing communities of health interests, delegates make decisions jointly and on an equal footing on all matters of health care and development of health activities. In that way, a new, very significant step was made in the development of socioeconomic relations in the field of health.

Planning and programming of health care

The basic principles of planning are determined by the Constitution of the Federal Republic and are worked out in detail in the Federal Law on Social Planning. In Yugoslavia, there exists the uniform system of social planning on the following principles. The working people associated in working organizations have the right and duty to adopt plans and programmes of development, independently. Self-managing communities of interest also adopt independently plans and programmes. The planners (working organizations and self-managing communities of interest) adjust their plans and programmes in accordance with the common interests and objectives. In the commune, autonomous province, republic and federation social plans are adopted on the basis of agreement of common interests and the objectives of economic and social development. The common development, organizational and economic policies provide conditions for implementation of the plans that are also determined by those plans. The planners are responsible for the accomplishment of the plans.

In accordance with these principles and on the basis of the scientific knowledge and appraisal of the development possibilities, each health institution adopts its own plan of work and development. The plan of work and development of self-managing community of health interests represents a consensus of the interests and aims of the general working people and those in the health field.

Plans and programmes are adopted for five year periods (medium-term). Annual plans and programmes represent a part of the medium-term plan for that period. Long-term plans are also made.

Organization of health care

At the Federation level there is a Committee for Health, Labour and Social Security chaired by a president who is a member of the Federal Executive Council. At the level of a republic and equally in an autonomous province there is a secretariat responsible for health and social security, headed by a Secretary who is a member of the Executive Council of the Republic or the Autonomous Province. Sanitary inspection is organized by these state bodies which are responsible mainly for the implementation of health protection activities provided for by legislative acts, ordinances and laws of the country.

Health work organizations are independent associated labour organizations that provide health care to the workers and other citizens, on the same principles as other work organizations. Health organizations of associated labour may be: basic, working or composite.

As they perform an activity of a special importance, their self-managing organs also include representatives of social community. The following types of health organizations exist: health centres, medical centres, clinics, hospitals, (general, special and clinical), institutes of public health and other independent institutes, natural health resorts, pharmacies, dispensaries for occupational medicine.

These types of health organizations work either as independent or combined services and are responsible for various other health services.

In 1976, there were 898 independent health institutions, namely 275 health centres, 117 medical centres, 134 general and special hospitals and natural health resorts, 139 pharmacies, 22 institutes of public health, and 211 other independent institutions.

Hospital services

Hospital services are organized by general and special hospitals, medical centres, clinics and special institutes.

The total hospital capacity in 1976 was 129 112 beds, that is 6 beds per 1000 inhabitants.

There were 83 017 beds in general hospitals and centres, 37 363 in special hospitals, clinics and institutes, and 8732 in natural health resorts.

Out of the total number of beds, 8360 were available for tuberculosis patients, 11 250 for mental patients and 9020 for rehabilitation.

In all, there were 1960 hospital wards and the hospital service employed the following types of health workers: physician-specialists (6769), other physicians (3156), stomatologists (150), nurses (25 871), midwives (3604), other health workers with intermediate or advanced training (4450) and health workers with primary education (6940).

Other services

Most of the other services are delivered through the health and medical centres but some services are also provided through special institutes or dispensaries. The following table gives the services available, the number of organizational units providing in 1976 the various services and the type of staff employed.

General practice provides an outpatient health service, in towns mainly to adult population, but in the rural areas to the total population.

Occupational medicine service is also provided through independent dispensaries for occupational medicine.

Child health care provides outpatient care to preschool children.

Health care for schoolchildren provides outpatient forms of health care.

The maternal health care service provides both preventive and curative outpatient health care.

	General practice	Child health care	School health care	Maternal health care	Tuberculosis control	Cancer control	Mental health	Dental	Pharmaceutical	Emergency	Occupational medicine	Hygiene and epidemiology
Number of organizational units	3923	1131	623	982	460	60	310	2673	1565	120	1165	1565
Type of staff employed												
Physician-specialists	946	778[a]	430	528[b]	365	174	224[c]	—	—	73	682[d]	290[e]
Other physicians	4021	567	451	126	55	65	25	—	—	297	1084	156
Stomatologists	—	—	—	—	—	—	—	4707	—	—	—	—
Dentists	—	—	—	—	—	—	—	430	—	—	—	—
Pharmacists	—	—	—	—	—	—	—	—	2784	—	—	64
Chemists	—	—	—	—	—	—	—	—	—	—	2052	—
Nurses	5000	2838	1391	495	1055	244	263	1347	—	—	—	—
Midwives	—	—	—	1627	—	—	—	—	—	—	—	—
Dental technicians	—	—	—	—	—	—	—	4775	—	—	—	—
Medical technicians	—	—	—	—	—	247	—	—	—	—	—	643
Nurses and medical technicians	—	—	—	—	—	—	—	—	—	640	—	—
Pharmaceutical technicians	—	—	—	—	—	—	—	—	2876	—	—	—
Pharmaceutical laboratory technicians	—	—	—	—	—	—	—	—	615	—	—	—
Dental assistants	—	—	—	—	—	—	—	3061	318	—	—	—
Other health workers with advanced education	196	—	—	—	—	—	—	—	—	—	191	—
Health workers with primary education	1276	—	—	—	—	—	—	—	—	164	225	—

[a] Paediatricians.
[b] Gynaecologists.
[c] Psychiatrists.
[d] In occupational health.
[e] In preventive medicine.

The *tuberculosis control service* provides outpatient health care (prevention, early detection, and outpatient treatment).

The *cancer control service* is organized to provide measures for prevention of malignant disease, its early detection and devotes considerable attention to health education.

The *dental service* is provided through the health centres and medical centres.

The *emergency service* provides urgent medical aid, in case of sudden illness and other urgent conditions, to the diseased and injured, at the place where disease or injury occurred and during the transport to the appropriate health organization. In addition to the centres, the service is provided through independent health organizations and institutes or stations for urgent medical aid.

The *pharmaceutical service* is provided by the independent pharmacies within health centres and medical centres.

The *hygiene and epidemiological service* is provided by institutes of public health, medical centres or health centres. Main tasks of this service are undertaking the necessary measures for prevention and control of communicable diseases and environmental control.

The *mental health service* is concerned with the prevention and control of mental diseases. It operates through 44 dispensaries for mental health, 13 dispensaries for alcoholism and 253 psychiatric offices.

Health manpower and training

Physicians. The total number of physicians in 1976 was 27 150, or one physician per 794 inhabitants. Out of this number 14 637 were specialists and 12 513 general practitioners or specialist trainees. There is one physician for 664 inhabitants in urban areas, and one for 1208 in rural areas. The unequal distribution of physicians in the developed as compared with the underdeveloped areas, and the proportionally large number of specialists compared with the number of general practitioners, represent problems.

Stomatologists. In 1976 there were 5141 stomatologists, that is one stomatologist per 4500 inhabitants.

Pharmacists. In 1976 there were 4571 pharmacists, or one pharmacist per 4800 inhabitants.

Other health workers. There were 11 916 workers with advanced education, 72 321 with intermediate education and 13 812 with primary education.

Training schools. In 1976 there were 9 medical, 6 stomatological and 4 pharmaceutical faculties.

The total number of students in the medical faculties was 14 493, in the stomatological faculties 4542 and in the pharmaceutical faculties 2372.

In the course of the year 1737 students graduated from the medical faculty, 580 from the stomatological faculty and 317 from the pharmaceutical faculty.

There were five postbasic nursing training schools with 3660 students leading to senior nurses positions, and 485 students leading to similar positions in preventive branches of medicine. There were also 96 intermediate training schools with 34 416 pupils.

Organization of scientific medical research

Scientific research is organized primarily within the medical faculties and special institutes. Basic research is usually financed by communities for research work, while the research in health service organization is financed by self-managing communities of health interests and communities for disability-pension insurance. A number of projects is conducted jointly with the World Health Organization (regionalization of health service, comprehensive cardiovascular care, disability in the working population).

Cost of health care

In 1975, 30 840 million dinars were spent on health care—6.7% of the national income. The real annual increase of costs amounted to 5.7%.

Of the total allocation, the costs of outpatient health care amounted to 29.1%, hospital treatment costs to 40.1%, the cost of drugs to 17.1%, dental care service to 5.9%, and other costs to 7.8%.

EASTERN MEDITERRANEAN REGION

AFGHANISTAN

Major health problems

Major health and health-related problems noted during the period under review were: high infant and child morbidity and mortality, maternal mortality, and labour force morbidity; and limited coverage of the population by health care services, particularly in rural and remote areas.

The most common diseases recorded during the period were: bacillary dysentery and amoebiasis, enteritis and other diarrhoeal diseases, tuberculosis of the respiratory system; internal obstruction and hernia, psychoses and nonpsychotic mental disorders, bronchitis and emphysema, pneumonia, cataract, appendicitis and tuberculosis other than that of the respiratory system, including late effects.

Action taken

Health policy

Control of communicable diseases is considered the first priority of the national health programme, including mass immunization, which is expected to give good results. Less prevalent causes of morbidity and mortality will be tackled through the regular work of health care services.

The environment, the major cause of the spread of communicable diseases, is the second priority programme area, and especial importance is given to safe water supply and excreta disposal.

Together with measures to combat malnutrition, effective and easily accessible health care services are conceived as the most powerful instrument in the hands of the Ministry of Public Health to control disease and reduce mortality. The improvement and expansion of the whole system to provide optimal health care is the subject of a set of objectives of the national health programme, the essential elements being: a team approach in which health professions are integrated and coordinated; a spectrum of services that includes education, prevention, diagnosis, specific treatment and rehabilitation; a coordinated community and regional system incorporating these services and providing for coordinated care from primary contact through the various levels of treatment; and a continuing programme of evaluation of and research on the quality of the services provided and their adequacy in meeting the needs of the patient and the community.

Health manpower has also been given high priority.

Health legislation

No new legislation had been brought into force during the period.

Health planning and programming

The health plan forms part of the national development plan. The present plan covers the period 1976–1982. The annual per capita government expenditure under previous health plan was 23 afghanis and the per capita allocation of the current plan has been 36 afghanis.

Health planning and programming being a continuous process, the implementation of the national health programme is preceded by detailed tactical planning of health projects and programmes every year. For this purpose objectives to be achieved, technology to be applied, activities to be performed, the aims likely to be met and the resources needed are clearly identified and documented.

Organization of the health services

The Minister of Public Health, who is the head of the Department of Health, is responsible for health services. All statutory powers are vested in the Minister, who issues orders and supervises the activities of the entire Department and other agencies for the provision of health services. The functions of the Department of Health include preventive and curative health care, the treatment and care of the physically and mentally ill and their rehabilitation; regulation and control of training; control of appointments and conditions of service of medical officers, nurses and other health staff; research; food safety; pharmaceutical production and quality control; collection, analysis, publication and dissemination of health information;

improvement of environmental sanitation; and inoculation, vaccination and the issue of health certificates.

The Minister of Public Health is assisted by a Deputy Minister of Public Health, a General Director of Health, directors of curative medicine, preventive medicine, foreign relations, planning, administration, and nursing, and a number of other directors, and a Health Planning Board of which the Minister is the Chairman. Provincial administration is carried out through the provincial governors and provincial health officers.

The Minister also exercises some measure of supervisory control over certain professional bodies, such as the Afghan Family Guidance Association.

Biomedical and health services research

Research has been given due importance in the national health programme and is conducted mainly by the technical support services in large hospitals, and by organizations responsible for the vertical health programmes.

Education and training of health manpower

Professional training of doctors is provided at the universities. Training of nurses, postgraduate and other paramedical staff is the responsibility of the Ministry of Public Health, but under its existing programme insufficient numbers are trained to meet the requirements of the health care programme. This deficiency will be corrected in order adequately to staff existing institutions and to supply additional manpower needs for new and expanded facilities. A few categories of personnel will be sent abroad for specialized training, while the great majority will be trained locally through the expansion of current, and development of new training programmes.

Health resources

Health establishments

The health establishments functioning during 1977 were: 68 general hospitals with 3031 beds (including 19 with 1400 beds not administered by the Ministry of Public Health); six specialized hospitals, with 535 beds; 122 basic health

centres, 78 subcentres, 35 maternal and child health centres, and 7 other institutions.

Health manpower

There is a shortage of nurses and auxiliary medical staff. There were 4717 posts including doctors and nurses under the Ministry of Public Health in 1977, of which 50% are in hospitals and basic health centres and the rest in the technical support services and public health and specialized (vertical) programmes.

Satisfaction of effective demand for health manpower is the target for the seven-year plan, to be achieved by improving health manpower management, increasing the supply of categories that are in short supply, and training primary health workers.

Production and sale of drugs and pharmaceuticals

It is proposed to promote production and use of generic named drugs, and the Government aims at using only generic named drugs by the end of the seven-year plan period. In order further to increase production, the Government intends to complete a pharmaceutical factory during the period, and drugs produced will be sold at lower profits. A new institute for vaccine and sera will also be put into operation in March 1979.

Health expenditure

General government expenditure for health during the financial year 1976 was 796.6 million afghanis, and the plan outlay for health during 1977 was 834.0 million afghanis.

Appraisal of progress made between 1972 and 1977

An all-round increase was achieved in the health facilities with the extension of health care services to remote and difficult areas which were previously underserved. The facilities increased as follows during the period:

	1972–1973	1977–1978	Increase
Hospitals	48	55	14.6%
Hospital beds	1492	2166	45.2%
Basic health centres	70	122	74.3%
Doctors	561	719	28.2%
Nurses	766	946	23.5%

Outlook

The health goals for the next 5–10 years are:
(1) to improve the health of infants and children and reduce infant and child mortality;
(2) to improve the health of expectant mothers;
(3) to improve the health of the labour force, reduce the number of days lost due to sickness, increase production and improve socioeconomic conditions;
(4) to ensure balanced development of health care services and make facilities available to the entire population within a reasonable distance from their homes (increasing contacts will be provided under the family guidance programme);
(5) to improve health education and environmental health, especially safe water supply and excreta disposal, which are given high priority in the national health programmes (sewerage systems will be established in urban areas by stages);
(6) to control communicable diseases as a high priority, especially malaria, leishmaniases, trachoma, tuberculosis and leprosy, with the ultimate aim of eradicating malaria;
(7) to bring all infants and children under the expanded immunization programme;
(8) to promote primary health care and basic health care as an integral part of the total health care system;
(9) to upgrade the facilities for the provision of optimal medical care in provincial hospitals and to increase their utilization;
(10) to develop large regional hospitals capable of providing high-quality, moderately specialized medical care, increase the bed/population ratio and provide a more equitable bed distribution; and
(11) to improve specialized hospital care at the central level.

Health manpower development

Apart from the universities, the professional training of the health manpower is in the Public Health Institute, the Schools of Nursing and Midwifery, the Institute of Radiology, the Institute of Child Health and other institutes of the Ministry of Public Health. Coordination of the activities of the institutes and of in-service, postgraduate and advanced training will be pursued intensively. Existing training organizations for health care personnel will be strengthened and new training programmes will be developed where necessary to provide manpower with special skills required to operate existing health care delivery programmes and supply additional manpower needs for new and expanded facilities, and thus to achieve a balance between the demand and supply of health manpower.

Drugs and biologicals

Great importance is attached to the production and supply of drugs and biologicals, including sera and vaccines. A new pharmaceuticals factory and a vaccine and sera institute will be established in order to make available and control the required quantities of all vital drugs with the ultimate aim of self-sufficiency in drugs, biologicals, sera, vaccines, infusion fluids and culture media for diagnostic tests. A national formula with generic names of drugs will be established, and medical and veterinary students will be instructed in the use of the generic names of drugs.

Drugs prices will be controlled, and storage facilities will be improved.

Further aims include:

– development of a functional ambulance service, first at the periphery and district levels and subsequently at the provincial, regional and central levels;
– balanced increases in the numbers of support establishments such as laboratories, blood banks and X-ray units;
– expanded health insurance coverage;
– new health legislation and the establishment of a Medical Court;
– improved collection, analysis and dissemination of health information;
– improved health administration to facilitate the implementation of the national health programme;
– development and improved organization of transport, logistic communications, construction and supply services of the Ministry of Public Health;
– improved cooperation between the departments of the Ministry of Public Health and close coordination with all sectors of the Government and with agencies for health and health services development.

BAHRAIN

Major health and health-related problems

The major problems in the period 1973–1977, by order of priority, were:

– the continuing prevalence of diarrhoeal diseases and infections and infestations contracted by the faecal-oral route of transmission;
– environmental sanitation problems following in the wake of extensive land reclamation from the sea and the rapid growth of the building industry which strained the already inadequate drainage system in urban areas;
– indigenous transmission of malaria from a sizeable reservoir of imported cases in 1976 and 1977;
– the strain on health and welfare facilities consequent upon a large influx of immigrant workers;
– a shortage of medical and auxiliary health staff, in particular family physicians and community health doctors, public health nurses and other national nurses;
– the need to reorganize and develop ambulance services;
– the need for proper coverage by primary health care services for the whole population;
– drug control as there is no drug analysis and control laboratory in the country;
– the need to increase the hospital bed/population ratio from 3.5 per 1000 to 7 per 1000, i.e., to double the number of hospital beds;
– medicosocial problems of geriatrics;
– training and rehabilitation of the handicapped and the mentally retarded.

Action taken

Health policy

The main aims of current policy are:
– control of important communicable diseases by concerted attack, including an expanded programme of immunization, better surveillance, improvement of environmental sanitation, and specific action to deal with specific problems;
– expansion of health care facilities commensurate with rising population figures and higher expectations of service;
– the provision of free primary, secondary and tertiary health care to all nationals, with minimal charges for specialized services (partial support by employers for primary health care of their employees is part of current practice);
– a "family physician" system of health care for the whole population is envisaged as a long-term goal.

Health legislation

Legislation introduced during the period under review included: the Public Health Law (1975); the Organization of Pharmacy (Profession and Pharmaceuticals) Act (1975); the Labour Law (private sector), including health, welfare and safety provisions (1976); the Social Security Law, with disability and compensation clauses (1976); the Communicable Diseases Law (1977); and the Midwifery Law (1977).

Health planning and programming is in operation in all fields of medical care. The programmes completed in the period under review include rural latrines construction, subsidized and supervised by the Directorate of Public Health. This project was started in September 1973 and completed by end of 1977. A total of 3051 latrines were constructed or modified in rural areas to improve sanitation and reduce transmission of bowel infections and infestations. Indirect evidence that the objectives are a step nearer attainment was provided by the absence of cholera in 1977 in spite of the fact that large numbers of travellers arrived from cholera-infected areas at the height of epidemics in a number of neighbouring countries.

The objective of providing safe water supplies throughout the State was achieved.

On-going programmes include the improvement of surveillance and control of important communicable diseases, including typhoid and paratyphoid fevers, poliomyelitis, viral hepatitis, diphtheria, meningococcal infections, tetanus, malaria and leprosy; the expanded programme on immunization; the improvement of food hygiene; the improvement of environmental sanitation (construction started in 1977 on a comprehensive and modern sewerage system for the safe disposal of human waste from the main population centres), and the collection and disposal of dry refuse.

Pest control, especially control of *Anopheles*

mosquitos, flies, cockroaches and rodents, is a continuing struggle. In recognition of the fact that a better informed public will ease the burden on health services, health education programmes are being constantly modernized. Occupational health and workers' health and welfare problems are being tackled.

The coverage of primary health care services is constantly increasing; there were 14 health centres at the end of the period under review and it is planned to have 20 by 1982.

Two new hospitals are planned, to increase the bed population ratio from 3.5 to 7 per 1000 by the 1980s.

Studies on the medicosocial problems of geriatrics are proceeding with the Ministry of Labour and Social Affairs in order to define the magnitude of the problem and to elaborate plans. Measures for the training and rehabilitation of the handicapped and the mentally retarded are also being studied in cooperation with the Ministry of Labour and Social Affairs, as well as the Ministry of Education.

Education and training of health manpower

A plan for training of Bahraini doctors in the field of family practice, as the backbone of a proper primary health care service, is under consideration. The importance of health coverage using public health nurses and Bahraini general nurses is recognized. Programmes are being implemented to prepare the required number of nurses and to encourage Bahrainis to attend the College of Health Science.

A study was made in preparation for the development of ambulance services.

Health resources

Health establishments

There were the following government establishments and services for health care and administration in 1977:

General hospital	1
Specialized hospitals	4
Health centres	14
Child welfare teams	9
Environmental health offices . .	7
Port health offices	6
Public health directorate	1

There was also one private general hospital.

Health manpower

In 1975 there were the following health professionals:

Physicians	177
Dentists	21
Nurse-midwives	455
Nurses	566

Production and sale of pharmaceuticals

No pharmaceuticals were produced in the country. The Council of Arab Ministers of Health for the Gulf area has studied a project for the construction of a well-equipped drug analysis and control laboratory in the area.

Health expenditure

The cost of medical care in the period under review, expressed also as a percentage of total public expenditure by the Ministry of Health, were as follows:

	Total (in Bahraini dinars)
1973	3 473 000 (10.8%)
1974	5 377 177 (6.0%)
1975	9 294 009 (6.9%)
1976	9 434 000 (4.9%)
1977	11 770 000 (4.7%)

Appraisal of progress between 1973 and 1977

With increased continued surveillance of diarrhoeal diseases (cultures of stools sent to the Bacteriological Laboratory for any reason are made as a routine measure throughout the year for cholera detection), and some improvement in general sanitation with the construction of rural latrines, as well as the emphasis on personal hygiene, cholera has not been reported in Bahrain since 1974, after the 72 cases and four deaths in 1972 and 37 cases with no deaths in 1973.

Surveillance and control measures against other important communicable diseases were continually strengthened.

Inspection of all items of perishable imported food has become a routine health measure. All items of imported food including nonperishable food, have been inspected as a routine measure since early 1978. Hygiene control in the national food industry has also improved.

Environmental sanitation measures include stricter sanitary control of water and improvements in refuse disposal, and pest control activities are being steadily improved despite constraints.

Outlook

Health goals for the next five to 10 years include the elimination of the malaria risk; vaccination coverage of susceptible groups so as to eliminate poliomyelitis, diphtheria, tetanus, pertussis and measles; and the establishment of complete occupational health services.

CYPRUS

Introduction

The achievement of a high standard of health has long been recognized in Cyprus as constituting a very significant factor in economic and social development and an essential prerequisite for the attainment of individual happiness. This recognition has led to the incorporation of health development in the five-year general development plans.

The long-term objectives in the field of health are: the provision of the best possible medical care and attention to all citizens, and the minimizing of the incidence of disease through effective preventive measures.

The general strategy for the pursuance of the above-mentioned long-term objectives consists in the quantitive and qualitative improvement of medical, nursing and auxiliary personnel; the increase in the capacity of hospitals and other medical and health institutions; the supply of modern equipment; the strengthening of primary health care services so that such care can be given as near as possible to the patients' home; the strengthening of the public health services for sanitation and prevention of disease, food control and drug control; and assistance and guidance in the private medical sector. The development plans further envisage the introduction of a general integrated health care scheme and of the required organizational and operational changes in the interest of effectiveness and efficiency.

Health situation

Up to mid-1974 considerable progress had been made in the attainment of objectives in the health sector. Human and material resources had been increased and the services provided to the people has been considerably extended and their quality improved. Higher living standards had been attained and had helped to raise the general level of health. Among the projects for which plans for further development had been prepared were the erection of a new modern general hospital at Nicosia, a new hospital for Kyrenia and two rural hospitals and improvements and extensions to existing hospitals and rural health centres. It had been decided to introduce an integrated State-controlled health services scheme; considerable work had been done in elaborating a suitable scheme on the basis of the social, cultural and economic conditions. The various health indicators showed that the level of health had been rising yearly; morbidity had been reduced, the crude death rate had fallen to 9.5 per 1000 population, infant mortality had decreased to about 28 per 1000 live births and maternal mortality to 0.6 per 1000 births. The main causes of death (other than advanced age) were road accidents, cardiovascular diseases and malignancies. Action had been taken with a view to reducing deaths due to the first two of these causes and, in the case of malignancies, facilities had been introduced to enable early detection and appropriate treatment. A special programme had also been prepared to combat the special problem of thalassaemia, an indigenous genetic disease in the Mediterranean area.

After mid-1974 progress was halted by the hostilities in Cyprus in that year and the establishment of a separate administration for about 40% of the territory. About one-third of the population were displaced as a result of the invasion and this created serious social, economic and health problems not only for those displaced from their homes and work places, but for nearly the whole population. Planned development projects, including those in the health sector, had to be postponed, modified, or abandoned and efforts directed towards the satisfaction of more immediate serious needs. With the assistance received from various overseas sources and with the planned use of local resources, it became possible to alleviate the difficulties, and by the end of 1977 economic and social progress was resumed, although not at the previous level.

Major health and health-related problems and action taken

After the eradication of malaria from the island and the steady decline of infectious and parasitic diseases, the major health problems were the following: (1) Nearly 16% of the total population have the thalassaemia gene, and at least one child in 200 is born with the disease. Special services are being organized in the form of clinics in all general hospitals of the Island for the treatment of children suffering from the disease, and preventive efforts are being made to enlighten the public through the mass media. (2) There has been an increase in degenerative or metabolic diseases (cerebrovascular disease, ischaemic heart disease, malignant diseases, diabetes mellitus, etc.) and the leading causes of death in 1976 were cardiovascular diseases, road accidents and malignant diseases. Special departments were created in the Nicosia General Hospital to meet the needs of the whole Island: an intensive coronary care unit was established for patients suffering from ischaemic heart or cerebrovascular diseases; a haemodialysis department was established for patients suffering from acute or chronic renal failure, and a neurosurgical department for patients suffering from cerebrovascular diseases or other diseases of the central nervous system and those involved in road traffic accidents. A radiotherapy department was established for the treatment of patients suffering from malignant diseases. Medical rehabilitation departments exist in all the general hospitals. (3) Until 1970 the incidence of hydatidosis (echinococcosis) in man in Cyprus compared with other countries was considered to be rather high, due mainly to the absence of proper slaughterhouses in all communities, inadequate meat inspection services, the large numbers of stray dogs and the lack of proper information of the public about the disease. The Government, in its efforts to reduce and ultimately eradicate this disease, introduced appropriate legislation and launched an anti-echinococcosis campaign, which has been very satisfactory and has achieved significant results in reducing the causes of the disease. It may be predicted that the disease will be ultimately eradicated from Cyprus. (4) Most foodborne diseases were due to bacterial food poisoning. Chemical food poisoning cases were sporadic and the chemicals implicated were those used for spraying fruit trees. For the elimination of the hazards arising from foodstuffs, the existing food legislation was amended and food hygiene regulations were drawn up. The legislation applies to all food manufactures, to the sale of food and to the addition of preservatives and colouring agents. Health education draws attention to the numerous risks due to unhygienic food and the proper way of avoiding them.

Targets of health policy

The following are some of the targets set by the Government in its health policy:

(1) to extend to all the population urban and rural care and to upgrade the primary health care already available in an effort to provide a uniformly high level of health services;

(2) to extend the school services started in 1977 to cover the whole school-age population in urban and rural areas;

(3) to establish old people's homes and small geriatric units—previously there were no geriatric hospitals in Cyprus or separate geriatric departments in general hospitals (the situation has been made worse by the hostilities, as a result of which hundreds of old people have been forced to leave their homes);

(4) to prevent and eliminate diseases which are a threat to the health of the whole population, in particular thalassaemia and pneumoconiosis;

(5) further to reduce infant mortality by improving the maternal and child health services.

Health legislation

The following laws concerning health were enacted during the period under review:

– a law ratifying the Protocol amending the Single Convention on Narcotic Drugs, 1961;

– the Convention on Psychotropic Substances Ratification Law;
– the Agreement on the Transfer of Corpses Ratification Law;
– European Agreement on the Exchange of Tissue-Typing Reagents Ratification Law;
– Convention on the Elaboration of a European Pharmacopoeia Ratification Law;
– the Corneal Grafting Law, 1976.

Health planning and programming

The specific projects and programmes in the field of health include the creation of a new general hospital in Larnaca, better equipped and staffed so as to serve the increased needs of the Larnaca area, the expansion of the existing hospitals in other districts, and the erection of new rural health centres to serve after upgrading as small general hospitals.

There is a project for the erection and establishment of thalassaemia clinics in all general hospitals for early detection, better treatment and prevention. It is also planned to change the curriculum of the school of nursing and midwifery in such a way as to produce polyvalent health workers capable of providing health education, home visiting, immunization, school health service, and midwifery including home confinements.

Further plans are aimed at the elaboration and introduction of a complete integrated health care scheme to replace the existing partial and uncoordinated schemes of the public and private sectors.

Organization of the health services

At the head of the organization of the Health Services is the Minister of Health who, together with the Director-General and other senior officials of the Ministry (administrators as well as specialists), is responsible for the formulation and review of policy and its implementation, the control and coordination of the operational health units and services throughout the country, and generally for the management of the health services.

The hospitals (general and specialized) and the rural health centres are organized on a district basis. In each district there is a District Medical Officer who is responsible for the hospital services and health services in his district. In Nicosia District the hospital services are the responsibility of the Medical Superintendent of the Nicosia General Hospital. Some services such as those of psychiatric institutions, the sanatorium and the chemical laboratory, operate as independent units and report directly to the Ministry of Health and not to the District Medical Officer.

A reorganization of the public services, including the services under the Ministry of Health, was proposed in 1976, but the changes recommended have not yet been approved.

Biomedical and health service research

None.

Education and training of health manpower

All scientific personnel, including doctors, dentists, chemists and pharmacists, receive their education and training abroad; Cyprus does not yet have a University. However, the practical training of newly qualified medical graduates, who are required by law to undergo a training of 18 months duration in an approved hospital, can be done in the Nicosia General Hospital or in any other Cyprus hospital as may be approved for this purpose.

Nursing personnel and health inspectors receive their education and training locally. A school of nursing and midwifery is operating at the Nicosia General Hospital, with branches in Limassol Hospital. A school for psychiatric nursing is in operation at the psychiatric hospital in Nicosia. Finally, a school for the training of health inspectors operates according to needs.

Postgraduate training of health personnel takes place in overseas institutions.

Health resources

Health establishments

At the end of 1977 there were six general hospitals, one for each town, a psychiatric hospital in Nicosia, a tuberculosis hospital in the Troodos mountains, and a small leprosy hospital in Larnaca. There were also 18 rural health centres serving an average of 10 000 people each. They provide primary health care. However, the general hospitals remain the main medical institutions providing preventive, diagnostic, curative and restorative services; they are adequately equipped and staffed.

Health manpower

Health manpower is growing gradually. Numbers of health workers currently employed in the public health sector are as follows:

Doctors	200
Dentists	35
Nurses and midwives (all grades)	1 273
Health visitors	42
Radiographers	40
Laboratory technicians	27
Physiotherapists	15
Pharmacists	78
Health inspectors	66

The private sector, which offers mainly curative services, employs far smaller numbers of staff.

Production and sale of pharmaceuticals

With a view to ensuring strict control over the importation, preparation, storage and sale of dangerous drugs and poisons and compliance with the Narcotic Drugs Law and Regulations and the Pharmacy and Poisons Law and Regulations, regular inspections are carried out. Local manufacturing of drugs is very limited. The bulk of the drugs used are imported from abroad. The importation and distribution of drugs is effected through specially authorized wholesale dealers who are subject to inspection and control by the Inspector of Pharmacies. The Pharmaceutical Quality Control Law was enacted in 1967 for the purpose of facilitating the exercise of quality control over pharmaceutical preparations manufactured locally or imported.

Health expenditure

The following figures show in summary form the level of government expenditure on health for the year 1976; the annual health expenditure for each of the years in the period under review has been approximately of the same level as that of 1976:

Capital expenditure	Cyprus pounds
Extensions to hospital buildings	96 611
Equipment	52 361
Mobile dental units	7 158
Sub-total—Capital expenditure	156 130
Recurrent expenditure	
Personal emoluments	3 113 306
Maintenance	977 194
Pharmaceutical supplies	642 009
Prevention of diseases	171 925
Sponsored patients abroad	89 818
Health inspectors' training	1 691
Repairs	1 912
Office expenses	2 940
Sub-total—Recurrent expenditure	1 887 489
Grand total	5 156 925

Outlook

As already indicated, the activities of the Ministry of Health (as was the case with the entire State services) have, since the summer of 1974, been geared to the solution of problems created by the hostilities and the establishment of a separate administration for about 40% of the territory. As long as these problems persist health activities will be carried out in such a way as to give special emphasis to the satisfaction of the needs of displaced persons and other needy members of the population. At the same time, and within economic and financial potentialities, efforts will continue to be made towards the maintenance of a high standard of health and the further development of the health services in order to make it possible not only to maintain high health standards but also to respond to new situations and needs which may arise in the modern, changing society.

EGYPT

Major health and health-related problems

Population estimates for the years 1973–1977 were 35 619 000, 36 488 000, 37 358 000, 38 228 000, and 39 099 000 respectively. The population, with the predictable rapid increase, is expected to be nearly double by the year 2000, which will have repercussions on the size and quality of present and planned health services.

Environmental sanitation for both urban and rural communities poses additional health problems, with special reference to occupational hazards. Further problems are malnutrition and its effects on all ages, but especially on certain more vulnerable groups, and endemic and communicable disease control.

Action taken

Health policy

The availability and provision of free health services to the whole population is a general condition guaranteed by the Constitution. In addition, there is the fee-for-service private practice for those who desire it. Community participation in planning, administration and supervision is encouraged. Priority is given to provision of basic and primary health care for both rural and urban populations through an extensive network of rural health units, rural health centres and urban health centres. All of them deliver the service through an integrated system including compulsory vaccinations, treatment and control of endemic and communicable diseases, maternal and child care, birth control and school health, in addition to normal care services.

This first level of care is considered to make the best use of the limited resources. Relatively low allocations give a high expectation of effectiveness. Priorities are the provision and upgrading of health services for mothers, children and school-age groups to reduce the high infant and child mortality; the greater emphasis on the field of occupational health, to minimize hazards and provide rehabilitation services; efforts to upgrade emergency medical services, which are expected to lower case fatality rates due to accidents and acute medical conditions, including those requiring surgery; manpower as a vital factor for delivery of health care services—good organization of available manpower, inservice training, education and supervision are essential elements for better utilization and greater efficiency; increase and improvement of drug and vaccine production for self-reliance and in order to satisfy local and regional needs.

Health legislation

New laws have been introduced, either dealing with new topics or modifying old legislation, including:

– control and regulation of utilization of narcotic and hypnotic drugs, tranquillizers and analeptics;

– at least two years' compulsory government service for new graduates (physicians, dentists, pharmacists, nurses, sanitarians, health technicians and other health professions), with priority for service in rural and remote areas;

– food control regulations, including the use of preservatives and colouring agents;

– regulation of medical practice of physicians, midwives, nurses and dentists;

– regulations for nursing education (requirements, length of training and curriculum);

– compulsory immunization against measles (in addition to smallpox, diphtheria, poliomyelitis and tuberculosis);

– resistration of new pharmaceuticals;

– regulation of the importing of pharmaceutical and medical equipment;

– decentralization of responsibility for health care delivery to governorate levels;

– protection against importation of human and zoonotic diseases; and

– compulsory registration of births and deaths.

Health planning and programming

A five-year health plan forms part of the national plan and is divided into yearly plans which are readjusted according to achievements and remaining allocations. Suggestions for the plan are made at the peripheral level, studied and approved at the governorate level, and finally analysed, processed and harmonized at the central level for implementation by the governorates.

All services and activities are run by governorate and local health authorities in an integrated system. In addition, some vertical programmes are carried out and implemented centrally in one or more governorates because they are of nation-wide importance or are still in the experimental phase. These include activities of the family planning and birth control services; nutrition surveys; the schistosomiasis control programme under-way in four governorates, with systematic snail control and mass treatment of infected persons; filariasis control; and the strengthening and upgrading of rural health services in four governorates, with more facilities for transport and communications, equipment and continuous training of work teams.

	Number	Graduates (in academic year)				
	(1977)	1972/73	1973/74	1974/75	1975/76	1976/77
Faculties of medicine	9	2 686	3 200	3 550	3 523	—
Faculties of dentistry	4	422	400	443	438	—
Faculties of pharmacy	6	878	889	1 007	1 164	—
Higher institutes of nursing	2	160	177	125	139	—
Secondary technical nursing schools	134	—	—	3 760	3 730	3 817
Former nursing schools	—	470	460	42	—	—
Schools for assistant nurse/midwives . .	4	748	403	104	92	87
Health visitor schools	9	551	446	504	435	337
Institutes for health technicians	6	658	786	783	699	1 365

Organization of health services

At the central level there are sectors for preventive measures, curative measures, for basic services and endemic diseases control, and public health laboratory services and environmental sanitation.

Each of the sectors is headed by one of the under-secretaries. Sanitation—the provision of safe potable water supply, sewerage and refuse disposal, and control of industrial effluents—is the responsibility of different bodies and ministers. The Ministry of Health is responsible for quality control, and supervision and detection of sources of pollution.

At the governorate level a similar organization exists and each section is headed by a senior health administrator.

Urban services are provided separately by hospitals (general or specialized), health bureaus, maternal and child health centres, and school health units. Rural services are integrated in the rural health unit and delivered by a health team headed by a fully qualified physician.

Education and training of health manpower

In 1977 there were the training institutions shown in the table above (numbers of graduates are given for the period under review).

Internal scholarships for degree programmes of the Ministry of Health were awarded as shown in the table at the bottom of the page.

In addition, scholarships abroad for degree programmes of the Ministry were awarded to 139 candidates in 1975, 308 in 1976, and 263 in 1977.

Those attending in-service training and continuous education programmes of the Ministry included:

	1975	1976	1977
Medical and technical courses . .	735	734	6 721
Administration courses	1 724	631	660
Conferences	745	1 379	299

Health resources

Health establishments

There were the following establishments of the Ministry of Health for inpatient and outpatient care in the period under review (private hospitals numbered 138 in 1973, 166 in 1974, 171 in 1975, 177 in 1976 and 177 in 1977).

	1972/73	1973/74	1974/1975	1975/76	1976/77
Physicians	425	436	551	1 060	800
Dentists	43	58	53	23	37
Pharmacists	29	24	55	31	14
Other health workers (chemists, veterinarians, nutritionists, psychologists, social workers)	30	49	64	28	24
Nurses	301	401	282	489	463

	1973	1974	1975	1976	1977
General hospitals	167	184	185	169	167
Specialized hospitals	214	210	201	200	202
School health units	185	195	199	234	236
Rural health centres	587	587	588	588	588
Rural health units	1 453	1 487	1 551	1 612	1 661
Maternal and child health centres	214	215	216	216	223
Health bureaus	300	302	305	307	311
Dental units	*	*	*	813	1 131
Tuberculosis control units	85	61	46	58	60

* Figures not available.

Total beds numbered 77 078 in 1973, 76 254 in 1974, 78 928 in 1975, 79 896 in 1976 and 78 425 in 1977.

Health manpower

Health personnel in the period under review included:

	1973	1974	1975	1976	1977
Physicians	23 725	25 797	28 837	31 969	35 489
Dentists	3 045	3 428	3 823	4 204	4 631
Pharmacists	8 368	9 298	10 228	11 256	12 314
Nurses[1]	27 805	28 750	30 590	35 583	40 578

[1] Including assistant nurses, nurse/midwives and nursing supervisors.

Production and sale of pharmaceuticals

In 1977 the production of drugs represented approximately 116 870 000 Egyptian pounds, and sales 131 618 000 pounds.

Health expenditure

The only available figures are the yearly budgets of the Ministry of Health and four of the health organizations under its direct supervision, for which expenditure in the period under review was as follows (in thousands of Egyptian pounds):

	1973	1974	1975	1976	1977
Ministry of Health . . .	54 553	60 347	71 036	87 908	96 852
Health organizations . .	8 030	8 425	9 294	20 701	26 773
Total	62 583	68 772	80 330	108 609	123 625

Appraisal of progress made between 1973 and 1977

The following service indicators are given as evidence of the progress achieved in the period under review (registered manpower figures were used to calculate the rates), with ratios expressed in numbers of inhabitants to one health professional:

	1973	1974	1975	1976	1977
Physician/population ratio	1 500	1 405	1 293	1 196	1 102
Dentist/population ratio	11 693	10 576	9 755	9 093	8 445
Pharmacist/population ratio	4 255	3 899	3 646	3 396	3 176
Nurse/population ratio	1 280	1 261	1 219	1 074	964
Physicians per 10 000 population	6.7	7.1	7.7	8.4	9.1
Dentists per 10 000 population	0.86	0.95	1.0	1.1	1.2
Pharmacists per 10 000 population	2.4	2.6	2.7	2.9	3.1
Nurses per 10 000 population	7.8	7.9	8.2	9.3	10.4
Hospital beds per 10 000 population	21.6	21.0	21.2	20.9	20.

The crude death rate fell from 13.1 in 1973 to 12.7 in 1974, 12.2 in 1975, 11.7 in 1976, and 11.7 in 1977 (the figures for the last three years are tentative).

Life expectancy at birth was as follows:

	1965	1970	1975
Males	47.8	50.2	52.3
Females	51.2	53.3	55.2

The extension of coverage of health services in the period under review is reflected in the following figures:

	1973	1977	Increase (decrease)
Rural health units and centres	2 040	2 227	9.2%
Rural population (per unit or centre)	10 000	9 466	(5%)

Outlook

The aims for the next five years included (in 1978) the following measures for the development of primary care and basic health services:

– establishment of 300 new rural health units covering all villages with up to 3000 inhabitants;

284

– establishment of 100 rural health centres, each covering about three rural health units;
– establishment of 140 urban health centres, including maternal and child health and school health services;
– introduction of dental services in 500 rural health centres and units in addition to those already available;
– extension of the schistosomiasis control programme to cover all upper Egypt and the western part of the Nile Delta;
– intensification of family planning activities in collaboration with IBRD in order to reduce the crude birth rate, infant mortality and maternal mortality;
– measures to protect the environment against pollution, with the establishment of a national centre for relevant research and planning;
– expansion of secondary and tertiary care facilities;
– an increase in the number of hospital beds by about 3000 in order to keep the ratio constant at about 2.1 per 1000 population;
– upgrading of existing hospitals by introducing appropriate logistics and technical equipment, with special emphasis on emergency services;
– training and continuous education of different categories of personnel in order to improve the quality and extent of all services;
-- development of self-reliance in drugs and pharmaceuticals.

IRAN

Major health and health-related problems

One of the major health problems in Iran is the difficulty of reaching the rural population— the majority of the total population—which is sparsely scattered over vast areas. The situation is further complicated by the fact that the new approach calls for a team of trained health and medical workers to provide an adequate standard of health care, and that there is a lack of such personnel.

Environmental health problems, including those related to the provision of safe water supplies and difficulties in providing health education, are also serious in rural areas, and result in high morbidity rates for infectious and parasitic, respiratory, and gastrointestinal diseases. The fact that the infant mortality rate is 120 per 1000 in rural areas compared with 62 per 1000 in urban areas is an indication of the extent of these problems.

Inadequate coordination of the activities of the various organizations delivering health services has resulted in a decrease in the efficiency of personnel and insufficient attention to priorities.

The administrative responsibilities assigned to physicians have demanded much of their time, thus aggravating a situation that was already difficult because of the shortage of physicians. In addition, the fact that physicians were more involved in the decision-making process resulted in priority being given to curative services at the expense of preventive activities.

Action taken

Health policy

The health policy concentrates on removing the gap between rural and urban areas regarding the provision of health and medical care services. The major features of this policy are as follows: the aim is to establish a comprehensive network of health and medical care providing services to the population throughout the country. The decentralization of the Ministry of Health and Welfare was begun in 1977, and is still in progress. Administrative and financial powers have been delegated to the regional (provincial) executive directors, who are in charge of the regional health and welfare departments and are responsible for all aspects of health and welfare in the province.

The newly introduced system is to be coordinated at the country level by a council of health and at the provincial level by a council of health and welfare and a council for coordination.

The establishment of a health network and introduction of a health insurance scheme are parts of this coordinated and comprehensive system. The rural health subcentres are the basic units of the network, functioning in the remotest rural areas, supported and supervised by health centres and district and regional hospitals which provide all types of medical care to the population.

In view of the shortage of trained manpower, it is vitally important that coordinated administrative measures be adopted in order to improve

285

the efficiency of the personnel and facilities available. Since it is difficult to secure trained manpower, particularly physicians, whose training requires a long time, special emphasis is given to the training of auxiliaries, mainly primary health workers who can be trained in a much shorter period.

Responsibility for the provision of safe water supplies and the improvement of environmental health in rural areas has been transferred from the Ministry of Agriculture and Rural Development to the Ministry of Health and Welfare.

In the implementation of programmes the full participation of the population is sought and community and local resources are utilized.

Health legislation

Major items of health legislation passed during the period under review were: a law regarding the integration of the former ministries of health and social welfare into the new Ministry of Health and Welfare; a regulation regarding a scheme for the decentralization of the Ministry of Health and Welfare and the creation of the regional health and welfare organizations; amendment of the penal code regarding plastic surgery, transplantation of organs, abortion and sterilization, providing more liberal measures on sterilization and abortion; amendment of the Family Protection Law to raise the age of marriage; a decree for expansion of the maternal and child health and family planning services and the provision of supplementary food for children under two years of age; a decree for the provision of supplementary food for schoolchildren; a decree for social insurance schemes covering the whole population; a decree regarding the provision of health services emphasizing case-finding, the control of communicable disease, eradication of those diseases which can be prevented through mass vaccination, environmental health, and health education; and a decree concerning the provision of health identity cards for all citizens.

Health planning and programming

Within the framework of the above-mentioned policies, the major health programmes and plans, in order of priority, are as follows:
(1) Free public health services to the whole population, including the improvement and up-

grading of environmental health, mainly in the rural areas; the development of health education through the utilization of all existing formal and informal channels for the dissemination of information in order to increase the public's awareness; the eradication of communicable disease through well-organized preventive efforts; and the expansion of maternal and child health programmes.
(2) Expansion of the clinical care services, mainly in the rural areas, and a balanced distribution of health and medical personnel throughout the country.
(3) Development of hospital services by establishing regional and provincial hospitals and increasing the efficiency of existing hospitals.
(4) Manpower development at all levels, including the training of primary health workers and rural midwives to meet the need for rapid expansion of the health network in rural areas; increasing the capacity and number of nursing schools, particularly those providing short-term training; the training of health technicians, increasing the capacity of institutions for technologists and expanding medical schools; and the adoption of measures for both quantitative and qualitative coordination of the training curricula with the new system and the future needs of the programme.

Organization of health services

The organization of health services is undergoing a substantial change. A new scheme is being introduced which provides preventive, curative, rehabilitation and environmental services to the whole population through a countrywide health network. The lowest level of this network, which functions even in the remotest rural areas, is the *khaneh behdasht*, which provides primary health services to 2000 people in rural areas, or 8 villages (the average population of a village is 250 persons). These rural subcentres are supervised and supported by the health and welfare centres. Each rural health and welfare centre is responsible for 10 000 people, and each city health and welfare centre for 20 000. These centres provide clinical treatment and public health services in the population under their coverage. They refer patients needing more specialized clinical treatment to polyclinics attached to district hospitals. For still more specialized services the district hospitals refer to regional hospitals.

At the headquarters level, at the Ministry of

Health and Welfare, the Environmental Health Unit is composed of a group of specialists for planning, supervision and consultation, and at the regional level it consists of an enforcement group including specialists and technicians. Between 1973 and 1977 the following personnel were trained and employed: 64 sanitary engineers; 40 sanitarians; 193 sanitary engineering aids; and 397 sanitarian aides. In addition to the above-mentioned graduates who are employed to carry out environmental health activities at the country level, 32 schools in Iran have included environmental health in their academic curricula, and at present 1781 students are being educated in this field. Following completion of their military service they can be employed as environmental health staff if they so desire.

Biomedical and health services research

Of the several research projects undertaken, the most important is that on the service delivery system carried out in West Azerbaijan with the cooperation of WHO, the School of Public Health and the Institute for Health Studies, University of Teheran. This is a significant effort of the Ministry of Health and Welfare to find a practical solution to the country's health problems.

Priority areas for biomedical and health services research for the Sixth Plan (1978–1982) are malaria, schistosomiasis, gastrointestinal diseases, tuberculosis, brucellosis, evaluation of the health services system and a survey of causes of mortality.

Training of health manpower

In view of the lack of the trained personnel required for the new health system, high priority is being given to education and training. Although emphasis is placed on the development of training medical, nursing and other professional health personnel, the training of auxiliaries and primary health workers is also receiving considerable attention.

Health resources

Health establishments

In 1975 outpatient care and public health services for the rural population were offered through 1658 centres, and in urban areas these services were available to the low-income population through 1805 centres. Other sectors of the population pay for these services from 6912 private clinics. The total number of hospital beds increased from 48 800 in March 1975 to 55 500 by the end of 1976; it is expected that there will be 13 600 more beds by the end of 1979.

Health manpower

The manpower active in health programmes in 1975 totalled more than 62 000 persons (of whom 14 000 were in administrative posts), the doctor/population ratio was 0.35 per 1000, and the ratio of nursing staff (nurses and nurse aides) to doctors was 1.6 to one.

Production and sale of pharmaceuticals

At present more than 3600 drug items are available, 50% of them locally manufactured. All these items have recently been grouped into four broad categories according to the degree to which they are necessary. The use of pharmaceuticals has been increased threefold in the period 1970 to 1976.

Health expenditure

In 1975 allocations for health, medical care and nutrition amounted to 56 700 million rials (equivalent to US $810 million, and representing 3.4% of the country's total budget). The per capita budget for the above services was 1700 rials (equivalent to US $24.30), and the per capita health expenditure was 3000 rials (equivalent to US $43).

Appraisal of progress made between 1973 and 1977

Following the passing of the decree for free health services in 1973 a serious campaign was started for mass immunization and the prevention of communicable diseases, and efforts were increased fourfold during this campaign. To obtain information on the health and medical problems of the population, health identity cards were issued to the population under 18 and to parents for their children, and health histories were recorded.

The number of vaccinations against poliomyelitis increased from 2 146 293 in 1973 to 6 807 012 in 1975, and the number of cases of this disease decreased during the same period from 572 to 178. The number of vaccinations against measles was 1 460 855 in 1973, 2 584 673 in 1974, and 1 958 510 in 1975, and the number of cases decreased from 42 994 in 1973 to 14 269 in 1975. The number of vaccinations against diphtheria was 6 666 234 in 1973, 12 129 929 in 1974, and 10 808 870 in 1975, and the number of cases decreased from 2598 in 1973 to 587 in 1975. Similar progress has been made with regard to tetanus, pertussis and other diseases.

Following decrees concerning the provision of supplementary food for schoolchildren and for children under two years of age, free nutrition programmes in schools were expanded to cover 6.1 million children in 1975/76 (compared with 450 000 in 1972/73). The coverage of the maternal and child nutrition programmes was also extended during the same period from 5000 mothers and 5000 children to 39 000 mothers and 39 000 children.

Outlook

The basic objectives of the health programmes for the five years starting in 1978 as stated in the Sixth Five-Year Plan are to ensure the physical, mental and environmental wellbeing of the population, and to improve the quality of life, as a human right, within the context of socioeconomic programmes, which have a great impact on the achievement of the desired objectives. These objectives have been defined as follows:

— to increase life expectancy at birth to 60 years or more (65 in urban areas and 55 in rural areas);
— to decrease the crude birth rate to less than 31 per 1000 (urban 22 per 1000 in urban areas and 40 per 1000 in rural areas):
— to decrease the net population growth rate to less than 2.3%:
— to reduce the mortality rate for children under one year of age to less than 60 per 1000:
— to decrease morbidity rates of various diseases through mass immunization programmes;
— to decrease the prevalence of disabilities caused by communicable diseases through

expanded immunization programmes and improved environmental sanitation;
— to ensure and improve the proper growth and development of children; and
— to decrease morbidity and infirmity caused by other diseases, and their complications.

In order to achieve the above-mentioned targets, the following operational objectives have been identified, bearing in mind the increased demands during the national development plan and constraints, especially that of manpower shortage:

— to ensure an average of five visits per year for rural inhabitants to receive medical and primary health care at rural centres;
— to extend services for dental and mental health, the prevention of cardiovascular diseases, diabetes, goitre and occupational diseases, and the early detection and treatment of cancer;
— to expand school health services to cope with 27 million visits a year, including one million complete medical check-ups of students at the time of first school entry;
— to provide medical and health services to 12 million infants, 9.5 million children of 1–2 years of age and 8 million children of 2–5 years of age;
— to provide health and nutrition education, in coordination with other health activities through the national health network system;
— to conduct research to identify the national health problems and priorities, evaluate medical and preventive services, and establish a fully satisfactory system for the collection and analysis of health and vital statistics;
— to establish the necessary framework for delivering the best possible preventive and medical services to the population of both urban and rural areas, and also to improve the management system so as to ensure the optimum utilization of health manpower and facilities;
— to ensure an average of one visit per year for rural inhabitants to receive medical and preventive services at rural health centres:
— to ensure an average of 0.2 visits per year for rural inhabitants to receive medical and preventive services at a polyclinic or specialized health centre;
— to ensure facilities with an average of 5.5 visits per year for medical and preventive services for urban inhabitants;
— to provide adequate hospital bed facilities (approximately 0.45 bed days per year for

inhabitants of rural areas and 0.85 for inhabitants of urban areas by the end of the development plan);

— to provide prenatal and postnatal care for 30% of mothers in rural areas and 78% of those in urban areas, and with further expansion of such services through the health network system;

— to provide adequate maternity services in the hospitals and maternity centres for 25% of the pregnant women in rural areas and 75% in urban areas;

— to provide facilities for all types of vaccinations in urban and rural areas, especially for the most vunerable sectors of the population;

— to implement active malaria eradication programmes in rural areas and expand intensive surveillance programmes in urban areas;

— to control tuberculosis through the early detection of active cases and the provision of adequate medical treatment at outpatient clinics and hospitalization where necessary with the provision of 1.8 million bed days and the administration of 19 million BCG vaccinations and 5 million tuberculin tests;

— to expand urban and rural health services, improving the drinking-water supplies, sewage systems, public health, and control of foodstuffs, constructing drinking-water supply systems in 10 000 villages and establishing health institutions in 5000 villages;

— to control communicable eye disease (especially trachoma), brucellosis, leprosy and venereal diseases, and improve immunity levels against diseases such as diphtheria, tetanus, pertussis, and poliomyelitis;

— to provide health insurance coverage for 90% of workers both in urban and rural areas, including industrial and agricultural workers. In the rural areas the aim is to increase the bed capacity of the health and clinical services tenfold, and the hospital services 2.6 times during the next five-year programme. For urban areas the proposed increases are 120 and 160% respectively. By the end of the sixth five-year plan there should be 9500 rural health subcentres, 1970 rural health and welfare centres and 537 urban health and welfare centres.

IRAQ

Population and other statistics

The last national census of population was conducted on 17 October 1977. The preliminary results of the census, give a total population for 1977 of 12 029 760 (males 6 224 195, females 5 805 565, the sex ratio thus being 107 males to 100 females).

The urban population was 7 640 674 (or 65.5%), the rural population 4 389 085 (or 34.5%). The average density was 28 inhabitants per km^2.

Other vital statistics for the period 1973–1977 are given in the following table:

	1973	1974	1975	1976	1977
Mean population	10 412 586	10 765 442	11 124 253	11 505 234	12 171 480
Birth rate (per 1000 population)		42.6[*]			
Death rate (per 1000 population)		10.6[*]			
Infant mortality (per 1000 live births)		88.7[*]			
Natural increase rate		32.0[*]			
General fertility rate (per 1000 women of childbearing age)		198.1[*]			

[*] Sample registration system and survey figures.

289

Of the 51 775 deaths recorded in 1975, the main causes were: ill-defined conditions (19 692), chronic rheumatic heart disease, hypertensive disease, ischaemic heart disease and other forms of heart disease (9304), accidents (4533), pneumonia (3027), malignant neoplasms (2185), tuberculosis, all forms (1781), cerebrovascular disease (1349), congenital anomalies, birth injury, difficult labour and other anoxic and hypoxic conditions, other causes of perinatal mortality (1058), bronchitis, emphysema and asthma (477), meningitis (456), enteritis and other diarrhoeal diseases (284), intestinal obstruction and hernia (250), anaemias (237), cirrhosis of liver (212).

The communicable diseases most frequently notified in 1976 were: trachoma (130 292), mumps (41 381), measles (37 884), tuberculosis, all forms (20 060), pertussis (19 472), common cold (18 407), malaria (8109), chickenpox (5423), typhoid and paratyphoid fevers (2319), cerebrospinal meningitis (2175), gonorrhoea (2042), bacillary dysentery (1752), poliomyelitis (1416), tetanus (1221), infectious hepatitis (1202), diphtheria (1027), leishmaniasis, cutaneous and visceral (699), viral pneumonia (304).

Organization of the public health services

The Ministry of Health is responsible for preventive and curative medical care. The Ministry is divided into five departments with a director-general in charge of each, two other establishments, and a health inspection office.

The country is divided administratively into 18 governorates (*muhafadas*), each governorate is divided into districts (*qadas*), which in turn are divided into subdistricts (*nahiyahs*). In each governorate there is a Chief Medical Officer responsible for all health services and institutions located within the governorate. He is assisted by a medical officer for rural health services and one for endemic diseases programmes including the malaria eradication programme.

Hospital services

In 1977 Iraq had 191 hospitals with 24 031 beds, of which 23 663 were in 179 government hospitals. The bed/population ratio was 1.98 per 1000. The beds in government hospitals were distributed as follows:

Category and number		Number of beds
General hospitals	110	14 822
Rural hospitals	31	780
Maternity hospitals	7	922
Paediatric hospitals		1 486
Tuberculosis hospitals	9	2 472
Emergency hospitals for surgery	2	477
Mental and neurology hospitals	2	1 547
Children's and welfare hospitals	3	72
Ophthalmic hospital	1	134
Brain surgery hospital	1	105
Leprosy hospital	1	360
Nuclear medicine and radiology hospital	1	108
Hospital for cardiac surgery and medicine	1	194
Physiotherapy establishment	1	36

Outpatient care facilities were provided at 165 hospital outpatients departments, 56 polyclinics, 501 evening clinics and people's clinics, 1077 rural health centres, 292 dispensaries, and 182 mobile health units.

Medical and allied personnel and training facilities

In 1977 Iraq had 5233 doctors, of whom 4923 were in government service. The doctor/population ratio was one to 2297. Other medical and auxiliary personnel in 1977 are shown in the table below:

Dentists	771
Pharmacists	1 456
Nurses (qualified)	4 121
Health officials	2 875
Dressers	4 057
Laboratory technicians	1 351
Pharmacy assistants	1 035
X-ray technicians	961
Health visitors	289
Health inspectors	1 297
Midwives	1 743
Ophthalomologists	66
Physiotherapists	190
Dental assistants	54
Other health personnel	318

There are five medical colleges at the Universities of Baghdad, Mosul, Basra, Mustansria (in Baghdad City) and Sulaimaniya, which provide a six-year medical training course. The existing legislation makes it compulsory for new graduates to serve for one year in rural health services immediately after qualifying. The Universities of Baghdad and Mosul also have a college of pharmacy. In addition, the University of Baghdad has a dental college, a veterinary college and a college of nursing.

There are six nursing training schools, at which students are given three years of training. Each of these schools accepts 30–50 students yearly. Training of auxiliary personnel is undertaken at the high institutes of health in Baghdad, Basra and Mosul. Two-year courses are subsequently given to train 11 categories of such personnel. About 1000 students a year are accepted.

Communicable diseases control and immunization

Among the leading diseases in 1976 were cerebrospinal meningitis, measles, tuberculosis, mumps, trachoma, malaria, pertussis and tetanus. Preventive measures will be given priority by the Government in the National Health Plan, with a wide range of activities, programmes and projects for disease prevention: nutritional and epidemiological surveillance, quarantine, school health examinations, tuberculosis control, maternal and child health services, and prevention, control, surveillance and eradication of malaria, smallpox, poliomyelitis and schistosomiasis and various other diseases. The control of schistosomiasis and trachoma is effected though the endemic disease services in all provinces, and periodical prevalence surveys are undertaken in schools and urban and rural communities.

Since June 1973 BCG vaccination has been compulsory for children under 10 years of age, and especially important when they enter school.

In 1976 the following immunizations were carried out.

Diphtheria/pertussis/tetanus	525 942
Poliomyelitis	891 884
Smallpox	621 147
Cholera	165 384
Typhoid	206 816
Measles	85 250
BCG	305 084

Specialized units

In 1976 there were 101 maternal and child health centres; 111 325 pregnant women, 176 577 infants, and 115 701 children aged 1–6 years availed themselves of their services. Of all deliveries in 1975, 44 782 (or 23%) were attended by a doctor and qualified midwife in hospitals, 146 706 (or 75%) were attended by a qualified midwife at home. In 1976 there were 35 school health units, 16 tuberculosis outpatient clinics, 3 venereal diseases centres at outpatient clinics, and a leprosy outpatient clinic.

Environmental sanitation

There is a Directorate-General of Human Environment, established in 1975 under the Ministry of Health. Plans and activities related to the human environment as a whole are coordinated through the Supreme Council of Human Environment, in which 18 ministries are represented.

The Supreme Council will continue to coordinate environmental health matters, including applied research, air pollution monitoring and control, food safety and occupational health and other subjects concerning the environment. Air and water pollution, basic community sanitation, community water supply and disposal of wastes will remain among the major government concerns in the National Plan.

ISRAEL

Major health and health-related problems

Environmental health: increasing air, water and soil pollution; urban planning; solid waste and waste-water disposal; noise and radiation exposure; drinking-water and general food hygiene and sanitation; control and surveillance of cariogenic and other toxic substances in food water and environment.

Communicable diseases: despite virtual elimination and control of infectious diseases such as poliomyelitis, malaria, trachoma, and tuberculosis, monitoring and surveillance of these diseases must continue. There is excessive morbidity and mortality from enteric infectious diseases (viral hepatitis, and dysenteries) compared to other developed countries. The rate of hospital infection is also causing growing concern.

Geriatric and chronic diseases: a growing elderly population (9.2%) requires development of adequate community and institutional support services. There are severe shortages of manpower and facilities for such services.

Drug abuse: Israel has the highest rate of prescription of drugs per patient in the world. Excessive consumption of drugs is both an economic and a health problem. A related problem is the increase in the number of drug addicts over the past few years.

Hospital bed distribution: although the overall ration of hospital beds to population (6.8 per 1000) seems adequate, some imbalance exists in the geographical distribution and in the distribution of beds for different types of care. There is a need for good systematic planning and rationalization.

Health care costs: rapid growth of health care costs is essentially the result of hospital costs, which represent 43% of all the health expenditure, but is due to waste and duplication of services and lack of effective coordination of resources.

Noncommunicable diseases: the incidence of cardiovascular diseases (in particular ischaemic heart disease), cancer and road accidents is continuing to increase and they constitute the principal factors in mortality and morbidity.

Organization and delivery of services: the existence of two parallel health providers—the Ministry of Health and the Sick Fund—creates a bureaucratic maze, with duplication of services, lack of coordination and planning, lack of continuity of health care for patients, and gaps in certain fields. In addition to the lack of reliable and flexible health information data systems, there is no effective mechanism for planning of health services based on the population's needs and resources.

National health insurance: although 90% of the population is covered by voluntary health insurance provided by various sick funds, the insurance coverage is not universal nor is it comprehensive. There is a need for a national health insurance mechanism to provide a uniform comprehensive insurance programme to all residents.

Dental health: severe manpower shortages and extremely high costs for treatment affect adversely the dental health status of the population. There is a need to develop dental and

auxiliary dental manpower and to increase preventive care programmes using measures such as fluoridation of drinking-water.

Manpower planning: shortages in some medical professions, and severe shortages of nurses and workers in some auxiliary medical professions, hamper proper delivery of health care. The creation of a health manpower development, planning and training mechanism constitutes a first priority.

Action taken

Health policy

The highest priority is the establishment of a new national health insurance to provide a uniform comprehensive insurance programme to all residents. Other priorities are: integration of curative, preventive and health promotion services at the regional and national level in order to avoid duplication and wastage of resources as well as to improve the health status of the population by reducing the main causes of mortality and morbidity (comprehensive programmes for atheriosclerotic cardiovascular diseases, cancer and road and work accidents); establishment of regional health authorities, and of priorities for the distribution of resources to underserved population groups and areas; further development of comprehensive community-based geriatric and mental health, providing diagnostic, curative and preventive and promotive services, establishment of a statutory authority for all aspects of food hygiene, production and marketing as well as nutrition problems; establishment of a national authority for all the intersectoral aspects of the environment; setting-up of a reliable and flexible information data system for management and planning purposes; control of health care costs by developing further preventive programmes and primary health care and by assessment of the increase in medical specialities, as well as by assessment of the use of existing and new technologies; rationalization and integration of the process of planning for health services and health manpower; dental health programmes based on prevention and treatment of high-risk groups.

Health planning and programming

There is no health planning authority at the national or local level. Health planning, is, however, carried out by some public bodies and Ministry of Health departments. A hospital planning and construction authority under the chairmanship of the Minister of Health was set up to coordinate and plan hospital construction. Building of all medical instructions now requires a licence from the Ministry.

The Association for the Planning and Development of Services for the Aged is a public body funded by several ministries and other agencies and is responsible for long-term planning and development in the geriatric field.

A health manpower planning programme is scheduled to start as of June 1979.

Organization of health services

The Ministry of Health has overall authority for the planning and supervision of health care services, licensing for health professions, provision of direct preventive, curative and rehabilitation services and environmental and public health. The Ministry is entrusted with the administration of public health law, and at present functions through two main sections at the national level: the medical section, including six divisions for public health, hospitalization services, mental health, chronic diseases, nursing and pharmacy, and the administration section, which is responsible for all management units.

At the regional level the Ministry operates through a network of six district and 14 subdistrict health offices dealing essentially with public health. Certain health areas are under the jurisdiction of ministries other than the Ministry of Health; veterinary health is under the Ministry of Agriculture; occupational health and custodial care of the mentally deficient come under the Ministry of Labour and Social Welfare.

A new interministerial committee, headed by the Deputy Prime Minister and comprising the ministers and directors-general of the social service ministries (or their representatives), is working for a better coordination of services.

The Ministry of Health directly operates 33 hospitals, with 9860 beds, or 40% of total bed capacity. It maintains two-thirds of the 810 family health centres (or mother and child health stations), nursing schools, public health laboratories, child guidance and mental health clinics, rehabilitation centres and two physiotherapy schools.

The medical system is based on a voluntary health insurance system which covers over 90% of the population and operates through a variety of so-called sick funds. Those insured are entitled to pre-paid treatment at clinics, at home or at the home of a physician, free hospitalization and drugs, facilities for convalescence, and reduced rates for dental care.

The largest sick fund, run by the *Histadrut* (General Federation of Labour) with approximately two and one half million members (73% of the population), employs 50% of the doctors in the country and maintains over 1200 ambulatory clinics, 14 hospitals and other facilities.

Education and training of health manpower

It is estimated that there are approximately 7000 active physicians, or one to 490 inhabitants. There are four medical schools, from which about 200 students graduate yearly. Students who have obtained their high school matriculation certificate may apply for admission. The course of study is six years, with one additional year for internship.

The School of Health Sciences in Beersheba, which opened in 1974, encourages the development of health practitioners with an orientation towards community-based work.

In 1976 there were approximately 14 750 nurses, or one nurse to 235 inhabitants; 65% are practical nurses and 35% are registered nurses. At present there are 19 schools for registered nurses, from which about 500 graduate annually; 15 courses for practical nurses which about 450 students pass each year, and recently 15 comprehensive high schools have introduced specialization in practical nursing. Those completing these high school programmes are now beginning to enter the working force. With the departure of nursing schools from their traditional dependency on hospitals, there has been a change in the scope and content of nursing education, with growing emphasis on community nursing, psychiatric nursing, and nursing for the chronically ill and the elderly, necessitating new courses of instruction in gerontology, psychiatry, cardiology, and the behavioural sciences. The increasing academic character of nursing education is reflected in the establishment of a degree of Bachelor of Nursing at Tel Aviv University and the Hadassah Hebrew University. Plans for establishing similar degrees are now planned for the Beersheba and Haifa Universities. The tendency has likewise raised the educational levels required for entrance to nursing schools; completion of junior high school is required of candidates for schools for practical nurses, and completion of high school for those enrolling in registered nursing programmes. Duration of studies is one and a half years for practical nursing and three years for registered nurses.

In 1977 there were approximately 1830 working dentists licensed and registered by the Ministry of Health, or one dentist to 1191 inhabitants. The duration of studies is six years, after which the student becomes a Doctor of Dental Medicine. Students must have matriculated from high school. At present there are two dental schools: The Hadassah Dental School, from which about 35 students graduate each year, and the new Tel Aviv University Dental School, from which a first class of 24 students will graduate in 1979.

There are approximately 360 qualified dental assistants. Duration of studies is one academic year, after which the student receives a certificate of studies. All students must have completed high school, but a matriculation certificate is not required. Courses are offered in four institutions, from which a total of about 80 students graduate each year.

The first course for dental hygienists opened in 1978 with an enrolment of 12 students. The duration of studies is two academic years, after which the student is awarded a certificate of studies. High school graduates are accepted for the programme.

Courses for dental technicians have opened at various technical high schools in recent years. In addition, two new courses will open in 1979 for about 40 students. The duration of studies will be two academic years. In 1977 there were 1479 pharmacists and 813 assistant pharmacists. The School of Pharmacy in Jerusalem, connected to the Hadassah Medical School, has about 65 graduates a year. Enrolment is being increased and it is estimated that approximately 80 students will graduate annually in the near future. Students with matriculation certificates are accepted for a four-year course of studies.

There are two schools for physiotherapists from which 50–60 students graduate each year. A new school at the Tel Hashomer Hospital will have a first class of 20 in 1979. A fourth school is planned at the Beersheba Medical Centre. The duration of studies is three years. A fourth year internship has been initiated at the Tel Hashomer School for Physiotherapy. Applicants must be holders of a school matriculation certificate.

There is one school for occupation therapists at the Hadassah Medical Centre from which about 30 students graduate each year. The duration of studies is three years. In 1978 Haifa University opened a School of Occupation Therapy for students with a B.A. degree in the humanities or social sciences. This retraining course will be for two academic years, and applicants must have a high school matriculation certificate.

There are two kinds of courses for dieticians. One is a nonacademic course which offers a certificate of studies, and the other is an academic course at the Rehovot School of Agriculture of the Hebrew University, which offers a B.Sc. degree in nutrition. Both courses are for three years and about 30 students graduate each year.

There are four schools for X-ray technicians, and the duration of studies is two years. A total of 50 students graduate each year.

There are three courses for medical laboratory technicians which a total of about 60 students pass each year. Applicants must have a high school matriculation certificate. The duration of studies is two years, with an additional year for practical work.

There are two kinds of courses for sanitarians: one for three years (including practical work) and one for practical engineers in environmental health, lasting two academic years. About 20 students a year pass each course. Applicants must have high school matriculation.

Health resources

Health establishments

In 1977 there were 126 hospitals; 810 family health centres; and 1200 clinics for ambulatory and specialists care; 11 child development centres; 83 outpatient mental health facilities; 6 drug addiction centres; 206 dental clinics serving schoolchildren; 7 public health laboratories; 22 pulmonary disease prevention centres; and 4 comprehensive medical health centres.

Health expenditure

Expenditure on health in the budgetary year 1976/77 constituted approximately 6.6% of the gross national product, as compared with 6.1% in 1975/76. The figure was expected to rise slightly to 6.9% in 1977/78, and then remain stable for the following years.

In 1976/77 the expenditure increased by only 1% over the previous years (at constant prices), compared with an average annual growth rate of 9.2% since 1971, the result of the sharp reduction in investment in construction of hospital buildings, especially government hospitals, in keeping with the Goverment's aim of maintaining existing services without further spending on construction of new hospitals. Thus in 1976/77 current expenditure, i.e., the value of health services and goods which are supplied to the public, increased by 6% over the previous year (at constant prices); while fixed capital formation, i.e., expenditure on construction of buildings and purchase of equipment, decreased by 25%.

The current expenditure on hospital services in 1975/76, as in the previous two years, represented 43% of the total current expenditure on health. The proportion of expenditure on hospitals increased steadily over the years (from 38% in 1962/63 to 43% in 1975/76). Over the same period the proportion of total health expenditure taken by the services of clinical and preventive medicine decreased from 40% to 37%.

Appraisal of progress made between 1973 and 1977

The health status of the population improved considerably in the period under review. The infant mortality rate for the total population declined from 24.2 infant deaths per 1000 live births in 1973 to 17.8 deaths per 1000 live births. Among the Jewish population the rate dropped from 18.1 to 13.8; and in the non-Jewish sector the rate fell from 37.1 to 30.4. In 1977 life expectancy for the Jewish population reached 71.9 for males and 75.4 for females, and for the non-Jewish population 68.5 for males and 71.3 for females.

Mortality and morbidity from infectious diseases have continued to decrease with the virtual elimination or control of various infectious diseases. Mortality due to infectious diseases accounted for about 10.4 deaths per 100 000 inhabitants.

Voluntary health insurance today covers nearly 93% of the population, providing extensive health care for almost all citizens. Certain restrictions applying to those insured in the various sick funds have been removed so that most insured members today receive complete health coverage. The Ministry of Labour and Welfare and the Ministry of Finance provide health insurance coverage for those receiving welfare payments.

The addition of numerous hospital beds has maintained an adequate bed/population ratio and has helped to reduce the waiting time for admission. The development of alternative community-based facilities and day hospitals has contributed to reducing hospital occupancy rates.

Services for geriatric and chronic illnesses have been expanded to meet the growing needs. The Ministry of Health, in conjunction with the Association for the Planning and Development of Services for the Aged—a public body funded by the various ministries and a distribution committee, embarked on its second five-year national plan including the construction of old peoples' homes, community day-care centres and clubs, geriatric wards in hospitals and numerous other community programmes and services.

The Ministry of Health and the Sick Fund of the General Federation of Labour reached an agreement to regionalize all psychiatric facilities to ensure the provision of comprehensive care and continuity of treatment regardless of affiliation to any health insurance scheme. A collaborative master plan has been elaborated covering deficit expenditure. Two new 400-bed mental hospitals have been constructed, one at Beersheba serving the Southern District, and the other at Tirat Ha-Carmel for the Northern District. In addition, six new drug abuse and rehabilitation centres have been opened and have proved highly successful; a network of such centres is planned to deal with the new health problems.

New services for mother and child health care and services for the prevention and early detection of diseases in the elderly, as well as follow-up treatment for those with mental or chronic illnesses, have been added to the other functions of the family health centres. Other programmes, such as family planning and counselling, eye and ear tests for infants, and home visits for the handicapped, have been initiated in a growing number of centres.

The health goals for the comming 5–10 years are:

(1) *The organization and delivery of services* including: the establishment of a national health insurance plan to provide comprehensive and universal health coverage for the entire population: the regionalization of health services

through the creation of comprehensive health units; and the linking and integration of various providers of health service in order to ensure continuity of treatment and to eliminate duplication and waste, as well as the creation of planning mechanisms for the coordination and rationalization of development of services.

(2) *Environmental health*, with increased monitoring, surveillance and enforcement of present regulations and laws in hygiene and ecology.

(3) *Dental health*, with greater emphasis on prevention, through such measures as fluoridation of drinking-water, and the development and training of dental and auxiliary manpower.

(4) *Communicable and noncommunicable diseases control*, especially to reduce mortality and morbidity from food-, milk- and waterborne sources, with health education and preventive health measures to combat the increasing incidence of heart disease, cancer, road accidents, and occupational health hazards.

(5) *Hospital services*. Priority will be given to the completion of hospitals under construction and the addition of new wings and departments. Old buildings will be renovated, new equipment will be installed. There will be rationalization of the type and distribution of hospital beds to alleviate shortages of beds and overcrowding.

(6) *Geriatric services*. The need to develop community-based services, home care and day hospitals and the addition of geriatric wards and other facilities for the elderly, including counselling clinics, will continue to be stressed.

(7) *Psychiatric services*. Alternative community mental health services will be developed in order to reduce hospitalization as much as possible.

(8) *Manpower development*. Sufficient medical teams of high quality, and auxiliary personnel will be trained in all fields according to the needs of the population, through the expansion and opening of new schools, programmes and in-service training courses.

JORDAN

Major health problems

The major health and health-related problems can be categorized as follows:

The basic health services suffer from maldistribution and variable quality of services in rural and desert areas, shortage of professional and auxiliary health manpower, overlapping of curative services and limited coordination between the public and private sectors.

In hospitals the number of beds per 10 000 population is 17 (27 in Amman, 7.5 in the Balka Governorate). There is poor communication between those working in basic health services and those working in hospitals; a referral system is needed. Hospitals in each sector have their own administrative procedure.

There is a shortage of professional and auxiliary health manpower, and migration of health manpower to neighbouring countries.

Environmental sanitation suffers from the shortage in quantity and the unsafe quality of water supplies, and the distribution network is incomplete and obsolete. Sewage disposal and garbage collection and disposal of industrial wastes pose further problems, as do air pollution

and food control. There is a need to strengthen food control.

In health insurance the main problem is that the individual pays only one dinar for health insurance and the coverage is incomplete.

There is duplication of responsibilities and of tasks among providers of health services.

Some 3600 drug items are found in Jordan, imported from 302 different companies. There is insufficient evaluation and analysis of the drugs for efficacy.

There is a need for health research, particularly in the fields of health management, administration and evaluation, and to adapt technology to local health services needs.

Action taken

Health policy

The objectives of the Ministry of Health have been fixed and active steps are being taken to achieve them.

More weight is to be given to community health services rather than to health services to the individual, the family being recognized as the basic unit of the community. A balanced curative and preventive health care system is to be established with comprehensive health services that include rural and desert areas, starting with the comprehensive health centres that provide all outpatient health care at the focal point of several basic health centres, each containing a general medical clinic and maternal and child health services as a minimum. Basic health centres can then be developed with tuberculosis control units and health inspectorates.

Preventive health services

Emphasis on prevention will be ensured by increasing the number of maternal and child health centres to provide health care to mothers during pregnancy and delivery and after delivery and child care up to school age, as well as health and nutrition education to mothers and supplementary foods to the mother and the child.

There were during the period under review some 50 centres, whose services were utilized by 41% of the population. Simple evaluation confirms the need for several times this number of centres to protect the health of present and future generations. The main difficulty is the shortage of midwives; an increase in the number of midwifery graduates is impossible under the present training system requiring 24 months of training for a candidate completing secondary school. Also graduates prefer to work in urban rather than rural communities.

Current policy is to provide the students of assistant nursing schools, which require 18 months training, with some midwifery training so that they can act as nursing-midwifery assistants in maternal and child health centres in rural areas and provide the dual function of nurse/midwife as a step towards integration of these centres with the village clinic, using the least manpower possible.

The school health programme was established in 1975. School health services provide periodic medical examination of students and supervision of schools, environmental sanitation (the Ministry of Health provides such services on behalf of the Ministry of Eduction). Only 5% of students are covered by eight medical teams and four dental teams, whereas the actual need is for 30 medical teams and 20 dental teams.

No more than one-fourth of eligible children are immunized against communicable diseases. A special section was established in the Ministry of Health, with units in governorates, in order to apply a comprehensive plan of compulsory immunization in collaboration with school health services.

The increase in the quantities of foods destroyed is one indication of the strengthened control and food inspection. But cooperation between different authorities concerned with food quality control in the Ministry of Health, Ministry of Agriculture, Ministry of Trade and Industries, Ministry of Finance and Customs and Amman Municipality is still needed. Legislation on this subject is being prepared.

Environmental sanitation is not the responsibility of the Ministry of Health alone, the main burden lies with other official bodies. A decision was made by the Cabinet, after cholera broke out in Jordan last year, to establish the Supreme Safety Council as a permanent body to supervise environmental health control, particularly safe water and wastes disposal and any condition hazardous to health. Its efforts were tremendous.

A health education section was established in the Ministry of Health to prepare publications and information pertaining to health education and to exploit the mass media for this purpose, with the participation of the Ministry of Education in updating health curricula for the schools and literacy centres.

A plan for the improvement of curative services is based on providing medical care at three levels, through basic health centres, comprehensive health centres and hospitals. Hospital services are to be modernized and expanded.

Ambulance and emergency services are lacking, or are limited to transport of casualties without special equipment. Emergency centres in cities and along main roads, with trained personnel and ambulances, are needed to guarantee proper management of casualties and their rapid transport. According to instructions from His Majesty King Hussein, and as part of an extended microwave project, emergency telephone points were installed at intervals of 10 km, by which police, fire brigade and emergency rescue services can be called by any person in need. Information was being collected on this emergency system so that it might be installed throughout the country before the end of 1978.

Health legislation

A Supreme Health Council has been established which is responsible for health legislation.

It deals with health services in general, and with specializations; some of the most important subjects are:

— defining responsibilities and duties, and strengthening cooperation and coordination between the public and private health sectors;
— studying and coordinating all matters concerning the drug industry and commerce;
— establishing the basis for delivering health services, in their various forms, to all areas and increasing health services promotion;
— defining the requirements of health manpower; providing incentives for staff to obtain the qualifications that are needed in the health sector, and increasing numbers of staff to cover all areas;
— encouraging wider medical scientific research.

The Council is headed by the Prime Minister and the membership includes the Ministers of Health and of Finance, so that political and financial support are ensured.

Health planning and programming

A directorate of planning was established in the Ministry of Health; contracts with foreign companies in this field resulted in a preliminary survey whereby the goals and assumptions, important parameters in the health sector, proposed composition and schedule of a health planning team and major recommendations for the pre-planning team were studied as a first phase in September 1977. In the second phase the physical and human environment, health status, nutrition, water supply and sanitation, the existing health care system, and manpower were studied and recommendations made. The last phase started with an inventory of manpower and facilities, and was to continue into 1978, completing the work in 30 months.

Organization of health services

Three important sections were established in the Ministry of Health: the vaccination section, the school health section (which started in 1975), and the health education section. A section of environmental sanitation controls the quality of water and ensure that water is adequately treated before it reaches the public. Water from the King Talat Dam is intended for domestic use, and the section is prepared for the

new problems which arise. The sewage disposal plan in Amman was expanded, the plant in Salt was renovated, and three new plants were under study. Each industrial establishment is obliged by law to treat its waste. Refuse disposal is by open dumping and burning.

Biomedical and health services research

With the discovery of imported cases of schistosomiasis, a survey was carried out which showed that the snail *Planorbis* is present in the Jordan Valley.

Education and training of health manpower

Support continued to the existing colleges of nursing. The Ministry of Health opened three schools for nurse aides, and the School for auxiliary health personnel started, and the University of Jordan opened colleges of medicine, nursing and pharmacology in 1973. A nursing curriculum was introduced in girls secondary schools by the Ministry of Education. The total numbers of graduates during the five-year period was 255 nurses, 58 midwives, and 262 auxiliary health technicians, not including the sectors not covered by the Ministry of Health.

Health resources

Health establishments

There are 16 government hospitals with a total of 1362 beds, and 17 private hospitals with a total of 647 beds, 45 governmental health centres, 260 village clinics, 51 maternal and child centres and 31 dental clinics. In the non-governmental sector there are 36 health centres, 11 maternal and child health centres, 532 private medical clinics and 168 dental clinics.

Health manpower

The health manpower consists of 1460 physicians (892 government-employed, 568 private), 270 dentists (98 government-employed, 172 private), 504 pharmacists, 838 registered nurses and 216 midwives.

The following table compares manpower, hospital beds and other health institutions, under the Ministry of Health and in all sectors.

	Ministry of Health		All sectors	
	1972	1977	1972	1977
Physicians	217	408	688	1 460
Dentists	23	44	112	270
Pharmacists	20	31	203	504
Senior nurses	175	263	331	838
Midwives	94	145	181	216
Total hospital beds	1 274	1 349	1 896	3 530
Clinics	251	342	313	895
Dental clinics	29	31	106	212
Blood banks	8	11		
Maternal and child health centres	32	51		
Total budget (in thousands of dinars)	2 333	8 630		

Pharmaceuticals

Control of drugs is the responsibility of the pharmacy and supplies directorate in the Ministry of Health. The number of imported drugs has been reduced by nearly 30%. All those excluded are nonessential drugs. The development of a drugs industry is highly encouraged by the Ministry; the Arab Pharmaceutical Manufacturing Company has received government support, representing 18% of the total drug production companies now under development.

Financial resources

The budget of the Ministry of Health increased more than threefold during the period 1973–1977 (in 1973 it was 2 576 065 dinars, in 1977 it was 8 763 700); the per capita health expenditure was four dinars; other government sectors concerned with health have their own budgets.

Outlook

The current five-year plan aims:

— to expand and improve preventive services with special attention to student health and mother and child care;
— to develop and expand curative medical services in hospitals, health centres and clinics;
— to organize the manufacture, distribution and export of pharmaceutical drugs;
— to place emergency and first aid services within the reach of all citizens; and to upgrade the rural medical services as a requisite for community development and integrate these

services with health services in the urban centres.

The projects in the five-year plan are:

(1) a health centre project to establish 11 health centres, each comprising a medical and dental clinic, a maternity and child care section and other units for student health care, control of infectious and endemic diseases, as well as environmental and health extension services;
(2) a polyclinic project to establish five polyclinics in remote areas where medical services are insufficient to cope with cases of disease, accidents or emergencies (each polyclinic will be organized along the lines of a health centre);
(3) a basic medical centre project to establish six basic medical centres in sparsely populated areas with difficult access to medical or health centres, including a general medical clinic, a maternal and child care unit and first aid services:
(4) a hospital project to establish four hospitals in areas with difficult access to central hospitals of the governorates and large cities, and to expand certain hospitals in the main cities to cope with the increase in demand for hospital services;
(5) a pharmaceutical control laboratory project to build a laboratory for the quality control of the various kinds of drugs on the market; and
(6) a psychiatric hospital project to establish a hospital in a suburb of Amman for the treatment of mental cases.

KUWAIT

Population and vital statistics

At the last census, taken in 1975, the recorded population was 994 837, of whom

522 749 (54.7%) were non-Kuwaiti. The total estimated population in 1977 was 1 066 400. The annual growth rate for the Kuwaiti population was 6.4% compared with 5.9% for the

	Population			Birth rate	Death rate	Natural increase	Net increase	Total growth
	Male	Female	Total			(rates per 1000 population)		
Kuwaiti	236 600	235 488	472 088	51.1	6.1	45.0	21.1	66.1
Non-Kuwaiti	307 168	215 581	522 749	36.9	3.5	32.0	23.9	55.9

non-Kuwaiti population. Population density was 60 per km². The substantial increase in the population was mainly due to immigration. The components of population growth in 1975 are shown in the table above.

In 1977, the infant mortality rate was 39.3 per 1000 live births compared with 44.0 per 1000 in 1973.

Major health problems

Like many other countries, Kuwait is faced with the dilemma of how to maintain a healthy environment in an urbanized pre-industrialized society. It thus encounters some of the public health problems facing developing countries. The major health problems are therefore gastrointestinal infections including parasitoses, respiratory diseases, motor-vehicle accidents, heart disease, mental diseases, environmental sanitation and overcrowding.

The major causes of death in the years 1975–1977 (in order of their importance in 1975 and by section or category of the International Classification of Diseases) were as shown in the table below.

The most important causes of death were as follows (in order of importance): enteritis and other diarrhoeal diseases, respiratory diseases, ischaemic heart disease, motor-vehicle accidents, diseases of infancy and congenital anomalies.

Among the communicable diseases, the following were those most frequently notified: measles (2162), infectious hepatitis (1345), mumps (1201), salmonellosis (1152), chickenpox (1028), streptococcal sore throat (435), and typhoid fever (397).

Organization and administration of health services

Medical services provide care free of charge for all persons living in Kuwait regardless of their nationality. These services, which include

Cause of death	1975		1976		1977	
	Number of deaths	% of all deaths	Number of deaths	% of all deaths	Number of deaths	% of all deaths
Enteritis and other diarrhoeal diseases	564	12.0	510	10.7	674	14.5
Diseases of respiratory system (other than pneumonia)	416	8.9	501	10.5	494	10.6
Diseases of the circulatory system (ischaemic heart disease)	381	8.1	460	9.6	1 077	23.1
Symptoms and other ill-defined conditions	357	7.6	238	4.9	390	8.4
Accidents (motor vehicles)	302	6.4	344	7.8	557	12.0
Anoxic and hypoxic conditions	223	4.8	227	4.8	128**	2.7
Other causes of perinatal morbidity and mortality	205	4.4	156*	3.3	423	9.1
Cerebrovascular diseases	188	4.0	193	4.0	126*	2.6
All other congenital anomalies	163	3.5	174	3.6	252	5.4
Malignant neoplasms of other and unspecified sites	120	2.6	199	4.2	351	7.5
Total	2 919	62.3	3 002	63.4	4 472	95.9
Other causes	1 767	37.7	1 733	36.6	191	4.1
Grand total	4 686	100	4 735	100	4 663	100

* Diseases of the nervous system.
** Diseases of the digestive system.

the private sectors, are administered by the Ministry of Public Health.

At present the technical services of the Ministry of Public Health form seven major departments, for public health and planning, hospital administration, research, community care administration, central technical service, and dental and paramedical administration, each independent in the conduct of its administrative and technical affairs; they report to the Under-secretary. Other divisions which are not under the above-mentioned departments, such as the drug manufacturing plant and the drug control laboratory, also report to the Undersecretary.

Communicable disease control

Intestinal infections are common and preventive sanitary measures against anthrax are compulsory.

Vaccination of infants against smallpox, diphtheria, pertussis, tetanus and poliomyelitis are obligatory, and the medical control of travellers and pilgrims is functioning well. In 1977 the following immunizations were carried out: cholera (132 474), smallpox (158 714), measles (30 085), poliomyelitis (91 029). Moreover, following WHO recommendations, all necessary precautions for cholera control are being taken through frequent inspections, chlorination of water, health education and other sanitary measures.

Health education

In 1977 there was great activity in the health education of the public. The health education centres and guidance section spread knowledge of social and personal health subjects through the different mass media and by other audio-visual means throughout the country. During the year 1977 there were 29 104 attendances at the centres in the course of 1215 district visits.

Maternal and child welfare

In 1977 there were 284 537 antenatal consultations; this constituted a substantial increase since 1973. The number of births attended by qualified doctors or midwives amounted to 17 966 (i.e., over 95% of the total births in the

country). This shows remarkable progress since the year 1973 in the utilization of available medical facilities.

Rehabilitation

Mental health programmes attracted increasing public and professional attention during the period under review. In order to extend the service to the mentally retarded and handicapped, the Ministry of Public Health is collaborating with the Ministry of Education and the Ministry of Social Affairs and Rehabilitation in providing health services to persons in psychological difficulties, as well as to those suffering from mental disorders, in the institutions run by those Ministries.

Environmental sanitation

There was a progressive improvement in the general sanitary conditions of the country. This may be attributed both to frequent inspection by health personnel and to the campaign of health education.

There are direct piped water supply systems as well as a sewage disposal system that functions well.

Health establishments and manpower

In 1973, there were 11 hospitals and sanatoria with 3731 beds, 12 preventive health centres, 42 clinics and polyclinics and 270 school clinics. The hospital bed/population ratio was approximately 3.5 per 1000.

In 1973 there were 800 doctors, 355 pharmacists and assistant pharmacists, 2987 nurses and 399 other technical staff assigned to the different departments of hospitals, health centres and private medical centres. By 1977 there were 1359 doctors, 475 pharmacists and assistant pharmacists, 3353 nurses and 454 other technical staff. There were thus 1.3 doctors per 1000 population. The total number of patients (inpatients and outpatients) treated in government and private hospitals was 1 266 916. The total attendances at dispensaries and polyclinics numbered 6 619 520 in 1973 and 7 759 919 in 1977. The production of the drug manufacturing plant totalled 35 784 361 batches in 1973 and 47 976 114 in 1977.

Education and training of health manpower

Lack of health manpower is the major problem facing the developing countries, in which respect Kuwait is no exception. The Faculty of Medicine at Kuwait University was established in 1976 and students are now in training there. The Ministry of Public Health collaborates, through joint boards, with the School of Medicine in providing professional training, speciality training and continuing education for general practitioners and newly employed physicians; and with the School of Medicine and the Ministry of Education in giving courses in medical technology, medical records and X-ray and radiography at the associateship degree and bachelorate levels. There are also nursing training institutions providing three-year courses, as well as postgraduate courses in obstetrics, and producing a minimum of 70 nurses each year.

Above all, nationals are sent abroad under national and international sponsorship to be trained in different branches of public health, depending upon the needs of the country.

Medical and public health research

A number of research projects are in progress, including studies in smoking, hypertension, anthropometric measurement, as well as other health practice research.

Long-term plan

In future national health planning, the main programmes will be the systemization of the administration, the improvement of hospital organization, the establishment of additional public health centres, the development of health manpower and prevention and control of communicable and noncommunicable diseases.

In the next few years, the Ministry of Public Health plans to establish a well-organized, efficient and comprehensive health service with easy access for all people to all health facilities throughout the country.

Government health expenditure

Total government expenditure on health increased from 8 million Kuwaiti dinars in 1963 to 60 million in 1976/77, 6.5% of the total government outlay.

LIBYAN ARAB JAMAHIRIYA

Epidemiological surveys and studies carried out over five years showed that the occurrence of outbreaks of communicable, endemic, water- and foodborne diseases could be greatly reduced by strengthening the community health programmes in general, and in particular by the implementation of environmental health programmes. Consequently a preliminary investigation of gaps and priority needs in the field of environmental health was performed, and short-, medium- and long-term measures were devised. Close collaboration and cooperation with the Secretariat of Municipalities was envisaged with a view to implementing the programmes at municipality level. Simultaneously, great efforts were directed towards the further development of health establishments and health manpower and training facilities. The basic health services gained momentum and their ability to provide an integrated complex of preventive, promotive, curative and rehabilitative services for the individual, the family and the community was enhanced.

The emphasis on measures to improve sanitation and public and environmental health resulted in the widespread provision of adequate and safe water supplies; proper sanitary disposal of liquid and solid wastes in most of the rural and urban settlements and by new individual installations; control of vectorborne diseases; and food control. Specific legislation was drafted and enforced.

Some 80% of the population are served by piped public water supply systems and about 65% are covered by water-carried sewage disposal facilities.

A countrywide programme for drinking-water quality monitoring and surveillance has been in progress since 1969, and since 1974 is availing itself of 18 well-equipped and well-staffed laboratories for bacteriological and chemical investigation.

Desalination has been introduced on a large scale in order to supplement conventional public water supplies. About 20 of the 46 municipalities were to be served by desalination units by mid-1979.

Biological waste water treatment plants are functioning in some 15 municipalities. The plants serving the major towns include tertiary treatment in view of the reuse of treated effluents, mainly for agriculture irrigation.

The prevalence and potential danger of vec-torborne diseases have been substantially reduced as a consequence of the improvement in environmental factors and the proper use of insecticides.

Health education plays a fundamental role in the promotion and implementation of the community health programmes.

Control of foodborne diseases is being achieved through the inspection of food processing establishments, marketing places and food handlers, and by routine sampling and bacteriological and biochemical analysis of food specimens.

The programme is supported and speeded up by the promulgation of the public health law (1973) and by recent *ad hoc* regulations (1975) issued by the Secretariat of Health.

OMAN

Major health and health-related problems

The major problems in the period under review were those of water supply, sewage disposal and vector control, and the communicable diseases posing a particular threat were malaria, gastroenteritis, trachoma and influenza and upper respiratory tract infections.

Action taken

Health policy measures were taken for the expansion of public health services and the integration of preventive and curative services.

Various laws and ministerial decrees were passed during the period, and comprehensive health laws are in the process of being issued.

Health planning and programming were included in the five-year plans covering the whole Sultanate. The health services were organized according to available facilities and resources, which increase yearly.

Biomedical and health services research is still limited. Some education and training of health manpower is local. There is a School of Nursing.

Outlook

Health goals for the next five years include programme development and coordination with neighbouring countries and with international agencies; development of primary health care and integration of both preventive and medical services, especially at the rural level; development of maternal and child health services, health education, disease prevention and control, covering particularly malaria, trachoma, enteric diseases and respiratory diseases; nutritional survey and services; a mass immunization programme; promotion of environmental health (including water supply, sewage disposal and vector control); health manpower development; and development of a health statistical system.

SAUDI ARABIA

Health policy

Health is one of the basic foundations of the country's socioeconomic development plan. A clean environment, disease prevention and satisfactory provision of a high standard of curative services are recognized as fundamental to health and for raising labour productivity. The Ministry of Health has laid down health policy, which may be summarized as follows:

(1) to maintain the close relationship between health and development, treatment being required to safeguard its population and to promote productivity, since it transforms the nonproductive patient into a productive, healthy person whose efforts contribute to development;

(2) to increase the accessibility of health services by linking families closely to health units and by gaining the confidence of the citizen in order to improve his education in matters of health and so raise his level of health;

(3) to increase the efficacy of health services through improved manpower efficiency, employing highly qualified workers in health units affiliated to the Ministry, and benefiting by their continuing training, in addition to providing modern scientific appliances and equipment;

(4) to give due emphasis to preventive medicine and preventive programmes by taking an interest in the relevant studies and encouraging those undertaking studies of epidemic disease control in general, with special reference to tuberculosis, ophthalmias, malaria and schistosomiasis (preventive medicine is the concern of one of the main departments of the Ministry of Health);

(5) to maintain coordination between the various ministerial departments working in fields relating to health making use of available human and material resources, and to promote the quality of treatment and set up a minimal level of performance, thus assisting in the provision of a coordinated high-level and fully beneficial service.

Health planning and programming

The objectives of the plan covering the period under review were as follows:

(1) improvement of the standard of curative services, vertically and horizontally, by increasing the bed/population ratio to 2.5 per 1000 inhabitants;

(2) strengthening of preventive services, especially programmes aiming at decreasing morbidity from communicable diseases, thus reducing infant mortality rates;

(3) control of communicable diseases;

(4) review of the country's basic health problems;

(5) extension of the coverage of curative and preventive services through dispensaries in underserved sectors such as rural areas and nomad populations;

(6) provision of the human and material resources required to raise the doctor/population ratio to one doctor to 2000 inhabitants, and to increase the percentage of Saudi doctors to at least 15% when the plan is completed, in addition to strengthening training institutions;

(7) promotion of nursing, encouraging Saudi girls to join nursing schools, and increasing the number of male and female nurses in general by providing incentives for entering the profession, with a view to achieving a staffing rate of one nurse to no more than three beds;

(8) attention to statistical and planning studies and research as a basis of health plans;

(9) provision of drugs to hospitals and private pharmacies and investigation of the possibility of preparing certain pharmaceuticals in the country;

(10) establishment of an office to coordinate health services among ministries and government departments concerned with the common weal such as those of education, agriculture, the interior and social affairs;

(11) support for health education, its extension to rural areas and nomad populations and its coordination with the mass media, i.e., radio, television and the press;

(12) delegation of further responsibilities to directors of health affairs and decentralization of health care;

(13) strengthening of equipment maintenance capacity, its decentralization, and development of medical supply units in various provinces;

(14) increase in the efficiency of emergency aid services through the provision of the necessary ambulances in agreement with the Red Crescent;

(15) investigation of the possibility of developing a health card for every citizen;

(16) activation, support and control of the private health services sector.

In order to achieve these general objectives, the Ministry's different sectors set up secondary plans, each including a group of programmes and projects arising out of a study of health problems and reflecting the present status of every sector and its needs in this respect, as specified hereunder:

(1) *Curative services sector*

– programmes increasing the number of hospitals and beds in order to achieve a bed/population ratio of 2.5 per 1000 inhabitants, while raising the relevant capacity according to every specialization and district needs;
– programmes for polyclinics and the introduction of curative services therein; for the coordination of preventive and curative services in rural areas; and for the establishment of rates for the services to be rendered by the polyclinic to inhabitants, in addition to the development of health education;
– programmes for laboratories and auxiliary equipment, such as X-ray and medical rehabilitation equipment, and establishment of peripheral laboratories in the provinces;
– programmes for district polyclinics to relieve the burden on hospitals;
– programmes for nomads.

(2) *Preventive services sector*

– programmes for communicable disease control, increasing the number of health offices and establishing additional health units as a part of a system using offices at three levels—rural, urban and district;
– programmes for maternal and child care;
– programmes for health education development;
– programmes for environmental health and epidemiological research;
– programmes for endemic, chronic and chest diseases.

(3) *Administrative development and organizational services sector*

– programmes and projects for planning;
– programmes and projects for organization and administration;
– programmes and projects for medical supply;
– programmes and projects for engineering;
– programmes and projects for health education and health manpower training.

Health manpower

There are 31 851 workers in the health sector serving a population of 7 200 000. Physicians account for 19% of the total, while dentists account for 1%, technicians 3%, health auxiliaries 58% and administrative staff 19%.

The Ministry of Health structure comprises 60% of the workers in the health sector; 8% of all practising physicians are Saudi nationals.

There are one physician to 1800 inhabitants; one dentist to 32 000, and one health auxiliary to 890. There are 2.1 health auxiliaries per physician.

Statistical information

The tables below were supplied by the Ministry of Health statistics unit through the Directorate General of Preventive Health.

The following vaccinations were performed by the services of the Ministry of Health during the year 1976:

Vaccination	Number
Cholera	943 458
Smallpox	587 311
Cerebrospinal meningitis	192 531
Diphtheria/pertussis/	
tetanus	177 847
Poliomyelitis	137 983
Tuberculosis	84 208
Typhoid	20 200
Measles	6 019
Yellow fever	1 501
Total	2 151 058

The activities of the Ministry of Health blood bank in 1976 were as follows:

Analyses	Number
Blood grouping	71 702
Rhesus factor	62 855
Identification	22 447
Haemoglobin test	22 294
Compatibility testing	13 810
Other examinations	1 810
Blood supply management:	
Blood donors, unpaid	19 915
Blood donors, paid	268
	20 183
Number of blood transfusion	
requests	19 948

The number of attendances at Ministry of Health hospital outpatient departments, dispensaries and health posts and the number of inpatients admitted to Ministry of Health hospitals in the years 1972–1976 were as follows:

	Outpatient consultations	Inpatients
1972	14 397 098	162 877
1973	16 766 815	187 139
1974	19 617 842	220 628
1975	21 082 054	244 559
1976	22 550 503	265 253

Laboratory examinations performed in the Ministry of Health laboratory and hospitals during the period 1972–1976 were as follows:

	Number of examinations
1972	1 214 481
1973	1 530 888
1974	1 888 385
1975	2 093 610
1976	2 185 827

X-ray department activities in Ministry of Health hospitals and dispensaries in 1976 were as follows:

Radiography:

Number of films	696 888
Number of patients	439 972

Radiotherapy:

Malignant tumours	799
Other tumours	485

Electrical treatment

Number of patients	37 641
Number of sessions	66 537

Physiotherapy and massage

Number of patients	66 209
Number of sessions	85 719
Other examinations or treatment	358

Health expenditure

The following table shows the budget of the Ministry of Health for the last four years:

	Amount (rials)
1974/75	1 162 997
1975/76	3 197 333
1976/77	2 972 726
1977/78	3 684 075

SYRIAN ARAB REPUBLIC

Population and other statistics

According to the last census, taken in 1970, the population of the Syrian Arab Republic was 6 304 685. The table below gives the estimated population and other vital statistics for the period 1973–1976.

Of the 30 842 deaths recorded in 1976 the main causes were symptoms and ill-defined conditions (16 465), diseases of the circulatory system (3835), infectious and parasitic diseases (1797), emergency cases, poisoning, and accidents (1462). Causes coming under the heading of geriatrics were: mental disorders (1242), cerebrovascular diseases (909), diseases of the digestive system (863), acute respiratory diseases (720), malignant tumours (524), genital

	1973	1974	1975	1976
Population	6 889 948	7 120 953	7 355 000	7 596 000
Births	406 314	351 990	361 183	345 356
Birth rate (per 1000 inhabitants)	59.0	49.4	49.1	40.0
Deaths	24 258	25 368	28 277	30 842
Death rate (per 1000 inhabitants)	3.5	3.6	3.8	4.1
Natural increase (%)		32.8		
Infant deaths	4 557	4 800	5 165	5 299
Infant mortality rate (per 1000 live births)	11.2	23.6	11.2	15.3
Deaths, 1–4 years	3 549	3 750	4 032	4 964
Maternal deaths	33	57	58	45
Maternal mortality rate (per 1000 live births)	0.02	0.03	0.03	0.01
Death rate. 1–4 years (per 1000 population at risk)	8.7	10.7	11.2	11.5

and urinary diseases (368), and diseases of the endocrine glands and nutritional and metabolic diseases (252).

The communicable diseases most frequently reported in 1976 were: mumps (3319), and cholera (1459), pulmonary tuberculosis (1187), chickenpox (1108), measles (1054), typhoid and paratyphoid fevers (783), hepatitis (564), meningitis and meningococcal infections (143—tubercular meningitis, 13), malaria (158), leishmaniasis (158), tetanus (120), puerperal fever (66), poliomyelitis (20), scarlet fever (18), encephalitis (12), schistosomiasis (10), rabies (8), rubella (4), leprosy (2).

Organization of the public health services

The Ministry of Health is responsible for the preventive and therapeutic health services, while the Ministry of Higher Education is responsible for a certain number of teaching hospitals. The central directorate of the Ministry of Health is subdivided into 10 departments. These are responsible for preventive medicine, medical services, pharmaceuticals, laboratory services, research, planning, and various specializations.

There are 14 provinces (*mohafazats*), each divided into regions. A provincial director is responsible for the health services provided by all the health institutions of a province.

Health resources

Health institutions

In 1976 there were 111 hospitals, with 7626 beds, including 35 governmental hospitals with 6071 beds—equivalent to about one bed per 1000 inhabitants—distributed as follows:

Category	Number	Number of beds
General	27	4 241
Surgical	51	1 260
Obstetrics and gynaecology	20	375
Infectious diseases	2	113
Tuberculosis	3	580
Leprosy	1	209
Ophthalmology	2	28
Psychiatry	2	660
Ear, nose and throat	2	150

There were 296 dispensaries and health centres.

There are three medical faculties, three dental schools, three pharmaceutical schools, 11 nursing schools, three schools of midwifery, and four schools for assistant nurses. There is also a training school in Damascus for medical technicians.

In 1978, two other institutes were inaugurated, at Homs and Deir-ez-Zor.

Manpower

In 1976 there were 2824 doctors (one to 2690 inhabitants), 822 dentists (one to 9241), 1277 pharmacists (one to 5948), 918 qualified midwives (one to 4361), and 1513 qualified nurses (one to 4961).

Preventive services

The important aspects of the preventive services receiving greatest emphasis are maternal and infant care and family planning, vaccination programmes, environmental health, and health education.

Maternal and infant care and family planning

The centres provide services for children and pregnant mothers, and organize periodic training courses for their staff in order to improve the standard of the services offered. The centres also coordinate seminars with the Ministry of Higher Education, the responsible medical faculties of the country's universities, with a view to introducing courses on family care and planning into the medical curriculum.

Communicable diseases

The main endemic and infectious diseases are: intestinal infections—bacterial dysentery, typhoid and paratyphoid fevers—malaria, tuberculosis, schistosomiasis, diphtheria, pertussis, measles, tetanus, and poliomyelitis. Cholera epidemics have recurred during the past few years, the last in 1977.

In cooperation with the other governmental authorities responsible, the Ministry of Health provides drinking-water for a large number of people. The Ministry also ensures the general disposal of liquid sewage. However, since it will be a long time before the sanitation policy is fully successful, it continues to pursue the course of health education and preventive immunization—for example, against poliomyelitis and typhoid fever—for a certain number of social groups exposed to these diseases. At the same time, with the help of UNICEF, the Ministries of Health and of Higher Education have been able to train hospital staff in rehydration techniques, and have provided the necessary equipment to treat children suffering from dehydration, thus reducing infant mortality due to that condition caused by intestinal infections.

In recent years a negative trend has been recorded in the incidence of malaria. Malaria is still actively spreading among inhabitants in the North, and there is significant danger of a major outbreak. The Ministry of Health has consulted experts from WHO in order to draw up an interim plan for 1978 in the hope of halting the spread of malaria. This interim plan was only a stop-gap until a three-year general plan, starting in 1978, could be prepared.

The campaign against tuberculosis has continued normally, the most important weapon against it being BCG vaccination, which it is planned to extend to the majority of children during the five years of the national immunization programme. Statistics of recent years have shown that the number of recorded cases of tuberculosis has remained constant. It is hoped that the number will be further reduced in the coming years.

The campaign against schistosomiasis has continued along the lines laid down in the plan elaborated in conjunction with WHO. These plans cover all the northern and eastern provinces: Deir-ez-Zor, El Haseka and Ba'quba. All areas of infection are to be isolated to prevent the disease from developing further.

Immunization programmes

With help from the WHO and UNICEF the Ministry of Health has been engaged in a national immunization campaign against tuberculosis, diphtheria, pertussis, tetanus, measles, poliomyelitis and smallpox.

In close cooperation with the Ministry of Education, the Ministry of Health has been carrying out another programme for the vaccination of all primary schoolchildren in their first and second years of schooling. These include immunization against smallpox, tuberculosis, poliomyelitis, diphtheria and tetanus. The programme covers about 90% of all schoolchildren in each year and is considered to be one of the most successful of the Government's projects.

The vaccinations given in health centres run by the Ministry of Health are: smallpox (61 456 in 1976), poliomyelitis (181 350), BCG (42 940), measles (55 433).

Environmental health services

In cooperation with the Ministry of Housing and Services on the one hand, and the directorate for water pollution control of the Ministry of Public Works on the other, the Ministry of Health is running several projects through its environmental health services to combat water pollution. These involve the periodic testing of water samples taken by investigation teams from all the water supply systems. The Ministry of Health's central and provisional laboratories analyse the samples in order to ensure the water's fitness for drinking.

Health education

The Department of Health Education prepares various programmes designed to supply the public with the necessary health information to encourage it to modify behaviour and traditions and observe hygiene requirements. The information is publicized through conferences, meetings, and televised interviews, and further reduction of 55 000, will probably be achieved notices and patrols.

Outlook

The fourth five-year plan aims at providing means of prevention and treatment for all citizens by increasing the number of hospital beds throughout the country. In this way it is hoped that it will be possible to provide:

- one bed to 600 inhabitants towards the end of the period;
- balanced distribution among the provinces of health institutions and specialized departments.
- a complete network of health services through health centres.
- gradual application of the principle of health insurance;
- training of the technical staff indispensable for the smooth running of existing health institutions, as well as of institutions to be built in the future. This will depend on the Ministry of Health's undertaking to train auxiliary technical staff, nurses, and midwives, building new schools and enlarging the existing ones.

TUNISIA

Health status

In recent years, there has been a marked improvement in the health status of the population. Life expectancy at birth is much the same for women as for men, since women's health is closely linked with the high fertility rate and childbirth-related problems. It rose from 47 years in the early 1950s to 52 years in 1965 and 57 years in 1975. The progress is attributable to:

– the reduction of overall morbidity and mortality (the gross mortality rate decreased from 14.1% in 1965 to 10% in 1976);
– the decrease in the incidence of endemic diseases due to communicable disease control campaigns and a marked improvement in sanitary conditions;
– the consolidation of the structures for preventive and curative health care, as shown by an increase in hospital beds and improved ratios of medical and auxiliary health personnel to population;
– the rapid growth of State expenditure on health and the improvement of health conditions (the operating budget of the Ministry of Public Health rose from 16.105 million dinars in 1972 to 31.259 million in 1976, and the equipment budget rose from 2.245 million dinars to 7.829 million, including expenditure on family planning).

However, despite the progress achieved, the health care system is still impaired by several inadequacies. The health care delivery system is still much more oriented towards cure than prevention.

The uneven distribution of health care services and medical and auxiliary personnel throughout the country is still an acute problem; 56.5% of medical personnel are concentrated in Tunis, which has only 17% of the total population. A similar imbalance can be seen in the regional distribution of hospital beds, 5250 (39%) of which are in Tunis. Certain governorates, especially the new ones, still have inadequate health care systems. The governorates of Sidi-bou-Zid, Siciliana and Kasserine, for instance, have 61, 117 and 176 beds respectively, i.e., 2.65% of all existing beds between the three of them. The renewed spread of certain infectious and endemic diseases is one of the major problems facing the public health authorities. Tuberculosis is one of those giving rise to the greatest concern— its incidence is reported to have increased by 50% in some governorates, in particular Mahdia, Monastir and Sousse. The recrudescence of viral hepatitis in 1975, especially in the southern governorates (Gabès and Médenine), seems to be connected with problems of sanitation and environmental health. New or aggravated risks include: traffic and occupational accidents, which are a more acute health problem than ever before, especially from the points of view of prevention and establishment of emergency services and of occupational and road safety services. Expanding industry and tourism, as well as the development of agricultural techniques relying more and more on pesticides, give increasing urgency to the problem of pollution and environmental nuisance control and protection. In all these areas, the results achieved during the 1973–1976 quadrennium will have to be consolidated and improved upon during the period covered by the next Plan.

Action taken during the Fourth Plan

The Fourth Plan allocated 20 million dinars for capital investment in the public health sector, as against 10 million dinars invested during the decade 1962–1971. Actual investment reached about 21 million dinars, of which 1 857 000 was for preventive medicine, 8.2 million for infrastructure, 5.5 million for equipment and almost 6 million for family planning. This total does not include the funds invested by certain public and private bodies (estimated at 5.5 million), investment in hydrotherapy establishments (3.9 million dinars), or funds for rural development programmes (one million dinars). In all, capital investment in the health sector, including hydrotherapy establishments, between 1973 and 1976, amounted to nearly 31.5 million dinars.

The hospital bed/population ratio remained the same throughout the Fourth Plan period at 2.4 beds per 1000 population, although the actual number of beds increased from 12 700 in 1972 to 13 350 at the end of 1975. This slight rise in bed capacity was brought about, for the most part, by the extension of certain existing hospitals. However, the funds allocated under the Fourth Plan enabled a start to be made on the construction of three university hospital centres (Tunis-Thameur, Sousse and Sfax); four regional hospitals (Médenine, Gabès, Mahdia and Jendouba), and five auxiliary hospitals (Djerba, Nefta, Ras-el-Djebel, Moknine and Menzel-Temine). The family planning programme includes, in addition, the construction of 29 new maternal and child health/family planning centres, scheduled to become operational at the end of 1976, the reorganization and equipment of 71 existing centres of this type, as well as the construction of two rural maternity hospitals at El-Hamma and Mareth, and four urban maternity hospitals with 510 beds at Tunis, Bizerta, Sousse and Sfax.

Apart from the new maternal and child health/family planning centres, almost all these projected facilities will become operational during the Fifth Plan. They will increase the number of beds to about 17 000 in 1981 and raise the bed/population ratio to 2.7 per 1000.

Communicable disease control

The activities carried out under the Fourth Plan met with varying degrees of success. In the case of cholera, after the 1973 recrudescence, 1974 and 1975 were almost totally cholera-free owing to sanitation activities and mass vaccination of persons at risk (4 481 000 vaccinations in 1973; 1 875 000 in 1974 and 1 861 681 in 1975). Malaria and schistosomiasis are in process of eradication. Six malaria cases were reported in 1973, four in 1974 and 28 in 1975. Whereas continued surveillance is all that is required for these diseases, more energetic measures are needed for some others. During the Fourth Plan there was a marked resurgence of tuberculosis; incidence is thought to have increased by 50% in some governorates, such as Monastir, Mahdia and Sousse, making for renewed infectivity, especially among adolescents and adults. This situation clearly shows one of the shortcomings of the Fourth Plan that the Fifth Plan will have to make good.

Health manpower

Some of the major achievements of the 1973–1976 quadrennium in the field of professional manpower development included the establish-

ment, under the Fourth Plan, of two new medical schools—at Sousse and Sfax a faculty of pharmacy and a school of dental surgery at Monastir, as well as the extension of some public health administration schools, including the *Ecole Avicenne* in Tunis.

The number of medical students increased from 977 in the academic year 1972/73 to 2079 in 1975/76, so that, with the return of the young doctors trained abroad, the total number of doctors rose from 847 in 1972 to 1215 in 1976. The number of Tunisian doctors increased from 405 in 1972 to 686 on 1 January 1976, 340 intern and resident trainees not included. Thus the doctor/population ratio rose from one doctor to 6250 inhabitants to one to 4700 over that period (for Tunisian doctors the ratio rose from one to 13 000 to one to 8300).

As regards auxiliary personnel, the total number of students training in public health administration schools increased overall during recent years, as follows:

	Students
1972/73	1 366
1973/74	1 339
1974/75	1 661
1975/76	1 975

Over a similar period, the number of graduates showed the following pattern:

	1973	1974	1975
Specialized auxiliaries	258	456	494
Senior auxiliaries (including midwives)	135(43)	260(44)	243(58)
Other health auxiliaries	248	223	248
Total	641	949	985

The larger number of graduates made it possible, to improve the ratio of auxiliary personnel to population from 1.2 per 1000 in 1972 to 1.35 at the end of 1975 and, at the same time, to obtain a better auxiliary personnel staffing structure as shown in the following table of statistics from the public health administration staffing survey of 31 December 1972 and the regional survey of April 1976 by the Ministry of the Plan:

	1972	1976
Specialized auxiliaries	34.3%	34.2%
Senior auxiliaries	6.7%	17.4%
Other public health auxiliaries	59.0%	48.4%

Under the Fourth Plan the senior technician training currently offered by the Tunis and Sousse schools of medicine was also improved.

The specialties now offered include physio-therapy, biochemistry, anaesthesiology and environmental sanitation. The numbers of students in training were 142 (70 male and 72 female) in 1974/75, and 269 (139 male and 130 female) in 1975/76.

As regards the allied professions, the number of dental surgeons rose from 70 in 1972 to 130 in 1976, while some 160 Tunisian pharmacists returned from their studies abroad during the quadrennium.

Family planning

Where family planning is concerned, after the 1973 shortfall in the achievement of demographic objectives, 1974, 1975 and 1976 saw more rapid progress. The consolidation of administrative structures and intervention techniques (the establishment of the National Family Planning and Population Bureau in March 1973), the liberalization of abortion in September of the same year and the development of the first contact and human resources infrastructure brought about a marked increase in the practice of contraception. The reduction in the expected number of births specifically attributable to the family planning programme went from 15 000 in 1972 to 17 000 in 1973 and 29 000 in 1975. The target set by the Fifth Plan, i.e. a reduction of 55 000, will probably be achieved before that date.

In 1975 the gross birth rate stood at 36% as against 37% in 1971 and 45% in 1964. The overall fertility rate decreased from 162% in 1971 to 147.7% in 1975, an annual decrease of 3.57 births per 1000 women of childbearing age.

In the area of drug supplies, the moderate pricing policy for supplies to the public was maintained under the Fourth Plan, as also the establishment of new pharmacies in rural areas (80 are already open) in application of the policy of bringing the drugs to the patients; existing pharmacies are sold as private enterprises. Between 1972 and 1975, 34 pharmacies were sold to young pharmacists.

During the Fourth Plan, national drug production was as follows:

	Value (in dinars)
1972	1 442 000
1973	1 560 000
1974	1 613 000
1975	1 613 000
1976	1 090 000

Although this production, in volume, repres-ents almost 55% of current hospital consumption, it accounts for only 15% of current private consumption. In value, it amounts to less than 15% of total drug sales, mainly because of the price-freeze on drugs since 1968.

In view of the relative stagnation in hospital consumption of drugs in recent years, the Central Pharmacy is concentrating its production activities on better coverage of national needs in the private sector, broadening its range of current products and manufacturing more drugs under licence.

In 1975 national drug consumption came to almost 15 million dinars. The 1975 consumer expenditure survey showed that the average annual per capita expenditure on drugs amounted to 2.205 dinars in 1975 compared with 0.539 dinars in 1966. As national production accounted for less than 15% of drug sales in terms of value, drug imports rose by 15% in 1973, 17% in 1974 and 20% in 1975, placing a heavy burden on the balance of payments.

This increase in drug consumption seems to be due to the rise in national income, the increase in the number of mutual benefit societies and group insurances, the opening of new medical practices in the cities and the increase in self-medication. While it certainly reflects a growing will to combat disease among the population, some drug abuse cannot be excluded; this calls for better education of patients and those who prescribe for them.

Action during the Fifth Plan (1977–1981)

The Fifth Plan sets three main objectives for the health sector:

(1) *Development of preventive activities*

Analysis of the results of the Fourth Plan showed the need for strengthening and better organizing the control of communicable diseases, some of which have shown a considerable recrudescence. The measures to be taken during the Fifth Plan will be mainly along the following lines:

The central departments of preventive and of social medicine will have to be restructured and their fields of activity redefined. They will be progressively freed from executive duties in order to concentrate on the development of a preventive policy, the drafting of new legislation on prevention and the centralization of all information on preventive activities. They will also act as technical support bodies for the proposed interministerial committee on prevention that is to ensure better coordination in this sector. The implementation of preventive policy will be decentralized and entrusted to the regional health centres, which will be responsible in future for all the general and specific preventive activities (school medicine and industrial medicine) of the Ministry of Health. The intention is gradually to transform rural and urban district dispensaries into basic preventive health care centres in order to avoid the development of a hiatus between preventive activities and the health care system. This integration of activities is the best way of incorporating preventive activities in a permanent framework permitting the more sustained and better integrated approach that should gradually take the place of mass campaigns.

These measures make an increase in the preventive health services' financial and human resources a priority requirement. The magnitude of medical and auxiliary personnel requirements itself confirms the need for the introduction or development of preventive health in study programmes for these personnel, since current study programmes do not seem to promote awareness of their role. The establishment of departments of preventive and of social medicine in the university hospital centres will provide confirmation of the privileged place and the important role of prevention in the health care system.

In financial terms, the share of preventive medicine in the total public health budget will have to be increased to 15%.

(2) *Better control over health expenditure and improvement of its effectiveness*

The first steps towards ultimate rationalization of health expenditure are the optimal utilization of the existing infrastructure and equipment and better control over consumption of health care, including drugs.

Optimal utilization of the existing infrastructure. Achieving this, especially in the case of auxiliary hospitals and dispensaries involves improving their equipment and providing them with more numerous medical and auxiliary health personnel. Measures to be taken include improving the equipment and staffing of the regional hospitals, which will gradually be provided with speciality and outpatient consultation services, thus increasing the speed and effectiveness of their action. Except where construction is already under way, no new auxiliary hospitals will be built and the existing ones will be gradually reoriented towards preventive activities and better coverage for their areas. Side by side with the strengthening of regional hospitals, the Fifth Plan includes an increase in the number of ambulances and mobile clinics, to meet the needs of the rural population. As the Fourth Plan already explicitly acknowledged, the effectiveness and quality of health services is judged less by the bed/population ratio than by the technical equipment and expertise, efficiency and speed of action of the basic health networks.

The greatly increased first-contact capacity that will be achieved during the Fifth Plan will make it necessary to train enough medical and auxiliary personnel. The 1220 doctors who will be trained in Tunisia between 1976 and 1981 will make it possible to ensure the better distribution of personnel among regions and specialties that will result in better utilization of this capacity. Requirements for auxiliary staff have been estimated at nearly 5500, not including replacement of personnel currently in service (retirements, departures and deaths). The output of the public health administration schools is estimated at 6791 graduates during the Fifth Plan. Where hospitals are concerned, the Fifth Plan will earmark 5 million dinars for equipment and 2.5 million for the maintenance of existing buildings and equipment, for which there will be special technician training courses.

The inadequate funding of public health care establishments (which has remained unchanged for the past few years at about 2.3 million dinars per annum) and the limits of the current nomenclature seem to have hampered the smooth running of hospitals and dispensaries during the Fourth Plan. The revision of the nomenclature currently under consideration and the increase expected in the funds set aside for hospital drug supplies should bring about an improvement in this area during the Fifth Plan.

Health care establishment charges for fee-paying patients will have to be increased in accordance with the increase in the cost of hospitalization per day if the cost/benefit ratio of these establishments is to improve. Current charges entail the State's assuming part of the expenses which should be discharged in full by paying patients and their insurances (occupational accident schemes and mutual benefit societies, etc.).

Better control of health care consumption, including drugs. Comparison of the results of the 1966 and 1975 consumer expenditure surveys shows that the average annual per capita expenditure under the heading "hygiene and health care" rose during that period from 3.098 dinars to 8.042, an increase of 160% at current prices. This represented 4.3% of total expenditure in 1966, rising to 5.6% in 1975.

By comparison with 1966, national drug expenditure has increased almost three-fold. Although this reflects a concern for better health, some abuses of drug consumption and self-medication extremely dangerous to health cannot be excluded. During the Fifth Plan solutions to this problem will be sought in the better education of patients and those who prescribe for them, the increase of national pharmaceutical production and restriction of imports, and the elimination of the most expensive products when there is an acceptable and less expensive substitute.

(3) *Improved regional distribution of public health care services*

Activities aimed at improving the infrastructure and quality of care in the least favoured regions during the Fifth Plan will include:

– intensification of the training of medical and auxiliary personnel for and overall improvement in the doctor/population ratio and a better balance between regions and activities;

– establishment by 1981 of three health service centres to cover the north, south and centred regions;

– development of integrated family health care in the rural areas by the establishment of small health centres combining maternal and child health/family planning activities with health care and the preventive activities of the dispensaries (close coordination will be sought between health programmes undertaken in the course of rural development, Ministry of Health programmes and those of the Family Planning Bureau, in order to foster the installation of facilities for the same area in the same place and progress towards integrated medicine).

– the activities carried out in the Nabeul governorate during the Fourth Plan will gradually be extended to other regions (multipurpose mobile clinics and teams will have to be encouraged in order to extend preventive and diagnostic activities, as well as health care, to scattered populations);

– finally, in order to bring drugs to the patient, the Fifth Plan will maintain a moderate public price policy, and the establishment of pharmacies in isolated areas will continue.

UNITED ARAB EMIRATES

The Federal Ministry of Health assumed its functions as from April 1973. The health facilities and health manpower have made great progress since that date and are still working to assure the highest standard and availability of health services to the community.

Major health and health-related problems

One of the major health problems is the recruitment of health manpower—mainly nursing and technical staff—for whom the country still depends mainly on expatriates. The second health problem is that of occupational health hazards and health hazards due to the vast amount of construction, agriculture and industry, depending mainly on expatriate labour.

Health policy

The main aims are to provide one doctor for every 600 people, one hospital bed for 200 people and one qualified nurse for two beds.

Health legislation

A number of health acts were issued concerning the organization of the Ministry of Health; the registration of births and deaths; the practice of medicine, licencing and registration of physicians; laboratories, clinics, and private hospitals; duties and responsibilities of physicians; registration of drugs; drug distribution and private pharmacies.

Many other health acts covering communicable disease control, occupational health and environmental sanitation were in preparation.

Health planning and programming

The health plan of the Ministry aims at providing coverage by preventive and curative facilities free of charge to the whole population.

Organization of health services

The health services are organized to cover all aspects through departments for preventive medicine, curative medicine, pharmacies and planning and research.

Biomedical and health services research

In the national plan it is proposed to start medical research at the Faculty of Medicine to be established in the early 1980s. Some research is carried out on specific medical problems such as nutrition and accidents.

Education and training of health manpower

There is no formal education of health manpower, but in-service training of staff is carried out regularly. One nursing school has been functioning for four years, and another is due to open in 1979.

Health resources

Health establishments

The available health establishments are general hospitals, and specialized hospitals mainly for gynaecology and obstetrics and for chest diseases. The total beds available number 2200. There are a good number of outpatient clinics, both general and specialized, and 8 maternal and child health centres, 8 preventive medicine centres, and 8 central school health clinics.

Production and sale of pharmaceuticals

The Government imports the majority of the required pharmaceuticals from different sources, and the private sales distribution is under the control of the Ministry of Health. There is a registration section in the Ministry for approval of drugs and control of their distribution on the private market.

Health expenditure

The health services are free of charge for all the population. The total budget for the Ministry of Health for 1978 was about 800 million dirhams.

Appraisal of progress between 1973 and 1977

Clear progress is noted in the quality of health services: health manpower increased fourfold; the total number of hospital beds increased fourfold; that of central and rural clinics increased fivefold and a good coverage was assured in remote areas; 8 maternal and child health centres and 8 central school health clinics were established, and the number of preventive medicine centres was increased from 2 to 8.

Outlook

It is planned to establish health centres according to optimal geographical distribution in the next five years in order to offer health services throughout the country. The plan includes: comprehensive programmes for training staff, including in-service training, mainly for the local staff; health education programmes; research programmes for the identification of major health problems, including especially nutrition, parasitic diseases, infectious diseases, accidents, and noncommunicable diseases, particularly heart diseases and dental conditions; establishment of hospitals for maternity, psychiatry, and chest diseases and other specializations; establishment of facilities for deep X-ray therapy, nuclear medicine and more developed curative services; a rehabilitation programme, and educational programmes (establishment of the Faculty of Medicine and strengthening of nursing schools and nursing education).

WESTERN PACIFIC REGION

AMERICAN SAMOA

Major health and health-related problems and action taken or planned

Infantile gastroenteritis and diarrhoea were identified as high priority problems in 1976 and a special plan was developed by the Office of Comprehensive Health Planning, containing goals, objectives and an action strategy. As a result a special project was initiated under the maternal and child health programme of the Public Health Department in 1976. Other action taken included: the drilling of 12 wells to provide safer drinking water; a stepped-up programme of water quality monitoring; ongoing medical education for the improved management of dehydrated infants; and increased emphasis by the Health Education Section on informing the public about the importance of sanitary preparation of infant foods and utensils and improved household sanitation, and public notification of contaminated water sources, with recommendations to boil water from those sources.

The amount of resources contributed directly to this effort cannot be determined; however, it is felt to be more a matter of increased emphasis than a massive infusion of additional resources. It is too early to determine the results of the most recent action. However, over the four-year period 1973 to 1976 the problems appeared to be steadily lessening: outpatient infantile gastroenteritis and diarrhoea cases decreased from 330 per 1000 live births in 1973 to 196 per 1000 in 1976; hospital discharges increased slightly from 116 to 128 per 1000 live births; and mortality decreased from 4.8 to 0.9 per 1000 live births.

The five-year objectives listed in the Plan for Health are: to reduce the infant gastroenteritis and diarrhoea mortality rate to 1.7 per 1000 live births, or less, by January 1983; to reduce the hospital discharge rate to 95 per 1000 live births, or less, by January 1983; and to reduce the reported incidence of infantile gastroenteritis and diarrhoea to 245 cases per 1000 live births, or less by January 1983.

Infectious hepatitis has been identified as a high priority problem in the Plan of Health. There were 45 new cases per 100 000 population in 1973, 83 in 1974, 149 in 1975, and 47 in 1976. Action taken to improve the quality of

drinking water should also have an impact on the situation, but the new case rate does not indicate any general trend in reducing the seriousness of the problem. The five-year objective is to reduce the incidence of infectious hepatitis to 60 per 100 000 population, or less, by January 1983.

Heart disease is the leading cause of death. A territory-wide survey in 1975–1976 showed over 1000 persons aged 35 years or over in an estimated population of 29 000 to have high blood pressure. A hypertension detection, treatment and follow-up programme was initiated in 1976. No new personnel or training element has been included in the programme. Patients discovered by the survey are being referred on a scheduled basis to the hypertension clinic. Over the last three years health education has been emphasizing heart disease and its relationship to lack of exercise, obesity, and smoking. An emergency medical services plan was developed in 1976 which, when implemented, should improve the capability to respond to emergencies, including heart attack and stroke. Five-year objectives given in the Plan for Health are: to reduce the mortality rate for heart disease for persons aged 35 years or over from 400 to 360 per 100 000, or less, by January 1983; and to reduce the heart disease hospital discharge rate from 14.2 per 1000 discharges in 1973 to 12 per 1000, or less, by January 1983.

Similar action has been taken with regard to *cerebrovascular disease.* The five-year objective given in the Plan for Health is to reduce the mortality rate for cerebrovascular disease from 51 to 44 per 100 000 population, or less, by January 1983.

Diabetes mellitus has been recognized as a high priority problem for several years, but no direct action has been taken to reduce it. The Plan for Health recommends that a special diabetes detection and control programme be started as soon as possible. The five-year objective is to reduce the mortality rate for diabetes as a direct or contributing cause of death from 16 to 10 per 100 000 population, or less, by January 1983.

Accidental and intentional trauma are leading causes of death and disability. Steps taken to reduce this problem are the Highway Safety Plan developed in 1976, the Emergency Medical

Services Plan developed in 1976, the Disaster Plan developed in 1977, the Child Abuse and Neglect Act passed in 1977, the Child Abuse Programme started in 1977, the Emergency Medical Services Programme started in 1976 with funding of US $50 000 per year, the training of 12 health staff in emergency medical technology in 1977, health education directed at reducing home and village accidents, and the purchase of a new ambulance. As a result annual deaths from car accidents fell by 29% between 1973 and 1976, the number of reported car accidents fell by 30% in the same period, the number of hospitalizations following car accidents fell by 17%, and between 1974 and 1976 the number of outpatient visits following car accidents fell by 12%.

The objective given in the Plan for Health is to reduce the accident mortality rate from 49.7 to 38 per 100 000 population, or less, by January 1983.

Manpower development

Suitable high-school graduates are being encouraged to continue their education to become physicians, nurses, physical therapists, and laboratory and X-ray technicians. Scholarships are made available for qualified individuals. In addition to physicians and nurses the Public Health Department has 14 sanitarians.

Health care delivery and costs

Health care is provided at the Lyndon B. Johnson Tropical Medical Center and by the Public Health Department, with two outlying dispensaries on the island of Tutuila, one on Aunu'u and four on the three-island Manu'a group. The Center consists of a 181-bed hospital (including 36 bassinettes) with wards for paediatrics, internal medicine, surgery, and gynaecology and obstetrics. There are two major operating rooms, two delivery rooms, nursery, intensive care unit, clinical laboratory, X-ray and physical therapy departments, pharmacy and outpatient clinics for surgery, internal medicine, paediatrics, ophthalmology, ear, nose and throat, dentistry, family practice, mental health and emergencies.

The hospital has a general surgeon, an internist, three paediatricians, one ophthalmologist, one gynaecologist/obstetrician, one anaesthesiologist, one nurse anaesthetist, three family medical practitioners and 17 American Samoan physicians who received their medical education at the Medical School in Suva, Fiji.

The Public Health Department has viable programmes for maternal and child health and crippled children, control of contagious diseases, venereal diseases, filariasis control, mental health, and a public health laboratory for monitoring water samples.

With inflation and the provision of increased services, the cost of medical care increased by an estimated average of 10% a year from 1973 to 1977.

Appraisal of progress made between 1973 and 1977

There has been a significant improvement in major health parameters over the period under review. The infant mortality rate dropped from 25.7 per 1000 live births for 1972–1974 to 19.0 per 1000 live births for 1975–1977. The estimated population in 1975 was 29 000. The neonatal mortality rate dropped from 14.6 per 1000 live births for 1972–1974 to 9.9 per 1000 live births for 1975–1977. The crude death rate for 1972–1974 was 5.5 per 1000 population. The rate for 1975–1977 was 4.3 per 1000 population. Deaths occurring at 50 years of age or later accounted for 49.1% of all deaths in the period 1972–1974 and for 52.4% in 1974–1976.

Considerable progress was made between 1973 and 1977 in the number of children aged 1–5 years immunized against contagious diseases, in the detection and treatment of cases of pulmonary tuberculosis, hypertension and microfilaria, and in mosquito control. Prophylactic dental services were expanded.

Outlook

Goals for the next five to ten years are:
(1) to train additional national personnel to be physicians, nurses and sanitarians, and for other paramedical positions;
(2) to install two artificial kidney machines (funding has been obtained and the project will be accomplished by the end of 1978);
(3) to provide full-time physician services for the Manu'a islands (project started in January 1978);
(4) to add the following additional specialists

to the Lyndon B. Johnson Medical Center staff: an additional general surgeon, an orthopaedic surgeon, two internists, one for cardiovascular diseases and one for gastroenterology one paediatrician, two family medical practitioners, a full-time optometrist, and 20 registered nurses (a full-time pathologist joined the staff in March 1978);

(5) to provide for additional educational meetings and seminars for medical staff members;

(6) to improve the family planning programme;

(7) to improve dental prophylaxis; and

(8) to pursue with vigour improvement of sanitation and water supply.

AUSTRALIA

Major health and health-related problems

During the period under review there were significant structural changes and developments in the delivery of health care in Australia and broader social and economic issues have become more prominent in the strategies to improve health. A major change in the financing of health care occurred with the introduction of compulsory universal health insurance, so that financial barriers to necessary access to care are removed. Escalating costs of health care, and the need for effective and efficient management of resources so as to promote and restore health are major issues. Health expenditure has grown from \$A 1922 million (5.9% of the gross domestic product) in 1970–1971 to a preliminary estimate of \$A 6254 million (7.7% of the gross domestic product (GDP) in 1976–1977). Important factors in this increase are the changing patterns of disease and the increase in health personnel costs. The demand for medical, pharmaceutical and hospital services, often involving highly expensive sophisticated technologies, has to be weighed against demands for other preventive and social expenditures that have as significant effects upon health status.

There is an increased awareness that a system of acquiring and communicating information about the people who are most in need and most at risk must be built into the health service structure. Those at risk include the poor, the near poor, the aged and infirm, culturally deprived minorities such as Aboriginals and some migrants who are poor and do not understand how to use health systems, the handicapped (both physically and mentally), and those who lack access to services in the outskirts of large cities and in remote rural areas. It is also recognized that a large amount of disease and disability, including that due to emotional disorder and social malfunctioning, can be prevented. As in other developed countries, there is a high incidence of chronic disability that could be reduced by preventive measures requiring more active responsibility by the individual. Preventable conditions that have a behavioural base relate to the use of alcohol (including social violence relating to road and other accidental deaths), use of drugs (prescribed, nonprescribed and illegal), ischaemic heart disease and chronic bronchitis. There is a high prevalence of psychosocial malfunctioning, which is reflected in interpersonal and marital breakdown, child abuse, alcoholism, accidents, venereal disease and illicit drug-taking. Health surveillance and preventive programmes, including health education, are being investigated and developed in an attempt to influence behaviour that is harmful to health. There is increasing recognition of the need to give strong emphasis to concepts of prevention and early rehabilitation in the education and training of all health professionals. Diversified means of providing a wide range of medical and health services in the community or work place have been developed under the community health programme. There is also an acceptance of the need to provide occupational health services at work. In the rehabilitation field there is a need to rationalize services in facilities such as hospitals and rehabilitation units on a regional basis. Rural areas suffer on account of the comparative lack of health personnel willing to work there and the need to upgrade communication facilities.

Although there is no formal or specific health plan at the present time, the emphasis in the coming decade will be on the financing of activities concerned with the prevention of illness and disability, and with early rehabilitation

	1972	1973	1974	1975
Mean population	12 922 241	13 168 454	13 777 459	13 539 716
Number of live births	264 969	247 670	245 177	233 012
Birth rate (per 1000 population)	20.4	18.8	18.3	17.2
Number of deaths	109 760	110 822	115 833	109 021
Death rate (per 1000 population)	8.5	8.4	8.7	8.1
Natural increase (%)	1.19	1.04	0.94	0.92
Number of infant deaths	4 430	4 085	3 958	3 325
Infant mortality rate (per				
1000 live births)	16.7	16.5	16.2	14.3
Number of deaths, 1–4 years	883	882	865	779
Death rate, 1–4 years (per				
1000 population at risk)	0.9	0.9	0.8	0.8
Number of maternal deaths	33	28	28	13
Maternal mortality rate (per				
1000 live births)	0.1	0.1	0.1	0.1

where illness and injury are inevitable. Community support and voluntary initiatives will be stressed. Focus on the identification of those whose health is particularly at risk, and the development of services tailored to their particular needs will be emphasized. As a first stage, existing services will be studied and evaluated to determine their accessibility and utilization in sufficient detail to plan and cost steps to overcome the areas of comparative neglect, and as a basis for planning demonstration and evaluation projects designed to incorporate proposals for the relief of these areas of neglect. The operation of health insurance arrangements and other methods of financing, organizing and managing health services will be carefully studied in a bid to ensure equity for the health consumer and the best value in the face of limited resources.

In 1975 ischaemic heart disease caused 30.02% of all deaths in that year, or 241.7 deaths per 100 000 mean population. In 1975, 48.9 deaths per 100 000 mean population were due to malignant neoplasms of the digestive organs and peritoneum. The number of deaths from malignant neoplasms of the trachea, bronchus or lung (lung cancer) continues to rise and accounted for 3.67% of all deaths in 1975. Mortality from these chronic and degenerative diseases in 1971–1975 is shown in the table below. The number of cases is in each case

followed by the rate per 100 000 population (mean population in the first two, total population for the last).

Organization of health services

Australia is comprised of six states and two mainland territories. The system of government is based on the federation (or Commonwealth) of the six states. At the government or public level, responsibility for health care is shared between the Federal Government, six state governments and one territorial government. A second territorial government is being created in 1978.

At the national level, health services are controlled by the Federal Government located in Canberra, which appoints a Federal Minister for Health, who exercises political control of the Federal Department of Health, headed by a Director-General. The Federal Department of Health has functional divisions for medical insurance services, hospital insurance, nursing, national health and medical research, medical services, health services, policy and planning, therapeutics, public health, quarantine, national biological standards laboratory, and management services (internal). The Department directly administers 14 pathology laboratories in various parts of the country, and certain

	1971	1972	1973	1974	2975
Ischaemic heart disease	33 572 (262.7)	33 156 (255.2)	32 988 (250.5)	34 629 (258.9)	32 731 (241.7)
Malignant neoplasm of digestive					
organs and peritoneum	6 004 (47.0)	6 167 (47.5)	6 319 (48.0)	6 467 (48.3)	6 623 (48.9)
Malignant neoplasm of the					
trachea, bronchus or lung . . .	3 406 (26.7)	3 474 (26.8)	3 643 (27.7)	3 865 (28.9)	4 002 (29.1)

laboratories for special purposes, e.g., radiation, acoustics, ultrasonics. The School of Public Health and Tropical Medicine, the Institute of Child Health, and the Institute of Anatomy are also controlled by this Department. The Federal Department of Health has offices in each state and in the Northern Territory it is charged with certain duties that in the states are carried out by the state health authorities. It is also represented overseas. The Australian Capital Territory, the other mainland territory, has a Capital Territory Health Commission, which commenced operation on 1 July 1975. The Federal Government is responsible for national aspects of health, such as quarantine, health insurance, provision of financial support to the states and selected providers of care for a number of health activities through legislation, such as the National Health Act, the Nursing Homes Assistance Act, and the Health Insurance Act.

The direct provision of health services is the responsibility of the state governments. Each state has a Minister of Health who is responsible to his state government for the administration of that state's health authorities. The trend is towards a unified health commission responsible for all aspects of health, organized on a regional basis. In the states of New South Wales, South Australia and Victoria, health commissions have come into existence, replacing hitherto divided areas of responsibility in health care in those states.

A significant proportion of health care delivery in Australia is provided on other than a governmental basis. Health care is also delivered by local government, semigovernmental agencies, private professional practitioners, voluntary agencies, and profit-making nongovernmental organizations.

Hospitals

In 1977 Australia had 2369 hospitals and nursing homes, providing 177 017 beds (or 12.6 per 1000 population), including 78 mental institutions which in 1972 had 28 861 beds.

The state governments have traditionally met the cost of hospital building and renovation programmes. However, in 1974 a hospitals and health services commission was established by the Federal Government with the role of ascertaining the health care needs of the community, providing the planning and delivery of adequate health services, and making grants for health care and related research. The commission de-veloped three new funding programmes to promote improved community health services, national hospital development and more effective health services research and planning.

In 1975–1976, with the major trends of the programmes established, it was recognized that the states should assume more responsibility for them. The consequent moves to reduce Federal involvement have minimized duplication of administrative overlap while maintaining joint Commonwealth/state consultation and collaboration.

Communicable disease control

The continued growth of air travel has meant that the risk of importing diseases into Australia has not abated. Outbreaks of certain "quarantinable" diseases included several outbreaks of typhoid fever which occurred in 1976 and 1977. It has been found that food handlers are particularly liable to contaminate prepared meals served on aircraft with typhoid (and other) organisms. Increased numbers of outbreaks of gastroenteritis also occurred among airline passengers arriving in Australia from overseas. Vaccination against smallpox is no longer recommended for international travel. Lassa fever and Marburg disease have been made "quarantinable" diseases.

Quarantine stations were established many years ago to protect the public by isolating people suffering from various exotic diseases, in particular smallpox. With WHO's smallpox eradication programme nearly complete, and because of the emergence of new viral haemorrhagic diseases that require intensive-care standards of treatment, existing quarantine stations are no longer adequate. Quarantine stations are being progressively closed and a central facility is being set up at Fairfield, Victoria, to which quarantinable cases will be flown from all parts of the country.

The number of cases of malaria continues to increase. Three introduced cases were notified in 1977 as well as 278 imported cases. The Government is concerned about the danger of malaria being re-established. To combat this, vigorous antimalaria measures are being promulgated. There is an increasing number of cases occurring in the southern states amongst people who have travelled from other countries or from northern states. There have been 35–45 new cases registered each year for the years 1975–1977 inclusive.

Gonorrhoea continues to be by far the most common of notifiable communicable diseases; a total of 11 479 cases was notified in 1976, followed by syphilis with 3182 notified cases. South Australia and the Northern Territory recorded increases of over 50% in syphilis notifications due to increased numbers of positive serological tests, mainly in longstanding asymptomatic cases. The third most frequently notified communicable disease was hepatitis A, which increased by approximately 8.5% in 1976 compared to the 1975 figure. However, there continued to be a more significant increase in hepatitis B notifications, with an increase in 1976 of 49% compared to 1975.

Federal Government funding of the nationwide tuberculosis campaign was discontinued from 31 December 1976. However, tuberculosis has not been completely eradicated and control programmes may again be necessary at a future time. A total of 1496 new or reactivated cases was notified during 1976–1977. There were increases in notifications in four states.

Poliomyelitis has ceased to be a problem. Sabin vaccine has been used in the last few years to combat the disease.

Concerted efforts are still being maintained against rubella. Rubella immunization is aimed at women who are of childbearing age and also schoolgirls. The results of the rubella immunization programme have not yet become evident, but should become apparent in the near future.

Medical and public health research

Direct Federal Government support for medical research rose substantially for the financial year 1976–1977—an indication of the importance placed on the need for a sound financial basis for medical research. For 1977 approximately $A 9.2 million were distributed by the National Health and Medical Research Council for the support of research projects, postgraduate and undergraduate scholarships and overseas travelling fellowships, and for the scientific establishments of two research institutes (the Walter and Eliza Hall Institute of Medical Research and the Howard Florey Institute). The role of the Council in research has become more active and directive in certain fields. Special investigations into specific areas of research include rheumatology, allergic diseases, renal diseases, cardiology, and drug evaluation. Council grants make up approximately one-third of the

total identifiable medical research expenditure and enable the Council to exercise a leading influence in the development of research. The largest grant given in 1976–1977 was $A 984 409, made to the Walter and Eliza Hall Institute in Melbourne. The Government also indirectly supports medical research through general grants to universities and special departmental institutions and laboratories. Thus, the John Curtin School of Medical Research in Canberra is entirely supported by grants to the Federal National University. The School of Public Health and Tropical Medicine at the University of Sydney is part of the Federal Department of Health. At this School three areas of research are being developed: health services, health education and preventive medicine, and health surveillance. The Institute of Child Health (the Department of Child Health at the University of Sydney) is also part of the Department of Health and undertakes some research activities.

Other funds for medical research are provided by state governments and a number of nongovernmental organizations such as the Australian Medical Association, the Life Insurance Medical Research Fund of Australia and New Zealand, the National Heart Foundation, the Australian Postgraduate Federation in Medicine, the Children's Medical Research Foundation, and a number of anticancer councils. Additional funds are also provided by private bequests.

Medical and allied health personnel

In December 1976 there were an estimated 21 400 doctors in active practice, which represents a doctor/population ratio of one to 654. Other health personnel in terms of full time equivalents included:

Ambulance officers	3 700
Chiropodists	950
Dentists	4 900
Ancillary dental personnel	7 500
Health surveyors (public health inspectors)	1 900
Medical laboratory personnel	3 900
Professional nurses	95 000
Auxiliary nurses	25 000
Occupational therapists	670
Optometrists	1 000
Ancillary optometrical personnel	2 400
Pharmacists	14 000
Physiotherapists	2 400
Radiographers	1 800
Speech therapists	350

Increasing attention is being given to the development of long-term plans for the supply of individual occupational categories. Plans have been completed for doctors and dentists and work is currently under way on nursing personnel.

Health costs and insurance

In the face of escalating health costs (some 7.67% of gross domestic product was devoted to the health sector in 1976–1977) various initiatives are being taken on quality assurance, utilization review and cost containment. This has obvious implications for the organization and composition of the health work force and particularly for doctors, for whom the feasibility of introducing systems of peer review of professional standards is being explored.

The health insurance programme, Medibank, commenced on 1 July 1975. It is noncontributory, being financed from Government consolidated revenue, and replaced the previous voluntary health insurance arrangements. Medibank provided universal coverage for the benefits available. In relation to medical services it provided cash benefits at the rate of at least 85% of schedule fees with the maximum patient contribution being $A 5 where the schedule fee was charged for the service. The schedule fees are included in the Health Insurance Act (1973) and Regulations. Payment of benefits is the responsibility of the health insurance commission. Australians were able to insure with nonprofitmaking private health insurance organizations for benefits additional to those offered by Medibank, including insurance for the difference between the Medibank medical benefits and the scheduled fee.

Following a comprehensive review of Medibank early in 1976, it was decided to modify operations, with effect from 1 October 1976. Under these modified arrangements, residents are covered automatically for standard Medibank benefits as before, unless they choose to insure themselves for basic medical and basic hospital benefits with a registered nonprofitmaking private health insurance organization, including the government-operated Medibank (Private) organization. Registration of these organizations is governed by a Federal statute, the National Health Act, 1953. Any Australian resident not appropriately privately insured is automatically covered by standard Medibank.

The modifications also provided for a health insurance levy equivalent to 2.5% of personal taxable income, with a maximum levy payment of $A 300 per annum for a family and $A 150 per annum for a person without dependants. Those on the lowest incomes, most pensioners, certain Defence Force personnel and veteran pensioners, and those who choose private health insurance for basic medical and basic hospital benefits, are exempt from the levy. Privately insured persons contribute to health insurance organizations, which operate separate, financially self-supporting hospital and medical benefit funds. There is no government financial support for medical benefit funds, so that rates of contribution are fixed to meet the liabilities of the fund.

Basic medical benefits for privately insured people are identical to the medical benefits outlined above for people covered by standard Medibank. This is a statutory requirement. Additional benefits for ancillary services such as physiotherapy and dental may also be offered, but an additional premium must be paid. Private insurance organizations may also offer supplementary coverage for the gap between basic medical benefits and schedule fees as part of these packages of additional benefits. The types and rates of all benefits offered by registered health insurance organizations and all contribution rates charges are subject to Federal Government approval in accordance with the National Health Act, 1953.

CHINA

Background

The Government of the People's Republic of China, consistently attaches importance to the improvement of the health of the people. Soon after the founding of the People's Republic, the Communist Party and Chairman Mao mapped out and issued four cardinal principles as guidelines for medical and health work in China. They are: (1) to orient the medical and health services towards the workers, peasants and soldiers; (2) to lay stress on preventive work; (3) to unite the practitioners of Chinese traditional medicine and of Western medicine; (4) and to promote participation by the masses in health work. These principles are centred on and embody the fundamental orientation of our health work, namely to serve the overwhelming majority and safeguard the health of the people. In the last 30 years, with the continual development of socialist revolution and socialist construction in the country, the medical and health service has been making progress and the health of the people has been improving unceasingly.

Organization of health services and health resources

Against a background of poverty and emptiness, the legacy of the old China, a primary network of health services has been established in the urban as well as the rural areas. In particular the stress laid in the programmes on health work in the rural areas has brought about a great change from the previous underprivileged situation and lack of adequate medical care. In each of the approximately 2000 counties, a hospital (with, on the average, 120 beds per hospital), a sanitary and anti-epidemic station and a maternal and child health care centre have been established, and in each of the approximately 50 000 communes a health centre has been set up with, on the average, more than 10 beds. There are also more than 500 000 cooperative health centres scattered through villages in the rural areas. The number of medical and health personnel had been gradually increased. At the end of 1977 there were in all about 1 700 000 regular hospital beds, 26 times the total beds in preliberation days, without taking into account a number of simple beds for the sick of various kinds in hospitals and in households.

There are altogether more than 2 900 000 professional medical, pharmaceutical and health personnel in the whole country, about 1 800 000 barefoot doctors and a total of some 4 million health aides and midwives. Remarkable progress has also been made in medical education. From 1949 to 1977 there were in all more than 350 000 graduates from medical and pharmaceutical colleges, equivalent to 37 times the total number of graduates over a period of 20 years (1928–1947) before liberation.

The production of pharmaceuticals, biological products and medical instruments and apparatus is in the main self-sufficient. At present more than 700 kinds of crude pharmaceutical materials, some 3000 varieties of pharmaceutical preparations, more than 40 kinds of antibiotics, and 110 biological products and more than 1400 kinds of medical instruments and apparatus are produced. The price of pharmaceuticals has been decreased several times since liberation and it now averages 80% less than the price before liberation. Various kinds of biological products used for immunization and compounds used for the chemoprophylaxis and chemotherapy of endemic diseases, as well as contraceptives and contraceptive devices, are supplied free of charge.

Soon after liberation, changes in sanitation were rapidly brought about in urban and rural areas throughout the country by the persistent launching of large-scale hygienic campaigns in which both the professionals and the community were involved. Acute communicable diseases, such as smallpox, cholera, plague and venereal disease—the main scourges which seriously threatened the life and the health of the people in preliberation days—were eradicated soon after liberation. The incidence of other infectious, parasitic, endemic and occupational diseases was also substantially reduced. In old China, schistosomiasis, endemic throughout the southern half of the country, was thought to be an incurable disease and was a terrible scourge, but now two-thirds of the patients have been radically cured and restored to health, and in two-thirds of the areas that harboured *Oncomelania* snails it is now hardly possible to find any.

Traditional medicine and pharmacology

The Chinese heritage embodying rich practical experience accumulated over a long history of several thousand years and regarded by Chairman Mao as a great treasure house, has been handed down and developed thanks to the Party's policy on traditional medicine. Traditional doctors scattered everywhere as private practitioners have been organized and put on the staff of hospitals. They have the same status as doctors trained in Western medicine. Unity between traditional and Western medical practitioners is advocated and they are encouraged to learn from their counterparts, stressing especially the importance of the study of Chinese traditional medicine for doctors of Western medicine. Departments of traditional medicine have been set up in general hospitals and special institutions for traditional medicine created such as research institutes and colleges and medium-level schools of traditional medicine. To traditional doctors and pharmacists who are very learned or outstanding in certain specialities or techniques, young traditional doctors or Western doctors who have studied Chinese traditional medicine are assigned as assistants so that they may classify and inherit their experience. The principle of integrating Chinese traditional and Western medicine is being tenaciously pursued and efforts are under way to create a school of new medicine and pharmacology to unify the two as a contribution to all mankind.

Maternal and child health

Emphasis is laid on maternal and child health care. More than 2000 institutions specifically for maternal and child care have been established throughout the country since liberation. Large-scale mass surveys and mass treatment for gynaecological diseases have been repeatedly carried out, and the occupational protection of women workers has been strengthened. Various kinds of vaccination are universally administered to children free of charge throughout the country in both urban and rural areas. The infant mortality rate has dropped remarkably. For instance, in Peking City proper, the infant mortality rate fell from around 120 per 1000 in 1949 to 10 per 1000 in 1977. The health level of children has risen remarkably.

China, as a country with a large population, pays serious attention to family planning and has effectively controlled population growth; for instance, the natural increase rate in Honan and Kiangsu province decreased from 2.5% in 1965 to 1.0% in 1978. In Shanghai and Peking, it has been brought below 0.6%.

Research and technology

The Government consistently stresses the development of medical science and technology; it has formulated a series of principles and policies and adopted measures to support and promote their implementation. The main emphasis in scientific research is laid on those diseases that are highly prevalent and detrimental to the health of working people; priority is also given to the development of new and emerging sciences. In the last 30 years a number of remarkable achievements have been made and special characteristic features are taking shape in China's research in the medical sciences. Acupuncture anaesthesia, the treatment of large-area burns, regrafting of severed extremities, combined traditional and Western therapy of fractures, and combined treatment of acute abdomen are examples of these achievements.

Under the leadership of the Central Committee of the Party headed by Chairman Hua, the people are striving hard to modernize agriculture, industry, defence, and science and technology by the end of this century and to transform the country into a strong modern socialist State. Compared with the advanced level elsewhere in the world, medical science and technology in China are still lagging behind, and in order to achieve modernization within this century, it must exert great efforts and persist in the tradition of self-reliance and hard struggle. At the same time, in view of the current situation, it must endeavour to acquire from other countries advanced experience and technology while strengthening international cultural exchanges and technical cooperation.

In modernizing medical science and technology, China still stresses work in the rural areas; readjusting, consolidating and improving the "grass-roots" health structures in rural areas and giving further training to barefoot doctors so as to raise their technical level. In the meanwhile, health services in the urban areas, factories and mines are being strengthened, readjusting, consolidating and restoring the existing units, in order gradually to expand some of the medical and health institutions in a planned manner, increase hospital beds, promote scientific research and education and increase the production of pharmaceuticals, as well as medical instruments and apparatus. The building-up of urban health undertakings will, in return, afford better assistance to the rural areas and ensure an overall improvement in health work.

COOK ISLANDS

Major health and health-related problems

The major health problems are respiratory diseases (bronchitis, pneumonia and asthma), particularly among children; diarrhoeal disease, again particularly among children; hypertension, diabetes mellitus and obesity; tropical ulcers; filariasis; influenza; and dengue. Major health-related problems have been, and continue to be, those pertaining to the organization and management of services (extending to 12 inhabited islands scattered over about 1 367 500 km² of ocean), logistics, and the training and supervision of staff.

The development and implementation of the health services are based on the recognition of the right of all inhabitants to a life of dignity and wellbeing; the belief that the Government has a responsibility to promote the total welfare of the entire population; the provision by the Government of free health services to all inhabitants, including permanent foreign residents; the right and obligation of the community to participate in the planning and programming of activities related to health and the health services; the provision of comprehensive health services which are fully integrated with other community and national programmes; the appropriate decentralization of provisions to permit the delivery of services at the community level to the greatest extent possible.

Action taken

Measures were taken to increase the quantity of well-child services on all islands, with restructuring of activities to permit more frequent services of improved quality both in clinics and through home visiting and to expand the immunization programme.

Increased attention and financial assistance was given to housing to relieve overcrowding and provide safe, hygienic living quarters. The rubbish disposal system was improved. Open water intakes were replaced by underground galleries on Rarotonga and Aitutaki, and artesian wells were constructed on Mauke and public catchments on other islands: a comprehensive water supply system was begun for Rarotonga, together with a study to determine the most suitable water supply systems for all islands.

Hypertension, diabetic and obesity clinics were established. Mosquito control activities were increased and the filariasis treatment programme extended. Postgraduate education for medical officers and postbasic training for nurses and other health professionals were provided.

Health resources

The total number of health establishments during the period under review was: one principal general hospital, 7 general hospitals on the outer islands, 4 dispensaries or clinics on the outer islands, 2 outpatient departments other than in hospitals (Rarotonga), one principal dental clinic and 4 on the outer islands, one principal public health office, and 4 on the outer islands, 32 child health clinics on Rarotonga, and 33 on outer islands.

The total health manpower of the national health services was comprised of the following.

Medical officers	18
Medical assistants (dressers)	4
Dentists	9
Nurses and nurse/midwives	57
Nurse aides	17
Dental nurses	5
Dental hygienists	2
Assistant dental nurses	3
Pharmacists	2
Dispensing assistants	2
Veterinary assistant	1
Physiotherapist	1
Medical laboratory technician	1
Assistant laboratory technicians	6
Radiographer	1
Assistant radiographers	2
Health inspectors	20
Hospital dietician	1
Health statistician	1
Medical record technicians	2

The percentage of the national budget which was spent on health services averaged 7.3%, with an expenditure over the years as follows (in New Zealand dollars):

1973	714 500
1974	784 000
1975/76*	1 065 014
1976/77	956 120

*15 months' expenditure.

Assessment of progress made in the period 1973–1977

During the period under review, progress made included reduction in infant and childhood mortality and morbidity; containment of infectious diseases; increase in the provision of safe water supply and in refuse disposal facilities; improvement in the quality of the health facilities, and extension of ancillary services; and development of a small cadre of health personnel with specialized and intensive postgraduate and postbasic training.

Outlook

Within the coming five to ten years efforts will be channelled towards the achievement of the following goals:

(1) streamlined organization and management of the health service delivery system, particularly as related to personnel policies for the outer islands, and to logistics;

(2) the institution of a comprehensive, national health information system;

(3) production of a well-qualified cadre of health personnel for service, through the provision of formal, basic training locally (at the School of Nursing, Rarotonga), in-service training locally (for all categories), and postgraduate and postbasic training abroad (for senior professionals);

(4) equitable distribution of personnel and material resources;

(5) provision of maternal and child health and outpatient services at the district level, preferably within multipurpose community centres, and improvement of the quality of these services;

(6) complete immunization coverage of the preschool population; control of environmental factors in disease, including improvement of housing, of water supply, sewage and refuse disposal systems, and control of mosquitos;

(7) the institution of a systematized programme of supervisory visits to the outer islands.

FIJI

General information

Fiji is an archipelago of some 320 islands, of which 100 are permanently inhabited, scattered over 424 760 km^2 of the South Pacific Ocean. The total land area is only 18 272 km^2. The largest islands are Viti Levu (10 386 km^2) and Vanua Levu (5535 km^2). There are about 2576 km of roads, mainly on the two bigger islands. Few islands are served by internal air services; most interisland transport is by small ship. Radiotelephone services are fairly satisfactory and provide the main means of communication from remote areas. Fiji is basically an agricultural country. Main sources of income are sugar, tourism, timber, gold, copra and a few other smaller industries.

The estimated population of Fiji at the end of 1977 was 601 594. Some demographic data for the period 1973–1977 are given in the table below.

Organization of health services

The Ministry is under the overall control of the Minister for Health, who is responsible for the formulation of health policies. the Permanent Secretary for Health is responsible to the Minister for the professional and administrative functioning of the Ministry. He is assisted by two directors: the Director of Curative Medical Services and the Director of Preventive Medical

	1973	1974	1975	1976	1977
Total births	16 131	17 048	16 794	17 706	18 295
Total deaths	3 084	3 197	3 493	3 367	3 285
Birth rate (per 1000 population)	29.3	30.3	29.3	30.0	30.6
Crude death rate (per 1000 population)	5.6	5.7	6.1	5.7	5.5
Infant mortality rate (per 1000 live births)	41.2	42.2	41.4	36.8	31.9
Maternal mortality rate (per 1000 live births)	1.3	1.2	1.4	1.2	0.8
Family planning protection rate	23.8	23.3	23.6	23.4	27.8

Services. He is also assisted by the Principal Health Inspector, the Controller of Nursing Services and clerical staff.

For ease of administration the country is divided into four divisions, each headed by a divisional medical officer, responsible to the Permanent Secretary for Health. Under the divisional medical officer there are 15 subdivisional medical officers-in-charge of subdivisions. The subdivisions are further divided into "areas" with area medical officers. The "area" is the basic medical unit, composed of one or more district zones under a district nurse.

In the curative service, the administration of the major hospitals is carried out by medical superintendents of hospitals, who are senior clinicians. They are responsible to the Permanent Secretary for Health; in the same way the medical officers-in-charge of area hospitals are responsible to the subdivisional and divisional medical officers. The subdivisional medical officer forms an important link between the divisional medical officer in the upper echelon and the area medical officer at the lower end of the scale. It is at this level of administration that integration of curative, preventive, nursing and environmental services is carried out.

Health policy and programming

The national health policy is based on the relation of health to overall national development, and emphasizes the development of rural areas, the desire to slow down urban shift of the population, the need for intersectoral coordination, the role of government as the chief provider of health services, and community participation. The main national health objectives are:

(a) to make available the necessary health manpower to staff the health facilities of the country;

(b) to improve the coverage of basic health services;

(c) to continue to protect the population against communicable diseases;

(d) to improve services for noncommunicable diseases;

(e) to develop and maintain at a satisfactory level basic sanitary facilities in both urban and rural areas;

(f) to ensure that the population growth rate is brought to a level that is harmonious with the growth of the economy.

The guiding principles followed in developing a health programming strategy include:

(a) the Government's as well as the people's responsibility for safe-guarding the health of the nation;

(b) due regard to the culture, traditions, beliefs, religion, and political ideology of the country;

(c) permanent availability of primary health care to the people;

(d) emphasis on preventive and promotive services; as far as curative services are concerned, preference will be given to outpatient management of cases over institutional care;

(e) close intersectoral coordination; and

(f) integration of external assistance, when sought, within the context of the national health plan of the country.

National health planning started in 1976. The first priorities of the plan are health manpower development, basic health services and family health. The second priority area includes communicable diseases, environmental health and hospitals.

Major health and health-related problems

The leading causes of death are heart diseases, senility, immaturity and early diseases of infancy, pneumonia and neoplasms.

Apart from pregnancy, the leading cause of admission to hospital is complication of pregnancy, childbirth and puerperium. The risk of sickness is highest in infants, followed by children of 1–4 years, then those of 5–14 years, and finally persons of 45 years and over, the age group 15–44 being at lowest risk.

The pattern for mortality is somewhat different in that after infants the age group 45 years and over is at greatest risk. Although the most productive age group (15–44) has the lowest morbidity, its leading causes of death are hardest to prevent.

About 50% of infant deaths are caused by diseases which are highly susceptible to preventive measures. Prematurity and other causes of diseases in infancy head the list, followed by diarrhoeal conditions and pneumonias.

The leading causes of morbidity are respiratory infections, gastrointestinal diseases, skin infections, wounds and lacerations, and noncommunicable diseases among which diabetes, hypertension, malignancy and accidents feature prominently.

To specify major health problems in order of priority is difficult. The following is a broad statement of problems to which certain specific points have been added.

Some of the main problems of concern under maternal and child health care services are:

(*a*) the high infant mortality and the number of low birth weight babies;

(*b*) risks and abnormalities associated with pregnancy and childbirth, including maternal mortality;

(*c*) nutrition, anaemia and malnutrition;

(*d*) family planning and associated problems related to family health in general;

(*e*) the birth rate;

(*f*) traditional birth attendances; and

(*g*) general factors concerned with physical, mental and social wellbeing of the mother and the child.

Other major problems include general morbidity and mortality and related preventive measures and control; environmental sanitation problems or associated health hazards contributing to general ill-health in the community; problems of "urban drift", motor vehicle accidents, cardiovascular diseases, diabetes, malignant neoplasms and physically and mentally handicapped children; health manpower development, the need for national health planning and other socioeconomic factors. Control of tuberculosis, leprosy, sexually transmitted diseases and other infectious diseases present special problems. There is a general shortage of doctors to work in rural areas. If doctors are sent to work in certain health centres, they may not be able to use their skills. Heavy workloads await nurses in areas where there is no medical officer; and difficult access to the health centre may deter the most isolated people from seeking assistance. There is growing concern over dental health. Personnel resources, training and costs, and supplies, combined with capital development programme costs, represent further problems.

Health establishments and health manpower resources

In 1977 there were 4 divisional hospitals, 3 specialized hospitals for tuberculosis, leprosy, and mental diseases, 10 subdivisional hospitals, 4 maternity units, 4 area hospitals, 2 private hospitals, 46 health centres, 86 nursing stations, 18 dental units, and 21 health offices. The total number of beds is 1573, giving a bed/population ratio of 2.6 per 1000.

The best guide to the health manpower situation is a comparison of total approved strength in 1973 and 1977 (actual working strength at any one time varies due to several factors):

	1973	1977
Doctors	244	237
Dental officers	32	29
Nursing staff	1 003	1 193
Technical staff	210	357
Clerical staff	126	194

Total numbers of all categories of personnel, excluding non-established staff employed by the Ministry, were 1800 in 1973 and 2238 in 1977.

The doctor/population ratio was one to 2399 in 1973 and one to 2279 in 1977. The target is to provide one doctor to about 2000 by 1980. Due to the general topography of the country, population concentration and problems of accessibility, etc., the distribution of doctors is uneven, but nevertheless satisfactory.

In 1977 there were 1193 nurses in government service and 29 in private hospitals, making a total of 1222. The actual nurse/population ratio was one to about 550.

There were 25 dental officers in government practice (actual working strength) and 10 in private practice, giving a total of 35, and a ratio of one to 17 200.

Health inspectorate staff numbered 108, which gives a ratio of one to about 5700.

National health plans

Fiji has a long history of planning, concerned with providing the people with a service of the highest possible standard within the limited resources available, and general development plans have almost become a tradition. The basic philosophy behind the planning has been to choose from amongst the many needs and demands those which have the greatest priority in producing the greatest benefit for the greatest number of people—health manpower development, basic health services, family health, communicable diseases control, environmental health and improvement in hospital services.

A national health advisory committee was set up to prepare a national health plan, the first phase of which was completed in 1976. A draft plan of the second phase with definite objectives for implementation is awaiting Cabinet approval and release.

Production and sale of pharmaceuticals

The Government is sole distributor of all narcotic drugs, antisera and vaccines. There is no local production.

Health expenditure

Since 1973 the operating budget of the Ministry, $6 242 610 in 1973 and $12 915 331 in 1977, has represented 9.35% of the total operating budget of the country. Almost two-thirds goes towards salaries and wages (personal emoluments) of the staff. The net per capita expenditure on medical services was $10.14 in 1973, $12.70 in 1974, $15.42 in 1975, $19.84 in 1976 and $22.12 in 1977.

Appraisal of progress made between 1973 and 1977

This includes the health services coverage of previously underserved population groups and areas.

Communicable diseases

Fiji is free from malaria and quarantinable diseases. The infectious diseases control measures against poliomyelitis (no cases since 1967), diphtheria (no cases since 1970), pertussis (25 to 30 cases per annum), tetanus (2 to 3 cases per annum) and tuberculosis (0.40 per 1000 population) all speak of the success of the expanded immunization programme.

The filariasis control programme covered about 200 000 people in 1968. From initial microfilaria rates of between 17.7%, and 6.7%, the rate is now below 1.0% (0.9% to 0.4%). The main emphasis is on follow-up of all positive registered cases at four-monthly intervals, radical treatment of remaining positive cases, and strict vigilance or surveillance of all foci through regular blood sampling and special surveys.

The new P. J. Twomey Memorial Hospital for leprosy patients, with 83 beds, is situated in the best residential area at Tamavua, Suva—an important factor in removing the stigma of "leper" and outcast. The numbers of new cases registered in the period are as follows: 62 in 1973,

77 in 1974, 28 in 1975, 37 in 1976 and 30 in 1977.

An epidemic of dengue occurred in Fiji between January and July 1975. All laboratory evidence indicated that type 1 dengue was the only prevalent dengue virus. This type had probably not been seen in Fiji for 30 years, and over 70% of the population was susceptible. *Aedes aegypti* appeared to be the major vector in urban areas, but circumstantial evidence indicated that *Aedes rotunae* was a vector in at least one remote area. All forms of the clinical spectrum of dengue, including haemorrhagic manifestations, were seen and reported in all age groups. The total number of cases officially reported was 16 203. A very large number were either self-treated at home or treated by private practitioners and not notified to the Ministry.

The problem of sexually transmitted diseases includes all features except drug-resistance, which has not yet developed in Fiji. The growing numbers of syphilis cases, including congenital syphilis, are of great concern as this disease was virtually unknown, particularly among the Fijian population, in the past.

Noncommunicable diseases and allied problems

The problems of malnutrition, maternal anaemia, the epidemic proportions attained by motor vehicle accidents in recent years, urban drift and cardiovascular and metabolic diseases are leading causes of the demand for health services.

Environmental sanitation programme

The UNICEF-aided school sanitation programme, water seal latrine programmes, and village water supply schemes in rural areas have shown very satisfactory progress during the period. The various activities in the health sector including food control, vector control, pollution control, quarantine services at sea and airports, and local authority work, have all contributed enormously to the improvement of the general health of the people. But the lack of safe water supplies in rural areas continues to be a major public health concern. The setting up of new industries demands that greater attention be given to pollution, occupational health and safety. The main objectives have been improvement of environmental health facilities, promotion of safety in industrial establishments, management of industrial waste, and control and prevention of vectorborne diseases.

Family health

The general development of the country has reached a level at which a new approach has to be given to health care policy, directed not only to the health of the individual but to the health of the family as a whole. A family health programme of the Ministry funded by UNFPA was started in November 1976, for which WHO is the executing agency.

The Family Health Unit organized field visits in November 1976 and April-May 1977 to assess the field situation. A questionnaire was prepared and sent to all field workers, to assess maternal and child health, attitudes of health workers to their work, and difficulties encountered. Analysis of existing data has been carried out since January 1977.

Four special cars for land transportation of nurses have been acquired, and there is to be a floating clinic.

The family planning training centre, which is to be part of the new Anderson maternity unit, is under construction. Posters on family planning, nutrition and infant feeding have been prepared and distributed to all health centres and hospitals. Contraceptives to the value of $20 000 were received in 1977.

To improve the recording and follow-up system, family health record cards, maternal death record folders, hospital discharge and follow-up slips, and obstetric ward record charts were prepared and sent to the field for testing.

A total of 300 nurses have been trained in the use of Sahli haemoglobinometers and treatment of anaemia. Sahli haemoglobinometers have been issued to all nursing stations. Some 172 nurses in the western and northern divisions have had refresher training in antenatal, natal and postnatal care of the mother and child. Family Health Unit staff gave lectures on family health to medical students, medical assistants and public health nurses.

Guidelines on high risk pregnancy, postpartum haemorrhage, pre-eclamptic toxaemia, treatment of anaemia in pregnancy and childhood anaemia and care given to the newborn were prepared and distributed to nurses and doctors to facilitate their work and improve the care given to mothers and children.

Three fellowships have been awarded for study overseas in the field of family health for a doctor and two nurses.

Education and training of manpower

Fiji trains its own medical and health personnel to meet the needs of the country. Recruitment of doctors on short-term contracts continued during the period, but this is now being phased out. The problem of filling consultant posts and posts in teaching faculties may take longer to solve. The two principal training institutions are the Fiji School of Medicine, at Suva, and the Fiji School of Nursing, at Lautoka. The training of doctors, dentists, nurses and medical assistants is free. The ancillary staff, e.g., laboratory technicians, X-ray technicians, physiotherapists, dieticians, dental therapists, dental assistants, assistant pharmacists and assistant health inspectors, are given on-the-job training (of the apprenticeship type) and paid the normal salary.

Postgraduate training in postbasic public health and in midwifery for nurses in Fiji, together with postgraduate training overseas in other fields for all cadres of staff, provides the main avenue for manpower resources development in the country. There are various supplementary seminars, refresher courses, visits and lectures.

Like the work of the Family Health Unit, and the growing emphasis on developing primary health care services, the training of medical assistants, dental therapists and dental assistants is aimed at increasing the coverage of the rural health services.

The need to upgrade the technical staff of the many supportive services for the health delivery system and to improve the management capabilities of the technical and supervisory staff, are areas which need special attention.

Outlook for the next 5–10 years

Policies and programmes, 1976–1980

The broad objectives are to promote the physical, mental and social wellbeing of the nation; to protect young and old people from illnesss and disease; to provide adequate clinical facilities and staff to satisfy the medical and dental needs of both rural and urban populations; and to promote a better standard of living, with lower birth rates.

In health policy, the emphasis has been redirected: clinical services must be maintained at an adequate level, but a slightly greater trend towards the preventive services will probably be seen, as preventive medicine and family planning, which are more labour-intensive, grow in contrast to curative medicine, whose emphasis is more on buildings, equipment and drugs, and as the services to the rural people are strengthened.

Government will watch closely the rise in the number of cases of noncommunicable diseases such as anaemia, diabetes, cancer, and of malnutrition and heart disease, by means of an active registration programme. Leprosy is a declining menace, but government will continue pressure to identify cases early in order to achieve eradication.

The control of mosquito-borne diseases, such as filariasis and dengue (haemorrhagic) fever and other virus diseases has certain special problems, and it may be necessary during the plan period for government to undertake a much more aggressive public health plan of attack if those diseases are to be kept at an insignificant level or eradicated. To control filariasis, government plans to carry out a survey, complete blood film examinations and follow up positive samples. While attempts will be made to isolate dengue virus strains and to find a suitable antidote, stronger immediate measures will be investigated such as legal prosecution for unsanitary living conditions, and regular spraying in urban areas by city councils. People in urban areas will be responsible for keeping drains clear outside their compounds.

The growth in tourism, transport and trade anticipated in the region will increase the need to prevent the introduction of quarantinable diseases. Government will continue control measures at airports and ports in accordance with international health requirements, and health inspectorate staff will carry out malarial spraying and other types of disinsecting and disinfection on incoming aircraft and shipping, where necessary.

The importance of good sanitation must also be stressed if health hazards are to be avoided. Government will promote fluoridation of drinking water in major urban areas and speed up the provision of piped water to villages and settlements. Water seal latrines will be provided to rural schools, and better sanitation will be encouraged in villages and settlements. The prevention of other major environmental and pollution problems will also be given emphasis during the plan by the health inspectorate staff.

For hospital services the policy will be to reduce overcrowding at existing hospitals, to rationalize hospital management, to improve staff accommodation at hospitals and to maintain hospital food services. It is planned to increase the number of general hospital beds. The demand for psychiatry beds is also likely to increase with the growth in urban populations and consequent social tensions. This will mean either extension of St. Giles Hospital, or the removal of psychiatric facilities to other buildings.

Replacement of the remaining old rural dispensaries and nursing stations for rural health services, construction of new stations and renovation or replacement of hospitals in rural areas will be a continuing policy. Consideration will continue to be given to proximity to centres of population, accessibility of the site, and other economic and social factors, before a site for a health centre or nursing station is chosen. The rural development committees will also continue to play a major part in the selection of sites.

A major aspect of policy will be the reorganization of the medical subdivision structure to increase population coverage and to ensure that the basic health needs of rural people are met by the health services, particularly in isolated areas such as central Viti Levu and the outlying islands. Area health centres with the poorest utilization records are all located in such remote areas.

Measures will also include the development of health teams to assist in the treatment of patients at health centres and nursing stations; more nurses, both male and female, will be trained to work in rural areas. Incentives will be introduced to encourage a greater number of qualified personnel to undertake medical duties in the rural areas.

Training of health workers will be further strengthened and their duties more precisely defined. It is estimated that by 1980 about 30 health assistants will be ready to join health teams working in rural areas. Their function will be to take over certain duties of the medical officer, leaving him free to use his more specialized skills; and to provide a more effective coverage of the community. They could be posted to small centres or stations where doctors' skills are not fully employed, or to places where a doctor is overworked; they may also go to nursing stations so that nurses can give the community service for which they are trained. Most health assistants will be recruited from rural areas for training, and an equal number of men and women students will be trained.

At the same time, it may also be possible to provide extra training to nurses who already do much of this work at nursing stations or health centres and to increase the number of nurses serving in rural areas.

The target of the services for family planning, maternal and child health is to reduce the birth rate to 22 per 1000 population by 1980, with a view to improving maternal and infant health and family care. The achievement of this target will require an increase in the number of acceptors of family planning protection to 40% per annum from the present 24%, a tremendous challenge, bearing in mind the failure to reach the previous planned target. Efforts will therefore have to be redoubled. Maternity services being thus complementary to family planning services for women, the aim is to develop and emphasize the interrelationship at all maternity hospitals, wards and clinics, improving on the present 90% attendance rates at antenatal and postnatal clinics and working towards 100% coverage of deliveries by medically trained staff by 1980. District and urban nurses will be trained to conduct personal interviews, to provide advice to mothers on spacing of pregnancies and to follow up patients regularly as a routine measure.

The major policy of dental services will be to prevent tooth decay, in particular among children, and to ensure that the scattered communities are fairly covered, especially with school preventive services. The number of mobile school dental clinics will be increased. Fluoridation of water supplies will also be carried out during the plan period to help to prevent tooth decay in young children. Consideration will be given to new forms of treatment, including low-cost denture services for the poorer sections of the community. One of the biggest problems regarding the overall standard of dental services is knowing whether the basic needs continue to be met. Government recognizes that a shortage of dentists exists. The number of dentists and therapists will be increased and, where necessary, expatriate dentists will be recruited. Dental statistics will be developed as a means of gauging more accurately the availability and quality of dental services.

FRENCH POLYNESIA

Major health problems

In determining health priorities, it is necessary to recall the geographical and demographic context of French Polynesia, which is comprised of two types of archipelagos: the Windward Islands, with Tahiti, where 74% of all inhabitants are located, where the health infrastructure is well developed and the way of living is similar to developed countries; and the other archipelagos, some quite isolated and sparsely populated where life-styles are less advanced and resemble those of developing countries. There are certain diseases common to both areas and some aspect particular to each.

The health problems common to both areas consist especially of metabolic diseases: obesity is widespread, linked to bad eating habits, as the Polynesian diet is high in energy foods and carbohydrates; diabetes occurs fairly frequently and is identified when complications have arisen (the diabetes encountered is plethoric and rarely requires insulin—infantile ketoacidic diabetes is exceptional); gout is encountered frequently in its arthropathic form.

Alcoholism especially due to beer, is widespread in all environments and in all areas. It is characterized by chronic liver ailments and acute neuropsychic manifestations. Nicotinism is highly prevalent among both men and women.

Cardiovascular diseases brought on by metabolic diseases are dominated by permanent arterial hypertension, idiopathic and neglected, and revealed through vascular, particularly cerebral complications. Peripheral arteriopathy is usually caused by diabetes; coronary diseases are increasing progressively; valvular diseases after rheumatism are widespread and are detected most frequently at school age or at adolescence; acute articular rheumatism is usually neglected; heart failures are consequently of high incidence, linked to these numerous and severe causes.

Dental caries, affecting nearly all children, is caused by the high-sugar diet and weak teeth.

Among infectious diseases, only measles causes widespread epidemics about every four years. Acute lung diseases of viral and bacterial origin are encountered frequently in seasonal epidemics; ear, nose and throat infections are related and numerous. Among viruses, the most frequent are those causing rhinopharyngeal and pulmonary disorders. Dengue develops sporadically, with some epidemics. A particularly extensive epidemic occurred in 1975 and affected the entire population, causing some haemorrhagic complications.

Illness due to poisonous fishes (ichthyosarcotoxism) occurs throughout the entire territory except on the southern islands.

The health problems more particular to Tahiti include, in addition to the above, road accidents, usually linked to alcoholism; venereal diseases (the incidence of syphilis and of gonorrhoea is rising progressively and is affecting lower age groups); psychological conditions which are accompanied by numerous psychotic neuroses.

The health problems of the archipelagos also include frequent infantile gastroenteritis with dehydration (due to delayed consultation), dermatosis, and frequent lung diseases and ear, nose and throat infections.

Action taken

Proven methods of health care, including widespread immunization, have practically eradicated epidemics and endemic diseases such as tuberculosis, leprosy, and particularly filariasis. New types of health care are now being developed to deal with the problems mentioned above.

Health policy

The health care policy has been developed in order to combine harmoniously individual medical treatment sufficient to allow the majority of the population to benefit from medical, surgical and obstetric care, without being highly developed, rare cases requiring specialized treatment being evacuated to facilities elsewhere; and collective preventive medicine for which development efforts are required to expand existing facilities and create new urgently required services in order to improve the health environment, to increase preventive care of mothers and children, and to develop health education.

Health legislation

Laws and regulations which are the responsibility of the health services are enacted progressively, adapting a combination of French and other, foreign health legislation. Priority areas are environmental control, and regulation of the medical and pharmaceutical professions. Texts already existing concern the following: housing hygiene and urban development (sanitary regulations for new buildings and sanitary installations); drinking-water hygiene (a draft text is being adopted); hygiene of food, food stores and food-handling personnel; and eradication of mosquitos.

Legislation on poisonous substances is being drafted.

Health planning and programme development

Plans are made according to policies adopted for a five-year period. Financial support is determined annually in view of current priorities.

Organization of health services

The Health Service of the Territory comprises, as its central organs, the Service Directorate (charged with administration, planning, elaboration of sanitary legislation, coordination and orientation of various public health activities, direction, orientation and control of training for nursing personnel, updating of statistics, and relations with outside services); the pharmaceutical service (charged with sanitary supplies and pharmacy inspections); and the school for nursing personnel.

Organs for collective preventive medicine comprise the territorial services, including an infantile protection service reinforced by a dispensary for maternal advice, vaccinations, etc.; a medical service for schools backed up by a dispensary for medical inspections of schools, vaccinations, regulation of cafeterias; a dental hygiene service charged with caries prevention; a service for territorial hygiene and quarantine charged with the control of the sanitary environment—health police at borders, housing hygiene, hygiene of water and waste products, food hygiene, etc.; and a mental health service. These preventive organs are centralized on Tahiti but are represented in the archipelagos by travelling and static agents or the medical service of the disstrict.

State services comprise an endemic diseases service charged with combating tuberculosis, leprosy and filariasis.

There are also the organs for individual medical treatment represented by three sectors: the primary sector, comprising urban and rural communal dispensaries, first aid units on atolls or in isolated valleys, and island infirmaries; the secondary sector, comprising specialized care centres (a medical centre for schools, an infant care centre, and a tuberculosis control centre), and secondary hospitals in major areas on archipelagos and hospital infirmaries on important islands; and the tertiary sector, comprising the territorial hospital establishments of Papeete, Mamao Hospital with its polyvalent services, and the Vaiami specialized hospital for mental illnesses.

The circulation of patients among different sectors is assured by primary referral or sanitary evacuation arrangements. Secondary evacuations from tertiary sectors are made to foreign or metropolitan hospitals.

Research

Research is carried out by an autonomous body, the Louis Mallarde Institute of Medical Research, which has a medical oceanographic, a medical biology and a medical entomology unit.

Training of health personnel

Training of nursing personnel in the Territory is provided by the School of Nursing. There are two levels of studies, one leading to a French State diploma, and the other for the training of nurses' aides, laboratory personnel, health agents and dental hygienists. Personnel in first aid units are drawn from the general population and given practical training.

Health resources

Health establishments

Establishments are distributed according to the health sectors: in the primary sector there are 45 first aid units, 15 urban and rural communal dispensaries, and 24 infirmaries; in the secondary sector, 4 central specialized dispensaries, 1 dental centre and 6 secondary hospitals of archipelagos; in the tertiary sector, 1 polyvalent territorial hospital, 1 psychiatric hospital, 1 hospital centre for leprosy, and 1 geriatric reception centre.

Health personnel

There were in 1977, 56 doctors, 3 pharmacists, 14 dental surgeons, 350 nurses or nurses' aides and 78 health agents (36 doctors are in the private sector).

Production and sale of pharmaceutical products

There is no local manufacture of pharmaceutical products. All products are imported, the great majority from France. The sale of medicaments is not carried out by the public sector but by 11 private offices and 6 storehouses. Sales are subject to legislation based on French laws.

Health expenditure

Territorial health budget for 1973 is 488 million CFP francs and for 1974, 648 million CFP francs.

Evaluation of progress made between 1973 and 1977

Substantial progress was made in the organization of services; all health structures were regrouped by Territorial Decree into the framework of a Public Health Service with two sectors of activity, for individual medical care and collective preventive medicine. Individual care was reorganized into a hierarchical structure with primary, secondary and tertiary levels.

Health coverage was extended to areas previously insufficiently covered by increasing the number of rural dispensaries on the island of Tahiti, Tahaa, Huahine, by establishing a medical centre at Tuamotu-Gambier on Rangiroa, by improving the system of health evacuations (particularly on the Tuamotu atolls), by improving the quality of first aid workers, transforming them progressively into community health agents, and by increasing the number of medical and paramedical personnel.

Outlook

A project for a Territory health policy to provide coherent services is planned, to maintain the current level of medical care in tertiary hospital sectors by improving equipment progressively without creating highly specialized services, by improving the autonomy of diagnosis and treatment in the archipelagos' secondary sector by multiplying communal first aid units transformed into medicosocial posts; and to develop the sector of communal preventive medicine by expanding existing services, establishing a real protection service for mothers and children—especially by establishing a health education service—and by improving penetration into the outer islands of the archipelagos.

Research is to be adapted to the changing pathological picture including research on metabolic diseases, on cardiovascular diseases, on causes of lung diseases, and diarrhoea. Surveys have been planned to improve the health environment. Efforts to enact or reactivate health legislation will be continued.

In all, a progressive improvement of health possibilities has been obtained which ensures a valid health coverage. Efforts must now be concentrated on disease prevention and health education, taking into account the different structures of development in the various geographical and demographic sectors.

GILBERT ISLANDS [1]

The Government's objectives for health as stated in the Third Development Plan were: to develop unified and effective preventive health services in all islands, to maintain curative services at the present per capita level in real terms, and to establish an influential national body to advise on matters affecting population growth.

Organization of health services

The plan period has seen a number of significant steps taken which have unified the health services and which will contribute to their effectiveness in the Islands. Each of the outer Islands services continued to be staffed by at least two Government health personnel with the exception of Kuria, Aranuka and the Line Group. The personnel consist mainly of nursing officers or medical assistants in the remote areas and, periodically, physicians. As important as the number of personnel has been the organizational change made to integrate the tasks of these workers. The emphasis is now on team work in an attempt to break from the tradition of separating preventive from curative work. The goal of a completely integrated service has not been completely achieved. The initial changes have been encouraging and with the proposed plan for the future a unified health service can be developed in the islands.

In addition to Government staff, the island health services are supported by maternal and child health aides and sanitary aides, who are paid by the local councils. Over 90% of the villages have a maternal child health aide and each island council employs one sanitary aide. They are supervised by the Government staff on the island or from headquarters. The number of aides has been continuously supported by the local councils and is gradually increasing. This fact alone is evidence of the importance that the councils attach to the health service. A great deal has been done by aides, but their potential is far greater, and the present plan will see improvements in their effectiveness to carry out the primary health care activities of the islands.

The later part of the plan period has seen a countrywide extension of water supply, and sanitary improvements. Following the successful pilot experiences in Nikunau, Tamana, and Arorae—where nearly all households have an improved water supply and a sanitary latrine—the Ministry has initiated similar projects on all islands. In the last year alone, 15% of the target for improved wells and 5% of that for sanitary latrines have been achieved.

The objective of stabilizing the cost of curative services was nearly achieved. The overall health budget has remained the same proportion of the total government budget. The percentage of the health budget for curative services has increased by 3% over the past few years. Curative services consume over 60% of the health budget, and the central hospital consumes approximately 80% of the allocation for curative services. The cost of running a modern hospital increases at a rate greater than for some government services—drugs and supplies account for much of this increase.

The establishment of a national body to advise the Ministry on population matters has not

---

[1] The Gilbert Islands became the Republic of Kiribati on 12 July 1979.

materialized. The overall national policy on population growth is to limit the natural increase. An explicit overall growth policy, given the uncertainties of the variable economic and social conditions, is hardly feasible. There are and will continue to be important interactions affecting population growth due to mobility caused by the declining phosphate industry, the attempt to increase the cash economy, the movement of workers to Tarawa, and the health aspects of malnutrition. This does not mean that population growth can be ignored. The overall policy must clearly be to limit natural growth. However, in terms of health policy the immediate concern must be the health of the family.

The previous plan period saw two events which caused major disruption in the Government's health services. The separation of Tuvalu, and the cholera outbreak; with the separation of Tuvalu, there was a mass exodus of health personnel from the Ministry's services which created loss of service effectiveness. A number of senior posts became vacant.

The entire health service as well as other Government services were mobilized to combat and successfully stop the 1977 cholera epidemic. The immediate effect was that apart from emergency work many other services were curtailed. For a health service which was already exiguous, it took many months to regain the losses. However, the team spirit which developed is being used to initiate further improvements. The awareness of the need for improved sanitation and water supply has never been higher, and this has been used to great benefit.

Programme assessment

Family health

With so many urgent social and economic development problems and malnutrition the children suffer. It has been clearly shown that retarded child development is related to economic conditions (insufficient food or the lack of certain growth foods), sanitation (increasing incidence of diarrhoeal and parasitic infections) and social conditions (introduction of solid foods and early weaning practices). In all parts of the country at least one of these conditions exists and in most parts all are at play, with the result that many of the youngest people are in very poor health.

The leading cause of morbidity at Tungaru Central Hospital in 1977 (excluding abnormal deliveries and cholera) was diarrhoea in infants. The tenth and fifteenth leading causes of morbidity were malnutrition (60% of cases being less than two years old) and parasitic infections. These data would suggest that one out of 15 children between six and 12 months old in South Tarawa had a serious enough growth problem to have to be hospitalized. It is recognized that the record system is not sufficiently developed to provide a completely accurate health status assessment. However, for this problem the signs are apparent from many sources. A number of recent studies on the development of children show that at least 10% of the children under five years old suffer from malnutrition, and in some areas the level is as high as 80%. The records from the island dispensaries for 1977 showed 1600 first-time outpatient visits for diarrhoea. It is estimated that in 50–70% of those cases the child was between six and 12 months old. From a list of reported causes of death from the island nurses it appeared that 25% of all deaths were due to diarrhoea.

It is clear that many children are facing the compounding problems of not having proper solid foods introduced early in life, suffering from diarrhoea and parasitic infections in the weaning period.

The nature of this problem necessitates the involvement of more than just the health resources. The Government has recognized the urgency of this problem and is seeking the assistance of the World Food Programme (WFP). Through WFP, as a temporary measure, the children and certain mothers will receive protein and energy supplements. This assistance will give time to develop long-term solutions. The Ministry of Health and Community Affairs is taking the initiative to mobilize the Government's resources in order to prepare the island communities for combating malnutrition in the long term.

Family planning

The planning of families and the health of children are recognized to be closely related. Infant mortality is estimated to be about 10% and must be reduced to about 3% before a family planning programme can be effective over the long term.

As recorded in a number of Government reports, there is concern that the very successful initial family planning efforts may be losing momentum. Each year it appears that the total number of family planning users continues to increase; there has, however, been a trend away from the use of intrauterine devices, (IUD) in favour of the pill or depot preparations, which need not necessarily cause concern, but it appears that these contraceptives are only used intermittently and the result is less reliable family planning. In addition, the number of "new users" in recent years has included more and more women resuming the use of the pill—in 1977 they accounted for over 50% of the total increase in family planning users. However, it is encouraging to see that a large number of families remain interested in preventing unwanted pregnancies. The fact that some island communities have a 100% higher use of family planning services than the average encourages also new initiatives in family planning.

Maternal health is not a serious concern. More and more staff are being better trained to detect potential problems such as risk pregnancies, and better facilities are planned in all islands to cope with those conditions that require special attention.

Environmental health

The pilot projects in Nikunau, Tamana and Arorae provided invaluable experience on how to provide the most appropriate protected drinking-water supplies and sanitary latrines for the outer island communities. The cholera outbreak gave added impetus to these programmes by prompting external financial assistance and internal motivation. It is already clear that in those areas with the most improved water supply and sanitation there is a lower rate of childhood morbidity. The Environmental Sanitation Section has been very active in seeing that the appropriate supplies and equipment are provided to island councils, assisting with the selection of wells to be protected and the locating of latrines. In addition, the health inspectors have been training council sanitary aides and supervising the aides in their work on the islands. The initial target for the present project of drinking-water well protection was 488 wells—one for every 10 households. As of November 1978, 185 had been completed. At this rate the project will easily be completed within the two-year plan period. With regard to the target of one sanitary latrine for every rural household, as of November 1978, 455 latrines had been constructed using only the resources of the Ministry

and island councils. The priority concern for most villagers is a protected water supply. However, with the acceptance of external assistance for the latrine project it is anticipated that the rate of latrine construction can be significantly increased.

A sanitation coordination committee composed of a number of government agencies concerned with the improvement of sanitation was formed after the cholera outbreak. It has proved useful in mobilizing the ideas and resources needed to make a real and lasting impact on improving sanitation in the islands.

Tuberculosis and leprosy

The control programme of the last plan period has improved the efficiency of activities with their integration into the basic health services. Incidence has remained relatively stable over the past few years, with approximately 150 and 15 new or relapse cases of tuberculosis and leprosy, respectively, each year. However, many of the new cases were detected by special teams and it is quite likely that other cases remain undetected. The objective is to continue to reduce the incidence of these diseases, with, for tuberculosis, immunization of all children below the age of 15 years and early detection of new cases and in order to render them noninfectious.

The coverage of BCG immunization has not been as high as desired. In some areas the number of new tuberculosis cases among children is of concern for reasons related to the viability of the vaccine cold chain. It is anticipated that with the new shipment of refrigerators to the outer islands the situation will improve.

For leprosy, the strategy is to up-grade the knowledge of health service staff in diagnosis and treatment, with emphasis on the consistent supervision of infectious cases and their contacts, especially child household contacts. Surveillance can only be achieved through the efforts of the island health workers. Assistance from WHO has been used to train staff and to improve the records that are required to monitor the status of patients. A medical assistant has been selected further to assist the island workers to improve follow-up and treatment.

Curative services

The curative services are provided through the central hospital, the small Betio hospital and the 21 dispensaries—most of them with inpatient wards—dispersed throughout the islands. Tungaru Central Hospital consumes the vast majority of the curative service resources, as is necessary to maintain the level of care required of a national hospital of such size.

Its facilities' expansion programme will be completed in the near future. The minimum level of professional and technical staffing has been achieved and can be maintained. The Hospital has approximately 80 beds in general wards (medical, surgical, private, obstetrics and paediatrics) and 60 in speciality wards (tuberculosis, leprosy, mental and infectious diseases). The supporting facilities (outpatients, pharmacy, laboratory, X-ray, dental, laundry and kitchen) have been increasing their effectiveness in order to meet the increasing demand. There is an increasing admission rate each year as more people move into the South Tarawa area. There has been a slight decrease in the average length of stay for the general wards; this trend will be maintained in the future as the hospital effectiveness improves. The leading causes of admission over the past years have been diarrhoeal diseases, normal delivery, accidents, complications of pregnancy, tuberculosis, respiratory illness and conditions of the urinary system. The 10 leading causes produce approximately 60% of the total hospital admissions. However, only 35% of the deaths in the hospital are due to these causes. The leading causes of death in the Hospital in 1977 where diarrhoeal diseases and

pneumonia, most of the victims were small children.

The recent cholera outbreak illustrated the hospital's ability to mobilize all resources to care for the masses in a disaster situation; one of the weak areas was laboratory support, and steps have been taken to solve this problem.

The curative services for people outside South Tarawa are minimal. There are no longer any medical officers posted in the outer islands. This gap continues to be partly filled by the medical teams that make regular visits and by the increasing number of medical assistants being trained. The rate of outpatient visits to the dispensaries by the people of the outer islands is quite reasonable. This is of course related to the expansion of dispensaries and their accessibility for the communities. There are a few instances where distance still precludes ready access to a minimum level of care. The outer island dispensaries have a minimum of drugs and supplies; in very few instances are there sufficient supplies for distribution to the maternal and child health aides in the villages.

The adult population is relatively healthy. There has been no significant change in the morbidity and mortality pattern as represented by the data at Tungaru Central Hospital over the past few years (with the exception of cholera in 1977). Therefore the majority of the new resources for curative services will be used to increase the level of care by other services than the Hospital.

GUAM

Major health and health-related problems

Health care costs have almost tripled during the period under review and are placing an ever increasing financial strain on the patient, medical care insurers and government. As a result of the increasing trend towards private sector medical care together with the pressures of trying to control costs, there is growing evidence of a breakdown in the quality of care provided to the patient. This is particularly apparent where expensive diagnostic work is deemed necessary or where hospitalization may be necessary. Although Guam Memorial Hospital has sufficient

bed capacity adequately to serve Guam's civilian population, a private hospital has also been built, almost doubling bed capacity and placing a great financial burden on the medical care system.

Guam was recently identified as a centre of illicit drug traffic between South-East Asia and the mainland of the United States of America. Drug addiction on Guam is estimated to have tripled in the last three years with a concurrent increase in social problems.

Under the influence of federal legislation, control of sewage disposal and the protection of the drinking water supply were transferred from

Public Health to the Environmental Protection Agency. Subsequently, enteric diseases, particularly shigellosis, vibriosis and salmonellosis increased substantially. Epidemiological investigations have revealed that *Vibrio* and pathogenic salmonellas are now relatively common in the environment. Active tuberculosis cases have risen for the past three years, partly due to an inadequate control programme and partly to imported cases among immigrants. The influx of people from surrounding countries entering into or passing through Guam has increased dramatically during the past five years, bringing arbovirus and other vectorborne diseases. For instance, an estimated 5000 cases of dengue were imported from Viet Nam.

Teenage pregnancies have increased dramatically in the last five years, and with this increase have come the almost overwhelming problems of increased birth anomalies, premature births, illegitimate births and fetal deaths. Although food is abundant, the accessibility and general acceptance of non-nutritional food products in the daily diet of most individuals continues to cause health problems. The number of individuals suffering from hypertension, diabetes, arteriocardiac and other diet-related diseases is well beyond acceptable levels. Neurological disorders, particularly anterolateral sclerosis and Parkinson's dementia, remain major unresolved health problems, and the incidence of these diseases remains higher than in almost all other areas of the world.

Action taken

The point has been reached where specific legislation has become necessary to respond to particularly critical problems in the health field. As more direct patient care is provided by the private sector, government controls become more necessary to avoid duplication of services, profiteering, poor quality care and excessive costs. Legislation developed or being developed includes the following:

(1) The certificate of need requires that any proposal that substantially changes the delivery of health services or that involves a major expenditure of money for equipment or facilities shall receive appropriate review and approval.

(2) Hospital cost containment legislation establishes ceilings for the rate at which hospital costs can rise and provides guidelines on the number of hospital beds per capita population permitted.

(3) Laws on health facilities and health professionals licensure have been developed to ensure that individuals offering health services have the necessary educational and technical expertise to provide quality care, and to ensure that hospitals, nursing homes, laboratories, pharmacies, hearing evaluation centres, vision centres, etc., have adequate facilities, equipment and technical expertise to provide quality services.

(4) Family planning legislation permits minors (under 18 years) to seek family planning (birth control) services without parental consent and permits the medical profession to provide such services to minors without parental consent.

Health policy

In response to the changes that have occurred in the delivery of health care, and in response to the problems cited in this report, the following changes in policy have been made:

(1) Direct patient care services provided by the public sector, such as maternal and child health services, are now directed specifically to those unable to support their own health care.

(2) More financial and manpower resources have been directed to the drug abuse programme for the education and rehabilitation of addicts, and additional resources have been made available to stop the illegal importation and sale of illicit drugs. The Department of Public Health and Social Services has established a narcotics and dangerous drug unit to control pharmacies and physicians in the dispensing, prescribing, inventorying and securing of restricted drugs and medications.

(3) The licensure of all health professionals and health facilities is being placed under the control of a separate bureau within the Department of Public Health and Social Services.

(4) A professional standards review organization is being established to review the hospitalization of Medicaid patients to determine whether it is necessary and to ensure that duration is not excessive.

(5) The Department of Public Health and Social Services has strengthened epidemiological evaluations of communicable diseases in

response to the appearance of pathogenic vibrios and the increase in pathogenic salmonella infections.

(6) The territory has actively pursued a closer relationship with the WHO Regional Office for the Western Pacific in an effort to participate in intercountry health problems such as arbovirus and enteric disease control.

(7) A larger portion of the financial and manpower resources within public health has been directed towards the tuberculosis control programme in an effort to provide better treatment and more effective follow-up of contacts.

Health planning

Health planning was reviewed in 1974 resulting in a revision of the approach to the health planning process. More emphasis was placed on eliminating duplicate services, manpower utilization, cost containment and consumer participation in the planning process. Public health programmes have been adjusted in the light of these new concepts. Other providers of health services will need to reassess their roles in the near future.

Education and training

With the assistance of WHO, health professionals are receiving advanced training in health education, environmental health, nursing administration and laboratory administration. This greatly assists the Government in establishing the middle management capabilities necessary to develop effective preventive and control programmes in chronic diseases, environmental health and other priority areas. Technical training in the control of specific diseases is being provided by WHO and the United States Center for Disease Control.

Many workshops and short courses have been provided within the territory to increase the competence and skills of auxiliary medical personnel.

Research

Basic health care research activities are limited by the lack of research facilities and personnel. Therefore, research activities have been directed towards the diseases that are uniquely prevalent on Guam: anterolateral sclerosis and

otitis media. A recent research breakthrough led to the discovery of the probable dietary and environmental factors that trigger the former in susceptible individuals. The development of new screening methods has permitted identification of infants who are most apt to develop otitis media. Both discoveries provide a base for the development of preventive programmes for these two diseases.

Appraisal of progress made in the period 1973–1977

There has been a major change in the delivery of health care in that the improvement in the quality and quantity of care available in the private sector has permitted the Government to redirect its health services. However, the gradual transition of patient care from the public to the private sector has increased the need for government, specifically the Department of Public Health and Social Services, to become more regulatory in nature. Legislation relating to the licensure of health professionals and health facilities has become increasingly necessary to protect the community from fraudulent or deceptive health care practices.

While the government continues to provide traditional direct care services to the public, such as maternal and child health and crippled children services, these are now being redirected specifically to the medically indigent. Further, concentration on basic primary health care services has ensured that the medically or financially indigent now have the opportunity to enter into a comprehensive health care system.

During the period under review, health care has been influenced by United States Federal health care concerns, which have centred around cost containment and adequate health planning. There is a substantial drive to encourage more public involvement in the entire health planning and health care process. United States Federal laws and regulations have also affected control of traditional programmes intended to prevent the spread of diseases through the environment.

Outlook

In the area of direct patient care, the following trends are anticipated:

(1) Some form of mandatory nation health insurance will be implemented to ensure that

every individual has access to a health delivery system that will meet his basic health needs.

(2) Almost all, if not all, patient care will be provided by licensed health maintenance organizations or other prepaid health insurance organizations.

(3) Outpatient care procedures will be formalized and criteria regulating inpatient services will be developed to prevent over-utilization of inpatient services and to control the cost of health care.

Health departments will become increasingly regulatory in nature in order to assure that quality health care is not sacrificed in the attempts at cost containment. Education projects will be developed to promote awareness of personal health, health planning and physical fitness. Greater emphasis will be placed upon disease prevention through regulation, education and research. Mental health services will become a standard part of routine outpatient and inpatient health care.

HONG KONG

There have been considerable improvements in the control of communicable diseases. Except for one imported case of cholera reported in 1976, no quarantinable diseases were reported during the period. Poliomyelitis was eradicated by 1974 as a result of immunization campaigns. Only one case of diphtheria was reported in 1977. The incidence of measles is on the decline. Tuberculosis, with an incidence of 159.3 per 100 000 population in 1977, remains a community health problem.

Noncommunicable diseases are on the increase—the leading causes of death are cancer, cardiovascular diseases, cerebrovascular diseases and pneumonia. Control measures are aimed at prevention, early detection and treatment. Attention is also being directed at providing care for the aged and disabled and improv-

ing the environmental and housing conditions of the community as a whole.

Population and other statistics

Population estimates and other vital statistics for the period under review are given in the table below.

The main causes of deaths in 1977 were: malignant neoplasms (24.1%), cardiovascular diseases (17.6%), cerebrovascular disease (10.3%), pneumonia (9.9%), accidents (4.2%), bronchitis, emphysema and asthma (3.9%), congenital anomalies, birth injury, difficult labour and other anoxic and hypoxic conditions, other causes of perinatal mortality (3.7%), suicide and self-inflicted injuries (2.7%), tuberculosis, all

	1973	1974	1975	1976	1977
Mid-year population	4 212 600	4 319 600	4 395 800	4 443 800	4 513 900
Number of registered live births	80 147	81 879	78 200	76 342	78 807
Birth rate (per 1000 population)	19.0	19.0	17.8	17.2	17.5
Number of registered deaths	21 360	22 050	21 191	23 195	23 459
Death rate (per 1000 population)	5.1	5.1	4.8	5.2	5.2
Natural increase (%)	1.39	1.39	1.30	1.20	1.23
Number of infant deaths	1 345	1 421	1 173	1 092	1 093
Infant mortality rate (per 1000 live births)	16.8	17.4	15.0	14.3	13.9
Number of deaths 1–4 years	337	348	248	271	249
Death rate 1–4 years (per 1000 population at risk)	1.07	1.10	0.77	0.84	0.78
Number of maternal deaths	8	13	2	14	13
Maternal mortality rate (per 1000 live births)	0.10	0.16	0.03	0.18	0.16

forms (2.3%), nephritis and nephrosis (1.6%), and cirrhosis of the liver (1.5%).

The communicable diseases most frequently notified in 1977 were: tuberculosis, all forms, new cases (7191), measles (1537), viral hepatitis (1008), chickenpox (899), food poisoning (555), typhoid and paratyphoid fevers (389), bacillary dysentery (322), leprosy (73), scarlet fever (28), amoebic dysentery (26), meningococcal infections (10), malaria, new cases (28, of which 26 were imported).

Environmental sanitation

The water supply in Hong Kong is surface water, collected and stored in reservoirs, augmented by a supply of river water from China and by desalinated water in times of drought. A central water authority supplies water to consumers through individually metered piped water connexions and, to some 5% of the population, through about 1000 public standpipes dispersed throughout the rural areas and, within urban areas, to meet the needs of the population living on boats and in temporary housing. An estimated 80% of the total population live in houses connected to the water-borne sewerage system.

Organization of the health services

Health services in Hong Kong are provided by the Government, government-subsidized voluntary agencies and the private sector. The government services are administered by the Medical and Health Department, which provides primary care, preventive health services, specialized and inpatient services, free or at a nominal charge. The Department works closely with other bodies or departments with statutory responsibility for safeguarding public health, such as the Urban Council, the Urban Services Department and the Labour Department. Medical officers are seconded to these departments.

Hospital services

In 1977 Hong Kong had 82 establishments for inpatient care providing a total of 19 277 beds, of which 8679 were in 33 government institutions, equivalent to 4.3 beds per 1000 population; 532 000 patients were admitted during the

year. The 19 277 beds were distributed as follows:

Category	Number of institutions	Number of beds
General hospitals	31	14 671
Rural hospital	1	18
Maternity hospital	1	296
Tuberculosis hospitals	2	692
Mental hospitals	2	2 281
Cancer hospital	1	150
Children's orthopaedic hospital	1	200
Medical rehabilitation centres	3	230
Hospitals for the mentally sub-normal	2	236
Maternity/nursing homes	38	503

Outpatient services

In 1977, outpatient services were available at 11 hospital departments, which recorded 2 886 435 attendances, and at 48 polyclinics and clinics, which recorded 6 879 104 attendances.

In 1977, maternal and child health services were available at 38 centres, and 28 831 pregnant women, 78 961 children aged under one year and 38 132 aged 1–5 years attended these units. The School Medical Service, which is administered by a statutory board, provided medical and health care to 106 193 schoolchildren. Dental treatment was given at 32 dental clinics. Other specialized units include 7 psychiatric outpatient clinics, 23 tuberculosis clinics, 16 venereal diseases clinics, 6 leprosy clinics, 16 ophthalmological clinics, 10 dermatological clinics, 7 ear, nose and throat clinics, 15 physiotherapy centres and 11 occupational therapy centres.

With effect from October 1973, the Medical and Health Department assumed direct responsibility in the provision of family planning services and commenced a three-phased operation to integrate family planning clinics hitherto run by the Government-subsidized Family Planning Association. The takeover was successfully completed on schedule in 1974. A total of 41 family planning clinics are operated by the Medical and Health Department's Family Health Services and another 24 clinics by the Family Planning Association.

Medical and allied personnel and training facilities

In 1977 Hong Kong had 3558 registered doctors (including 202 provisionally registered house physicians), of whom 864 were in government service. The doctor/population ratio was one to 1720. Health personnel in 1977 included:

Registered doctors	3 558	Pest control officers	3*
Unregistrable doctors[1]	389	Physiotherapists	86*
Dentists	633	Medical laboratory technicians	135*
Dental therapists	18*	Laboratory assistants	64*
Dental technologists	2*	Physicists	9*
Dental technicians	47*	Chemists	26*
Dental surgery assistants	90*	Radiographers	119*
Pharmacists	284	Occupational therapists	22*
Dispensers	221*	Speech therapists	2*
Veterinarians	13	Clinical psychologists	5*
Midwives	982	Optical technicians	5*
Registered nurses	8 919		
Registered psychiatric nurses	302		
Enrolled nurses	643*	[1] Persons with 6 years' training in medical schools not registrable
Enrolled psychiatric nurses	109*	with the Hong Kong Medical Council.
Health inspectors	558*	* In government service.

Arrangements for the training of professional and other health personnel are as follows:

Category	Duration of study (years)	Number of schools (government only)	Total enrolment (1977–1978)	Number of graduates in 1977
Doctors	5	1**	763	141
General registered nurses	3	2	750	297
Registered psychiatric nurses	3	1	142	14
General enrolled nurses	2	1	174	49
Enrolled psychiatric nurses	2	1	91	8
Nursing midwives	1	1	103	82
Midwives	2	1	12	10
Dental technicians	3	2	12	—
Dispensers	3	1	46	7
Laboratory assistants	2–3	1	10	3
Medical laboratory technicians	3	1	48	26
Health laboratory technicians	3	1	1	1
Physiotherapists	3	1	38	13
Prosthetists	3	1	2	—
Radiographers	3	1	42	14
Health inspectors	2	1	63	39

* In government service.
** Hong Kong University.

Social and economic developments of significance for the health situation

Economic growth was rapid in the period under review, and has significantly raised the standard of living in Hong Kong. The housing programme is being expanded rapidly. Primary education is being provided free of charge. Special attention has been paid to environmental pollution.

National health planning

The development programme of the Medical and Health Department has made rapid progress. Between 1973 and 1977, 52 projects were completed, were under construction or were being planned for the improvement and expansion of the health services in urban and rural areas.

The government plan for the development of medical and health services for the period 1973–1982 was stated in the 1974 Medical White Paper. The Medical Development Advisory Committee undertakes to advise on the phased implementation of the development programme and to review progress and update the programme every year.

Medical and public health research

Research activities are carried out by the various units of the Medical and Health Department and in collaboration with local and international agencies. Subjects studied during the period under review included viral hepatitis, tuberculosis, bronchogenic carcinoma and nasopharyngeal carcinoma. Clinical, biochemical and bacteriological studies are also being carried out on different therapeutic and anaesthetic agents.

Government health expenditure

In the financial year 1976/77, total government expenditure amounted to 6639.3 million Hong Kong dollars, of which HK $648.2 million were spent on the public health services. Recurrent expenditure was HK $633.7 million and capital expenditure was HK $14.5 million. The per capita expenditure on health was HK $146.

JAPAN

The health status of the Japanese nation has shown a remarkable improvement through successful public health activities, in particular, the extensive programme carried out for the control of tuberculosis and acute communicable diseases, along with the advancement of medical science and technology, progress of research in the development of pharmaceuticals such as the powerful antibiotics, etc.

Thus, the conspicuous prolongation of average life-expectancy has been achieved during the past post-war period which made it possible to place Japan in the group of countries now recording greatest longevity.

infectious diseases have been brought to a low level. However, a steady yearly increase has occurred in the death rates of those degenerative diseases like cancer, cerebrovascular and heart diseases, hypertension, etc., which are now the leading causes of death and are constituting a major problem because the lives of those people who are the nuclei of the productive society are heavily affected. Cerebrovascular diseases account for 25% of deaths, followed by cancer, which has increased from 16.8% in 1970 to 19.4% in 1975, and heart diseases, which caused 12.5% of deaths in 1970 and 14.1% in 1975. Much attention is therefore being paid to preventive programmes for the degenerative diseases.

Change in the major health problems

Change in the pattern of causes of death

In spite of such remarkable improvement made in the health of the people on the whole, there are many critical problems yet to be solved. Although the situation in Japan is now by no means inferior to the other advanced countries in terms of infant death rates, it is not satisfied with the extent of improvement in the neonatal death rates when compared with that of infant death rates as a whole. To overcome this, measures and programmes are being intensified within the maternal and child health service.

The death rates of those communicable diseases like tuberculosis, the malady which was once called a national disease, and other acute

Aging of population

Another problem Japan faces is the aging of population that has been accelerated by the remarkable decrease in the birth rates and general death rates, phenomena common to other developed countries in this latter half of the twentieth century. The problem of the aged population is now one of the most serious social problems in Japan.

Environmental pollution

In the Basic Law for Environmental Pollution Control enacted in 1967, as amended partially in 1970, "environmental pollution" is defined to apply to situations where human health or its living environment is damaged by air, water or soil pollution, noise, vibration, ground subsidence, and offensive odours, which occur over a considerable area as a consequence of industrial or other human activities. However, in addition to such environmental pollution, the problem caused by the urban activities has become quite severe in view of the rapid urbanization and improvement of people's living conditions between 1955 and 1965. Namely, the air pollution caused by sulfur oxides, nitrogen oxides, and photochemical oxidants created a serious problem, the pollution of neighbouring rivers and streams has worsened, and a new problem of eutrophication in the inland sea and lakes has emerged. In addition, there has been the problem of polychlorinated biphenyl contamination of foodstuffs.

A further serious problem is dealing with industrial wastes. During the 1973 fiscal year the total amount of industrial wastes produced by the manufacturing industry is said to have amounted to 340 million tonnes. It is therefore a task of considerable magnitude to ensure proper management of those wastes by organizing and completing the system and facilities for their proper disposal.

Attention has recently been directed towards the possible environmental pollution due to public enterprises such as construction of airfields and roads, reclamation of public water areas, construction of waste and nightsoil disposal facilities, and expansion of air-traffic and super-express national railways, etc. However, a wide range of pollution control measures have been introduced to cope with the environmental pollution mentioned above. As a result of such efforts, remarkable improvement has been made in various fields of pollution control, i.e., sulfur oxides, photochemical oxidant, sus-

pended particulate, etc., in air and hazardous chemicals in water. Japan is thus continuously making further efforts to maintain a comfortable living environment.

Medical care service

In addition to the changed pattern of main causes of deaths, there has been a general rising tendency observed in the morbidity ratio as shown by the National Health Survey and in the numbers of people who received medical treatment obtained through a patient survey. This tendency has been brought about by various factors, such as the increase of health consciousness in the general public by extensive health education campaigns through mass media as well as mass health examinations, and the increasing opportunities for the people to undergo medical treatment through the improvement and expansion of medical care facilities. The extensive delivery of medical care has been encouraged by the development of the nationwide health insurance scheme and the increased provisions by the Government for medical care expenses. Another factor has been the occurrence of new diseases or health hazards due to environmental deterioration or pollution.

Statistical data

Vital statistics

The population of the country rose by 5 million between 1973 and 1976, to 113 million. Some other vital statistics for the period under review are given in the following table with 1970 as a comparison year:

	1970	1973	1974	1975	1976
Number of live births	1 934 239	2 091 983	2 029 989	1 901 450	1 832 617
Birth rate (per 1000 population)	18.8	19.4	18.6	17.1	16.3
Number of deaths	712 162	709 416	710 510	702 281	703 270
Death rate (per 1000 population)	6.9	6.6	6.5	6.3	6.3
Natural increase rate %	1.18	1.28	1.21	1.08	1.00
Number of infant deaths	25 412	23 683	21 888	19 103	17 105
Infant mortality rate (per 1000 live births)	13.1	11.3	10.8	10.0	9.3
Neonatal deaths	16 742	15 473	14 472	12 912	11 638
Neonatal mortality rate (per 1000 live births)	8.7	7.4	7.1	6.8	6.4
Maternal deaths	1 008	801	700	546	474
Maternal mortality rate (per 1000 total live and still births)	0.49	0.36	0.33	0.27	0.26
Stillbirths	135 095	116 171	109 738	101 864	101 930
Still birth rate (per 1000 total live and still births)	65.3	52.6	51.3	50.8	52.7

Health establishments and health manpower resources

At the end of 1975 there were 8294 hospitals comprising 7235 general hospitals, 929 mental hospitals, 27 communicable disease hospitals, 87 tuberculosis sanitoria and 16 leprosaria. At the end of 1974 there were also 73 047 general clinics and 32 011 dental clinics.

The health manpower situation for the years 1974–1976 was as follows:

	1974	1975	1976
Medical doctors[a]	122 096	125 970	128 448
Dentists[a]	40 088	41 951	42 704
Pharmacists[a]	74 431	77 084	79 242
Public health nurses[a]	15 596	15 962	16 212
Midwives[a]	28 964	28 927	26 804
Nurses and assistant nurses[a]	372 880	395 663	375 738
Physiotherapists[b]	1 772	1 849	1 951
Occupational therapists[b]	507	558	623
Orthoptists[b]	322	374	470
Nutritionists[c]	13 343	13 928	14 472
X-ray and radiotherapy technicians[c]	14 655	15 348	11 698[d]
Clinical and health laboratory technicians[c]	28 130	23 594[d]	21 866[d]
Dental hygienists[a]	9 928	11 440	12 701
Dental technicians[a]	12 295	13 622	14 900

[a] Number engaged in practice.

[b] Number licenced.

[c] Number in medical facilities.

[d] Number working in hospitals only, not including those in clinics.

Environmental sanitation

The proportion of the population served with a piped water supply rose from 80.8% in 1970 to 87.6% in 1975 and the proportion benefiting from sewerage disposal facilities rose from 22.9% in 1970 to 24.6% in 1976.

Health expenditure

The following table shows an increased expenditure on health and welfare services:

	1973	1974	1975
Gross national medical expenditure (in thousand million yen)	3949.6	5378.6	6477.9
Percentage increase	16	36	20
Amount spent on medical care per capita (in yen)	36 332	48 875	57 871
Percentage of gross national medical care expenditure to gross national product	3.42	3.95	4.33
Percentage of total budget of the Ministry of Health and Welfare, for public and environmental health, medical care, social welfare, and social insurance to total national budget	14.7	16.8	18.4

MACAO

Population and other statistics

At the last census, taken in December 1977, the population of Macao was about 250 000. Some other vital statistics for the period under review based on the population of 250 000 are given in the following table:

Of the 1424 deaths recorded in 1977, the main causes were: malignant neoplasm (244); chronic rheumatic heart disease, hypertensive disease, ischaemic heart disease, other forms of heart disease (232); senility without mention of psychosis (154); cerebrovascular diseases (150); tuberculosis, all forms (128); disease of arteries,

	1973	1974	1975	1976	1977
Number of live births	2 686	2 781	2 583	2 369	2 532
Birth rate (per 1000 population)	10.6	11.1	10.3	9.4	10.1
Number of deaths	1 410	1 579	1 398	1 517	1 424
Death rate (per 1000 population)	5.6	6.3	5.5	6.0	5.7
Natural increase (%)	0.5	0.48	0.48	0.34	0.44
Number of infant deaths	59	57	59	61	53
Infant mortality rate (per 1000 live births)	22.0	20.5	22.8	25.7	20.9
Number of deaths, 1–4 years	18	27	10	12	17
Death rate, 1–4 years (per 1000 population at risk)	0.9	1.3	0.5	0.6	0.8

arterioles and capillaries (86); accidents (80, including 10 in motor-vehicle accidents).

The communicable diseases most frequently notified in 1977 were: tuberculosis, all forms, new cases (1070); infectious hepatitis (125); measles (72); influenza (23); typhoid fever (22); chickenpox (13).

Hospital services

In 1977, there were two general hospitals with 1272 beds, and 2 mental hospitals with 436 beds including those for drug addiction cases, making a total of 1708 beds, of which 479 were in government hospitals. The bed/population ratio was 6.8 to 1000.

Medical and allied personnel and training facilities

In 1977 Macao had 146 doctors, or one doctor for 1712 inhabitants. Other health personnel included:

Dentists	53
Operating dental auxiliaries	—
Pharmacists	20
Pharmaceutical assistants	—
Midwives	19
Assistant midwives	2
Nurses	291
Assistant nurses	51
Veterinarian	1
Auxiliary sanitarians	25
Auxiliary laboratory technicians	43
X-ray technicians	2

The Health and Welfare Services operate a technical school for the training of nurses, midwives, laboratory technicians and X-ray technicians. There are also 2 nursing schools run by missionaries, and a Chinese hospital.

Immunization services

The following vaccination procedures were carried out in 1977:

Cholera	27 358
Smallpox	4 781
Diphtheria	1 253
Poliomyelitis	5 888
BCG	2 458
Tetanus	1 259
Typhoid and paratyphoid fever	—
Duplex (diphtheria, tetanus)	449
Triplex (diphtheria, pertussis, tetanus)	2 098

Specialized units

In 1977 Macao had one prenatal and two child health centres. Other specialized units included a school health service, a dental health unit, a hospital rehabilitation outpatient department, a tuberculosis clinic, an ophthalmological clinic, an otorhinolaryngological clinic, a venereal diseases clinic and three laboratories.

MALAYSIA

Health and health-related problems

With the rapid economic development since independence in 1957, health problems are undergoing a change. Communicable diseases, although on the decline, are still a public health problem, and noncommunicable diseases and conditions, such as cardiovascular diseases and neoplasms, and accidents are rapidly increasing.

Other health-related problems were inherited on independence: the health services were almost wholly urban-based and almost wholly

curative; the specialist services in hospitals were mainly manned by expatriate officers, with very few Malaysians holding key positions; the few preventive measures existing, such as malaria control, maternal and child care services, safe water supply and sanitary facilities, were mostly concentrated in the urban areas or limited to the larger estates and mines which were foreign-owned; except for those visited by a few travelling dispensaries, the rural people, who constituted more than 70% of the population, were grossly underserved; and there were no specific health programmes designed to tackle many of the major endemic communicable diseases, such as tuberculosis, malaria, yaws, leprosy and filariasis, on a countrywide basis.

Population and other statistics

The estimated population and population density in 1977 were as follows:

	Estimated population	Density (per km^2)
Peninsular Malaysia	10 540 000	80
Sabah	870 000	11
Sarawak	1 120 000	9
Total	12 530 000	38

Mortality rates since independence have fallen as shown in the table below.

The proportional death rate (for those dying at over 50 years of age) increased from 32.8% in 1957 to 55.85% in 1975. The life expectancy at birth for the male and female population, which was 56 and 58 years respectively in 1957, had increased to 65.4 and 70.7 years by 1975. The crude birth rate was 31.7 per 1000 population in 1976 as compared to 46.0 in 1957. The rate of natural increase therefore declined from 33.7 in 1957 to 25.5.

Appraisal of progress

The general health status of the population continues to improve and the various mortality indicators are continuously on the decline. With the sustained expansion and improvement of the health services, there is every likelihood that complete coverage of the population in Peninsular Malaysia will be achieved by 1985. In the interim period, primary health care in the form of the community health movement is being introduced (see section on Primary health care, below). In Sabah and Sarawak, however, due to lack of a good communication system and to cultural factors, total coverage will take longer. For groups of population accessible by air, a flying doctor service and radiotelephone system have been introduced. With expanding health services of steadily improving quality, rapid economic growth and political commitment, the standard of living and quality of life has improved from year to year. There is every likelihood that this improvement will be sustained in the years to come.

Health policy

When the Ministry of Health assumed responsibility it was faced with the gigantic task of correcting the deficiencies of the past and the imbalance in the distribution, quality and quantity of the health services between the states and between the urban and rural areas of each state In developing and expanding the medical, health and dental services, major policy changes designed to overcome most of the obvious deficiencies as rapidly as possible were adopted. The highest priority was given to the establishment of a rural health service to correct the imbalance of distribution between the urban and rural areas. National programmes were established for the control or eradication of major communicable diseases that were the cause of high morbidity and mortality; e.g., yaws, filariasis, tuberculosis, malaria and leprosy. Greater emphasis was given to preventive services, using the rural health service infrastructure. Urgent steps were taken to develop and intensify the training of medical manpower locally by

	1957 (year of independence)	1976 (latest available data)	% decline
Crude death rate (per 1000 population)	12.4	6.2	50.0
Neonatal mortality rate (per 1000 live births)	30.0	19.0	36.6
Infant mortality rate (per 1000 live births)	75.5	30.7	59.3
Mortality rate 1–4 years (per 1000 population at risk)	11.0	2.6	76.7
Still birth rate (per 1000 live births)	24.0 (1959)	16.9	29.6
Maternal mortality rate (per 1000 live births)	2.8	0.8	72.3

the establishment of medical and dental faculties, and also training centres and schools for the training of nurses and other auxiliary staff. Local doctors received postgraduate training overseas to enable them to take over the specialist services from expatriate officers. Plans went forward for the expansion and modernization of existing hospitals and the establishment of new hospitals to bear the brunt of referred cases from the rural health services.

Health legislation

Existing health legislation is being reviewed and updated, and a public health act is being drafted to consolidate the various enactments and ordinances that existed in the various states. Health acts have been passed on State hospital assistants' registration (1965), midwifery (1966), dangerous drugs (amendment, 1966), nursing (1969), dental health (1971), private hospitals (1971), malaria eradication (1971), medical service (1971), destruction of disease-bearing material (1974).

Health planning and programming

The future of health services in Malaysia is embodied in the Government's overall development plans. The Health Plan is part and parcel of the Government's total socioeconomic programme based on the New Economic Policy. It is a prospective plan for the period up to 1990, designed to improve coverage and attain equitable and balanced distribution. The provision of improved health services will not only lead to a better qualty of life through general improvement of health conditions but, by reducing loss of working hours through illness, will increase labour productivity. Family planning, leading to the desired rate of growth of population, will also contribute to the development objectives of improving living standards.

The more detailed objectives of the Health Plan are:

(1) to promote the health of the individual and of the nation as a whole in order to measure up to the needs of the country's economic development and continuing social progress;

(2) to develop a training capability within the country so that the training programmes can be appropriately designed to suit local needs, and that dependence on foreign sources for training can be reduced;

(3) to achieve a well-balanced and well-distributed health service which is consistent, resilient, and alert to the changing pattern of health problems and demands resulting from an improving socioeconomic environment;

(4) to eradicate or control communicable diseases which are endemic and reduce human suffering and wastage;

(5) to support and complement the family planning programmes;

(6) to provide high-quality diagnostic and curative services so that maximum recovery is achieved in the shortest possible time;

(7) to provide high-quality preventive, restorative and curative dental care to the people;

(8) to strengthen the pharmaceutical and medical supplies services in order to provide adequate support for the achievement by all the other services of their stated objectives and goals; and

(9) to continue and expand clinical research in local health problems.

The Health Plan aims basically at consolidating the existing services, upgrading and updating facilities and services to ensure better standards of health care and distributing new facilities equitably so as to ensure that they reach the areas and population groups that need them most.

Since the launching of the Government's community development programme in 1966, increasing emphasis has been given to joint collaboration between the people and the Government in the improvement of the community and individual health. This principle is incorporated into the various health programmes and activities carried out in the field.

Satisfactory progress was achieved in the implementation of the health development plans during the first two years of the plan period; 529 out of a total 1769 projects (29.9%) were completed by the end of 1977, costing some 101.1 million Malaysian dollars; 304 (57.5%) of the completed projects were public health projects, 115 medical, 64 dental, 8 training and 38 projects for medical stores, construction of premises, and other related subjects.

Organization of health services

Rural health services

The original basic rural health unit as planned comprises one main health centre, four health subcentres and 20 midwife clinics, to serve a rural population of 50 000. As a result of a study using operational research technique in 1971–1972 it was decided to convert the three-tiered system (main health centre, health subcentre, midwife clinic) to a two-tiered system (main health centre, rural community clinic). This will upgrade the level of service at the periphery as there will be one doctor and one dentist per 15 000–20 000 population, not per 50 000. The scope of service at the midwife clinic level will be expanded to provide rudimentary ambulatory patient care, maternal and child health care, family planning, etc., in addition to the present domiciliary midwifery service.

In Peninsular Malaysia, 65 main health centres, 254 health subcentres, 1193 midwife clinics and 190 rural community clinics (*kelinik desa*) have been established since 1956.

The rural health service in Sabah is a two-tiered system comprising rural dispensaries and village group subcentres. The latter constitute the backbone of the maternal and child health services in the rural areas. Rural dispensaries are provided with beds for simple inpatient care, and in most places maternal and child health care is also available.

The rural health service in Sarawak is a modified version of that in Peninsular Malaysia. In concept it is a two-tier system consisting of a health subcentre serving a population of 5000 and a community health centre serving a population of 2000.

The demands made on the rural health service in Peninsular Malaysia have tripled since its inception, as shown below:

Year	Total attendances	Home visits	Domiciliary deliveries
1960	1 808 796	843 073	44 759
1970	2 645 332	1 729 296	76 455
1976	5 587 462	2 166 991	87 952

Primary health care

The existing basic rural health service is estimated to be serving some 80% of the rural population in Peninsular Malaysia, but less in Sabah and Sarawak. Although the Government is giving the highest priority to the development of basic rural health services, it is estimated that complete coverage of the rural population can only be achieved by 1985. In the interim it has been decided to provide the unserved and underserved population with health care based on an adaptation of primary health care principles to suit the local situation. In the Malaysian context the proposed health measures will be known as the community health movement.

An intersectoral approach is being adopted in the planning and later implementation of the community health movement programme. Special emphasis is placed on direct community involvement and participation in the planning and implementation of this programme. A survey of 44 administrative health districts started in September 1977 revealed that 2315 villages, with about 12% of the population covered, were underserved by the existing basic health services. Detailed studies are being made of the health and health-related problems in these underserved areas, after which health programmes will be formulated for implementation.

In the meantime, 46 mobile rural health teams have been created to provide basic curative and preventive services in the rural areas. Their functions and locations are being reviewed in the light of the survey results and the studies of the health problems in the underserved areas.

Medical care service

The medical care service is designed on a centripetal system with primary medical care at the periphery, secondary medical care at the intermediate level and tertiary medical care at the centre. Whilst secondary medical care is being decentralized to district hospital level, tertiary medical care is being regionalized in selected general hospitals to serve the population of a region (2 to 3 million).

The referral system has been reorganized so that a patient can receive expeditiously the appropriate level of effective care which the condition dictates.

The overall bed/population ratio is 2.7 beds per 1000 population, and the acute bed/population ratio is 1.8 beds per 1000 population in Peninsular Malaysia. The admission rate per 1000 population is 55.4. The average occupancy rate is 67.23% and the average length of stay is 8 days. The overall bed/population ratio for Sabah is 2.1 and the acute bed/population ratio 1.8 beds per 1000 population. In Sarawak the overall bed/population ratio is 2.46 beds per

1000 population and the acute bed/population ratio is 1.76 beds.

The growth of specialist departments providing high quality service since 1957 in Peninsular Malaysia, and in Sarawak and Sabah since 1963, has been most impressive. From 47 they have increased to 296. With the postgraduate training of more local doctors and the recruitment of foreign specialists on short-term contracts in fields where there is a dearth of local specialists, many more specialist departments will be established.

It is planned to establish an integrated diagnostic and public health laboratory service for the country. There will be four levels of laboratory service varying in the scope of examinations and tests. The lowest level will be established at health centres and outpatient departments, the next two levels at district hospitals and the highest level at the general hospitals. In this way it is hoped that the limited staff resources will be used to the maximum and duplication of services minimized.

The psychiatric service will be decentralized through the establishment of mental health units in selected district hospitals and all the general hospitals. This will reduce the need for maintaining large psychiatric institutions. The decentralization programme has the added advantage of providing wider coverage, and ensuring treatment for those requiring it in the early stage of the illness.

Dental service

The dental service is also patterned on a centripetal system. Using the rural health service facilities and schools as the base, this service has deeply permeated into the rural areas. For schools with enrolments too small to employ fully a resident dental nurse, and for isolated concentrations of population where no health facility is provided, mobile dental squads have been established.

The objective is to provide adequate preventive and promotional services and high quality dental care for the whole population.

There are 674 dental clinics with 1104 chairs and 22 mobile dental squads in Peninsular Malaysia, 35 dental clinics with 52 chairs in Sabah and 89 clinics with 134 chairs in Sarawak.

A dental epidemiological survey of 15 000 schoolchildren in 1971 showed that almost 90% of the children examined had at least one tooth with dental caries (the mean number of dental caries being 1.9 for all ethnic groups) and that 1 in 5 children had dentofacial anomalies.

Field work for the epidemiological dental survey of adults in Peninsular Malaysia has been completed. The sampling size of the population involved 9000 randomly selected people.

In Peninsular Malaysia almost all the public water supply systems have been fluoridated. Similarly, the public water supply system for Kota Kinabalu in Sabah has been fluoridated, as have 15 public water supply systems of the various townships in Sarawak. The programme of water fluoridation is estimated to cover some 6 million people, about 50% of the population.

Maternal and child health services

Continuous review and evaluation of the maternal and child health services are being carried out and the programmes and activities are being modified accordingly. Stress has been placed on the need for health staff to adopt a more positive and dynamic attitude towards health care and to move away from the clinic to the community concept. Although routine procedures and norms have been laid down, the staff are urged to take into account the health and health-related problems faced by the local community.

Family planning

Integration of family planning has been achieved in 34% of the maternal and child health service delivery points involving a total of 1237 maternal and child health clinics, main health centres, health subcentres, midwife clinics and rural community health clinics; 2862 assistant nurses and midwives, or 97% of the auxiliary staff, have already been trained in family planning work. Integration can thus proceed rapidly. The numbers of new acceptors and of follow-up visits increased from 2963 and 28 519 respectively in 1971, to 22 891 and 500 401 in 1976.

Communicable diseases

Under the impact of eradication and control activities, the incidence of *malaria* in Peninsular Malaysia fell from 2.75 per 1000 population in

1970 to 1.24 per 1000 in 1977; 62% of the population in Peninsular Malaysia are now living in transmission-free areas. In Sabah and Sarawak, despite the malaria control programme, the incidence of malaria is still high.

Pulmonary tuberculosis is still a public health problem, although its incidence fell from 0.92 per 1000 population in 1970 to 0.72 per 1000 in 1976.

A national survey of *sexually transmitted diseases* carried out in 1976 showed a rising trend in their incidence, particularly the incidence of gonorrhoea and syphilis. A national control programme is being elaborated.

The aim of the *leprosy* control programme is to reduce the incidence of the disease so that it is no longer a public health and social problem. The programme was launched in 1969, and 23 skin clinics have been established throughout the country. A central registry of cases has been set up at the national control centre and 7480, about half of the estimated number, have been registered. Of these, 1129 have been released from control and 940 have since died.

The *yaws* control programme, which started in the 1950s, has reduced the incidence of yaws considerably so that it is no longer a public health problem. The programme, now in the maintenance phase, is totally integrated into the basic health service.

The *filariasis* control programme, which started in the 1960s, has been expanded to cover all the known endemic areas in the country. There are at the moment 10 trained control teams, to be increased to 20 for more effective control.

Cholera outbreaks have occurred sporadically in certain foci in each of the past 10 years. Long-term remedial measures are being taken in urban slums and rural kampongs, in addition to vigorous interim measures.

Typhoid has been showing a rising trend since 1973, occurring in sporadic focal outbreaks in small estates, villages and towns.

The incidence of both *viral hepatitis A* and *B* is approximately twice that of typhoid, and it is rising with that of typhoid. Improvements in serological diagnosis and disease surveillance are needed. A WHO interregional seminar on viral hepatitis was held in Kuala Lumpur in December 1977.

The incidence of *dengue haemorrhagic fever* has been kept in check; from 2201 cases with 104 deaths in 1974, it fell to 773 cases with 37 deaths in 1977. Further attempts are being made to lower the morbidity and mortality.

A special unit has been established to gather and disseminate epidemiological information. The unit will also study and forecast impending epidemics and advise on the measures to be taken to avoid or overcome an epidemic.

A *vector control* unit has been established to carry out surveillance of disease-bearing insects, monitor resistance to insecticides and provide expertise in the control of vector-borne diseases.

Noncommunicable diseases

Studies and surveys are being planned to provide accurate epidemiological information on cancers and cardiovascular diseases so that a comprehensive programme for treatment, control, prevention and rehabilitation can be planned.

Environmental health

Environmental sanitation and rural community water supply

Many of the communicable diseases commonly occurring in this country are due to poor sanitation and improper water supply. Every emphasis is being placed on improved sanitation and water supply services in the rural areas and urban slums. In 1977 a total of 600 protected wells, 34 310 sanitary toilets and 21 gravity-feed water supply systems were completed in Peninsular Malaysia, providing 173 000 more people with sanitary facilities. In Sabah 80 rural water supply systems and 1438 sanitary toilets were completed; and in Sarawak, 156 rural water supply systems and 7402 sanitary toilets were completed.

Occupational health service

This service will produce and maintain the highest possible degree of physical, mental and social wellbeing of workers in all occupations, and prevent illnesses due to their working conditions. It will carry out environmental monitoring and control, control of occupational diseases, and surveillance of fitness to work, early treatment and rehabilitation.

Food sanitation and quality control service

This service aims at protecting consumers against health hazards and toxicity of food, as well as against misleading food advertisement.

Education and training of health manpower

In view of the critical shortage of trained and qualified manpower in the medical, health and dental services, the Ministry has intensified its training programmes as a matter of the highest priority. The critical shortage of staff is due to the ever-increasing demands made on the various services which are being continuously and rapidly expanded and upgraded.

New public health programmes, some on a national scale, are being embarked upon, and all these require trained medical manpower to be effectively operational. A two-pronged strategy was adapted to provide crash training programmes, and long-term programmes for the development and expansion of training facilities to increase local training capability and reduce dependence on foreign training sources.

Facilities for basic training of auxiliary and technical staff have been developed and expanded so rapidly that the stage has now been reached where the country is no longer dependent on foreign sources for such training. Two medical faculties, a dental faculty and a school of pharmaceutical sciences have been established in the local universities.

Continuing medical education for the professional, technical and auxiliary staff has not been neglected. Numerous postgraduate and post-basic courses have been established locally in conjunction with the universities, training institutions and professional organizations on a permanent basis.

Pharmacy and medical supplies

The scope and operation of the pharmaceutical and medical supplies services have been broadened from a mere procurement, storage and distribution service to include manufacture, analytical testing and quality control, phar-

maceutical research and product development, control and prevention of illegal sale of scheduled poisons and drugs and of substandard drugs (a drug inspectorate has been set up and is in operation). The aim is to provide adequate support for all the health services in the attempt to achieve their stated goals and objectives. To keep up with the requirements of the expanding service, the manufacturing capability of the Central Medical Store has been further expanded. It was found necessary to establish a pharmaceutical research and product development unit in the Central Medical Store to provide "in-process" quality control; monitoring involves a greater degree of innovation and applied research oriented towards solving processing problems and developing new formulations and packaging methods.

With the rapid growth of drug manufacture in both the public and private sectors, a national pharmaceutical control laboratory has been established to control, test and register all drugs manufactured locally or imported into the country and those offered for sale.

Medical research

The primary medical research centre in the country is the Institute for Medical Research, based in Kuala Lumpur, with branch laboratories in Penang and Ipoh. The Institute, which was founded in 1900 to conduct research in tropical diseases, is the national central reference laboratory. It is also the WHO reference centre for surveillance programmes on influenza, salmonella and shigella, food-borne diseases, oral cancer, and other diseases. For many years it has accommodated the United States Army Medical Research Unit and the International Centre for Medical Research of the University of California, and has actively participated in various international research projects.

Health budget

The health budget for 1977 was 562.0 million Malaysian dollars (M $459.8 million for operating expenditure and M $102.2 million for development expenditure). The operating expenditure for health was 7.29% of the total operating budget; the development expenditure was 2.27% of the total development appropriation. The per capita health expenditure was M $44.63.

NEW CALEDONIA AND DEPENDENCIES

Population statistics

At the last census, on 23 April 1976, New Caledonia and Dependencies had 133 233 inhabitants. Some other statistics are given below:

	1973	1974	1975	1976
Mean population	127 500	131 500	133 000	134 500
Number of live births	4 393	4 202	4 057	3 902
Death rate (per 1000 inhabitants)	7.8	7.9	7.0	7.8
Birth rate (per 1000 inhabitants) .	34.5	32.0	30.5	29.0
Natural increase (per 1000 inhabitants)	26.7	24.1	23.5	21.2
Infant deaths (per 1000 live births)	39.2	41.0	34.0	33.9
Number of deaths, 1–4 years . .	141	105	144	135

Organization of health services

The health services are supervised by a Director of Health and Public Hygiene, who is directly responsible to the Governor of the Territory. He is assisted by a technical deputy director, who is a physician, and an administrative deputy director. New Caledonia is divided into 16 medical districts, each under the authority of a chief medical officer.

Health establishments

In 1977 the Territory had 34 hospitals and hospital establishments with a total of 1677 beds (1357 of them in 31 public establishments), distributed as follows:

Category	Number	Number of beds
General hospitals	4	870
Rural hospitals	15	278
Medical centres	13	82
Psychiatric (and geriatric) hospital . . .	1	299
Leprosarium	1	156

Outpatients are seen at the Gaston Bourret Hospital, at 29 dispensaries (24 in the interior and five in Nouméa—four of them for preventive medicine), and by a mobile team.

In 1977 the maternal and child health centre provided services for 4867 pregnant women, 13 703 infants under one year of age, and 8127 children aged 1–4 years. 3027 deliveries reported in the same year took place in the presence of a physician or a qualified midwife (3000 in hospital and 27 at home). The entire school population (43 056 children) was under the supervision of the School Medical Centre in Nouméa and the chief medical officers of the medical districts.

In 1976 four dental health dispensaries attended to 7658 patients, 40% of them children under 16.

A leprosy dispensary and a tuberculosis dispensary were responsible for coordinating leprosy and tuberculosis control respectively. The mental health dispensary recorded 1159 consultations in 1977.

The Municipal Health Office supervised the general sanitation plan of the town of Nouméa (mosquito control), surveillance of water, sewage purification plants, etc.).

In 1976 the Sports Medicine Centre performed 4411 check-ups on athletes throughout the Territory (schoolchildren and others).

The two public health laboratories performed 414 965 tests in 1977.

The main tasks of the Health Surveillance Office are the treatment of sexually transmitted diseases, epidemiological surveys of contagious diseases, and the vaccinations required for international travel.

Sanitation

Facilities in dwellings improved substantially. In 1969 56% of dwellings had running water (87% in Nouméa). By 1976 the figures had risen to 72% for the Territory as a whole and to 97% for Nouméa. In 1976, 66% of dwellings had indoor toilets (compared with 43% in 1969).

Health budget

In 1976 the local budget of New Caledonia was 11 402 770 000 CFP francs, of which 1 358 420 000 CFP francs was allocated to the health services.

Health manpower

In 1976 there were the following numbers of health personnel:

Physicians	131*
Dentists	36
Pharmacists	35
Midwives	11
Nurses with State diploma	138
Nurses with local diploma	128
Assistant nurses and nursing aides	210
Public health technicians	4

*Including 55 employed by the Administration.

In 1976 the interior islands had 0.33 physicians per 1000 inhabitants, Nouméa had 1.87 per 1000, and the whole Territory 0.98 per 1000.

A nursing school opened in 1969 prepares students either for the local diploma in two years (8 graduates in 1977) or for the State diploma in three years (11 graduates in 1977).

Immunization

The following vaccinations were performed in 1977:

Smallpox	8 610
BCG	11 361
Diphtheria and tetanus	1 084
Cholera	2 768
Typhoid and paratyphoid fever,	
diphtheria and tetanus	2 681

Poliomyelitis	479
Typhoid and paratyphoid fevers	498
Diphtheria, tetanus and poliomyelitis.	701
Yellow fever	118
"Tétraco" (DPT + poliomyelitis)	3 549
Diphtheria, tetanus and poliomyelitis	8 398
Tetanus	903

Outlook

The hospital infrastructure is to be strengthened by the establishment of a modern hospital centre for the Territory. The phasing-out of unqualified paramedical posts will continue. In health technology emphasis will be placed on the prophylaxis of the social diseases by early detection and use of drugs or vaccination, particularly for tuberculosis and leprosy.

NEW HEBRIDES

Major health problems

The main medical and public health problems, in a population with a high proportion of infants and children below the age of 15 years living in unsatisfactory sanitary conditions, are those associated with communicable diseases. Common conditions reported are sores, fevers, (including malaria), scabies, diarrhoeal disorders, anaemia, helminthiasis, conjunctivitis and respiratory infections. During the period under review, yaws recurred on some islands and there were widespread outbreaks of dengue and influenza, and of gastroenteritis thought to be of viral origin.

Nutritional surveys conducted by South Pacific Commission staff and by hospital and health centre staff indicate that serious protein-energy malnutrition is uncommon; there is however a significant incidence of undernutrition among children seen at clinics and at school inspection.

Malaria is the major public health problem, with an estimated 23 000 cases in 1974, before control measures were implemented. Filariasis is a related problem. Surveys have shown prevalence to vary from nil on some islands to about 19% on the west coast of Santo. Mass treatment is being organized in highly infected areas.

In 1977 the incidence of all notified cases of tuberculosis was 1.42 per 1000 population, that of confirmed cases 0.82 per 1000; 253 active cases of leprosy were registered at the end of 1976, and incidence of new cases during 1977 was 0.16 per 1000 population.

Gonorrhoea is an increasing problem; in 1977, 616 cases were reported, the majority in urban centres or in certain rural areas with close communications with the two major towns.

Regular reporting of morbidity data from all health institutions is progressing and most outlying dispensaries now submit returns to their district centres and to Vila.

Although improvements are being made, most people in rural areas still live in unsatisfactory environmental conditions. Housing should be improved, while sanitation and waste disposal in most villages should be organized.

A systematic plan to provide piped water supplies to rural communities is being implemented by the Mines and Hydrological Service, and a water-seal latrine scheme is being promoted by the Health Inspectorate of the Medical Department.

Another health-related problem is the administrative organization of the Medical Department, with health services being provided by the French administration, the British administration, the Condominium administration and various religious organizations. With the establishment of a new Hebridean Ministry of Social Services (including Health) at the beginning of 1978, integration and unification of services is expected to take place soon.

Action taken

The general policy of the Government during the last few years has been to improve services given by dispensaries in rural areas through better training and refresher-training of staff, improving supplies and logistics, and organizing a regular and effective supervisory structure.

There is no formal comprehensive health plan at present. Various programmes to deal with major health problems have been organized and have been functioning for many years.

A WHO-assisted malaria control campaign has been under way since 1972. One round of residual spraying has interrupted transmission of malaria on the main island of Efate. Similar programmes have been extended to Santo, Malo and Malekula in 1975, and further extension of these programmes to other islands is intended.

Scar surveys undertaken in 1974 showed an 80% coverage of the population by BCG immunization in all age groups and very high BCG coverage in small children. WHO supports the tuberculosis control programme as well as the leprosy control programme, which is also assisted by New Zealand. Both involve training rural dispensary staff in case detection and management by ambulatory treatment.

A pilot mass filariasis drug administration programme begun in 1970, was extended in 1975 to areas with high parasite rates in Erromango and Aniwa. UNICEF is giving assistance in the purchase of diethylcarbamazine.

A programme for the development of health services was organized in cooperation with WHO and UNICEF. Refresher training of nurses and dressers has been given, a basic inventory of equipment was provided by UNICEF, logistics were improved, and supervision by touring teams was organized.

The main emphasis in the provision of health services is placed on family health services, including nutrition, immunization, and health education, through the promotion of primary health care and the training of community workers. A first course for training of village sanitarians to be employed by community councils was completed in May 1977.

Organization of health services

Administratively the country is divided into four districts. Primary health care and preventive services are provided by the dispensaries scattered over the islands. For some activities, assistance is given by the staff of the central office of the rural health service. Patients in need of more specialized care are referred to the rural hospitals or referral hospitals. It is estimated that nobody is more than six hours (by road or by boat) from a health institution.

The number of nursing schools has been reduced to two, one with teaching in French and one in English. Teaching is geared to community health practice and is beginning to provide dispensary staff of a high level of competency.

Health resources

By mid-1977 there were 112 health institutions: 3 referral hospitals, 8 community hospitals, 18 maternity centres, and about 80 dispensaries or aid posts. Total bed capacity was about 700.

There were 28 doctors, 20 of whom had French metropolitan qualifications, 240 qualified nurses, and about 28 paramedical staff. There were also 11 village sanitarians, and 79 student nurses.

Total expenditure (recurrent costs) by the three administrations and the various missions on medical services in 1976 was about 330 million New Hebrides francs, or NHF 3386 per head of the population. Salaries account for over 60% of total expenditure.

Outlook

Great progress has been made in the last five years, both in quality of services given and in coverage of the population. Difficult communications are the main problem and some small population groups will remain difficult to reach. It is estimated however that about 80% of the population are regularly covered by family health and other preventive programmes.

Efforts will continue to strengthen health, and especially primary care services, through development of health manpower. Most of the senior medical and nursing staff are at present expatriates, and there is an urgent need for training of more national health staff.

On the administrative side, the main emphasis in the near future will be on coordinating the various existing medical services under the new Ministry of Social Services.

NEW ZEALAND

Health planning—programming and reorganization

The organization of health services underwent reappraisal between 1973 and 1977. In 1974 the then Labour Government's White Paper, "A Health Service for New Zealand", proposed sweeping changes aimed at integrating the administration of public hospitals with that of other aspects of health services. This was not carried through because the Government changed at the end of 1975, but the widespread debate sparked off by the White Paper has continued and broadened, especially in the areas of health care costs and the provision of services in the community rather than in an institutional setting. In 1976 the Government established a Special Advisory Committee on Health Services Organization which developed a pilot scheme for restructured local health administration for the Northland area. This scheme is now being discussed in the local community prior to implementation.

At local levels there have been moves towards coordination between the district offices of the Department of Health responsible for environmental and preventive health, and the hospital board, in response to reforms proposed by the central Government and to community health proposals financed by additional duty on tobacco and alcohol.

The development of improved health planning mechanisms is also seen as an important facet of health service reorganization, both at national and regional levels. Study of the concept of planning for user-oriented services is now in progress.

Health legislation

New legislation passed in the period under review included:

– the Clean Air Act 1972, whereby industrial air polluting processes are licensed within certain prescribed limits;
– the Misuse of Drugs Act 1975, which consolidates the provisions of the previous Narcotics Act 1965, controls the use of, possession of and dealing in scheduled drugs;
– the Plumbers, Gasfitters and Drainlayers Act 1976, the Optometrists and Dispensing Opticians Act 1976 and the Nurses Act 1974 which provide for the registration of persons qualified in the occupations referred to and maintain controls over those occupations.

There have also been a number of amendments to existing statutes and regulations to ensure that they are relevant to current developments:

– the Food Hygiene Regulations, specifying minimum standards for the maintenance of premises and clothing and the conduct of food handlers were revised in 1974;
– Radiation Protection Legislation was introduced in 1973 and regulations providing for controls in the use of lasers and microwave ovens are in preparation;
– a code of practice for the safe use of lasers was issued in 1977.

Developments in the provision of public health services

Occupational health

Regional specialist teams are being recruited to investigate occupational health problems beyond the resources of the local medical officer of health; for example, occupational diseases in the timber and agriculture industries. Public health nurses' services are more generally available to industries too small to employ a full-time nurse, and a further six occupational health centres are planned, the first to be operational by mid-1979.

There was a reduction in the number of cases of vision permanently damaged by accident. A major zoonosis investigation is being undertaken in an attempt to eradicate leptospirosis and brucellosis, which still occur particularly among freezing plant workers, although the number of notifications of these two diseases has been reduced.

Toxic substances

There have been few large-scale problems with toxic chemicals, However, the number of instances in which toxic chemicals have been spilled during transportation has resulted in the establishment of Hazardous Substances Technical Liaison Committees in each of the 18 health regions, bringing together representatives from police, health, fire and other agencies.

New laws were expected to be passed in 1978 to control the labelling, packaging, availability and transport of toxic substances and to permit the setting-up of a computerized register of toxic substances imported or manufactured.

Public health engineering services

The number of approved water supply and sewage, reticulation, treatment and disposal schemes has risen from 250, valued at 9.9 million New Zealand dollars, to 484, valued at NZ $81.8 million in the four years under review. In 1975 all public water supplies were surveyed to see how many met the international standards for drinking-water. Although there had been a significant improvement, 5% of the total population still had water supplies that did not meet the international standards.

Two solid waste disposal site surveys have proved the effectiveness of this method of dealing with waste. Investigation of thermal pools has revealed the need to control naturally-occurring amoeba by preventing the contamination of pools from surrounding soil. This investigation followed seven fatal cases of primary amoebic meningoencephalitis associated with hot pools. The pools are to be surveyed periodically.

Food and nutrition

Large areas of in-shore waters in which rock oysters and mussels are farmed are monitored for contamination. The standards of the United States National Shellfish Sanitation Programme are being used.

The National Food Surveillance Programme has been expanded, and a marked reduction has been achieved in the lead content of canned beverages and infant food. Fish with a mercury level in excess of 0.5 mg/kg fresh weight (0.5 ppm) are no longer harvested for human consumption.

Two new, independent advisory committees, a Food Standards Committee and a Nutrition Advisory Committee were formed to advise the Minister of Health on all matters related to food and nutrition and to recommend proposed amendments to the Food and Drug Regulations.

Pollution control

In recent years noise has become a public health concern. The Department has instituted a noise control programme in all government workshops and investigates many environmental noise problems in order to advise local authorities, Under the Clean Air Act which became effective in 1973, all major sources of air pollution are controlled by the local authorities who establish clean air zones. The Department is represented on councils and committees of the National Water and Soil Conservation Authority which is responsible for the control of water pollution.

Radiation protection

At present studies are being made of radiation doses in patients exposed to mammography and chiropractical and dental radiography. Studies of genetically significant doses to the population from the unsealed sources used in medical practice, and from external beam radiotherapy, have been published. An investigation into X-ray emission from television receivers and associated equipment has been undertaken and continuing attention is being given to the reduction of accidental over-exposure in industrial radiography, especially in pipeline work.

Disease control

Most common communicable diseases occur at minimal levels. Health educators have been primarily concerned with problems of child and maternal health including antenatal care, alcohol, drug dependence, tobacco smoking and associated diseases, coronary heart disease, sexually transmitted diseases and the problems associated with the settlement of Pacific Islanders. The number of free confidential venereal disease clinics has been increased from 10 to 14, and 24-hour venereal disease answer phones have been installed in four cities. Advisory bodies have been established to advise the Government on the most effective means of expanding educative preventive and remedial work on the public health problems posed by cigarette smoking and alcohol consumption.

Family health

The New Zealand Family Planning Association (Inc) has expanded its activities to cover 36 clinics. Six additional clinics are situated in public hospitals. A revised method of subsidizing the Association's activities was implemented during 1976–1977. Three courses per year for the postgraduate training of doctors in family planning were financed by the Government in the period under review. A Royal Commission of Inquiry into Contraception, Sterilisation and Abortion heard submissions from the public and other organizations concerned in 1975 and 1976. A report was issued in 1977 with recommendations for the amendment of existing legislation.

In the field of child health care, special clinics have been established to combat the increase in ear infections, and in 1974 public health nurses undertook to test the general development of infants and preschool children. In 1975, new obstetrics regulations made provision for the notification of all births and congenital anomalies to medical officers of health, with the introduction of a handicapped children's register to ensure full use of services available to handicapped children.

An obstetrics facilities survey covering the period 1969–1974 produced a report on maternity services. This and other reports, together with the Regulations of 1975, provided for improvements in the field of maternal health.

Postneonatal mortality rates caused concern. A survey is being undertaken and infants are being examined at nine months of age. A pilot study in schools is to be undertaken this year whereby a nurse will be attached to some primary schools, and a committee on child health has been set up by the Board of Health.

A Conference on Women and Health was held in February 1977.

The National Health Institute

The Institute has become increasingly involved with the general welfare of the community and in disease prevention.

The virus laboratory provides a diagnostic service for a substantial area and is especially involved with influenza, measles and rubella surveillance. Preparations are being made for hepatitis investigation. An increasing amount of work is directed at the industrial environment, especially industries that use toxic chemicals or produce dangerous dusts or fibrous particles.

The food laboratories are expanding rapidly as the demands for the investigation of the microbiological quality of imported and exported foods, the security of water supplies, and food poisoning outbreaks increase.

Epidemiological studies of streptococcal diseases and the distribution and medical importance of types of coliform bacteria have been initiated recently. Other units which contribute a useful service to community health are concerned with streptococcal, staphylococcal and enteric bacteria (including phage-typing services), mycology, serology, biological standards, bacteriological taxonomy, and a serum bank. An endeavour is made to balance routine service work with relevant research projects.

The Institute has been called upon to help in the control of a cholera epidemic in the Gilbert Islands and an investigation of the incidence of typhoid in Tonga.

Biomedical and health services research

Data processing for the health services has been reorganized. Two major computers have been installed and they and all users are connected by a telecommunication network. Three core systems are being developed—payroll, clinical laboratory processing, and hospitals admissions and discharges.

Increased efforts have been made to develop in providers and consumers of health care an interest in and appreciation of the part that management services and research should play in the planning and management of health services. With continuing economic restraint people are beginning to appreciate the need for priorities and the contribution that health service research has to make. Recently a joint committee of the Medical Research Council and the Department of Health has been formed to foster and administer health services research.

At the community level efforts are being made to encourage the active involvement of providers and users of health care in the development of their own health services.

The hospital design and evaluation unit was established in 1971 to obtain greater efficiency in health service buildings and, in so doing, to achieve economies in both capital and maintenance costs. Hospital buildings must provide a safe environment for patients and staff and be compatible with other fields in the community such as education and housing. The design emphasis should be on flexibility to meet changed functions during a building's existence.

Health resources

Health establishments

In 1977, inpatient medical care was available in 358 hospitals, and other health establishments, providing a total of 32 762 beds of which 27 910 were in 202 Government maintained establishments. The 32 762 beds were distributed as follows:

General and maternity hospitals	18 978
Psychiatric hospitals and hospitals for the mentally retarded	8 932
Private hospitals	4 852

In the year ending on 31 March 1977, 384 567 patients were admitted to Government maintained institutions, and a total of 3 399 863 attendances at outpatient departments were recorded.

Health manpower

In 1974 a small manpower planning section was established within the Department of Health. The functions of the section are: to develop and maintain a comprehensive manpower planning data base to cover all professional and technical staff in the delivery of health care; to forecast the manpower requirements for stated health planning objectives; to devise and recommend measures to ensure that existing manpower resources are used effectively and efficiently and that required resources are available when and where they are needed; to develop and maintain liaison with organizations involved in any way with the recruitment, training and development of health workers. Despite initial difficulties, data on 27

health occupations were published in October 1974. Questionnaires are sent out each year with the annual practising certificates issued by professional registration bodies. This is a very successful way of collecting health manpower information. An expanded and updated report on health manpower has been published.

Manpower planning workshop reports include recommendations on medical migration and manpower, nursing manpower, women in medicine, the distribution of specialists, general practice, psychiatry, paediatrics, hospital staffing and community medicine. Further workshops are planned.

The education of doctors has always been university-based but, in contrast, most of the other health professions have developed through a hospital-based programme on the apprenticeship pattern. The widening needs of health care, the increasing accent on community care and the obvious advantages of the medical type of education have encouraged many of these professions to seek a comprehensive basic programme in the educational system. Gradually the responsibility for the education of health professions is being transferred to the Department of Education. Several universities are now offering courses in nursing studies towards a bachelor degree. One has a diploma nursing course, and an important innovation is a multidisciplinary graduate diploma course in health administration. Continuing education programmes are conducted by a number of hospital boards, mainly in the nursing area. A review of administrative training in the health service is at present being undertaken.

Production and sale of pharmaceuticals

The pharmaceutical industry is almost entirely concerned with formulation and packaging. There is no manufacture of bulk active ingredients but the first synthesis of some ingredients in New Zealand is now imminent. All manufacturers are subject to the Department of Health's Code of Good Pharmaceutical Manufacturing Practice which is based on the recommendations of WHO, modified where necessary to meet local conditions. The industry has cooperated fully with the Department of Health in its endeavours to achieve uniformly high standards. The Department's drug testing programme has been increased.

Although there is a combined purchasing scheme for many medicines used in hospital boards the purchase of medicines in bulk or the arrangement of contracts for medicines in the private sector is not undertaken. Medicines are normally sold through 1200 retail pharmacies from which a full range of pharmaceuticals is available including over-the-counter items as well as prescription-only medicines. However, most, medicines are available, free of charge, to patients under the pharmaceutical benefits scheme. A limited number of simple remedies can be sold in premises other than pharmacies.

Health services expenditure

The gross and net expenditure for the financial years in the period under review were as follows (in thousands of New Zealand dollars):

	1973/74	1974/75	1975/76	1976/77
Gross expenditure . . .	401 880	493 598	606 404	690 460
Less: departmental receipts	785	1 292	796	1 354
New expenditure . . .	401 095	492 306	605 608	689 106

These figures include all benefits administered by the Department of Health. Other benefits are available in respect of disabilities arising from age, sickness and other exceptional conditions and these are the responsibility of the Department of Social Welfare.

Extension of health services to groups in special need

Medical benefits have been restructured in an attempt to help most those whose health needs are greatest. In 1974 benefit rates for pensioners, social security beneficiaries and children were raised. The higher rates were also extended to those with chronic illnesses requiring frequent medical attention. In 1977 benefit rates were increased considerably for children in an attempt to minimize any financial deterrent to low-income families obtaining primary medical care for children. As a result of these changes these special groups of patients are making better use of general practitioner services.

The advent of accident compensation legislation in 1974 has also meant an increasing use of general practitioner and other health services, as no cost is borne by the person injured. The Accident Compensation Act also provides for the rehabilitation of accident victims.

In 1976 subsidies paid to general practitioners employing registered nurses were extended. Of the 1650 doctors in general practice, about 600 now work with registered nurses. The amended subsidies were designed to increase the use of these nurses in the domiciliary setting.

A family medicine training programme has been promoted under the registration of the New Zealand Council for Post-Graduate Medical Education.

The development of health centres and other forms of group practice has continued. There are now nine health centres, and all have attracted a full team of doctors and allied health professionals. About 30% of general practitioners now work in some form of group practice arrangement.

The rehabilitation departments of public hospitals have continued to be developed and upgraded. In 1973 a second school of physiotherapy was opened, doubling the intake of students to 120 per year. In 1974 an Aids and Appliances Unit was established by one hospital board to work in the field of design, adaptation and development of aids and equipment for disabled persons.

Outlook

For several reasons—economic, labour intensity and, most important, humanitarian considerations—there will be increasing emphasis on community health services in the next 5-10 years. These will alleviate the demand on institution-based services. Health care teams will develop, working from custom-built health centres and providing a community base for growing extramural services from the community and base hospitals.

There will be increasing cost-benefit analysis of expensive high-technology super-speciality medicine. Health education will be emphasized as part of the work of all health professionals. Professional health education will provide training to the medical professions.

There will be a progressive devolution of decision-making to regional health boards who will have greater autonomy in priority determination for their area of responsibility.

Health services research will have greater personnel and fiscal support and lead to the provision of more effective practical data. Health manpower planning and professional education programmes will be emphasized and considered together. Community participation in health promotion and the setting of local and national priorities will be encouraged.

Emphasis in health services will be on re-

habilitation, care of the elderly, social diseases such as alcoholism, and mental health and occupational health.

NIUE

Population and other statistics

Population and other vital statistics for the period under review are given in the following table:

	1971	1972	1975	1976
Population (mid-year)	5 115	4 541	3 969	3 843
Number of live births	156	154	98	90
Birth rate (per 1000 population)	30.5	33.9	24.6	23.4
Number of deaths	28	51	24	25
Death rate (per 1000 population)	5.5	11.2	6.0	6.5
Natural increase (%)	2.50	2.27	1.86	1.65
Number of infant deaths	6	3	3	—
Infant mortality rate (per 1000 live births)	38.5	19.5	30.6	—

Of the 25 deaths recorded in 1976, the main causes were: head injury due to motor vehicle accidents (3), urinary tract infection (2), asthma and emphysema (2), ischaemic heart disease (2), congestive heart failure (2), cerebrovascular disease (2), intestinal obstruction (1), bronchitis (1), influenza (1), meningitis (1), infectious hepatitis (1), aplastic anaemia, leukaemia (1), hepatoma (1), carcinoma of the cervix (1).

Organization of health services

Preventive and curative medicine, obstetrics, maternal and child health, school health and dental health services are integrated in the Health Department headed by the Director of Health. He is responsible to the Minister of Health on matters of policy and to the Secretary to the Government on the organization of health services and staff establishment.

There are two units for public health services, namely the public health team and the child welfare team—which is also known as the public health nursing section.

The first is led by the Health Inspector assisted by the Assistant Public Health Inspector.

The team is responsible for village health inspection (for which it works with the Women's Club), water safety, vector control, rubbish disposal, port and airport health activities, excreta disposal, meat inspection, inspection of food manufacturing premises and food handlers.

The child welfare team consists of a public health nurse, a staff nurse, and a nursing aide. They are in charge of the maternal and child health programme and the care of the elderly and the infirm. A mobile unit provides a service for all new-born babies and their mothers weekly until the babies are a month old, then fortnightly until they are three months old, then monthly up to school age.

Hospital services

There is one hospital with 42 beds and there are two district clinics. The Director of Health, the Senior Medical Officer and two other medical officers, together with the nursing section, provide the services. The Principal Dental Officer and three other dental officers provide the dental services. A mobile team consisting of a doctor and a staff nurse provide medical care to the people four days a week. There is a "lifeline" linking the villages to the hospital at all times for emergencies.

Medical and health personnel and training

Doctors	4
Dentists	4
Dental hygienist	1
Dental mechanic	1
Chairside assistant	1
Nurses (New Zealand registered)	4
Nurse/midwives (New Zealand registered) . .	2
Staff nurses	12
Senior nurses	2
Health inspector	1
Assistant health inspectors	2
Laboratory technician	1
X-ray technician	1
Dispenser	1

There is one nursing school which gives a nursing aide course of one year. There is continuing education for trained aides.

Communicable diseases control and immunization services

In 1976 there was an outbreak of influenza; 287 cases were reported; there were 1283 cases of bronchitis, and preschool children were affected. Mild outbreaks of pertussis occurred from July to November; 583 cases were recorded in all.

The following immunization procedures were carried out in 1976:

	1976	1977
DPT	182	170
Diphtheria and tetanus .	99	143
Poliomyelitis	258	185

Maternal and child health programme

Antenatal clinics are set up once a week in the hospital; pregnant mothers attend the hospital. In 1976 there were 90 deliveries, of which 13 took place at home and 77 in the hospital. The postnatal clinics are set up in the hospital, and child welfare clinics are set up during the regular visits of public health nurses in the villages.

Dental services

Two mobile dental units are fully equipped to provide treatment to school- and pre-school children; 1292 were treated in 1976. Plans have been made to provide routine conservative treatment for the adult.

Government health expenditure

During the fiscal year 1976/77 total government health expenditure amounted to about 331 000 New Zealand dollars, of which NZ $325 000 were spent on current account. The per capita expenditure on health was NZ $84.

The current government health expenditure included NZ $258 700 for administration and government personnel, NZ $10 000 for environmental services, and NZ $30 000 for general hospitals and clinics.

PAPUA NEW GUINEA

Major health and health-related problems

The health situation in Papua New Guinea is typical for an area at a very early stage of social and economic development. The most important problems are: acute respiratory diseases, malaria, gastrointestinal diseases, malnutrition, tuberculosis, leprosy, accidents and injuries, complications of pregnancy, and diseases of the newborn. The important diseases have a number of common features which are significant in health planning: they are easily treated by staff with low-level training, are mostly infectious and caused by, or related to, the low standard of the environment in which people live; they can be prevented by immunization, by improvement in dietary habits, food, or water supplies, or by spraying of houses in the case of malaria; they especially affect groups at risk such as young children and pregnant women. Accurate figures are not available on infant mortality but it is estimated at 90 per 1000 live births. Maternal mortality is estimated at 9 per 1000 live births.

A number of important health-related problems in the design and trend of health services have been given priority in the National Health Plan covering the five-year period 1974-1978. These are: the poor coordination and integration of present services; unrealistic and inappropriate standards of health technologies applied; inequalities in the distribution of health services; and the increasing demand for urban hospital services. In most rural areas the low density of population with poor communications and in a rugged terrain makes delivery of health services difficult. Inadequate transport and housing, over which the Department of Health has little control, remain major constraints to the expansion of services.

Action taken

Health policy

The current National Development Strategy published in October 1976 recognizes that the health of individuals and communities has an important effect on their ability to participate and contribute to economic and social development. It also endorses that the health policy outlined in the National Health Plan covering 1974–1978 will continue to be followed, providing comprehensive basic health services through health centres and aid posts and referring cases needing more specialized attention to hospitals. Future expansion of health services will concentrate on improving primary health care in rural areas. No new major hospitals are planned and there will be only limited expansion of existing hospitals. Improved training of health personnel in line with the concept of primary health care is essential.

Health legislation

The individual right of man to his own customs and beliefs is recognized by law. However, magicoreligious practices that do not conform to the general principles of humanity are prohibited. In general, the legal system follows both the principles and practices of the English and Australian systems, and there are various acts related to medical practice, control of food and drugs, control of communicable diseases, sanitation, registration of births, deaths and marriages, and quarantine services, most of which were enacted by the former colonial government. Since the country gained independence, legislation on baby feed supplies has been enacted with a view to promoting breast feeding.

Health planning and programming

The five-year National Health Plan is linked with overall national development policy and is directed towards: equalization of services, improved rural services, decentralization, integration, self-reliance and simplification. The objectives of the plan provide for assistance to rural areas with particular attention to the following problems and solutions:

(1) the relatively worse health conditions in rural areas and the vulnerability of children; rural health services will be given priority and better nutrition will be emphasized;
(2) increasing population; family planning facilities will be improved;
(3) excessive demand, particularly in urban areas, for hospital services; some hospital funds will be redirected to rural needs;
(4) inequality in the distribution of health services; resources will be redistributed to the provinces at present poorly served; and
(5) poor integration of present services; integration of services and resources will be promoted.

Organization of health services

The Department of Health, under the Minister for Health, and technically headed by the Secretary for Health, is responsible for most of the health services. Additional contributions are made by religious missions and by a comparatively small private medical sector. The church health services, which provide most of the rural health services, are fully integrated with the national health administration. The Secretary for Health is aided by two First Assistant Secretaries, by specialist staff in various disciplines including training, planning, research and malaria control, and by provincial health officers in charge of peripheral services. There is an active integrated nursing service.

In each province primary health care is provided by a large number of aid post orderlies. At the intermediate level care is provided by health centre staff, health extension officers (medical assistants) and trained nurses. Each province has one hospital staffed with doctors and providing more complex diagnostic and nursing procedures. The person of first contact for the great majority of population is the aid post orderly, the only health worker living and working in the village, amongst the people. Of very limited training and technical capability, the aid post orderlies are nevertheless crucial as they can save lives by relatively simple procedures, such as the injection of penicillin to pneumonia cases and the administration of chloroquine to malaria cases, and can assist in such vital activities as immunization, family planning and sanitation. There is no chance whatever in the forseeable future of doctors becoming available in sufficient number to become the first contact for the population. Health extension officers and nurses help to bridge the gap between the supervising provincial health officers and medical officers, and the aid post orderlies. The top and intermediate levels still rely heavily on expatriate medical officers. Localization is a firm policy and a number of national medical officers, nurses and health inspectors have been appointed to senior positions.

The high incidence of diarrhoeal diseases and skin diseases as well as the high infant mortality rate (estimated to be 90 per 1000 live births) are evidence of environmental sanitation problems. It is estimated that approximately 80% of the rural population lack adequate water, and a similar percentage lack sanitary toilets. A considerable number of national health inspectors are engaged in constructing simple rural water supply systems, mainly for demonstration purpose. Concern for environmental health has been overshadowed by more glamorous physical development projects like the construction of health centres and training institutes. More research and pilot projects are needed to find out how simple sanitary facilities are to be provided, especially when dealing with very sparsely populated rural areas.

Biomedical and health services research

Biomedical research is being carried out in association with three major governmental institutions, the Institute of Medical Research, the Faculty of Medicine of the University of Papua New Guinea, and the Department of Health. All biomedical and health practice research is coordinated and approved by the Medical research Coordinating Committee, which is responsible to the Minister of Health. Some projects are conducted in close cooperation with research institutions overseas. Certain criteria are used in considering research proposals for approval by the Committee, namely, whether the subject to be studied is of benefit to the community and whether the studies are in line with the national health development strategy. Training of national research workers has so far been negligible although national teaching staff in the medical faculty now have research opportunities.

Education and training of health manpower

Localization is a firm national policy. The National Health Plan recognizes the need to train a sufficient number of health workers with as broad a range of skills as possible. Employment of national personnel is increasing rapidly, but adequately trained workers are still urgently required at all levels.

The Government, with assistance from religious missions and WHO, has established basic training courses for physicians, dentists, nurses, health extension officers, health inspectors, laboratory technicians, dental therapists, aid post orderlies and other allied health personnel. Enrolment of medical and dental students and output of graduates are still at a low level but are expected to rise steadily. Postbasic courses in nursing have been established with WHO assistance. Training of orderlies for aid posts, a priority under the health plan, is in progress, but it must be improved in order to meet the objectives of national health development strategies. The general education system cannot yet meet the demand, either in quality or quantity, and this shortcoming has to be taken into account in health manpower training.

Health resources

Health establishments

The number of health establishments at the end of 1977 were as follows:

Hospitals, general	19
Hospital, specialized	1
Health centres	174
Health subcentres	191
Aid posts	1681

The hospital bed/population ratio was one to 670. The total bed/population ratio (including beds in health centres) was one to 220.

Health manpower

The numbers of health workers by category (with numbers of expatriate staff in brackets) at the end of 1977 were as follows:

Doctors	209 (147)
Health extension officers	204 (16)
Dentists	18 (4)
Nurses	1476 (193)
Nurse aides	1063
Aid post orderlies	1615
Health inspectors	86 (2)
Dental therapists	92
Pharmacists	12 (12)
Health educators	23
Health engineer	1

Production and sale of pharmaceuticals

There are no government activities in this field and there is no facility for production of pharmaceuticals within the country. There is no national who is a qualified pharmacist.

Health expenditure

Total government expenditure on health and health-related activities in the fiscal year 1976/77 was 39 271 716 kina of which 85% was accounted for by the Department of Health and about 15% by other government departments. Department of Health expenditure in the financial year 1976/77 was K33 251 800, which is about 8% of total government expenditure, giving a per capita expenditure of K11.90. In 1973/74, the per capita expenditure was K8.30. Hospitals and urban health centres accounted for 46.6% of the total health expenditure, followed by rural health services 25.0%, malaria control 9.7%, policy and administration 9.5%, training 5.8%, and other health activities 3.4%.

Appraisal of progress made between 1973 and 1977

Comparison of numbers of basic health facilities in July 1973 and December 1977 is as follows:

	1973	1977	National Health Plan target
Hospitals	29	20	20
Health centres	137	174	178
Health subcentres	198	191	
Aid posts	1547	1681	

There has been unequal development of health centres, with 10 provinces not reaching the target, 7 passing it and 3 on target. In general, development efforts for the expansion of aid posts were in line with the policy stated in the National Health Plan.

Comparison of the current staff profile with that in 1973, and with that proposed as the target by 1977 in the National Health Plan, shows the following:

	1973	1977	National Health Plan target
Doctors	207	200	226
Dental officers	26	18	31
Nurses	1544	1476	1228
Health extension officers	180	204	278
Dental therapists	61	74	114
Health inspectors	62	86	80
Aid post orderlies	1547	1615	

With the exception of nurses and health inspectors, manpower output lags behind the target.

The increase in expenditure from the fiscal year 1974/75 to 1976/77 in real terms (at constant price) was 10.4%. From the fiscal year 1974/75 to 1976/77, the expenditures on hospitals and urban health centres increased, in real terms, by 31.6%, much faster than for total expenditure of the Department of Health. This means that a large share of health department budgetary increase went to hospitals and urban health centres and that the priority objective to fix hospital expenditure and to direct increased budgetary funds to rural areas has not been attained.

No attempt has been made to assess the improvement of health status by using health indices. Normal delivery was the leading cause of admission to hospital (20.1%), followed by accidents and injuries (10.4%) and pneumonia (9.7%). In 1976, only 23.6% of births were supervised; the target is 44% by 1978. The number of first consultations for prenatal care was 43.3% of total expected births (10 provinces were below the national average). Maternal and child health services were attended by 52.3% of children under one year of age (9 provinces below the national average). Periodical indoor spraying with DDT is undertaken for 50% of the population. Spraying coverage has been expanded to include 2 more provinces. In general, no marked reduction of malaria incidence has been seen because of the low standard of spraying operations resulting from managerial problems. The routine schedule of immunization for children under 5 years old includes BCG and diphtheria/pertussis/tetanus. In 1977, the coverage of immunization for this age group was estimated to be about 30%.

Outlook

The present National Health Plan expires at the end of 1978. It has been decided to embark on country health programming with a view to reviewing the performance of different services and against the targets set in the National Health Plan and, using this, to formulate the solutions to the identified problems for the next 5 years. Specific health goals for the next 5–10 years can only be established through the country health programming exercise, the first phase of which has already been started.

SAMOA

Major health problems

Despite some progress the incidences of pneumonia, gastroenteritis, tuberculosis, leprosy and malnutrition still give cause for concern. Further efforts are needed to improve environmental sanitation and water supplies.

Action taken

Health policy

The basic health policy objectives of the Government are to make available effective and reliable health services to the whole population and to increase the general wellbeing and economic productivity of the people. In addition the Government aims to improve environmental conditions to assist in the prevention of ill health. An equitable balance of health services between urban and rural areas is considered to be of major importance. To achieve these goals there will be continued encouragement of the traditional relationships in rural health and of local community support through the women's committees and other agencies.

Health legislation

Legislation enacted during the period includes: (1) the Pharmacy Act 1976, regulating activities of pharmacy services and practitioners; (2) the Narcotics Act 1976, increasing penalties for drug abuse; and (3) the Medical and Dental Practitioners Act 1977.

Health planning and programming

Health planning is carried out by a planning and evaluation unit headed by a medical officer. The unit initiates plans and programmes in association with staff in the various fields and in conjunction with other relevant ministries and departments. Public reaction to new proposals affecting their interests is taken into account.

A revised country health programme is being prepared, with the assistance of WHO advisers, which will be coordinated with developments in other sectors.

Organization of health services

The Health Department under the Minister of Health includes a Public Health Division with sections for family welfare, communicable disease control, health education and sanitation, a Nursing Division and a Health Planning Information Unit. The family welfare section has provided services in maternal and child health (including antenatal and postnatal care and school health), family planning and nutrition. The section is based in Apia but works through public health nurses and women's committees to give national coverage.

Biomedical and other research

Filariasis control commenced in 1965, with the support of WHO and UNICEF. In 1977 the project's work was expanded by the addition of a research project with generous financial assistance from the Sasakawa Memorial Health Foundation, Japan, as part of the WHO Special Programme for Research and Training in Tropical Diseases. Project activities include determination of the number of the population infested with microfilariae and field studies on the vectors to determine mosquito population dynamics, resting habits and breeding site preferences.

Education and training of health manpower

Health workers in the higher grades, such as medical officers, dental officers, pharmacists, radiologists and dental and medical nurses, normally obtain their basic and postgraduate training overseas, with the help of fellowships, mainly in Fiji and New Zealand. Local programmes provide training for hospital and public health nurses and assistant health inspectors. A variety of in-service training programmes are conducted for nursing staff, dental assistants/hygienists, laboratory assistants and pharmacy assistants.

Training has been provided for new categories such as traditional birth attendants and village health aides, with a view to increasing local participation in rural districts. Some 60 health aides have so far completed training and are assisting public health nurses in the field.

Further courses are being held to extend the system throughout the country.

Health resources

Health establishments

The capacity of the Western Samoa National Hospital, which has 298 beds from 1973 to 1976, increased to 311 in 1977 with the opening of a new paediatrics ward; the opening of the new Palauli-i-Sisifo Hospital in 1976 to replace Foaluga Hospital resulted in an increase from 24 to 30 beds, giving a total of 172 beds in rural hospitals on Savaii Island, while that for Upolu Island remained constant at 191 beds from 1973 to 1977. The totals for the country thus increased from 655 in the first three years to 661 in 1976 and 674 in 1977.

While the number of doctors (51 in 1977), radiographers (9), health inspectors (22), laboratory staff (31), nursing sisters (15), public health nurses (54), nurse aides (58) and pharmacists (18) remained almost stationary during the period, there were increases in dental staff from 23 in 1973 to 34 in 1977, medical records officers from 2 to 21, staff nurses from 163 to 252, and administrative staff from 81 to 99.

Production and sale of pharmaceuticals

Figures are not available for sales by commercial concerns. The value of items dispensed from government hospitals and centres was: 15 944 Western Samoa talas in 1973, WS $15 729 in 1974, WS $14 253 in 1975, WS $15 934 in 1976, WS $20 077 in 1977.

Health expenditure

Figures for total government and Health Department expenditures, together with per capita expenditures on health, are given below:

Year	Total government expenditure WS $	Health Department expenditure WS $	Per capita expenditure on health WS $
1973	9 335 761	1 342 504 (14.4%)	8.9
1974	11 693 180	1 373 576 (11.7%)	9.1
1975	13 579 750	1 689 039 (12.4%)	11.2
1976	16 847 526	1 918 120 (11.4%)	12.6
1977	19 438 354	2 764 560 (14.2%)	18.0

Progress 1973–1977

Although the major capital investment, using foreign aid and national funds, was the rebuilding of the national hospital, there was an increasing emphasis in this period on improving health standards in areas outside Apia. New health subcentres were opened at Falealupo, Lotofaga, Amato and Apolimatai. An old people's home was established by one of the churches at Mapuifagalele. As a step towards strengthening primary health care, training programmes have been instituted for traditional birth attendants and health aides.

In the public health field, assistant health inspectors were posted to four districts in Savaii and five in Upolu in this period. With assistance from UNDP and UNICEF the water seal latrine project was continued and it is estimated that about 70% of the population is now served by water seal latrines and water closets; 2338 water seal latrines were contructed in 1973, 2330 in 1974, 2146 in 1975, 2028 in 1976, and 599 in 1977, making a total of 10 985 since 1970.

A piped water supply was extended to approximately 80% of the population in the period under review.

With considerable aid from New Zealand, a water and sewerage scheme is gradually being implemented in Apia.

Outlook

Health goals in the current Third Year Plan are:

(1) to improve the quality of all preventive and curative health services;
(2) to strengthen the national structure of health services delivery, and to render access to preventive and curative health care on a more equal basis to both the rural and the urban populations;
(3) to increase the awareness and participation of the people in health promotion activities; and
(4) to enhance the productivity of local and aid resources applied to health section development.

In view of the shortage of funds and the lack of trained manpower in health fields, the Government is aware that to achieve real gains in the health sector its most efficient long-term strategy should be: to emphasize development of the less costly primary health care, utilizing less trained staff and less elaborate facilities to bear the major burden of health service delivery; and to develop specialized secondary level

health care, including inpatient treatment and personal attention by physicians, only as problems grow too complex to be dealt with at the primary level.

SINGAPORE

Major health and health-related problems

The health status of the population is relatively high, as reflected in the low infant mortality rate of 12.2 per 1000 live births and a maternal mortality rate of 0.3 per 1000 live-births in 1977. The infant mortality rate has declined from 20.3 in 1973 while the maternal mortality rate has remained around 0.1–0.3 per 1000 since 1973. Disease patterns as reflected by mortality and morbidity statistics are changing as the population grows older and as modern life styles emerge.

The major causes of death in the period 1973–1977 were malignant neoplasms, ischaemic heart disease, cerebrovascular disease and pneumonia. Together they accounted for nearly half of all deaths in 1977. The death rates in 1977 for lung cancer and coronary heart disease were 22.0 and 72.0 per 100 000 population respectively, representing a 37% and 41% increase of these causes of deaths respectively since 1973.

The incidence of mental illness has increased, resulting in an increase in hospital admissions for mental illness from 2707 in 1973 to 4229 in 1977, while psychiatric outpatient attendances rose from 28 138 to 62 214. At the primary health care clinics, upper respiratory infections accounted for the highest number of visits. There have been annual influenza outbreaks in April to July from 1974 to 1977.

The most severe infectious diseases such as malaria, diphtheria and poliomyelitis are now under control, about 95% of the malaria cases are imported, while there has been no local case of laryngeal diphtheria or poliomyelitis since 1974 and 1973 respectively. Of the four diseases subject to the International Health Regulations, only cholera continued to be reported sporadically—11 cases were reported in 1977. Tuberculosis continued to be a health problem, with 2747 notifications in 1977 compared with 3037 in 1973. The incidence of venereal dis-

ease, which became notifiable in August 1977, increased from 6211 cases reported in 1973 to 12 020 in 1977. This apparently sharp rise is due to better reporting of cases and can be attributed to educational campaigns urging early diagnosis and treatment.

Action taken

Health policy, planning and programming

Keeping the population healthy, efficient and productive is crucial to the total national development strategy. In order to prevent illness, greater emphasis is being placed on preventive medicine and health promotion. This strategy is also being adopted in the attempt to alleviate the problem of government health expenditure, which rose by 80% between 1972 and 1976. In 1976 outpatient, maternal and child health and school health services were integrated, in order to control rising expenditure, into the Primary Health Care Division. With these services under one administration, a more flexible and efficient utilization of existing manpower and material resources was effected. Primary health care services provide all members of the family with good preventive and therapeutic care as well as screening those acutely ill for selective institutional care, thus alleviating the pressure on high-cost hospital services.

A nurse-practitioner scheme was instituted in 1977 whereby specially trained nurses at primary health care clinics screened patients for minor ailments to assist doctors in managing the large numbers attending the clinics. A Home Nursing Foundation was launched in 1976, through which volunteer and service nurses provide nursing care to the aged, sick, disabled and chronically ill in their own homes.

Health education, an important arm of preventive medicine, has been intensified. More systematic health education activities in the form of mass national health campaigns, regular talks, film shows and exhibitions have been organized, aimed particularly at schoolchildren.

Major improvement programmes have been implemented for the existing hospitals in order to provide better accommodation and facilities in keeping with rising public expectations and to upgrade patient care in hospitals. A major project is the complete redevelopment of the largest acute hospital, the Singapore General Hospital. The total number of beds in the 13 government hospitals numbered 8574 in 1977.

A programme was initiated in 1975 to provide comprehensive dental health care for primary school children through dental clinics within the school compound. To complement the expansion of the dental health services, the Institute of Dental Health, completed in 1977, will train more dental therapists and dental nurses.

Environmental sanitation and antipollution measures continued to be upgraded. The environmental health services kept the Republic remarkably clean and maintained an adequate standard of personal hygiene among food establishments and food handlers. Street cleaning and refuse removal were increasingly mechanized, while refuse collection routes were streamlined. Construction of an incinerator capable of burning 1200 tonnes of refuse per day (of a total of 1300 tonnes generated each day) began in July 1976. The sewerage system was extended.

The national family planning and population programme continued to be implemented vigorously, leading to a fall in the total fertility rate about two children per woman in 1975. This was maintained in 1976 and 1977. It is the demographic goal of the Government to maintain replacement level, thereby reaching zero population growth in about 50 years, when the population will have grown from its present 2.3 million to about 3.5 million.

Health legislation

The new Medicines Act, introduced in 1975, provides for a licensing system for the manufacture, importation, sale and supply of all medicinal products, based on their safety, efficacy and quality. It also provides for all medical advertisements and clinical trials to be approved by a licensing authority.

The 1969 acts legalizing abortion and sterilization were repealed and replaced by the Abortion Act, 1974, and the Voluntary Sterilization Act 1974, which further liberalized abortion and sterilization.

The Nurses and Midwives Act, replacing the Nurses Registration Act and the Midwives Act, 1975, brought the nursing and midwifery professions under one controlling body, the Singapore Nursing Board.

Organization of health services

Responsibility for curative, promotive and rehabilitative health services rests with the Ministry of Health. The curative services are provided through 13 government hospitals and the network of outpatient, school health and dental clinics. The promotive services are provided through the maternal and child health services, school health services, the Training and Health Education Department and the Family Planning and Population Board.

Established in 1975, the Rehabilitation Medicine Services, comprising three component sections for physiotherapy, occupational therapy and speech therapy, operate in most of the major government hospitals with staff of clinical disciplines and the medical social workers.

The Ministry of the Environment fulfils its responsibility for protection and improvement through the Environmental Public Health Division and the Environmental Engineering Division. Their programmes include quarantine and epidemiology activities, food quality control, vector control, sewerage and solid waste disposal.

The Industrial Health Unit of the Ministry of Labour provides advisory services on occupational health problems to industries and government departments.

In the private sector, medical services are provided by registered private practitioners and about 10 private hospitals, which have a total bed complement of 1007.

Biomedical and health services research

Studies carried out during the period 1973–1977 included:

— in clinical research, fertility control agents such as metabolic effects of contraceptive pills and trials on prostaglandins, and different regimes in the treatment of pulmonary tuberculosis;
— in epidemiological research, the epidemiology of cardiovascular diseases, hypertension, renal diseases and tuberculosis, road

traffic accidents, morbidity patterns, and the epidemiology of nasopharyngeal carcinoma;

— in biomedical research, normal values for serum proteins, iron, calcium and immunoglobulin amongst infants and children, the biochemistry of wounds, and the immunological aspects of diseases;

— in health services research, the factors responsible for optimum ward administration, the pattern of utilization of medical services, and the utilization of doctors, nurses and dentists.

Education and training of health manpower

Training of health manpower was continually reviewed to upgrade the quality of medical and paramedical personnel. The University of Singapore has a Faculty of Medicine (five-year course), a Faculty of Dentistry (four-year course) as well as a School of Postgraduate Medical Studies. The latter offers postgraduate training in anaesthesia, internal medicine, obstetrics and gynaecology, paediatrics, public health and surgery.

Training in general nursing, postbasic nursing and midwifery, dental therapy and dental nursing, and radiography continues to be conducted by the School of Nursing, the Institute of Dental Health and the School of Radiography respectively.

Health resources

Health establishments

During the period under review the total number of beds in the 13 government hospitals increased from 8031 in 1973 to 8574 in 1977. Including the 1007 beds maintained by the 8 private hospitals, the total of 9581 beds at the end of 1977 represented a ratio of 4.2 beds per 1000 population.

Hospital facilities exist for internal medicine, general surgery, orthopaedic surgery, ophthalmology, paediatric medicine, otorhinolaryngology, dermatology, obstetrics and gynaecology, haematology, pathology and radiology. Specialist hospitals cater for treatment of infectious diseases, skin and venereal diseases, tuberculosis, leprosy and care of the chronically sick and the mentally ill.

The tertiary specialities have developed over the past five years. Cardiothoracic surgery now includes open-heart surgery, and nephrology has progressed to renal transplants. The Plastic and Reconstructive Surgery Unit and the Department of Neurosurgery and Neurology are fully operational.

Primary health care is provided through 26 outpatient dispensaries, 40 maternal and child health centres and family planning clinics, 4 polyclinics and the school health services. A large number of private general practitioners augment the government services.

Operating a total of 123 dental clinics (increased from 94 in 1973), the public dental services provides a full range of dental treatment facilities.

Health manpower

Over the 10-year period 1967–1977, the overall doctor population ratio improved from one to 1799 to one to 1250 (registered medical practitioners only).

In the case of registered nurses the ratio was one to 339 in 1977 as compared with one to 564 in 1967.

Production and sale of pharmaceuticals

There were 16 pharmaceutical factories in the private sector and one operated by the Government. While some of the products of the factories in the private sector were exported to neighbouring countries, all products manufactured by the government factory were for use in government hospitals and clinics only. In addition, Singapore imported large quantities of medicines for local use.

Health expenditure

Health expenditure has been rising steadily, and the total expenditure of the Ministry of Health increased from 102 570 000 Singapore dollars in 1973 to 177 540 000 in 1977 (provisional figure). The per capita health expenditure rose from S $46.94 in 1973 to S $76.92 in 1977.

Appraisal of progress and outlook

Progress has been made in both quality and quantity of health services to cater to the demand created by the public's rising expectations and the growing population. All arms of health care, preventive, curative, rehabilitative, environmental and industrial have been upgraded and mobilized to meet the needs of the population, whether these needs are imposed by population shifts, by the ageing population or by greater health awareness. Improvement in the health indicators reflected the general progress.

Health policies for the next decade will take cognizance of social, economic, environmental and demographic changes and morbidity and mortality trends. The integrated primary health care services will be strengthened with the building of more new polyclinics in major housing estates, bringing preventive health services, general curative and dental treatment under one roof.

Of increasing concern is the growing incidence of lung cancer, ischaemic heart disease, hypertension and mental illness precipitated by the habits and stresses of modern life styles. Health education programmes for the population, in particular to militate against these harmful life styles will be intensified. Systematic general health education activities will be organized to reach all strata of society. In order to upgrade the quality of patient care, further improvement schemes for major existing hospitals will be implemented. Changes in the population age structure will necessitate the development of geriatric medicine and expansion of the home nursing scheme. Rehabilitative medicine will also be given added emphasis so that those with degenerative conditions, the chronically ill, and mental patients, may be returned to society as useful citizens wherever possible.

Crucial to the qualitative and quantitative development of the service is the adequate supply of medical and paramedical personnel. The Ministry of Health will need to resolve the problem of the shortage of doctors and explore avenues for retaining the services of experienced consultants. The nurse-practitioner scheme, which uses experienced and specially trained nurses to record clinical history of patients and to undertake routine examination and simple medical treatment, will be extended and institutionalized.

SOLOMON ISLANDS

Major health problems

Malaria

Malaria still ranks as the major health problem in terms of health expenditure and national effort. Once the main cause of mortality and morbidity, it has since 1962 been considerably reduced under the malaria eradication programme. In the period under review the situation continued to improve, but since 1977 a reverse has been suffered especially in the main areas of population and development in Guadalcanal and Malaita. In 1973 there were 7725 positive cases; in 1974, 3681; in 1975, 3554; in 1976, 2489; and in 1977, 10 591.

Tuberculosis

Tuberculosis is widespread throughout the Islands and is responsible for more protracted ill-health and death than any other communicable disease. There has been a steady decline in the number of cases: in 1973, 324; in 1974, 319; in 1975, 261; but 1976 saw the commencement of an upward trend with 331 cases, 382 in 1977. The increase was most marked in the under-5-year age group, suggesting that the BCG immunization programme was failing.

Antenatal care and conditions of the newborn

The Solomon Islands have one of the highest rates of increase of population in the world, 3.4%. The crude death rate has been estimated at 9 per 1000 population and the crude birth rate at 43 per 1000. The mid-year population in 1977 was 207 090, so that there may be estimated to have been some 8905 births; 19% of the population are women in the 15–45 year age group. The maternal mortality rate is not high (estimated at 2 per 1000 live births), but the expectation of life of women is much less than for men. After the age of 35 years the ratio of women to men falls from one to 0.8. The perinatal mortality rate is estimated at 35 per 1000 and infant mortality rate at 20 per 1000 live births.

Leprosy

Leprosy, once a serious problem, is now well contained. In 1972 and 1973 a consultant leprologist visited the Islands, and after extensive search placed a number of unregistered cases on the register bringing the total in 1973 to 112 cases; but since then there has been a progressive decline of new cases discovered; in 1974, 52 cases; in 1975, 35; in 1976, 42 and in 1977, 33.

Gastroenteritis

One of the commonest causes of attendance at clinics—especially of children—gastroenteritis has yet received little attention. There are no accurate figures for the prevalence of this disease, but one survey in 1974 in a population of 37 917 found 8825 cases, or 6% of all people attending clinics and hospitals. The causes are mainly associated with poor sanitation.

Bronchopulmonary conditions

A group of upper respiratory infections including influenza, pneumonia, and bronchitis are the leading cause of outpatient attendance. Influenza is not an important element, and there is no specific feature amenable to preventive methods.

Accidents

Accidents are the leading cause of hospital admissions, domestic accidents associated with gardening and village life being more important than road traffic and industrial accidents.

Tetanus

In 1977 the Solomon Islands had the highest rate of tetanus for any Pacific country; 20 cases were recorded. The cases are mainly neonatal tetanus with high mortality.

Measles

Epidemics of measles occur at three-year intervals, there having been outbreaks in 1974 and 1977. During the period of the report mortality was low.

Gonorrhoea

So far the only venereal disease of any importance, gonorrhoea is mainly a problem of urban life.

Action taken

Health policy

Recognizing that 90% of the population live in rural areas, the policy of the Government has been to strengthen the rural health services by improving the network of clinics, ensuring that they are staffed, and improving supervision and referral by encouraging regular touring by senior staff. Combined with this has been a national policy of decentralization to councils, which has further improved local administration.

The malaria eradication programme has suffered a number of technical and other difficulties: change in vector behaviour, partial tolerance to DDT, failure of the rains which normally destroy breeding places, increased mobility, resistance by householders to house-spraying, a lowering of morale and poor supervision of workers. Many of the problems are centred on an area of persistent infection in North Guadalcanal.

Immunization is a function of the multipurpose workers at the rural health clinic. Unfortunately there is evidence that coverage has not been complete. Difficulties of supply and storage of vaccines confront the nurses; more effort and more active support from senior staff are needed.

A family health programme to upgrade the existing services commenced in 1973, supplying needed equipment, especially canoes and outboard motors, giving greater mobility to staff visiting different areas. Child health clinics for "under fives" are held on a regular basis, but attendance in many areas is poor; the services will have to be brought to the people.

Antenatal care is provided at clinics, as are the services for normal deliveries. Approximately one-third of all deliveries take place in clinics, another third in hospitals and the remainder are unattended by qualified staff. Family planning is still rudimentary and the object of much uncertainty and suspicion.

Health legislation

No major health legislation has been enacted in the period of the report.

Health planning and programming

The existing clinics cater for some 1500 to 2500 persons each, but with difficult terrain and adverse weather conditions health care is still not easily available to a large segment of the population. The Government has been planning a village health aide programme; by the selected community, the aide will receive three months training and be supplied with medicines for prevention as well as curative services. This scheme was to start in 1978.

A hospitals feasibility study is planned to review the existing hospital and clinics, especially the National Hospital in Honiara, as well as the primary health care level. An intermediate category of health centre will also be considered, and established clinics will be upgraded.

Two special campaigns are planned to strengthen the malaria eradication programme in the area of persistent infection in North Guadalcanal: a combined larviciding and mass drug administration programme, and a trial of a nonirritant insecticide.

Staff shortages have been a continual problem. Increases in the numbers of nurses are proposed, as well as the introduction of health extension officers to assist doctors. The latter are in short supply, especially nationals.

The importance of health education is recognized, and great expansion in this section is proposed in the next plan period.

The low level of sanitation and the pollution of natural water sources have been a major concern; a large project to bring safe water and sanitation facilities to the whole population by 1990 is to commence in 1979.

Organization or health services

With the devolution of health services to councils, the Ministry of Health and Medical Services retains mainly a coordinating, planning and advisory role. The central hospital and Honiara urban nursing service are still administered by the Ministry, but all other services are controlled at council level. The council has a health committee made up of elected members, with the medical officer-in-charge acting as an advisor. Each council has a base hospital (Guadalcanal and central islands using the central hospital and a complement of medical staff who ensure preventive as well as clinical services within their council area. Each council area is sub-divided into clinic areas in which there is a permanent building with at least one registered nurse. The registered nurse is a multipurpose health worker who is expected to tour the area regularly, performing immunizations, advising on environmental hygiene, supervising maternal and child health, following up tuberculosis and leprosy patients as well as treating patients. Aid posts provide a rudimentary service to smaller groups of people and are supervised by the registered nurse in charge of the clinic area.

Each council has an assistant health inspector who acts more as an adviser anticipating village cooperation in the provision of water supplies and latrines. The malaria eradication programme is still controlled centrally and has its own staff, but the medical officer in charge in each council area is delegated for local supervision. It is hoped to integrate the programme with the rural health services, as special programmes are found not to have a sustained effect.

Biomedical and health services research

The country is too small to have its own research organization, but some research has been done in the course of normal duty. Most research interest is centred around the malaria programme with various combinations of drug regimes being attempted to overcome persistent *Plasmodium vivax* infection. On vector studies, the change of *Anopheles farauti* from a night feeder to an early evening and early morning feeder has helped to explain many of the difficulties encountered. A seven-year study on filariasis has shown that *Wuchereria bancrofti* has been eradicated from some areas by vector control measures against *A. farauti* alone. A small study of goitre was conducted with good success using an iodine preparation. New surgical techniques in the treatment of elephantiasis have been developed.

Education and training of health manpower

Medical officers are trained either in Fiji or in Papua New Guinea, but during the period 1973–1977 there was no increase in national staff, because as many retire as enter service. The nursing school in Honiara conducts a three-year comprehensive course, the average number qualifying per annum being 21. A single course to train nine new health inspectors was held in 1977. Malaria staff are trained initially in short in-service courses, which are also a feature of continuous nursing training.

Medical officers, some nurses and supervisory malaria personnel attend appropriate courses of further study overseas.

Health resources

Health establishments

There are one central hospital and 5 council hospitals. Two further hospitals are run by missions. There are 2 area health centres, 79 clinics and 44 aid posts. A few of the clinics and the majority of the aid posts are run by churches or commercial concerns.

Health manpower

The number of doctors is about 36, only 16 being nationals; 4 are mission doctors. A private practitioner transferred from Government service towards the end of 1977. There are 3 dental officers and 2 hygienists, 338 registered nurses, 51 of which are employed by churches or commercial companies, 121 nursing aides, most of whom are directly employed by councils, churches or commissions and 22 environmental

health workers, all employed by the Government. There are only 2 trained health education staff. Ancillary staff number 6 pharmacy workers, 8 laboratory technicians, 1 physiotherapist, and 6 X-ray technicians. The malaria eradication programme employs 319 staff. There are shortages of suitably educated and motivated students of medicine or prospective ancillary staff, and financial constraints prevent the employment of more nurses or health inspectors.

Production and sale of pharmaceuticals

None.

Health expenditure

From 1975 to 1977 the recurrent expenditure on health was 4 073 000 Australian dollars or 11.9% of the budget. Capital expenditure (mainly foreign aid) was A $2 921 000 or 15% of the capital budget. The malaria eradication programme is a capital aid project and accounts for a large part of the capital expenditure. An estimate of the per capita expenditure on health is A $7.76.

Of the health budget 63.6% is spent on personnel emoluments and wages. A breakdown of expenditure reveals that 11% is spent on headquarters, 36% on the central hospital and only 53% in the council areas where the majority of the population live.

TONGA

Major health and health-related problems

As in most developing countries, the major problems in Tonga are those related to rapid population growth, manpower shortage, poor environmental sanitation, especially limited availability of a safe and potable water supply, poor housing and overcrowding, poor personal hygiene and the lack of understanding of nutrition.

Action taken

There has been a change of approach, with a shift of official policy from the curative towards

strengthening of public health services. This has meant increasing the public health budget and the manpower—in particular, by training public health workers.

One of the objectives of the Third Development Plan, 1975–1980, is the continued reduction in the rate of growth of population by a lowering of the birth rate. Although demographic data are incomplete and suspect, there is some evidence that the rate of growth is beginning to slow down. After a limited start in 1958, family planning became part of government policy in 1962 and was intensified in 1972 with assistance from WHO and UNFPA. The Government recognized the urgency of solving the population problem, continuing to give family planning a high priority in the Third Development Plan.

An intensive programme of developing safe and potable water supplies for the people of Tonga was initiated in the early 1960s, based on community participation, with each village, the Government and UNICEF bearing a third of the cost of each scheme. The programme has been such a success that by the end of 1977 all villages in Tongatapu had access to a safe and potable water supply and the two main towns of Nuku'alofa in Tongatapu and Neiafu in Vava'u had reticulated water supply to homes. 'Eua island also has a safe water supply. The programme is being continued with the hope of providing adequate and safe water to all villages and islands in Tonga. Unfortunately, the development of water seal latrines has failed to keep up with the development of water supply. Consequently, the improvement in the standard of health has failed to reach expectations.

Legislation has been enacted to govern the operation of village water supplies.

One of the major developments in the Public Health Division has been the formation of the Health Education Section, which, although still understaffed and underequipped, has made its presence felt with the education of the public in family planning, nutrition, filariasis control, immunization, tuberculosis control and other health subjects.

The Public Health Division has the responsibility of developing all these programmes. The environmental section, under a senior health inspector, is responsible for the development of adequate and safe water supplies and the proper disposal of sewage. The Maternal and Child Health Section, under a medical officer, is responsible for family planning, nutrition and immunization. The Health Education Section, under the health education medical officer, carries out all health education activities associated with programmes. The actual field workers are the public health nurses who are responsible for antenatal care, midwifery and postnatal services, nutrition, immunization, motivation for family planning and so on.

To achieve the desired improvements, increased education and training of professional and technical staff are required. Some staff require overseas training, while others receive in-service training. Regular seminars for nurses and other medical and auxiliary staff have been held. Training seminars for group leaders, community leaders and teachers have also been held, with the hope that dissemination of information will be quicker.

Health resources

There are three hospitals with a total capacity of 290 beds, seven rural dispensaries and 19 maternal and child health clinics. Medical officers and medical assistants in dispensaries are also responsible for the public health activities in their district. During the period under review, the manpower responsible for these programmes consisted of 6 medical officers, 5 medical assistants, 2 nursing sisters, 28 public health nurses, 9 health inspection staff, 2 health education assistants, 2 public health assistants and 20 daily paid labourers. The total health expenditure in 1976 amounted to T $750 600, which was 11.2% of total national expenditure for the year and approximately T $7.9 per head of the population. Of this amount T $90 557 were allocated for public health services.

Appraisal of progress made in the period 1973–1977

The achievements over the past five years have been small but definite. The official estimated birth rate has been steady at around 25.5 per 1000 population. A more realistic figure for the last five years would be a fall from 35 to around 33 per 1000. The Public Health Division of the Ministry has been strengthened and a qualified health education medical officer has been employed since January 1977. The maternal and child health and family planning programme became fully fledged in 1973 with the appointment of a WHO medical officer. The village water supply projects have continued, with more emphasis over the past two years on activities in Vava'u.

Outlook

To maintain and improve the achievements of the last five years, the following long-term objectives and strategies have been approved by the Government:

(1) to reduce further the rate of natural growth of the population through the

strengthening of the maternal and child health, family planning and health education programmes;

(2) to reduce the morbidity and mortality from preventable diseases to the lowest possible level;

(3) to improve the early diagnosis and prompt treatment of disease, through strengthening of medical care programmes in outpatient units and hospitals, health education and staff education and training;

(4) to improve the capability at all levels of health services in terms of physical and manpower resources and to improve effective utilization of those resources;

(5) to develop rural health services with particular emphasis on the provision of fully integrated health facilities as close as possible to where people live;

(6) to improve and maintain the safety of the environment by expanding and strengthening environmental health programmes, with emphasis on provision of more safe water supplies, the promotion of personal hygiene and sanitation, safe and proper disposal of refuse and sewage, control of insect vectors and prevention of environmental pollution; and

(7) to give the highest priority to the education and training of nationals (both at undergraduate and postgraduate levels).

TUVALU[1]

Population and other vital statistics

The 1973 census showed a population of 5 888. In 1977, after separation of Tuvalu (then the Ellice Islands) from the Gilbert Islands in 1976, the estimated population was 6 500. The return of an estimated 712 civil servants and other nationals contributed to the significant increase in population. The actual number of deaths in 1977 was 46, live births numbered 145, giving a birth rate of 22.3 per 1 000 population, the death rate was 7.1, and the natural increase 1.52%.

The following communicable diseases were recorded in 1977: influenza, 1 320; infectious hepatitis, 6; bacillary dysentery, 36 and tuberculosis, 5.

Major public health problems

Basic primary health problems arising from inadequate sanitation remain the most important public health problems, apart from the diseases already mentioned. Urgent measures are needed to safeguard the urban environment against overcrowding and epidemic diseases introduced through air or sea communications. Improvement of sanitation will inevitably reduce the infant mortality rate.

National health planning

In the first development plan (1978–1980) the health objectives are: to develop and maintain unified preventive health services on all islands; maintain basic curative services at the present level and maintain and support motivational and promotional activities in family planning. These objectives are already being pursued, but in the long-term the aims are: to raise the standard of sanitation throughout the territory, to integrate and consolidate the various preventive health services and to maintain and improve existing hospital and curative health services.

Organization of the public health services

All public health services are controlled by Government through the Senior Medical Officer, assisted by two medical officers and one dental officer. One medical officer is responsible for preventive health services and also assists the other medical officer in curative health activities in the hospital. The dental officer is responsible for dental health services. There is a small inspectorate under the direction of a medical officer. The nursing service is now being developed to cater for hospital services and family health services in outer islands.

The only hospital in Tuvalu is based on the main island of Funafuti, headquarters of the

---

[1] Formerly the Ellice Islands.

country where approximately 21% of the population live. Medical stations on outer islands are staffed by a medical assistant and a staff nurse for islands with larger populations, and either a medical assistant or a staff nurse for islands with smaller populations. In addition there are maternal and child health aides, one for each island, who have been trained locally to assist the staff nurse.

Hospital services

In 1977 Tuvalu had one hospital and seven outer island dispensaries for inpatients, providing a total of 64 beds (30 at the main hospital and 34 in the seven medical centres or dispensaries). The bed ratio was 9.8 per 1 000 population.

Outpatient facilities were available in 1977 at the outpatient department of the main hospital which recorded 9336 attendances, and at the seven medical centres, staffed by a medical assistant or a staff nurse or by both, and which provide limited inpatient and outpatient services to island populations ranging from 350 to 960.

Medical and allied personnel and training facilities

At the end of 1977 Tuvalu had three physicians, all in government service. The doctor/population ratio was thus one to 2166. Other health personnel included:

Dentist	1
Pharmacist	1
Nurse/midwives	17
Nursing auxiliaries and maternal and child health aides	8
Health inspector	1
Sanitation aides	8

There are no training institutions in Tuvalu; training of medical, dental and ancillary staff is undertaken mainly in Fiji.

Communicable disease control

Tuberculosis and filariasis are the most important public health problems in Tuvalu. An antituberculosis campaign started in 1961 with the assistance of WHO continued after the territory separated from the Gilbert Islands. However, due to a shortage of trained staff it was only possible to concentrate on BCG vaccination and to rely on case-finding by a touring medical

officer and the medical staff on each island. A total of 43 patients were under treatment in 1976, and 38 in 1977. The total number of registered patients from 1961 to the end of 1977 was 273, including those who died or contracted the disease whilst in the Gilbert Islands.

A filariasis control programme started in 1972 and continued until the end of 1975. Before the campaign between 12% and 40% of the population on the islands were affected by the disease, but by the end of it the carrier rate had decreased to 1%–3%. A full course of drug therapy has been administered to repatriated Tuvaluans from the Gilbert Islands since separation.

Since 1976, five cases of leprosy have been reported (all members of two family units) from one island; they were isolated for initial treatment on their own island.

Although there has been no major outbreak of diarrhoea since separation, diarrhoeal diseases are still common and can only be reduced by providing safe water supply and hygienic waste disposal.

No cases of yaws have been reported since after the yaws campaign two decades ago. In 1977 no cases of sexually transmitted diseases were reported.

The following immunization procedures were carried out in 1977:

Smallpox	40
Poliomyelitis	21
BCG	123
Cholera	1197
Diphtheria/pertussis/tetanus	112
Tetanus toxoid	89

Specialized units

Tuvalu provides maternal and child health services at eight antenatal and child health units—one for each island. In 1977 there were 151 deliveries (including four stillbirths and two perinatal deaths); deliveries are attended if necessary by a doctor, but mostly by a qualified midwife, either in hospital or at home. Family planning remains, as in the preseparation period, one of the Government's priorities. Although the number of acceptors decreased from 365 in 1976 to 341 in 1977, there was an increase in the number of acceptors among young mothers. Trained maternal and child health aides provide extra assistance in extending basic maternal and child health services. For every island there is a school health service provided by the maternal and child health team on each island. In 1977 dental treatment was given to pupils and to general patients.

Environmental sanitation

Fresh water is normally plentiful throughout Tuvalu, and with the assistance of WHO and UNDP a project is now being launched to improve water supply for all islands. There is no piped water supply in the urban area of Funafuti. In rural areas fresh water is used mainly for drinking purposes and well water for general use.

A programme to provide every household with a water-seal latrine was launched in 1976 as a British aid project.

VIET NAM

An examination of statistics relating to the health situation in Viet Nam during the period 1973–1977 should take account of the following historical facts:

(1) Between January 1973 and 30 April 1975, Viet Nam was made up of three States: the Democratic Republic of Viet Nam, the Republic of Viet Nam and the Republic of South Viet Nam.
(2) The statistics for 1973, 1974 and 1975 refer to the Democratic Republic of Viet Nam and have been retained in full as such;
(3) from July 1976, date of the foundation of the Socialist Republic of Viet Nam, the statistics refer to the whole of Viet Nam during the first year of reunification.

Population and other statistics

The figures for the period under review are as follows:

Major health problems

In spite of the difficult and unstable conditions over the past 30 years caused by war and foreign intervention, the Vietnamese health service has progressed steadily and is becoming an increasingly essential factor in any economic and social activity, and in the life of the population, in times both of war and peace.

In the five-year postwar economic restoration and development plan (1976–1980), the responsibilities assigned to the health service are extremely heavy. The priority aims of the health programme have been defined as follows:

— to improve the sanitation of both the living and working environment for the working population;
— in rural areas promotion of the three-part rural sanitation scheme, i.e., the construction of two-compartment latrines, protected wells and washrooms will continue; in the

	Democratic Republic of Viet Nam			Socialist Republic of Viet Nam
	1973	1974	1975	1976
Population (in thousands)	22 065	22 596[*]	23 235	48 060
Birth rate (per 1000 population)	33.8	34.4	31.3	31.0
Death rate (per 1000 population)	7.0	7.2	5.5	5.5
Natural increase rate (per 1000 population)	26.8	27.2	25.8	25.5
Infant mortality rate (per 1000 live births):				
Premature	—	11.4	11.2	—
Neonatal	—	17.1	17.0	—
Infant	—	30.5	32.6	—

[*] Census figure, 1 April 1974.

towns and industrial areas, particularly the southern provinces, measures will be taken to reduce noise and toxic gas levels in factories (an environmental protection programme will be drawn up for industrial establishments to be constructed);
— the prophylaxis and effective control of dangerous communicable diseases still prevalent in the southern provinces, such as cholera, plague and dengue fever, and social diseases with a high incidence such as malaria, venereal diseases, tuberculosis, goitre and trachoma;
— the promotion of family planning, using all acceptable methods;
— to promote the cultivation of medicinal plants and the rearing of animals that provide basic drugs; increase the production of medicinal preparations based on local vegetable and animal substances; gradually develop chemical pharmacy and the production of antibiotics, and take measures to ensure the economic, safe and rational use of medicinal preparations;
— to reform the teaching system in order to extend, accelerate and improve the training of health personnel, particularly with regard to university-level and specialized personnel, technicians and administrators;
— to acquire knowledge of and utilize the experience of traditional medicine in prophylaxis and therapy; to link traditional medicine closely with the socialist Vietnamese system of medicine; and
— to promote the strengthening of basic and district health networks which will effectively support agricultural development and the creation of new economic areas.

Action taken and measures recommended

Health policy

With a view to protecting and improving the health of the population, the Communist Party of Viet Nam has defined the following five basic principles for the health service:

(1) the building and defence of socialism should coincide with the happiness of the people. Public health should benefit productivity, life, national defence and the working population;
(2) a public health system based on preventive medicine;

(3) the combination of modern and traditional national medicine and development of a Vietnamese system of medicine;
(4) the use of popular support and of the people's capacities, to build up and develop public health trying at the same time to obtain foreign aid and widen international cooperation in the medical field. Development of the abundant materia medica available in the country, rapidly building up a pharmaceutical industry and increasing the production of medical supplies and instruments;
(5) impetus to the training and improvement of professional medical and pharmacy workers in the spirit of the late President Ho Chiminh's teaching that the physician should also be a good mother.

On the basis of these principles the health service has defined five objectives to be realized under the Second Five-Year Plan:

(1) to persevere in the development of the patriotic movement for health and physical culture; to complete the "three-part rural sanitation scheme"; to prevent the outbreak of epidemics and take measures to ensure the rapid suppression of any epidemics that do occur;
(2) to improve the quality of medical examinations, treatment, care provided in sanatoria, and the prophylaxis and control of social diseases, primarily malaria, goitre, venereal diseases and tuberculosis; to find a solution for the aftereffects of war wounds; and to give particular attention to health management, outpatient services and primary care;
(3) to publicize family planning in order to reduce the natural increase rate; to make every effort to exceed the forecast family planning index; and to promote the prevention and treatment of gynaecological disorders, medical assistance during confinements and prenatal visiting;
(4) to resolve all pharmaceutical problems (materia medica, pharmaceutical production, the distribution and use of medicinal preparations), giving priority to the cultivation and use of medicinal plants at the rural level; and to increase the cultivation of medicinal plants and the breeding of animals providing basic drugs so as to avoid any shortage of medicinal preparations, in particular those used in the prevention and control of epidemics, in general use, or for children.

(5) to improve the health organization at provincial level; to concentrate efforts on developing district and community level health services; to build up a highly specialized medical system at central level which will support agricultural development and the creation of a new socialist rural area; and to mobilize the forces of the entire health service, institute examples of advanced care systems, multiply them and rapidly raise the whole country to an equal standard of health.

Health legislation

Between 1973 and 1977 the Communist Party of Viet Nam and the Government of the Socialist Republic of Viet Nam announced guidelines and decisions on the following matters:

— exemption from hospital fees as a first step in the rapid progress towards free treatment of diseases;
— strengthening of health activities within the framework of the new policies;
— improvement of provincial health organization;
— integration of management in the health service;
— strengthening of guidelines concerning hygiene, prophylaxis, prevention and control of epidemics, and health protection of the population;
— reform of the private medical and pharmaceutical system in the southern provinces;
— a number of technical standards regarding pharmaceutical products; and
— regulation of hygiene and health protection measures.

The Ministry of Health has also distributed medical legislation documents to ensure enforcement of the legislation throughout the country.

Health plan and programme

The health plan is part of the economic construction and cultural development plan for the whole country. There are two kinds of plans: a long-term (five-year) plan and short-term, annual plan. The Second Five Year Plan (1976–1980) is under way and is put into concrete form in the annual plans.

The Five-Year Health Plan aims to resolve the urgent problems cited above. The major objectives, to be achieved by the end of 1980, are as follows:

— for every family in rural areas, a trench latrine meeting the hygiene requirements;
— for every inhabitant, an average of three medical visits per year;
— 30 hospital beds for 10 000 inhabitants;
— reduction of the rate of the natural population increase to 2.1%;
— one physician for 3600 inhabitants;
— eradication, to the greatest possible extent, of malaria and the suppression of dangerous communicable diseases.

Organization of the medical and health network

The state controlled medical and health network is divided into four organizational levels from the capital to the provinces.

The basic level includes the communities in rural areas, town neighbourhoods, industries, schools, offices and work places. Each unit has a health post responsible for encouraging the population to build sanitary facilities, the prevention and control of epidemics, health management, the promotion of family planning, making regular medical visits, providing prenatal supervision and regular obstetric care. The progressive health coverage of a certain number of people and the supervision of a certain number of chronic patients will eventually result in the health coverage of the entire population.

The district level (towns and boroughs) includes the health office, the hospital, the regional polyclinic, the health team responsible for hygiene and the prevention of epidemics and malaria control (in the mountainous provinces there are still mobile health teams), and pharmacies.

The central level includes medical and pharmaceutical research institutes, hospitals, specialized clinics, sanatoria, advanced medical and pharmacy schools, a school for the training of health administrators, pharmaceutical factories, companies, medical publications, and the Central Medical Library.

The Ministry of Health of the Socialist Republic of Viet Nam is responsible to the Government for the efficient management of the physical, scientific and technical facilities available to the medical health service so as to ensure improvement in the people's health.

The Minister of Health is a member of the Government Council. The deputy Ministers, the secretariat and various technical, supply and personnel management departments assist the Minister in his duties. Finally there is also a Scientific and Technical Council, which acts as a consultative body to the Minister, and the Medical Association of Viet Nam.

Research

Scientific research is undertaken on a wide scale in all health establishments.

Research is focused on the public health status, diseases and the biological constants of the Vietnamese people; the materia medica and the production of preparations from medicinal plants; the aftereffects of war wounds; the eradication of communicable, parasitic and social diseases; environmental sanitation; the application of new examination, diagnostic and therapeutic techniques; the production of new vaccines; and the surgical treatment of liver cancer combined with immunotherapy. Scientific and technical cooperation with foreign countries has been initiated and is developing.

Training and refresher training of professional personnel

The training and refresher training of professional personnel is seen as one of the main long-term tasks of the health service. The provinces are responsible for the training of intermediate level professional personnel (admission requirements, 7–10 years of general studies; duration of studies, three years). At the end of 1977 there were 21 secondary health schools in the provinces and towns. Approximately 2000 nurses, midwives, technicians and medical auxiliaries graduate annually from secondary health schools.

The Ministry of Health is responsible for university-level training of personnel. There are six advanced medical and pharmacy schools. Candidates for advanced schools must hold a higher school certificate and take an entrance examination. Medicine is a six-year and pharmacy a five-year course. Approximately 1000–1200 physicians and 200–270 pharmacists graduate from the advanced schools every year.

Postgraduate training and refresher training courses are also provided both at home and abroad. The School for Medical Administrators was created in 1976, with a branch in Ho Chi-minh City. It provides refresher training for management and administrative personnel working in the health sector.

Facilities

Health establishments

These were the following health establishments in the period under review:

	Democratic Republic of Viet Nam			Socialist Republic of Viet Nam
	1973	1974	1975	1976
General and specialized hospitals	443	447	437	540
Regional hospitals	698	760	672	978
Sanatoria	92	99	82	93
Community health posts	5 673	5 566	5 785	8 215
Advanced medical schools	3	3	3	6
Pharmacy schools	1	1	1	1
Secondary medical and pharmacy schools	31	27	28	34
Hygiene and epidemiology units	26	26	26	38
Tuberculosis units	21	21	21	33
Dermatology and venereal disease units	21	21	20	32
Malaria control units	25	25	25	37
Ophthalmology units	19	21	19	20
Maternal health and family planning units	26	26	26	38
Leprosaria	17	17	16	25

The hospital beds were distributed as follows (figures in brackets indicate the number of beds per 10 000 population):

	Democratic Republic of Viet Nam			Socialist Republic of Viet Nam
	1973	1974	1975	1976
Total	101 379	105 619	107 988	159 088
	(45.9)	(46.7)	(46.5)	(33.1)
	54 938	58 071	59 201	98 362
Number financed from national budget	(24.9)	(25.7)	(25.5)	(20.5)
	46 441	47 548	48 787	60 726
Number in community services	(21.0)	(21.0)	(21.0)	(12.6)

Inpatient and outpatient services

The following items of treatment and examination were recorded for the period under review:

	Democratic Republic of Viet Nam			Socialist Republic of Viet Nam
	1973	1974	1975	1976
Persons examined	14 727 976	17 234 132	18 028 905	27 028 905
Medical examinations	15 784 706	18 730 410	20 842 642	32 844 642
Outpatients	2 619 366	2 898 656	2 663 478	3 920 227
Inpatients	2 616 826	2 905 805	3 336 082	4 836 082
Persons (obstetrics) examined	653 103	776 731	854 488	1 086 165
Obstetrical examinations	964 208	1 127 980	1 218 140	1 678 140
Confinements in health establishments* .	423 530	492 616	489 806	668 951
Women fitted with coils	54 145	114 610	124 103	377 272

*Incomplete data.

The numbers of communicable diseases cases recorded in the period under review were as follows:

	Democratic Republic of Viet Nam			Socialist Republic of Viet Nam
	1973	1974	1975	1976
Cholera				1 068*
Plague				593*
Dengue fever	905	111	13 998	21 361
Diphtheria	819	955	1 119	1 740
Poliomyelitis	211	104	306	617
Typhoid	217	419	502	5 168
Measles	42 365	185 520	81 805	98 362
Pertussis	63 704	94 301	42 528	50 623
Malaria	79 391	110 714	233 735	276 936
Trachoma	705 885	1 040 861	746 369	1 041 020
Tuberculosis	18 482	48 153	30 639	55 026
Leprosy	15 255	14 219	14 939	26 652
Syphilis	—	—	305	5 190*
Gonorrhoea	—	—	92	3 969*

*Confirmed cases.

Immunization

The following vaccinations were administered in the period under review:

	Democratic Republic of Viet Nam			Socialist Republic of Viet Nam
	1973	1974	1975	1976
Cholera and TAB	10 049 300	11 081 100	16 229 992	34 801 992
BCG	568 700	622 900	403 928	1 285 876
Poliomyelitis	3 082 300	3 252 500	2 958 335	4 291 857

Health personnel

There were the following health personnel in the period under review:

	Democratic Republic of Viet Nam			Socialist Republic of Viet Nam
	1973	1974	1975	1976
Physicians	5 352	6 256	6 419	9 006
Auxiliary physicians	21 156	21 686	21 902	26 347
Second level medical technicians	1 315	1 320	1 375	1 728
Pharmacists	1 776	2 117	2 297	3 041
Auxiliary pharmacists	3 196	3 408	3 367	4 645
Second level pharmacy technicians	110	138	199	251
Nurses	41 108	43 258	42 513	50 143
Second level nurses	237	664	1 116	4 315
Midwives	10 063	9 290	8 281	11 378
Second level midwives	127	206	278	647
Dispensers	9 984	9 839	8 503	11 239
Laboratory technicians	1 138	1 055	1 092	1 570

The doctor/population ratios and the ratios of auxiliary physicians to population are given below expressed as one doctor and one auxiliary physician to so many inhabitants):

	Democratic Republic of Viet Nam			Socialist Republic of Viet Nam
	1973	1974	1975	1976
Doctor	4 260	3 611	3 816	5 278
Auxiliary physician	966	946	1 118	1 824
Doctor or auxiliary physician	780	763	865	1 355

Production and sale of medicinal preparations

The production and sale of medicinal preparations in the period under review developed as indicated by the following figures for turnover and cost (1973 is taken as the base year at an index of 100):

	Turnover	Value of production
1973	100	100
1974	99	107
1975	103	116
1976	131	185
1977	179	214

The production and distribution of medicinal preparations is a government monopoly. The private pharmaceutical production centres and pharmacies in the southern provinces are in the process of being reorganized and restructured so as to provide the best possible health services.

Public health expenditure

In the Socialist Republic of Viet Nam all public health expenditure is met by the State. Over and above the national budget, the agricultural and craft cooperatives also contribute part of their income to help in constructing the medical health posts and paying the permanent personnel for the community health network.

WALLIS AND FUTUNA

Major health problems

Filariasis is practically the only tropical disease encountered in this area; it is, however, extremely widespread both in its common form, such as lymphangitis, and in more complex forms, such as elephantiasis.

Apart from tuberculosis, the dominant form of pulmonary pathology is bronchial asthma, which occurs at all ages and in all degrees of severity. The most varied forms of lung disease are frequently encountered, and their incidence is so high that some experts suspect that the population is particularly susceptible to pleuropulmonary illnesses. Nicotinism, which is widespread among both sexes, would appear to be a contributing factor to these conditions.

Rheumatic conditions are also seen frequently in medical consultations. The most common condition is usually osteoarthrosis, which thrives in the hot and humid climate. Rheumatic fever is treated at an early stage; only a few severe cases of carditis occur. Dermatological conditions are largely limited to staphylococcal infections of all kinds, and to mycoses, particularly pityriasis versicolor and circinata. Treatment of cutaneous mycoses is still unsatisfactory despite the use of new therapy, and there are inevitable relapses due to the prevailing climatic and hygienic conditions.

As a result of new laboratory methods, the detection rate for diabetes is improving. The incidence of diabetes is already high, and the current process of adopting the Western diet can only worsen the Polynesians' genetic predisposition to diabetes. Their traditional diet is high in glucose, and the excessive intake of energy foods, along with an almost total lack of exercise, particularly among women, leads to obesity which is a major factor in the etiology of diabetes. Chemotherapy, using oral hypoglycenic agents, is normally sufficient, and the use of insulin is rarely necessary. Finally, diabetes does not appear to lead to other diseases to a significant degree apart from arterial conditions and their classic complications.

Hygiene and sanitation problems are essentially limited to housing and the surrounding environment, and to drainage and septic treatment of faeces.

Organization of the health services

The reorganization of the Health Service is progressing gradually and in accordance with plans. To date the following have been established:

— a health service headquarters at Mata-Utu with administrative and managerial capacities;
— a medical treatment service divided into two medical regions, one on Wallis using the Territorial Hospital which provides medical and surgical hospitalization for the whole of the territory (there are two district dispen-

saries, one at Mua and one at Hihifo); the other service, located on Futuna, also has two units, one at Sigave and the other at Alo;
— a service for hygiene, disease prevention and endemic disease control which, due to more regular interisland transport and communications, is starting to cover the entire territory and is thus gradually assuming its mobile and efficient vocation; and
— a service of basic health education is at present attached to the Service for Hygiene, Disease Prevention and Endemic Disease Control. It was established on Wallis in 1977 and has a branch on Futuna.

Antifilarial chemoprophylaxis has been extended to cover the whole population, with haematological control and entomological studies in conjunction with the Louis Mallarde Institute of Tahiti.

Numerous wells have been sunk on the island of Wallis, and a network for the distribution of piped water has been set up. The total population now has access to fresh drinking-water.

Health resources

Health care units

A new territorial hospital was commissioned in July 1975 and includes modern X-ray, laboratory, surgical and dental equipment. Two modern maternity units have been set up, attached to the two medical centres on Futuna.

Health manpower

The four doctors practising in the Territory are all employed by the State administration. There is no private medicine. The local nursing staff is highly dedicated but lacks specialized technical competence. There are certain rare exceptions to this, mainly among new, younger staff. In order to encourage and promote talented young staff members, career development and refresher courses in the various disciplines are held at Noumé. Traineeships are also offered periodically at the Wallis Hospital for younger staff-members practising on Futuna.

There is a shortage of qualified nursing staff in specialized areas such as radiology, anaesthesia and laboratory work, and traineeships have been arranged for radiographers and laboratory personnel at the Pasteur Institute and Gaston Bourret Hospital, New Caledonia.

Health expenditure

All care provided by the Territory's health service is free and is financed by the French Government.

Medicine is imported either from New Caledonia or from France and is distributed free of charge.

Major development in the period 1973–1977

Over the five-year period the general public became more aware of health problems. More advanced technical methods were instituted, and a preventive health system which benefits the whole population.

The campaign for installation of flush toilets is making encouraging progress.

Outlook

Efforts will now be concentrated on environmental control and further housing sanitation.

Over the next few years, sanitary engineering (which affects several professional fields) will play a significant role in the areas of urbanization, road construction, rural development and in routine sanitary projects.

ADDENDUM

MALI

Population and health statistics

According to the most recent census, the tentative results of which were published in March 1978, the total population was 6 308 320 at the beginning of 1977, 50.94% female, 49.06% male. The estimates for the preceding years are:

1973	. . . . .	5 407 407
1974	. . . . .	5 543 821
1975	. . . . .	5 680 000
1976	. . . . .	5 822 000

Population numbers and density by region in 1977 were as follows:

	Area (km²)	Population	Inhabitants per km²
Kayes	119 815	871 871	7.2
Bamako	90 100	1 320 170	14.6
Sikasso	76 480	1 171 861	15.3
Ségou	56 127	984 613	17.3
Mopti	88 752	1 236 172	15.9
Gao	775 111	725 653	0.9
Total	1 204 021	6 308 320	5.2

The birth rate in 1977 was 55 per 1000, the gross mortality rate 30 per 1000, the natural growth rate 2.5%, the infant mortality rate 188 per 1000 live births, and life expectancy at birth 37.2 years.

Communicable diseases

The number of cases of communicable diseases during the period 1973–1977 were as follows:

	1973	1974	1975	1976	1977
Smallpox	—	—	—	—	—
Yellow fever	—	—	—	—	—
Cholera	23	618	—	—	—
Meningitis	1 401	824	200	224	267
Measles	37 654	42 618	37 828	30 673	25 624
Tetanus	709	522	539	739	475
Poliomyelitis	624	363	763	581	527
Diphtheria	80	25	81	29	42
Pertussis	11 527	12 640	9 943	8 066	5 555
Trypanosomiasis	201	105	164	105	105
Leprosy	3 505	3 907	4 237	2 845	2 922
Treponematosis	39 108	31 844	37 331	31 446	21 833
Onchocerciasis	5 950	4 087	5 150	5 868	4 997
Trachoma	3 444	2 405	8 575	2 378	3 235
Tuberculosis	1 616	1 357	1 507	2 039	1 408
Schistosomiasis	. . .	. . .	19 449	20 069	20 670
Malaria	479 365	505 290	408 934	383 663	319 411

Hospitals and specialized establishments

In 1978 Mali had the following establishments for inpatient and outpatient care (numbers of beds in brackets):

National hospitals	2	(715)
Regional hospitals	6	(1 255)
County (cercle) health centres	42	(679)
Marchoux Institute	1	(79)
Institute of Tropical Ophthalmology . .	1	(80)
Administrative maternity clinics	52	
Rural maternity clinics	238	
Rural dispensaries	387	
Dental care centres	11	
Maternal and child health care	52	
Sanitation and health centres	19	
Rehabilitation centres	2	
Village pharmacies	150	

Health manpower development

The increases in health manpower levels between 1973 and 1977 were as follows:

	1973	1974	1975	1976	1977
Physicians	135	168	178	—	237
Surgeons	—	—	—	—	17
Dental surgeons	7	—	—	—	12
Pharmacists	11	17	17	17	18
Sanitary engineers . . .	1	2	2	2	18
Water supply assistants .	4	—	—	—	4
Prosthetists	4	4	4	4	5
Midwives	152	168	206	224	268
State nurses	351	466	488	518	575
Public health nurses . .	1 012	1 255	1 308	1 359	1 415
Sanitarians	21	47	54	66	80
Laboratory technicians .	40	46	49	67	76
X-ray technicians . . .	6	10	17	17	17
Social workers	—	61	61	61	61
Auxiliary nurses	—	—	—	—	556
Auxiliary social workers .	156	156	156	156	156
Rural midwives	—	123	205	318	400
Traditional birth attendants	—	—	—	—	75

There are four training schools run by the Ministry of Public Health and Social Affairs: the Basic Training School, the Secondary Health Training School, the National School of Medicine, Pharmacy and Dentistry, and the Training School for Community Development Workers.

The arrangements for training of the different categories of staff are as follows:

	Number of establishments	Training period (years)	Capacity
Medical doctors	1	5	236
State nurses	1	3	204
State midwives	1	3	31
Laboratory technicians .	1	3	24
Sanitarians	1	3	15
Pharmacists	1	5	68
Nurses with basic training	1	3	277

There are also facilities in each region for the training of auxiliary nurses, and in each provincial capital for rural midwives.

The categories and numbers of staff trained in the four special schools between 1973 and 1977 were as follows:

	1974	1974	1975	1976	1977	Total
Physicians	—	8	13	17	25	63
State nurses . .	37	36	32	38	49	192
State midwives	19	14	12	19	17	81
Laboratory technicians .	7	7	3	5	9	31
Sanitarians . .	11	11	5	7	10	44
Nurses with basic training .	67	54	58	54	58	291

Health expenditure

Changes in the national budget allocations for health in the years 1973–1977 were as follows (in thousands of Mali francs):

	National budget (1)	Increase (%)	Health budget (2)	(2) as a percentage of (1)
1973	28 134 933	9.2	2 418 898	8.59
1974	31 823 348	13.10	2 598 115	8.16
1975	32 129 004	19.81	2 909 410	7.63
1976	50 199 768	31.65	3 465 234	6.90
1977	56 387 590	12.32	3 520 599	6.24

The funds for health manpower in the national health budget were distributed as follows (in thousands):

Section/programme	1976	1977	Increase (decrease)
Ministerial cabinet and national health administration	166 417	196 218	29 801
Health service physicians	961 383	900 058	(61 325)
Professional and technical instruction	131 370	127 375	(3 955)
Social and preventive medicine . .	380 934	385 834	4 900
. . . .	66 424	69 467	3 043
Tuberculosis control	52 178	45 753	(6 425)
Supply pharmacy	64 636	61 579	(3 057)
Vehicle maintenance	26 489	28 144	1 655

The funds for equipment were distributed as follows (in thousands):

Section/programme	1976	1977	Increase
Ministerial cabinet and national health administration	1 011 889	1 013 535	1 646
Health service medicine . .	88 908	104 042	15 134
Food for hospitals	193 353	217 100	23 747
Professional and technical instruction	28 500	31 000	2 500
Social and preventive medicine	41 154	45 903	4 749
Environmental health . . .	12 311	16 869	4 558
Tuberculosis control	13 164	18 670	5 506
Supply pharmacy	6 044	7 470	1 426
Vehicles	6 589	16 000	9 411
Institute for Traditional Medicine	2 905	3 500	595
National health inspection .	—	1 980	—

Major health and health-related problems

Mali has all the health problems characteristic of the developing countries: a high incidence and significant predominance of communicable diseases (especially malaria, measles, and enteritis), attributable in part to the poor living conditions in the rural communities where 85–90% of the people live (the severity of the problems is illustrated by the statistical tables in the section on "Communicable diseases" above); inadequate personal and environmental hygiene; undernourishment and malnutrition; insufficient health education; and poor housing conditions.

The living conditions are related to the low income of the population. The drought which started in 1973 has only aggravated the situation, especially in the northern regions. Mention must also be made of the fact that the health infrastructure and the health service system are still not well adapted to the real needs of the population and to the geographical and climatic conditions. Certain manpower categories are in short supply and are, in particular, poorly distributed, the geographical area is vast, and the rural population widely dispersed, without sufficient means of communication and transport.

The health budget is insufficient and inappropriately distributed, and there are other problems due to difficulties with supplies, organization and health management.

Action taken

Health policy

The 1971–1973 programme for economic and financial recovery, the main goal of which was to stimulate the economy and correct basic imbalances, the five-year plan for 1974–1978 which followed it and which was aimed at providing fuller coverage of the rural population, and the conclusions of the first national conference on primary health care in November 1976 together give the following definition of health development strategy for the period:

— to provide the most efficient and the most basic health services (with emphasis on health promotion activities and disease prevention) to people living on the outskirts of society;
— to build up the health infrastructure in order to promote such coverage;
— to continue to give priority to communicable disease control within preventive medicine (especially for tuberculosis, leprosy, onchocerciasis and bilharziasis) and to establish a broader immunization programme for common childhood diseases;
— to promote family health by better protection of the mother and the child through the development of a rational nutrition policy;
— to train and improve the skills of all manpower categories at all levels;
— to integrate all socio-medical activities into large-scale development projects, thus encouraging integrated development;
— to promote and rationalize research work in community health development; and
— to aim at self-sufficiency in all fields.

Health planning and programming

At the end of the third year of the five-year plan it was decided to evaluate it, and the evaluation was completed on 31 December 1976 for the field of public health and social affairs. The findings were that, considering the projects planned (at 1974 prices), then 20.5% of the financing was assured—40.3% if the projects for which financing had been agreed upon in principle were included, and as much as 60% if the projects not included in the plan were considered to be, in fact, as "bankable" (in terms of health development efficiency) as the projects initially included in the plan.

Health legislation

Health legislation is drafted by the national and judicial health administration, voted upon by the Military Committee for National Liberation, and enforced by the Judiciary.

Organization of health services

National level. Health services come under the jurisdiction of the Ministry of Public Health and Social Affairs. The Minister is responsible for implementing the policy outlined by the Government concerning the health and social protection of the people. The Minister and his cabinet determine the main areas in which work must be carried out, and the planning and programming which must be implemented.

Attached to the Minister's cabinet are: the Institute of Human Biology, which is in charge of promoting vaccines and serum, of supervising biological products, and of training management staff and laboratory technicians; the Research Institute for Pharmacopoeia and Traditional Medicine, whose task it is to study medicinal plants and other products or methods used in traditional medicine; and the General Public Health Administration, which is responsible for implementing, supervising and evaluating the programme. It has four divisions, for social and preventive medicine, family health, medical care, and supplies.

Regional level. In each of the seven administrative regions a regional health administration has been established under a physician who acts as regional health director, has overall jurisdiction, and whose main function is to coordinate activities. He serves as public health adviser to the governor of the region. In each of the 46 counties (*cercles*) there is a health area directed by the head physician for the county. Each of the 286 districts (*arrondissements*) has a rural dispensary and a rural maternity clinic directed by a State nurse. In the large villages, village health teams are working to implement the policy of primary health care.

Communicable diseases

The mass BCG vaccination campaign which started in 1968 continued throughout the period under review; 10 000 villages were visited and 2 510 889 vaccinations administered. A tuberculosis control study involving 2% of the population showed that there was 79% overall coverage in the 0–20 year age group. Since 1975, when the follow-up campaign was launched, it has been conducted in 68 centres (maternity clinics and maternal and child health centres) and by mobile teams.

Mass vaccination programmes for other diseases are administered each year by teams dealing with major endemic diseases and by various institutions, mainly dispensaries, medical centres and maternal and child health centres.

A measles study was conducted during an epidemic outbreak in Bamako in 1976.

Family health

A family health division was set up in 1975 and a head physician appointed to direct it. The division published a family health handbook designed for midwives and medico-social manpower with State diplomas. Three physicians were assigned to Mopti, Sikasso and Ségou to take charge of the family health programme in those regions. A training course in family planning and two refresher training courses for 76 midwives and nurses in the field of family health and nutrition were given in 1977. Health card files and records for the supervision of children and pregnant women were established as part of maternal and child health activities. Several maternal and child health centres were equipped. Various surveys were conducted on child nutrition.

As malnutrition is the sixth most common cause of death and as Mali is one of the countries which has been hardest hit by the drought of the last few years, the Ministry of Public Health and Social Affairs has a nutrition programme which is carried out by the national nutrition service. This programme consists basically of manpower training, the education of mothers, and the coordination of food aid to the people.

Environmental health

A public health and sanitation service was set up for the entire country; 18 public health and sanitation offices were established, covering the regional capitals, the communes and the capitals of the major counties.

Water supply projects were completed during the period for Ségou, Kati, Mopti Sevaré, Koutiala, Djenné, Goundam, Douentza, and Diré; 177 wells were drilled in the county of San by the *Aqua Viva* Project (a private Catholic organization).

Biomedical and health services research

A rural health research and training centre has been set up in the district of Massantola (in the county of Koloni), under the jurisdiction of the National School of Medicine and Pharmacy.

Outlook

The goals of the Government's health development strategy continue to be those stated in the section on "Health policy" above. The entire strategy is centred around primary health care which aims at correcting the current uneven distribution of health services. In order to achieve this goal, the following activities have been planned:

— A village health team, including 2–4 traditional midwives who have received proper training and 2–4 village health workers, will be sent to each village and a small village pharmacy established there, with the corresponding infrastructure, a rural maternity clinic with 8–10 beds and a first-aid station.

— A team including 2–4 traditional midwives, four village health workers and one rural midwife will be sent to each basic sector (7–10 villages with a total of 4000–7000 inhabitants), with the corresponding infrastructure, one rural midwifery centre with 8–10 beds and a first-aid station.

— Water supply will be provided for the people by digging wells near each school and rural maternity clinic.

— Each school and rural maternity clinic will be equipped with latrines meeting basic hygiene requirements.

The construction costs (both for materials and labour) for equipment for maternity clinics are borne in their entirety by the rural population, as are the wages of rural midwives (self-financing through rural cooperatives).

The strategy which has been decided upon for the next 10 years is to give the country a strong health service structure including 10 368 village health teams, 1300 basic sector health teams, 286 health centres in the districts (10 000 to 30 000 inhabitants); 47 county health centres directed by a head physician and officials in charge of treatment services, preventive medicine, and the public health, sanitation and communicable diseases service; six health reg-ions, each managed by a regional health physician who is technical adviser to the Government of the region, administering, coordinating, and supervising all health activities in the region.

High priority will be given to traditional medicine and medicines in the framework of primary health care, and the work of the National Research Institute for Traditional Medicine is proceeding apace.

MAURITANIA

Background information

The total area of Mauritania is 1 288 000 km^2. The country is divided into three ecological regions: the Sahara region covers seven-eighths of the total area and has less than 100 mm of rain annually—water points are scarce; the Sahelian region stretches from the valley of the Senegal River to a line passing through Nouakchott, Tamchakett, Aioun el Atrous and Néma, and has between 100 mm and 250 mm of rain annually. Water is scarce and the water-table very low. The coastal region also has little rain; the climate is tempered by the cool winds from the Atlantic; there are no water points.

Population

In the following table population figures based on 1976–1977 census results are compared with the statistical services' estimates for the year 1970.

	1970	%	1976–1977	%
Total population	1 124 326		1 481 000	
Rural nomads	810 000	72%	539 000	36.5%
Rural sedentary population	157 653	14%	565 319	38.5%
Urban population (regional capitals and prefectures) . . .	156 673	14%	369 813	25%

Migration of the nomadic populations towards the south is to be noted, with gradual sedentarization in the vicinity of large population centres and important road axes; there has also been a marked exodus from rural areas. These two phenomena appear to be chiefly due to the drought in recent years and to the economic situation.

The population density is approximately one inhabitant per km^2 for the country as a whole. Some seven-eights of the population live in the Sahelian region, which accounts for only about one-eighth of the national territory.

The percentage distribution of the population by age groups was as follows in 1977:

Years	Urban	Rural sedentary	Rural nomadic	Total
0–5	19.2	20.6	19.3	19.9
6–14	23.7	24.6	24.7	24.4
15–44	45.8	39.6	37.6	40.3
45–59	7.2	8.8	11.5	9.4
60 and over . .	4.1	6.4	6.8	6.0

The average family size varies between 4.8 persons (in Nouadhibou) and 7.2 (in Sélibaby).

There are 16 towns or localities with 5000 inhabitants or more, plus the regional capitals of Dakhla and F'Dérick, whose population falls just short of 5000 inhabitants, making 18 towns in all qualifying as centres of urban population.

There are 13 administrative regions, plus the District of Nouakchott. Each region comprises one or several departments; the departments are in turn subdivided into *arrondissements*. Each region has a governor, who is placed under the authority of the Ministry of the Interior.

The gross birth rate is estimated at 43 per 1000, the gross mortality rate at 27 per 1000, the growth rate estimated at 20–25 per 1000, and the infant mortality rate at 169 per 1000. The per capita gross national product is less than US $150.

Health development strategy

The Government's objectives in the field of health are subject to a number of imperatives dictated by the constant concern to extend public health coverage to those living in rural areas and those living on the periphery of large towns—essentially, nomads and rural inhabitants who have abandoned their homes as a result of the drought prevailing in recent years and who are completely destitute and unprepared for urban life; these imperatives are:

(1) the extension of the public health system and its decentralization (regionalization), mainly through the implementation of new social and health development projects, especially in distant and poorly equipped areas and on the periphery of large towns;
(2) the training of the medical and auxiliary personnel needed for the smooth operation of the services set up to extend public health care to all inhabitants of the country, aiming at self-sufficiency within the shortest possible time;
(3) the continuous search for maximum efficiency and the constant improvement of the services which provide the population, in an integrated manner, with essential health care; namely, therapy and prevention, including vaccination, mother and child health care, advice on nutrition, protection of the environment, and health education;
(4) reform of the former policy, which was based on a multiplicity of "heavy infrastructure" projects to the detriment of units better adapted to the needs and resources of the country. Priority will be given to the setting up of smaller units which will make it possible to extend the network of fixed outposts on which the primary health care scheme for the communities must rely.

This new national health policy is in conformity with the directives of WHO.

Major health problems

Health situation

Despite a still inadequate system of notifications and of supply of statistical information, the Government is convinced of the need to give priority to communicable and parasitic disease control which constitutes the major public health problem, to which must be added malnutrition and undernourishment of the most vulnerable group, namely, children.

Malaria, tuberculosis and measles head the list of diseases. In children, enteric diseases are extremely frequent and are responsible for a high mortality. Complications arising from measles, pertussis and bronchopulmonary disorders follow, in that order, as the most frequent childhood diseases.

Schistosomiasis and dracunculiasis affect large numbers in certain areas of the country. Trachoma and conjunctivitis of the ordinary kind are very common. Sexually transmitted diseases are widespread. Leprosy is to be found in the south; the number of patients is estimated at 2500.

Only the south is infested by the anopheline mosquito; malaria is thus endemic in the most densely populated area; it is responsible for a high infant mortality as well as a high degree of morbidity in all age groups.

Pulmonary tuberculosis constitutes a major public health problem. Its propagation is due to the rapid sedentarization of the nomadic populations and also to the poor hygiene, housing and nutrition conditions. The estimated number of tuberculosis patients is 9000–12 000, and the annual number of new cases, 3300. The Government has intensified all preventive activities since 1968 in the form of systematic BCG vaccination of the 6–20 year age group. In 1976 the national antituberculosis programme was launched, making use of the existing infrastructure for the national antituberculosis service and strengthening its activities, with detection by bacilloscopy.

Measles has caused deadly epidemics, especially in rural areas which have a poor infrastructure and where the action of mobile teams is inevitably tardy. Vaccination has been given priority, but it is hampered by difficulties in obtaining supplies of vaccine, by logistic problems and by problems connected with the refrigeration equipment.

Gastrointestinal and pulmonary infections are extremely common among the 0–5 year age group; the lack of hygiene contributes to the spread of these infections, which are very common among children in rural areas and on the periphery of Nouakchott and the other large towns.

No less than 80% of the population has always been chronically undernourished; but since the drought the resulting socioeconomic upheavals have greatly increased the incidence both of undernourishment and of malnutrition, particularly among the most vulnerable groups. Public health units are daily confronted with this problem. The services for recovery and nutritional education—at present there are four centres in the city of Nouakchott—are to be extended to the rural areas; it was planned to establish 10 centres by the end of July 1978.

Health legislation

The Government's priority programme for the extension of social and health coverage to the whole population has recently been strengthened by the entry into force of a decree of 11 July 1977 providing for the reorganization of the regional public health units with the aim of decentralization in terms of infrastructure, personnel and resources.

The preventive function of the prefectoral health centres and of the health posts of the *arrondissements* has been clarified. The reorganization of the mobile polyvalent teams is under way.

With the opening in November 1976 of the National Hygiene Centre—where a Chinese team and WHO staff cooperate—the development of social and preventive medicine will be facilitated. The general objectives of the Centre have been clearly defined in a decree of 17 March 1978. The Centre has been designated by WHO as a national centre to cooperate in the African regional network for the training of personnel and in research in the general field of epidemiological surveillance and communicable disease control.

Planning and programming

The Government's priority projects all have as their common goal the extension of social health coverage to the most remote and the most vulnerable sectors.

The new infrastructure projects have as their common objective the strengthening of the networks to support public health activities in rural areas, which extend also to the periphery of the capital:
— the part of the family welfare projects dealing with infrastructure covers the creation of mother and child centres in the regional capitals, an increase in the number of centres and of rural maternity and recovery centres, and the setting-up of 450 "health huts" in small villages and fixed encampments over a period of five years;
— the project for the extension of social health coverage aims to set up 150 public health posts in larger villages and fixed encampments over five years, and lays stress on

the best use to be made of human resources in the villages selected;
— the infrastructure of the regional prefectoral units is being adapted to their new role in the framework of regionalization through specific projects; the maintenance of these units has once again been ensured.

Training of personnel

Further projects are directed towards the training of personnel adapted to the real needs of the country. The medical personnel are trained in friendly countries; the auxiliary personnel are almost all trained locally. Professional nursing staff are trained at the National School of Nursing and Midwifery. Other auxiliary staff are largely trained on the actual site of activities. They are to play a predominant role in the projects relating to the activities of maternal and child health and primary health care. Voluntary personnel complete the network of public health workers.

Friendly countries and the international organizations grant fellowships for the specialized training of medical and paramedical staff.

It must be stressed that the family welfare project, the project for the extension of social health and the project supported by USAID which is in the course of formulation, all give an important place to the training of personnel and to health education of the population.

Disease control

The campaign against communicable diseases has taken a new turn with the expanded programme of immunization, which has started in the capital and in the Trarza Region. With the arrival of a large consignment of vehicles the programme is to be extended to the country as a whole, using the resources of the mobile teams which have been reorganized and made operational.

The campaign against tuberculosis continues within the framework of the activities of the National Antituberculosis Service.

The recently opened National Hygiene Centre lends its support to the activities connected with the campaign against communicable diseases by training specialized personnel, undertaking research relating to epidemiological surveillance and working to improve the environment.

The campaign against noncommunicable diseases is developing, with the training of specialized personnel in dietetics, buccodental health, and mental health.

Environmental health

Environmental health is a matter of special concern, particularly with regard to water supply, the removal and treatment of refuse and waste water, the sanitary control of foodstuffs, and vector control, owing in particular to the lack of qualified personnel and of a national sanitation plan, and the poor quality of sanitation services, chiefly in the rural areas and the peripheral areas of large urban centres.

Since the arrival of a WHO sanitary engineer, the preliminary draft of a national plan of sanitation and health legislation has been prepared and submitted to the Government.

Public health resources

Institutions

The following medical care institutions are in service in the Nouakchott District: the National Hospital, with 460 beds (the construction work to double the capacity of this hospital has just been completed); a polyclinic completed in 1976; 5 prefectoral dispensaries in the town; 4 maternal and child health centres; a school medical centre; 2 communal factory clinics; and the National Hygiene Centre inaugurated in November 1977 with credits from China.

The maternal and child health centre in the first *arrondissement* has recently been completed with financing by the Fonds d'Aide et de Coopération and the World Lutheran Federation, but is not yet open. A 50-bed tuberculosis hospital is in the course of construction with financing by Sheik Nasser. Financing is under way from the African Development Bank for the enlargement of the National School of Nursing and Midwifery. Studies for the setting-up of dispensaries are being financed by Iraq.

Regional hospitals in Nouadhibou, Akjoutj, Kaédi, Atar, Dakhla, Rosso and Ales are in service, with a total of 320 beds. In the regional capitals, the existing health units are quite old and no longer sufficient; they are being gradually replaced by hospitals. Hospitals are under construction at Kiffa, Néma and Sélibaby (all three with Chinese financing); the construction is expected to be completed in 1979–1980. Regional hospitals have 25–150 beds for treatment, specialized services for pathology, surgery, maternity, and an X-ray laboratory. The mobile teams are directly under the authority of the chief physician of the medical subdivision.

A hospital is under construction at Tidjikja, financed by Kuwait; work was expected to be completed in May 1979. Two interregional hospitals are in the planning stage: the Kaédi hospital, with 80–120 beds, and the Aioun el Atrous hospital (with financing by Saudi Arabia). Enlargement and renovation of the Atar hospital with financing by the Fonds d'Aide et de Coopération is also planned.

A project is taking shape to set up at Nouadhibou a hospital unit suited to the needs of this important economic centre.

There are, further, 40 prefectoral health centres, 48 ward (*arrondissement*) health posts, and 20 maternal and child health centres. The number of these centres will gradually increase. A health post includes premises for consultations and medical attention (stores, medicaments, archives) and is headed by a qualified male nurse. Rural maternity posts are planned. In addition, 15 mobile teams are based on the regional capitals.

The substantial financial support extended by Saudi Arabia will make it possible to modernize and to improve the equipment of a larger number of health units in the regions.

	Néma	Aioun	Kiffa	Kaédi	Aleg	Rosso	Atar	Nouad hibou	Tid- jikja	Séli- baby	F'Dé- rick	Ak- joutj	Dakhla	Nouak- chott	Total
Regional health centre .	1	1	1	1	1	1	1	1	0	1	0	1	1	*	11
Mobile teams	3	2	2	1	1	1	1	1	1	1	0	0	0	1	14
Maternal and child health centres	1	1	1	3	2	3	1	1	1	1	0	1	0	4	20
Departmental health centres[1]	6	4	4	4	4	6	3	1	3	1	4	1	4	5	49
Health posts (*arrondisse- ments* and main towns) . .	4	1	1	7	7	12	3	1	3	6	—	1	2	—	48

[1] A departmental health centre includes premises for consultations and medical attention, a maternal and child health centre, premises with beds for patients under observation, a small maternity clinic directed by a doctor and with a midwife in attendance.

* Nouakchott has a polyclinic.

Health manpower

Comparative figures for public health personnel in government services in 1973 and the first half of 1978 were as follows:

	1973		1978		Nationals being trained
	Nationals	Total	Nationals	Total	
Physicians . . .	8	64	18	95	97*
Pharmacists . .	1	2	1	4	...
Dentists	1	3	1	4	...
Midwives . . .	10	15	12	19	37
State-qualified nurses . . .	99	99	192	195	42
Auxiliaries and assistants . .	204	204	246	246	...
Auxiliary midwives . .	17	17**	...	...	...

*Medical students are trained abroad.
**There are also 83 traditional midwives being retrained.

Professional paramedical personnel (midwives, state-qualified nurses, certified nurses) are almost all trained at the National School of Nursing and Midwifery. The Government has encountered many problems in this field, among them a certain lack of interest on the part of young men for the public health professions, with the result that the students admitted and trained for these professions are of a rather mediocre level.

Fellowships granted by international organizations and by friendly countries have made it possible for numerous personnel to specialize in various fields considered by the Government as having priority.

The training of personnel has been the subject of attentive and realistic planning.

Developments in the period 1973–1978, and future prospects

Although, because of the persistent drought which has seriously hampered the efforts at planning the socioeconomic development of the country, and also because of the difficulties arising from the war, the progress made in the last few years with regard to infrastructure and to staff coverage has been comparatively mediocre, a marked improvement in the situation is noticeable following the important public health policy decisions taken in the last few months.

It is the Government's deliberate policy to develop preventive medicine as a priority; with the launching of the projects centred on the strengthening of maternal and child care activities, health education, the training of auxiliary personnel, the expanded programme of immunization and the planning of improved environmental hygiene, this will make it possible—with the cooperation of international bodies and friendly countries and the willing effort of the population—to bring health to a satisfactory level within the coming 20 years.

Prospects up to the year 2000

The general objectives in the long term are to promote and settle policies and programmes for a healthy environment, and to evaluate, control and help to make better known the conditions and risks connected with the environment that can influence human health. The detailed objectives are: to cooperate in the planning and final formulation of policies and programmes for a healthy environment, integrated with the nationwide planning policies and projects for economic development; to promote the national planning of public water supply services and the disposal of refuse, and to cooperate in such planning; and to promote the preparation and implementation of programmes for the rapid detection and control of factors causing pollution (chemistry, physics and biology of the environment).

RWANDA

Major health and health-related problems

The major problems, in order of priority, are tuberculosis and other bronchopulmonary diseases, diarrhoeas, intestinal parasitic diseases, malaria, recurrent fever, exanthematous typhus; problems of environmental hygiene; undernourishment and malnutrition, particularly in the 2–5 year age group; endemic measles; population growth; and mental health problems.

Action taken

With regard to public health, the Second Five-Year Economic, Social and Cultural Development Plan (1977–1981) provides for the development of mass medical care, preference being given to preventive medicine, and to improving the efficiency of the health services, bearing in mind their importance in the socio-economic structure of the country.

National health policy and health planning

The national health development strategy has been formulated in the overall context of the Five-Year Plan. The Government's objectives are the following:

(1) to develop the public health infrastructure so as to have three reference hospitals with a total of 5000 beds at least, as well as three reference laboratories; one 250-bed hospital in each prefectorial district; one health centre in each commune; two mental health centres—one in the North, the other in the South of the country—as outposts for the Ndera (Kigali) psychiatric centre;

(2) to integrate the health and social services in the medical units;

(3) to develop the capacity for planning, coordination and evaluation of public health authorities;

(4) to develop primary health care in the framework of community development;

(5) to organize programmes for communicable disease control, and promote the expanded immunization programmes;

(6) to train the health personnel needed at all levels; to train Rwandese teaching staff for the Faculty of Medicine of Butare; to bring up to date the medical and auxiliary personnel training programmes; to create a school for assistant sanitation technicians and a school for assistant laboratory technicians;

(7) to provide the population of Kigali and Butare with safe potable water, and to recondition 5500 small rural water sources;

(8) to set up a factory for the packing of pharmaceutical products; and

(9) to set up public municipal pharmacies.

In order to deal with the demographic and malnutrition problems, a number of intersectoral measures have been taken under the auspices of the Ministry of Social Affairs and of the Cooperative Movement assisted by the Secretary-General of Public Health. There are, within this Ministry, a general directorate of basic health services, a general directorate of pharmacies, a directorate of hospitals and medical sectors, a directorate of hygiene and a bureau of health statistics and health education.

The country is divided into 10 prefectoral districts, five of which fall under the direction of the prefecture. There are three reference hospitals and there is at least one rural hospital in each prefectoral district; there are 143 communes having a health centre and/or a dispensary.

Preventive medicine is integrated with curative medicine. With regard to preventive medicine, however, there is a central national epidemiological service which deals with communicable diseases and vaccinations, at the periphery there are itinerant vaccinators.

There is a rehabilitation centre for the handicapped; and there is a psychiatric centre at Ndera.

The Hygiene Service deals with the problems of the environment and sanitation.

Medical research

There is a research centre which has started work on traditional medicine, particularly medicinal plants.

Education and training of health personnel

Medical practitioners are trained in the Faculty of Medicine of Butare. Medical assistants are trained in the schools for medical assistants at Kigali and Butare. Hospital nurse/midwives are trained at the Rwamagana Nursing School, other nurse/midwives at the Kabgayi Nursing School, assistant nurse/midwives at the Mugonero School and assistant nurses at Kirinda.

There are in-service training courses for all categories of personnel of health teams. Specialized training for medical and pharmaceutical staff is generally obtained abroad with the aid of fellowships. These activities will be further developed in the future.

Health resources

Health care institutions

In 1977 there was one hospital in the capital. In the rest of the country there were 22. Health centres and dispensaries totalled 243. There was one sanatorium, one psychiatric centre, and one centre for the physically handicapped.

Health personnel

In 1977 there were 27 medical practitioners in the capital. In the rest of the country there were 94, giving a total of 121.

Medical assistants numbered 226; male nurses, 74; female nurses of all categories, 318; and assistants, 313.

Promotion and sale of pharmaceutical products

There is no production of medicaments locally; the State Pharmaceutical Organization purchases medicaments and distributes them to the various health units. A nongovernmental organization purchases medicaments and sells them to the approved health units (mission units). UNICEF and other bilateral and multilateral organizations cooperate in this sector.

Public health expenditure

Public expenditure in the health sector amounted to 450 million Rwandese francs in 1977, or 7% of the total State budget, representing an average expenditure on health of 105 francs per inhabitant.

Evaluation of progress made between 1973 and 1977

Public health coverage substantially improved during the period, which corresponded to the advent of the Second Republic. The central organization was strengthened by the setting-up of a general directorate of basic health services and a directorate of hospitals and medical sectors. The number of hospital beds rose from 3227 in 1973 to 4028 in 1977. The number of health centres increased from 28 to 63. The number of dispensaries increased from 155 to 180. The general hospital bed/population index rose from 0.81 to 0.90 per 1000 population. The bed/population index of health centres and dispensaries rose from 0.42 to 0.63 per 1000 population.

The doctor/population ratio rose from one to 51 000 to one to 37 000. The medical assistant/population ratio rose from one to 23 000 to one to 20 000. The nurse/population ratio rose from one to 11 736 to one to 7 352.

The infant mortality rate fell from 127 to 126 per 1000 live births. The maternal mortality rate based on deaths in hospital fell from 4.7 to 3.1 per 1000 live births.

There was a resurgence of malaria, measles and relapsing fever; at the same time there was a regression in exanthematous typhus. The eradication of smallpox was officially declared. A mental health centre came into operation in the South. A total of 2390 small rural water sources were opened.

Outlook

In order to achieve the declared objectives, the Government proposes to develop planning and management of the health services, country health programming, primary health care, essential drugs, technical cooperation among developing countries, the expanded programme on immunization, and training of personnel for the health services, including teacher training.

TOGO

Major health and health-related problems

The Government of Togo's highest priority is to make medical care available to the greatest number of people.

There are nearly 2 400 000 people living in Togo's 56 785 km^2, giving a density of 42 inhabitants per km^2; 15% of the population lives in the city, with 9.6% in the capital and 5.3% in the other cities. The rural population is thus 85%. The 1971 census showed an infant mortality rate of 91 per 1000 compared with 125 per 1000 in 1961, and a general mortality rate of 19 per 1000. Life expectancy had risen to 42 for men and 50 for women.

Measures taken

Health policy

Health policy is aimed to give greater priority to ambulatory care over outpatient care by fixed health units; to give greater emphasis to the primordial role of preventive medicine; to improve the existing health units rather than build new ones; and to develop and implement a vaccination campaign for the most fatal infant diseases, thus reducing the infant mortality rate and thereby the general mortality rate.

Health legislation

The piecemeal health legislation which dates back to the colonial period is under study with a view to the need to correct all existing international and national situations.

Health planning and programming

In June each year the progress made in the past year is reviewed and the changes that need to be made for the following year are determined.

Organization of health services

Health services are organized so that all forms of medical care (prevention, treatment, rehabilitation, re-education, health education, basic health measures, protection of the environment, family planning, nutrition) are integrated into one health unit with a health team consisting of a doctor, a nurse, a midwife, a health assistant, a sanitarian, a laboratory technician, a travelling health worker and a social worker.

Curative medicine

Hospital care. The table below gives a breakdown of the number of persons hospitalized and the length of their stay, for the period 1973–1978. These data are only estimates, owing to the difficulties encountered by the National Service of Health Statistics in establishing the total number of patients hospitalized at the National Teaching Hospital in Lomé. The table clearly shows that the number of persons hospitalized is increasing steadily, the average length of stay being 12 days.

Outpatient care. The table also refers to the level of activity of outpatient clinics, in this case the health centres. Statistics on their activities are more reliable than those on hospital care. The table shows that the number of patients consulting outpatient clinics is also rising steadily. On the basis of these statistics, the estimated ratio of outpatients to the total population was 80.8%, 76.3%, 78.8%, 84.6%, 77.6% and 78.2% for the years 1973, 1974, 1975, 1976, 1977 and 1978 respectively. The irregular pattern makes any trend impossible to establish. The average number of visits for medical care per outpatient was 3.51, 3.51, 3.21, 3.07, 3.23 and 3.26 for the same years respectively.

Preventive medicine

Sanitary education must be decentralized as far as possible so that the village nurse may have the necessary authority to work in depth on the urban fringes. The same goes for the state sanitarian as well as for the travelling health worker, since both the illiterate mother and father must be included in education measures to make vaccination and health coverage as broad as possible. The solution of the problems of refrigeration and of the price of the vaccines remains a condition *sine qua non* for the success of the expanded programme of immunization.

	1973	1974	1975	1976	1977	1978
Hospital establishments	17	18	18	18	18	18
Beds	3 010	3 010	3 124	3 124	3 418	3 451
Admissions*	90 300	90 300	93 803	93 803	102 540	103 530
Days hospitalized*	1 083 600	1 083 600	1 125 640	1 125 640	1 230 480	1 242 360
Health centres	226	227	250	249	285	288
Inhabitants per health centre	9 684	9 685	9 019	9 206	8 216	8 457
Outpatients	1 704 896	1 678 465	1 778 061	1 957 854	1 819 184	1 907 206
Visits	5 992 966	5 894 283	5 717 061	6 023 374	5 880 307	6 225 240

*Estimates.

	Number of hospitals		Inhabitants per hospital	Bed/population ratio (one to ...)	Health centres	Inhabitants per centre
		Beds				
Lomé	1	1 062	277 200	261	19	14 589
Aného-Vo	2	329*	153 650	934	27	11 381
Tabligbo	1	115	87 500	761	6	14 583
Tsévié	1	82	189 700	2 313	23	8 248
Notsè	1	75	99 000	1 320	8	12 375
Kloto	2	202**	101 350	1 003	37	5 478
Atakpamé-Akposso . .	1	306†	307 000	1 003	39	787
Tchaoudjo-Sotouboua .	1	281†	198 800	707	27	7 363
Bassar	1	94	109 100	1 161	14	7 793
Bafilo	1	28	33 500	1 196	4	8 375
Lama-Kara	1	317	110 500	349	8	6 139
Pagouda	1	88	51 200	582	9	5 639
Niamtougou	1	159	60 300	379	7	8 614
Kantè	1	24	50 700	2 113	11	4 609
Mango	1	53	69 800	1 317	10	6 980
Dapaong	1	236	217 200	919	29	7 483
Total	18	3 451	131 739	687	288	8 234

* Including one private hospital with 136 beds.
** Including one private hospital with 81 beds.
† Including beds in adjoining dispensaries.

Biomedical research

Biomedical research has just been initiated and is devoted above all to work on medicinal plants in collaboration with traditional practitioners.

Education and training of health personnel

There are internships and refresher training programmes for public health officials at all levels every year. There is also an annual meeting of all the doctors in charge of the various health units to evaluate the health situation in the past year and to establish a further plan of action for reaching the defined objective of health care for the greatest number of people.

Health resources

Hospital establishments

Togo has 18 hospitals: one teaching hospital in Lomé, four regional hospitals in the chief towns in the regions of Atakpamé, Sokodé, Lama-Kara and Dapaong, 11 secondary hospitals, including the regional hospital clinics, and two private hospitals—one in the coastal area and the other in the plateau area (Afagnan and Agou-Nyogbo). The distribution, with details of coverage and numbers of beds, is shown in the table above.

In 1978 the hospital bed ratio was one to 687 inhabitants.

For outpatient care Togo has 288 health centres, or one to 8234 inhabitants—which is still far from the goal of one to 5000.

Health personnel

If health personnel are divided into three groups, doctors, "paramedicals" and auxiliaries, for the period 1973–1978, according to their duty station in or outside the capital, the figures are very significant: the doctor/population ratio is increasing, both in Lomé and in the interior. Lomé has a number of private practitioners, who cannot be found in any other part of the country, widening the gap between the capital and the interior. In 1973 there was one doctor to 81 965 inhabitants outside the capital; by 1978 there was one to 48 680. Thus, in 1973, the ratio between the number of doctors per inhabitant in Lomé and outside the capital was of the order of one to 15, while in 1978 the ratio was one to 17, so that the gap is not narrowing to any appreciable extent.

Starting in 1980, the Medical School of the University of Bénin will train 20 doctors a year. It is hoped that this will improve the trend in favour of the urban fringes.

"Paramedical" staff include medical assistants, public health technicians, midwives, public health nurses, public laboratory technicians, and public sanitarian assistants. From 1973 to 1978 the paramedical staff/population ratio in Lomé increased from one to 472 to one to 345, while outside Lomé the paramedical staff/population ratio increased from one to 4098 to one to

403

2922. The ratio of the number of paramedicals per inhabitant in Lomé to those outside the capital was of the order of one to nine in 1973 and one to eight in 1978. These figures show an improvement in favour of the urban fringes. If the National School of Health Auxiliaries is able to meet the demand, a clear improvement in the present trend in favour of the rural population can certainly be expected. The same may be said for the Teaching Institute of Health Technology and the National School for Health Assistants.

The situation outside the capital is better than within Lomé for other auxiliary personnel. The School for Health Aides in Sokodé will certainly improve this situation quantitatively and qualitatively.

The Government is endeavouring to give standardized training to a large staff at every level, to distribute personnel more evenly across the nation, authority being given at all levels in the spirit of the conclusions, drawn on the occasion of the Ministry of Public Health's last round-table conference at the beginning of 1979, in favour of a sound management of available funds.

Health expenditure

Between 1973 and 1976, the per capita gross national product rose from 42 024 to 57 400 CFA francs, the per capita available income from 40 407 to 56 366 CFA francs, and the per capita national income from 39 779 to 55 280 CFA francs.

The part of the general budget reserved for the Ministry of Public Health is increasing, as shown in the table below (in thousands of CFA francs).

Production and sale of pharmaceuticals

"Togopharma", incorporating five State pharmacies and 69 drug dispensaries, to which seven more are soon to be added, does its best to make drugs easily available to the rural population, but its efforts are limited by inflation.

Outlook

There are still many problems to be solved. The group of infectious and parasitic diseases will continue to head the list of priorities. An effort must be made to eradicate, or at least to reduce, the diseases in this group which can be most easily avoided. There is hope that just as smallpox has been eradicated, so tetanus, measles and pulmonary tuberculosis will be eradicated one by one, since a vaccine exists against these blights; the same political will, the same continental and world strategy and the same aid from developed countries will put an end to these few preventable diseases.

Meanwhile, an effort will be made to pool existing knowledge on the health infrastructure by giving the National Teaching Hospital, the regional and secondary hospitals everything they need, so that the referrals may be kept to a strict minimum.

In 1979 a special list of the International Classification of Diseases and Causes of Death (1975 Revision) will enter into force, replacing the "Basic List of Tropical Diseases" which has been used up to now for the compilation of health statistics by outpatient clinics.

The donation of a dual key entry data recorder by the WHO Regional Office for Africa to

	1973 Amount	1974 Amount	Increase %	1975 Amount	Increase %	1976 Amount	Increase %	1977 Amount	Increase %	1978 Amount	Increase %
General budget . . .	3 434 166	16 244 600	20.92	30 514 684	87.84	50 018 859	10.3	55 280 829	10.36	60 593 000	9.77
Health budget (operational) . . .	880 056	1 090 751	23.94	1 441 328	32.14	1 846 367	10.2	2 044 863	10.75	2 911 087	42.36
Ratio (%)	6.55	6.72		4.72		3.69		3.70		4.80	
Health investment budget	25 000	101 920	307.7	191 902	88.2	65 000	13.4	159 822	145.8	56 000	64.8
Independent budget of the Lomé Teaching Hospital	438 100	557 500	27.2	770 000	38.1	886 100	15 08	1 067 800	20.50	1 217 340	14.00
"Togopharma" aid . .	10 000	10 000	0.00	10 000	0.00	10 000	0.00	10 000	0.00	10 000	0.00
Total State expenditure for public health . .	1 353 156	1 760 171	30.08	2 413 230	37.10	2 826 336	17.12	3 282 485	16.14	4 194 427	27.78
Total per capita expenditure (in CFA francs) . . .	641	801	24.96	1 070	33.58	1 222	14.21	1 402	14.73	1 722	22.82

the National Service of Health Statistics will make the Ministry of Public Health autonomous in the filing of health statistics in a form which can be used directly on the computer of the National Data Processing Centre.

ZAIRE

Major health problems

The health problems which are felt most acutely in Zaire and which the public health officials are trying to solve are: (1) communicable diseases; (2) health services in rural areas; and (3) the very high rate of natural population growth.

Communicable diseases

These diseases are quite widespread, and mainly affect pregnant women, mothers, and pre-school children. This is not to say that communicable diseases spare the other groups in the population, but rather that they have a much weaker impact and a much lower mortality rate for these other groups. All of these diseases can be prevented. The high incidence of disease is due to environmental factors—the inadequacy of health and sanitation infrastructures—and the lowering of the people's resistance through malnutrition and undernourishment.

Health services in rural areas

The problems in this field are a result of the social structure. The proportion of people living in rural areas, estimated at 75%, is expected still to be around 65% in 1980. It is unclear whether urban health problems differ greatly from those in rural areas or not.

Solutions cannot be found unless the health infrastructure is altered to suit the needs of urban and rural areas, taking into account the fact that the population is spread over a large area.

Natural population growth

There has been a population explosion (the population growth rate is 29.5%). Special attention must be given to protecting the resulting large child population; the necessary measures will consume a substantial proportion of health resources.

Conclusion

The implications of these issues for health are too great to be ignored. In drawing up health policy, the Department of Health has taken them into account, considering the scope for action, and, in particular, the possibility of increasing it.

Action taken

Health policy

The National Council for Health and Welfare was set up in 1974 in order to draft health policy. It set the following main goals for health:

(1) raising the population's level of health and welfare;
(2) organizing health activities mainly for the high-priority category of mothers and children;
(3) integrating curative, preventive, and educational activities, with special emphasis on prevention and environmental sanitation;
(4) developing basic services and activities, especially those benefiting the community;
(5) incorporating community health care training in the training programme for health manpower at all levels; and
(6) promoting wide participation of the population in health development, by stages.

In order to achieve these goals, more activities will be carried out within the framework of the so-called community health structure and system.

Health legislation

Legislation has remained the same as under colonial rule, although there are plans to revise it. The legislation covers the following subjects:

— practice of medical and related professions (physicians, dentists, pharmacists, nurses, birth attendants, *agents sanitaires*, and other);
— regulations governing pharmacy (practice of pharmacy; toxic substances, soporifics, poisonous narcotic drugs, antiseptics, and biological substances);
— teaching in medical and allied professions;
— international health regulations;
— health policy for immigration;
— public health and sanitation (immunization, diseases requiring quarantine measures, environmental health and occupational health).

Health planning and programming

Health planning is still in its initial stages. There is a shortage of statistical data which the Government is trying to remedy.

Organization of health services

The services for curative, preventive and community medicine are becoming increasingly integrated by means of fixed centres which are responsible for all three and mobile teams entrusted with screening for diseases and providing the people with nutritional and health education.

Biomedical and health services research

A contract has been signed with the Institut Pasteur with a view to setting up a biomedical research unit in Kinshasa. At present, the Scientific Research Institute is conducting research solely on health services.

Education and training of health manpower

For training physicians, Zaire has a faculty of medicine within the National University which trains most of its medical professionals. A number of physicians come from foreign universities. Higher-level auxiliary staff are trained by the Higher Medical Technical Institute. The other categories of health manpower receive their training at the medical technical institutes throughout the country.

Health resources

Health care establishments

Health care services are provided by the Executive Council, the public sector, and the missions.

In 1977 there were the following establishments for health care (numbers of beds in brackets):

	State	Mission	Other
General hospitals . . .	163 (28 758)	101 (16 764)	68 (12 387)
Clinics	13 (1 344)	—	6 (156)
Sanatoria	5 (948)	—	—
Psychiatric centres . . .	2 (740)	—	—
Leprosaria	10 (444)	14 (421)	5 (47)
Isolated maternity- clinics	89 (2 375)	221 (8 546)	20 (508)
Health centres	8 (110)	4 (—)	12 (110)
Dispensaries	2 946 (3 596)	288 (622)	419 (1 062)
Total	3 236 (38 315)	628 (26 353)	518 (14 160)

Thus Zaire has 332 hospitals, 19 clinics, 330 maternity clinics, 3653 dispensaries, 12 health centres, 29 leprosaria, five sanatoria, and two psychiatric centres, with a total of 78 828 beds.

Health manpower

As of 31 December 1978, Zaire had 1723 physicians, including 572 foreigners. The following table describes the situation as regards medical and allied personnel:

	Nationals	Foreign	Total
Physicians	1 151	572	1 723
Pharmacists	378	159	537
Dentists	—	—	53
Health engineers	7	1	8
Assistants and medical graduates . .	136	—	136
Hospital administrators	289	—	289
Nurses	3 408	259	3 667
Childbirth nurses	802	—	802
Laboratory technicians	160	—	160
X-ray technicians	52	—	52
Sanitary technicians	170	—	170
Anaesthetists	40	—	40
Physiotherapists	85	—	85
Auxiliary nurses	10 144	—	10 144
Auxiliary birth attendants	1 905	—	1 905

Health expenditure

The following table shows gross domestic product, national budget, and public health budget at current prices:

	Gross domestic product	National budget[1] (1)	Public health[2] budget (2)	(2) as a percentage of (1)
1973	. . .1 357.7	450	11.4	2.53
1974	. . .1 675.2	745.2	14.8	2
1975	. . .1 670.7	596.1	8	1.34
1976	. . .2 477.4*	807	36.7	4.55
1977	. . .3 224.3	995.7	36	3.61

[1] Including ordinary expenditure and investment expenditure.
[2] Including ordinary expenditure and investment expenditure, plus spending by the Presidency on specific projects.
* Revised.

Evaluation of progress between 1973 and 1977

Some of the pilot centres for community health care have met with the full satisfaction of all health authorities. At the end of 1977 work was started to establish such centres on a larger scale. The community health programme has been introduced in all the medical and nursing schools.

INDEX TO COUNTRIES AND AREAS

CURRENCIES

A list of national units of currency and US dollar equivalents is given below. The rates are those that prevailed at 31 December 1977, the end of the period covered by the report.

Owing to variations in exchange rates any attempt to express national expenditures over the whole of the five-year period covered by the report in terms of a single currency might give rise to certain anomalies.

Country or area	Units of currency per US dollar (December 1977)		Country or area	Units of currency per US dollar (December 1977)	
Afghanistan	44.50	afghanis	Greece	36.00	drachmas
Albania	4.10	new leks	Guam	1.00	US dollar
American Samoa	1.00	US dollar	Guatemala	1.00	quetzal
Argentina	590.00	pesos	Honduras	2.00	lempiras
Australia	0.89	dollar	Hong Kong	4.65	dollars
Austria	16.15	schillings	Hungary	20.83	forints
Bahamas	1.00	dollar	Iceland	210.00	kroner
Bahrain	0.395	dinars	Indonesia	415.00	new rupiahs
Bangladesh	15.00	takas	Iran	70.35	rials
Belgium	35.00	francs	Iraq	0.295	dinar
Bermuda	1.00	dollar	Ireland	0.55	pound
Bolivia	20.00	pesos	Israel	15.15	pounds
Botswana	0.828	pula	Italy	880.00	lire
Brazil	15.43	cruzeiros	Japan	240.00	yen
Bulgaria	0.972	leva	Jordan	0.322	dinar
Burma	7.34	kyats	Kenya	8.17	shillings
Canada	1.10	dollar	Kuwait	0.284	dinar
Cayman Islands	0.833	dollar	Liberia	1.00	dollar
Central African Republic	242.00	CFA francs	Libyan Arab Jamahiriya	0.296	dinar
Chad	242.00	CFA francs	Luxembourg	35.00	francs
Chile	25.67	pesos	Macao	5.00	patacas
China	1.85	yuan	Madagascar	242.00	FMG francs
Colombia	37.37	pesos	Malawi	0.88	kwacha
Cook Islands	1.00	New Zealand dollar	Malaysia	2.37	ringgits (formerly Malayan dollars)
Costa Rica	8.57	colones			
Cuba	0.825	peso	Maldives	3.93	rupees
Cyprus	0.398	pound	Mali	484.00	francs
Czechoslovakia	11.24	korvnas	Malta	0.418	pound
Denmark	6.10	kroner	Mauritania	48.40	ouguiya
Dominican Republic	1.00	peso	Mauritius	6.60	rupees
Ecuador	26.00	sucres	Mexico	22.64	pesos
Egypt	0.70	pound	Monaco	4.85	francs
Equatorial Guinea	69.50	ekuele	Mongolia	3.26	tughriks
Ethiopia	2.0545	birr	Morocco	4.50	dirhams
Fiji	0.889	dollar	Netherlands	2.40	guilders
Finland	4.13	markka	New Caledonia	91.00	CFP francs
France	4.85	francs	New Hebrides	81.00	NH francs
French Polynesia	89.77	CFP francs	New Zealand	1.00	dollar
Gambia	2.20	dalasis	Nicaragua	7.00	cordobas
German Democratic Republic	2.25	marks	Niue	1.00	New Zealand dollar
Germany, Federal Republic of	2.22	marks	Norway	5.42	kroner
Ghana	1.15	cedis	Oman	0.345	Oman riyal
Gilbert Islands	0.89	Australian dollar	Panama	1.00	balboa

Country or area	Units of currency per US dollar (December 1977)		Country or area	Units of currency per US dollar (December 1977)	
Papua New Guinea	0.769	kina	Tuvalu	0.89	Australian dollar
Paraguay	126.00	guaranies	Uganda	8.17	shillings
Peru	115.00	soles	Union of Soviet		
Poland	19.92	zlotys	Socialist Republics . .	0.722	rouble
Portugal	40.50	escudos	United Arab		
Romania	12.00	lei	Emirates	3.95	dirhams
Rwanda	92.00	francs	United Kingdom of Great		
Samoa	0.80	tala	Britain and Northern		
Saudi Arabia	3.52	riyals	Ireland	0.55	pound
Senegal	242.00	CFA francs	United Republic		
Singapore	2.37	dollars	of Cameroon	242.00	CFA francs
Solomon Islands	0.903	dollar	United Republic		
Sri Lanka	16.00	rupees	of Tanzania	8.17	shillings
Suriname	1.77	guilders	United States		
Sweden	4.78	kroner	of America	1.00	dollar
Switzerland	2.17	francs	Upper Volta	242.00	CFA francs
Syrian Arab			Venezuela	4.28	bolivares
Republic	3.90	pounds	Viet Nam	3.78	dongs
Thailand	20.15	bahts	Wallis and Futuna	91.00	CFP francs
Togo	242.00	CFA francs	Yugoslavia	18.35	new dinars
Tonga	0.9075	pa'anga	Zaire	0.86	zaire
Tunisia	0.423	dinar	Zambia	0.78	kwacha
Turkey	19.25	liras			

ALGERIA	Société Nationale d'Edition et de Diffusion, 3 bd Zirout Youcef, ALGIERS
ARGENTINA	Carlos Hirsch SRL, Florida 165, Galerías Güemes, Escritorio 453/465, BUENOS AIRES
AUSTRALIA	*Mail Order Sales :* Australian Government Publishing Service Bookshops, P.O. Box 84, CANBERRA A.C.T. 2600 ; *or over the counter from :* Australian Government Publications and Inquiry Centres at : 113–115 London Circuit, CANBERRA CITY A.C.T. 2600 ; Shop 42, The Valley Centre, BRISBANE, Queensland 4000 ; 347 Swanston Street, MELBOURNE, VIC 3000 ; 309 Pitt Street, SYDNEY, N.S.W. 2000 ; Mt Newman House, 200 St. George's Terrace, PERTH, WA 6000 ; Industry House, 12 Pirie Street, ADELAIDE, SA 5000 ; 156-162 Macquarie Street, HOBART, TAS 7000 — Hunter Publications, 58A Gipps Street, COLLINGWOOD, VIC 3066
AUSTRIA	Gerold & Co., Graben 31, 1011 VIENNA I
BANGLADESH	The WHO Programme Coordinator, G.P.O. Box 250, DACCA 5 — The Association of Voluntary Agencies, P.O. Box 5045, DACCA 5
BELGIUM	Office international de Librairie, 30 avenue Marnix, 1050 BRUSSELS — *Subscriptions to World Health only :* Jean de Lannoy, 202 avenue du Roi, 1060 BRUSSELS
BRAZIL	Biblioteca Regional de Medicina OMS/OPS, Unidade de Venda de Publicações, Caixa Postal 20.381, Vila Clementino, 04023 SÃO PAULO, S.P.
BURMA	*see* India, WHO Regional Office
CANADA	*Single and bulk copies of individual publications (not subscriptions) :* Canadian Public Health Association, 1335 Carling Avenue, Suite 210, OTTAWA, Ont. K1Z 8N8. *Subscriptions : Subscription orders, accompanied by cheque made out to the* Royal Bank of Canada, Ottawa, Account World Health Organization, *should be sent to the* World Health Organization, P.O. Box 1800, Postal Station B, OTTAWA, Ont. K1P 5R5. *Correspondence concerning subscriptions should be addressed to the* World Health Organization, Distribution and Sales, 1211 GENEVA 27, Switzerland
CHINA	China National Publications Import Corporation, P.O. Box 88, PEKING
COLOMBIA	Distrilibros Ltd., Pío Alfonso García, Carrera 4a, Nos 36–119, CARTAGENA
CZECHO- SLOVAKIA	Artia, Ve Smeckach 30, 111 27 PRAGUE 1
DENMARK	Ejnar Munksgaard Ltd., Nørregade 6, 1164 COPENHAGEN K
ECUADOR	Librería Científica S.A., P.O. Box 362, Luque 223, GUAYAQUIL
EGYPT	Nabaa El Fikr Bookshop, 55 Saad Zaghloul Street, ALEXANDRIA
EL SALVADOR	Librería Estudiantil, Edificio Comercial B No 3, Avenida Libertad, SAN SALVADOR
FIJI	The WHO Programme Coordinator, P.O. Box 113, SUVA
FINLAND	Akateeminen Kirjakauppa, Keskuskatu 2, 00101 HELSINKI 10
FRANCE	Librairie Arnette, 2 rue Casimir-Delavigne, 75006 PARIS
GERMAN DEMOCRATIC REPUBLIC	Buchhaus Leipzig, Postfach 140, 701 LEIPZIG
GERMANY, FEDERAL REPUBLIC OF	Govi-Verlag GmbH, Ginnheimerstrasse 20, Postfach 5360, 6236 ESCHBORN — W. E. Saarbach, Postfach 101 610, Follerstrasse 2, 5 COLOGNE 1 — Alex. Horn, Spiegelgasse 9, Postfach 3340, 6200 WIESBADEN
GREECE	G. C. Eleftheroudakis S.A., Librairie internationale, rue Nikis 4, ATHENS (T. 126)
HAITI	Max Bouchereau, Librairie " A la Caravelle ", Boîte postale 111-B, PORT-AU-PRINCE
HONG KONG	Hong Kong Government Information Services, Beaconsfield House, 6th Floor, Queen's Road, Central, VICTORIA
HUNGARY	Kultura, P.O.B. 149, BUDAPEST 62 — Akadémiai Könyvesbolt, Váci utca 22, BUDAPEST V
ICELAND	Snaebjørn Jonsson & Co., P.O. Box 1131, Hafnarstraeti 9, REYKJAVIK
INDIA	WHO Regional Office for South-East Asia, World Health House, Indraprastha Estate, Ring Road, NEW DELHI 110002 — Oxford Book & Stationery Co., Scindia House, NEW DELHI 110000 ; 17 Park Street, CALCUTTA 700016 (*Sub-agent*)
INDONESIA	M/s Kalman Book Service Ltd., Jln. Cikini Raya No. 63, P.O. Box 3105/Jkt, JAKARTA
IRAN	Iranian Amalgamated Distribution Agency, 151 Khiaban Soraya, TEHERAN
IRAQ	Ministry of Information, National House for Publishing, Distributing and Advertising, BAGHDAD
IRELAND	The Stationery Office, DUBLIN 4
ISRAEL	Heiliger & Co., 3 Nathan Strauss Street, JERUSALEM
ITALY	Edizioni Minerva Medica, Corso Bramante 83–85, 10126 TURIN ; Via Lamarmora 3, 20100 MILAN
JAPAN	Maruzen Co. Ltd., P.O. Box 5050, TOKYO International, 100–31
KOREA, REPUBLIC OF	The WHO Programme Coordinator, Central P.O. Box 540, SEOUL
KUWAIT	The Kuwait Bookshops Co. Ltd., Thunayan Al-Ghanem Bldg, P.O. Box 2942, KUWAIT
LAO PEOPLE'S DEMOCRATIC REPUBLIC	The WHO Programme Coordinator, P.O. Box 343, VIENTIANE

WHO publications may be obtained, direct or through booksellers, from:

LEBANON	The Levant Distributors Co. S.A.R.L., Box 1181, Makdessi Street, Hanna Bldg, BEIRUT
LUXEMBOURG	Librairie du Centre, 49 bd Royal, LUXEMBOURG
MALAYSIA	The WHO Programme Coordinator, Room 1004, Fitzpatrick Building, Jalan Raja Chulan, KUALA LUMPUR 05–02 — Jubilee (Book) Store Ltd, 97 Jalan Tuanku Abdul Rahman, P.O. Box 629, KUALA LUMPUR 01–08 — Parry's Book Center, K. L. Hilton Hotel, Jln. Treacher, P.O. Box 960, KUALA LUMPUR
MEXICO	La Prensa Médica Mexicana, Ediciones Científicas, Paseo de las Facultades 26, Apt. Postal 20–413, MEXICO CITY 20, D.F.
MONGOLIA	see India, WHO Regional Office
MOROCCO	Editions La Porte, 281 avenue Mohammed V, RABAT
MOZAMBIQUE	INLD, Caixa Postal 4030, MAPUTO
NEPAL	see India, WHO Regional Office
NETHERLANDS	N.V. Martinus Nijhoff's Boekhandel en Uitgevers Maatschappij, Lange Voorhout 9, THE HAGUE 2000
NEW ZEALAND	Government Printing Office, Mulgrave Street, Private Bag, WELLINGTON 1. *Government Bookshops at :* Rutland Street, P.O. 5344, AUCKLAND ; 130 Oxford Terrace, P.O. Box 1721, CHRISTCHURCH ; Alma Street, P.O. Box 857, HAMILTON ; Princes Street, P.O. Box 1104, DUNEDIN — R. Hill & Son Ltd, Ideal House, Cnr Gillies Avenue & Eden Street, Newmarket, AUCKLAND 1
NIGERIA	University Bookshop Nigeria Ltd, University of Ibadan, IBADAN — G. O. Odatuwa Publishers & Booksellers Co., 9 Hausa Road, SAPELE, BENDEL STATE
NORWAY	Johan Grundt Tanum Bokhandel, Karl Johansgt. 43, 1010 OSLO 1
PAKISTAN	Mirza Book Agency, 65 Shahrah–E–Quaid–E–Azam, P.O. BOX 729, LAHORE 3
PAPUA NEW GUINEA	The WHO Programme Coordinator, P.O. Box 5896, BOROKO
PHILIPPINES	World Health Organization, Regional Office for the Western Pacific, P.O. Box 2932, MANILA — The Modern Book Company Inc., P.O. Box 632, 926 Rizal Avenue, MANILA
POLAND	Składnica Księgarska, ul Mazowiecka 9, 00052 WARSAW *(except periodicals)* — BKWZ Ruch, ul Wronia 23, 00840 WARSAW *(periodicals only)*
PORTUGAL	Livraria Rodrigues, 186 Rua do Ouro, LISBON 2
SIERRA LEONE	Njala University College Bookshop (University of Sierra Leone), Private Mail Bag, FREETOWN
SINGAPORE, REPUBLIC OF	The WHO Programme Coordinator, 144 Moulmein Road, G.P.O. Box 3457, SINGAPORE 1 — Select Books (Pte) Ltd, 215 Tanglin Shopping Centre, 2/F, 19 Tanglin Road, SINGAPORE 10
SOUTH AFRICA	Van Schaik's Bookstore (Pty) Ltd, P.O. Box 724, 268 Church Street, PRETORIA 0001
SPAIN	Comercial Atheneum S.A., Consejo de Ciento 130–136, BARCELONA 15 ; General Moscardó 29, MADRID 20 — Librería Díaz de Santos, Lagasca 95, MADRID 6 ; Balmes 417 y 419, BARCELONA 6
SRI LANKA	see India, WHO Regional Office
SWEDEN	Aktiebolaget C.E. Fritzes Kungl. Hovbokhandel, Regeringsgatan 12, 10327 STOCKHOLM
SWITZERLAND	Medizinischer Verlag Hans Huber, Länggass Strasse 76, 3012 BERNE 9
SYRIAN ARAB REPUBLIC	M. Farras Kekhia, P.O. Box No. 5221, ALEPPO
THAILAND	see India, WHO Regional Office
TUNISIA	Société Tunisienne de Diffusion, 5 avenue de Carthage, TUNIS
TURKEY	Haset Kitapevi, 469 Istiklal Caddesi, Beyoglu, ISTANBUL
UNITED KINGDOM	H.M. Stationery Office : 49 High Holborn, LONDON WC1V 6HB ; 13a Castle Street, EDINBURGH EH2 3AR ; 41 The Hayes, CARDIFF CF1 1JW ; 80 Chichester Street, BELFAST BT1 4JY ; Brazennose Street, MANCHESTER M60 8AS ; 258 Broad Street, BIRMINGHAM B1 2HE ; Southey House, Wine Street, BRISTOL BS1 2BQ. *All mail orders should be sent to* P.O. Box 569, LONDON SE1 9NH
UNITED STATES OF AMERICA	*Single and bulk copies of individual publications (not subscriptions) :* WHO Publications Centre USA, 49 Sheridan Avenue, ALBANY, N.Y. 12210. *Subscriptions : Subscription orders, accompanied by check made out to the* Chemical Bank, New York, Account World Health Organization, *should be sent to the* World Health Organization, P.O. Box 5284, Church Street Station, NEW YORK, N.Y. 10249 ; *Correspondence concerning subscriptions should be addressed to the* World Health Organization, Distribution and Sales, 1211 GENEVA 27, Switzerland. *Publications are also available from the* United Nations Bookshop, NEW YORK, N.Y. 10017 *(retail only)*
USSR	*For readers in the USSR requiring Russian editions :* Komsomolskij prospekt 18, Medicinskaja Kniga, MOSCOW — *For readers outside the USSR requiring Russian editions :* Kuzneckij most 18, Meždunarodnaja Kniga, MOSCOW G-200
VENEZUELA	Editorial Interamericana de Venezuela C.A., Apartado 50785, CARACAS 105 — Librería del Este, Apartado 60337, CARACAS 106
YUGOSLAVIA	Jugoslovenska Knjiga, Terazije 27/II, 11000 BELGRADE
ZAIRE	Librairie universitaire, avenue de la Paix Nº 167, B.P. 1682, KINSHASA I

Special terms for developing countries are obtainable on application to the WHO Programme Coordinators or WHO Regional Offices listed above or to the World Health Organization, Distribution and Sales Service, 1211 Geneva 27, Switzerland. Orders from countries where sales agents have not yet been appointed may also be sent to the Geneva address, but must be paid for in pounds sterling, US dollars, or Swiss francs.

Price : Sw. fr. 28,—   Prices are subject to change without notice.